W9-BUI-812

SB
415
.L3
*1968

Laurie, Alexander,
 1892-
 Commercial flower
forcing.

LIBRARY/LRC
OUACHITA TECHNICAL COLLEGE
P.O. BOX 816
MALVERN, ARKANSAS 72104

COMMERCIAL
FLOWER FORCING

ALEX LAURIE, B.S., M.S.
Professor Emeritus, The Ohio State University

D. C. KIPLINGER, B.S., M.S., Ph.D.
Professor of Floriculture, The Ohio State University

KENNARD S. NELSON, B.A., M.S., Ph.D.
Formerly Extension Specialist in Floriculture, The Ohio State University

COMMERCIAL FLOWER FORCING

*The Fundamentals and Their Practical Application
to the Culture of Greenhouse Crops*

SEVENTH EDITION

OUACHITA TECHNICAL COLLEGE

McGRAW-HILL BOOK COMPANY

New York   St. Louis   San Francisco   Toronto   London   Sydney

COMMERCIAL FLOWER FORCING

Copyright renewed 1969 by Alex Laurie.
Copyright © 1958, 1968 by McGraw-Hill, Inc.   All Rights Reserved.
Copyright renewed 1962, 1967 by Alex Laurie.
Copyright 1934, 1939, 1941, 1944, 1948 by McGraw-Hill, Inc.
All Rights Reserved.   Printed in the United States of America.
No part of this publication may be reproduced, stored in a retrieval system,
or transmitted, in any form or by any means, electronic,
mechanical, photocopying, recording, or otherwise, without
the prior written permission of the publisher.

Library of Congress Catalog Card Number: 67–25355

ISBN 07-036632-2
67890 HDMM 75432

SB
415
23
1968

PREFACE

The basic format for *Commercial Flower Forcing* was established over thirty years ago, and it has remained essentially unchanged through the years and several revisions. The objectives have been to describe thoroughly all phases of the industry of producing and marketing flowers and plants grown in the greenhouse, and to relate the practices and techniques used to the scientific principles involved. Although the book is written primarily for use as a college text in undergraduate and graduate instruction in floriculture, the presentation is clear and uninvolved enough to be a valuable reference book for commercial greenhouse operators and students in trade and vocational schools.

With each edition, changes in details must be made to keep abreast of this dynamic industry. Knowledge is gained, concepts change, mistakes are recognized, equipment is developed, social customs vary, new plants are hybridized, economics fluctuates, transportation improves, and chemicals are manufactured; these and other factors profoundly affect the producing and marketing of greenhouse flowers and plants. Equally important has been the large increase in the amount of time and effort devoted to the scientific investigation of greenhouse crops and their environment, which has led to new learning and new understanding. Although the same general format is used, it has been necessary to completely reorganize and rewrite the entire text in order to provide the proper relationship of principle, concept, and practice.

In the course of this work the authors became indebted to many colleagues in education, research, and the industry for information and valuable suggestions. Their help is appreciated and gratefully acknowledged.

Alex Laurie
D. C. Kiplinger
Kennard S. Nelson

CONTENTS

COMMERCIAL FLOWER FORCING

1

STATUS AND DEVELOPMENT OF THE INDUSTRY

Commercial flower growing in the United States is of comparatively recent origin. It is thought to have had its inception in the early part of the nineteenth century in the vicinity of Philadelphia, which then was considered the social center of the country. At first the products were grown outdoors and were of poor quality and limited variety. Gradually, however, with the erection of greenhouses to meet the increasing demand, commercial flower growing developed to such an extent that retail stores began to handle the output. Gradually the public became accustomed to buying from stores devoted exclusively to flowers, and thus the separation of production and marketing of flowers was established.   Further development necessitated the introduction of the middleman, or wholesale commission florist.

The production of flowers and plants.   The producers are either retail growers who sell directly to the consumer or wholesale growers who sell to individuals or firms who resell the flowers and plants.   Retail growers usually have a relatively small area (25,000 square feet or less) devoted to greenhouses in which they attempt to produce a varied selection of flowers and plants to satisfy the requirements of their customers.   Some of the greenhouses may be used solely for the display of pot plants for holidays or bedding plants in the spring. Most of the retail growers cannot produce all the flowers and plants which they need for their retail sales, and additional produce is purchased directly from wholesale growers or from wholesale commission houses.   Although the greenhouse area should and often does contribute income in proportion to the space involved, its size does not necessarily indicate the total amount of retail business which is done, as the dollar volume in the retail shop may be increased greatly from merchandise which is bought and resold.   Wholesale growers often specialize in one crop or just a few crops; and because their income is based largely on the amount of production area, their greenhouse ranges may be large (25,000 square feet and up).   Some wholesale growers sell their entire production directly to operators of retail stores.   This method of selling is more common for pot plants than for cut flowers.   Many wholesale growers consign all their flowers or plants to wholesale commission houses, and some of them operate their own commission establishments in which they not only sell the produce from their greenhouses but from other production areas as well.

Retail greenhouses are distributed throughout the country uniformly in proportion to population, since the need for them is directly related to local sales. The location of wholesale greenhouses may be related partly to population but also has been determined by weather conditions and transportation.   Initially, large wholesale greenhouses were established in the vicinity of the large cities, but as transportation improved, the proximity to market became of lesser importance. In more recent years several production areas have developed because of more suitable climatic conditions.   One of the earliest of these was in the New England states where carnations are produced because of high light intensity in the winter and cooler temperatures in the summer than in several midwestern locations. Because of the high light intensity in the winter in the vicinity of Denver, it has also become an important area for the production of carnations.   Chrysanthemum, rose, and carnation production in the San Francisco area has increased tremendously because of cool summer temperatures and generally good light conditions the year-round.   The uniformly mild climate and the good light conditions of southern California have influenced growers of Chrysanthemums, poinsettias, carnations, and foliage plants to locate in that area.   Gladiolus, Chrysanthemum, and foliage plant growers have located in Florida because of the mild temperatures the year-round. Operations in Florida are largely outdoors, and greenhouses are used only for specific purposes such as propagation.

The greenhouse area in the United States increased about 19 percent from 1949 to 1959. According to the 1959 census the area covered by greenhouses which produce flowers and plants increased from 159,917,237 square feet in 1949 to 190,425,469 square feet in 1959. Approximately half of this increase took place in the state of California. The smallest greenhouse area reported per state was 15,800 square feet for Nevada. Some greenhouse area for the production of flowers and plants was reported for each of the 48 states, and California had the largest area in greenhouses. About one-half of the total greenhouse area used for the production of flowers and plants in the country is located in only five of the states.

Table 1-1. *Greenhouse Area in Square Feet for Flowers and Plants in the Five Leading States*

	1949	1959
Total in the United States	159,917,237	190,425,469
California	13,950,352	28,525,642
Pennsylvania	16,953,480	17,183,822
New York	17,578,411	16,426,310
Ohio	12,315,203	15,587,518
Illinois	16,363,246	14,716,036

Some flower and plant crops are produced in outdoor areas. For census purposes cloth houses, plastic screen houses, lath houses, and frames are classed as outdoor areas along with fields that have no coverings. In some climates the crops may be grown in the outdoor area only in suitable weather during a portion of the year, but in favorable climates they may be grown outdoors throughout the year.

The main areas of outdoor production of flowers and plants are Florida, 11,744 acres; Georgia, 7,660 acres; and California, 6,290 acres. The leading states for the production of bulbs are Washington, 1,588 acres; Michigan, 1,296 acres; Illinois, 1,163 acres; and Oregon, 1,155 acres. Just about the entire acreage of seed production is located in California, 3,069 acres.

Table 1-2. *Outdoor Area in Acres for Production of Flowers and Plants*

KIND OF CROP	AREA IN ACRES
Total in the United States......	54,843
Flowers and plants	41,350
Bulbs	10,362
Seeds	3,131

Approximately a 53 percent increase was reported in the value of flower and plant crops at wholesale prices from 1949 to 1959. In the 1959 census the value of the flower and plant crops produced in greenhouses and outdoors in the United States at wholesale prices was reported to have increased from $190,909,-456 to $292,302,771 in the 10-year period from 1949 to 1959. It is believed that this increase resulted primarily from greater production rather than from higher wholesale prices per unit.

Table 1-3. *Total Reported Value for Some Flower and Plant Crops at Wholesale Prices*

	1949	1959
Bedding plants including geraniums	$22,079,171	$51,024,541
Chrysanthemums—cut flowers plus rooted cuttings	19,130,320	44,636,024
Foliage plants including cacti and succulents	13,157,771	34,109,126
Carnations including rooted cuttings	20,344,079	31,361,762
Roses—cut flowers only	30,582,022	30,942,064
Gladiolus—cut flowers only	14,868,387	15,473,799
Pot Chrysanthemums—pot plants only	No record	11,733,853
Poinsettias including rooted cuttings and plants	4,878,538	9,351,483
Azaleas including growing-on plants	5,428,329	8,508,841
Cattleya orchids—cut flowers only	7,169,354	6,276,016
Lilies—pot plants only	3,555,517	5,779,511
Snapdragons—cut flowers only	No record	4,562,007
Hydrangeas including rooted cuttings and plants	4,566,974	4,409,532
Cymbidium orchids—cut flowers only	No record	1,841,070

There were some very interesting developments in the production of flowers and plants from 1949 to 1959, and the values reported in the census indicate some of these. The value of bedding plants including geraniums more than doubled; this can be attributed to the development of better varieties, greatly improved containers and methods of handling, more sales promotion, improved sales outlets, a greater number of homes established, and more emphasis on effective gardening.

Chrysanthemums were grown commercially the year-round for a few years before 1949, but the big surge came later. Some existing greenhouse crops were dropped in favor of year-round mums, new greenhouses were erected for new mum programs, some mums were produced outdoors during the summer in the North, and many acres of spray mums were grown outdoors for the major portion of the year primarily in Florida. The tremendous increase in Chrysanthemum production was made possible by two factors: (1) commercial adaptation of the effect of day length on flowering mums, pioneered by Laurie at The Ohio State University and Post at Cornell University, and (2) the breeding of improved varieties along with methods for producing good-quality, disease-free rooted cuttings, developed by Yoder Bros., Inc.

The increased use of foliage plants in the home and in public buildings was coupled with the establishment of large production areas for foliage plants in Florida, California, and Puerto Rico. A greater variety of plants were available, and the selection and quality of plants were greatly improved.

The reported value of carnation production was approximately 50 percent greater in 1959 than in 1949. About one-half of this income was caused by the expansion of carnation production areas in California and Colorado and greater activity in sales promotion. The balance was due to general growth in several areas of the country.

The values reported for poinsettias, azaleas, and lilies for 1959 are sizable advances over those reported for 1949. This increase appears to be general over the country.

The reported value of flower and plant crops produced in greenhouses and outdoors is greatest in California. As reported in the 1959 census, approximately 56 percent of the total value of flower and plant crops grown in greenhouses and outdoors in the United States was produced in six states—California, Florida, Pennsylvania, New York, Ohio, and Illinois. Certainly there are other production areas of tremendous importance, but the greatest production volume comes in these states. The biggest change in areas of production from 1949 to 1959 was in the increase of greenhouse and outdoor growing in California and in outdoor crops in Florida.

This is a dynamic industry. The history of the floriculture industry through the years has been one of change and improvement. Continued advancements will be made as long as interested individuals constantly strive to provide better products for the consumer. There are several approaches to the improvement of flowers and plants. Breeding of better varieties and the selection of more desirable strains or sports is very important. These are activities best handled by the specialist; his work must be encouraged and well supported.

Better control of the plant environment will improve quality and quantity of the product. Many phases of the industry are involved in this. The universities and experiment stations have been instrumental through the years in uncovering truths and developing commercial applications based on them. Qualified educators should be urged to continue their important work, and the education and research facilities should be increased. In many instances improved control of the environment is directly related to new products, machines, or tools. Some of these are adaptations from other industries, and others are made specifically for the flower and plant crops.

Table 1-4. *The Total Value at Wholesale Prices of Several Flower and Plant Crops Produced in Greenhouse and Outdoor Areas in the United States, and a Comparison of Crop Values in the Six Leading States*

	CALIFORNIA	FLORIDA	PENNSYLVANIA	NEW YORK	OHIO	ILLINOIS
Total	$46,042,804	$33,107,962	$22,112,074	$21,804,593	$21,798,783	$17,480,679
Azaleas (1) $8,508,841 at $1.35 per pot	994,206	10,620	818,991	1,210,432	511,012	657,991
Bedding plants and geraniums (2) $51,024,541	8,850,023	579,844	3,510,005	3,535,928	3,977,899	3,140,887
Carnations (3) $31,361,762 at $0.07 each	6,466,488	54,977	2,757,683	1,919,535	1,674,896	1,298,273
Chrysanthemums—sprays $23,409,079 at $0.79 per bunch	1,993,511	5,694,802	1,827,747	1,570,338	3,995,748	1,096,488
Chrysanthemum—standards $21,225,945 at $0.18 each	4,680,089	1,053,536	1,675,534	1,326,697	4,536,419	1,229,927
Chrysanthemums—pot (4) $11,733,853 at $1.20 per pot	656,821	557,956	590,002	602,013	813,964	876,360
Foliage (5) $34,109,126	4,690,732	12,639,416	2,035,649	1,530,043	1,596,405	1,566,540
Gladiolus $15,473,799 at $0.55 per dozen	1,377,033	7,981,793	289,367	390,460	348,587	444,467
Hydrangeas (6) $4,409,532 at $1.35 per pot	197,110	55,156	489,489	278,789	318,462	303,707
Lilies $5,779,511 at $1.40 per pot	406,270	63,131	515,888	439,522	238,286	519,308
Orchids—Cattleya (7) $6,276,016 at $0.82 each	803,481	286,652	330,549	668,324	420,846	671,685

Table 1-4. (Continued)

Orchids—Cymbidium (8) $1,841,070 at $0.54 each	750,519	15,140	477,108	72,642	29,746	13,526
Poinsettias (9) $9,351,483 at $1.31 per pot	636,198	133,266	696,577	903,253	665,899	706,517
Roses (10) $30,942,064 at $0.09 each	4,928,653	113,762	3,336,924	3,787,001	1,092,348	3,490,255
Snapdragons (11) $4,562,007 at $1.09 per dozen	113,448	39,487	600,639	462,952	487,673	309,608

OTHER AREAS OF PRIMARY IMPORTANCE IN SPECIFIC CROPS:

(1) Azaleas—New Jersey, $872,315
(2) Bedding plants including geraniums—Michigan, $3,189,497
(3) Carnations—Colorado, $5,970,328; Massachusetts, $3,427,574
(4) Pot Chrysanthemums—Texas, $1,003,325; North Carolina, $620,860; Alabama, $465,955; Oklahoma, $460,003
(5) Foliage—New Jersey, $1,419,931; Texas, $1,385,636
(6) Hydrangeas—Texas, $290,957; New Jersey, $272,882
(7) Cattleya orchids—New Jersey, $1,132,169; Connecticut, $504,525
(8) Cymbidium orchids—New Jersey, $128,447
(9) Poinsettias—Wisconsin, $491,321; New Jersey, $441,350; Michigan, $414,739
(10) Roses—Indiana, $2,503,106; Connecticut, $1,696,914; New Jersey, $1,303,378; Michigan, $1,279,886; Massachusetts, $1,101,973
(11) Snapdragons—Massachusetts, $353,218

Transportation is particularly important with highly perishable products such as flowers and plants. It can be expected that transportation will continue to improve, but the individuals in the flower industry must be alert to make the best use of it.

Public relations and effective sales promotion need to be continued with increased effort. Some of the best men in the industry must be encouraged to work on this. The Society of American Florists represents the entire industry in public relations and political matters. This organization may be effective if its objectives are well outlined, the staff is capable, and the entire industry backs the group.

Many area or local organizations have been very effective in public relations and sales promotion. They are usually called "allieds" or "uniteds." These groups can do an excellent job, and local units should function in each area of the country.

The Florists' Telegraph Delivery Association pioneered in the handling of flower sales by wire, and this was an important step in sales promotion. Since that time some similar organizations have been established. These organizations have been instrumental in the promotion and sale of flowers and plants. They make the consumer more aware that flowers are available and that they can be supplied conveniently in any location.

Continued efforts must be made to make flowers and plants available to consumers in the form that they desire them and at the right time. The possibilities in the industry are limitless if this objective is pursued.

2

GREENHOUSES AND RELATED STRUCTURES

Greenhouses are used so that flowers and plants can be produced continuously throughout the year. They should be located and constructed in such a way that the maximum amount of sunlight is available and that controls are provided for temperature, moisture, and air movement. Thus greenhouses make it possible to realize improvement in quality of flowers as well as year-round production.

Location of greenhouse. Consideration needs to be given to the potential market. This is of particular interest with pot plant production as it usually is not economical to transport pot plants long distances. If it is desired to locate the greenhouse a distance from the market, the effect of transportation on costs should be evaluated.

Climate varies considerably over the country. It is advisable to locate in an area where the climate is most suitable for the crops that are going to be produced. With most crops the amount of sunlight is the limiting factor during the winter. During the summer high temperatures can reduce the quality or quantity of the crop. Fuel costs are higher in the North than in the South. Some areas are plagued with storms that can damage structures and crop. The effect of climate must be considered carefully before locating the greenhouse.

Operating costs may be quite different depending on location. Labor probably will make up about half of the operating costs. The availability and the going rate of pay for labor in the area under consideration is important. Some of the other items that may vary considerably with area are taxes, fuel, water, and electricity.

Once the general area for locating the greenhouse is selected, the particular site should be chosen to allow for full benefit of the sun. Air movement and water drainage should be adequate, and the area should be essentially level so that wheeled vehicles can be used to advantage. The quality and quantity of water must be good, and there should be ready access to the site for shipping.

Size and arrangement of houses. The requirements of the crops should be considered first. Pot plant crops are grown more easily in smaller houses that have easy access to a central headhouse and shipping room. In such a situation the varied temperatures can be provided that are needed for pot plant crops; and

2-1. The smoke stack is the landmark of the greenhouse range.

movement to and from the potting area, greenhouses, and the shipping room is direct and convenient.   Cut flower crops are often grown better in larger houses; however, with crops such as mums there is an advantage in having units that can be handled separately.

Economy of construction is important.   Ridge and furrow type construction is usually more economical, and it does require less land area.   Some disadvantages are excessive shade from the gutters, lack of temperature control of

2-2.   Various arrangements of greenhouses are used depending on the crops to be grown and the land available.   Separate greenhouses require more land than gutter-connected (ridge and furrow) ones, but they can provide better light, ventilation, and temperature control. (*Lord & Burnham photograph.*)

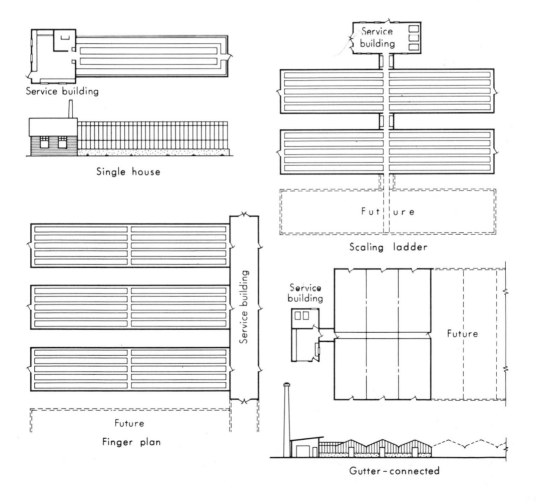

Service building

Single house

Finger plan

Future

Service building

Service building

Scaling ladder

Service building

Future

Gutter-connected

individual houses, and no side ventilation. If forced-air ventilation is used, the lack of side ventilators may be no problem.

The houses should be arranged so that labor is conserved and the crop is handled most efficiently. Consideration should be given to the ease with which flowers can be cut and moved to the grading area, and pot plants moved from area to area or to the shipping room.

The benching arrangement as well as the heating and cooling system should be planned while the general layout for the greenhouse is being made. This is much easier than trying to fit them into the established range after it is up, and it may very easily change preconceived ideas on the best arrangement of houses.

Types of framework. The framework of the greenhouse consists of side posts—or gutter posts in the case of connected houses—at about 10-foot intervals, to support the roof trusses. The eave or gutter extends from post to post at the point where the truss joins the side post. The ridge extends from truss to truss at the peak of the house. Midway between the ridge and eave a purlin extends from truss to truss. If the house is wide, two or more purlins may be spaced equidistant between ridge and eave. For narrow houses or houses with adequate trusswork this is the basic framework of the house. For wider houses or for trusses that need additional support, posts are provided at each truss from the purlin to the ground.

2-3. Typical dimensions of a 35-foot clear-span greenhouse. This is a separate house with both ridge and side wall ventilators. This benching arrangement would be suitable for pot plants. For cut flower crops there should be six 3½-foot benches either on the ground or slightly elevated. (*Lord & Burnham drawing.*)

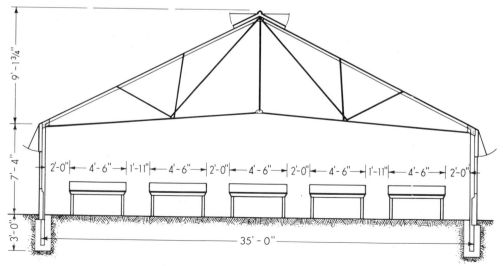

Usually a curtain wall of concrete or transite is used for about 3 feet at the base of the side walls of the greenhouse. For glass houses roof bars are installed approximately 2 feet apart from ridge to purlin to eave, and wall bars are placed from the eave to the sill of the side wall. These bars provide the base for the glass. Houses that are to be covered with film plastic may have bars or rafters spaced about 4 feet apart with wire fabric installed beneath the plastic film to support it. Corrugated plastics should be applied to framework members that run lengthwise to the house (purlins). These should be installed about every 3 feet across the width of the roof depending on the weight of the corrugated plastic and the pitch of the roof.

The post and truss designs for greenhouses may be the same whether they are to be covered with glass, film plastic, or rigid plastic; but the purlin and bar arrangement should be made specifically for the type of material that will be used to cover the structure. Usually it is not possible to switch from one type of covering to another without making the necessary changes in bars or purlins first. However, in replacing glass with corrugated plastic in old, wooden bar houses,

2-4. Connected (ridge and furrow) greenhouses in the process of construction. These are clear-span greenhouses—the roof is supported solely by the trusses which extend from side post to opposing gutter post. (*Lord & Burnham photograph.*)

it is possible to remove the glass, clean and paint the bars, and then apply the corrugated plastic directly to the bars at a slight angle.

The choice of materials for the framework of a greenhouse is based on structural strength, durability, initial cost, and maintenance costs. Wooden framework is used primarily for temporary or semipermanent structures. The most durable wood with the least maintenance cost is redwood. Steel framework has been used widely. This does require frequent painting to prevent rust, but it is very satisfactory in other respects. Steel frame houses may have redwood or aluminum roof and wall bars as well as ventilator sash.

Aluminum has become increasingly popular for the greenhouse framework. The roof and wall bars and ventilating sash all are made of aluminum. The corrosion problem with aluminum is slight, and the structure does not

2-5. The supporting framework for greenhouses is side or gutter posts with trusses extending across the house between opposite posts. The trusses join with the ridge at the peak, the eave or gutter at the side, and one or more purlins spaced equidistant between ridge and gutter. The roof bars which hold the glass extend from ridge or ventilator header to purlins to gutter or eave. (*Lord & Burnham photograph.*)

require painting.   It should be kept in mind, however, that the glazing procedure and maintenance are approximately the same for wood, steel, or aluminum.

Types of glazing.   The greenhouse must be glazed with as clear a material as possible to provide the maximum amount of sunlight for the plants.   This is the primary requisite of the structure.   The durability of the glazing material, the initial cost, and the maintenance costs then determine the desirability of the material.

Light transmission through glass is excellent, and for that reason it has been the primary glazing material used through the years.   The initial cost of glass is reasonable, but it is difficult to install and the periodic reglazing that is required is costly.   It is subject to considerable breakage in areas subject to hail storms.   In fact, hail damage is such a threat in certain locations that wire netting is installed above the glass to protect it from the hail.

Glass is placed on the greenhouse in much the same manner as shingles on a home—except that the panes are not lapped as much, and they are held in place by glazing points placed at the bottom of each pane, on each side, and also at the top surface at each side.   To make the house watertight the glass is set in bedding compound on the bars, and after the glass is in place glazing compound is run along each side of the bar and then painted to complete the seal.   The exterior of a glass house needs repainting every 2 to 4 years to maintain a good seal between bar and glass.   Occasionally, loose glazing compound will need to be replaced before repainting.   If the seal between bars and glass becomes loose, it is then necessary to reglaze the house.   In reglazing, all the glass is removed

2-6. Roof bars are designed so that the glass can be placed in bedding compound on each side, and there are drip grooves toward the bottom to conduct the condensation to the sidewall.   The barcap covers the bar to preserve the glazing.   (*Lord & Burnham photograph.*)

from the house, the bars are cleaned, and the glass is relaid.   This is an expensive procedure but a necessary one if the best growing conditions are to be maintained in the greenhouse.   This glazing procedure is virtually the same whether the bars are wooden, steel, or aluminum, but wooden or steel bars must be painted before the bedding compound is applied.

To reduce the frequency of painting and reglazing that is necessary, aluminum bar caps are used.   As the name indicates, they are aluminum caps or strips that are installed over the bar.   They protect the seal from the weather and reduce the amount of maintenance that is needed.

The use of plastic films for glazing greenhouses is controversial.   Several of these have suitable light transmission, and in addition they are economical in material and installation costs.   The problem lies in durability.   However, continual improvements are being made in plastic films, and it is possible that a completely satisfactory glass substitute may be available eventually.

Polyethylene film has been used quite extensively.   It has some features that are very good and a few that are very objectionable.   The initial cost is low, and the installation cost is favorable.   The film is available in widths that allow the covering of a roof or possibly an entire structure with a single sheet of film. This can be quite an advantage in installation.   Light transmission, although not as satisfactory as that of glass, is adequate for most crops.   However, polyethylene degrades in sunlight, becomes brittle, and then tears or cracks easily. This occurs more rapidly during the summer.   A house covered in the spring may not be intact by fall, but an October application of polyethylene usually can be expected to last until spring.

Because of these properties, polyethylene is used primarily on semipermanent structures or for seasonal protection.   Florida foliage plant growers cover their slat sheds with film for 3 or 4 months during the winter.   This not only prevents freezing but also increases production because of the higher temperatures that can be maintained.   Northern growers may cover structures only in the spring in order to increase their growing area for bedding plants, or they may apply the cover in the fall and produce under polyethylene during the winter. Then in the spring they may replace the cover with plastic screen for summer production.

Vinyl film (polyvinyl chloride, PVC) is more durable than polyethylene. It can be expected to remain intact for a year and possibly longer.   It costs approximately twice as much as polyethylene and is produced in widths to 6 feet. It may transmit more light than polyethylene when new.   It does become dirty more readily, and the light transmission may be less after several months.   Because of its increased durability, vinyl is usually considered more suitable than polyethylene for year-round structures.

Mylar polyester film is clear and it remains clear.   Light transmission approximates that of glass.   It costs several times as much as vinyl, but it is more

2-7. PVC film house, with a wooden, A-frame framework structure and a single purlin midway between eave and ridge.   There are neither ridge nor sidewall ventilators in this house.   Ventilation is provided by exhaust fans in one endwall and ventilators in the opposite wall. (*Stylon, Inc. photograph.*)

durable.   The initial cost of Mylar approximates the cost of glass, but the installation and maintenance costs may be less.   Everything considered, the costs of glazing with glass and Mylar are probably quite similar.

The framework for plastic film houses is most often made of wood.   This is more suitable for temporary or semipermanent structures, and the initial cost is lower.   The lower initial cost of plastic film houses has caused them to become a means of expanding production areas with a lower investment.   Then as funds are available the plastic houses may be replaced with glass houses.

Rigid or semirigid plastics have gained some acceptance for glazing greenhouses.   In most situations they are considered a permanent type of installation, and usually the framework is much the same as that used for glass houses.   Fiber glass (glass fibers imbedded in acrylic resin) is being used with apparent success, and more recently sheet or rigid polyvinyl chloride has been

2-8. Wooden frame structure covered with clear, corrugated PVC. Between gutter and ridge, the PVC is attached to purlins spaced 3 feet apart. (*Jednak Floral Co. photograph.*)

installed on some greenhouses. Several years of use will be needed before the worth of these materials can be fully evaluated. Fiber glass material costs are as much as or more than glass, but the installation costs are less and the maintenance costs may be less. Rigid vinyl costs less than fiber glass, and it can be a clearer material. The outlook for it is really quite hopeful, but more experience with weathering qualities and durability is needed. What is already known is that at least some of the fiber glass products erode in time and expose the fiber. Then dust and dirt remain on the surface, reducing the light transmittance. For this reason it may be necessary to recoat fiber glass with acrylic resin periodically.

Houses glazed with plastic, whether film or rigid, provide a different environment than houses glazed with glass. Plastic houses are tighter houses. There are few if any cracks in the glazing, and the exchange of atmosphere with the exterior is slight. In glasshouses there is a continual air leakage through the glass laps except when the glass is covered with frost or ice. It is common knowledge that a glasshouse heats much more easily during cold spells when the glass is frozen over than when it is clear.

2-9. Connected quonset structures covered with clear, corrugated PVC. There are no ventilators. Ventilation and cooling are by exhaust fans in one end wall and wet pads in the opposite end. Note the steam mains which service these and other houses. They are sufficiently elevated to give adequate clearance for trucks, and they are insulated to conserve heat. (*Jos. W. Vestal and Sons, Inc., photograph.*)

The humidity is higher in plastic houses. This can be an advantage, but there are some objectionable features. Typically there is more drip in plastic houses. This is due partially to the higher humidity, and partially to the nature of the glazing materials and the way it is applied to the structure. Condensation on the inside of glass in glasshouses is common, yet there is usually very little drip since the condensate flows down the drip groove of the roof bar to the eave. Film plastic, of course, is flexible, and the condensate scatters off it as the film is jarred or rippled. In fiber glass or rigid vinyl houses the condensate flows down to the bottom of the corrugation, but it then collects at each purlin or cross member of the structure and drips from that. Excessive dripping can be a nuisance and may encourage some disease. Aluminum spacers should be used in applying

2-10. Quonset-type structures covered with clear, corrugated PVC. Continuous air circulation is provided by Nivola Dutch Mills, and the primary heat source is from the aluminum-fin Orbital Heaters. (*Jos. W. Vestal and Sons, Inc., photograph.*)

2-11. Wooden frame structure covered with clear, corrugated PVC used for azalea production in Alabama. The minimum heat requirements are supplied by pot, oil burners. Irrigation is by the sprinklers located at regular intervals throughout the house. (*Blackwell Nurseries photograph.*)

2-12.   Quonset-type structure being covered with fiber glass.   (*Lord & Burnham photograph.*)

corrugated plastic to the roof.   The spacers are placed between the crest of the corrugation and the purlin, and they are high enough so that the valley of the corrugation does not touch the purlin.   Condensation flowing down the valley then can proceed uninterrupted to the side wall.

The plastics are not as transparent as glass, and some are really only translucent.   Light transmission through plastics is generally less than through glass.   However, direct comparisons are somewhat questionable.   The light that comes through plastic is diffused, which may result in the irradiation of portions of the plant that normally are shaded by its leaves in direct sunlight.   Growth of plants can be as good under plastic as under glass.

Ventilating equipment.   A means of exchanging air with the outside is needed to regulate the temperature and humidity in the greenhouse.   Recently there has been concern with ventilation in relation to the carbon dioxide content of the air in the greenhouse.

Usually the greenhouse has had ventilator sash located at the ridge.   In separate houses ventilator sash may be located also just below the eave of the

2-13.   Air-supported structure.   The 12-mil PVC film is anchored at the base and entirely supported by air introduced into it by the fan located to the left of the doorway.   The fan operates continuously and is rated to replace the air loss.   Ventilation and temperature control may be a problem in this type of structure.

2-14.   Ridge ventilators for the control of temperature, air circulation, and humidity in the greenhouse.   (*Lord & Burnham photograph.*)

2-15. Ridge ventilators and equipment for manual operation. (*Lord & Burnham photograph.*)

sidewall. The principle involved is that the hot air, being lighter, rises and passes through the ventilator. The cold air from the exterior, being heavier, flows toward the base of the greenhouse after it enters the ventilator. This provides air movement as well as temperature adjustment in the greenhouse. Usually the ventilators are operated manually by crank-type units located approximately every 100 feet in the greenhouse. The object is to coordinate the ventilator operation with the amount of heat that is used so that the greenhouses are maintained at the correct temperature and, at least in some instances, at the best humidity. In recent years motor-driven units have been designed for automated ventilator operation. These are controlled by thermostats, and with proper installation it is possible to have automatic ventilator operation and good temperature control in the greenhouse without personal supervision.

Early in the 1950s the pad and fan method of ventilating and cooling greenhouses was developed in the southwestern United States. Since that time these systems have been used widely throughout the country. They involve the installation of moistened fiber pads on one wall of the greenhouse and exhaust fans on the opposite wall. During warm weather the ventilators are closed, the exhaust fans are operated, and air enters the greenhouse through the moistened pads. The temperature of the air that is introduced into the greenhouse is reduced by this method.

Initially pad and fan systems were installed on existing structures by making necessary minimum modifications. Subsequently attempts have been made to alter the greenhouse design to allow for the most efficient pad and fan installation.

The exhaust fans are permanently mounted, but the fiber pads must be installed each season in order to provide for maximum air entry during hot weather and a tightly closed greenhouse during the cold season. There is an

2-16. Sidewall ventilator with operating equipment. One of the advantages in separate houses is increased ventilation, possible because of sidewall ventilators. This photograph also shows the attachment of the truss to the side post and the roof bars to the eave. (*Lord & Burnham photograph.*)

2-17. Power-operated ridge ventilators make automated ventilation possible. (*Lord & Burnham photograph.*)

2-18. A greenhouse without ridge ventilators. Hot-weather ventilation and cooling are provided by a fan and pad cooling system. Cool-weather ventilation is supplied by the perforated, plastic ventilation tube and exhaust fans. The primary source of heat in these houses is from overhead heating lines hung by chains from the trusses. Note that the supporting members for the grids that keep the plants erect are perforated metal straps hung from the trusses. (*Lord & Burnham photograph.*)

advantage, particularly during spring and fall, in providing an option in the structure for pad operation or an entirely closed greenhouse from day to day depending on the weather. This can be done by installing the pad on the inside of the side or end ventilators.

There is interest in year-round exhaust fan ventilation in the greenhouse, in order to make better use of the fans, eliminate ridge ventilators, and possibly provide better air movement and temperature control. For cold-weather operation a method needs to be provided for distributing the incoming cold air uniformly. This can possibly be done with plastic film baffles or with perforated polyethylene tubes connected to the opening and running the length of the greenhouse. Actually in cold weather it is possible to get some air exchange in glasshouses by operating the exhaust fans only. There is air seepage at the glass laps, and that will provide some ventilation. An automated system for cold-weather operation can be designed for control by thermostat so that the exhaust fans are started first, and then as further temperature reduction is needed the shutter for the perforated polyethylene tube is opened.

Air circulation. The air in the greenhouse should be in constant motion, to assure even temperature and humidity throughout the air mass, reduce the incidence of disease, and distribute carbon dioxide equally. Air circulation occurred in greenhouses in the past only if there was a temperature differential. It has been good, common practice to provide some ventilation even while operating heating lines. This assures air circulation because the heated air rises and the cool air from the exterior flows toward the bottom. This method can be used during a considerable period of the year. However, in extremely cold weather it may not be possible to open the ventilators, and during the summer there may be many occasions when there is no temperature differential between outdoors and within the greenhouse. A mechanical means for circulating the air at those times especially is needed.

Two fans, the Nivola Dutch Mill and the Acme Turbulator, have been designed for the purpose of providing positive air circulation in the greenhouse. These air-circulation fans are suspended, 30 to 50 lineal feet apart, from the ridge of the greenhouse along the length of the house. The blades are about 10 feet above the soil in which the plants are growing. They are designed to operate continuously and establish an airflow pattern from the blades toward the eave of the house. From that point the air returns to the fan in two streams: one flows just below the roof and then feeds into the fan from the top; the other flows along the base of the greenhouse and then feeds into the fan from the bottom.

Greenhouse benches. There are two reasons why benches are used in the greenhouse. They make it possible for better control of the environment around the plants, and they allow the work to proceed more efficiently.

The greenhouse bench for cut flowers needs to be level or very nearly level and deep enough to hold at least 6 inches of soil. It should provide excellent water drainage and isolation from disease or insect infestation. If the bench is constructed on the ground, the bottom and sides must be a solid piece. Concrete is the only material suitable for such a bench. To assure good drainage a V-bottom is used, with the bottom of the V at least 1½ inches below the side. A half tile is placed over the bottom of the V, and the bottom is then filled level with coarse gravel. Lengthwise the bottom of the bench must fall 1 inch per 100 feet.

Raised benches may be constructed from wood, concrete, or transite. Regardless of the material, water drainage must be perfect. The reasons for using raised benches are better drainage, isolation from pests and disease without solid construction, and easier and more efficient height for work. For most cut flower crops it is considered now that the bench should be close to the ground. There was a time when it was thought necessary to have heating lines under each bench. This is no longer desired, and underbench space is not needed for this reason. Many crops are grown tall, and sufficient head room is an advantage. The width of a concrete block makes about the right elevation for a raised cut flower bench. The bench width is usually 3½ or 4 feet.

2-19. Wooden benches for cut flowers. These are elevated enough to assure isolation from pests and diseases as well as to provide good drainage. Benches for pot plants should be higher for ease in handling plants. (*Yoder Bros., Inc., photograph.*)

Cut flower benches are steamed often. For steaming it is best to have benches without posts so that they can be covered easily, and concrete benches must be constructed carefully to prevent cracking. Most cut flower crops require some overbench structure to support cloth or wires. The method for attaching such support should be considered when the bench material is selected.

The requirements for pot plant benches are quite different. They should be raised to about 30 inches for convenience in working. If they are going to be worked from both sides, the most efficient width is about 6 feet. Ideal drain-

2-20. The boards in the bench bottom must be well spaced as illustrated to assure complete and immediate drainage of water from the bench. (*Yoder Bros., Inc., photograph.*)

2-21. Concrete, ground bench for cut flowers. Benches of this type have sides and bottoms poured in one piece for good control of pests and diseases. The bench bottom is V-shaped for adequate water drainage.

age is needed, and there is interest in perfect air circulation around pot plants. Pot plant benches are often constructed without sideboards and with their bottoms as open as possible. A very good pot plant bench bottom is 14-gauge, 1-by 1-inch welded wire fabric. This allows the ideal air circulation around pot plants that is needed.

The arrangement of the benches can affect working conditions in the house considerably. In building a new structure it would really be best to plan

2-22. Transite bench construction. Corrugated transite must be used on the bottom for strength. To provide good drainage, the bottom should be pitched from one side to the other. If this cannot be done, drainage holes must be drilled in each valley. (*Lord & Burnham photograph.*)

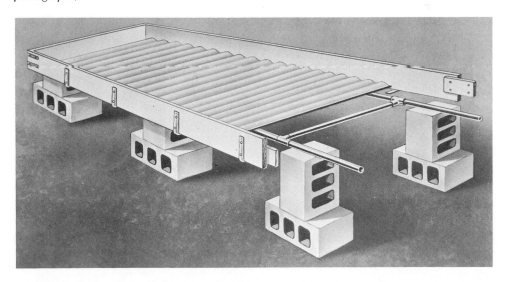

OUACHITA TECHNICAL COLLEGE

2-23. Welded wire fabric can be used as bottoms for pot plant benches. This provides maximum drainage and air circulation. The 14-gauge wire fabric has 1-inch spacing. (*Jednak Floral Co. photograph.*)

the work area and bench arrangement, and then choose the structure to properly enclose it. Too often the greenhouse is all erected before thought is given to how the benches fit.

Traditionally benches have been installed lengthwise in the greenhouse. This has been based to some extent on convenience and efficiency of working, but another reason for it is that this orientation has seemed to be the best solution for supporting bench heating lines and water lines without interference to walking. Long benches, however, are not always the most efficient size. With some crops, cut flowers for example, long benches necessitate frequent trips through narrow walks, and long benches can be even more of a problem with pot plants. There also is an advantage in having crop-size benches, which often means that the unit should be shorter than the length of the house.

There is a trend away from installation of heating lines on the bench. Overhead heating systems do perform satisfactorily, and they are not nearly as costly to maintain as bench lines. With the heating lines overhead, the ground area can be benched for the most efficient use. One such arrangement is peninsular benching or cross-benching. A walk wide enough to accommodate wheeled carts is provided the length of the house, either at the side or in the middle, depending on the width of the house. The benches are installed across the width of the house and butt on the wide walk. Such an arrangement can increase the efficiency of a pot plant house, and it may be an advantage in some cut flower houses, depending on the situation.

Greenhouse walks are usually minimum width and for good reason. Production space in the greenhouse should be utilized to the best advantage, and it is apparent that no flowers can be grown in the walks. It is possible to use 18-

2-24. Cross-benching in a greenhouse.   The principal advantages are crop-size benches and the use of wheeled carts in the wide walk to service all benches.   Note that the primary source of heat is overhead unit heaters but that heating lines are provided on the sidewalls as well. (*Lord & Burnham photograph.*)

to 24-inch walks; however, at least one walk in the house should be wide enough to handle wheelbarrows, sprayers, or wheeled carts.   Walks should be level and should have a satisfactory surface in order to promote the best movement of workers or vehicles.

Workroom.   The workroom should be located, if possible, at the north end of the greenhouse, in order to provide some protection from cold prevailing winds.   Its size and design are largely dependent on the size and number of greenhouses it is to serve and the type of crops being grown.   If separate from the greenhouse, the workroom should be near enough to minimize walking and make transportation of plants between the two structures simple and convenient.

The workroom should be heated, well lighted, and equipped with tables and storage bins for soil, manure, sand, peat, and other similar materials.   A cooler is necessary for the storage of cut flowers.   Storage for cut flower boxes, flats, tools, insecticides, fungicides, fertilizers, and other items necessary for the production of plants should be provided.   A steam-sterilizing box or unit in the workroom is a desirable asset.

The table space for grading, bunching, and wrapping of cut flowers and space for pot plants should be ample for all occasions such as holiday periods when a large volume of stock is handled.   Substantial potting benches at the proper height for ease in working are necessary.   Potting benches on wheels can be rolled to the desired location, which eliminates moving of pots in the workrooms.

The workroom is often a part of the building where cut flowers, plants, pots, and other materials are received or loaded for shipping out.   If such is the case, the room should be wide and long to accommodate one or more large trucks. Cut flowers and plants for holiday delivery may be loaded inside the warm workroom, which somewhat reduces the wrapping and insulation necessary for protection from cold.   Doors should be high and wide to accommodate trucks.

Conveyors.   The use of some type of conveyor is widespread in industrial plants where mass-production methods are in vogue.   The florist industry, with some exceptions, has been slow to recognize the advantages of such labor-saving devices.   This is partially due to the lack of knowledge of the costs of various operations, and also to the reluctance of many growers to change with the times.   Conveyor systems are probably most useful where pot plants are grown.   The use of conveyors to move plants for the purpose of potting, shifting from one house to another, or moving finished plants out of the houses for delivery eliminates hours of drudgery.   Initial costs are high, but conveyor systems save time and money in addition to increasing the efficiency of every employee.

Cloth houses.   The purpose of a cloth house is to expand production area for the period when weather conditions are favorable for culture of plants without benefit of a greenhouse.   Although cloth houses are no longer as popular as they once were, good-quality asters and mums can be produced under cloth.

The side posts may be of wood, 3-inch pipe, or old boiler tubes and should be set deep enough in the ground so that they will not be heaved out by freezing and thawing.   Because of the weight of the cloth, guy wires should be attached to a "dead man" support.   Usually No. 9 galvanized wire is fastened to the tops of the posts, and the cloth is sewn to it.   Posts within the cloth house need not be very heavy since they are subject to far less strain.   The cloth covering is itself generally plastic screen rather than cotton, which lasts only one year.

Lath houses.   The precision growing of such plants as azaleas and Hydrangeas may require the use of lath shade during the summer months in many localities.   Cold frames with lath covering in place of glass sash are useful, although the inconvenience of frames often limits their use for this purpose. Snow fence is commonly used by supporting it 30 inches above 4-foot beds.

In the South slat sheds are used for growing *Asparagus plumosus,* and stock of *Philodendron, Nephthytis,* and other tropical foliage plants.   The 12-foot posts of 4- by 4-inch pine, pressure treated with copper naphthenate, are spaced

2-25. Cloth house to provide partial shade and protection from pests for crops grown outdoors during the summer in the North and the year-round in the South. This house is covered with cotton, tobacco cloth, but plastic screen is commonly used.

2-26. Azalea plants in a large, plastic screen house in central Florida.

13 feet apart with 3 feet buried in concrete in the soil.   The stringers are 2- by 6-foot pressure-treated pine boards 14 feet long, nailed on alternate sides of the posts at the top.   The slats on the roof are ½- by 2- or 3-inch rough cypress spaced 1 inch or less apart.   Most crops are grown under 75 percent shade, but *Aglaonema* is best under 90 percent shade while *Peperomia* should be in 50 percent shade.   Plastic screen of the proper density may be substituted for the roof slats. The south side is slatted the same as the roof, and the other sides are boarded solid.

One of the best types of structure consists of a permanent frame of pipe or wood at least 7 feet high, on top of which snow fence can be unrolled or lath sash placed when it is needed.   When no longer needed, the snow fence is rolled together or lath sash removed, and the plants are exposed to full sun.   A permanent structure made by nailing 1- by 2-inch lumber 2 inches apart on a wooden frame is useful, but the plants must be moved in and out, which is not as satisfactory as rolling or unrolling snow fence.

Bulb storage.   Bulbs are very commonly stored outside in beds especially reserved for this purpose, but cold-storage buildings, erected for the sole purpose of storing bulbs to condition them for forcing or hold them back for late flower-

2-27.   Lath house to provide partial shade for crops grown outdoors in the summer in the North and the year-round in the South.   Southern structures usually are constructed to provide more shade and commonly are called slat sheds.

ing, are preferred.   A storage in the form of a naturally cool structure such as a cellar or an insulated, refrigerated structure is very satisfactory.   The uniform conditions that prevail in these structures are ideal.   Although they are more expensive to construct than outside beds, cool storages are more convenient, can be equipped with shelves spaced about 18 inches apart to accommodate a large number of pots, and in general give more satisfactory results.   When shelves are used, a layer of peat on the shelf reduces the danger of drying out.

Outside beds for bulb storage consist of nothing more than shallow pits dug in the soil in which the pots or flats are placed.   The variations in temperature in outside storages, the inconvenience during extremely cold weather or the muddy conditions in mild weather, and the difficulty of proper labeling are against the use of outside beds for bulbs, but because no special equipment is needed, they are common.

General storage.   For storage of cut flowers and potted plants that are fully developed in advance of the time they are wanted, some type of structure, either naturally or artificially cooled, is necessary.   Refrigerated storages are ideal, as a uniform temperature may be maintained, but a shed or heavily shaded greenhouse may be used for this purpose.

3

GREENHOUSE HEATING
AND COOLING

Accurate temperature control in the greenhouse is of great importance since the desired, best growth of plants occurs within a limited temperature range. The degree of temperature control must be much more precise than just keeping the plants from freezing or keeping them warm enough. For each kind of plant and the type of growth desired, the best results are obtained only at the proper temperature. Variations in this temperature may result in a complete lack of growth or extremely excessive development.

Plants grown in the greenhouse are classed by the night temperature at which they are grown. The day temperature provided is 5 to 10°F higher than night temperature depending on whether the day is cloudy or bright.   Such crops as carnation and snapdragon are grown at 50°F, and some of the 60°F crops are rose, poinsettia, and *Chrysanthemum*.   Either of these night temperatures is suitable for many of the greenhouse crops, with the notable exception of most of the foliage plant crops, which require a 70°F night temperature.   There are many specific effects of temperature on plant growth; but for a statement on growth in general, plants develop and grow slower in cooler temperatures and more rapidly in higher temperatures.   There are specific variations, too, in the quality of growth, but in general the plants are shorter and heavier at lower temperatures and taller and thinner at higher temperatures.

There is merit in establishing the greenhouse in an area of the country with a suitable outdoor climate so that the least possible adjustment needs to be made in temperature.   Unfortunately, outdoor temperatures vary considerably from one season to the other, and a desirable outdoor temperature for one time may be a definite problem for another season.   Temperatures in Florida from fall to spring may be more suitable than those in northern states, but from spring to fall they are too warm for satisfactory growth of many kinds of plants.   Even in Florida the winter temperatures are lower than desired for good plant growth. On occasion this results in the freezing and loss of some plants, and in less severe weather it results in delays and harmful effects in quality.   In central Florida, foliage stock plants are grown in slat sheds or plastic screen houses, and the plants are propagated in greenhouses which are heated in the winter and may be cooled during the summer.   For years the stock plant sheds were heated only by temporary means to prevent excessive damage from freezing, but after some years of loss, the structures were modified so that they could be covered by plastic film during the winter and heated more effectively.   In fact, many of the growers installed steam heating systems.   These changes in structures and heating systems not only prevented damage from freezing but provided better growing temperatures during the winter so that growers reported from 50 to 100 percent increase in production.

Sensing temperatures.   Thermometers must be located in the greenhouse at plant level and in sufficient numbers so that they reflect accurately the temperature for the entire house.   Placing a single thermometer in a house is not sufficient to determine temperature differentials from end to end or side to side. Thermometers located at eye level are easy to read, but the readings are proper only if the plants are also at that level.   For young plants in ground beds, the thermometer should be placed at the ground level.

Thermometers must be mounted so that the direct rays of the sun do not shine on the bulb.   A suitable method of mounting thermometers is to attach them to a wooden board and orient them so that the thermometer is facing north. The proper location of thermostats which operate the ventilators or steam valves is even more important. For more precise temperature control, aspirated units are used in which a small fan draws a low volume of air through the thermometer or thermostat, providing a more representative sample of the air in the greenhouse.

Thermometers and thermostats sense air temperatures, and within limits it can be assumed that the plant temperatures are approximately the same as the air temperatures. If practical methods of sensing plant temperatures directly were available, they would be preferred. When a variable heat source is used, plant temperatures change more rapidly than air temperatures, and if plant temperatures could be sensed as rapidly as the changes occur, corrective action could be taken faster.

Sources of heat. The primary source of heat in the greenhouse is the sun. Unfortunately it is not available for the entire 24 hours of a day, and even during the daytime the amount of heat transmitted from the sun to the plants in the greenhouse varies tremendously. During the summer days the sun causes too high temperatures in the greenhouse, and various methods are used to reduce the intensity of the rays entering the greenhouse, or cooling systems are used to reduce the temperature. On clear winter days even when the outdoor temperature is low, no supplementary heat may be required, and some ventilating may have to be used to reduce the heat.

Coal, oil, and gas are used as supplementary sources of heat in greenhouses. The choice of fuel in each greenhouse depends on the cost per Btu of heat, the availability of the fuel, transportation costs, equipment costs, possibilities of automation, and labor costs. No single fuel is best for all greenhouses. A careful study must be made at each location to determine which fuel is best suited for that situation. In many localities coal may be the most economical fuel per Btu, but because it is more difficult to handle, more labor may be required. In considering the availability and transportation of a fuel, special scrutiny should be given to the coldest period of the year. In extremely cold weather, shutdown of the heating system for even a short period of time can be disastrous, and any fuel, regardless of its economy, is worthless if it is not available.

Methods of distributing heat. Most commonly the greenhouse heating systems are either steam or hot water. The fuel is burned in a boiler, and the hot water or steam is piped to the greenhouses in mains and heating lines in such a way as to distribute heat evenly throughout the entire area. The cool water and condensate from the heating lines are returned to the boiler for reheating.

3-1. Many greenhouses use gas-fired boilers because they are more easily automated and require less labor.   The units are compact and need no fuel-storage space or handling equipment. Typical boiler rooms: coal-fired, left; gas-fired, right.

Some of the possible advantages of the two systems are:

STEAM	HOT WATER
1. Because of the higher temperature of steam, smaller mains and heating lines can be used	1. The water temperature can be adjusted as needed.
2. Heating lines can be heated or cooled more rapidly.	2. Less water treatment is required as no makeup water is added.
3. Steam can be transported more efficiently over long distances.	3. No traps are needed.
4. Steam will be available for sterilization.	4. The temperature of the heating lines is more uniform.
	5. A licensed engineer may not be required.

Steam has been used primarily in larger ranges, and hot water in the smaller greenhouses, but it is possible to use closed-system hot water at high pressure and high temperature as efficiently as steam in large ranges.

Boilers for the greenhouse heating system. Improvements are made in boilers continuously, and it is best to seek the latest information and expert advice at the time of choosing a boiler. There are many variations, but boilers are made of either steel or cast iron. The steel boilers may be fire tube, in which the heat and flue gases pass through the tubes that are surrounded by water, or water tube, in which the heat and flue gases pass around the tubes that are filled with water. Each type has some advantages depending on the specific situation and how they will be used.

The capacity of a boiler is referred to in terms of horsepower, and 1 boiler horsepower equals a heat output of 33,475 Btu per hour. In order to know what size boiler is needed, the heat requirement of the greenhouse must be determined; it is based primarily on the square foot area of surface of the greenhouse exposed to the outdoors, the desired temperature to be maintained within the greenhouse, and the lowest temperature to be expected outdoors. Without making this calculation it is impossible to know the exact boiler size needed. For general conditions a boiler rated at 200 horsepower should be adequate to maintain a 60°F temperature in a greenhouse covering 50,000 square feet of ground when the temperature outdoors is −10°F. Instead of one boiler of the maximum capacity, two boilers are often used with about that total maximum capacity; thus either boiler can be used separately to heat the entire place in mild weather or the two boilers can be used in conjunction to provide the maximum heat in the coldest periods. A two-boiler installation is an excellent safeguard as even in the most severe weather either boiler could prevent a freeze-up in the event of the failure of operation of one of them.

Operation of the boiler. In order to have good combustion of fuel, the right amount of air must be supplied in the boiler. In some instances the air is furnished together with the fuel, and additional air is provided at the burner. Different methods are employed depending on the fuel and the boiler, but regardless of the method the amount of air must be carefully regulated. There must be a continuous draft that provides the new air supply to support combustion and to remove the smoke and products of combustion from the boiler. Natural draft can be established with a chimney or stack of adequate size and proper construction. The principle involved with the natural draft produced by a stack is that the column of hot air in the stack is lighter than a corresponding column of air outside it, and the hot air rises and is replaced by cool air, thus establishing the draft. In cold weather it takes some time to heat the stack, and this is important as a natural draft system will not operate unless the proper stack temperature is maintained. For good draft a stack temperature of about 500°F is needed. If the stack temperature is lower than that, the draft will not be enough; and at higher stack temperatures heat is wasted.

The stack is an integral part of the heating system, and it must be designed for the specific type of boiler and operating equipment. The advice of a specialist should be sought in erecting a new stack or in connecting a different boiler to an existing stack. The requirements of the stack for a boiler that has a mechanically induced draft are different from those of the stack that produces draft by natural thermal action.

The amount of draft is not only influenced by the diameter and height of the stack but also by the kind of flues and the material from which the stack is constructed. For natural thermal action a brick or concrete stack holds heat better than a metal stack, and this is an advantage at times when the boiler is not being operated continuously.

The greenhouse stack frequently is a landmark in the community, and in trying to find the location of a greenhouse in a strange place, it is often possible to sight the stack from a distance.

In addition to the natural draft furnished by means of a stack, many boilers use forced draft which consists of a fan that increases the air supply directly to the fuel.

In some boilers the induced draft system is used which consists of a fan placed on the stack side of the boiler. The size, arrangement, and temperature of the stack are of less concern with induced draft than with natural draft, as the draft is directly related to the mechanical efficiency of the fan located between boiler and stack. Since more positive draft control is possible with the induction system, and since a tall, costly stack does not have to be provided and maintained, there is increased use of the induced draft system. It should be acknowledged that the induced draft is entirely dependent on electrical power, and if there is a power failure, the boiler does not operate. Since most boilers are dependent on other electrical controls, this just emphasizes the need for an adequate, emergency, standby power generator in the greenhouse boiler room.

The water that is used in the boiler must have the right properties, and it is best to seek advice from boiler water specialists about the treatment that the water may need. If the water is not right, it may cause undue scaling in the boiler or deterioration of the mains and the heating lines.

Operation of the boiler varies all the way from completely manual operation to highly sophisticated systems that are entirely automated. The choice of the method of operation of the boiler is based on the efficiency and the costs involved.

Emergency, standby power.   Several essential operations in the greenhouse are dependent on electrical power; and since power failures are possible, it is necessary to provide an emergency, standby power unit of sufficient size to handle these operations. The need for a continuous power supply is often associated only with the winter season as most boilers operate with electrical controls. An interruption in power for a few hours during cold weather can cause loss of all the stock by freezing. However, continuous power may also be essential at other times of the year, as ventilation may be dependent on exhaust fans, water may be available only from pumps operated by electric motors, and electric power may be needed for refrigeration. An emergency power unit must be large enough for all the essential operations, and in figuring the power needs, it must be remembered that more power is required to start motors than is needed to keep them operating. When there is a power failure, motors will have to be started; and the emergency power supply will have to be great enough to handle this peak load.

After an emergency power unit is obtained, a routine must be established to assure its readiness for operation in any situation. In most areas power failures seldom occur, and therefore if the generator were operated only during an emergency, there would probably be a long delay in getting the unit started. Hence it is wise to develop a routine for starting and operating the emergency power unit regularly every week in order to be sure that the equipment operates satisfactorily.

Figuring the heat requirement of the greenhouse. The direction of movement of heat is from high temperature to low temperature, and the greater the temperature differential, the faster the heat movement or heat loss. During the heating season the direction of heat movement or loss is from the interior of the greenhouse through the roof and walls to the cooler air outdoors. The warmer the indoors temperature and the colder the outdoors temperature, the greater the transfer of heat will be—and the greater the heat requirement will be for the greenhouse. To determine the heat loss, it is necessary to know the total square foot surface area exposed to the two different temperatures, the rate or coefficient of heat transfer through the material of which the exposed area is made, and the temperature differential between indoors and outdoors.

Since the exposed area of greenhouses is almost entirely glass, it is best to begin calculations by converting concrete, wood, or transite wall areas to the equivalent amount of glass area. The transmission of heat through those materials is considered to be one-half that of glass. If the length of the roof bars is known, the area of the roof is readily calculated. If the roof bar length is unknown and cannot be measured easily, it can be computed readily. The standard pitch of a greenhouse is 26½°, which is 6 inches rise for every 12 inches in width across the greenhouse. With such a pitch the height of the ridge above the eave or gutter will be one-fourth the width of the greenhouse. The ridge of a greenhouse 36 feet wide with a standard roof pitch will be 9 feet above the eave. By calculation of right triangles, the roof bar length is determined to be just over 20 feet, as the length of the roof bar is equal to the square root of the sum of the squares of one-half the width of the greenhouse (18 feet) and the height of the ridge above the eave or gutter (9 feet).

Table 3-1.   *Equivalent Distances over the Roof for Greenhouses of Various Widths*

(Based on a standard pitch of 26½°, which is a rise of 6 inches for every 12 inches across the width of the house)

TYPICAL GREENHOUSE WIDTHS	DISTANCE OVER ROOF, EAVE TO EAVE
18 ft 0 in.	20 ft 0 in.
21 ft 6 in.	23 ft 11 in.
24 ft 11 in.	27 ft 9 in.
28 ft 5 in.	31 ft 7½ in.
31 ft 10 in.	35 ft 6 in.
35 ft 4 in.	39 ft 4 in.
42 ft 3 in.	47 ft 1 in.
49 ft 2 in.	54 ft 6 in.

If it is desired to find the heat requirement of a greenhouse that covers a 40- by 200-foot ground area, is of standard pitch, and has 7-foot sidewalls consisting of 3 feet of concrete and 4 feet of glass, the size of the various exposed areas must be calculated and totaled. To find the area of the roof, the distance from eave to ridge to eave is multiplied by the length of the house. In many instances the length of the roof bar is known, and the roof area is then calculated by multiplying the length of the bar by 2 and then by the length of the greenhouse. If the length of the roof bar is not known, it is computed as described above. Since our example has a standard pitch roof, the height of the ridge above the eave is 10 feet (40 times ¼), and the length of the roof bar is equal to the square root of the sum of 100 (the square of the height of the ridge above the eave) and 400 (the square of one-half the width of the greenhouse). The length of the roof bar is approximately 22.4 feet (the square root of 500).

> 8,960 square feet area of roof (2 times 22.4 times 200)
> 1,600 square feet area of glass sidewalls (2 times 4 times 200)
>   600 square feet glass equivalent area of concrete sidewalls (½ times 2 times 3 times 200)
>   720 square feet area of glass gable end (2 times 4 times 40 plus ½ times 2 times 10 times 40)
>   120 square feet glass equivalent area of concrete end walls (½ times 2 times 3 times 40)
> 12,000 square feet total glass or glass equivalent exposed area

Although this 40- by 200-foot greenhouse covers 8,000 square feet of ground area, it can be seen that the total glass and glass equivalent area exposed is considerably greater—in this instance 1½ times as much.

Any surface of the greenhouse that is attached to another structure which is operated at the same temperature is not included in computing the exposed area because of an equal exchange of heat. If one end of the greenhouse is attached to a headhouse or one sidewall is attached to an adjoining greenhouse, these areas are not included in the exposed area totals.

The rate of transmission of heat through glass varies with the temperature, but the heat transmission coefficient commonly used is 1.13, which indicates the transmission by glass of 1.13 Btu of heat per square foot per hour per 1°F temperature differential from one side of the glass to the other.

The total heat loss by transmission through the exposed surfaces of the 40- by 200-foot greenhouse if it is going to be maintained at 60°F at −10°F outdoors would be 949,200 Btu per hour (12,000 times 1.13 times 70).

In addition to the transfer of heat from the inner surface of the exposed area to the outer surface, there is some heat loss in the greenhouse due to infiltration caused by the movement of heated air through openings, ventilators, glass laps, and doorways. Heat loss due to infiltration varies considerably with the structure and the wind velocity, and at best only an estimate is possible. During periods of high winds there is considerable leakage of air—and heat—through the glass laps, but fortunately during extremely cold weather the glass laps are often sealed closed by frost. During cold, windy weather the greenhouse operator can hasten the sealing of the laps with frost by spraying water on the heating lines in the house.

If the greenhouse structure is in poor condition or if high winds are common in the area, some allowance should be made for heat lost by infiltration; however, in most greenhouses the heat lost by infiltration is not of great enough significance to be included in the calculation of the heat requirements.

Methods of distributing heat in the greenhouse. The heat must be transported from the boiler to the various greenhouses and then distributed throughout the greenhouses evenly. The steam or hot water from the boiler is piped to the greenhouses in large pipes called mains, and the cool water is returned to the boiler in large pipes called returns, or return mains. Since steam or hot water is lighter than cool water, it is possible to get adequate flow in mains and returns if the boiler is at a lower level than the greenhouses. The light steam or hot water rises up to the greenhouses in overhead mains, and the cool water will flow back to the boiler in returns located at ground or just below ground level. Such a system operates because of the difference of weight between hot and cool water or the effect of gravity on less dense (steam or hot water) and denser materials (cool water). These systems are commonly called "gravity systems."

Mechanical devices—circulators or pumps—can be used to distribute steam or hot water through the mains, heating lines, and returns, and their use is increasing. This provides a more positive method of control over the movement

Table 3-2.   *Main Sizes* °

HOT WATER		STEAM †	
CAPACITY IN LINEAR FEET OF 2-IN. PIPE	APPROXIMATE MAIN SIZE, IN.	CAPACITY IN LINEAR FEET OF 1¼-IN. PIPE	APPROXIMATE MAIN SIZE, IN.
65	¾	115	¾
100	1	200	1
175	1¼	375	1¼
300	1½	575	1½
600	2	1,150	2
1,100	2½	2,200	2½
1,600	3	3,450	3
2,100	3½	5,450	3½
2,900	4	7,500	4
4,800	5	12,200	5
6,400	6	17,800	6
12,800	8	29,300	8
19,200	10	43,700	10

° This table shows the approximate linear feet of steam or hot water heating pipe which mains will supply.   The main sizes shown in this table are approximate.   Capacities are dependent on many factors, such as length of main, number of fittings, depth of cellar, elevations of greenhouses, and other factors.   The exact size should be determined by an experienced heating engineer.

† These steam main sizes are for use where the condensation returns to the boiler by gravity.   If the condensation is pumped back to the boiler, the main capacities (linear feet of 1¼-inch pipe) in the table should be multiplied by 2.

of heat and eliminates the need for a cellar or basement.   In addition, the heating system operates more efficiently.   In a steam heating system the returns are pitched toward a receiving tank that is located below the greenhouse level, and a pump is used to bring the condensate from the receiving tank to the boiler.

Hot water systems may use either accelerators or circulators.   An accelerator can be used with a gravity system, and it is located in the return main close to the boiler to increase the circulation of the water.   It is a motor-driven impeller that causes increased circulation when in operation and does not impede normal flow created by gravity when the motor is not turned on.

The circulation of water in hot water systems can be handled completely by mechanical means, using circulators.   A single circulator can be used that provides circulation throughout the whole system, or circulators can be provided for individual houses or zones.   When circulators are installed, the boiler may be on the same level as the greenhouse, since the flow of water is entirely independent of gravity.   The water flows when the circulators are operating and does not flow when they are turned off.

Mains may be pitched up or down depending on the situation. However, steam mains must have drip pipe and traps at each low point to pass condensate to the returns, and hot water mains must have air vents installed at the high point in the main to allow the escape of trapped air.

With steam systems the steam is produced at higher pressure in the boiler and is reduced to lower pressure before circulation in the greenhouse. The pressure regulator may be located in the vicinity of the boiler so that the steam is distributed in the mains at low pressure, or pressure-regulating valves may be located at each house so that the steam is transmitted at the higher pressure in the mains. The amount of steam pressure produced depends on the type of boiler equipment and the way in which it is operated. Although terminology varies in different areas, boilers operated at 10 to 15 pounds of pressure per square inch are commonly known as "low-pressure systems," and those operated in excess of 15 psi are called "high-pressure systems." High-pressure boilers may be operated at pressures up to 90 pounds per square inch and more. Regardless of the boiler operating pressure, the steam pressure is usually regulated so that it is distributed in the greenhouse at 1 to 5 pounds per square inch.

The traditional radiators in the greenhouse are lines of black iron pipe that are installed the length of the house and distributed across the house in a way to produce even heat throughout. The heat transfer from black iron pipe is satisfactory, and the cost of material is comparatively low. If heating lines are painted, black paint should be used. Galvanized pipe or pipe painted with aluminum or light colors does not transfer heat as readily as black pipe.

In some instances finned pipe is used for heating lines, and of course the area for the transference of heat to the surrounding air is greatly increased by the addition of fins to pipe. Iron pipe is not used much for fins because it cor-

3-2. Heating lines often are hung on the sides of benches. The heating line on the right is supplied from a header above, and the line on the left enters a steam trap connected to a return main.

rodes readily in the moist greenhouse atmosphere and is difficult to repair. Finned copper or aluminum pipe is used commonly in the greenhouse in unit heaters or in areas where a greater concentration of heat is needed.   Transference of heat from either copper or aluminum is rapid, and there is the added advantage that these metals do not corrode as readily as iron.   There is a possibility of some deterioration of copper or aluminum pipes by electrolysis when they are used in conjunction with iron pipes, but authorities differ in their opinions of the practical significance of the problem.

In steam systems 1¼-inch pipe is used, and in hot water systems 2-inch pipe is used most commonly; however, in high-pressure water systems smaller diameter pipe may be used.   Air and the surrounding objects in the vicinity of the pipes are heated, and convection currents are established, with hot air rising and cool air descending.   The air circulation that results from the hot pipelines in the greenhouse serves the double purpose of distributing heat throughout the greenhouse and giving air motion.   Unless fans are used to move the air mechanically, air movement in the greenhouse is entirely dependent on the establishment of a temperature differential with the resulting convection currents. Air movement not only helps distribute heat evenly, but continuous air circulation assures uniformity of relative humidity and carbon dioxide throughout the air mass in the house.

Heat is lost in the greenhouse primarily through the surface areas of the house that are exposed to the outdoors, and the largest area is the roof, about three-fourths of the entire exposed surface in the greenhouse.   Since hot air rises, the temperature differential at the roof will normally be greater than it is at the walls; and the rate of heat transfer will be faster than through the walls. The air that is cooled at the roof surface does not descend directly to the base of the greenhouse but flows along the inner surface of the roof.   Because of the location of the cool air return along the inner surface of the greenhouse roof, it is essential to have heating lines located on the sidewalls to heat this descending, cool air before it reaches the plants and soil.   The heat supplied by these lines is often referred to as "perimeter heat."   Regardless of how the other heating lines in the house are located and operated, the side lines should be used whenever heat is introduced into the house.   Within limits, the greater the proportion of sidewall heating lines to the total number, the better.   Because of physical limitations, however, it may not be possible to place more than about one-fourth of the total heat requirement at the sidewalls, which should be sufficient.

The location of heating lines at the sidewalls is indispensable, but the balance of the heat requirement can be located in several different ways and still produce even heating.   Heating lines may be located under the benches, at the sides of the benches, or above the benches; or unit heaters may be used above the benches.   If handled properly, equally good results can be obtained with any of these methods.   There is more interest in overhead installations, however, as they are put in more easily and do not deteriorate as rapidly. There is some objection to the possible shade caused by overhead lines or heating units. The shade is not significant with steam heating lines or unit heaters as they do not cast that much shade, but if the heating system is hot water with 2-inch lines, it is virtually impossible to install the pipes overhead because of extreme shade.

At a steam pressure of 1 psi, 1¼-inch black iron pipe will give off heat at the rate of about 180 Btu per hour per linear foot of pipe in a 60°F house, and 2-inch hot water pipe will transfer 160 Btu per hour per linear foot of black iron pipe when the water temperature is 180°F. The heat output of unit heaters is listed by the manufacturers.

To satisfy the heat requirement of 949,200 Btu per hour for the 40- by 200-foot house discussed earlier, approximately 250,000 Btu should be furnished in sidelines. If three 1¼-inch lines with a steam heating system were located at the sides and ends of this greenhouse, there would be a total of 1,440 linear feet of pipe; and these side heating lines would provide approximately 259,200 Btu per hour (1,440 times 180). The balance of the heat to be furnished from heating lines around the benches or overhead would be 690,000 Btu (949,200 minus 259,200), which would necessitate about 3,800 feet of 1¼-inch iron pipe or 19 heating lines the length of the greenhouse. If this were an 8-bench house and heating lines were placed around each bench, there would be 16 heating lines; and the additional heat could be furnished with additional overhead lines or additional sidelines (snow-melting lines at eave or gutter). Depending on how the piping is arranged, some additional heat may be expected from mains and headers.

If the heat in addition to the sidelines were going to be furnished overhead, nineteen 1¼-inch heating lines could be provided above the benches; or the overhead heat could be furnished by seven unit heaters that are rated at 100,000 Btu per hour per unit. The unit heaters would be installed about 15 feet from each end of the 200-foot greenhouse and then spaced equally about 30 feet apart the length of the greenhouse.

If the 40- by 200-foot greenhouse is to be heated with hot water at a temperature of 180°F, four 2-inch heating lines on each side and the ends would provide 307,200 Btu per hour (1,920 times 160); and the balance of the heat would need to be furnished from heating lines on the benches, from overhead units, or from a combination of the two. Placing 2-inch lines around each bench would provide an additional 512,000 Btu per hour (3,200 times 160), and the balance of 130,000 Btu could be furnished from four overhead heating lines or two additional heating lines on each side of the house.

Some 2-inch hot water heating lines can possibly be installed overhead, but to place all but the side heating lines overhead would cause a shade problem. It would be possible, however, to provide overhead heat with hot water unit heaters. In order to supply the additional 642,000 Btu per hour needed

(949,200 minus 307,200), 10 unit heaters of 70,000 Btu capacity could be installed at about 20-foot intervals the length of the 200-foot greenhouse.

Arrangement and placement of heating lines.   The heating lines must be supported sufficiently so that there are no sags, but because pipe expands and contracts with changes in heat, the pipe hangers must allow for free movement of the pipe.   The side heating lines are suspended from the side walls one pipe above the other, and the bench heating lines are hung from the sides or underneath the bench.   Overhead heating lines are hung from the trusses or from purlin posts.   If unit heaters are used, they are suspended from the trusses.   Heating lines are more efficient if air can circulate freely around them, and for this reason the pipe should be hung so that it is not directly in contact with the bench, the wall, or the ground.

The heating lines must be arranged so that uniform and sufficient heat is furnished by using only a few lines during mild weather and most of the heating lines in cold weather.   If too many heating lines are used for the existing outdoor temperature, the steam or hot water may not flow the entire length of the house before the thermostat causes the supply to be shut off.   This produces a very unsatisfactory temperature differential lengthwise in the house.   If several heating lines are positioned on the sidewalls or overhead, it is best to use a continuous (trombone) coil that will produce a single pipe of heat the length of the greenhouse when steam or hot water is available for a short period of time, and heat in several pipes the length of the greenhouse if the steam or hot water remains on.   If the same number of pipe lines is supplied from a common header (box coil), the steam or hot water will enter all the heating lines at the same time, but in mild weather the lines will not become heated for the full length of the greenhouse.

3-3. Heating lines are hung by various means, but the hanger must allow for freedom of movement of the pipe as it expands and contracts with change in temperature.

For the most efficiency, steam lines must be trapped.   A steam trap does just what its name implies—it traps the steam in the heating lines, but it allows water to pass on to the returns.   The two types of traps that are used are thermostatic and bucket.   In a thermostatic trap the bimetal element is affected by temperature; it opens the outlet when water (from condensed steam) is in the trap and closes the outlet when the higher temperature steam enters the trap. The bucket trap has an inverted float bucket that opens or closes the outlet. When water enters the trap, the bucket sinks, the outlet is opened, and the water passes to the return pipe, but when steam enters, the bucket floats and the outlet stays closed.   Steam traps should have screens on the inlet side to prevent the entry of dirt or scale that would interfere with the operation of the trap.

Traps that malfunction and do not allow the passage of water to the return main cause water to be backed up in the heating line, and the line remains cool.   Traps that pass steam as well as water can be identified by the hot return in the vicinity of the errant trap.

Each coil of steam heating lines in the greenhouse should be provided with a trap that is large enough to take care of the water produced in the coil, Approximately 1 pound of water is produced per 1,000 Btu of heat per hour. A 1¼-inch steam pipe 200 feet long would require a trap that would handle at least 36 pounds of water an hour (200 times 180 times 0.001).   The capacity of steam traps is rated by the manufacturer, and the size of trap that will be large enough for the amount of water produced in the coil should be chosen.

The control of the heating lines can be manual or by thermostat.   With manual control of the heating lines, hand valves are used for regulation.   By checking the thermometer regularly and activating heating lines as needed by

3-4. Water can be returned to the boiler room by gravity if the boiler is lower than the return lines, or the return lines can be pitched to a tank as illustrated and from there pumped to the boiler room. With such a system the boiler may be on the same grade as the greenhouses.

opening valves, the greenhouse can be kept within the proper temperature range. A manual system of operation does require the presence of some dedicated workers day and night—workdays and holidays—to open or close valves as needed.

The steam heating lines in many greenhouses are either fully or partially controlled by thermostats and power-operated valves, which may be operated by electric motors, compressed air (pneumatic), or electric solenoid, or may be self-contained. The electric motor and the pneumatic valves are used more often than the other types of valves, and they are available as either two-position (open or closed) or modulating types. The modulating-type valve opens and closes gradually as it is activated by the thermostat, giving a more even control of temperature.

Temperature control in the greenhouse with a hot-water heating system is attained by regulating the temperature of the water and by the use of electric, motor-driven water circulators. In mild weather, water temperatures of approximately 145°F may be used, and in cold weather the water temperature may be increased to 180°F in an open system or higher temperatures in a closed system. The water circulators are activated by thermostats, and when heat is required in a given area, the circulator pumps the hot water through the pipes in that area.

The control of the heating system must be carefully coordinated. The boiler must be operated so that there is a sufficient supply of steam or hot water when needed but no great excess at any time. This is a problem when the weather changes rapidly or the sun varies in intensity on partly cloudy days.

3-5. Better control of hot-water heating is provided with circulators in the various areas to be heated. (*Lord & Burnham drawing.*)

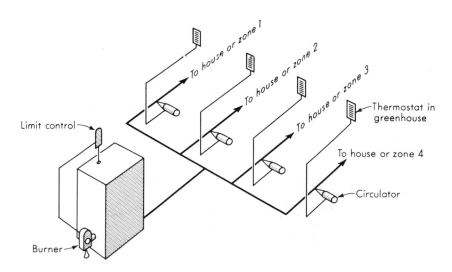

3-6. Various types of unit heaters are available. These are gas units with horizontal air movement and vented to the exterior. The quonset-type house is covered with polyethylene film. (*Lord & Burnham photograph.*)

The demand for heat must be anticipated far enough in advance so that the boiler is prepared to furnish the quantity of heat that is needed at the right time.

Temperature control in the greenhouse during the heating season is provided by good coordination and regulation of heating lines and ventilation. Whether the operation of the heating lines and ventilators is manual or automated, it must be carefully supervised to produce the proper temperature range and even heating.   No matter what controls are used, they must operate equally effectively during the night, day, holidays, weekends, and workdays.

Special heat requirements.   Higher temperatures are used for the propagation of plants. Propagation benches for rooting cuttings and grafting benches or cases are maintained about 10°F warmer than the temperature used for growing the crop.   Seed flats also are kept in warmer temperatures for the best germination of seed.   In spite of the relatively small area concerned with propagation, there is a large number of plants involved; and the temperature requirements are critical.

The propagation areas may be in shaded locations so that they do not receive direct light or heat from the sun. Flower production areas are always in full sun, and if the heating system is operated solely for them, some provision must be made for furnishing heat solely to the propagation area on sunny days.

Some plants are propagated at the time of year when the heating system is not normally used for the production areas. The heating system must then be put in operation just for the propagation area or an alternate heating system must be used. Thermostatically controlled electric soil-heating cable is an excellent means of furnishing the uniform, warm temperatures needed in propagation areas.

With some crops, temperatures need to be varied at certain stages of growth to produce the desired kind or amount of growth. The size of structure and the control of the heating system that will provide the conditions needed for the specific crop are required. There is an advantage in having "crop-size" houses so that the temperature can be controlled as needed for the crop without affecting a crop at another stage of growth. In the early stages the quality and rate of growth of snapdragons are better at 60°F than at 50°F, but it is not possible to provide these different temperatures if young plants and flowering plants are grown in the same structure. In many instances there is an advantage in growing Chrysanthemums at a warmer temperature during the early stages of growth than at the time of flowering, and the timing of holiday production of cut flowers and pot plants is adjusted by the regulation of temperature. This is possible only if the supply of heat can be controlled as needed for the crop.

The problem of proper temperature is not just a matter of producing more or less growth, but also of producing the kind of growth desired. With many varieties of *Chrysanthemum*, flower buds form and develop properly only within a limited temperature range, and the azalea forms flower buds in warm temperatures but develops or matures them in cooler temperatures. There are many other examples of the effect of temperature on flowering.

Because several disease organisms may grow and thrive in the same temperature and moisture conditions that are furnished for the greenhouse crop plants, it is essential that they be eliminated from the surroundings. Steaming soil, tools, benches, and surroundings is the best method of eliminating disease organisms, and it also controls soil pests and the growth of weeds in the soil. A source of steam is needed the year-round for this purpose; if the steam boiler cannot be used, a steam generator should be provided just for this purpose.

Providing steam for sterilization of soil and equipment. Steaming soil is the best method of controlling disease organisms, pests, and weeds. In addition it gives many soils a better structure which promotes better soil drainage and improved root growth. For proper steaming of soil all portions of it must be heated to 180°F and maintained at that temperature for a minimum time of 30 minutes. This will require about 3,500 Btu of heat per hour (about 3.6 pounds of steam) per cubic foot of soil, or, in a bench, per 2 square feet of soil. Since there is approximately a 50 percent loss of heat between the boiler and the soil to be sterilized, twice the amount of heat must be generated at the boiler as will be used efficiently in heating the soil: 7,000 Btu or about 7 pounds of steam per hour. A boiler rated at 200 horsepower would produce about 6,695,000 Btu or 6,900 pounds of steam per hour, which would be capable of steaming approximately 36 cubic yards of soil or 2,000 square feet of 6-inch-deep bench soil (three benches 3½ by 200 feet).

If steam is not available from the heating system, a steam boiler or generator should be obtained just for the purpose of providing steam for sterilization. Such a boiler would be smaller than those used for heating systems, but a 40-horsepower unit would furnish enough steam for sterilizing a single bench 3½ by 100 feet. Portable steam generators, or oil-fired units on wheels, are available also. There may be an advantage in being able to move them to the vicinity in which they are needed, but because of their small size they can sterilize only about a 50-foot bench at a time.

Either low-pressure or high-pressure steam can be used for soil sterilization because, regardless of the pressure at which the steam is piped to the bench, the pressure drops immediately when the steam is released into the soil. The only advantage in using high-pressure steam is that smaller pipe for the same quantity of heat can be used in transporting the steam from the boiler to the bench. High-pressure steam generators for industrial cleaning are usually not satisfactory as a source of steam because they produce only a low volume of steam despite the high pressure.

Reducing temperatures in the greenhouse. As noted earlier, plants produce the best growth within a fairly narrow temperature range. Heating systems are used to increase the temperature during cool weather, and cooling systems may be used during the time of the year when the temperatures are too high. Since heat is removed from the surroundings as water changes from the liquid to the vapor state (evaporates), it is possible to cool greenhouse air and plants by introducing some water into the greenhouse atmosphere. The amount of heat removal (cooling) that is possible depends on the temperature of the air indoors and outdoors and the relative humidity of the air. Maximum cooling is possible when the relative humidity of the air is low and the temperatures are not extremely high. In most areas it is found that greenhouse air temperatures can be reduced about 10 to 20°F, which is sufficient to allow a definite improvement in plant growth. Greenhouse air temperatures often are 100°F and may reach a maximum of around 110°F during the heat of the summer. Since the growth of many types of plants is adversely affected at temperatures above 90°F, the temperature reduction that is possible with cooling systems is sufficient to bring the greenhouse temperatures within a suitable range.

Moist pad, mist, or combinations of the two are used for cooling greenhouses. With the moist pad system (fan and pad), exhaust fans are placed in one wall of the greenhouse, and the moist pad in the opposite wall. All other air entries are closed during the operation of the fan and pad system, and as the exhaust fans evacuate some of the air from the greenhouse, air from the outdoors enters through the moistened pad. As the air passes through the moistened pad, some of the water changes from the liquid state to the vapor state, removing heat from the air. Then as the cooled air passes across the greenhouse, heat is transferred to it from the warm plants and the surrounding air.

If mist systems are used for cooling, the mist must be very fine—much like fog—so that it readily changes from the liquid state to the vapor state. Mist that is too coarse will fall out as moisture on the plants and surroundings. To supply fine mist, water at high pressure is ejected through nozzles that are spaced equally throughout the greenhouse. Maximum ventilation should be used with the high-pressure mist system, and the system is even more efficient if air-circulation fans are provided in the greenhouse for continuous air movement. In some instances high-pressure mist is used in conjunction with exhaust fans; in this case, mist nozzles are placed at the opposite sidewall from the fans as well as throughout the house.

Regardless of which cooling system is used, the same degree of cooling can be realized with fan and pad or high-pressure mist systems if they are properly installed. The high-pressure mist system, in addition to being used as a cooling system during the summer, can be used at any time of the year to increase the relative humidity in the greenhouse.

Design of the fan and pad cooling system. When possible, it is best to locate the exhaust fans in one wall with the moist pad in the opposite wall, and the pad should be on the windward side. With separate houses the airflow is established lengthwise if possible, as this can be done more efficiently than across the rather short width of the house. With ridge and furrow ranges the airflow may be either lengthwise or across the houses depending on how they are situated, but there is an advantage in moving the air across the houses, as the gutters between the houses then function as baffles to keep the airflow at the plant level. In making the decision on the direction of airflow through the greenhouse, it is also necessary to consider whether the necessary size and number of fans can be located in the wall and whether the opposite wall will accommodate the required size of pad. It is not possible to plan to move air farther than about 225 feet, as the pad required for such a distance would be too large for the opposite wall. A distance of 150 feet is considered the maximum for greatest efficiency in

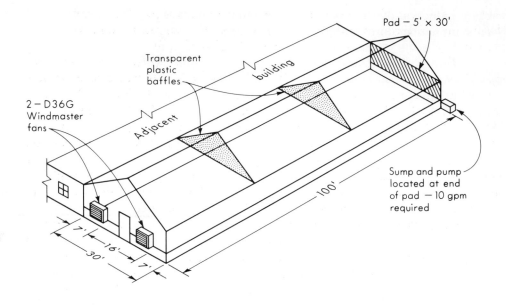

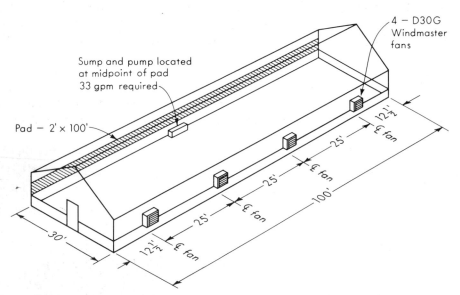

3-7.   Two kinds of fan and pad cooling systems for a 30- by 100-foot greenhouse.   (*Acme Engineering and Manufacturing Corp. drawing.*)

cooling. Because of the many different greenhouse designs, the installation of the fan and pad systems has to be adjusted for the particular situation, and in some instances fans are mounted in the roof instead of in the wall.

The rate of airflow should be from 7 to 10 cubic feet per minute per square foot of ground covered by the greenhouse. The higher rate of airflow is used in situations in which the distance from pad to fan is short, and in areas of the country in which the humidity is comparatively high. For a greenhouse 40 by 200 feet, the air would have to move at the rate of 56,000 (8,000 times 7) to 80,000 cubic feet per minute (8,000 times 10), depending on the circumstances. Since approximately 1 square foot of moist pad is required per 150 cubic feet of air moved per minute, from 373 square feet to 533 square feet of pad would be needed. This need could be satisfied by a pad about 10 feet high in one end wall or by a pad about 3 feet high the length of one sidewall.

For a 40- by 200-foot house without other obstructions around it, a 10-foot pad would be provided in the windward end wall; in the other end wall would be four exhaust fans with a capacity of about 15,000 cubic feet per minute each. If it were necessary to establish air movement across this house, a pad about 3 feet wide could be installed the length of the windward sidewall; and eight exhaust fans with a capacity of about 10,000 cubic feet per minute each would be located in the opposite sidewall. A pad only 3 feet high would provide a narrow stratum or band of cool air, and the crops could grow above it. Hence the pad height should be greater than the minimum for a larger area of cooled air in the greenhouse.

Since the air enters the greenhouse through the pad, there is some resistance. Fans should therefore be selected according to their rating at 0.1-inch static pressure. The fans are mounted in boxes that are provided with automatic shutters that open when the fan operates but remain closed during nonoperation

3-8. Exhaust fans for a fan and pad cooling system. Note the ridge ventilators are closed during the operation of this system. (*Acme Engineering and Manufacturing Corp. photograph.*)

of the fans.   In order to provide uniform air movement throughout the green-house, the exhaust fans should be spaced no further apart than about 25 feet. Exhaust fans are available with either 110- or 220-volt motors, and 220-volt motors are generally used if that power is available.

Pads must be uniformly porous enough so that the air will flow through them evenly, and absorbent so that they will retain some water.   Shredded wood serves this purpose well.   It is fashioned into pads about 2 inches thick and in lengths and widths for convenient installation in various situations.

The pad is moistened by water trickled through it from a trough installed above the pad.   The excess water may be wasted or it may be collected in a tank and pumped up to the trough for recirculation through the pad.   A sufficient amount of water must be supplied to keep the pad uniformly moist, at least ⅓ gallon of water per minute per linear foot of pad regardless of the height of the

3-9.   Wet pad for a fan and pad cooling system.   The water returns to the tank at the midpoint and is pumped from there to the trough over the pads.   (*Acme Engineering and Manufacturing Corp. photograph.*)

pad.   Water loss in the pad is approximately 3 percent.   In a system that recirculates the water, the make-up water is added to the tank by a float-operated water valve.   If the water is recirculated through the pad, it is possible to treat the water for improved operation.   Some detergent should be added to the water in the tank to facilitate the wetting of the pad.   Any of several household detergents can be used satisfactorily, and the amount to use depends on the hardness of the water.   Do not use so much that excessive foaming is produced.   For the control of algae growth in the pad, Phygon 50 gives good results if it is added to the pad water at the rate of 1 tablespoon per week per 200 gallons of water.   It is possible that insects and other small pests may be swept through the pad along with the air from outdoors, and every effort should be made to keep the area outside the pads free from pests.   In addition to this control, there is an advantage in using pesticide for thrips in the pad water as they have the ability to soar from considerable distances.   For thrips control use dieldrin 18.5 percent emulsion at the rate of 1 quart per 100 gallons of water in the tank.

The pad deteriorates with use and should be replaced yearly to ensure the best results from the cooling system.   It becomes plugged with dirt, minerals, debris, and algae, causing a reduced airflow.   The wood fibers rot gradually, allowing some sagging and producing holes in the pad that permit the entrance of uncooled air.   Washing the pad from the inside with a forceful stream of water directed through the pad will often dislodge foreign matter and improve the efficiency of the system.

There is a big advantage in having the pads installed in the greenhouse in such a way that they can be placed in or removed from operation on very short notice, to provide for the use of the cooling system at will during the unpredictable temperature fluctuations in the spring and fall.   The best solution seems to be to provide large wall ventilators with the pad located inside the wall.   Then the greenhouse can be opened or closed rapidly by simply opening or closing the ventilators.   If the installation of the pad necessitates the removal of the greenhouse wall, it is almost impossible to guess when the wall should be removed in the spring and when it should be replaced in the fall.

Greenhouse cooling with high-pressure mist.   In order to provide cooling with high-pressure mist, water at 500 to 600 pounds of pressure per square inch is ejected through nozzles spaced uniformly throughout the greenhouse and about 10 feet above the soil in which the plants are growing.   The essential components of the high-pressure mist system are water that is free of sand, silt, and dissolved minerals; a pump capable of delivering water at 500 to 600 pounds of pressure per square inch; a control system to automate the activation of the system as needed; and nozzles that deliver high-pressure water at about 0.6 gallon per minute.

Most water supplies are too hard—contain too much dissolved mineral matter—and can cause clogging of the nozzles and accumulation of undue residue

3-10. Whenever possible the wet pad should be located within the greenhouse so that the house can be opened or closed as the weather demands. This type of sidewall ventilator operating equipment allows the wet pad to be inside the wall.

on the plants in the greenhouse. Such water can be treated by the inexpensive method used in ice plants to produce clear ice. The calcium and magnesium salts that are dissolved in the water are precipitated by adding liquid sodium aluminate and hydrated lime to the water in a tank. The water and additives are thoroughly mixed for about 30 minutes and allowed to settle for about 4 hours; the precipitate has then settled to the bottom and the mineral-free water can be drawn from the top of the tank. Filters are used to remove any undissolved material such as silt in the water supply that might cause clogging or malfunction of valves or nozzles.

In addition to furnishing water at pressure of 500 to 600 psi, the pump must have the capacity to furnish the amount of water needed to supply the total number of nozzles used in the system. Several types of high-pressure pumps are available, and the choice should be based on performance and cost. Maintainance costs are much higher on some types than on others.

The control unit should provide misting for approximately 30 seconds, alternating with a period of no misting for at least 30 seconds, to allow the air moisture to increase gradually. It is convenient to handle the total area to be misted as two units, with mist being furnished alternately to the units at 30-second intervals. A humidistat is used in each area to sense the amount of air moisture and activate the pumping unit on demand.

3-11. The Mann Hi-pressure Mist System provides for air cooling in the summer and for raising the relative humidity at any time.   (*E. G. Hill Co., Inc., photograph.*)

Stainless steel oil-burner-type nozzles are installed directly on copper pipe for the misting lines.   The most adaptable method places the nozzle on a short "rat tail" on the copper pipe, allowing the position of the nozzle to be adjusted to the best direction for uniform coverage of mist in the house.   The nozzles are installed every 5 feet on the copper pipe, and houses up to 20 feet wide can be properly serviced by a single mist line the length of the greenhouse. Two mist lines are used the length of the house in houses 25 to 45 feet in width, three mist lines in houses 45 to 60 feet wide, and four mist lines in houses 60 feet wide.   If the house is between the one- and two-line capacity, two lines are used, but some of the nozzles are replaced with plugs.

The mist lines should be installed approximately 10 feet above the soil in which the plants are growing, and each line should serve an equal area.   As the nozzles need to be cleaned periodically, the lines should be installed in accessible positions and, if possible, over walks.

Continuous air movement increases the efficiency of the high-pressure mist system. Whenever possible both ridge and eave ventilators should be fully open during the operation of the misting system, and it is also helpful to use air-circulation fans as they assure good, continuous air movement at all times independently of outdoor temperature or air movement.

With either cooling system, moisture is added to the air. If conditions are such that this moisture evaporates readily, the temperature of the air in the greenhouse is reduced; and there is no deposition of moisture on the surface of the plants. When too much moisture is introduced into the air or conditions are such that the moisture does not evaporate readily, some moisture will be deposited on the plant surfaces. This may establish a suitable environment for the germination and growth of some disease organisms. Cooling systems must be designed and operated so that excessive moisture is not introduced into the greenhouse atmosphere.

Cool storage. Many greenhouse crops require cool temperatures at some stage of development. Cut flowers should be stored overnight in water in refrigerators maintained at about 45°F or lower. Some cut flowers can be held satisfactorily for several days in storages operated at 33°F, and some rooted and unrooted cuttings can be kept in good condition for several weeks at that temperature. Some bulbs and plants require a period of cool storage in order to flower satisfactorily in the shortest time. And some holiday pot plants can be held in cool storage when they flower before the scheduled time.

Refrigerated storage may not be an absolute necessity at each greenhouse, but there are few greenhouses that could not use it to good advantage if it were available. Reliable companies specializing in refrigerated storages should be consulted in order to obtain the most economical construction and operation. Cooling units that are "frostfree" and without strong drafts are most desirable.

4

FACTORS INFLUENCING PLANT GROWTH

For a clearer understanding of the manner in which plants grow, it is desirable to describe their structure and development together with some of the more important metabolic processes.

The plant. The plants that a florist commonly cultivates are composed of roots, stems, leaves, flowers, fruits, and seeds, but some plants exist that do not possess all these organs. Anyone familiar with plants is aware that there is considerable variability in these organs among different species and varieties. The various organs of a plant consist of well-organized tissues, which in turn are composed of tiny boxlike units called cells.

Cells.   The basic unit of the plant is a many-sided compartment called a cell.   It is within these cells that the metabolic processes take place.   Cells vary considerably in shape, from those which are almost cubical to those which are considerably elongated.   Surrounding the cell is the cell wall.   It is relatively rigid and is composed of pectic compounds and cellulose, which originates by secretion from the rest of the cell.   Cytoplasm, composed of several organic substances such as amino acids, proteins, and other organic compounds made by the plant, are within the cell and line the cell wall.   In the cytoplasm are plastids, small bodies which may contain the green pigment chlorophyll, as well as some of the yellowish pigments found in many plants.   Mitochondria, important in the vital process of respiration, are also in the cytoplasm.   The nucleus, containing the chromosomes that determine the heritable characteristics of the plant, is in the cytoplasm.   Together all these parts are called the protoplasm, which is the part of the cell having the property called life.   The protoplasm is an exceedingly complex system which contains the enzymes that regulate the many diverse processes occurring in plants.

In the center of many cells, surrounded by the differentially permeable layer of the cytoplasm, is the vacuole which contains water, dissolved mineral salts, and other soluble materials, which are referred to collectively as the cell sap.   Certain red pigments (anthocyanins) are found in the vacuole.

Tissues.   The cells are organized into larger units called tissues.   The kinds of processes which occur in various regions of the plant are in part determined by the structural features of the cells in the tissues.

The innermost portion of the stem and some roots contain the pith, which is composed of thin-walled, loosely arranged cells.   Surrounding the pith is the xylem tissue through which water and soluble fertilizer materials move from the roots to the aerial portions of the plant.   The xylem is the "woody" part of a stem and is important in support.   Just external to the xylem is the vascular cambium, which divides to form additional xylem to the inside and phloem to the outside.   Continued division of the vascular cambium results in an increase in diameter of the stem and root.   The phloem is the tissue through which soluble foods, such as carbohydrates and amino acids, and other materials are transported. The pericycle, which usually is the tissue from which new roots originate when a stem or root cutting is made, is located outside the phloem.   Endodermis is found in some stems and roots and, when present, is external to the pericycle.   Surrounding the endodermis is the cortex, which may help to support young stems as well as serving as a food-storage tissue.   In older stems or roots a cork cambium originates in the cortical tissue and by repeated divisions forms corky cells such as the "bark" on rose plants.   In young stems cork is not present, and the external tissue is a single layer of cells named the epidermis, which protects the inner tissues.   The epidermis of petals contains the color pigments which are important for the eye appeal of the various flowers that are produced.

Meristems.   Groups of actively dividing cells are known as meristems, and the principal areas where these are found are the apical tissues at the tips of the root and stem, as well as the vascular cambium, which is a lateral meristem. The increase in length of roots and stems is brought about not only by the greater number of cells resulting from divisions in the apical meristems but also by enlargement of the cells longitudinally.   The various tissues result from the differentiation of the cells formed by the apical meristem.   Secondary xylem and phloem are formed from the vascular cambium.

Surrounding the stem tip are numerous very young leaves which envelop the growing point.   The apical meristem of a stem gives rise to new leaves and buds in the axils of these leaves.   The apical meristem may continue to grow vegetatively, but under certain conditions it will form a flower bud at the tip or in the axils of the leaves.

The root.   The root serves as the principal area for absorption of water and mineral salts and also as an anchor or support for plants.   Water enters the plant through the root hairs and other root surfaces not enveloped in cork. The life of a root hair is relatively short, and new ones develop as the root grows through the soil medium.   Exposure to air or sun, insufficient oxygen, or overabundance of water kills the root hairs and hence checks the growth of the plant. New root development is dependent upon the food supply from the leaves, good aeration of the soil, and adequate moisture; and a continued extension of the root system is vital to the development of a good-quality plant.   As the root system grows, new branch roots arise from the pericycle.   In their early growth these branch or lateral roots rupture the outer surface of the main roots.   These injuries can serve as places of entrance for soil microorganisms that cause certain diseases of florist plants.

The arrangement of the vascular tissue near the root tip is different than in older root tissue.   Instead of a cylinder of vascular tissue with the phloem covering the cambium and xylem, the xylem and phloem are side by side in a ring or circle.   Water enters through the root hairs and diffuses directly into the xylem, the principal water-conducting tissue, since it is not covered in the very young root tissue by the cambium and phloem as it is in older roots.

The stem.   The stem furnishes support for the leaves and flowers, and contains the conducting tissues through which water, mineral salts, foods, hormones, and other materials move through the plant.   These conducting tissues branch within the stem, entering the petioles (leaf stems), leaves, and petals as veins.

Many plant stems will not branch unless the tip is removed (by pinching), and then the axillary buds at the base of the leaves will start development to produce a multistemmed plant.

The vascular system (xylem, cambium, and phloem) exists in a cylindrical form immediately within the outer layer (epidermis) and is continuous from near the root tip to near the stem tip in plants with two seed leaves (dicotyledons). The stem becomes larger in diameter by division of the cambium, laying down secondary xylem and phloem. In monocotyledons, which have one seed leaf, such as the lily, the vascular elements are in scattered bundles. Since there is no vascular cambium, the stem does not continue to increase in diameter.

The leaf. A leaf consists of the petiole (leaf stem), the blade, and stipules, which are small leafy growths at the base of the petiole and are found on relatively few florist crops (one is geraniums). The petiole supports the blade, which is the seat or origin of many of the most important physiological processes that take place in the plant, among them photosynthesis or manufacture of sugars. At the base of the petiole next to the stem is an abscission layer. In the few woody plants that florists grow (Hydrangeas, roses), the abscission layer disintegrates either with leaf age or with change in environment, and the leaf falls because of dissolution of the middle lamella of the abscission cells. Herbaceous plants (poinsettia) also have this abscission layer, and age or an unfavorable environment causes leaf drop. The presence of certain unsaturated hydrocarbon gases (ethylene) often hastens the disintegration of this layer or else causes elongation of cells on the upper side of the petiole, resulting in the leaf's bending downward, a phenomenon called "epinasty."

The leaf blade (Fig. 4-1) has an upper epidermis which may contain varicolored pigments (coleus). Underneath it are palisade cells, so named because of their position in columns or rows. These cells have considerable chlorophyll, and much of the photosynthesis that occurs takes place in the palisade cells. The spongy mesophyll cells under the palisade layer consist of loosely arranged thin-walled cells which also contain some chlorophyll. Carbon dioxide diffuses through this area to the palisade layer. Carbon dioxide enters through the stomates, small porelike openings that are most often found on the lower epidermis of the leaf. The turgidity of two guard cells surrounding the stomate governs the degree of opening of the stomate. Plants whose guard cells are flaccid or wilted carry on reduced photosynthesis or sugar manufacture because the stomates are nearly closed. When hydrated, the stomates are wide open because of the curved nature of the adjacent guard cell walls. Water vapor diffuses from the leaf to the external atmosphere through the stomates.

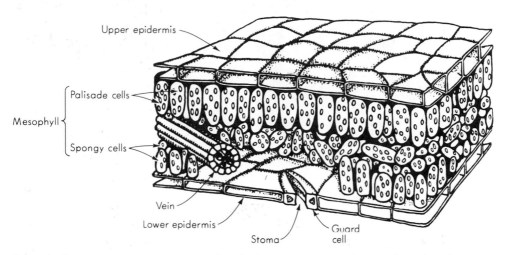

4-1. A diagrammatic representation of a leaf cross section. Note epidermis with stoma, mesophyll with numerous chloroplasts in each cell, and veins with xylem and phloem conducting cells. (*From "The Life of the Green Plant," by Arthur W. Galston, Prentice-Hall, Inc., Englewood Cliffs, N.J.*)

The flower. The sepals, petals, and reproductive parts are called the flower. Sepals cover the petals of the bud; they may be green as with a rose or carnation or colored as with a lily, tulip, or orchid. The petals are the main reason for growing many ornamental plants because their diversity of form and color are attractive and eye-appealing. The petals, collectively called the corolla, generally have the color in the epidermal cells. In some flowers (poinsettia), the petals are inconspicuous, and it is the bracts or colored leaves which are attractive. In the *Hydrangea,* on the other hand, the sepals form the colorful head and the flowers are borne underneath.

The pollen-bearing organs are the stamens, consisting of an anther and the filament which supports it. In the center of the flower is the pistil, and at the top of the pistil are the stigma, which receives the pollen, and the style, the tube that connects the stigma to the ovulary. The ovulary contains the female organs, which are fertilized by the pollen and then form the seed. The nectaries, which are closely associated with the pistil, secrete various aromatic substances that cause flower fragrance. Following fertilization, the flowers may wilt (orchid) or abscise (snapdragon), but the florets of Chrysanthemums remain in good condition for some time. Flowers age and petals fall through the dissolution of the middle lamella of the abscission layer, similarly to the leaves. The flowers remaining on the plant keep better than those cut and placed at room temperature in water, probably because the water-conducting vessels of cut flowers are plugged and the available food supply is depleted.

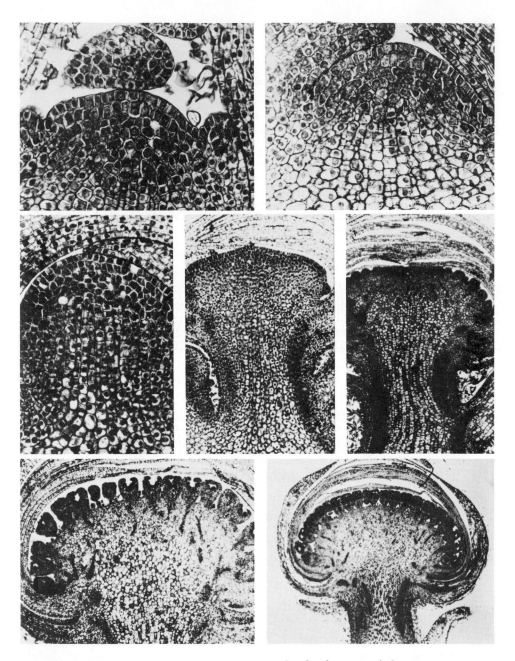

4-2. Photomicrographs showing various stages in the development of the stem tip or apex of the Chrysanthemum Bittersweet following short-day treatment. Left to right: Top, in long days the typically flattened appearance of the vegetative stem apex; after 5 short days it is beginning to become rounded or humped. Middle, after 9 short days there is pronounced elongation of the central cells; after 14 short days the formation of head or capitulum is very evident; after 20 short days flower primordia are evident at outer edges. Bottom, after 26 short days flower primordia are differentiated in central as well as outer areas of head; after 30 short days the flower head is well differentiated.

Flowers form in aerial plant meristems when favorable conditions exist. They may form in either the terminal or lateral buds. Stems form leaves and increase in stem length until the stimulus for flowering occurs, and then flower buds form. In some plants the first flower buds may form in the stem tip (rose, carnation, and azalea), followed by flower bud formation in the lateral meristems in the axils of the bracts or leaves immediately below the tip. This is known as cymose or determinate inflorescence since the growth in stem length terminates with the formation of the terminal flower.

4-3. The parts of a flower. The ovary develops into a fruit when stimulated by fertilization or an auxin spray. Development of an ovule into a seed occurs only after fertilization. In this process, the egg and polar nuclei are both fertilized by sperms produced in the pollen tube to form, ultimately, the embryo and endosperm of the seed. (*From "The Life of the Green Plant."*)

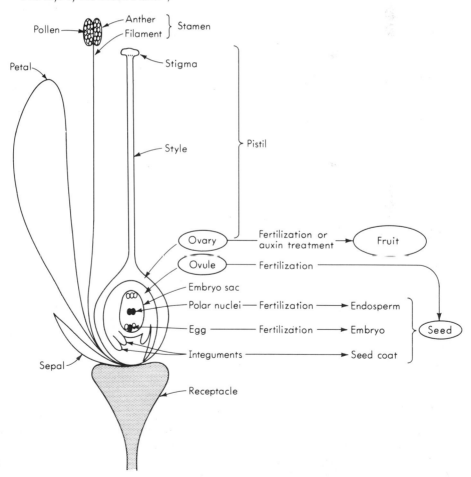

Some plants form flowers only in lateral meristems in the axils of bracts or leaves. This is known as racemose or indeterminate inflorescence because the stem has the potential of continued growth in length. In some such plants, after the flowering stimulus occurs, leaf formation at the stem tip is replaced by bract formation, and flowers form in the axils of the bracts (*Chrysanthemum*, snapdragon, and *Gladiolus*). Although growth from the stem tip continues after lateral flowering starts, it terminates subsequently; the most mature flowers are toward the base and the more recently formed flowers toward the tip. Because the Chrysanthemum stem tip produces very compact growth as the flowers form, the inflorescence is compact and is known as a head. The stem tips of snapdragon and *Gladiolus* continue to elongate as bracts and flowers form resulting in a spike type of inflorescence.

Geraniums, African violets, Petunias, and Begonias form flowers only in lateral meristems in leaf axils. With these plants the stem tip continues to form leaves after the start of lateral flowering, and succeeding flowers are formed in these leaf axils. Growth of the stem tip continues indefinitely.

Flower stems are called peduncles, and the tip where the flower is borne is known as the receptacle. If each flower of the inflorescence is on a stem, the individual stems are known as pedicels. Some flowers (*Chrysanthemum*, snapdragon, *Gladiolus*) are attached directly (sessile) to the peduncle. Various flower inflorescences differ in the length and arrangement of pedicels, resulting in flower clusters which are characteristic of those particular plants.

If the inflorescence consists of more than one flower, each one is properly called a flower, although the individual flowers are commonly called florets. Possibly the most common misunderstanding of flower terminology is with *Chrysanthemum*, which is often considered a solitary flower rather than an inflorescence of flowers (florets). Actually Chrysanthemums have two types of flowers in the inflorescence—disk flowers which may be rather inconspicuous and ray flowers which are commonly referred to as petals.

PLANT GROWTH

The processes taking place in a plant are very complex. The following is a brief account of some of the more important ones that are of concern to the florist.

Absorption. In the absorption of water, the concentration of soluble materials dissolved in the water within the root is usually greater than the concentration in the water outside the root. Thus the water can diffuse into the root —from a region of higher to lower concentration. The diffusion of water into roots through the cytoplasmic membranes is called osmosis. Water may also enter the roots because of reduced water pressure within the plant caused by evaporation of water from the foliage (transpiration).

4-4. Longitudinal section of the apical-stem tip of coleus. The apical meristem appears between the first two, only partly developed leaves. Just below, appearing as shoulders on the sides of the stem, are bases of the second pair of leaves, which are borne opposite to the first pair. Farther below is the third pair of leaves, which have in each of their axils a young lateral bud. Distance from the top of the apical meristem to the base of the section is 0.86 mm. (*Photomicrograph by Tillman Johnson. From "Introduction to Plant Physiology," D. Van Nostrand Company, Inc., New York.*)

Roots that have been injured by too high a concentration of fertilizer or insufficient air may continue to absorb water. The plant will then remain turgid provided there is a low rate of evaporation of water from the leaves. If the rate of evaporation increases, however, because of increased air or leaf temperature, the plant will wilt severely since the rate of absorption cannot keep pace with the rate of evaporation from the foliage.

The mechanism of absorption of minerals cannot be a simple diffusion phenomenon since the concentration within the root is usually greater than in the soil solution. The greatest amount of absorption of fertilizer materials appears to take place in the area of most active cell division. The energy of respiration is apparently used in absorption of minerals.

Oxygen enters the root system as a gas dissolved in the soil solution or directly from the soil atmosphere. The chemical combination of oxygen with certain foods results in a release of energy, which is used in certain metabolic processes. The root systems of plants which are continually overwatered or are in too heavy a soil grow poorly because of limitations of the oxygen supply.

Translocation. The movement of water, soluble organic materials synthesized within the cells, and fertilizer materials from one part of a plant to another is termed translocation. The water and fertilizer materials move from the roots to the top of the plants through the xylem tissue. Fertilizer materials sprayed on the foliage, however, move from the leaves to the stem, and then in either direction in the stem through the phloem tissue. It appears that organic materials move in either direction principally through the phloem.

Transpiration. Transpiration is the loss of water from the plants in vapor form. Most of the transpiration occurs from the leaves by way of the stomates, but about 10 percent is through epidermal cells directly. A waxy layer of cutin on the surface of the epidermis prevents greater loss of water directly through the cell walls.

Light is an important factor governing transpiration in that stomates are generally closed in darkness and the water loss at night is markedly reduced. In the daytime the stomates are open unless there is a water stress causing wilting. When light from the sun or other sources falls on a leaf, the temperature of the tissue is raised. This increases the pressure of the water vapor that is evaporating from the spongy mesophyll layers, and in so doing increases the rate of transpiration. Even though the relative humidity of the atmosphere outside the leaf may be very high or at saturation, transpiration will still occur because the vapor pressure is greater in the leaf than in the air outside the leaf, due to the tissue's being warmer than the air.

Movement of air will dissipate the pocket of high relative humidity that accumulates around a leaf or petal as a result of transpiration, hence increasing the rate of water loss. Normally this is not an important factor to consider in a greenhouse unless an improperly installed form of forced air circulation is used, causing undue air movement in local areas.

Photosynthesis. Photosynthesis is the synthesis or manufacture of sugar in the presence of light. The sugar is made in the chloroplasts from carbon dioxide and water. The characteristic green color of the chloroplasts is from the pigment chlorophyll. Photosynthesis can occur in any living cell containing chlorophyll, but the leaves are the principal organ where the process occurs. Light is the energy source bound in the sugar during the photosynthesis process, and although sunlight is the usual source of energy for plants, visible light from any source may be effective in photosynthesis.

The more important factors influencing the rate of photosynthesis are light, carbon dioxide, water, temperature, and phosphorus. Since the oxygen released in photosynthesis comes only from the water supplied, water is both a raw material and an end product in the process. The chemical equation representing photosynthesis is written as follows:

$$6CO_2 + 12H_2O \xrightarrow[\substack{\text{chlorophyllous} \\ \text{tissue}}]{\text{light energy}} C_6H_{12}O_6 + 6H_2O + 6O_2$$

Carbon Water   Sugar   Water Oxygen
dioxide

It should be realized that this equation in no way indicates the complex nature of the photosynthetic process. The mechanism of photosynthesis is only partially understood. Light is absorbed by the pigment, which then becomes activated. Blue and red light, 420 and 670 millimicrons (Table 4-1) in wavelength, respectively, are most effective in photosynthesis, and green light, 500 to

Table 4-1. *Wavelengths of the Various Components of Solar Radiation*

	Range in angstrom units *	Radiant energy as kind of light or ray
	0.0005	Cosmic
	0.01–1.4	Gamma (uranium, radium)
	10–150	X-ray
	150–3,900	Ultraviolet
Visible Light	3,900–4,300	Violet
	4,300–4,700	Blue
	4,700–5,000	Blue-green
	5,000–5,600	Green
	5,600–6,000	Yellow
	6,000–6,500	Orange
	6,500–7,000	Red
	7,000–7,600	Far-red
	7,600–26,000	Infrared
	26,000–1,000,000	Electric, or radio, waves

* Divide by 10 to convert to millimicrons.

600 millimicrons, is the least effective. The activated pigment reacts with water and organic constituents in such a way that energy is chemically released for the formation of adenosine triphosphate (ATP), which is rich in energy. The energy in ATP supports various chemical reactions; among them is the formation of sugar from carbon dioxide, which can occur in light or darkness. The presence of phosphorus and magnesium is essential since they are the mineral elements that directly influence the photosynthetic process.

Sugar is formed by a series of chemical reactions and may be changed in the leaf to starch, a storage form of carbohydrate, or translocated as sugar through the veins of the phloem tissue which permeate the leaf to other parts of the plant.

Pigment formation. The various pigments found in the flowers as well as the leaves of certain ornamental plants are important to florists because they are the basis for the wide diversity of color found in the many species and varieties of plants.

Chlorophyll, a green pigment, is most important in the photosynthetic process which is basic for all growth. It is found in leaves, stems, and young flower buds, but that in the leaves contributes by far the greatest amount of total photosynthate for plant growth.   There are several kinds of chlorophyll in plants, and all are found in the chloroplasts.   Chlorophyll contains carbon, hydrogen, and oxygen as well as nitrogen and magnesium, the only mineral element constituent.   Deficiencies of mineral elements such as iron, boron, manganese, sulfur, and others, however, inhibit chlorophyll synthesis and cause development of chlorosis, the absence of normal amounts of chlorophyll; the upper leaves then quickly turn yellow.   Affected leaves may never regain their normal green color even when the deficient minerals are supplied and normal growth resumes.

Carotenoids are yellow, orange, red, or brown pigments found in the chloroplasts together with chlorophyll.   They consist of carbon and hydrogen, and some contain oxygen.   Unlike chlorophyll, the carotenoids have no minerals. Carotene, a well-known carotenoid, is an orange-yellow pigment.   Lycopene, a red pigment, is closely related chemically to carotene.   Xanthophylls, which are chemically similar to carotene, are yellow or brown pigments found in the chloroplasts of the leaves or petals.

Anthocyanins are red, blue, or purple pigments found in the vacuole or cell sap.   Formation of these pigments is associated with an accumulation of sugars within the plant tissues, and factors which favor this—low temperature, drought, or low nitrogen—generally result in greater anthocyanin formation. When the pH of the cell sap is acid, anthocyanins are reddish colored; but as the sap becomes less acid, the color changes to violet or blue.

Anthoxanthins are colorless or yellowish and cause the yellow color of aging flowers.   They are found in the cell sap with anthocyanins to which they are closely related chemically.

Amino acid and protein synthesis.   Nitrogen is absorbed by the plant primarily as nitrates, though ammonium can also enter some plants, especially if the soil medium is well aerated.   Most of the nitrate is chemically reduced to amides and amino acids in the roots of many plants, while in others this process takes place in the leaves in the presence of light.   The amides, amino acids, and nitrates are translocated to other parts of the plant primarily in the xylem.   Some amino acids are synthesized in the leaves from inorganic nitrogen and carbohydrates.   These reactions take place slowly at cool temperatures which is one of the reasons for the rather specific night temperatures at which florists grow plants to obtain the desired rate of growth.

Proteins are formed by condensation of numerous amino acids into a chemically complex, long chain molecule through the action of ribose nucleic acid (RNA).   This process occurs in the cytoplasm of all living cells on small bodies known as ribosomes or microsomes.   Amino acids are translocated freely within plants, but proteins are used in the area where they are formed.   New growth of plants can continue only if protein synthesis takes place without interruption or inhibition.

Enzymes.   In every actively metabolizing cell many chemical reactions occur, the direction and speed of which are controlled by enzymes.   Basically all enzymes are protein, and they may cause oxidation, reduction, or digestion depending upon their nature.   They act as catalysts, speeding the rate of a reaction without becoming a part of it.   Certain enzymes contain iron, copper, or zinc as part of the molecule—an illustration of the importance of trace elements for plant growth.

Hormones.   Hormones are growth substances made in minute amounts within the plant in a given area and translocated to another area where a specific effect takes place.   Auxins and gibberellins are the two most important plant hormones.

Auxins are produced in the tips of either stems or roots.   They are translocated from these areas to various portions of the plant where they may influence cell enlargement, formation of roots, and the dominance of certain parts of the plant over others.   Unequal amounts of auxin cause curvature of the tissue, allowing stems to bend toward light (phototropism) or roots to grow downward (geotropism).

Gibberellins also cause striking cell elongation, but gibberellin-caused elongation is always uniformly distributed, as opposed to that caused by auxin. Though all plants have gibberellins, the taller varieties are thought to have more than those that are dwarf or normal in size.   Gibberellin action is thought to be closely related to that of enzymes.

Growth regulators such as Cycocel and B-Nine are synthetic products not found in plants.   A discussion of their use is covered in Chap. 5.

Other metabolites.   In addition to the numerous compounds already mentioned, plants contain many others which are important in growth.

Starch is a storage type of carbohydrate formed in the chloroplasts and found in seeds, bulbs, tubers, etc.   Inulin, another storage product, is present in many members of the daisy family (Compositae).   Pectins are found in cell walls and give strength to the plant by holding the cells together.   Fats and oils are storage forms of food found in every living cell.   Phospholipids are fatty compounds with phosphorus that maintain the stability of the protoplasm.   Cutin, an oxidized fatty acid, covers the external surfaces of the plant and prevents excessive water loss, while suberin is chemically related but is found at the wound or cut surface of a cutting shortly after it is made.   Fragrance may come from essential oils, or terpenes, or from nectar, which is derived from sucrose.

Assimilation.   The dry matter of a plant is composed of various foods with sugar as a basic or raw material.   The process by which all these various foods are utilized in the formation of cell walls and cytoplasm is called assimilation. The cell walls are largely of carbohydrate nature, while cytoplasm is proteinaceous. As a result of assimilation, the plant increases in dry weight as it grows. Plants with greater dry weight are often of better quality or desirability.

Respiration. Respiration is the oxidation of food within a living cell, resulting in release of energy. This energy may be released as heat, which is largely wasted in plants, or as chemical energy, which is important in causing various processes such as cell division, absorption of minerals, movement of foods, and synthesis of amino acids and proteins.

The oxygen-consuming portion of respiration occurs in the mitrochondria of the cells and is a complicated process known as the Krebs cycle. Sugars or other simple foods are oxidized into carbon dioxide and water, and ATP is the "carrier" of the energy that is ultimately used in growth.

Respiration may be aerobic, where atmospheric oxygen is used, or anaerobic, where compounds within the cells are changed and the oxygen supply is from the compounds themselves. Both kinds of respiration are common within plants. Anaerobic conditions immediately external to plant roots are, of course, undesirable and inhibit growth.

Flowering. With the exception of foliage plants, most florist crops are produced for the beauty of their flowers. In some plants the development of flowers can be induced by exposure to the proper day length or photoperiod, and in others temperature is the controlling factor. However, flowers appear on some plants when they attain a given size or age, no matter what photoperiods or temperatures they are exposed to.

Though the mechanism of flowering has been studied, many facets are not well understood. Presumably one or more hormones may be involved, and the name florigen has been used simply for convenience, though such a substance has never been isolated or chemically identified.

Photoperiodism. The term photoperiodism refers to the effect of the daily length of the light period on the growth of plants. The outstanding work of Garner and Allard has formed the basis for regulation of the flowering of several florist crops. They classified plants into three groups: (1) short-day plants, those that flower only in relatively short photoperiods, (2) long-day plants, those that flower only in relatively long photoperiods, and (3) indeterminate, or day-neutral, plants, those that flower over a wide range of day lengths. Since then another group of plants has been added, called the intermediate plants, those that flower only in a specific range of day lengths and are vegetative at shorter or longer light periods.

Most of the original work with photoperiodism was concerned with flowering, but it is known that certain vegetative phases of plant growth are affected. Seed germination, elongation of internodes, enlargement of leaves, and storage organ development, as well as flower bud initiation and the subsequent development of buds, can be governed by photoperiodism. With respect to flowering, a somewhat more detailed classification than that proposed by Garner and Allard is desirable because the effect of photoperiodism on flower bud initiation may be different from the subsequent development of the same buds.

Phytochrome. When "white" light is passed through a prism, it can be separated into its component colors as shown in Table 4-1. Phytochrome, the blue-green pigment which has a controlling effect on the photoperiodic response, is affected by the following two specific wavelengths: (1) Orange-red radiation in the region of 660 millimicrons changes the phytochrome to the far-red absorbing form (Pfr) which promotes germination of light-sensitive seed, promotes internode elongation, reduces leaf enlargement, and inhibits flower bud initiation of short-day plants. (2) Far-red radiation in the region of 735 millimicrons changes the phytochrome to the red absorbing form (Pr) which inhibits germination of light-sensitive seed, reduces internode elongation, and promotes leaf enlargement. It does not as yet promote flower bud initiation on short-day ornamental plants, but it does promote development, and does not as yet prohibit flower bud initiation on long-day ornamental plants. How the phytochrome operates is not understood, but it probably affects enzyme and hormonal systems.

Optimum critical day length. For short-day plants the maximum number of continuous hours of light at a given temperature that will permit the most rapid flower bud initiation is called the optimum critical day length. Any increase in the length of day beyond this critical point will cause a delay in initiation: the longer the illumination, the greater the delay. The reverse is true for long-day plants.

For short-day plants, the optimum critical day length decreases as the temperature is raised. As an example, poinsettias initiate flower buds when the day length is 11 hours and 50 minutes at 60°F, but when the temperature is raised to 65°F, the number of critical hours of daylight is 10, and at 70°F it is only 9. In practical application, it is important to use black cloth shade when poinsettias are grown at 70°F in late September and early October to provide a sufficiently short day for flower buds to form.

Short day versus long night. The term short day was first used by Garner and Allard, and it has continued in use even though the term is no longer thought to be correct. If a short-day plant is grown under a short day, it will flower; but if the long night is interrupted with light and the length of the day is not changed, the plant will not flower. Thus it is the length of night that is important for photoperiodic plants. During a long night an interruption with orange-red radiation changes the phytochrome system from the Pr to the Pfr form which prevents initiation of flower buds. Lighting near the middle of the dark period is safer than either after sunset or before sunrise because the number of hours of continuous darkness will be two shorter periods rather than one longer period. In the latter case, the Pr system could permit flower bud initiation.

Inheritance. In the nucleus of the cell are the chromosomes which are the carriers of the genes, the units which govern the heritable characteristics of plants. Chromosomes consist of a complex chemical called deoxyribose nucleic acid (DNA) in long, spiral strands. Duplication of DNA is thought to be the means by which hereditary characteristics are transmitted as a cell divides, duplicating the chromosomes and producing two cells with exactly the same number of chromosomes as the one which preceded.

In the normal vegetative growth of plants, before the time of cell division, the chromosomes duplicate, and one duplicate moves to each of the opposite poles of the cell. When the middle lamella or primary cell wall forms between the two groups of newly duplicated chromosomes, each new cell has the same number of chromosomes as the parent cell and hence is similar to it. Such cell division is called mitosis, and it takes place in all areas of the plant except the sporogenous tissues (forerunners of the pollen grains and embryo sac). Plants have a specific number of chromosomes, and the cell division described above assures continuation of this specific number.

In the sporogenous tissue, the pollen grains and the embryo sac, only half the normal number of chromosomes are found. This is brought about by reduction division or meiosis. Here the complementary chromosomes pair (in a process called synapsis) rather than duplicate. They then migrate to opposite poles of the cell so that when the primary cell wall forms between them, each of the two new cells has only half the normal number of chromosomes. This is referred to as the haploid number of chromosomes. When two parents are different genetically, the two cells have chromosomes carrying different heritable characteristics, and when the sperm from the pollen grains fertilizes the embryo sac in the ovulary, a new generation begins which is genetically different from either parent.

Different combinations of characteristics may be obtained by crossing plants of the same species but of different varieties. This is one of the ways new varieties are produced. Individual varieties of many florist crops do not breed true when "selfed" (self-pollinated), and they are called heterozygous, which means they have unlike genes. By continued selfing of successive populations, it is possible to obtain "pure lines" which are essentially homozygous with the same genes for a given heritable character. Such inbred lines may not themselves have desirable form or appearance, but when crossed with other pure-line types of the same species they often produce plants of outstanding vigor and floriferousness, a quality which is called hybrid vigor or heterosis. Snapdragons and petunias are hybrids of this nature; pure line A crossed with pure line B gives seed C which when sown is often unlike A or B but is an outstanding type. Selfing plants produced from seed C results in a mixed population including less vigorous forms. Generally the members of the population are inferior because of the difference in the genes originating from the sperm and the embryo sac. Some plants cannot be selfed to procure pure lines because they so degenerate in vigor before the pure line is obtained (usually at least eight selfings) that they die or are otherwise unsuitable. Examples are Chrysanthemums, carnations, and roses; these and many others are composed of numerous types that have freely crossed and whose origins are lost in antiquity.

For a more complete treatment of the mechanism of inheritance, the reader is referred to any one of a number of books on the subject of plant genetics.

Mutations and sports. Not all varieties are produced by the kind of plant breeding briefly described above. Different chromosomal content of plants may occur spontaneously or may be induced chemically or by radiation. This is not infusion of new genes; rather, changes occur because of interference with the normal division of a cell (mitosis). One or more genes may be displaced or relocated or the chromosome content may be doubled (see Polyploidy). Such a cell will be different, and subsequent normal divisions will continue to maintain this difference.

The change in chromosomal content brought about by an aberration as described above, either natural or man-made, is called a mutation. Sometimes this is called a "sport" since it is a change from the normal plant in which it developed. There are countless examples of such mutations: the red rose, Better Times, mutated from a pink variety, Briarcliff; the numerous Indianapolis varieties of Chrysanthemums came from Indianapolis Pink; and the William Sim carnation gave rise to the exceedingly great number of "Sim sports" which are cultivated today.

Mutations probably occur rather commonly in plants, but they must take place at a position in which their effect will be noticed. Flower color is the usual basis in floriculture for determining whether a mutation has occurred. This means the mutation must have been in a cell in the epidermal layer in the meristematic region of the stem tip, resulting in a color change that causes the plastids in the epidermal layer of the petals to be of a different color. If a mutation occurred in a root or internal stem tissue, it would probably never give rise to an observable change.

Flower color is not the only factor that may change by mutation. Keeping quality, stem stiffness, floriferousness, or any other characteristic can be affected if the mutant cell happens to have been in the right position to effect the change.

Chimeras.   When a mutation occurs in a cell, the tissue becomes differ-ent from the cells adjacent to it.   The situation in which two genetically unlike tissues are growing within the same plant is called a chimera.   There are es-sentially three kinds of chimeras—mericlinal, periclinal, and sectorial.

If a cell in the epidermis mutates and gives rise to only a section of the entire epidermal tissue (Fig. 4-5), a mericlinal chimera results.   If the mutant has a different flower color from the original tissue, a change to a triangular or pie-shaped section of the flower results.   If the mutation occurred far enough down the stem so that the axillary, vegetative buds grew from the changed tissue, it is possible to propagate the mutant by vegetative means.   The bud in the mutant tissue can have the epidermal layer consisting entirely of the mutant type; it is a periclinal chimera (Fig. 4-5).

Such a periclinal chimera is not reproduced if the plant is propagated from root cuttings because the new shoot from it arises from internal tissues (pericycle) not affected by the mutation.   The origin of roots on roots, roots on shoots, shoots on shoots, and shoots on roots helps to explain some apparent anomalies such as just described.

Replacement or vegetative (somatic) segregation.   Replacement of tis-sue is not well understood, but it involves the development of mutant tissue into an area where it is normally not found.   This is how a sectorial chimera can develop, and it differs from a periclinal chimera in that it involves a section of the stem and not just the epidermis.   If the mutant tissue in the stem gives rise to a lateral bud, all the new stem tissue, not just the epidermis, consists of the mutant.   This is segregation of cells giving rise to a new type by vegetative means, rather than in the sporogenous tissue through the process of sexual re-production.

4-5. Diagrammatic representation of the development of a peri-clinal chimera on a stem having a mericlinal chimera. Upper series in cross section, and lower in longitudinal section.

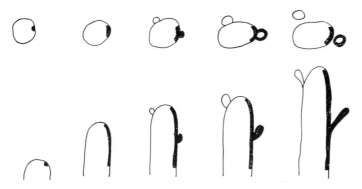

An example of replacement is the red variety of poinsettia, Paul Mikkelsen, which mutated to a colorless sport in the epidermal layer, producing plants with light-pink-colored bracts named Mikkelpink.   Then some of the second layer was replaced with mutated external tissue, resulting in the variety Mikkeldawn—a plant with bracts that are light pink near the midrib and whitish elsewhere. Still further replacement involving three colorless layers resulted in the variety Mikkelwhite, which has white bracts.

Variegated ivy occasionally produces an all-white or albino shoot, in another case of vegetative segregation.   It is believed that vegetative segregation or replacement may be a common occurrence.

Polyploidy.   When the middle lamella does not form during mitosis, the result is a polyploid cell with double the normal number of chromosomes.   This occurs naturally and can also be induced by treatment with the alkaloid, colchicine.   Seeds may be treated by soaking them before germination in concentrations of colchicine varying from 0.05 to 1.5 percent.   A solution of colchicine may also be placed on the tips of actively growing stems.   The solution is prepared by mixing 7.5 milliliters of glycerine (to retard drying) with 2.5 milliliters of water, adding several drops of wetting agent (to facilitate coverage), and finally adding the colchicine powder to make the desired concentration in the range indicated above.   Colchicine can also be dissolved in lanolin (wool fat) and applied to the stem tip, using concentrations of 1.0 percent or more.   Colchicine is a poison and must be washed off the skin immediately.

The usual effect of doubling chromosomes is a larger leaf and/or flower and greater substance, but often there are fewer flowers per plant.   When a normal or diploid (2n) plant is crossed with a tetraploid (4n), the progeny is triploid (3n) and is usually sterile with pollen from itself or from diploid plants. Sterility is often overcome by treating with colchicine to produce a hexaploid (6n).

Polyploidy can occur naturally or as a result of treatment with chemicals or radiation (x-rays or gamma rays).   It is not at all uncommon to find chimeras with 2n or 4n chromosome counts with as many as three different tissue layers or histogens involved.

Selections.   Florists may make selections of varieties in order to maintain vigor, early flowering, or other desirable characteristics.   This means they have been observant enough to see a superior characteristic resulting from mutation or vegetative segregation and have propagated from the improved type.

5

THE CONTROL OF ENVIRONMENTAL FACTORS INFLUENCING PLANT GROWTH

The previous chapter dealt with basic information regarding the development of a plant.   In this chapter the importance of this information in the actual culture of florist crops will be considered.

LIGHT

One of the most important factors influencing the growth of plants is light.   Light may vary in intensity, duration, and quality, and all these various aspects of light influence growth in one way or another.

INTENSITY

Intensity refers to the amount of light which the plants receive. Although there are a number of ways in which light intensity can be measured, the one most used by florists is foot-candles. A foot-candle is the density of light striking the inner surface of a sphere, all surface area being one foot away from a 1 candle-power source. Sometimes light is measured in lumens, and 1 foot-candle equals 1 lumen per square foot. There are various types of small light meters measuring light intensity up to 10,000 foot-candles which may be purchased as an aid in determining the existing light intensity at a given time. Light meters may also be used to measure the reduction of light intensity after application of a roof-shading compound as well as to measure the pentration of light through black shading cloth for photoperiodic control.

On a clear summer day at noon in Ohio the light intensity is approximately 10,000 to 12,000 foot-candles. The intensity varies greatly, however, depending upon the season, clouds, smog, haze, and similar factors. In the winter, for example, there may be only 300 to 500 foot-candles of light during the brightest part of the day.

In certain areas of the home where natural illumination is absent or very low, illumination for plants may be provided by artificial sources. Incandescent lamps generate considerable heat and in many situations are unsatisfactory except when located several feet from the plants. The large proportion of red and far-red radiation may cause excessive elongation of petioles (leaf stems) on some plants, making them unsightly. Fluorescent tubes are useful as the sole source of light for African violets, gloxinias, episcias, and many foliage plants which grow satisfactorily at low light intensities. Such plants grow exceptionally well in basements or other areas where sunlight is low or completely lacking, provided the 300 to 600 foot-candles is maintained for 12 to 18 hours per day. A two-tube industrial lighting fixture equipped with daylight or standard cool white tubes, suspended 12 inches above the plants, provides about 300 foot-candles. For areas where foliage plants are displayed in public buildings and the like, as little as 50 foot-candles from incandescent spotlights is sufficient for fairly satisfactory growth of a number of plants that withstand rather adverse conditions, although more light would be preferable. Newer types of fluorescent lamps with higher total energy (Power Groove) or greater energy in certain wavelengths (Gro-Lux) are useful also.

General effects of light intensity. Increasing light intensity usually results in greater photosynthesis in plants in which considerable mutual shading of leaves occurs. Since many leaves on florist crops are shaded by adjoining foliage because of close planting, as much sunlight as possible should be admitted to permit maximum photosynthesis without damaging the plants from excessive intensities. All other factors being equal, plants subjected to shade from gutters, eaves, adjoining building, and the like do not grow as much in dry weight as plants not shaded. The maximum intensity which can be used varies with the kind of plant (see later discussions of the individual crops). In this connection it should be pointed out that generally as light intensity increases, so does temperature, and this necessitates more frequent watering unless some form of greenhouse cooling is employed.

The applications of fertilizer should be regulated in relation to light intensity because of the effect of light on photosynthesis, which forms the carbohydrate used in the synthesis of amino acids and proteins. In periods of low light intensity, the carbohydrate supply is relatively low, and large amounts or frequent applications of nitrogen generally are wasteful and may even be injurious. However, in bright weather, frequent applications of nitrogen are necessary for the continued optimum rate of formation of the amino acid and protein which will become an integral part of the cells of the newly developing growth.

During periods of low prevailing outdoor temperatures, ventilation may be reduced to conserve fuel and maintain the desired air temperature. In areas where light intensity is high, this can result in a marked reduction in the carbon dioxide level in the greenhouse atmosphere, and additions of this gas may improve growth. Where the light intensity is low during late fall, winter, and early spring, carbon dioxide additions can be beneficial, but the results may not be as striking when compared to areas of better light.

Excessive light intensity destroys chlorophyll even though the synthesis of this green pigment in many plants is dependent upon light. Optimum growth and flowering of the African violet in the greenhouse are obtained when light intensity does not exceed 1,100 foot-candles at the brightest part of the day. At lower intensities the leaves are dark-green, but flowering is reduced. At intensities of 1,500 foot-candles or more, much of the chlorophyll is destroyed and the Saintpaulia leaves are yellow. Leaves on many foliage plants will be burned if exposed to light intensities in excess of 2,000 to 3,000 foot-candles. Flowers of Hydrangeas and geraniums may be burned in spring unless lightly shaded. This is probably due to the effect of light in raising the temperature of the tissues, which causes excessive transpiration, resulting in drying and death of the cells. In the high light intensities of summer, stems on roses and carnations may be shorter than desired. If the light intensity is reduced to some extent, leaves will be quite dark green, the stems somewhat longer, and the leaves thinner.

Bending of stems toward the source of light is commonly observed in many houseplants, and in the greenhouse, particularly in winter, on carnations and lilies. It is believed that light causes an unequal distribution of the growth substance, or hormone, which is essential for cell elongation. The side of the stem in direct light has been found to contain less of this hormone than the side of the stem not exposed to the direct light. Hence the side of the stem toward the light does not grow in length as much as the opposite side, resulting in curvature of the stem.

The formation of flowers in the African violet, cineraria, geranium, and some others is believed to be dependent upon the accumulation of sufficient carbohydrates. As will be pointed out later, light duration and temperature affect flower bud initiation of many florist crops, but development of the flower buds is also dependent on food supply. With African violets flower bud initiation will occur at intensities of 100 to 200 foot-candles, but development of the flower buds does not take place until there are several hundred more foot-candles of light.

In summer a heavy shade on the roof used to lower the temperature reduces the intensity of light to such a low level that development of the plant is retarded. In dark days of winter, growth of many plants is slow, and several days of sunshine will make a considerable difference in their rate of development.

Bright light fades the color of many flowers. This could be caused by partial destruction of the pigment due either to the light or indirectly to the higher temperature.

Reducing light intensity. Since excessive light is undesirable, intensity can be reduced by shading the glass with various materials. Although mud or lime suspensions can be brushed on the greenhouse roof, they are temporary at best, and lime causes the putty to dry out, thus shortening its life. Lime is also destructive to aluminum barcaps. Liquid shading compounds are preferred, and those most commonly used have latex paint as a base. These are sprayed on the roof, and a mixture of 1 part paint to 8 or 10 parts water applied to cover the glass completely will provide a very heavy shade. A 1 to 15 or 1 to 20 dilution is generally more satisfactory for most purposes. The shading compound is most easily removed by wetting it with water containing a detergent, and then brushing to loosen the paint, followed by flushing with clean water to wash off all residue. Where light intensities are very high, as in the South, and where foliage plants are grown, the glass is often painted with a mixture of white lead and gasoline since a relatively permanent shade is desired.

Cloth may be suspended inside the greenhouse to reduce light intensity. Very light weave cotton cloth will reduce the light by 10 to 15 percent, while muslin may reduce the light intensity by one-half. Saran varies in its reduction depending upon the weave, but it is the material most commonly used in the South.

Chrysanthemums grown under cloth structures are taller, with larger leaves and flowers, than similar plants grown in full sun. Furthermore, the tissues are somewhat softer, and, more important, the stem will absorb water more readily. The reduction in light intensity from the cloth (aster cloth, Saran, onion sacking, and others) is the primary cause of the differences in growth.

Greenhouse glass will reduce the light intensity about 8 to 10 percent, and dirty glass, obviously, will cut out considerably more.

Increasing light intensity. In most areas the use of artificial sources of light, substituting for or supplementing sunlight in the greenhouse, has never proved to be an economical or a practical means of increasing growth. A sufficient number of high-energy fluorescent lamps for intense illumination have been installed in greenhouses in Alaska for use during the extremely short days that prevail there in winter, but the economics of this method is somewhat questionable unless electricity is cheap and the price for the product is high. Lights are used in greenhouses generally for the purpose of regulating the flowering of plants, by photoperiod control, and the intensities (5 to 10 footcandles) are too low for any significant photosynthetic activity.

There are two practices which will ensure maximum light in the greenhouse. The first is keeping the glass clean to permit more light to enter, which is particularly important in winter when the intensity is low in many areas of the country. The other is making use of reflected light from sash bars, posts, and other structural members by painting them at regular intervals (every five years). Generally, plant growth is improved because of increased reflected light from the painted surfaces.

DURATION

Duration refers to the length of time the plants are exposed to light, regardless of the intensity.

Photoperiodism. This term refers to the effect of the length of the light (or more correctly, the dark) period on the growth of plants. Perhaps no other environmental factor has so drastically affected the florist business as the discovery that certain plants could be made to flower at any season by means of manipulation of day length together with the proper temperature control. The more important floral crops affected are Chrysanthemums and poinsettias, which are short-day plants. Some others that are subject to photoperiod manipulation are asters, azaleas, Begonias, Gardenias, Kalanchoe, lilies, and orchids. Carnations were long thought to be relatively unaffected by day length but may be cropped more easily under long-day conditions.

The optimum critical day length varies with the different plant species. Chrysanthemums will initiate or form a flower bud under any day length (even 24 hours of continuous illumination), but most rapid development of buds to flowering takes place when the day length is about 12½ hours. If the day length is reduced, for example to 9 hours, no hastening in development takes place as compared to the 12½-hour period. Flowering will take place as the day length approaches 12½ hours, for example 15 hours or less, but development is very slow, and there is likelihood of imperfect buds or flowers because of too many hours of day (Fig. 5-1). Specific information on other plants is presented later in this chapter or under the discussion of the individual crop.

5-1. Chrysanthemum crown buds can be caused by light leakage, day-length fluctuations, or high temperatures.   Left: normal flower buds.   Right: crown buds.   (*Yoder Bros., Inc., photograph.*)

Shortening the day.   The term short day has been used since Garner and Allard's original work, but it is interesting to note, as pointed out in Chap. 4, that a short day is also accompanied by a long night.   To make sure of obtaining the short-day effect, the night period must be uninterrupted; a short-day plant, then, might also be called a long-night plant.   However, the term short day is so common and so well understood that it will be used in this text.

To provide a short day when the day length is greater than the critical point, the plants are covered at an appropriate time with some material impervious to light, to make an artificially short day.   Black sateen cloth (64 by 104 mesh or closer) is very satisfactory, though light-impervious plastic films may also be used.   To achieve a short day, no more than 2 or 3 foot-candles should penetrate the cover when it is applied at 5 P.M.   At this time the light intensity in the greenhouse may be 2,000 or 3,000 foot-candles, so the covering must be quite impervious to light.   A light meter is useful in determining the effectiveness of the cover in excluding light.

The plants are generally covered at 5 P.M., and the shade cloth removed between 7 and 8 A.M. the following day.   Such a system provides a 9- or 10-hour day, which is well below the critical photoperiod and fits well into the routine of greenhouse operation.   In summer a considerable amount of heat may accumulate under the cloth, which can cause undesirable effects on growth.   This can be partially alleviated by covering only from 8 P.M. to 7 or 8 A.M., by raising the sides of the cover after dark and lowering them before daybreak, or by using washed-air cooling under the cover.

It is presumed that flowering is due to a hormonal influence, and it is known that the recently matured leaves are the most active in bringing about the flowering response.   Therefore, if the cloth covering allows a small amount of light to fall on the basal leaves, no delay in flowering will be observed.   How-

5-2. The effect of continuity of short days on the flowering of spray Chrysanthemums. Left to right: shaded 7 days per week; shaded 6 days per week; shaded 5 days per week; and shaded 4 days per week. (*Yoder Bros., Inc., photograph.*)

ever, if the cover is torn or not placed over the plants properly to exclude the light, flower buds may not form or flowering will be delayed considerably.

Age and exposure to weather will affect the covers used for shading. With ordinary care black sateen cloth will give good results for about 3 years, but the older the cloth, the less effective it becomes because of wear, which allows light to penetrate. For shading Chrysanthemums, or poinsettias in summer, new black sateen cloth or two layers of old cloth is recommended because of the high light intensity. A single layer of the older cloth can be used when the sunlight is not very bright.

Some short-day plants. *Chrysanthemum morifolium* is the classic example of a short-day plant; however, it is interesting to note that even under short photoperiods, flower buds will not form unless the night temperature is high enough. At cool night temperatures the growth often rosettes and the stems are "blind."

The date of flower bud formation in Chrysanthemums varies, depending upon the earliness of maturity of the variety. Those that flower normally in late October form buds in late August, those that flower in November initiate flower buds in early September, while those that flower in December form buds in mid-to late September.   The differences in time of flower bud initiation are probably due to differences in sensitivity to light intensity.   Late varieties are very light-sensitive, and 12½ hours of more than 1 or 2 foot-candles keeps them vegetative; therefore they initiate flower buds later in the season.   The earlier varieties are not as light sensitive, and flower buds may form and subsequently develop when there are 12½ hours of more than 10 foot-candles.   Even at day lengths of 15 hours, early varieties can form flower buds, though their rate of subsequent development may be reduced at this increased day length.   Prevention of initiation of flower buds on many early varieties is as yet an unsolved problem.

The *Chrysanthemum* is flowered on a year-round basis as a cut flower or potted plant simply by controlling the length of day and temperature.

The *Begonia socotrana,* or Christmas flowering *Begonia,* normally forms flower buds in early October.   For earlier flowering the black-cloth treatment should be started about 8 to 10 weeks before the plants are desired to be in flower.   The early growth of this plant takes place slowly until the days become long enough to permit vegetative development.   The tuberous-rooted *Begonia* is a long-day plant, and *B. semperflorens* is indeterminate, or day-neutral.

Gardenia grandiflora is a short-day plant, and if it is shaded July 21 to August 13 in central Ohio, a number of flowers generally mature for Christmas and early January.   If it is shaded for only two weeks, the desired effect on initiation is not obtained.   Longer periods of shading cause flower bud initiation at the terminus of nearly every shoot, but the buds fail to develop until the long days of the following spring.   Total darkness is essential during the 3-week shading period, and because of their size, 2-year-old plants give more satisfactory results in terms of number of flowers than do younger plants.   As many as 12 to 15 flowers per plant can be obtained from mid-December to January 1.

Kalanchoe blossfeldiana, flowers 12 to 14 weeks after short-day treatments are started if the temperature is about 60°F at all times.

The poinsettia, *Euphorbia pulcherrima,* forms flower buds between September 25 and October 1 in central Ohio.   Early propagated plants develop rapidly and should be lighted from September 23 until October 5 or 10 to prevent early maturity and overripeness at Christmas.   Night temperature is also an important factor in relation to the proper day length for flower bud initiation in poinsettias (see page 77).

Lengthening the day.   To provide a long day for promoting the flowering of long-day plants or maintaining the vegetative growth of short-day plants, lights are used when the day length is less than the critical number of hours.   Incandescent lamps are superior to other types because they emit more orange-red radiation than most other lamps, and the orange-red rays are more effective in photoperiodic phenomena.   Light from most fluorescent lamps does not have as much orange-red radiation, and these lamps must generally be operated for longer periods to obtain the same results.   However, pink fluorescent lamps have considerable orange-red radiation and they are superior to incandescent lamps for lighting florist crops.   The duration of lighting each night with pink fluorescent lamps can be half that recommended for incandescent lamps because of the great amount of orange-red radiation compared to the far-red.

As measured by a light meter, 10 foot-candles of incandescent light has enough orange-red radiation to cause the desired effect with all florist crops. Some plants, such as the aster and poinsettia, are affected by as little as 1 or 2 foot-candles, while Chrysanthemums may need as much as 8 or 10 foot-candles, depending upon the variety.   Because plants are placed close together, there usually is considerable shading of one plant by another, and it is best to supply slightly more light than necessary to ensure against failures.

For small installations, 60-watt bulbs spaced 4 feet apart and placed 2 feet above the tops of the plants will provide a minimum of 10 foot-candles at all areas of a 4-foot-wide bench.   Another possibility is spacing 100-watt bulbs 6 feet apart and 3 feet above the plants.   Suitable reflectors are needed to direct the light onto the plants, or bulbs may be purchased which direct the light downward.   Where entire houses are lighted, clusters of floodlight-type bulbs are placed uniformly in the upper regions of the greenhouse.   For such installations the local light and power company should be consulted, and 1½ watts of light per square foot of ground area covered is considered the minimum.

It has been shown that lighting in the middle of the night is more effective in promoting vegetative growth of short-day plants than lighting at the end or beginning of the day.   The reason is that the night is thereby divided into two shorter intervals, each of which is shorter than the minimum dark period needed to cause flowering.   Consequently, it is suggested that lighting start at 10 P.M. and continue for as many hours as necessary.   The effective number of hours of light per night for supplemental illumination of florist crops is shown in Table 5-1.

Table 5-1.   *Recommended Number of Hours of Lighting per Night*

Months	Hours of light
August and May	2
September–October and March–April	3
November–February	4

In order to take advantage of a reduced rate for electricity if its use is spread over a greater length of time at night, an area may be lighted in several different ways. Half the area can be lighted so that illumination ceases near or at midnight, and the other half of the area can be lighted from midnight on, using the hours given in Table 5-1.   Somewhat superior to this, however, is lighting all the area with half the number of total hours of light needed; the lighting ends near 11 P.M., and the balance of the light is started at 1 or 2 P.M.   This breaks the dark period into three small segments, no one of which is sufficiently long to induce flower bud initiation.

Cyclic lighting may be used effectively with incandescent lamps as well as with rapid start fluorescent lamps. One possibility is to give a flash of light every few minutes; however, it is better to light for a somewhat longer period, since a flash is not always effective with some plants, particularly Chrysanthemums. The recommendations are for the use of lights for a minimum of 20 percent of the time every 30 minutes for the duration of time suggested in Table 5-1. Thus in November, when 4 hours of light is suggested, lights would be turned on at 10:00 P.M., off at 10:06 P.M. (6 minutes is 20 percent of 30 minutes), on at 10:30 P.M., off at 10:36 P.M., etc., until they were finally turned off at 2:06 A.M. It is also possible to obtain equipment that will permit sequence lighting of areas. In this way one area would be lighted for 6 minutes, then another area for the following 6 minutes, and so on for another three successive 6-minute periods. Then the first area would again be lighted.

Some long-day plants. Many of the annuals which now are seldom grown under glass are long-day plants and will flower earlier when lighted. Specific suggestions are given below for some crops to which lighting is beneficial.

Calceolarias develop flowers in long days and can be matured earlier than is normal by lighting. Flower bud formation in this plant, however, is independent of day length. The China aster will flower at any day length, but long days increase the length of stems.

Azaleas and Hydrangeas are not photoperiodic with respect to flowering, but long days will increase the length of internodes. Thus in the vegetative growth of azaleas, long-day conditions together with night temperatures of at least 65°F are desirable to obtain a larger plant more rapidly. Hydrangeas for Mother's Day are taller than similar plants for Easter because of the effect of the longer day during the forcing period.

Some indeterminate plants. There are some florist crops which flower irrespective of the natural day length, and which obtain no beneficial effect from either supplemental illumination or short days. The rose and African violet are outstanding examples. Some indeterminate plants are influenced markedly by temperature, as discussed in a later section of this chapter.

Latitudes and day length. At the equator the days and nights are approximately of equal length at all seasons. In summer the length of day is greater as the distance increases north of the equator, and in the Arctic zone the day is 24 hours long. In winter the reverse is true, and in the Arctic zone there are 24 hours of darkness. On March 21, the vernal equinox, and September 21, the autumnal equinox, the length of day is 12 hours at any point on the earth.

Therefore, depending upon the latitude, the length of day varies except at the equinox periods. In summer the northern parts of the United States have a longer day than Florida, but in winter the days in Florida will be longer than in areas farther north. This has a bearing on the cultural practices of lengthening or reducing the day length by artificial means. For example, in production of Chrysanthemums in Florida, the days are seldom long enough to require the prolonged use of black cloth for flowering. In Hawaii, on the 20th parallel, the days are so short that lights must be used at all seasons to promote vegetative growth of Chrysanthemums.

QUALITY OR COLOR

The term quality is used to refer to the wavelength composition of light. Different sources of illumination have different levels of various wavelengths which will cause distinct manifestations of growth. Incandescent lights are rich in red radiation and are warm or even hot, whereas most fluorescent lamps have somewhat less red radiation and are cooler.

When sunlight passes through glass, most of the ultraviolet rays do not pass through. Red, on the other hand, does pass through, and hence solar radiation warms the greenhouse, undesirably so in summer. The various plastic materials, either rigid or film, have different transmission of the wavelengths of light, and growth of plants under plastics can be different because of this effect. Because plastic materials make a "tighter" greenhouse than glass, relative humidity, temperature, and other factors also may be quite different than in a glass greenhouse, and variations in growth may be due to these in addition to differences in the wavelengths of light.

It has been pointed out that orange-red radiation keeps short-day plants growing vegetatively. As yet it has not been possible to cause flower buds to form by irradiating florist crops with far-red or any other kind of light.

TEMPERATURE

Temperature is another important factor governing plant growth in the greenhouse. Because much of the time in many areas of the country the florist can control the air temperature in the greenhouse, growth and flowering of many plants can be regulated by that means.

Through its influence on the many processes occurring in the plant, temperature affects the quantity and quality of the plant or flower. For example, many rose varieties are grown at a night temperature of 60°F because at that temperature the number and size of flowers produced, coupled with the diameter and stiffness of stem, are that quantity and quality which the grower desires. At higher night temperatures, more flowers would be produced, but they would be smaller and lighter colored, they would lack "substance," and the stems would be thinner and weaker.   At temperatures lower than 60°F, the color of the flowers and thickness of the stem would be particularly satisfactory, but there would not be enough roses produced to be economically practical.   The same is true for other cut flowers and potted plants.   The term optimum temperature used in subsequent discussion refers to the temperature at which the florist can obtain from the plants the quantity and quality of growth he considers optimum or desirable for his business; there is no optimum, as such, for the plants themselves.

Temperature coefficient.   The rate of reaction of most chemical processes in a plant increases rather uniformly as the temperature is raised.   With many of these chemical reactions the rate is doubled for every 10°C (0°C equals 32°F, 10°C equals 50°F, 20°C equals 68°F, and 30°C equals 86°F).   Above 86°F, however, the rate may not only markedly slow down but may drop lower, though the reasons are not clear.   Hence, temperatures above 85°F are not beneficial to the plants.

Physical reactions increase only 10 to 20 percent as the temperature goes up 10°C.   The movement of foods and other physical changes take place at a much slower rate than those of a chemical nature.   This is referred to as the temperature coefficient and is expressed by the term Q_{10}.   The Q_{10} for many chemical reactions is 2, while for physical reactions it is 1.1 or 1.2.

Night and day temperatures.   Throughout this text references will be made to specific temperatures, and, unless otherwise stated, these will be night temperatures.   The temperature at night appears to have a greater effect on the growth than does day temperature, and it is well known that the night temperature is most important in governing the initiation of flower buds on certain types of plants.

This is not to imply that day temperatures are of minor importance, because either too cool or too warm a range will adversely affect plant growth. Whenever possible, it is generally the practice to maintain the day temperature about 5°F higher than night temperature on cloudy days and about 10 to 15°F higher on sunny days.   In the dark weather of winter, the day temperature for snapdragons is often not raised above that maintained at night, and if the cloudy weather persists, the night temperature may be dropped 1 or 2°F a night to a maximum of 5°F lower than the previously maintained night temperature.   When the light intensity improves, temperature is generally regulated as described previously.

The reasons for temperature variation between day and night will be discussed under the various topics which follow.

Photosynthesis. The rate at which carbohydrates are synthesized is dependent to a considerable extent upon the temperature. If no other factors are limiting, the initial rate of photosynthesis increases, within certain limits, with an increase in temperature. At still higher temperatures this increased initial rate is not maintained, and in a very short time it may drop to a value even below that at a lower temperature. In the greenhouse, for example, it has been observed that day temperatures above 85°F generally have a detrimental effect on the growth of the plant (see Temperature Coefficient), though probably other metabolic processes are also involved along with the photosynthetic rate.

When the light intensity is high, the maximum rate of photosynthesis occurs at a slightly higher temperature than under lower light conditions; therefore day temperatures are maintained at a higher level, which may result in an accelerated rate of photosynthesis and a net increase in food supply. If the light intensity is low, the day temperature should either be kept the same as at night or raised only 5°F since the rate of photosynthesis is limited by low light rather than by temperature.

Respiration. Temperature, along with food supply, influences the rate of respiration. Within certain limits an increase in temperature causes an increase in respiration. Since respiration occurs both day and night, an excessive rate caused by maintenance of high temperature will deplete the food supply of the plant, and growth will be unsatisfactory. In the field production of bulbs, such as hyacinths, Narcissus, and tulips, which are later used for forcing, best results are obtained in areas where nights are cool and day temperatures are not excessively warm even though the light intensity is high. These conditions favor accumulation of carbohydrates in the bulb so that they can be forced in the greenhouse.

Because respiration is very slow at temperatures of 31 to 34°F, some kinds of plant material can be stored successfully at this low range for rather prolonged periods as compared with temperatures between 50 and 60°F. Bulbs are stored at 33 to 35°F in order to provide the necessary conditions to bring the rest period (dormancy) to a close yet prevent them from growing. At 40°F, the rest period is diminished the most rapidly, but the bulbs sprout, which is undesirable for long-time holding. At temperatures of 65 to 75°F, bulbs of lilies, tulips, hyacinths, Narcissus, and others will remain in a *status quo* condition, that is, they will be dormant, and the various changes that occur when the bulb is kept cool will take place very slowly. If such a bulb has not been cooled, it will remain in good condition longer at the warm temperature range than near 33°F. This temperature is used with the Florida-grown Easter lily bulbs, which are harvested in August but not planted until late December or early January; however, a 6-week cooling period is necessary just prior to planting to permit rapid forcing.

Iris bulbs may be "retarded," that is, stored warm (around 86°F) after digging to maintain them in good condition and prevent sprouting. They are given six weeks of cooling prior to shipping and planting for late flowering. If stored cool, they would sprout or their vitality would be depleted.

Carnation cuttings may be removed from stock plants in fall and early winter and stored for propagation later on in the spring. They are either placed in polyethylene bags which are folded and stapled but not sealed, or in waxed or metal trays equipped with a lid that is reasonably airtight. The unrooted cuttings can be stored at 31 to 33°F for as long as a year. Rooted carnations may be stored for several weeks, but they will grow even at such low temperatures and eventually form a flower bud.

Unrooted Chrysanthemum cuttings can be stored at 31 to 33°F for about two weeks, but varietal differences are great. Terminal buds on some may be injured or killed by as short a storage time as one week, while only the lateral buds on others may be affected. Rooted Chrysanthemum cuttings should not be stored for more than several days since the terminal or side buds may be injured.

Seedlings of some bedding plants may be stored at 33°F for several weeks by overwrapping the flat with polyethylene. This is a means of holding the young plants at a desirable size when it is not possible to transplant them.

Flowers of roses, carnations, and Chrysanthemums may be stored at 31 to 33°F. They should not be placed in water prior to storage unless they wilt. Only the best-quality stock should be selected, graded, then placed in containers that will not absorb moisture from the plant tissue. There should be a minimum of empty space within the container since successful storage depends upon reduced respiration brought about by a reduced oxygen supply and an accumulation of carbon dioxide as well as a slower rate of respiration from low temperature. Roses may be stored from 5 to 7 days, carnations up to 10 days, and Chrysanthemums for several weeks. The greater the food supply in the plant material, brought about by a favorable environment for growth, the longer the material can be stored. When the stock is removed from cold storage, the ends of the stems should be cut and the stems placed in water at 80 to 100°F for rapid rehydration, and the containers should be placed in a temperature of about 50°F for several hours prior to shipping.

Amino acid and protein synthesis. In the formation of additional leaves, stems, petals, and roots, amino acids and proteins are vital constituents of the protoplasm of each cell. Temperatures affect the rate of synthesis of these materials in much the same manner as with photosynthesis and respiration. When the temperature is too low for a rapid rate of amino acid and protein synthesis, carbohydrates accumulate, and often anthocyanins and other pigments become evident by a change of color in the leaves or stems.   Older leaves on geraniums turn red in cool greenhouses, and white petals on many flowers will be tinged with pink.

High temperatures that may favor very rapid synthesis of amino acids and proteins, as well as depletion of the carbohydrate reserves, often cause development of tissues that are soft and may lack substance.   This is particularly noticeable in the prolonged dark cloudy weather common in winter.   Development of the plants can be hastened somewhat by raising the temperature during dark weather, but until there are a few days of sunshine to restore the carbohydrate supply, growth will be slow even if the day and night temperatures are maintained relatively high.   Therefore it is not beneficial to maintain high night temperatures in periods of very low light intensities.

Transpiration.   As the temperature within the leaf rises from either sunlight or the turning on of heating lines in the greenhouse, the amount of water vapor that transpires will increase.   If transpiration exceeds absorption, the tissues will wilt, which may in turn result in a partial closure of the stomates and resultant reduction of loss of water vapor.   In prolonged dark weather in winter, the soil temperature is generally close to that of the air, and when the sun shines brightly, the leaf temperature increases rapidly, resulting in rather severe wilting because the rate of transpiration is greater than that of water absorption.

Transpiration may also occur when the relative humidity is quite high. Since the temperature of the leaf is usually higher than that of the air during the day, the vapor pressure of the air in the intercellular spaces of the leaf is greater than that of the external atmosphere and more water molecules will escape from the stomates than will enter.   This phenomenon is commonly observed when flowers from the greenhouse are placed in a refrigerator and mild wilting of the tissues occurs.   It can be alleviated by placing the flowers in warm (100°F) water to speed water absorption and hydration of the tissues.

Net assimilation.   Assimilation is the use of foods to make new cell walls and protoplasm, which results in an increase in the dry weight.   The temperature at which a plant grows governs all the processes that are concerned with assimilation.

There is no one optimum temperature as a plant grows and develops from a small to a larger size.   It has been found with snapdragons and Chrysanthemums that the optimum night temperature decreases as the plant increases in size.   The reason is that the relationship of photosynthetic area to that of respiratory tissue changes as the plant grows.   In the early stages, much of the foliage is exposed to full sunlight and there is little shading of the lower foliage by the upper leaves or of one plant by another.   The amount of photosynthetic area is then large in comparison to that of respiration.   As the plant grows, only the upper leaves receive full sunlight, and the lower foliage is shaded by leaves above on the same plant as well as by adjoining plants. Therefore the photosynthetic area becomes smaller compared to the amount of respiring tissue, so that the temperature must be lowered if there is to be a continued gain in net assimilation. Translated to commercial practice, this means that the night temperature should be reduced as the plant grows in order to prevent undue loss of food from respiration, resulting in a product of inferior substance and quality.

With potted plants, it is possible to move the plants from one temperature to another or, if the houses are small and the plants are at a similar stage of development, to reduce the temperature as the plants develop. With cut flowers which are grown as similar-sized plants in one greenhouse or in a compartment, such as snapdragons, Chrysanthemums, and single-cropped carnations, the air temperature can be reduced as indicated. When plants of different ages are in one greenhouse or with roses or carnations which have different stages of growth on the same plant simultaneously, it is impossible to reduce the temperature as the plant increases in size.

Reducing the temperature near the end of the crop is a standard practice for many pot plant growers since this often intensifies flower color and conditions the plant for the rigorous environment of the retail store and the location where it will ultimately be placed for enjoyment.

Other metabolic processes. The numerous chemical and physical processes that take place within the plant, aside from those already discussed, are also affected by temperature in a manner similar to that of photosynthesis and respiration. Generally it is believed that the beneficial effects of raising the day temperature cease for most plants at approximately 85°F, based on observation of the quality and quantity of growth at higher temperatures (see Temperature Coefficient).

Soil temperature. The soil temperature will affect the rate of absorption of water, fertilizers, and other materials by the root system. If the soil is cold, absorption will be reduced, as evidenced by wilting of the plant if the leaf temperature is high. The absorption and effectiveness of systemic insecticides have been observed to be most pronounced on bright days when both soil and tissue temperatures are high. In prolonged cloudy weather when the soil is cooler, the effectiveness of such insecticides is reduced.

Growth of soil microorganisms is slow when the temperature of the soil is low. Organic fertilizers such as blood, tankage, and others are very slow to become available in winter because their conversion by microorganisms to a form that can be absorbed and utilized by the plant is retarded when the soil is cool. In spring, when the sunlight is brighter, the soil temperature in the greenhouse will rise, and occasional damage from excess fertilizer has been observed. This can often be traced to the rapid conversion of organic fertilizers, applied when the weather was cool and cloudy, to an available form which decreases the rate of water absorption by interference with root growth.

Excess heating of soil can be prevented in summer by the use of mulches. Generally peat or manure spread to a depth of an inch will suffice. Though the somewhat warmer soil temperature is probably not injurious to the roots, it promotes rapid drying of the soil, necessitating frequent watering. Heating the soil or the water even slightly above 70°F in winter may inhibit growth of some florist crops.

Leaf and tissue temperature.   The temperature of the leaf is usually higher than that of the surrounding atmosphere when light from the sun or artificial sources of illumination falls on it. Light rays are absorbed by the leaf, thereby raising the temperature, because of conversion of the light or radiant energy to heat energy. In bright sunlight the temperature of the leaves of plants growing outside may be as much as 15 to 20°F higher than that of the air. In the greenhouse the temperature of a leaf in bright sunlight may be only 5 to 10°F higher than the air, while a shaded leaf may only be 2 to 3°F warmer than the atmosphere. The higher the air temperature, the smaller the temperature differential, and at an air temperature of 100°F the leaf is only slightly warmer. Transpiration will be increased markedly by such temperature extremes because of vapor pressure differences, as explained earlier. This necessitates frequent watering of the soil in bright weather to retain an adequate supply of moisture to prevent wilting. In greenhouses with washed-air cooling there can be considerable difference in the air temperature compared to a non-air-cooled house. However, leaves exposed to full sunlight in a cooled house may be only 1 to 5°F cooler than those in a non-cooled greenhouse. The radiant energy warms the leaf tissue in spite of the cooler stream of air that is flowing around it.

After a period of dark weather, many plants will wilt severely on a bright day. This is particularly noticeable on the young growth of carnation plants. The tissues are soft, and they lose water vapor rapidly when heated by the sunlight even though the soil may be quite moist. Several days of bright weather will result in formation of sufficient carbohydrates and proteins so that the tissues have substance and do not wilt.

Injury to the leaves or petals is quite common during periods of bright weather. Patches of tissue may be "scalded," turning brown or black and then drying, by excessive loss of water vapor. Hydrangea leaves and geranium flowers are particularly subject to damage in the bright weather of spring.

Freezing can cause injury or death, but tissues of many plants do not freeze until 29 to 30°F because the dissolved minerals and organic constituents in the cell sap lower the freezing point. The formation of ice crystals in the cells during freezing ruptures the cells and causes disorganization of the protoplasm.   Freezing injury may also be due in some instances to drying of the tissue, resulting from the removal of free water in the formation of ice.

Whenever tissues are frozen, it is desirable to thaw them slowly so that there will be less danger of disruption of the protoplasm.   Frequent sprinkling with cold water keeps the tissue temperature low, which delays the rate of thawing.   This is particularly important because in many instances rapid thawing rather than the initial freezing has been found to be the cause of death.

Leaves and flower buds of plants kept outside in fall, such as azaleas and Hydrangeas, can be injured by chilling even though the air temperature may not reach 32°F.   The leaves and buds radiate heat energy at all times, and on nights when there are no clouds, radiation or heat loss is particularly rapid.   Under such circumstances the leaf temperature drops lower than that of the surrounding air, and injury from chilling can occur.   Placing black cloth covers over the plants on such nights is effective in reducing radiation from the leaves and will prevent chilling injury.   In the greenhouse at night, leaf temperatures may be lower than the air if the air temperature outside is considerably cooler than that maintained in the greenhouse.   Radiation is taking place from the warm leaf to the colder outside air.

Cold water on leaves of African violets causes a breakdown of chloroplasts in the palisade layer, with the resultant development of yellow rings or spots on the foliage.   It is the temperature of the water rather than the water itself that causes this disorder.   If the temperature of the water is as warm as the leaf, no damage occurs.   Contrary to popular opinion, water on the foliage of plants does not cause a burn or scald, but it may encourage growth of disease organisms.

Propagation.   It is usually desirable to maintain the temperature of the rooting medium 5 to 10°F higher than that of the air.   The healing of the wound and formation and development of roots are hastened by the warmer temperature through its effect on the rate of various processes in the portion of the stem or leaf in the rooting medium.   Since the air is cooler, there will be less depletion of food in the leaves by respiration as well as a reduced rate of transpiration from the foliage.   Propagation houses are often shaded heavily, unless some mist system is used, to prevent the sunlight from markedly raising the temperature of the air and the leaf.

When mist systems are installed in propagation houses, rooting may be somewhat delayed if the water is cold.   This is particularly true in winter when the water temperature is at its lowest range and an intermittent mist is employed which sprays the cold water on the cuttings.   Adequate bottom heat will keep the medium sufficiently warm to offset the cooling effects of the water.

When seeds are sown, the absorption of moisture and resumption of metabolic processes are dependent to a considerable extent upon the temperature. Generally, the temperature is maintained somewhat higher than that which is considered optimum for the mature plant since rapid germination and growth are generally desired in the early stages of the life of the plant (see Net Assimilation).

Development of certain plant parts.   The stems and flower buds of some florist crops will not elongate or expand until they have been exposed to cool temperatures (35 to 50°F) for several weeks.   Hydrangeas and azaleas will not force unless cooled, and bulbs of such plants as hyacinths, lilies, Narcissus, and tulips are placed in a cool location for some time before being taken into the greenhouse.   The cool temperature causes many chemical changes within the tissues, so that when the plant is brought into a warm greenhouse it will force rapidly.   One of the changes is concerned with the enlargement of cells.   Before exposure to cool temperature, the cells will not expand, but after a specified time in a cool location, the cells will enlarge and do so at a rapid rate in a warm greenhouse.   Just what changes occur that bring about a resumption of growth is not well understood.   Starch is digested to sugar by the enzyme amylase, and this occurs quite rapidly at 41°F.   This change in the kind of food results in accumulation of a soluble carbohydrate which is readily available for respiration and energy release or assimilation into proteins and other cell-building constituents, both of which are needed in the rapid growth that takes place when the plants are placed in a warm greenhouse.

This stem-elongation phenomenon is the chief reason why bulbs are placed in a cool location.   Many florists believe that bulbs are planted and placed at a cool temperature (35 to 50°F) for the purpose of developing a root system.   Actually, the roots have no dormancy and would grow faster at somewhat higher temperatures, but the processes that allow for later stem elongation would not occur.   If the temperature drops below 35°F, root growth is impaired.

Flower bud initiation.   The formation or initiation of flower buds on many plants is dependent upon temperature.   With such plants as *Calceolaria*, cineraria, *Cypripedium*, genista, *Pelargonium domesticum*, primrose, and stock, flower bud formation takes place at temperatures between 50 and 60°F, independent of photoperiod.   Gardenias form buds readily between 55 and 60°F.   However, a temperature range of 60 to 65°F is most favorable for initiation of flower buds with some short-day plants.   Most varieties of Chrysanthemums initiate flowers in short days only when the temperature is above 60°F, and with poinsettias a 58 to 65°F range is preferred for flower formation.   Such plants could be classified as thermophotoperiodic.   Other plants which are indeterminate form flower buds much more rapidly at 60 to 65°F than at lower ranges.   Most azalea varieties, some kinds of *Cyclamen*, and greenhouse Hydrangeas are examples.   Plants which form flower buds within any usual range of night temperature maintained in greenhouses are the African violet, carnation, and rose.   These could be considered nonspecific in regard to the effect of temperature on flower bud formation.

The various kinds of bulbs forced by florists differ in the optimum range of temperature for most rapid flower bud initiation.   Initiation of Iris, hyacinth, and Narcissus flowers is accelerated at temperatures between 70 and 80°F for short periods, while a 65 to 68°F range is best for tulips.   West Coast lilies will form buds at temperatures between 45 and 70°F, but not above 70°F, if they have not been cooled after digging from the field.

Flower bud development.   The development of flower buds is also affected by temperature.   At low temperatures of 35 to 50°F, growth is very slow, and as the temperature rises, growth increases (see Temperature Coefficient). There is an upper limit at which development will slow down, probably because of insufficient food for new tissues, and this is particularly pronounced in periods of very low light intensity.   The minimum, optimum, and maximum temperatures for development depend upon the desired quantity and quality of the particular plant.

The *Chrysanthemum* provides an interesting paradox with respect to effect of temperature on development of flower buds.   Some varieties will form and develop flower buds in a relatively wide range of night temperature (58 to 80°F).   Others exhibit a condition called "heat delay," a failure of the flower buds to develop, but the range at which it occurs differs with the variety.   On many of the late types which normally flower 12 to 15 weeks after flower buds form, a night temperature of 65°F is necessary for initiation, but this temperature will stop development.   Flower development, however, is most rapid on the 12- to 15-week varieties at 55 to 58°F.   On others, temperatures of 80 to 90°F for a few hours at night will curtail development of the flower buds.   When the initiated bud stops growing, axillary shoots below will develop and initiate buds, which in turn are arrested in development, giving rise to a series of branched

5-3. Uneven flower development or failure of Chrysanthemums to form flower buds in the proper photoperiod may be due to low temperatures. (*Yoder Bros., Inc., photograph.*)

shoots at the end of the main stem.   Heat delay is most serious in summer when the black cloth is used to provide short-day conditions, and again in winter when the 12- to 15-week varieties are flowered.   Cooling the greenhouse in summer by washed air or high-pressure mist has proved quite successful in preventing difficulties from heat delay.

Gardenia flower buds will not develop in short days at night temperatures above 65°F.   Attempts to force the plants into flower by raising the temperature usually cause severe bud drop.   Sweet peas drop buds in dark weather when the temperature is raised much above 55°F.

Flowers on genista and *Pelargonium domesticum* usually drop if the temperature is warm, and for this reason their popularity has decreased considerably.

Development of flowers on many bulbs will only take place after a period of cool temperature, as discussed earlier.

Leaf and flower color.   Temperatures too low for the desired rate of growth generally bring about the development of pigment in the leaves, stems, or flowers.   This is probably due to a reduced rate of nitrogen utilization, resulting in an accumulation of some forms of carbohydrates.   Lower leaves on many plants turn bronze or red if kept too cool, though this same condition may be induced by nitrogen deficiency.   White Chrysanthemums turn an undesirable pink at cool temperatures, and this same color develops when they become too ripe on the plant.

Cool temperature near the finishing of a crop can be used to advantage as discussed in the section on Net Assimilation.

Excessive heat causes loss of color of the flowers.   This can be due to prevention of pigment formation or to destruction after formation.   Bright light also "fades" flowers, which could be caused by the bleaching action of the sun or the raising of the temperature of the petals.   Bronze Chrysanthemums are often yellow in summer, while many pink or red varieties fade to a dirty white.

Too low a light intensity will limit the supply of material necessary for desirable pigment formation; this is most pronounced on crops forced in dark winter weather.   In the case of red or pink snapdragons or Gladiolus as cut flowers placed in a rather dark location in the home, the new flowers will be almost white because of depletion of food from which anthocyanins develop.

Temperature regulation.   The importance of maintaining closely regulated temperature has been stressed in this section in dealing with its effect on growth and flowering.

Heat should be used judiciously so that in periods of cool or mild weather the temperature of the greenhouse does not rise too high because of the use of too many heating lines, coupled with inadequate ventilation.   Although automatic valves and thermostats may be installed, some judgment must be exercised,

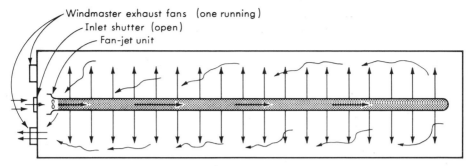

Fresh air ventilation

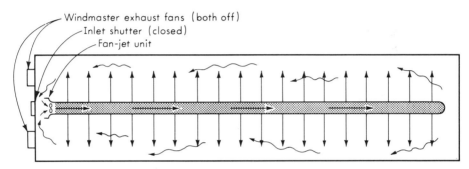

Continuous recirculation and air motion

5-4. In the Fan-Jet system the continuously operating fan discharges into a perforated polyethylene tube. When the greenhouse temperature becomes too warm, outside air is admitted through the motorized shutter in the gable wall as air from the greenhouse is expelled by an exhaust fan. (*Acme Engineering & Manufacturing Corp. drawing.*)

depending upon the expected weather conditions. It is best to use the minimum number of heating lines required to maintain the desired temperature, since this will provide a steady flow of heat. When only a few heating lines are needed, the heat should be distributed by using lines at scattered locations in the house rather than all on one side or in the middle.

When unit heaters are installed overhead, the heat may be more uniform because of the fans which circulate the air. Improper placement of heaters, however, can cause cold or hot areas which adversely affect crops.

Perimeter heating lines should be turned on first to provide heat near the plants where there is radiation from the side and gable walls. Additional heating lines or unit heaters may be used to provide more heat when needed. The last pipes to be turned off should be the perimeter heating lines.

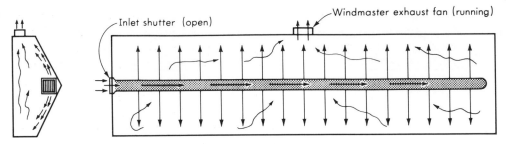

5-5. Perforated plastic tube ventilation. Air from outdoors is introduced into the greenhouse through the perforated tubing when the exhaust fan is operating. (*Acme Engineering & Manufacturing Corp. drawing.*)

In extremely cold weather the temperature in the greenhouse may drop below the desired point. Water applied to the heating pipes will rise as "steam" and will condense and freeze on the glass, sealing the laps and covering the glass with ice. Loss of heat will be reduced appreciably.

Heat loss can be reduced by fastening clear plastic material to the inside of the sash bars within the entire house. The light transmission of the plastic should be high or the crop will suffer from insufficient light. The dead air space between the plastic film and the greenhouse glass acts as an insulator.

Cooling greenhouses by means of washed air or mist has been discussed in Chap. 3.

MOISTURE

Plants grow luxuriantly and flower profusely only with an adequate supply of water. The fertilizer materials which are absorbed by the plant are in solution in the water in the soil. In the plant, water is essential because it is the medium, or "vehicle," in which the various metabolic or physiological processes take place.

The water absorbed by the root system moves upward through the roots and stems in the xylem. Branching of the xylem system into side branches, leaves, and flowers ensures a supply of water to all aerial parts of the plant. Proper regulation of the moisture supply enables the florist to regulate the growth of plants, and the more important phases of this are discussed below.

Cell division and enlargement. In order for cells to divide and make new tissue, they must have a plentiful supply of water. The less turgid the tissues, the slower the rate of cell division and the slower the growth. Plants that are carried extremely dry exhibit a high root-to-top relationship, because water is more limiting for the aerial portions, and the new stem and leaf growth is small.

Enlargement of newly formed cells is dependent upon water supply as well as upon hormones, food, and the inherent character of the plant. With optimum moisture the cells will enlarge, resulting in long stems, large leaves, and fully developed petals. The importance of cell enlargement can be more fully appreciated when it is realized that roses form flower buds when the shoot is approximately 1½ inches long, and the subsequent increase in length of the stem is due almost entirely to enlargement of the cells in that very short shoot. Soil in which geraniums are growing is often kept very dry, and as a result top growth is reduced, internodes are short, and flowering is delayed.

Loss of water can be reduced by several cultural practices. Increasing the humidity by means of wetting the walks and plants is effective, but only for a very short period since air movement quickly dissipates the atmospheric moisture. Both the high-pressure mist system and the washed-air cooling system raise the relative humidity in the greenhouse. Reducing the light intensity by shading the roof or by using cloth under glass reduces the temperature, resulting in a rise in the relative humidity, both of which conditions reduce the loss of moisture from the plant.

For the most rapid rate of cell division and enlargement, it is essential that the water supply not become limiting within the plant.

Photosynthesis. Although water is one of the materials that are used in this highly important physiological process, less than 1 percent of the moisture absorbed becomes an integral part of the synthesized carbohydrate. However, the rate of photosynthesis is materially reduced when plants wilt, partly because a decrease in turgidity causes closure of the stomates, thus limiting the entrance of carbon dioxide. Plants that have been allowed to wilt seldom carry on photosynthesis at as great a rate as before they wilted. Thus continued wilting will appreciably slow down the manufacture of food which is used in the development of new tissues.

Transpiration. Transpiration, or loss of water vapor from the leaf, is a normal process in the plant, and for every gram of dry matter produced by the plant as much as 500 grams of water may be lost. However, when the rate of loss exceeds the rate of absorption by the roots, wilting occurs even though there is an adequate supply of water in the soil. When the soil is dry, plants wilt quickly, and unless the soil is watered soon, severe injury can occur. The rate of transpiration is reduced when the plant is wilted because the guard cells surrounding each stomate through which the water vapor diffuses into the air become less turgid, making the stomatal opening much smaller. When the internal water supply increases, the guard cells become turgid, the stomates open, and the rate of transpiration increases.

Propagation.   Moisture is important in the rooting of cuttings.   At the time the cutting is made, it is desirable that the tissues be turgid, since water absorption will be limited because of severance from the root system, and since internal moisture is necessary for all the processes associated with root formation. Good contact of the rooting medium with the stem will prevent drying and allow for the entrance of a limited amount of water into the cutting.   Uniformity of moisture is desirable, and intermittent mist not only maintains moisture in the atmosphere but prevents undue drying of the medium as well.

In the germination of seeds, uniformity of moisture is desirable, and mist systems are ideal for this purpose.   Alternation of wet to extremely dry conditions will reduce or prevent germination.   The regulation of moisture is most critical in seed germination because failure to provide the proper conditions will result in loss of plants and time.

Time of watering.   There are no satisfactory rules which can be given concerning the time of watering since there are so many factors involved.   The appearance or "feel" of the soil may be used as a guide, and judgment in the matter will come largely from experience.

Usually the proper time to water is at the point where the soil will crumble easily and not form a wad, or ball, if compressed in the hand.   If large quantities of peat have been added to the soil, it may not form a ball unless excessively moist.   If an ordinary soil or soil mixture fails to crumble when compressed in the hand, it is probably moist enough.   The entire depth of soil in a bench or pot must be examined, since the surface may be rather dry, while the area where the roots are found is quite moist.

A clean trowel or bamboo cane may also be used as a guide for determining when to water.   If either of these is inserted in the soil and there is some resistance, or "grating," and upon withdrawal it is free of soil particles, the soil probably should be watered.

Tensiometers also have been used as guides to soil moisture.   This is a device consisting of a porous clay cup with a vacuum gauge attached.   The cup is inserted into the soil, and the entire apparatus is filled with water.   As the soil dries, water leaves the porous cup and exerts a tension or pull which registers on the gauge.   When the soil is considered dry enough to water, the tension can be recorded, and thereafter the soil can be watered whenever the needle on the gauge reaches this particular value.   Although it would appear that such a device would be quite useful, it is subject to some limitations.   Insertion of several tensiometers close together in a bench usually results in as many different readings as there are tensiometers because of lack of uniformity in drying and some variations in the clay cup.   Insertion in the soil can result in different degrees of compaction, which accounts for variation and failure to give a true picture of the tension in an area not so compacted.   The tensiometer must not be disturbed or continuity of the moisture in the cup with that of the soil will be broken and there will no longer be any tension. It appears that this device is something of a "gadget," and it has not found wide acceptance in the trade.

There are several other factors which must be considered when determining whether the soil is dry enough to water. Though the soil usually dries from the top downward, it may be drier at the bottom than at the surface in winter, with heating pipes underneath. Heavy clay soils will dry more slowly than the lighter sandy types, and in the same soil type large plants with an expanded foliage area will have to be watered more often than small plants with limited foliage. As the temperature rises the soil will dry more rapidly because of an increased rate of evaporation of water from the soil and the plants. Mulching is helpful in reducing the evaporational loss from the soil.

With pot plants, the soil generally dries rapidly because of the small volume in relation to the size of the plant. Within a group of plants, some growers allow a few to wilt and then water the entire group on the assumption that all of them will need watering. However, some of the plants can be easily overwatered if this system is used, especially if the root system is not well developed. The color of the soil usually becomes somewhat lighter when it dries, and it may be used as an indicator of the need for water application. As the soil dries it becomes harder, and pressing on the soil with the thumb or fingers may indicate the relative dryness. Soil shrinks as it dries, and the ball will pull away from the side of the pot. When the soil shows hair line cracks at the edge of the ball, the plants should be examined periodically because this is an indication that the soil is beginning to dry.

When a soil is thoroughly moistened, small changes in the moisture content may not cause any detrimental effects on the plants. However, as the soil becomes progressively drier, only slight changes in the amount of water may result in wilting and subsequent injury. It is therefore necessary to inspect the soil and the plants frequently when the soil reaches the state of being nearly ready to water. The lighter the soil mix brought about by additions of inorganic and organic diluents or additives, the less is the danger of overwatering and therefore the more satisfactory is the medium for general use.

Amount of water. In a bench where the soil is 4 to 6 inches deep, usually ½ to 1 gallon of water is applied per square foot of area to adequately moisten the soil and cause some drip through. However, more water is needed to wet a heavier, or finer particled, soil as contrasted to the lighter, or coarser particled, types.

Frequent light sprinklings are injurious in that the surface of the soil remains moist, and the lower strata may become very dry, thus restricting the development of the roots throughout the entire soil mass. Whenever a soil is watered, enough should be applied to cause some to drain through, whether it is in a pot, flat, or bench.

Leaching is the application of several gallons of water per square foot of area to wash out excessive fertilizer which may injure the roots. Leaching will occur any time the soil drips after watering, but the amount of fertilizer removed is rather small in a normal watering.

Growers have long observed that soils watered from below stay wet longer than the same soil watered overhead. In fact, many growers are reluctant to subirrigate in winter because the soil stays so wet for such a long time. The difference in drying is due to the effectiveness with which the capillary, or water-retentive, pores are saturated by the method of watering used. Water applied from above enters the capillary, or small, pores, as well as the noncapillary, or large, pores, which are the air spaces in the soil. In these large pores, water is pulled downward by the force of gravity, and the excess water escapes from the soil before it has saturated or completely filled all capillary pores. However, water applied from below rises in the capillary pores and generally saturates all of them. Thus the amount of water held in a given soil will be greater when it is subirrigated than when it is watered overhead. Movement of water in a soil is largely vertical, and since there is so little lateral movement, it is important to apply a sufficient quantity of water as uniformly as is possible over the surface in order to thoroughly moisten all the soil.

Breakers. If water is forcefully applied to the surface of soil, it often breaks down the granules to the individual soil particles or causes a compaction that impedes the infiltration and percolation of water. The various mechanical systems (described in subsequent sections) for application of water to soils for both cut flowers and potted plants are of such nature that the water is applied as droplets or small streams, neither of which will cause compaction.

For the initial watering of a well-prepared or light soil which will be subsequently watered by other than manual means, it may be desirable to use a breaker to reduce the forcefulness of the water stream, yet cause just enough compaction to permit capillarity to become established so that subsequent waterings will adequately wet the entire soil body.

Methods of watering. Soil may be watered overhead or from below, the overhead methods being the most common. In either case there are mechanical means of application which reduce the amount of labor needed.

OVERHEAD SYSTEMS

Manual. Water can be applied to either cut flower benches or pot plants through a hose in the conventional manner. The volume should be great enough to complete the job without a waste of time, yet slow enough to avoid washing the soil or splashing the plants unduly. Breakers, as previously described, are suggested. The disadvantage of this method of watering is that it is very costly from the standpoint of the labor required.

Ohio surface irrigation.   A galvanized pipe can be laid lengthwise on the soil in the center of the bench and connected at one or more points to the water-supply line.   The pipe is drilled and tapped every 3 feet for nozzles that throw the water in a flat spray in a complete circle several inches above the soil. The overlapping of the sprays from the nozzles permits uniform wetting of the soil, and since the spray of water is parallel with and very close to the soil, there is a minimum of foliage wetting.   Considerable pressure and volume are needed to operate more than 50 feet of pipe because the nozzles allow approximately 1½ gallons of water to pass through them per minute.   Splashboards at the sides of the bench are needed to prevent the water from being wasted in the aisles as well as to adequately moisten the soil at the edges of the bench.   The full-circle nozzles and pipe may be obtained from the Skinner Irrigation Company, Troy, Ohio.

Plastic tubes—bench crops.   There are several types of plastic tubes which can be used for watering bench crops.   The collapsible tube lies flat on the surface of the soil, but when water is introduced, it becomes nearly round because of the pressure.   Although there are several alternatives in the matter of their placement, the holes from which the water escapes are generally located opposite each other in the upper portion of the tube so that the water flows out like a small fountain.   Pairs of these holes are spaced approximately 4 inches apart, permitting many small streams of water to fall on the soil.   Two lines of tubes commonly are used in a 4-foot-wide bench, placed lengthwise in the bench, parallel to each other and about 2 feet apart.   This system of watering operates satisfactorily on 2 to 3 pounds of water pressure, but greater pressure causes the streams of water to shoot out too far.   The water is allowed to run from 5 to 30

5-6. Perimeter watering of bench-grown plants moistens the soil uniformly without compaction. (*From "Flower and Plant Production in the Greenhouse," Interstate Printers & Publishers, Inc., Danville, Ill.*)

minutes, depending upon how long it takes to adequately moisten the soil. Although algae control has been solved by use of black plastic, the small holes may become clogged, leaving dry spots in the bench.

In perimeter watering, plastic pipe is placed around the bench. Polyethylene pipe is soft whereas polyvinyl chloride pipe is quite rigid, and the latter is easier to hold to the top of the bench sides and ends because it does not stretch or sag. The plastic pipe is connected at one or more places to the water supply to provide uniformity of pressure. Nozzles that throw a flat spray of water in a half circle are simply twisted into the pipe at 2- to 3-foot intervals facing the bench. The overlapping of the sprays from the nozzles permits uniform wetting of the soil, with more water falling on the soil near the edges of the bench than on the center because the plants offer some obstruction to the passage of water. Since the soil at the edge of the bench usually dries out more rapidly than that in the center, the system is well adapted. When the bench is steam-sterilized, the piping must be removed, and it is wise to wipe off the pipe with a suitable disinfectant prior to replacing it. Pipes and nozzles may be obtained from florist supply houses or local sources.

Soil in benches may be watered also by "ooze" or "soaker" hoses. These are usually made of a polyethylene sheet, folded and sewed loosely so as to permit water droplets to fall on the soil and slowly spread down and outwards. Since the rate of "flow" of water is slow, considerable time is required to water an area, though no labor is required other than opening and closing the valve. The number of hoses per bench depends upon the type of soil—how well the water spreads laterally to moisten all areas uniformly. Three are suggested for a 4-foot-wide bench.

5-7. Bench crops may be irrigated with collapsible plastic tubing, in this instance the Greco system. Small streams of water are emitted from the pairs of holes spaced 4 inches apart the length of the tubing. Note the straw incorporated into the soil for improvement of drainage. (*From "Flower and Plant Production in the Greenhouse," Interstate Printers & Publishers, Inc., Danville, Ill.*)

Plastic tubes—potted plants.   The irrigation of potted plants, particularly the 4-inch and larger sizes, has been revolutionized in the last few years. There are numerous variations and adaptations, but all are based on a plastic water supply main in the bench; connected to it are small plastic leader tubes which run to the individual pots.   The main is usually a ¾-inch plastic pipe but may be as large as 1¼ inches, depending upon the number of pots to be watered. It may be placed in the center of the bench, but placing it along one side permits more flexibility in spacing the pots.   A ¾-inch main will supply enough water for 1,600 pots (800 each way when the water enters the middle) while a 1¼-inch main will handle 4,400 pots.   Leader tubes which are inserted into the main should be uniform in length since the longer the tube, the greater the friction, which reduces the water flow.   Long and short leader tubes from the same water main will result in different amounts of water being applied to individual pots.

To hold the leader tubes firmly in the main, a small metal fitting can be inserted into the main with a punch device and the leader placed in the fitting where it holds tightly.   At the end of the leader tube for each pot, a special lead weight or anchor holds the end of the tube in place on the soil surface and permits the water to flow out freely.   Although usually one leader tube is placed in a pot, with the larger pot sizes or baskets, several tubes per container may be needed to give uniform water distribution.

Where there are larger numbers of potted plants to be grown in a bench than one main can supply, an additional main or two can be installed with leader tubes to supply the needs.   The main and leader tubes with weights are not permanently fastened in the bench but can be moved to other benches if desired. If a portion of the bench is empty, some of the leader tubes can be removed. The lead weights or anchors are removed from those that remain, and the end is placed back into the main so that the water is returned to the main and not wasted.

The above-described system may be used for cut flowers also by placing one or more leader tubes per square foot of bench area depending upon how

5-8. Pot plants can be irrigated by small plastic tubes supplied from a water main on the bench. Fertilizer may be injected into the irrigation system to provide a uniform amount of fertilizer regularly to each plant. (*Chapin Watermatics, Inc., photograph.*)

rapidly the water will spread laterally in the soil. There is no spray of water to moisten the foliage as in perimeter watering.

Variations of the single main or the multimain consist of having a manifold or header of smaller plastic pipe, usually of a short length, to which a number of leader tubes are permanently fastened, each tube leading to a pot. This can be somewhat cumbersome when plants must be spaced. When a portion of the bench is empty, the manifold may be disconnected from the main and a plastic plug inserted to prevent the waste of water.

The above systems may be operated manually or by valves which must be turned on by hand but are shut off automatically when the desired amount of water is added or after a given length of time (Fig. 5-9). Even more automatic is a "scale" on which a pot is placed. As the soil dries, the weight decreases and the platform of the scale rises. At the desired point of soil dryness, an electrical contact is made as the platform rises, and this operates a circuit that opens a solenoid valve to permit water to flow into the main and into the leader tubes to the pots. A spring adjustment on the scale permits varying amounts of water to be added before the weight of the pot plant is sufficient to depress the platform and break the electrical circuit. Several benches of pot plants can be watered from a single scale provided the plants are of the same size and the soil dries at the same rate as that of the pot on the scale. With potted mums it is well not to place the scale on the outside row of pots in a bench because if the pot on the scale is knocked off by the application of shading cloth in the afternoon, the plants will be watered all night, which is detrimental.

The use of small plastic tubes to irrigate pot plants will apply the water much more uniformly per pot than can be done by hand. If one or more plants develop poor roots for any cause, they should be taken off the system to prevent them from being watered before needed. Any of the pot plants grown by florists can be irrigated by this method, provided the mixture in which it is used has

5-9. One type of control for automated pot plant watering. When the desired amount of water enters the glass container through the small plastic tube, its weight trips the valve, shutting off the water flow. Other types of controls are a small scale which weighs the potted plant and a timing device to regulate the irrigation. (*Chapin Watermatics, Inc., photograph.*)

sufficient lateral capillarity to moisten the entire soil mass. A mixture of 2 or 3 parts soil, 1 part peat moss, and 1 part perlite is an ideal combination for many potted plants and has the necessary lateral capillarity. Immediately after potting, it is strongly recommended that the soil be watered with a breaker to "settle" it and establish contact between particles so that subsequent irrigations through the tubes will moisten all parts of the soil mixture.

In addition to the small plastic tubes, short sections of soaker or ooze hoses may be useful for the larger-sized pots and bushel baskets. These hoses are connected to the plastic pipe serving as the water main by short lengths of small-diameter tubing, and when the water is turned on, the soil in each container is watered uniformly but at a very low rate.

The water system for the greenhouse should be equipped with a suitable filter to prevent clogging of the small plastic tubes, and the filter should be cleaned or replaced periodically. Fertilizer can, of course, be supplied through the irrigation water by means of injectors. The method of irrigation through the tubes in conjunction with fertilizer injection can greatly improve the quality of any crop which has been subjected to faulty watering practices and haphazard fertilization.

SUBIRRIGATION

Subirrigation has been used for many years, but one of the greatest problems is maintaining a bench in a watertight condition when it is steamed frequently.

Manual. A level watertight bench with a V-bottom equipped with a channel (inverted eave trough or half tile) to permit uniform spread of the water is a requisite for raised benches. Gravel is placed in the bottom of the bench, covering the trough, to aid in the lateral movement of water to the sides of the benches. Ground beds can be subirrigated successfully if there is a rather impervious layer of soil or hardpan relatively near the surface which will retain the water long enough to permit saturation of the capillary pores before it escapes. Tile lines are laid 1½ to 2 feet apart in such soil above the hardpan, and water is introduced through these lines.

Water is generally allowed to run into the channel in the bench or tile in the ground until parts of the surface of the soil become moist, indicating that capillary pores in that area are saturated. The water is then turned off, and the excess is allowed to drain away. The cost of erecting and maintaining the benches in a watertight condition is a factor to consider. Further, unless the soil is watered overhead periodically, fertilizer salts accumulate in the soil, particularly at the surface, and may damage or kill the plant.

Pot plants are seldom subirrigated since a large volume of water is needed because of the relatively large amount of space between the pots. If the water were reused, there would be danger of spreading soil-borne disease organisms if present. Plants can be placed on gravel in a watertight bench and the water allowed to rise an inch or so above the gravel. When most of the soil is moistened, the water is drained. Soil in different pot sizes dries at different rates, necessitating numerous small units for each pot size, which is not practical.

Constant-level. This method involves a watertight bench in which a constant level of water is maintained by a float valve, usually located in a small external tank connected to the bench. Great care must be exercised with soil in benches or it will become extremely wet if the water level is too high and the anaerobic conditions in the lower soil area will usually prove phytotoxic. Pot plants are placed on a layer of sand which is kept constantly moist. Only clay pots are suitable since they permit water to move by capillarity through the clay pot wall to the soil, keeping it wet. Loss of capillarity is common if the pots are not firmly set on the sand. Constant level is seldom used commercially.

WATER QUALITIES

Hard and soft water. Hardness of water is caused by dissolved calcium and/or magnesium carbonate. Treatment to remove these materials is generally rather expensive. When salt (sodium chloride) is used in the Zeolite softening process, there is always danger that some of the salt may be discharged into the water supply and cause trouble. Addition of Calgon (sodium hexametaphosphate) to the water-supply lines will materially decrease the residue left on the foliage of plants caused by the dissolved minerals precipitating out of solution when the droplets on the leaves evaporate. The addition of any acid to water only changes the pH and does not soften it.

Hard water usually causes a gradual rise in the pH of the soil because of the alkalinity of calcium and magnesium carbonates. Other than this effect, it is believed that hardness has no detrimental effect on plants. The scale of values in Table 5-2 indicates the relative hardness of water.

Table 5-2. *Hardness of Water*

HARDNESS AS PARTS PER MILLION	HARDNESS AS GRAINS PER GALLON *	RELATIVE DEGREE OF HARDNESS
0–50	0–3	Very soft
50–100	3–6	Soft
100–200	6–12	Moderately soft
200–300	12–18	Hard
300 plus	18 plus	Very hard

* One grain is equivalent to 17 ppm.

Acidifying water.   Because the water supply in many areas of the country is alkaline, it has often been advocated that the water be acidified before it is applied to the soil, to prevent undue alkalinity.   While it is possible to do this, the equipment is rather expensive, and addition of too much acid can corrode the water pipes to the point where they may break.

The alkaline effect of hard water can be counteracted by use of acidifying fertilizers.   Ammonium sulfate, ammonium nitrate, and most complete fertilizers have a gradual acidifying effect on soil.   If the use of fertilizers does not neutralize the alkalinity, periodic applications of sulfur or iron sulfate can be made.   The use of such materials is cheaper than and just as effective as acidifying the water.

Chlorination.   Chlorine is added to water to reduce the population of various microorganisms which cause diseases in humans.   The chlorine gas is dissolved in the water, but it readily escapes when the water is aerated.   The application of water to the soil in itself causes aeration to some extent.   The amount of chlorine added to water is very small, and even though the water may have a decided chlorine taste, it is still not harmful to plants.   It is only when so much chlorine has been added that it is no longer fit to drink that chlorine can be injurious to plants.

Fluoridation.   The addition of sodium fluoride to municipal water supplies has been shown to be beneficial in reducing the incidence of cavities in children's teeth.   Because sodium fluoride is a poison if taken in quantities, the belief has arisen that fluoridated water would be harmful to plants.   The amount added is usually 1 part per million, and in many areas of the country the natural fluoride content of the water is 3 to 5 parts per million.   There need be no fear that fluoridated municipal water will be harmful when used in a greenhouse.

Total salts.   Fertilizers are commonly referred to as salts, and the total amount of fertilizer dissolved in water is referred to as the salts content.   The term does not refer specifically to the sodium chloride (table salt) content of the water, but rather to the amount of dissolved mineral elements.   As the total salts content of the soil rises, absorption of water decreases, and damage has been known to occur if the concentration rises too high.

Analysis of the total salts content of water by means of a Solu Bridge Model RD-B15 apparatus (Beckman Instruments, Inc., Cedar Grove, New Jersey) can be made easily, and the scale of values in Table 5-3 and their interpretation are of interest.

Where well water has too high a total salts concentration, a new well should be drilled, tapping another vein of water.   Otherwise the salts concen-

Table 5-3.   *Total Salts Content of Water as Determined by a Solu Bridge*

Solu Bridge reading of water	Interpretation
0–0.25	Excellent
0.25–0.75	Good
0.75–1.50	Fair
1.50–2.00	Permissible
2.00 plus	Excessive (too salty)

tration will rise in the soil and crops will not grow properly. Changing soil periodically is an expedient but does not remove the cause of the trouble.

RELATIVE HUMIDITY

Relative humidity is the amount of water vapor in the atmosphere at a given temperature expressed as a percentage of the amount that could be held if the air were saturated. A relative humidity of 70 percent at any temperature indicates that the air is holding 70 percent of the moisture that it could hold at that temperature. Since warm air can hold more moisture than cold air, considerably more water must be evaporated at a high temperature to maintain a certain percentage of relative humidity in the atmosphere. As the temperature drops, the relative humidity will increase unless there is some means of allowing the air to escape from the greenhouse. A still lower temperature may result in condensation of the moisture as water on the plants, which may allow the development of certain disease organisms. At temperatures somewhat above freezing, the air next to the glass is cold enough so that the moisture it contains condenses on the glass in droplets. In severely cold weather, ice forms inside the glass from the freezing of the condensed moisture, and the relative humidity is reduced.

The maintenance of sufficient relative humidity in the daytime and its dissipation at night can become very important problems in the culture of florist crops. Plastic greenhouses, whether of rigid or film material, have fewer laps or places for air to enter or escape, hence excessive relative humidity becomes a problem particularly in relation to such diseases as Botrytis blight or powdery mildew.

Transpiration. Transpiration is the loss of water vapor from the plant from stomates, or pores through which carbon dioxide enters the leaf. It is governed by the humidity of the atmosphere and vapor pressure in the leaf. At rather low relative humidities, transpiration occurs by diffusion, which is the net movement of molecules from a region of higher concentration of molecules to one of a lower concentration of the same kind of molecules. If the relative humidity is near or at saturation, water vapor still escapes if the leaf is warmer than the air, because of the greater vapor pressure of the water in the leaves. If the relative humidity is kept high in the daytime, water loss is reduced and cells of plants are larger, generally giving rise to a higher quality product. Washed-air or high-pressure-mist cooling is an effective means of maintaining high relative humidity in the daytime.

Photosynthesis.   When a high relative humidity is maintained, the stomates remain open.   If the relative humidity drops, the stomates may almost close, thus limiting the formation of carbohydrates.

Reducing relative humidity.   Because certain disease organisms (powdery and downy mildew and others) flourish at very high relative humidities, it is decidedly advantageous to prevent the atmosphere from carrying too much moisture, which is likely to occur at night.   As the temperature drops, the relative humidity increases, and with transpiration continuing, a pocket of very high relative humidity can accumulate around the plant.   This pocket can be dissipated or prevented from forming by use of fans or ventilation with heat. Leaving the ventilators somewhat open at night is no insurance of adequate air circulation—at least not enough to prevent trouble from certain disease organisms.   Turning on a heating line or two in mild weather not only causes a slight rise in temperature, which in itself reduces the relative humidity, but also accelerates circulation, which prevents pockets of moist air from forming.   The use of heat alone, however, is not enough—it must be coupled with some ventilation. Proper regulation of these two factors will provide an unfavorable environment for the continued growth of powdery mildew so that a fungicide can be used to kill the organism and effective control may be obtained.   Use of a fungicide alone without regulation of the environment will not be effective.

Fans for air circulation dissipate pockets of high relative humidity around the plants and mix the air homogenously.   However, the use of fans alone may not be satisfactory because the relative humidity can rise if there is no ventilation. In fact, fans can spread spores of mildew and *Botrytis* very effectively.   When an exhaust fan is used, particularly in connection with perforated polyethylene tubing into which the outside air is conducted by means of a louver in a gable wall, excess relative humidity at night can be regulated through temperature control.   When air is constantly circulated through one or more polyethylene tubes in a greenhouse (the Fan-Jet method), more precise control of temperature and relative humidity is obtained.

Walks or aisles may be covered with a thin layer of concrete to reduce the surface area from which moisture can evaporate, resulting in a lowering of relative humidity.   Using all the heating lines in very cold weather dries the air, and this, coupled with freezing of the water on the glass, may actually cause a low relative humidity to develop which may be detrimental for normal stem elongation and flower enlargement.

Increasing relative humidity.   The air change in a greenhouse may be almost as frequent as once a minute if both the side and top ventilators are wide open.   With only the top ventilators open, a complete change may occur every 10 to 15 minutes since the entrance of air between the overlapping glass is somewhat slower.   In plastic houses the air change is even less frequent because of the limited number of places of entry for air unless side ventilators or louvers are used.

Syringing the foliage and walks by hand will temporarily raise the relative humidity, but in the hot summer weather with the ventilators wide open, this moisture is soon dissipated because of its quick evaporation and movement out of the house.   Unless the foliage and walks are moistened several times an hour, the increase in moisture is temporary.

A shade on the roof will reduce the temperature, which in itself will cause a rise in relative humidity.   Shading plus syringing is used by some florists to combat the effect of low relative humidity.

Washed-air cooling is an effective means of increasing atmospheric moisture.   The evaporation of moisture from the aspen pad reduces the temperature and increases the relative humidity, both of which are desirable for many plants in hot summer weather.

Maintaining a favorable relative humidity of the air can become a problem during cold weather when many heating lines are used.   The air is dried not only from the heat but also from the condensation and freezing of the atmospheric moisture on the underside of the glass in the roof.   The high-pressure-mist system can be used to advantage, day and/or night, to provide the desired relative humidity.

Water can be misted at either low (up to 100 pounds) or high (400 to 800 pounds) pressure.   Low-pressure misting is less desirable than high because the water is really not a mist but rather small droplets which quickly wet the foliage and run off on the soil, keeping it soggy.   The high-pressure misting systems fog the water so that the foliage only becomes wet if the system is improperly operated.   It is the more desirable of the two misting methods, but it requires the use of special pumps and filters, as described in Chap. 3.

For propagation, low-pressure misting is very suitable.   By keeping a film of moisture on the leaves of most plants, it is possible to greatly increase the light intensity without burning or injuring the foliage.   The cuttings root faster and do not become soft, as they often will in conventional propagation houses which are heavily shaded.   The most satisfactory control for mist consists of a time switch for control of the hours or time of operation, which in turn controls a timer, which governs the frequency of misting.   Timers are available for misting from as often as every minute to as infrequently as every 2 hours. Within this period, the apparatus is adjustable to operate the mist for as little as 3 seconds or longer as desired. Usually the mist is operated more frequently in the early stages of rooting or seed germination, then tapered off as the cuttings root or the seedlings develop.

A typical misting setup consists of a metal or plastic pipe over a propagation area which is generally a bench, although aisle space and heated frames may be used when space is at a premium. Nozzles that emit a full-circle mist spray are placed every 3 feet on the top of the pipe, and at this distance there will be sufficient overlapping of mist to cover the area uniformly. Placing a shutoff valve under each nozzle will permit greater flexibility in tapering off or completely shutting down mist. Dripping of the water from the pipeline does not appear to cause problems in a rooting bench from excess moisture unless the propagation medium is poorly drained; however, in seed flats it is troublesome. Entrance of the water into the overhead pipeline is governed by a solenoid valve that is controlled by the timer.

Some florists have several smaller sections of mist line rather than one large system. By having several timers on which the frequency of misting varies, they can plug in the electrical wires from the solenoid valve to a receptacle controlled by the appropriate timer to obtain the desired misting interval.

A mist propagation line with nozzles would not be very satisfactory for watering plants in soil because the droplets would be rather small and a considerable period of operation would be required to wet a bench or pot. Bedding plants in their shallower containers could conceivably be watered with a mist line. Where foliage on growing plants should not be moistened because of evidence of disease, a mist line would prove impractical. Mist propagation lines are unsatisfactory for overhead placement in a greenhouse to provide relative humidity because the droplets are too large and "fall-out" of moisture would make the soil too wet. This does not apply, however, to propagation and growth of tropical foliage plants in Florida.

AERATION

An exchange of air is desirable in a greenhouse to enable the plants to grow satisfactorily. Very often an experienced greenhouse operator can "feel" the air as he walks through the greenhouse and determine whether it is buoyant or stuffy.

Photosynthesis. The carbon dioxide content of the air is approximately 0.03 percent, and during periods of high light intensity and warm temperatures when the plants are well supplied with water, it is the limiting factor in photosynthesis. Generally, the higher temperatures associated with greater light intensity make it mandatory to provide ventilation, thus assuring the presence of as much carbon dioxide as is available in the atmosphere.

Addition of carbon dioxide to the greenhouse atmosphere is now a common practice though there is much to be learned about its use. At present there is insufficient information about the level to be maintained in the atmosphere and the time that carbon dioxide should be added. Despite this, there are some practices which are generally used that are successful with a number of crops. The practicability of its use depends on the costs of installation commensurate with higher quality or greater quantity of crops.

Carbon dioxide can be obtained from several sources; the compressed gas is stored in bulk tanks outside the greenhouse and the flow of the gas is regulated by means of flow meters. Carbon dioxide can be generated by burning various fuels such as propane, illuminating gas, or kerosene in specially designed equipment that provides complete combustion to eliminate formation of ethylene and other unsaturated hydrocarbons as well as carbon monoxide. Too hot a burner may cause formation of oxides of nitrogen which are detrimental. Dry ice has also been used by placing it in a chamber where the evolved gas can be metered through lines to the greenhouse. When a fuel is used that contains sulfur, the amount that is permissible should not exceed 0.02 percent for fuel oil, 10 grains per 100 cubic feet for propane, and 3.5 grains per 100 cubic feet for natural gas, or the amount of lethal sulfur dioxide may be too great.

The carbon dioxide from the compressed gas or dry ice is regulated by flow meters to each area where it may be introduced into the greenhouse through

5-10. This is a gas-fired carbon dioxide generator. In addition to carbon dioxide, heat and water vapor are also produced.

5-11. A refrigerated tank for the storage of carbon dioxide in liquid form. The flow of carbon dioxide into the greenhouse is controlled by regulating valves, and the carbon dioxide is dispensed into the greenhouses by means of small-diameter perforated plastic tubes. (*General Dynamics Liquid Carbonic Division photograph.*)

an overhead plastic tubing, ¼ inch in diameter, which has been pierced with a needle every 3 feet. The outlet may also be placed near a fan which will effectively distribute the gas. In fact, it is difficult to confine the gas to one greenhouse since glass partitions are not usually very tightly lapped or butted and carbon dioxide can diffuse through polyethylene. Normal circulation of air will distribute it quite readily.

5-12. The gas-fired-type carbon dioxide generator. It is located outside the greenhouse, and the carbon dioxide is cooled before it is introduced into the greenhouse. (*Tectrol Division photograph.*)

Carbon dioxide generators make use of fans or jet action to blow the gas into the greenhouse atmosphere where it spreads quickly. There must be sufficient oxygen in the air for complete combustion, which can be a problem in a plastic house or a new "tight" house. A duct to the outside must be installed to provide unlimited oxygen. If sulfur is used for control of diseases, a duct to the outside is also necessary to prevent excessive sulfur dioxide fumes from being generated.

Some carbon dioxide comes from the respiration of microorganisms in the soil as well as from the roots, and from organic mulches, which generate considerable quantities in the early stages of decomposition.

Early research indicated benefits from as little as 500 ppm of carbon dioxide maintained in the air, and since then considerably higher levels have been tested. A level of 5,000 ppm is the maximum permitted for human safety in submarines, and higher levels are not advised. However, the cost of maintaining more than 2,500 ppm will not be justified by the returns from the crop, indicating that other factors are limiting and damaging when the level is this high.

Under normal air movement a higher carbon dioxide level probably has to be maintained compared to the use of fans in order to have a similar amount of the gas around the leaf. In still air, a deficit of the gas could exist under the leaf caused by diffusion of carbon dioxide into the stomates. Fans would quickly replenish or maintain the supply by air movement, but without them, carbon dioxide would have to diffuse from surrounding air to replenish the atmosphere in the area of the leaf.

Carbon dioxide is generally used from November through early March in areas where the outside temperature dictates reduction of ventilation to maintain a favorable air temperature in the greenhouse. However, it seems possible that carbon dioxide might even be added in summer in washed-air-cooled houses where the air is pulled long distances and the level can get quite low by the time the air is exhausted through the fan.

Carbon dioxide is usually introduced slightly before sunrise to build up the level before photosynthesis starts. The flow meters or generators are started, and as the light intensity increases, the level of the gas will drop to the range at which it is desired to be maintained. If ventilation is needed because of a rise in temperature above the desired level, the carbon dioxide is usually shut off when the top vents are open more than 2 inches because of the loss of the gas.

Additions of carbon dioxide have proved beneficial where other environmental factors do not limit the growth of plants. This means that carbon dioxide is not a cure-all, but simply an aid to the grower. When it is used during the winter months with roses, production is increased and stems are somewhat stiffer. Carnation stems are generally stiffer, but flower size and color are not enhanced. Cut Chrysanthemums may mature slightly earlier, have somewhat larger flowers, and weigh more, but their color is generally unchanged. Snapdragons may flower

5-13. Some varieties of Chrysanthemum respond favorably to additions of carbon dioxide to the greenhouse atmosphere if other factors are also optimum. (*Yoder Bros., Inc., photograph.*)

as much as two weeks earlier and their stems may be stronger.   There has been less research or grower experience with pot plants, but somewhat larger plants and reduced crop time have been observed.   Keeping quality has not been materially affected on any crop, though dry weight has increased.

Limited experience indicates that the night temperature should not be changed if carbon dioxide is used.   If the day temperature rises above normal from the reduced ventilation when using carbon dioxide, the quality of the crop can be adversely affected, though this may depend upon the crop.   Carnations are reduced in quality in higher day temperatures while mums may be slightly benefitted.

Respiration.   Oxygen is needed for this vital energy-releasing process. Approximately 20 percent of the air is oxygen, which is sufficiently high so that it does not become limiting to respiration.   Soil aeration can be troublesome in heavy, poorly drained soils, and suffocation is the probable reason why seeds planted too deeply will not germinate, and roots die when the soil is kept too wet.

In the 31 to 33°F storage of cuttings and cut flowers in packages or containers, respiration is reduced by the continual decrease in oxygen level in addition to the cold temperature and increased carbon dioxide.   It is therefore important to have the package or container filled with the plant material with little empty space.

Relative humidity.   Stagnant air is undesirable in a greenhouse largely because the accumulation of atmospheric moisture is favorable for development of certain disease organisms.   During the day high relative humidity is seldom a problem except in "muggy" mild weather when the outside temperature is just high enough so that heat is not needed. Even with the ventilators open, air circulation is slow and the relative humidity can rise. This high relative humidity can be dissipated by use of a few heating lines to circulate and dry the air. At night some ventilation is needed, provided the weather is suitable, to allow for escape of the moist air. Heat will accelerate circulation and prevent dangerously high humidity. In extremely cold weather when ventilation is impractical, the freezing of the moisture on the glass is effective in preventing excessively high relative humidities.

Fans are ideally suited for circulating the air and preventing "dead" areas or stagnant atmosphere.

Ventilation. For many years greenhouses were ventilated by the use of top vents alone or in combination with side vents. With the introduction of washed-air cooling, it appeared logical to continue the use of some of the fans in winter for ventilation. This serves partially as a justification for year-round use of the equipment and also gives better temperature control. Until perforated polyethylene tubing or plenum was introduced, there was no satisfactory way of introducing the outside air into the greenhouse without cold drafts. Fans are being used increasingly for ventilation, because they can be controlled with a thermostat which maintains a more uniform temperature than is possible with manpower on conventional ventilators.

The preferred type of conventional top ventilation is continuous on each side of the ridge. Sometimes, for the sake of economy, only one top ventilator is installed on the side away from the prevailing wind in cold weather. The ventilators should be hinged at the ridge rather than at the header, because if they are hinged at the header, rain or snow will enter unless the ventilator is completely closed.

Side ventilators are very useful in promoting air circulation, although such pests as thrips, grasshoppers, and tarnished plant bugs can enter the greenhouse through the side vents and injure the plants. Side ventilators reduce heat considerably in summer.

There should be some ventilation in a greenhouse at all times except during unfavorably cold weather or storms or during fumigation. Heavy winds will often tear the ventilators from the greenhouse or cause such stress that the glass will break if the vents are only partially open. The ventilator opposite to the prevailing wind should be open the widest, and the amount of ventilation should be such that there are no strong drafts.

In bright, warm summer weather the ventilators are usually open all night except in stormy weather, and they should be raised early enough to prevent the temperature from becoming too warm. In winter, there is virtue in not raising the ventilators too early, in order to allow the accumulated carbon dioxide to dissipate.   However, it is foolhardy to keep ventilation reduced in winter to save carbon dioxide since quality will be adversely affected if the day temperature is allowed to become too warm.   Ventilation is reduced in the evening as the temperature drops, but some heat should be used when necessary to allow for air circulation.   Conserving fuel by clamping the ventilators in late afternoon and leaving them closed until the next morning is false economy because inhibiting air circulation may allow certain disease organisms to flourish.

Although power equipment is available for raising top ventilators, it is usually more satisfactory to use fans and polyethylene tubing and dispense with top ventilators except as an emergency.

Several systems involving fans may be used for late fall, winter, and early spring ventilation.   One or more of the washed-air-cooling fans which exhaust the air can be operated and a top vent used for admittance of fresh, cooled air; this usually results in a downdraft of cold air and uneven temperatures.   The same fans are preferred for use in conjunction with a polyethylene tube, which is usually 18 to 30 inches in diameter with holes at regular intervals on opposite sides.   The tubing is attached to a louver which opens when the exhaust fan operates and admits the fresh, cool air into the tubing.   The air flows from the small openings and mixes thoroughly with the greenhouse air before it strikes the plants.   An improved version of this is the Fan-Jet system in which a circulating fan, mounted 12 to 18 inches from the gable wall, blows into the polyethylene tubing.   This fan runs continuously and circulates the air night and day.   When the temperature of the air is greater than the thermostat setting, an exhaust fan begins operation, and a motorized louver installed in the gable end in line with the circulating fan opens.   Fresh cool air is thus introduced and the hot air is exhausted.   When the desired temperature is reached, the exhaust fan shuts off and the louver closes, but the circulating fan continues to operate.   Precise temperature control is possible with this system.

GROWTH REGULATORS

Growth regulators consist of a large number of organic compounds, which may be unrelated chemically, that have a pronounced effect on plant growth. Some may promote growth, such as the naturally occurring hormones that were briefly mentioned in the previous chapter.   Other regulators act as inhibitors of growth and serve the useful purpose of preventing plants from growing too tall.

Fatty acids of 8-, 9-, or 10-carbon chains, when applied as a spray to the upper portions of some plants cause the stem tips to die, and hence act as a chemical-pinching material.   Concentrations of 1 to 3 percent on Chrysanthemums and 3 to 4 percent on azaleas have been effective experimentally.   Other florist crops have been injured severely by these fatty acid sprays.

Benzene ring compounds such as naphthalene and related compounds show promise experimentally in the disbudding of standard Chrysanthemums. When it is applied as a spray or a fumigant to plants given 10 to 18 short days, the terminal bud is not affected, but the partially developed axillary flower buds are damaged by the material and do not continue in growth.

Undoubtedly, as research progresses, other chemicals will be found that will be more effective and safer as chemical-pinching and disbudding agents.

General effects of treatment. Most of the growth retardants used by florists cause a reduction in the rate of cell division in the meristematic area of the stem tip as well as a very marked reduction in cell elongation in the area immediately below the tip (subapical meristem). It is believed that the retardants may interfere with the action of the naturally occurring gibberellins, causing growth to be reduced.

The growth retardants usually make the leaves darker green. The palisade layer of cells in the leaf is much closer together in retardant-treated plants so that there is a greater concentration of chlorophyll per area of leaf surface. The number of internodes is the same on treated or untreated plants, but the internodal length is shorter on the treated plants. Because of the short internodal length, the stems offer better support for the leaves and flowers on most plants (except lilies) even though the stems are structurally weaker. Leaves of treated plants may feel thicker to the touch, but actually they are thinner. On poinsettias and Chrysanthemums the time of flowering is not affected, though the size of both leaves and flowers as well as the colorful bracts on poinsettias is slightly reduced. The growth of treated azaleas is so severely checked that flower buds form, and hence the materials are useful in promoting floriferousness. Treated azaleas usually must have a longer cooling period and be forced at a higher temperature than untreated plants. The method of application depends upon the material and the plant to be treated.

5-14. Spraying with B-Nine at the time of disbudding of some Chrysanthemum varieties will reduce the length of the flower stem or "neck" and may also cause the flower to be more incurved. (*Yoder Bros., Inc., photograph.*)

5-15. B-Nine sprays at the time of disbudding some Chrysanthemum varieties may adversely affect their flower form. (*Yoder Bros., Inc., photograph.*)

Phosfon. Phosfon (2,4-dichlorobenzyl tributyl phosphonium chloride) is a quaternary ammonium compound called a phosphonium. It is effective on azaleas, Chrysanthemums, Easter lilies. Petunias, and Rhododendrons, but inactive on China asters, geraniums, and poinsettias. The commercial product is a 10 percent formulation sold as Phosfon-D (dry) and Phosfon-L (liquid).

If stronger concentrations of Phosfon than recommended are used, the

5-16. Cross sections of leaves from Elisabeth Ecke poinsettia plants in short days. Top to bottom: untreated check, B-Nine sprayed, and Cycocel sprayed. Left to right: samples taken 2, 4, and 6 weeks after treatment. Treated leaves have smaller cells and are thinner, and both the palisade and the spongy mesophyll layers are more compact. The darker green appearance of treated leaves is due to more chlorophyll per unit leaf area.

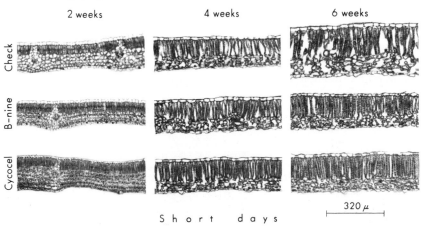

2 weeks   4 weeks   6 weeks

Check

B-nine

Cycocel

S h o r t   d a y s   320 μ

plants are severely stunted, and even at suggested concentrations its effect is long-lasting. Specific directions concerning its use are given for the various crops. Because it is a soil drench rather than a foliar spray, more time and precision are needed in its application and its use is giving way to other materials.

Cycocel. Cycocel (2-chloroethyl trimethyl ammonium chloride), formerly called CCC, is also a quaternary ammonium compound, and can be used on azaleas and poinsettias. It is available in liquid form as an 11.8 percent formulation which is diluted with water and applied as a foliar spray to azaleas and as a soil drench or foliar spray to poinsettias. The soil drench is preferred on the early-propagated poinsettias, because one application is more effective in reducing height than several foliar sprays.

B-Nine. B-Nine (N-dimethylaminosuccinamic acid), formerly called B-995, can be used on azaleas, Chrysanthemums—both as pot plants and cut flowers, pot Gardenias, Hydrangeas, and poinsettias; and also on bedding plants such as China asters, Cosmos, marigolds, Petunias, and Salvias. The commercial product is a 5 percent formulation with a self-contained spreader. It is applied as a foliar spray and is absorbed best when the plant is fully turgid. Therefore, application should be made in late afternoon on well-watered plants so that the maximum absorption can take place overnight. Sprayed plants should not be syringed or misted for several days following application or the effect will be diminished.

Others. Maleic hydrazide has been tried as a growth retardant but its effect is severe stunting rather than shortened normal growth. While the various weed killers, including 2,4-dichlorophenoxy acetic acid (2,4-D) and numerous related compounds, are often referred to as growth regulators, they have no place in the greenhouse. Accidental application often kills plants, or if they survive, they may be malformed and unsalable. Fumes of these compounds are also damaging as they may be carried some distance in the air and cause trouble. Water supplies occasionally are polluted with weed killers as a result of application to cultivated field crops or in brush-killing operations.

6
SOILS

Soil is a mixture of weathered particles of rock and decaying organic matter containing moisture and air that covers the earth in a thin layer. It is a dynamic and ever-changing system because of the physical, chemical, and biological changes brought about by the activities of numerous microorganisms. Thus the soil is a very complex medium, serving as a mechanical support of plants and also as a reservoir for a partial supply of fertilizer materials and moisture.

CHARACTERISTICS OF SOIL

About half of a given volume of soil consists of solids; the other half consists of voids, or openings, which contain water and air in varying proportions. Mineral matter comprises over 90 percent of the solid matter in most soils. However, the mineral content is less than 35 percent in peats and varies between 35 and 75 percent in mucks.

Texture. The term texture in reference to soil refers to the size of the individual soil particles, which are classified as sand, silt, or clay. The relative sizes and some other properties of these particles are shown in Table 6-1.

Table 6-1. *Some Properties of Individual Soil Particles*

TEXTURAL NAME	DIAMETER, MILLIMETERS *	NO. OF PARTICLES PER GRAM (APPROX. 1/30 OZ)	SQUARE CENTIMETERS/GRAM SURFACE AREA
Clay	Less than 0.002	90,260,853,860	11,342.5
Silt	0.002–0.05	5,776,674	453.7
Sand	0.05 –2.0	5,777	45.4

* As established by the U.S. Department of Agriculture.

Clay. It has often been stated that clay is the "active" part of the soil as opposed to the other mineral constituents, which are often referred to as the "skeleton" of the soil. Clay is composed largely of crystalline minerals which contain a high proportion of silicon, aluminum, magnesium, iron, and hydrogen, with much smaller amounts of calcium, potassium, and sodium. The minerals are composed of layers of silica (silicon dioxide) and alumina (aluminum oxide), which in turn are arranged in a definite manner. The kaolin group of clays is composed of one layer of silica and one of alumina. It is a rigid, or nonexpanding, crystal with limited internal space. The montmorillonoid group of clays is composed of two layers of silica and one of alumina. It has considerable internal space and possesses the property of great internal expansion and shrinkage during wetting and drying. The illite group of clays has a fixed, or nonexpanding, crystal of two layers of silica and one of alumina. While this group does not expand internally, there is some swelling and shrinkage upon wetting and drying because of the large amount of water that can be held by the clay.

Expansion and contraction of the clays, particularly montmorillonite, accounts for the appearance of cracks in soil when it becomes dry, followed by closure of the cracks when the soil is wetted. Sometimes water runs through these cracks so rapidly that the soil mass is not uniformly moistened. This condition necessitates a second watering to moisten all parts of the soil adequately. Generally, in the interval of time between the two waterings, the wetted clay colloids will have absorbed water and expanded so that the cracks will have been closed, reducing the rate at which water will percolate through the soil.

The clay particle is negatively charged at its "core," and it will adsorb positively charged fertilizer ions (cations such as potassium, calcium, magnesium, and others). These fertilizer materials are held rather tightly to the clay particle, and watering the soil will not dislodge them. By a process called "cation exchange (often referred to as base exchange)," some of the cations can be replaced upon addition of certain fertilizers to the soil. For example, if a solution of muriate of potash (KCl) is applied, the potassium will replace calcium held on the clay particles and the replaced calcium will form a calcium chloride solution in the soil. The calcium in calcium chloride then exists in an ionized (free) state rather than adsorbed to the clay particle. In the respiration process, roots and microorganisms form carbon dioxide, which can combine with water in the soil, giving rise to carbonic acid. This acid dissociates, and the hydrogen ions will replace those of potassium, calcium, ammonium, magnesium, and others, which were adsorbed on the clay colloid. These replaced fertilizer elements can then be absorbed by the root or can be leached away. Thus it is that clay soils eventually become acid and depleted of certain necessary elements when cropped for many years without addition of fertilizer or lime because of the absorption or leaching of the bases (calcium, potassium, and others). For this reason (the property of cation exchange) it is desirable to have some clay in a soil mixture, because many of the fertilizers will be adsorbed and will not leach. This cation-exchange phenomenon is most pronounced in the montmorillonite clay where the particles have a large internal and external surface area. In sandy soils the absence of any appreciable amount of clay necessitates the frequent application of fertilizers to maintain a rather uniform supply for the plants.

When a single application of lime is added to soils there is often little or no change in acidity. This resistance of soils to change in acidity is called "buffering," and the amount of resistance is called the "buffer capacity" of a soil. The buffer capacity of a soil is due to adsorption of the calcium on the colloidal particles rather than its existence in solution of "free" state. Until a large percentage of the adsorptive areas in the clay is saturated with calcium, free calcium will not be present in appreciable amounts in the soil solution. Until this occurs, there will be little change in soil acidity.

From the above presentation it is readily apparent that clay is a very important constituent of soil because of its effect on expansion and contraction, cation exchange, and buffer capacity.

Silt. Particles of silt, in general, are too large to have any marked effect on the process of cation exchange described for clay. Silt particles do not readily cohere or adhere to other mineral soil constituents, which gives rise to the expression that some silt soils "run like sugar." In the gradual decomposition of silt, some bases (calcium, potassium, and others) are liberated and can be adsorbed on the clay, absorbed by the plant, or leached from the soil.

Sand.   Because particles of sand are so large in relation to particles of clay, they have a small surface area in comparison and no chemical activity occurs on them as it does with clay.   The clay particles may adhere to sand, and as such the sand becomes a "framework" in the soil.   Sand will increase the size of the spaces between the smaller soil particles and facilitate movement of air and water.   Some soils containing large amounts of sand, however, can pack together tightly, forming a soil that may resemble concrete.

Loam.   Mixtures of certain desirable proportions of sand, silt, and clay are called "loams," that is, sandy clay loam, silty clay loam, and others.   The florist usually removes the top soil from an area of land and adds large quantities of organic matter as well as sand for some potted plants.   Thus the original soil generally loses its identity because of the addition of various materials far in excess of what would normally be added in nature or general farming practices.

Structure.   Structure refers to the arrangement of the primary, or individual, soil particles.   When the particles are loosely arranged, largely as primary particles, the soil structure is said to be "dispersed."   As such, the soil can become compact and not permit the rapid passage of either water or air.   A dispersed condition often occurs at the surface of soil in benches when subjected to the "pounding" of forceful streams of water applied manually from the hose over a period of time.   The water will stand on the soil for some time before penetrating the dispersed layer and percolating through the soil.   The use of breakers on the hose as well as mulches on the soil will prevent dispersion of the soil granules.   Irrigation of benches by nozzles on pipes and potted plants by small tubes to each plant reduces soil compaction and hence is preferable to hand watering.

Granulation is the grouping together of the primary soil particles into secondary particles.   It is desirable because it draws the particles into close contact, leaving spaces between the granules.   The importance of this will be emphasized later in relation to air and water in the soil.

Granules, or aggregates, vary in stability depending upon the nature of the forces holding them together.   Although these forces are not well understood, it appears that they are associated to some extent with the water content, organic matter, and clay content of the soil.   As the soil dries, granules become more stable because of attraction of the soil particles to each other.   When the soil is wet, the granules may partially disintegrate, and they may regranulate in a different pattern upon subsequent drying.   The gluelike secretions of microorganisms may also cement together the particles of soil at the surface of a granule in a more permanent manner than that of the colloids in wetting and drying.   The effect of secretions of microorganisms in granulating soils is much more pronounced if materials high in easily decomposed carbohydrate are added to the soil.   Corncobs, manure, sugar cane, straw, hay, and other materials that are fresh or not well decomposed will stimulate growth of microorganisms and increase the amount of material secreted.   Addition of peat will not cause granulation because peat resists decomposition by microorganisms.   Krilium is the trade name of a synthetic material which stabilizes the structure by its effect on the granules that exist in the soil.

Porosity, or pore space.   Between the primary soil particles as well as the granules are spaces which may be occupied by water or air, depending upon their size.

Within many granules and where granules touch each other, the pore spaces are small and are capable of holding water against the force of gravity. These are called capillary pores.   If the base of a column of soil is placed in water, the water will rise in capillary pores in the same manner as ink spreads in a blotter.   When applied from below, water will rise in the capillary pores of a clay soil to a height of about 20 inches in a day's time, or until the free water supply is exhausted.   When the soil is watered from above, the capillary pores will be saturated, provided sufficient water is applied and provided there are not so many large pores or cracks that the water drains through before the capillary pores are completely saturated.   The water that is absorbed by the roots of most plants is held in the capillary pores.   Because of the small size of the particles of clay there are many capillary pores, which is the reason why clay soils are wet and heavy.

The larger spaces usually found between granules are called noncapillary pores because water will not rise in them if a column of soil is placed in water. Normally the noncapillary pore space is occupied by air unless the drainage under the soil is impeded or water is being applied overhead, at which time most of the spaces would be temporarily filled with water.   Since these noncapillary pore spaces cannot hold water against the force of gravity, they provide the channels through which air can diffuse into or out of the soil as well as for circulation of air within.   Sandy soils usually have numerous noncapillary pores, and this is the reason why they dry rapidly.

There is no sharp line of demarcation at which a noncapillary pore becomes small enough to be called a capillary pore or vice versa since the pore spaces in the soil are irregular in size and are not necessarily continuous.   The ideal soil contains enough of each kind of pore space to supply adequate moisture and air for the root system and desirable microorganisms.

Soil water.   The noncapillary pores are so large that water applied overhead will drain through them by the force of gravity.   The water that passes through is called "gravitational water."   It is not absorbed to any degree by most florist crops because it is not in the soil for any length of time.

In the capillary pores, water is held against the force of gravity. The pores are so small that the cohesive force within the water and the adhesive force between the water and the soil particles are stronger than gravity, though the amount of capillary water is less at the top of a column of water than at the lower portion. This capillary water is available to the plant. Capillary water moves to a very limited extent in soils, mostly by evaporation and subsequent condensation in an adjacent area. In subirrigation, capillary water moves upward in soil by virtue of the presence of a water table under the soil. When the water table is withdrawn and all the "free" water has been absorbed, capillary movement will stop. When a soil is saturated and most of the gravitational water has escaped, the soil is said to be at field capacity. At this point the water is not held with as much tension as it is when the soil becomes drier. Eventually, as the soil dries, the force with which the water is held becomes as strong as that of the absorbing force of the root, and the plant wilts. This point is referred to as the wilting point, or wilting coefficient, because the plant will not revive if placed in a saturated atmosphere. Although at the wilting point the percentage of moisture varies with the soil type (more in clay and less in sand), all plants wilt at about the same percentage of moisture in a given soil. A plant is said to be at the incipient wilting point when it will recover when placed in a saturated atmosphere. In this case there may be available moisture at the roots, but the rate of transpiration exceeds that of absorption.

Hygroscopic water may be considered the moisture that exists in an air-dry soil, and it is not available to plants.

Movement of water through the soil is largely in a vertical direction. Thus it is important to apply water uniformly to the surface so that as it percolates through the soil, the entire mass will be moistened. Failure to apply water uniformly generally results in the development of dry spots or areas in the bench, and these may become difficult to wet unless the soil is watered daily for a period of several days. When water is applied overhead, field capacity may not be reached for some time, and as water evaporates from the soil surface, more water moves up by capillarity. In the water are carried various fertilizers, and these may accumulate to injurious levels in the top layer of soil in the bench. Some lateral movement of capillary water probably occurs when water is absorbed by the root.

Rapid drying of soils when the temperature is high necessitates frequent watering, which is laborious. Mulches applied to the surface of the soil will reduce the evaporational rate, but on some plants such as carnations the moisture at the soil surface may encourage growth of disease organisms which can damage or kill the plant.

Soil air. Air enters and leaves the soil through cracks in the soil, the noncapillary pores at the soil surface, and the capillary pores from which water has evaporated or has been absorbed. The presence of a layer of dispersed soil at the surface will limit the air exchange, as will a greasy residue from certain organic fertilizers. Mulches prevent soil dispersion by protecting the soil from forceful streams of water which may compact the soil. Breakers are also useful in this respect.

Oxygen in the soil atmosphere is used in respiration by roots and micro-organisms. The oxygen can enter the root as a dissolved gas in the soil solution or directly as a gas through the cell membrane. In soils which are overwatered, roots are injured or killed from a lack of oxygen rather than from too much water. However, disease organisms can impair the activity of roots when the soil is kept too wet, which severely reduces growth and yield. In tests with roses, where the composition of the soil atmosphere was controlled, it was found that oxygen concentrations as low as 5 percent were not detrimental to growth. It should be pointed out, however, that the air was flushed through the soil so that the total amount of oxygen was probably sufficient for normal root growth. Had the soil atmosphere not been renewed by changing the air, the plants would probably have been damaged.

Cultivation has long been advocated as a means of aerating soils, and some florists still cultivate the soil in benches to a depth of ½ to 1 inch with "scratchers" made of stiff wire. Tests have shown that the oxygen content of the soil atmosphere is very close to 20 percent, which is the same as the air above the soil. When soil is watered overhead, the oxygen content drops to 14 to 16 percent for a period of 24 to 36 hours, and then returns to its original range. In that period of time when the oxygen content is somewhat reduced, the soil is too wet to cultivate, and by the time it is dry enough to cultivate, the oxygen content is as high as it can be. The only reason for surface cultivation in a greenhouse is to break up a hard crust or a greasy film on the surface of soil to permit greater air exchange and intake of water.

The oxygen supply can become limiting in a soil if the drainage is inadequate. Wooden benches with boards too close together may swell shut, while concrete benches with flat bottoms may permit water to stand in between the drainage slots. Drainage, to allow for escape of water from the bench or bed, is important to keep crops from being injured by lack of oxygen at the roots.

Carbon dioxide in the soil atmosphere arises from respiration of roots and microorganisms. It can combine with water, forming carbonic acid, and the hydrogen from this dissociated acid can replace, by cation exchange, elements which are held on the clay particles, liberating some fertilizer materials. Excessive concentrations of carbon dioxide conceivably could damage plant roots by exerting a toxic effect.

Maintaining good soil structure with adequate air exchange at the surface, coupled with common sense in watering, will provide adequate air for the roots and microorganisms in the soil.

pH. The symbol pH is used to designate the degree of acidity or al-kalinity of soil. A pH of 7.0 is neutral, and readings of 7.5, 8.0, and higher indicate that the soil is progressively more alkaline, while readings of 6.5, 6.0, 5.5, and lower indicate that the soil is progressively more acid. Soil at pH 4.0 is 10 times as acid as a soil at pH 5.0, 100 times as acid as soil at pH 6.0, and 1,000 times as acid as soil at pH 7.0.

Soil acidity is a condition in which the basic elements such as calcium, magnesium, sodium, and potassium become soluble and leach away, leaving be-hind the iron, silicon, and aluminum with which they were combined. This undersupply of bases produces an acid reaction which may be injurious to plants. On the other hand, many plants are acid-tolerant, so that such a con-dition may be beneficial provided it is not extreme. Various forms of calcium are used to counteract acidity.

The direct effect of pH on the growth of plants is not clear, but indirectly it affects the availability of various fertilizer elements. At pH 6.0 to 6.5 most fertilizers are available to some degree, and that is why this pH range is recom-mended for most plants. Azaleas, Camellias, Gardenias, and Hydrangeas grow better in a soil at pH 5.5, primarily because there is more ferrous iron available, while sweet peas and other legumes grow better at a soil pH of 7.5 because there is a plentiful supply of calcium available. Foliage plants grow well in mixtures where the pH is 5.0.

Soil mixtures. Soil in the field has long columns of capillary water, and the pull of gravity makes the soil much wetter lower down than at the surface. Under these conditions roots of plants in the field will grow where the environ-ment is most favorable, which is in the upper strata because the soil there is aerated but still adequately moist. When such soil is placed in the bench or a pot, the effect of the pull of gravity on the shortened capillary columns is less than in the field so that the same soil is wetter in the bench or pot because of this. Though plants can be grown in soil in this situation, it is easy to over-water with resultant adverse effects.

Drainage of heavy soil in a pot is not improved by the time-honored placement of a handful of gravel in the bottom of the pot. This slightly shortens the capillary columns so that the soil will actually be somewhat wetter. Gravel, however, will provide a well-aerated, moist environment favorable for root development, and this is why much of the root system will be found there instead of in the heavy, wet soil above.

Dilution of most types of field soil with suitable inorganic and organic materials will reduce the water content of soil since such materials hold less water than the soil they replace. The soil will be more suitable for growing either potted plants or cut flowers. Some of the more commonly used diluent or additive materials are discussed in the subsequent sections.

The nature of the base soil will govern the amount of diluents or additives used, but in heavy silty clay or clay soils, the use of two or three parts soil to one part inorganic additive and one part organic additive will provide an excellent mixture for a wide variety of florist crops.

Inorganic materials.   Sand has been the most universally used inorganic additive for soil because it is widely available, cheap, and quite effective.   The coarser, sharp-edged types are preferred because round-particled, fine sand will pack and crust badly, and when added to many types of soils will make the mixture extremely hard and virtually impenetrable.   Sand is heavy, and when added in liberal quantities to pot plant soil makes the work of handling the plants very tiring.

Perlite is a volcanic rock heated to about 1,800°F, which causes it to expand and become porous.   It is neutral in reaction and is sterile in unopened bags.   Though it does not decay, the particle size can become smaller by fracturing as it is handled.   Perlite weighs 6 to 9 pounds per cubic foot and holds three to four times its own weight in water.   The special grade is fine and useful primarily for seed germination, while the coarser type or horticultural grade is best suited for mixing with peat, in equal parts, for propagation, or with soil for growing plants.

Vermiculite, a mica compound heated to above 1,400°F, is sterile as it exists in the bag.   It has a platelike structure that enables it to retain both water and fertilizer.   However, this structure can easily be destroyed by handling since the lumps of vermiculite are broken into smaller pieces or plates and thus some of the desirable properties are lost.   Moist vermiculite does not expand once compressed, and hence its air-holding capacity is reduced if it is handled roughly.   Vermiculite has an adsorptive capacity for fertilizer much like that of clay but to a lesser degree.   It has no nitrogen or phosphorus but contains considerable potassium and magnesium in an available form.

Calcined clay (Turface, Terra-Green, Arcillite) is a relatively new material which can be added to soil to improve the air-water relationship.   It is montmorillonite clay (a specific type) which is baked at a high temperature. It is porous and can hold water when the amount of moisture in the soil is relatively high.   As the soil dries, plants can obtain water from the baked clay particles.   In itself, it has no fertilizer value, but the water it can absorb may have a plentiful supply of fertilizer.   The particles are highly resistant to breakdown from mechanical handling of the soil.   It would appear that this material would be advantageous for use in heavier soil where abundant moisture prevails which could be absorbed by the baked clay particles.   Like sand, calcined clay is heavy, and mixing it with soil for pot plants increases the weight of the potted specimen.

Organic materials.   There are many kinds of organic materials available for use by florists to incorporate with soil or use as a mulch, and the effects of the organic material depend upon its nature, so much so that generalizations are not possible.

Manure is the time-honored source of organic matter for florists, but it is becoming scarcer each year, and in many areas of the country suitable manure is either unavailable or too high-priced. Fresh manure contains considerable amounts of nitrogen and, if added to soil, can damage the roots. This is particularly true if the soil is steamed, because ammonia is formed which can burn both roots and foliage. Well-rotted manure adds very little fertilizer to the soil because most of what is left consists of organic materials somewhat resistant to decomposition. Manure with straw in it may cause nitrogen starvation because as the straw decomposes, microorganisms will use the nitrogen in the soil and manure for their development. Dried, packaged manure is too expensive to consider for use under glass. Manure from dairies may have been chemically treated to keep down the objectionable odor, and the chemicals can be injurious to the roots. Manure, as can be seen from the above, is variable, no two sources being quite the same. Cultural practices must be varied, depending upon the kind of manure used, and often some damage may occur before proper steps are taken to remedy the difficulty.

Although manure can carry an appreciable quantity of fertilizer, particularly nitrogen, it should be considered primarily as a soil conditioner or additive. Application of manure water to plants has given way to the use of soluble fertilizers.

Peat is the successor to manure as one of the sources of organic matter for florists. Sphagnum peat is considered the best because it is resistant to decomposition, uniform in body, and acid in reaction. It comes from bogs where sphagnum moss grows, which are located principally in Maine, Michigan, Minnesota, Canada, and Europe, although there are local deposits in other areas. The coarse grades are preferable to the fine, which have been run through a hammer mill, in that the coarse types decompose more slowly and the lumps provide a favorable environment for roots. Sphagnum peats are usually light brown in color when dry. Year after year peat is essentially the same, so that it does not give trouble from variable composition as manure does. Continued use of peat on soil in benches may eventually lead to a reduction in crop yield. This appears to be due to the inability to wet the soil adequately because of the nature of the decomposition product of the peat. Consequently, alternative materials should be used on bench soils and peat added only periodically.

Peat from hypnum and other kinds of mosses breaks down rapidly, as compared with sphagnum, and is not as desirable. Peat from sedges, reeds, cattails, arrowheads, and other swamp plants decomposes rapidly and does not last long in the soil.

Muck can be described as peat that is farther along in the process of decomposition and generally has a higher content of mineral matter than peat. Because of its advanced stage of decomposition, it is not as effective in improving the soil as is peat. Generally muck is black, and often the particles are granular. When damp muck is rubbed between the thumb and forefinger, it will smear rather than roll, or "ball up."

Humus is generally well-decomposed organic material that is so well broken down that the original plant from which it came is no longer identifiable. It may be colloidal in nature, and it functions in a similar manner to the clay colloids in adsorption and cation-exchange phenomena. Often the term humus is used in advertisements for the sale of organic matter when the product is really muck.

Corncobs, either whole or ground, have been used primarily as a mulch for roses. When fresh they cause granulation of the soil but deplete the nitrogen, as explained previously in this section in the discussion of strawy manure. Well-rotted cobs may be incorporated with soil as a source of organic matter.

Leaf mold is occasionally used in the soil for African violets, Begonias, and a few other potted plants. It often consists of more than just leaves; forest litter of all sorts may be found in it. Leaves can be collected in the fall and saved, but they rot down rapidly and are not used widely because such a large volume is needed.

Peanut hulls, or shells, are fibrous, resist decomposition, and may be mixed with soil. They can be used to dilute peat in the culture of azaleas. Hulls of rice, barley, cottonseed, and other plants can be utilized if available at a reasonable price, but precautions must be taken to prevent nitrogen starvation of plants in soil in which the hulls have been either incorporated or mulched.

Sugar cane, or bagasse, has essentially the same effect as corncobs, but care must be exercised that the plants do not become nitrogen-starved in the early stages of breakdown of the material.

Straw and hay may be incorporated in soil but must be chopped into rather short lengths to facilitate their incorporation. They can also be used as a mulch. Straw will cause nitrogen starvation unless precautionary steps are taken, while hay (from a legume) may not materially affect the nitrogen content of the soil.

Sawdust and shavings are not used widely because of their alleged acidity and their possible content of toxic materials. Incorporating fresh sawdust or shavings in soil will result in a quick drop in the nitrogen level and lead to severe nitrogen deficiency. The persistence of these materials in the soil is such that nitrogen must be applied for quite some time or the crop will be stunted. Danger from tannic acid and other materials appears to have been overemphasized, and possibly the "toxicity" was little more than severe nitrogen deficiency. Sawdust and shavings aged or weathered for several months are used successfully in growing mediums for many plants, and as a mulch on any crop they are satisfactory.

The above and other organic materials, when either incorporated with or mulched on soils, have physical, chemical, and biological effects on the soil.

Physical effects of organic matter. Organic matter dilutes the soil, and this is an important consideration with florist crops as has been pointed out in the section on Soil Mixtures. With Gardenias, as much as 50 percent peat may be mixed with the soil, foliage plants may be grown in 100 percent peat, and with many other pot plants and cut flowers one-fourth organic matter by volume is usually added. As a mulch, a layer several inches thick is applied.

Dilution of a sandy soil with organic matter increases its water-holding capacity, while adding organic matter to a clay soil spreads the particles apart, allowing more air to circulate and reducing the moisture content. In either case the effect on the soil is beneficial for the crop.

Granulation of soil is brought about through the use of organic matter containing rapidly decomposing organic materials. In fresh corncobs there may be as much as 6 to 7 percent sugar, while in many kinds of organic materials there are starch, cellulose, and other easily decomposed organic substances. The microorganisms multiply rapidly when a supply of easily digested foods is added to soil, and in so doing they secrete a gluelike substance which cements the soil particles together into granules. Well-decomposed organic matter or materials like sphagnum peat, consisting largely of lignin which resists decomposition, do not bring about granulation but benefit the soil by dilution.

In sandy soils which dry rapidly, granulation brings some of the particles closer together, creating capillary pore spaces within the granule in which water can be retained. In clay soils which remain wet, the drawing together of the particles creates more noncapillary pores between the granules for added aeration. In each case the mechanism of granulation is the same, but the effects on the soil are opposite because of the differences in the physical properties of the soils.

Chemical effects of organic matter. If the added organic matter is acid, such as sphagnum peat moss, the soil will become more acid. The more readily decomposable organic matter, such as manure, leaf mold, and straw, has an alkaline reaction in the later stages of decomposition, because what remains is calcium, potassium, magnesium, and other bases. Even oak leaves eventually become alkaline when the acids that are present are leached.

The nitrogen level will change, depending upon the nature of the added material. Fresh manure causes quite a sharp rise in nitrogen, whereas sedge or reed peat and hay from legumes may cause only a slight increase. Nitrogen in the form of amino acids and proteins in the manure or peat is converted to nitrates through a complicated process of nitrification by microorganisms. In soils kept too wet, toxic nitrites are formed instead of nitrates because of the reduced supply of oxygen. Corncobs, straw, sugar cane, and other materials high in easily decomposable matter bring about a drop in the soil nitrogen level, caused by increased growth of microorganisms that are stimulated by the added food. In the development of these lower forms of plants, nitrogen is used for amino acids and proteins, and it is obtained from the soil if the supply in the organic material is low. Sphagnum peat additions have little observable effect on the nitrogen content of the soil.

Since all forms of organic materials were once plants, a wide range of fertilizer elements will be added by organic matter because these elements were once part of the plant, though usually in small amounts. Tobacco, however, has relatively large amounts of potassium.

As the organic matter from any source breaks down into humus, it becomes colloidal in nature, so that cation exchange and adsorption take place, as they do on clay colloids.

Biological effects of organic matter.   Addition of many kinds of organic matter stimulates growth and development of the microorganisms in the soil so as to greatly increase their numbers. The organic matter itself is generally teeming with numerous forms of plant and animal life, which add to the already existing population. Some kinds of organic materials sold under trade names may be "fortified" with various microorganisms with the idea that they will add "life to the barren soil." No matter how poor the soil may be for agricultural purposes, it is usually well populated with a wide variety of invisible plant and animal life so that purposeful additions usually mean little.

Organisms detrimental to florist crops are often introduced with organic matter. Soil-borne disease organisms such as Verticillium wilt of Begonias, Chrysanthemums, and cinerarias; bacterial wilt of carnations; and Fusarium wilt of asters are examples of this. Nematodes, either root-knot or root-lesion, are often brought in with organic matter. Numerous insects, worms, weeds, weed seeds, and other destructive forms of life may enter the greenhouse by way of organic matter. Sterilization of organic matter either before or after mixing with soil is the most effective control.

Mulches.   Mulching with organic materials has effects on the physical, chemical, and biological aspects of soil that are similar to the effects of incorporating the same materials into the soil.

Physically, mulches prevent rapid evaporation from the soil surface and reduce the rapidity of drying. The soil surface is protected from the dispersing action of water, and granulation occurs underneath if decomposable organic substances leach into the soil. Chemical and biological changes are the same as discussed in the section on organic materials.

Practically any type of organic material is suitable as a mulch provided it is properly managed with respect to the need for fertilizer applications, liming, and the watering practice.

Soil preparation in the field.   Soil as it exists in the field can be improved considerably in physical structure by proper methods of cultivation and growing of crops.   Ordinary addition of manure alone to a soil in the field is insufficient preparation.   Legumes have been advocated as crops to improve the soil, particularly because of the nitrogen they supply, but sod crops with their fibrous roots are now considered more valuable.   Specific information on the kinds of crops to grow should be obtained from the county agent or experiment station because conditions vary so widely.   It should be pointed out that little benefit will be obtained if the crops do not make adequate growth in the field because of insufficient fertilization, particularly with nitrogen.   Herbicides (weed killers) must not be used on soils to be used later in the greenhouse.

The compost pile.   Composting is not practiced as widely as it used to be because of the labor required to turn the pile and because soil in the bench is no longer changed.   In composting, alternate layers of soil and manure, each about 6 inches deep, are piled on top of each other until the heap is approximately 4 feet high.   The top should be dished to hold water to aid in decomposition of the manure.   Some florists have used plant residues from disbudding, stripped leaves, and other such material in place of manure.   The pile should be turned once by shoveling, which mixes the ingredients.   A compost pile made in spring and turned in late summer will be ready for use in fall or early winter.

Preparation in the greenhouse.   For crops grown in a bench or bed, the soil is generally brought in from the field, and inorganic and organic matter are added.   Generally in a soil with a depth of 4 to 6 inches, a 1- to 2-inch layer of an organic material is applied and a 1-inch layer of an inorganic material. Specific directions are given in subsequent discussions on the cut flower crops. Lime should be applied if the soil is acid, and particularly if acid peat is used. Superphosphate may also be broadcast on soil brought in from the field.   After the ingredients are thoroughly mixed either manually or with a Rototiller or similar instrument, the soil mixture should be sterilized.

Soil is seldom changed—that is, wheeled out of the greenhouse each year and fresh soil brought in—because often, from the standpoint of physical condition, better soil is taken out than brought in.   Sterilization plus improved methods of determining fertilizer excesses has made the practice of changing soil obsolete. Therefore, before a new crop is planted, additional organic matter should be applied and sterilized.   Many florists sterilize but once a year; however, im-

6-1. Adding straw to greenhouse soils and hand spading are good methods for maintaining coarse, porous soils. (*Yoder Bros., Inc., photograph.*)

proved growth and production will generally be obtained by steaming before planting each crop. The use of high-analysis liquid fertilizers has made the customary application of superphosphate unnecessary unless difficulty from ammonia burn has been experienced. Then either superphosphate or gypsum at 5 pounds per 100 square feet can be added; the sulfate or phosphate will combine with the free ammonia and alleviate the trouble. It cannot be emphasized too strongly that addition of organic matter before planting each crop is essential if a good physical condition is to be maintained in the soil.

For pot plants, soil from the field or from a bench or bed in the greenhouse is customarily used. In the case of the latter, residue of fertilizer applied to the previous crop can cause root injury if the level is too high. The necessary organic matter is added and mixed by shoveling over three times on the potting bench, by means of a soil shredder, or by use of a front-end loader on a tractor. Some florists use a concrete mixer to blend the added ingredients with the soil.

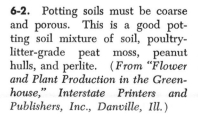

6-2. Potting soils must be coarse and porous. This is a good potting soil mixture of soil, poultry-litter-grade peat moss, peanut hulls, and perlite. (*From "Flower and Plant Production in the Greenhouse," Interstate Printers and Publishers, Inc., Danville, Ill.*)

6-3. Mulches keep rose soils in better condition. The mulch here is ground corncobs. Other materials used are manure, straw, and hay.

Lime is added if the mixture is too acid. Specific directions on soil mixtures are given in the subsequent discussions on the potted plants. The soil mixture should be sterilized.

SOILLESS CULTURE

Various methods have been devised through the years for growing plants in materials other than soil, and unquestionably more and possibly better means will be found in the future. Regardless of the method, the basic requirements of the materials are the same as they are for soil: they must provide moisture, air, and minerals to the plants uniformly and adequately. The main reason for using soilless materials for growing plants is that they can be reproduced exactly each time, and irrigation and fertilization practices do not have to be changed to ad-

6-4. Chlorosis of the terminal leaves is a symptom of poor root growth commonly caused by saturated soil because of poor bench drainage or too frequent irrigation. (*Yoder Bros., Inc., photograph.*)

just to differences in the various soils that are available. Other possible advantages of soilless mixtures are the ready availability of materials, ease in handling, and closer regulation of the mineral supply. Some of the possible disadvantages of using soilless materials are the critical regulation of mineral supply, too rapid drying of the material, and the need for more elaborate preparations. The possible advantages in supplying minerals in soils or soilless materials vary with the soils that are available and the methods that are used. Soils contain many minerals—sometimes most of the minerals that are required for good plant growth. With soils the problem is to add the deficient minerals or eliminate those that are present in excess. With soilless materials none of the required minerals may be present, and all of them may have to be added in the proper proportion. This presents an opportunity to provide just the right minerals for the plants, but it also presents a problem if the right minerals are not applied when they are needed. In addition most soils have the capacity to attract and hold minerals from the soil solution, which may prevent damage to roots from excesses. Most of the minerals in soilless mixtures dissolve readily and may cause damage to the roots if the right proportions are not used.

There is no question about the quality of plant growth in soilless materials, as excellent growth can be obtained. The decision on the use of soil or soilless materials must be based on the availability of materials, the capabilities of the individuals involved, the equipment that is available, and the methods of operation.

In some instances azaleas and tropical foliage plants are grown solely in peat moss, and these might be the earliest examples of the use of materials other than soil for growing plants. This practice no doubt arose because the use of peat moss to make such soils more acid led to the eventual use of it entirely. To ensure good drainage with the resultant good aeration and root growth, coarse peat moss must be used. Poultry-litter-grade German peat moss is the most desirable type to use. Peat moss should not be kept constantly wet nor should it be allowed to dry completely as it is almost impossible to wet it again once it becomes dry.

Sand culture was among the early developments in the use of soilless materials for growing plants. It was developed as a means of studying the mineral nutrition of plants, and later adaptations were made for its use in commercial production of several different crops. Commercially, coarser materials were used such as Haydite, gravel, or crushed rock; and the popular term for this method of culture is gravel culture. The use of sand or gravel culture both experimentally and commercially has added valuable information about the proper use of minerals whether the plants are grown in soil or other materials. Sand and gravel culture also effectively demonstrate the value of adequate aeration in the substrate (soil or soil substitute).

Although gravel culture was used as an experimental tool for growing pot plant crops as well as cut flower crops, commercially it is of value only for use with cut flowers, as pot plants in gravel cannot be handled successfully by the customer after purchase. The advantages of gravel culture are the degree of control of mineral nutrition and the automation of irrigation. Water and minerals are furnished in gravel culture by flushing the gravel periodically with a nutrient solution. This is done by using watertight benches, pumping the solution into the benches, and then allowing the solution to drain back into the solution tank. In gravel culture, irrigation may be required anywhere from several times a day to once a day or less, depending on the size of plants, kinds of plants, temperature, and light. The frequency of irrigation can be regulated by time clock; and regardless of the frequency, no labor is expended as the operation is entirely automatic. Since the gravel that is used is coarse, it drains readily and must be irrigated frequently. This is no problem as the operation is automated, and a feature of importance is that it is virtually impossible to irrigate too frequently as the aeration will be good in the coarse gravel. Overwatering then is not one of the critical problems that it can be with soils.

Minerals for gravel culture do need to be chosen wisely and supplied regularly. Many of the procedures for the commercial use of gravel culture were developed at the Ohio Agricultural Experiment Station and The Ohio State University, and the WP formula listed in Table 6-2 can be used successfully for many different crops. In addition to these materials, ferrous sulfate should be added weekly at the rate of 4 ounces per 1,000 gallons of water, and manganous sulfate should be added monthly at the rate of 1 ounce per 1,000 gallons of water.

Table 6-2. *Composition of the WP Formula* *

Chemicals	Per 1,000 gallons of water
Potassium nitrate	5 lb 13 oz
Ammonium sulfate	1 lb
Magnesium sulfate	4 lb 8 oz
Monocalcium phosphate	2 lb 8 oz
Calcium sulfate	5 lb
Total	18 lb 13 oz

* Developed by Arnold Wagner and G. H. Poesch of the Horticulture Department of the Ohio Agricultural Experiment Station and The Ohio State University.

The nutrient solution is usually used for the duration of the crop, and it must be tested regularly so that the additional minerals that are required can be added. Magnesium is not usually included in the test, and if the solution is used for several months without changing, the full amount of magnesium sulfate should be added to the solution about every 2 months.   In some instances it is necessary to use a higher concentration of minerals per 1,000 gallons of water.   Table 6-3 gives the amounts of minerals that should be maintained in the gravel culture solution as determined by soil tests.

Table 6-3.   *Nutrient Levels in Parts per Million*

	WP	2 WP
Nitrates	400	600 plus
Ammonium	25	50
Phosphorus	25	40
Potassium	100	200
Calcium	125	200

Some of the possible problems with gravel culture are the difficulty in sterilization of tanks and pipes between crops, the upkeep of watertight benches, and the necessity of providing exact amounts of minerals.

Several variations of mixtures with peat moss have been recommended in different parts of the country.   The ones that have received the most publicity are mixtures of peat moss and fine sand known as the U.C.-type soil mixes (as recommended in Manual 23, California Agricultural Experiment Station, Berkeley).   The U.C. mixes vary from fine sand only to peat moss only, but the mixes that are used more commonly contain from 25 to 75 percent fine sand and 75 to 25 percent peat moss.   All the required minerals must be added to these mixes, and some or all of them are added at the time of mixing.   Various sources of minerals can be used depending on the use to which the mix is to be put; but an example of the materials that can be used to supply the minerals in a mix made of 50 percent each fine sand and peat moss is the incorporation of ¼ pound potassium nitrate, ¼ pound potassium sulfate, 2½ pounds single superphosphate, 7½ pounds dolomitic limestone, and 2½ pounds limestone per cubic yard of U.C.-type soil mix.   As the crop grows, additional nitrogen and potassium fertilizer must be provided.

The use of mixtures of peat moss and either perlite or vermiculite have been recommended at Cornell University (New York State Flower Growers, Inc., Bulletin No. 209); these are called peat-lite mixes.   They are considerably lighter in weight than the U.C. mixes, as either perlite or vermiculite weighs about one-tenth as much as fine sand.   The peat-lite mixes are made from equal parts of sphagnum peat moss and either horticultural perlite or number 2 vermiculite. The required minerals are supplied by incorporating 10 pounds dolomitic limestone, 2½ pounds superphosphate, 4 pounds ammonium nitrate, and ½ pound potassium chloride per cubic yard of peat-lite mix.   If vermiculite is used in the mix, the potassium chloride is omitted as vermiculite contains about 5 percent available potassium.   Before the peat-lite mixes are used, they must be thoroughly wetted.

The principal advantage of the use of either U.C.-type soil mixes or peat-lite mixes may be that they can be reproduced in the same manner each time, and the same growing techniques can be used without making allowance for differences in soils from crop to crop.

SOIL DISINFESTATION (*Sterilization*)

Some method of disinfestation is necessary to control insects, disease organisms, weed seeds, and other pests that are found in soil, manure, leaf mold, and similar materials.   Serious damage is experienced yearly from the depredations of pests, not to mention the labor expended in weeding soils that are not disinfested.

Soil may be disinfested by heat or chemicals.   The equipment at hand, the area to be treated, and other factors govern the choice of method, but in any case disinfestation should be practiced to produce quality crops.

HEAT

Steam.   Steam is the most effective method of combating pests of all types in soil.   For greenhouses not heated with steam, it is possible to purchase portable or stationary boilers to generate steam for disinfestation.

The inorganic and organic matter should be added, and if superphosphate is desired, it can be incorporated before steaming.   The organic matter should be mixed uniformly either manually or with a Rototiller or similar cultivating tool.   A moderately moist soil is best, since either a very wet or a very dry soil heats slowly, and many objectionable organisms will not be killed in a soil that is very dry.   Dry soil may also be difficult to wet after steaming.   If the soil is somewhat dry, the soil surface should be moistened slightly just prior to steaming. After the soil is steamed, crops may be planted as soon as the soil is cool.

About 2 pounds of coal is needed to disinfest 1 square foot of soil in a bench, and 1 square yard of soil 6 inches deep can be steamed per boiler horsepower.   If the boiler is operated at an overload, a corresponding increase in area can be steamed.   The temperature at the coolest part of the soil should reach 180°F and remain there for 30 minutes.   Several points should be measured since the areas nearest to and farthest from the entrance of steam will most likely be the coolest.   An ordinary dairy thermometer is suitable.   A less accurate but satisfactory method is to place several potatoes in the bench at various locations; when they are baked, the soil is disinfested.   Soil should not be steamed for more than 4 hours because of the possibility of the formation or release of toxic substances.   If the steam pressure is too low or too great an area is being heated, the desired temperature may not be attained.   With tubing or steam conductors buried in the soil, it is suggested that the maximum distance to be steamed be not more than 50 linear feet on a 4-foot-wide bench.   However, with higher steam pressure a pipe header in the form of an H will supply steam for 100 linear feet, 50 feet on each side of the header.   A U-shaped header is used on shorter lines. Steam is admitted to each type of header by means of a connection in the middle of the crossbar.

Sometimes permanent tile lines are installed in ground beds, and they should be no more than 12 inches deep.   It is necessary periodically to reset some tile or replace broken sections to permit unobstructed flow of steam.

A covering is placed over the soil to confine the steam.   Some of the rubberized or plastic cloths with or without a fabric base are useful.   The plastic cloths should never be exposed to temperatures lower than 60°F since they become brittle and crack.   Newspapers are unsatisfactory except on very small areas, and many overlapping layers must be used.   Ordinary cloth is not suitable.

Whatever cover is used, it should extend over the outside of the bench so that the inner surface of the sidewalls will be steamed as well as the soil and the bench bottom.   Insects and disease organisms in the cracks and fissures of the sidewalls of both wooden and concrete benches can reinfest soil in the bench if the sidewalls are not steamed.

The conductor to carry the steam can be one of several kinds.   Formerly 3- or 4-inch agricultural tiles were used, but they are heavy and cumbersome and break easily.   Perforated, galvanized downspouting can be employed, but it rusts rapidly and its life is short.   Old boiler flues are too heavy and generally corrode quickly.   The most satisfactory material is 8- to 10-foot sections of aluminum

6-5. Steam treatment of soil for the control of disease organisms, pests, and weeds.   In this instance the steam will be introduced into agricultural tile buried in the soil. The bench is completely covered with the vinyl film during steaming.

alloy tubing since it will not corrode, is lightweight, and resists crushing. Aluminum tubing made of the 6061T6 alloy with a 2-inch outside diameter and an 0.049-inch wall is very satisfactory. To allow for escape of steam from the tubing, holes about ³⁄₁₆ to ¼ inch in diameter should be drilled 12 inches apart on opposite sides of the tubing. With a 4-foot-wide bench two lines of tubing should be buried in the soil approximately 2 feet apart, and with 5-foot benches three lines of tubing should be used. Burying the tubing so that there is about 2 inches of soil between the bench bottom and the tubing will prevent undue escape of steam through the drainage openings in the bench. The soil should be pulled away from the sides of the bench because otherwise it may not become hot enough in that area.

Instead of burying the tubing, it may be laid on the surface of the soil. Canvas hose is also a satisfactory conductor of steam if laid on the soil surface. The steamtight covering is placed over the conductor and held down by laying pipe near the edge of the bench. Some cloths cling to the side of the bench when wet and do not require fastening down. The steam is introduced, and at first it billows the cloth, but when pressure builds up, the steam is forced down through the soil. Very often steam penetration of the soil is not uniform with the conductor on the surface, and some parts may not be steamed adequately. Benches with posts in them are difficult to steam in this manner because the cloth cannot be made steamtight around the posts.

Because concrete benches crack easily when heated, the steam should be introduced slowly at first and increased in volume after 30 minutes. It is not necessary to maintain such high pressure that the steam forces the cloth away from the sides of the bench. This may burn crops in adjoining benches. Just enough steam should be admitted to keep the cloth billowed if it is the kind that clings to the bench side or is held down in some manner.

Aerated steam, obtained by combining air from a blower with the steam,

6-6. Steam treatment for disinfestation of soil and handling equipment. It is important to treat the tools which will be used on the soil. The steam conductor may be placed on the soil surface as indicated. This conductor is perforated aluminum tubing. (*Yoder Bros., Inc., photograph.*)

enables disinfestation of soil at a lower temperature. At a uniform soil temperature of 140°F the detrimental organisms are killed, yet many of the beneficial forms remain. The latter are helpful if a disease organism is accidentally introduced into the soil, because they prevent, by their competition, the rapid and widespread growth of the disease-causing organism. In the case of soils steamed at 180°F or higher, many beneficial organisms are killed and reinoculation with a detrimental organism may result in greater losses than if the soil had not been steamed in the first place.

Effects of steaming. Steam disinfestation causes certain physical, chemical, and biological changes to occur.

Physically, granulation occurs presumably because of the effect of heat, causing the soil colloids to shrink and to cement particles of soil together. One of the common mistakes after steaming is the failure to water heavily enough to wet all the soil. The water runs through the noncapillary pores rapidly so that many of the capillary pores may not be wetted. The first time steamed soil is watered, several applications should be made so that the soil colloids will swell, slow down the rapid exit of water, and cause wetting of all the soil particles.

Chemical changes are mostly concerned with some form of nitrogen. The nitrate nitrogen level drops for the first 3 weeks after steaming because

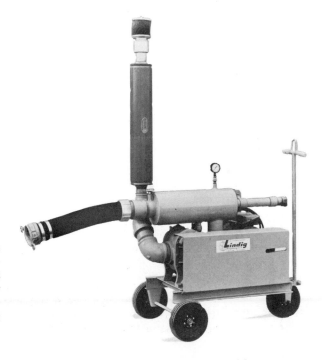

6-7. Lindig Steam Aerator—a means of adding air to either low- or high-pressure steam to adjust the temperature to approximately 140°F for steaming soil or equipment. (*Lindig Manufacturing Co., Inc., photograph.*)

ammonifying bacteria are changing it to ammonia. The ammonium nitrogen level reaches a peak in 3 weeks, and when the nitrifying bacteria population has built up in a matter of 5 to 6 weeks, ammonia is not present in any appreciable quantity. When fresh manure is added, ammonia can accumulate in rather large quantities and will burn roots and foliage. Broadcasting superphosphate or gypsum at 5 pounds per 100 square feet either before or after steaming, followed by a light watering, will furnish phosphate or sulfate which combines with the ammonia and thus prevents damage from this source. Nitrates may build up alarmingly in soils which had a rather high nitrate level before steaming and to which fresh manure was added. Heavy watering will remove excessive nitrates as well as wet all the soil, as has been discussed under physical effects. Too frequent watering on poorly drained soils can cause the formation of nitrites instead of nitrates.

Biological changes occur because of the effect of heat on the various organisms. Not all bacteria are killed with 6 hours of steaming, and it is doubtful if the mortality could ever be 100 percent in the conditions under which the soil is steamed. Nematodes, symphylids, grubs, and other similar pests are killed when the soil temperature remains at 180°F for 30 minutes. In ground beds, nematodes are killed in the steamed area, but the cooler areas below are a source of infestation. Symphylids usually migrate to cooler areas, and steaming ground beds for control of this pest is usually ineffective. In ground beds with a concrete bottom that is not badly cracked, control of these pests is as good as in raised benches.

Since the number of microorganisms is reduced by steaming, it has been recommended that a light mulch of fresh manure or soil be placed on the steamed soil to inoculate the soil with microorganisms. This could negate the original purpose of steaming because numerous undesirable organisms can be introduced. If the soil is left alone, sufficient reinoculation occurs by contamination from dust particles in the air and drips from the roof as well as by stimulation of the growth of the remaining organisms in the soil. If a poor job of steaming is done, competition among organisms is reduced to some extent, and occasionally some detrimental fungi or bacteria repopulate the soil so that susceptible crops are injured or killed when planted.

Unfortunately, some florists have the idea that steam disinfestation will take care of all disease problems in the soil. Since a commercial greenhouse can never be as aseptic as a hospital, contamination is bound to occur and steaming, together with care in watering and other good cultural practices, is necessary to keep soil-borne-disease problems at a minimum.

Hot water. Disinfestation of soil by this method is ineffective because the temperature does not remain sufficiently high long enough to do much good. Clay pots placed in vats or tanks of boiling water can be disinfested satisfactorily.

Baking.   Small amounts of soil can be disinfested by baking in any oven. The soil should be placed in a shallow pan with a medium-sized potato in the middle.   When the potato is baked, the soil is disinfested.   This method can be used with small lots of soil for starting seeds.

CHEMICALS

Formaldehyde drench.   Formaldehyde is a powerful disinfectant and can be used to disinfest outdoor soil where steam is not available.   The soil is loosened up well by spading and is then saturated with a solution made by diluting 1 gallon of commercial formalin with 50 gallons of water.   From ½ to 1 gallon of the solution should be applied to each square foot of the soil.   The amount that can be applied depends on the depth, dryness, and composition of the soil.   After treatment, the ground should be covered with a plastic or rubberized cloth for 24 hours and then allowed to dry and air out.   It may take from 10 days to 2 weeks for all the formaldehyde to escape so that the bed can be planted.   As long as any odor of formaldehyde can be detected in the soil, planting is unsafe.   This method of disinfestation is objectionable because some types of soil are badly puddled.

Tear gas.   Disinfestation of the soil with tear gas can be done when steam is not available; however, it is objectionable because of its noxious vapor, and fumes in the greenhouse will kill plants.   The soil is prepared in the usual way and treated with tear gas by injecting manually with a special applicator or a continuous-flow applicator pulled through the soil.   The soil should be medium moist, and the soil temperature at least 60°F.

The soil is marked in 10-inch squares, and from 2 to 4 cubic centimeters of tear gas is injected into each hole, placing the material 4 to 6 inches deep in the soil.   To prevent the escape of the gas, the holes are closed by stepping on them when using the manual injector.   The area should be covered with plastic or rubberized cloth for 3 days or sprinkled periodically with a fine spray of water to keep the soil moist to a depth of ¼ inch.   After 3 days the cover is removed, the soil allowed to dry, and when no tear gas odor is present, it is safe to plant. This usually takes at least 14 days after removal of the cover.

Piles of soil can be treated as outlined above, by treating layers approximately 10 to 12 inches deep.   Considerable time must be allowed for the fumes to escape from the center of piles 2 or more feet in height.   Turning the piles with a shovel is helpful in aerating them to allow the gas to escape.

Tear gas is toxic to plants, and it is virtually impossible to treat soil in a greenhouse unless it is empty of plants.   Tear gas controls soil insects, weeds, and nematodes in rotted roots.   High concentrations must be used for weed seeds, many disease organisms, and nematodes in unrotted roots.   When treating soil, a gas mask is desirable but unpleasant to wear for long periods in hot weather.

Methyl bromide. This fumigant is effective against soil insects, nematodes in unrotted roots, weeds, and many disease organisms. It is injected into soil in a manner similar to the injection of tear gas, and usually 8 cubic centimeters is placed on 10-inch centers. Methyl bromide is odorless and toxic to humans, and a gas mask is imperative. Any numbness of fingers, toes, or cheeks, or any staggering, double vision, nausea, or dizziness is an indication that fumes have been inhaled. The affected person should be kept warm and taken to a doctor at once.

DD. This chemical (no relation to DDT) is specific for nematodes and insects in the soil. It is nonvolatile and does not require a covering over the soil. The soil should be prepared as usual and injected with 2 to 3 cubic centimeters on 10-inch centers. Two weeks should be allowed after treatment before planting.

Vapam. This material is useful for control of nematodes and weeds and is fairly effective for killing various soil fungi. It is used at a rate of 1 quart to 100 square feet injected into the soil on 6- to 9-inch centers, or applied as a surface drench. A water seal for 10 to 14 days is maintained, and following this an aeration period of at least 2 weeks is usually allowed before planting.

SOIL TESTING

Slowly but surely the testing of soils is gaining a foothold among the growers. As the growing of crops becomes less haphazard each year, as the operation begins to depend upon scientific methods, as soil troubles multiply from year to year, as the ability to judge the quality of soils by appearance and feel disappears, it becomes evident that some method needs to be used which will be reliable enough to reduce failures. The testing of soils, for acidity as well as for the more important and limiting elements, is that method. In spite of the fact that absolute reliance cannot be placed on the tests, they are sufficiently accurate to be of considerable help. Soil tests are made by experiment stations as well as by private firms, so that florists can send soil samples periodically for analysis. Although it is possible for florists to test their own soil, lack of time for such tedious and exacting procedures, spoilage of reagents, and other difficulties may lead the florist to patronize a soil-testing laboratory unless his firm is large enough to hire personnel for this particular job.

The interpretation of soil tests is more effective if sufficient information on previous fertilizer practices, size and condition of the plants, and other such

6-8. Solu Bridge Soil Tester for rapid determination of total soluble mineral (soluble salts) content of soil or water. (*Beckman Instruments, Inc., photograph.*)

factors are known. The tests are designed to indicate the amount of available fertilizer elements in the soil. Soil tests should be used as a guide rather than a crutch, since too much dependence can be placed on the figures rather than on past experience and on appearance of the plants.

6-9. Junior Simplex Soil Test Outfit for the determination of pH and several minerals. (*Edwards Laboratory photograph.*)

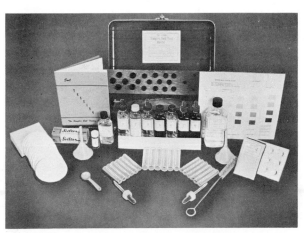

If each of several consecutive tests indicates a low reading on many of the fertilizer elements, several conclusions can be drawn: not enough fertilizer is being applied at any one time, the applications may be too infrequent, the watering practice may be such that most of the fertilizer is washed away, or some combination of these causes exists. Conversely, if the readings are consistently high, it may be that too much fertilizer is being applied at any one time, fertilizer is being applied too often, the watering is so light that there is little or no leaching action, or a combination of these is occurring. If the levels are in a suitable range, the fertilizer and watering programs are probably satisfactory.

7

FERTILIZERS

Fertilizers contain minerals that are essential for the growth of plants. In some instances minerals can be supplied to plants by applying a liquid fertilizer solution or spray to the leaves or the stems, but more commonly fertilizer is applied to the soil and subsequently the dissolved minerals enter the plants through the roots. Plants require many different minerals, but the amount that is needed of each one varies considerably.

Minerals are used in plants to form some of the building materials from which the plant is made, as catalysts whose presence is needed for some processes to occur, and to regulate the pH or buffer the cell sap. Some minerals are required in large quantities, and others, in small. Excess amounts may produce toxic conditions with some damage to the plant, while a lack of some necessary minerals may result in poor growth and the appearance of deficiency symptoms in the plant.   It is not uncommon to have excesses of some minerals and short-ages of others in the soil, and soils or plants must be tested regularly and proper action taken to adjust for these conditions.

The use of minerals by plants.   The minerals are often classed as major, minor, or trace elements according to the relative amounts that are used by plants, according to the amounts that need to be added to the soil, or according to the effect that their presence has on plants.   Such classifications do not really increase the understanding of the use of minerals by plants, and it is possible that they may cause some confusion.   Several minerals are of vital importance to plants whether they are commonly available, have to be supplied regularly, or are used in very small quantities.   Fertilizer labeling regulations may also cause misplaced emphasis on the importance of some minerals by requiring the analysis of only nitrogen, phosphorus, and potassium.   Certainly these three minerals are very essential, but such labeling can add to the impression that other minerals are not of consequence.   The role of each mineral that is used by the plant must be well understood.

Many soils are well supplied with the minerals that are needed for good growth of plants, but it is not possible to make all-inclusive generalizations be-cause soils vary greatly throughout the country.   Some mineral deficiencies may be common in Florida or southern California sands but rare in midwestern soils. The availability of minerals varies greatly with the acidity or alkalinity of the soils.   The acid eastern soils provide different mineral availability than the neutral soils of the Midwest or some of the alkaline western soils.

It is not unusual for greenhouse soils to be used for several years without change because steaming of soil gives control of disease organisms, but such intensive use of the same soil may develop some mineral deficiencies if adjust-ments are not made periodically.

In some instances plants are grown in materials that contain no soil, which may be composed of various mixtures of sand, peat moss, perlite, vermiculite, or other similar materials.   Minerals must be supplied carefully to such mixtures as they may be entirely devoid of some of the essential ones.

Nitrogen may not be classed properly as a mineral, but by association and use it is best discussed as such.   It occurs in plants as proteins, amino acids, amides, and alkaloids.   Nitrogen is used in large quantities since it is a constituent of the building materials (protoplasm) from which plants are made.   The ele-ment nitrogen is gaseous and is plentiful in the atmosphere, but it cannot be used by plants until it is combined into compounds with oxygen or hydrogen.   As a fertilizer, nitrogen may be used as nitrate (NO_3) compounds, ammonium (NH_4) compounds, or amide (NH_2 as in blood or urea), but regardless of the compound, it is referred to as nitrogen, and the analysis of the fertilizer is in terms of ele-mental nitrogen.   Most of the nitrogen that is absorbed by plants is in the nitrate form, and much of the ammonium and amide forms of nitrogen in fertilizers is changed to the nitrate form in the soil before entering the plants.   The conversion of ammonium compounds and amide in the soil to nitrates occurs more readily in warm temperatures, and for this reason fertilizers that contain the nitrate form of nitrogen are considered better for use, particularly during the winter. Another reason for using nitrate forms of nitrogen is that ammonium forms of nitrogen may cause injury when the carbohydrate supply is low in the plant (as in winter).

Because a deficiency of nitrogen limits the amount of protein and other building material in the plant, nitrogen deficiency symptoms are shorter or fewer stems, with small leaves and flowers, and less intense color of leaves and flowers. The presence of luxury amounts of nitrogen may produce elongated, weak stems and large, thin leaves.

Phosphorus is supplied to the plant only in the oxidized form (phosphate), but it is referred to in terms of phosphorus, phosphate, or phosphoric acid.   The fertilizer analysis has been in terms of P_2O_5, but in some areas it is now reported as phosphorus (P).   Because phosphorus is a component of the phospholipids and nucleic acids in the meristematic tissues, an adequate supply of phosphorus is needed for cell development and continuous growth of all parts of the plant and not just of the roots, which is a common misconception.   Phosphates act as catalysts for the action of some enzymes, and they may be involved in the hydrolytic change of starch to sugar in plants.   Large quantities of phosphorus are not used by plants, but it is essential to have a supply constantly available.   Phosphorus deficiency symptoms can be produced in carefully controlled experimental tests, but they are rarely observed in commercial plantings as the soils that are used are seldom devoid of phosphorus.

Phosphorus combines readily with calcium, aluminum, iron, and some other elements to form insoluble compounds, and it therefore translocates slowly in the soil.   Whenever possible, phosphorus fertilizers should be incorporated into the soil so that the phosphorus is distributed uniformly throughout before planting.

Potassium is the only one of the minerals used in quantity that does not become chemically combined with building materials in the plant.   It seems to be involved entirely as a regulator of processes or as a catalyst.   Apparently potassium is necessary for the synthesis of carbohydrates and proteins, and when the deficiency is severe, cells elongate but do not divide.   Potassium translocates readily within plants from older tissues to the newly developing portions of the plant, and the typical deficiency symptom is marginal chlorosis of the lower leaves, though this is easily confused with injury from sprays or aerosols.

As a fertilizer, only the salts of potassium are used, such as potassium nitrate, potassium chloride (muriate of potash), potassium sulfate, and potassium phosphate.   It is referred to as potassium or potash, but the fertilizer analysis has been in terms of K_2O.   In some areas it is now reported as potassium (K).

Calcium is a structural component of the cell walls, and it also has an effect on the permeability of some membranes and upon the hydration of colloids. Calcium does not translocate readily within the plant but does aid in the translocation of proteins and carbohydrates in the plant. A lack of calcium may produce stunted stubby roots, and this is the deficiency symptom that is associated with the lack of calcium, together with shortened growth at the stem tips.

Some calcium compounds may be used to make the soil more alkaline. $Ca(OH)_2$ (hydrated lime) can increase the alkalinity rapidly; $CaCO_3$ (limestone) or a combination of calcium and magnesium carbonate (dolomitic limestone) produces a slower change in alkalinity; while $CaSO_4$ (calcium sulfate or land plaster) has very little effect on the alkalinity of the soil. Calcium is often added to the soil when other fertilizers are used that contain calcium as a component part. For example, superphosphate is often used as a fertilizer source for phosphorus, and since it is composed of calcium phosphates and calcium sulfate, considerable calcium is added to the soil together with the phosphorus.

Iron is necessary for the synthesis of chlorophyll in green plants, and the typical deficiency symptom is chlorosis of the new leaves, while the older, lower leaves remain green, as iron does not move readily from one part of the plant to another. Iron is generally present in soils, but it may be in unavailable form in either soil or plants. If the iron is in unavailable form in the plant, iron deficiency symptoms may be exhibited even though there is a large amount present in the plant.

Ferrous sulfate ($FeSO_4$) has been the fertilizer most commonly used as a source of iron, but it is being replaced by iron chelate. Ferrous sulfate lowers the pH of the soil, while iron chelate does not affect pH. Iron combines readily with other materials in the soil to form insoluble iron compounds, and where this is a problem, chelated forms can be used in which the iron remains available.

Magnesium is the only mineral constituent of chlorophyll, and the deficiency symptom is interveinal chlorosis of the lower leaves. Magnesium translocates readily in plants moving to the younger portions. The magnesium supply of most soils is adequate; but if additional quantities are required, either dolomitic limestone or magnesium sulfate (epsom salts) can be used.

Boron affects development in the terminal portions of plants, and a boron deficiency produces such symptoms as malformed leaves or buds, stunted terminal growth, chlorosis of leaves, or death of terminal buds and shoots. Boron deficiency is more likely to occur in soils with high calcium content. Borax is used as a fertilizer source of boron, but it must be applied carefully as only small amounts are required; otherwise toxicity will result.

Manganese is required by plants in very small quantities, and slightly greater amounts can be toxic. It is believed that manganese affects the action of some enzymes and is related to the synthesis of chlorophyll, as a lack of manganese produces chlorotic leaves at the tip of the plant. The chlorosis is interveinal much the same as the chlorosis caused by a deficiency of magnesium, but it occurs first in the newly formed leaves rather than in the older leaves as with magnesium.   Manganese is generally present in soils, and it becomes more available in soils that are steamed excessively.   With some plants, toxicity symptoms appear after they are planted in soils that have been steamed for a long time.   If soils are deficient in manganese, small amounts of manganous sulfate can be added.

Sulfur is one of the essential minerals for plants because it is a constituent of some proteins.   Sulfur deficiencies are not common, however, because it is generally present in soils, and many of the fertilizers that are used are sulfate salts which add to the available supply.   Because of the widespread use of sulfate forms of fertilizers, soils may have to be changed periodically to reduce the amount of sulfur (salts).   In addition to its use in proteins, sulfur does acidify the soil and can be used to lower the pH.

Aluminum is present in most soils in quantity, but it is not in soluble forms except in acid soils.   The presence of calcium and phosphorus compounds in the soil decreases the solubility of aluminum.   Other than the effect that aluminum has on pigment development in plants, its use in them is not known.   Aluminum sulfate fertilizer is used on some hydrangeas to produce blue flowers, while its absence causes the flowers to be pink.

The choice of fertilizer is based on the minerals that are needed, the method of application that will be used, other effects of the fertilizer, and the relative costs.   One of the first considerations in choosing a fertilizer is the method of application and the effect it will have on the crop.   In some instances it is best to distribute a slow-release fertilizer throughout the soil so that a continuous supply of the minerals is available for a long time, and in other situations it is best to irrigate regularly with fertilizer solutions.   In most situations it is most satisfactory to use a combination of methods of fertilizer application.

The labeling of fertilizers is covered by governmental regulations, and it is required that the label declare the quantity of nitrogen, phosphorus, and potassium as a percentage of the total weight.   This is called the analysis of the fertilizer.   The nitrogen content is in terms of elemental nitrogen, but phosphorus may be reported in terms of P_2O_5 and potassium as K_2O.   This was standard labeling throughout the country for years, but there have been attempts to change the regulations so that phosphorus and potassium can be reported in terms of the element.   In some areas of the country this change has been approved, and in purchasing fertilizer it is important to know what label regulations are being used. A 20-20-20 analysis fertilizer that lists phosphorus as P_2O_5 and the potassium as K_2O would be approximately a 20-8.8-16.6 analysis fertilizer if the minerals were reported in terms of the elements N, P, and K.   The actual mineral content is the same in either case.

To convert from an analysis in terms of P_2O_5 to P, multiply by 0.44; or to convert from P to P_2O_5, multiply by 2.29.

To convert from an analysis in terms of K_2O to K, multiply by 0.83; or to convert from K to K_2O, multiply by 1.2.

In spite of the fertilizer label's declaring only nitrogen, phosphorus, and potassium, the fertilizer actually contains other materials that may or may not be beneficial to plants. Most of the mixed fertilizers for dry application contain calcium and magnesium that can be used to advantage by plants, but sulfates and cholorides may be of questionable use. Mixed fertilizers that are used for liquid application rarely contain calcium, magnesium, sulfates, or chlorides, and if these minerals are needed in the soil, they will have to be added separately.

Fertilizers for incorporation in the soil, and slow-release fertilizers. These are materials that can be mixed with the soil before planting to provide a safe, continuous source of minerals. Phosphorus and calcium fertilizers should be incorporated into the soil before planting because these minerals do not translocate readily throughout the soil. A single application is usually sufficient for the duration of most crops, and can be applied safely before planting, thus eliminating their insolubility in liquid applications.

All plants require a continuous supply of nitrogen, and if some nitrogen is not present in the soil at the time of planting, the plants may be damaged by its lack. For years several of the organic fertilizers have been used for incorporation in the soil. These are plant or animal materials or refuse from them that contain one or more minerals plus organic matter that may promote better soil structure and drainage. Organic fertilizers are generally safe to use in the soil before planting; but they do have the disadvantages of not being uniform, of being difficult to handle and obtain, and of being costly. More recently manufactured materials have been used for slow-release sources of minerals.

Blood is collected and dried at slaughterhouses, and it is an excellent source of nitrogen that ranges from 9 to 14 percent. The rate of application of blood is 2 to 5 pounds per 100 square feet.

Bone meal is another slaughterhouse product, and it may be obtained either raw or steamed. Bone meals contain approximately 20 percent phosphorus (P_2O_5), and the raw product contains about 3 percent nitrogen in addition. The phosphorus is very slowly available to plants, but in the finely ground meal it is more readily available than in the coarsely ground. Steamed bone meal contains practically no nitrogen. Bone meals should be applied at the rate of 5 pounds per 100 square feet, but because of its slow availability, other sources of phosphorus are preferred.

Cottonseed meal has an analysis of about 7-3-2, and it is somewhat acid in reaction. The rate of application is 2 pounds per 100 square feet.

Fish tankage is cooked and ground fish with an analysis of about 6-4-0.

It is more readily available in some areas of the country than in others, and it is used at the rate of 4 pounds per 100 square feet of area.

Fritted materials are manufactured products that contain minerals in a glasslike substance. Iron or potassium frits have been used to a limited extent, and the minerals are released over a long period of time. The manufacturer's recommendations should be used as a guide in choosing rates of applications.

Iron sulfate (ferrous sulfate or copperas) is the best material for rapid but safe acidification of soils, and in addition it supplies the iron which plants require. It is particularly useful in preventing iron chlorosis in such plants as azalea, *Camellia, Gardenia,* and *Hydrangea.* It is applied at the rate of 1 pound per 100 square feet or as liquid at 1 ounce per 2 gallons, to be used to cover about 6 square feet (1 pound to cover 100 square feet).

Limestone or hydrated lime is added to the soil to increase the calcium content of the soil or to make it more alkaline. The change in reaction is faster with hydrated lime ($Ca(OH)_2$). Limestone consists of calcium carbonates ($CaCO_3$) that are quite insoluble, while dolomitic limestone contains magnesium carbonate ($MgCO_3$) in addition. Only the more finely ground limestone should be used, as results are faster with it. Limestone or hydrated lime is applied at the rate of 1 to 5 pounds per 100 square feet.

Metal ammonium phosphates are chemical compounds composed of ammonium, phosphorus, and certain metals such as magnesium or iron that have the property of dissolving slowly. The magnesium compound has an analysis of 8-40-0, and it can be used as a slow-release mineral source but has not proved universally satisfactory.

Manures vary greatly in mineral content as well as in organic fiber quantity. It is preferable that their use be based on the effect of the fiber content on the soil rather than on the benefits that could be expected from the low amount of minerals. For these reasons the use of strawy manure is recommended, and it is applied at the rate of 1 to 2 inches on the surface of the soil and then mixed into the soil. The mineral analysis of manures may be about 1-0.5-1.

Sludge is treated sewage from municipal sewage plants, and it varies considerably with the processes that are used or the materials that are added to it. Sludge that analyzes about 5-3-0 is used at the rate of 5 pounds per 100 square feet.

Sulfur is used primarily to adjust the acidity of the soil. Finely ground dusting sulfur (325 mesh) or wettable sulfur should be used instead of flowers of sulfur (60 mesh) because their effect is more rapid. Sulfur is used at the rate of about 1 to 3 pounds per 100 square feet depending on the change in pH that is desired.

Superphosphate is the main source of phosphorus, and depending on how it has been prepared it has an analysis of 0-20-0 or 0-45-0. It is produced by treating rock phosphate with sulfuric and then phosphoric acids, and it contains calcium phosphates and calcium sulfate. It is applied at the rate of 5 pounds to 100 square feet. Superphosphate is commonly added to the soil before each crop is planted; however, if the same soil is reused year after year, such frequent applications of phosphorus will not have to be made as it will not be depleted that rapidly. The composition of superphosphate indicates that calcium is applied each time together with the phosphorus; and if regular applications of superphosphate are not made, calcium, if needed, should be added to the soil in the form of limestone or calcium sulfate (gypsum).

Tankage is cooked refuse from slaughterhouses with an analysis of approximately 5-15-0, and it is used at the rate of 4 pounds per 100 square feet.

Tobacco stems are a waste tobacco product that are used primarily as a source of potassium. The analysis may be about 2-0-5, and it is used at the rate of 5 pounds to 100 square feet.

Ureaform nitrogenous fertilizers have a coating that limits their solubility. They have an analysis of 38-0-0, and are applied at the rate of 1 to 2 pounds per 100 square feet. If ureaform fertilizer is mixed with potting soil, a level 3-inch potful is used per wheelbarrow (2½ bushels) of soil. In spite of its limited solubility, overdoses can cause severe burn or death of the plants because the material itself cannot be removed from the soil; and it continues to supply nitrogen whether needed or not.

Fetilizers for dry application. The organic fertilizers and some of the manufactured, slow-release fertilizers discussed earlier can be applied to the surface of the soil, and in addition several other fertilizers can be used in this way. To prevent root injury, the soil must be moist before application is made of a dry fertilizer, and then the soil must be irrigated afterwards. The fertilizers that are used for dry application may be completely soluble or only partially soluble, and they may contain one or more minerals. If nitrogen is one of the minerals present in the fertilizer, the rate of application is based on it. A 5-10-5 fertilizer is applied at the rate of 3 pounds per 100 square feet of soil, a 10-6-4 fertilizer is used at 1½ pounds per 100 square feet, and a 15-0-0 analysis fertilizer at 1 pound per 100 square feet.

These fertilizers may be chemical compounds that contain only one kind of material and usually only one or two minerals, or they may be mixed fertilizers that contain several materials and more than one mineral. Typically the mixed fertilizers are a combination of the minerals that commonly need to be added to the soil, and they are sometimes called complete fertilizers. The usual sources for the various minerals in mixed fertilizers are ammonium sulfate and ammonium liquors for nitrogen, superphosphate for phosphorus, and potassium chloride for potassium. The combined total declared analysis for mixed fertilizers for dry application is around 20 percent, and the undeclared remainder of the fertilizer contains some minerals that may or may not be needed, such as calcium, magnesium, sulfur, and chloride. Mixed fertilizers from different manufacturers may have various qualities that make them better for a specific use, and these qualities may be apparent from the labeling on the package or may be learned from experience and testing of the particular product.

It is possible to satisfy all the mineral requirements of plants using only dry applications of fertilizers, but in many instances it is best to use a combination of methods of application. Because of the limited solubility of some of these fertilizers, it is possible to provide a limited but continuous supply of minerals. In some situations there is an advantage in providing the allied constituents of the dry fertilizer such as calcium and magnesium. Some of the disadvantages in making dry applications of fertilizer are the lack of uniform distribution, more labor time required for application, the unavoidable damage of plants by placement of fertilizer directly upon them, and the fluctuation of mineral content in the soil between applications.

Fertilizers for liquid application. Some of the same fertilizers can be used for liquid application as for dry application, and this is determined by the solubility of the fertilizer. If it is completely soluble in water at the rate at which it will be used, the fertilizer can be used for liquid applications. Some of these fertilizers may be chemical compounds that contain one or possibly two minerals, but the mixed fertilizers may be made from several materials containing nitrogen, phosphorus, and potassium as well as other minerals. The commercially prepared and packaged fertilizers for liquid application often contain a total analysis of nitrogen, phosphorus, and potassium of about 60 percent. These are commonly called high-analysis fertilizers. In order to provide complete solubility together with high analysis, the manufacturer of these fertilizers may use urea, potassium nitrate, ammonium nitrate, or ammonium phosphate for the nitrogen sources; ammonium phosphate and potassium phosphate for the phosphorus sources; and potassium nitrate and potassium phosphate for the potassium sources. Various combinations of these materials can be used to produce fertilizers of different analyses. Depending on the manufacturer, these mixed fertilizers may also contain some chelated minerals that are used in small quantities as well as a dye that will indicate when fertilizer is present in the irrigation water.

If the proper materials are obtained and the mixing is done very carefully, it is possible for growers to prepare fertilizer mixtures themselves as they need them. The most useful materials for this purpose are potassium nitrate, calcium nitrate, ammonium nitrate, and di-ammonium phosphate (Table 7-2).

If phosphorus and calcium fertilizers are incorporated into the soil before planting, it is usually satisfactory to use fertilizers that contain only nitrogen and potassium during the production of most crops.

Methods for making liquid applications of fertilizer. Various methods may be used satisfactorily. One of the earliest procedures was to place manure in a tank and then pump manure water from the tank periodically or for each

Table 7-1.   *Analysis and Use of Some Common Fertilizer Materials*

| NAME OF FERTILIZER | ANALYSIS | RATE OF APPLICATION | | GENERAL REACTION |
		POUNDS PER 100 SQ FT	LIQUID	
Ammonium nitrate	33-0-0	½	1 oz–5 gal	Acid
Ammonium sulfate	20-0-0	1	1 oz–2 gal	Acid
Calcium nitrate	15-0-0	1	1 oz–2 gal	Alkaline
Sodium nitrate	15-0-0	1	1 oz–2 gal	Alkaline
Urea or Nu Green	45-0-0	½	1 oz–7 gal	Neutral
Superphosphate *	0-20-0	5	Insoluble	Neutral
Treble superphosphate	0-45-0	5	Insoluble	Neutral
Muriate of potash	0-0-50	1	1 oz–2 gal	Neutral
Muriate of potash (trona)	0-0-60	1	1 oz–2 gal	Neutral
Sulfate of potash	0-0-50	1	1 oz–2 gal	Neutral
Ammonium phosphate (mono)	11-48-0	1	1 oz–2 gal	Acid
Ammonium phosphate (di)	21-53-0	½	1 oz–5 gal	Acid
Potassium nitrate	13-0-44	1	1 oz–2 gal	Neutral
Chelated iron	Iron	Not recommended	1 oz–10 or 15 gal	Acid
Iron sulfate (ferrous sulfate)	Iron	1	1 oz–2 gal	Very acid
Lime or Limestone	Calcium	5	Insoluble	Alkaline
Gypsum (calcium sulfate)	Calcium	5	Insoluble	Neutral

* To add phosphorus to potting soil, incorporate a level 4-inch pot of superphosphate per 2½ bushels (one wheelbarrow) of soil. If there is sufficient phosphorus in the soil, nitrogen and potassium may be supplied by periodic additions of 1 ounce of nitrate of soda or 1 ounce of ammonium sulfate and ½ ounce of muriate of potash to 2 gallons of water when the soil is moist.

irrigation. The tank method is still in use but with chemical compounds instead of manure. It is an accurate method of supplying fertilizer to soils, and it may be one of the most economical systems to install. The primary equipment requirements for the tank method of making liquid applications of fertilizer are a tank large enough to provide the amount of water needed for the area involved, a large enough pump to deliver the rate of water flow that is needed, and piping from the tank to the areas to be irrigated. The tank method is used mainly for applying fertilizers periodically rather than with each irrigation. With a fertilizer containing approximately 20 percent nitrogen, about 3 pounds of fertilizer is used per 100 gallons of water in the tank. This liquid fertilizer should be applied to the soil at the rate of 1 quart per square foot.

Other methods of making liquid applications of fertilizer involve the use of some type of siphon or injector to add a fertilizer concentrate to the water as

Table 7-2. *Various Fertilizer Analyses from Combination of Some Common Fertilizers*

AMMONIUM NITRATE (33-0-0)	CALCIUM NITRATE (15-0-0)	DI-AMMONIUM PHOSPHATE (21-53-0)	POTASSIUM NITRATE (13-0-44)	FERTILIZER ANALYSIS
1 part	none	none	1 part	23-0-22
1 part	none	none	2 parts	20-0-30
none	1 part	none	1 part	14-0-22
none	2 parts	none	1 part	14-0-15
none	none	1 part	1 part	18-26-22

To assure good mixing the proper amount of each chemical compound should be added to the water in the tank and thoroughly mixed. If it were desired to use 1 pound of a 23-0-22 analysis fertilizer per gallon of water in the fertilizer concentrate, ½ pound ammonium nitrate and ½ pound potassium nitrate would be added per gallon of water.

it is being used in irrigation. The most reliable are the injectors as they add the same volume of fertilizer per volume of water regardless of varying conditions, and this ratio or proportion does not change. There really are only two problems with good-quality units: (1) The water motors can be damaged if the water source contains sand or silt. If a clean water source is not available, a strainer should be used. (2) Undissolved particles in the fertilizer concentrate may cause malfunction of the check valves in the injector.

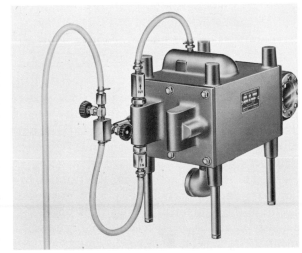

7-1. The Smith Measuremix fertilizer injectors are operated solely by the water passing through them, which gives positive, accurate injection of fertilizer concentrate into the irrigation water. Units in common usage vary in capacity from 3 to 15 gallons per minute for the portable model, R-3, to 20 to 100 gallons per minute for the 2-inch model, R-8. Larger models are available. (*Smith Precision Products, Inc., photograph.*)

The common proportions for injectors are 1 to 100 and 1 to 200. An injector with 1 to 100 proportion will inject 1 unit of fertilizer concentrate into the irrigation water in every 100 units that is dispensed, and an injector with 1 to 200 proportion will inject 1 unit of fertilizer concentrate in every 200 units of water that is dispensed from the injector. If the same amount of fertilizer is desired in the irrigation water, the fertilizer concentrate for the 1 to 200 injector would be twice as great as for the 1 to 100 injector. Most of the injectors are positive displacement hydraulic pumps or water motors, which are operated solely by the water that passes through them.

Injectors provide a convenient and reliable means of adding fertilizer regularly to the irrigation water, and their main use is in supplying fertilizer with each irrigation rather than periodically. If properly handled, this can provide uniform amounts of minerals in the soil at all times. When fertilizer is applied with each irrigation, the water should contain approximately 200 ppm each of nitrogen and potassium. Tables 7-3 and 7-4 list the amounts of several different fertilizers which can be used to obtain this concentration.

Table 7-3. *Amount of Nitrogen Fertilizer to Use with Potassium Nitrate for 200 ppm Each Nitrogen and Potassium*

Use 7.5 oz potassium nitrate (13-0-44) per gallon of concentrate water plus any one of these listed nitrogen fertilizers for 200 ppm each nitrogen and potassium with a 1 to 100 ratio fertilizer injector. For a 1 to 200 ratio injector use twice these amounts.

FERTILIZER	ANALYSIS	OUNCES PER GALLON OF CONCENTRATE WATER
Ammonium nitrate	33-0-0	5.0
Calcium nitrate	15-0-0	11.0
Ammonium sulfate	20-0-0	8.5
Sodium nitrate	15-0-0	10.5
Urea	44-0-0	4.0

When fertilizer is applied with each irrigation, heavy irrigation must normally be used—applying water at the rate of ½ gallon per square foot of soil. This will leach some of the fertilizer with each irrigation, but using lesser amounts of water will cause excessive amounts of minerals in the soil with resultant crop damage.

In selecting an injector, the features to consider are accuracy, reliability, capacity, and cost. Reliability is of great importance because no matter how accurate the equipment is when it is operating, if it malfunctions frequently or repairs cannot be made readily, that type of injector will not be a good investment. The injector must have the right capacity for the job because it must be

Table 7-4. *Amount of Nitrogen Fertilizer to Use with Potassium Chloride (Muriate of Potash) for 200 ppm Each Nitrogen and Potassium*

Use 5.5 oz potassium chloride (0-0-60) per gallon of concentrate water plus any one of these listed nitrogen fertilizers for 200 ppm each nitrogen and potassium with a 1 to 100 ratio fertilizer injector. For a 1 to 200 ratio injector use twice these amounts.

FERTILIZER	ANALYSIS	OUNCES PER GALLON OF CONCENTRATE WATER
Ammonium nitrate	33-0-0	8.0
Ammonium sulfate	20-0-0	13.5
Urea	44-0-0	6.0

able to handle properly the smallest rate of water flow and the greatest. Injectors are rated for the minimum and maximum water flow rates, and it must be determined whether the capacity of an injector will be suitable for the purpose intended before installing it. If not already known, the minimum and maximum water flow rate that will be used in the greenhouses ought to be established. They vary with the water pressure, piping, and other equipment. It is possible that the delivery from a single 50-foot, ¾-inch hose with faucet wide open will be about 12 gallons of water per minute. When the faucet is only partially open, as for watering pot plants, a single hose may deliver about 3 gallons of water a minute. In order to figure the water delivery from irrigation systems, it may be necessary to make readings with a meter. In some instances it is adaptable and economical to install two small capacity injectors in parallel rather than one larger capacity model. In this fashion one injector can then be used for low rate of water flow and both injectors can be used when increased capacity is needed.

There are many different types and sizes of siphons for adding fertilizer to irrigation water, but they all operate on the pressure differential produced by water as it goes through a restricted passage (Venturi). The ratio or proportion of fertilizer concentrate to water remains constant only if the rate of water flow stays the same. The proportion will vary with change in pressure or water flow rate of the water source, change in pressure on the discharge side by adding more or less hose, or change in the elevation of the hose on the discharge side when watering is shifted from crops on the ground to plants elevated on shelves. Siphon equipment may cost less but will be a real saving only if it results in suitably accurate performance.

Some mineral absorption occurs in the leaves. The primary means of entrance of minerals into the plant is through the roots, and without an actively growing root system the absorption of minerals may be seriously reduced. Some

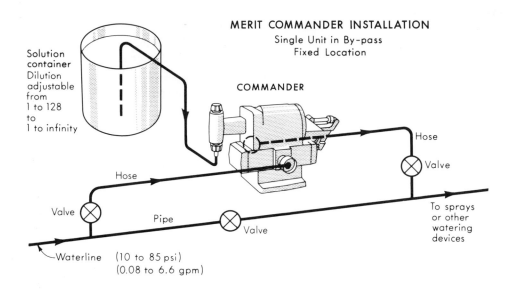

MERIT COMMANDER INSTALLATION
Single Unit in By-pass
Fixed Location

Solution container Dilution adjustable from 1 to 128 to 1 to infinity

COMMANDER

Hose

Valve

Hose

Valve

Pipe

Valve

To sprays or other watering devices

Waterline   (10 to 85 psi)
             (0.08 to 6.6 gpm)

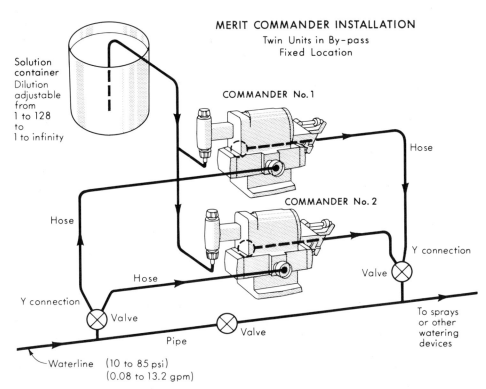

MERIT COMMANDER INSTALLATION
Twin Units in By-pass
Fixed Location

Solution container Dilution adjustable from 1 to 128 to 1 to infinity

COMMANDER No. 1

Hose

COMMANDER No. 2

Hose

Y connection

Valve

Hose

Hose

Y connection   Valve

Pipe   Valve

To sprays or other watering devices

Waterline   (10 to 85 psi)
             (0.08 to 13.2 gpm)

7-2.   The Merit Commander is operated by the water passing through it and injects fertilizer concentrate into the irrigation water in direct proportion of 1 ounce to each gallon of water (1 part to 128 parts).   This is a small, portable unit best suited for watering pot plants.   The maximum capacity is about 6½ gallons per minute.   For cut flower irrigation, double capacity can be obtained by using 2 units in parallel.   (*Merit Industries, Inc., photograph.*)

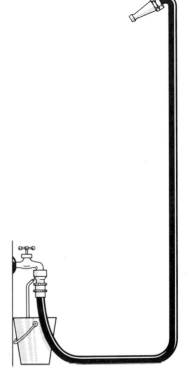

7-3. The Hozon Proportioner is a simple, economic, siphon-type device for adding fertilizer concentrate to the irrigation water. Because of its low capacity, it can be used only for watering pot plants. The rate of siphoning varies with the rate of water flow and pressure differential. (*The Hozon Co. drawing.*)

absorption of minerals can take place in the leaves and stems of plants, and in some special situations fertilizer solutions are sprayed on the leaves. It is generally considered that foliar applications of fertilizer are not as reliable and effective for greenhouse crops as are soil applications, except perhaps for correcting deficiencies of some of the trace elements.

Adjusting the soil reaction. The reaction of the soil is of concern because the solubility of some of the minerals is affected by it. Alkalinity or acidity is expressed in terms of pH whose values extend from pH 0, the most acid, to pH 14, the most alkaline, with pH 7 indicating neutral reaction. Many plants grow best in soils that are slightly acid in reaction because more elements are available to some degree in this range. Thus the soil reaction is maintained at approximately pH 6.3 to 6.8. There may be no adverse effect on plants in the range of pH 5.5 to 7.5, but if the soil reaction drifts toward either extreme, adjustments should be made.

The soil reaction is usually stable and does not fluctuate rapidly; however, faster changes can be expected in sandy soils than in clay because of the greater

Table 7-5.   *Lime Requirements of Various Soil Types*

Existing pH of soil	Pounds of agricultural limestone needed per 100 sq ft to raise:					
	Sandy loam soil		Silt loam soil		Silty-clay loam soil	
	to pH 6.0	to pH 6.5	to pH 6.0	to pH 6.5	to pH 6.0	to pH 6.5
6.0	0.0	2.0	0.0	4.0	0.0	5.0
5.5	2.0	4.0	4.0	7.0	5.0	10.0
5.0	4.0	6.0	7.0	11.0	10.0	15.0
4.8	4.5	7.0	8.0	12.0	12.0	17.0

surface area of the smaller clay particles.   It should be realized that a greater amount of the corrective material is needed to adjust the pH of clay soils than of sandy soils and that the change will be slower.

Table 7-6.   *Approximate Amounts of Sulfur Necessary to Lower the pH of a Silt Loam Soil*

pH	Pounds per 100 sq ft	Pounds per acre
8.0–6.5	3.0	1,300
8.0–6.0	4.0	1,750
8.0–5.5	5.5	2,400
8.0–5.0	7.0	3,000
7.5–6.5	2.0	870
7.5–6.0	3.5	1,525
7.5–5.5	5.0	2,175
7.5–5.0	6.5	2,830
7.0–6.0	2.0	870
7.0–5.5	3.5	1,525
7.0–5.0	5.0	2,175
6.5–5.5	2.5	1,090
6.5–5.0	4.0	1,750

Calcium compounds such as limestone are used primarily for raising the pH; however, it would be helpful in some cases to use sodium nitrate or calcium nitrate as these are two nitrogen sources that have an alkaline reaction.   For lowering the pH, either sulfur or iron sulfate is used, and ammonium sources of nitrogen will also help as their reaction is acid.   In some instances the pH of soils can be adjusted more effectively by adding neutral or alkaline soils or organic matter to soils that are too acid and adding acid soils or acid peat moss to soils that are too alkaline.

The status of minerals can be determined by soil tests, plant analysis, and observation of the plants. It is best to use a combination of methods to evaluate the mineral status of the soil and plant. The soil should be tested before planting to ensure proper corrective action and proper programming of fertilization. After planting, the soil should be tested often enough to assure that the proper minerals are available, and this will require testing once a month or more often until it is established that the fertilizer program is right. Careful observation of the plants during this period is essential in order to verify the soil-test reports.

Timeliness is very important. If it takes several weeks to receive the soil test report from a complete soil analysis, it will be necessary to use, in addition, some less detailed tests that produce immediate reports.

Plant analysis is a detailed laboratory procedure that has been used to a limited extent more recently. It does furnish information on the status of minerals right in the plant, and it may be particularly helpful when some unusual mineral situations exist.

Different methods of soil testing are used throughout the country, and the values that are reported by one testing method will not necessarily be comparable to the values used in another. Methods for determining pH are standard, and the values reported from any testing service should be the same for a given soil. Most soil-testing services give reports on the quantity of available nitrogen (expressed as nitrate nitrogen), phosphorus, potassium, and calcium in parts per million. Each soil-test report should be recorded and compared with previous tests of the same soil, as observation of the status of each mineral from test to test may give more useful information than the results from a single test. Phosphorus, pH, and calcium values should be quite stable and not change rapidly. If the tests indicate a general progression either way, some corrective action can be taken before trouble is encountered; usually, however, it is possible to make adjustments in the soil for pH, phosphorus, and calcium before planting that will satisfy the requirements for the entire crop. If a single test indicates values that are radically different from those in previous tests, another test should be made as quickly as possible to determine whether a mistake was made in sampling or the soil was given some unusual treatment between tests. Nitrogen values—and to a lesser degree potassium values—can fluctuate considerably between tests, and tests should be made frequently enough to evaluate their status and take corrective action. If the pH, phosphorus, and calcium quantities were properly adjusted before planting, only nitrogen or potassium applications may have to be made during the production of the crop. As indicated earlier, for many crops the soil pH should be approximately 6.5. Some differences may be encountered in recommendations for amounts of minerals in soils, but there is some agreement that nitrogen, as nitrate nitrogen, should be 50 ppm, phosphorus 5 ppm, potassium 40 ppm, and calcium 150 ppm.

In addition to reports on pH and the amounts of minerals, most soil-test services include an analysis of the amount of soluble salts in the soil. The soluble salts value indicates the total quantity of minerals that are available in the soil; even though it does not specify which minerals are included in the total, it is essential to keep advised of the total quantity as plants will not grow in an excess of minerals. The amount of soluble salts in soil is assessed by an instrument called "Solu Bridge," which determines the amount of salts in the soil solution by the relative amount of conductance of electric current through it. Readings can be made rapidly with the Solu Bridge, and it is operated easily. Most greenhouse operators should have their own Solu Bridge for making quick determinations of soluble salts, and more detailed reports could be obtained periodically from a soil-testing service. In making the Solu Bridge determination, some testing services use 1 part of soil to 2 parts of water, and others use 1 part of soil to 5 parts of water. Table 7-7 gives the recommendations based on values reported by either method.

Table 7-7. *Interpretation of Solu Bridge Values*

Because Solu Bridge values may be determined using either one part soil to two parts water or one part soil to five parts water, both values are listed. About 1965 the manufacturer changed the scale of the Solu Bridge. Units manufactured before that time will indicate readings 100 times greater than those listed here (the reading 0.50 on new equipment is the same as 50 on older units).

Solu Bridge readings		Interpretation
1 soil to 2 water	1 soil to 5 water	
Below 0.15	0.08 to 0.30	Too low. May be all right for seed germination, but too low for seedlings or plants.
0.15 to 0.50		Satisfactory only if soil is high in organic matter.
0.50 to 1.80	0.30 to 0.80	Satisfactory range for established plants, but upper level may be too high for some seedlings.
1.80 to 2.25	0.80 to 1.00	Slightly higher than desirable.
2.25 to 3.40	1.00 to 1.50	Plants usually stunted or at least not growing rapidly.
3.40 and up	1.50 and up	Plants dwarfed severely with the crop often an economic failure.

High soluble salts, a common problem in greenhouse soils, are caused by the addition of large quantities of fertilizer, poor drainage conditions, or failure to apply a sufficient quantity of water at each irrigation.   If a high soluble salts condition exists before planting, the situation can be corrected by the addition of soil or organic matter that is low in minerals.   If the high soluble salts problem occurs after planting, the first step is to determine whether the drainage through soil and bench is adequate.   With good drainage, heavy applications of water (leaching) can then be made in a short period of time to remove the excess minerals.   In order to prevent the soil from remaining constantly wet for an extended time, successive heavy irrigations should be made immediately following each other on the same day.   It is also possible that the soluble salts problem can be decreased if the source of minerals is changed.   In many instances sulfates and chlorides that originate in ammonium sulfate and potassium chloride fertilizers cause most of the soluble salts, and they can be eliminated in the future by changing to such fertilizers as potassium nitrate, ammonium nitrate, and calcium nitrate as sources of nitrogen.

Extremely high salts content in water supplies is not common, but it does occur occasionally and can be determined by the Solu Bridge.   Table 5-3 lists guides that can be used in evaluating the suitability of water because of salts content.

Most greenhouse operators should do some of their own soil testing to provide a rapid means of determining the status of minerals in the soil.   The results may at times not be as accurate as soil testing by a regular service, but it is a helpful supplement.   The Junior Simplex Soil Test Outfit made by the Edwards Laboratory, Box 318, Norwalk, Ohio, provides tests for the most common minerals as well as a simplified determination for pH, and it could be used to advantage in many greenhouses.   The Solu Bridge manufactured by Beckman Instruments, Inc., 89 Commerce Road, Cedar Grove, New Jersey, is another valuable tool for proper management of minerals.   The procedures are not difficult, and they can be done rapidly.   It is a means of making an immediate decision on whether a soil mineral problem exists, and this can be followed by a detailed soil test to determine which minerals are involved.   The cause of poor plant growth in the greenhouse may not be apparent readily, and the appearance of the plants could indicate either mineral (soluble salts) excesses or mineral deficiency.   The Solu Bridge can answer such a question in a matter of minutes.

The status of minerals within plants can be determined by plant analysis (tissue tests).   This is a rather lengthy laboratory procedure that is used as a research tool but has been adapted for some uses on commercial crops.   It does assess the mineral situation directly in the plant, and it may be a valuable additional means of determining the kind and amount of minerals to be supplied to the plant.   Procedures vary, but commonly the plant sample is made from leaves recently matured toward the top of the plant.   The sample is dried and analyzed, and the mineral content is reported in percentage of dry matter or parts per million depending upon the element. The interpretation of results varies with the crop, the sampling procedures, and the experience of the individuals making the analysis; but there is some agreement that the optimum content for most plants is about the same. The more typical acceptable values are nitrogen, 3.0 to 5.0 percent; phosphorus, 0.4 to 0.6 percent; potassium, 2 to 4 percent; magnesium, above 0.3 percent; calcium, above 1 percent; and boron, above 30 ppm.

Aside from soil or plant tests and observation of deficiency symptoms, the use of fertilizers must be tempered by the general growth of the plant and the environmental conditions that are provided for the plants. Minerals cannot be used by plants until they are absorbed, and since the primary means of entry is through the roots, minerals will be absorbed into the plant only if the roots are active and growing. The grower must observe the root growth constantly and adjust soil, drainage, or irrigation so that the best root growth is obtained. Adding fertilizers to soils when root growth is poor will actually cause harm. The condition of root growth can be used as a means of assessing several conditions that have been provided for the plants. If good, active root growth (many white root tips) is observed, this is sufficient evidence that soil aeration, drainage, and irrigation practices are satisfactory and that there is not too much fertilizer in the soil. If the roots are not in active growth (few white root tips) or they appear to be damaged, it could be caused by a soil, water, pest, or fertilizer situation or a combination of them. Whatever the cause of poor root growth, it must be corrected before the fertilizer application is made.

The use of fertilizer must be coordinated with other environmental conditions. If light or temperature conditions are not satisfactory, the plant will not use as great a quantity of minerals as it would in better conditions. The addition of fertilizer should also be based on the size of plants, kind of plants, and stage of development.

Fertilizer injectors are highly recommended because elements are applied on the basis of existing light and temperature conditions. The mineral requirements of some types of plants are greater than others, and, in general, large plants use more minerals than small plants. Plants that are in vigorous vegetative growth should usually be more adequately supplied with minerals than plants during the flower-forming stage of growth.

8

REPRODUCTION

Plants grown by florists are propagated by various means, depending on the feasibility or the economy of the situation. Plants such as asters, snapdragons, Cyclamen, primroses, and various garden annuals are usually propagated by seed. Carnations, Hydrangeas, geraniums, Chrysanthemums, and others are propagated from stem cuttings. Roses and some Camellias and azaleas are grafted, and roses may be budded. Although one method of propagation commonly is used, occasionally certain plants are propagated by more than one method.

PROPAGATION BY SEED

Propagation by seed is an economical method of reproduction, but is used only when the seed will reproduce the type of plant wanted within a short period of time.   In most instances it is not possible to produce the desired plant type from seed collected from florist crop plants.   Most of these plants are heterozygous, and seeds will produce various kinds of offspring.

The production of seed is best left to the specialist because of the close supervision and thorough knowledge of the techniques involved.   In recent years considerable use has been made of F_1 hybrids.   This seed is produced by crossing pure-line (homozygous) plants that may have quite different characteristics themselves but will make seed that produces young plants with some very desirable qualities.

Seed germination.   Germination of seed may be dependent on conditions of the seed itself or on the external environment in which the seed is placed. Seeds used by nurserymen often require special treatment before they will germinate, but most of the seeds that are in common usage in the florist trade are capable of germination upon being placed in the proper surroundings.   Germination of seed is usually obtained in moist conditions if the temperature is suitably warm and the medium in which the seed is placed is well aerated.   In some instances light is also needed for successful germination.

The medium that is chosen for sowing the seed must provide for successful maintenance of uniform moisture and aeration conditions.   Light or sandy soils are much more easily managed than clay soils for seed germination.   Mixtures of soil or sand with peat moss or sphagnum moss can be used.   In some instances there is an advantage in using peat moss or sand alone, while vermiculite, perlite, and other mediums have been used successfully by propagators.   No matter what medium is employed, moisture must be provided uniformly without limiting the supply of air.

Seeds usually germinate more readily in warm temperatures, and favorable results are obtained at about 70°F.

Useful seed-sowing methods.   The medium for the seedbed must be well screened unless it is naturally fine textured.   The smaller the seed, the finer the medium should be, to provide for closer contact between the seeds and the particles of the medium.

The amount of seed to be sown will determine the size of container, but very often it is most convenient to use a wooden flat.   Soil, sand, or peat mixtures should be well firmed in the flat before the seed is sown.   Vermiculite and similar materials should not be firmed.   The amount of firming of any medium will determine the moisture and air relationship, and too much firming may create a situation of too much moisture and not enough air.

Seed must not be sown deeply, as the growth of the plant is dependent on the limited food supply within the seed until it is in the light and is able to produce its own food by the process of photosynthesis.   Large seeds may have enough food supply to support underground growth, but small seeds such as Petunia and snapdragon have so little food reserves that they must be sown on the surface where the young plant will be in light soon after germination so that it can produce food for growth.   Wherever the seed is sown, it must be kept uniformly moist and warm for germination to take place, and enough air must be supplied for adequate respiration to take place in the plants.   The reciprocal nature of the moisture and air relationship must be kept in mind in supplying suitable environment for seed germination, as providing too much moisture limits the amount of air available and increasing the air movement too much may make conditions too dry.

Because seed is sown on the surface or close to it, moisture conditions will be variable unless definite provisions are made.   Uniform moisture may be assured either by covering the seed flat to prevent the loss of moisture or by adding moisture periodically by means of mist.   Various means of covering seed flats may be used.   One of the most common is glass.   If the cover is placed directly on the seed flat, moisture conditions will be uniform, but there will be little if any air movement.   If a transparent cover such as glass is used and the seed flats are in direct sunlight, an opaque cover such as paper must be used over the glass while it is directly on the flat to prevent extremely high temperatures. As soon as the seed starts to germinate, the opaque cover must be removed so that light is available for the young plants.   In order to prevent unduly high temperatures in the seed flat when the opaque cover is removed, the glass must be propped up to provide ventilation.   This will not only allow for temperature regulation in the seed flat but will cause loss of water.   As more air is provided in regulation of temperature, the flat must be misted periodically to keep the surface moist.

Seed flats that are covered must be inspected carefully every day to determine whether germination has occurred or whether there is any evidence of growth of disease organisms.   If germination has started, the opaque cover must be removed so that the seedlings will have light, and the transparent cover must be adjusted so that there will be sufficient air movement for proper regulation of temperature but not so much that there will be undue drying at the surface of the seed flat.   This is a very critical time in the reproduction of plants by seed. Usually several adjustments of cover may be necessary during the day to assure that the proper temperature, moisture, and air conditions are provided.   As the seedlings grow, the transparent cover should be raised higher and higher until it is entirely removed a few days after germination.   Some misting must be done as the cover is being raised to prevent drying of the surface and desiccation of the young plants.   Some plant pathogens reproduce very well in the same warm and moist environment provided for the germination of seeds.   In spite of excellent sanitation, some infestation is possible, and the propagator must be alert enough to observe the first indications of it.   Very often a disease infestation

8-1. It is best to sow seed in rows, as that prevents overcrowding and improves air circulation and light for the seedlings. Upper left: the rows which have been sown were lightly covered with sand, and the label inserted in the flat identifies the seed. Upper right: the sowing of seed has been completed, the label was placed on its side in the flat, the soil was thoroughly watered by subirrigation of the flat, and the flat was covered with a pane of glass to assure uniform moisture at the soil surface. Lower left: if the seed flat is placed in sunlight after sowing, it must be covered with an opaque material, such as paper, in addition to the glass, to prevent excessive temperatures within the flat. Lower right: the seed has germinated, the glass has been removed from the flat, and the label has been placed upright for easy identification.

may be controlled by limiting the amount of moisture at the surface of the seed flat. This may be accomplished by providing greater air movement over the surface of the flat.

Instead of covering seed flats to provide uniformly moist conditions, periodic misting may be used. The misting should be done just often enough to keep the surface of the seed flat moist. It is possible that this could be accomplished by the propagator with hose in hand, but actually it is not probable that he would be able to spend the amount of time required. An excellent job of misting is possible with a mist system controlled by a repeating timer which provides approximately 5 seconds of mist at intervals from 1 minute to 30 minutes or longer. This is the type of mist system which is in common usage for rooting cuttings. The accurate regulation of temperature, moisture, air, and light can be provided more reliably with a mist system than with the manipulation of a cover.

Thorough sterilization of the seedbed is essential because it will eliminate most of the disease problems. Chance infestations are always a possibility, however, and they can usually be kept under control if some ventilation is provided to prevent stagnant, moist conditions at the surface of the soil. Sowing the seed rather thinly is also helpful. It is easier to provide for air circulation around the seedlings if they are sown in rows rather than broadcast. Treatment with Morsodren, Dexon, and Terraclor fungicides is also useful in preventing losses from damping-off.

If the seed flat is well watered at the time of sowing, no further watering may be needed until after the seeds have germinated and more air is being furnished. Watering by subirrigation is a good method of thoroughly wetting the soil without disturbing the seed sown at the surface. If surface watering is used, a fine spray should be provided.

Fertilizer application will depend on the kind of seed and the medium that is used. Seedlings in sand, vermiculite, or perlite will need a fertilizer application sooner than those in soil mixtures. As soon as leaves are formed, seedling growth will be much more rapid if there is an adequate supply of fertilizer in the medium.

Handling seedlings.   Very often in the early stages seedlings will need to be placed in partial shade. As soon as possible, however, the shade should be decreased because the higher light intensities will produce heavier, stockier plants.

8-2. A flat of Cyclamen seedlings. Because the seedlings are not transplanted until several leaves are well developed, the seed is planted individually on about 2-inch squares.

When the seedlings can be handled, they should be transplanted to assure faster and more uniform growth. The root system is damaged the least if the plants are removed from the seed flat by lifting them out with a wide-bladed knife. Bruising and injury to the stem can be prevented if the plants are handled by their leaves rather than by their stems.

Different methods of transplanting can be used depending on the crop, the time and labor involved, and the amount of space available. Seedlings are often dibbled off in flats on 1- or 2-inch squares, which conserves space but means that the plants must be shifted again before long. Frequent shifting is also required if the plants are placed in small pots. If labor is costly or in short supply, it is best to transplant to larger pots or even directly to the bench in which the plants are to be forced. This method can be used very successfully with snapdragons, but it is more difficult to handle small seedlings in large soil volumes. Watering is critical, and for the first week or two it is easy to water too often. When the plants are established, growth is rapid and they are more easily managed.

Plants in small pots or closely spaced in flats are very often underwatered and not fertilized often enough, resulting in slow growth and seedlings that are hard and stunted.

Plant bands can be used to good advantage. In some situations they are more easily managed than pots, and transplanting is handled more rapidly than with flats.

Pots made of a compressed mixture of peat and wood fiber are useful. The soil dries more slowly than with clay, and the roots permeate the side walls of the pot, often growing through them. At planting, the pot is placed in the soil together with the plant.

VEGETATIVE PROPAGATION

Vegetative reproduction is practiced because of the rapidity with which maturity is attained and because many florist plants do not come true from seed. Propagation from cuttings is used for a large number of florist plants because it is a rapid and accurate method of reproducing the parent plant. Grafting and budding are used with some plants, and the bulbous plants are reproduced by means of bulblets, corms, or tubers.

Propagation by cuttings. Stem tip cuttings are used most commonly; even though various parts of the plant may be used for cuttings, usually one type of cutting is more suitable than another. Stem tip cuttings are used for carnations and Chrysanthemums, leaf cuttings for Saintpaulias, leaf bud cuttings for Hydrangeas, and root cuttings for phlox.

The important environmental factors are temperature, moisture, aeration, and light. The success or speed of propagation can be determined by the manner in which these conditions are provided.   Careful control of the temperature of the rooting medium is essential.   It is usually beneficial to maintain the rooting medium from 5 to 10°F warmer than the air temperature.   It may be possible to provide adequate control of bench temperature with steam or hot water lines under the propagation bench, but it should be determined definitely whether proper, uniform temperatures are being maintained.   Enough soil thermometers must be placed in the propagation bench so that it can be observed that temperatures are correct throughout.   Whatever the source of heat, there must be provisions for its control specifically for the propagation bench.   If the heat source is the same as the one for heating the entire greenhouse area, some provision will usually have to be made for heat in the propagation area in addition to that normally used in the rest of the greenhouse.   During the heating season it is possible, if the boilers are operated solely for the flower production greenhouses, that they may be shut down on clear days even in cold weather.   Most propagation benches require supplementary heat, day and night.   Some propagation is done during the summer when the heating system is not normally operated.   The propagation of poinsettias is a good example.   They are propagated in August and September when the night temperatures may be as low as 40 to 50°F.   If heat is not supplied to the poinsettia propagation benches, the cuttings will not root or will root very slowly.   One of the best methods of heat control for propagation benches is with electric soil cables.   They are regulated by thermostat, and the uniform temperatures which are required may be provided.

An adequate and uniform moisture supply is needed in the rooting medium as well as in the air surrounding the cuttings.   High air-moisture content will reduce the amount of moisture loss from the cutting.   Various misting devices with water under low and high pressure can be used that will increase the amount of moisture in the air, but some of them may keep the rooting medium too wet.   Moisture loss from the cutting can be minimized also by controlling air movement.   In general, cuttings may be rooted in higher light intensities if the air-moisture content is high.

In order to provide uniformly moist conditions for the cuttings, a mist system should be installed over the propagation bench.   The mist line should

8-3. Chrysanthemum unrooted cuttings to be stuck in a propagation bench containing peat moss and perlite.

8-4. Unrooted poinsettia stem tip cuttings being stuck in a propagation bench. The rooting medium is a mixture of peat moss and perlite. It is lined at the proper distance, and the cuttings are stuck, firmed, and then watered thoroughly.

be about 24 inches above the bench or just high enough so that it does not interfere with working the bench. Several different types of nozzles may be used. The deflection nozzle is popular, as it provides a fine, full-circle mist and requires no maintenance. This type of nozzle has a wire positioned over the hole so that the fine stream of water emitted from the nozzle strikes the end of the wire and deflects as mist in a horizontal plane. Each nozzle delivers about 1 gallon of water per hour at 50 psi, and the nozzles should be spaced approximately 3 feet apart on the misting line. The mist system should be operated so that the leaves remain moist, which requires about 5 seconds of misting as often as once a minute in midsummer and sometimes as seldom as once every half

8-5. Some cuttings are rooted directly in pots. Here poinsettia cuttings are being rooted in peat pots in racks.

hour during the winter.   An electric water valve (solenoid) is used which is activated by an interval timer.   The timer must be adjustable so that various intervals can be selected, depending on the weather and the requirements for misting.

Because of the small water volume required, ½-inch iron pipe may be used for the mist line in most situations and either ½-inch or ¾-inch electric water valves.   At 50 psi the potential rate of water flow through 100 feet of ½-inch iron pipe should be about 540 gallons per hour.   The water requirement for 33 mist nozzles installed on 100 feet of pipe would be about 33 gallons per hour, leaving a large volume of water in reserve.

The mist line must be installed at the same level as the electric water valve or above it.   If this is not done, water will drip from the nozzles during the off cycle, causing areas below the nozzles to be too wet, as well as depleting the water supply in the mist line.   If the water supply is depleted, the mist line must be filled with water before misting can start on the on cycle, causing a delay in the start and causing misting to progress from the water-supply end as the pipe fills with water.   When a misting system is properly installed on the level, misting occurs from all nozzles the instant the electric valve opens and quits completely when the valve closes.

When the mist system is operated during the summer, it is used only in the daylight because the relative humidity is usually high at night, causing the cuttings to remain moist without the use of mist.   A 24-hour clock or "day-night" timer may be used to provide operation of the system for the period of the day desired.   During the heating season, on the other hand, the relative humidity in the greenhouse is lower during the night than it is in the day.   For propaga-

8-6. Propagation benches for rooting Chrysanthemum stem tip cuttings. Left: mist lines not operating. Right: mist line in operation. The misting system is activated by clock at regular intervals so that a film of moisture remains on the leaves.

tion at that time of year, the misting system should be operated both day and night in most instances.

The frequency of misting should be reduced as the cuttings root. When the cuttings are stuck, the potential for water loss is much greater than that for water uptake. As roots form, some water is taken into the cutting through the roots, and the need for misting is less critical. Whenever possible, it is best to design the misting system in a size to suit the units which will be propagated at one time so that the misting may be controlled for that unit in accordance with the stage of rooting.

The moisture content of the rooting medium must not be maintained at the expense of aeration. If the drainage is poor or if water is added too frequently, air supply is reduced in the rooting medium and actually prevents rooting. Both the propagation bench and the rooting medium must drain well. Sand has been used successfully as a propagation medium for years. Washed, sharp silica sand is very satisfactory. Bank or lake sand is often too fine or contains too much clay and does not drain properly. In some instances it is advisable to use peat moss in the rooting medium. Materials such as vermiculite or perlite can be used successfully, but whatever the medium used, it must retain moisture uniformly and also drain well.

It is possible that the amount of light is not critical until root formation starts; however, the quality of the cutting is best if the highest light intensity that produces no burn or drying of the plant material is used. Depending on the amount of moisture that is maintained in the air, some reduction in light intensity is usually needed unless a mist system is used. Shade is best supplied at some distance above the cuttings so that air movement is not restricted,

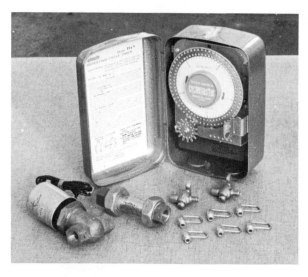

8-7. Electric water valve (solenoid), water strainer, petcocks, mist nozzles, and interval timer for a misting system. (*Jednak Floral Co. photograph.*)

and it should be adjustable so that it can be regulated as the light intensity varies.

There are several excellent root-promoting substances available containing indolebutyric acid, naphthalene acetamide, or other growth substances. Only a very small amount of such materials is needed to increase the amount of roots formed and reduce the length of time required for rooting. The dust form of the growth substance is often easier to use. If it does not adhere, the stem can be moistened a little. On the other hand, care must be taken to assure that not too much of the growth substance remains on the stem, as it can cause injury.

The importance of careful selection of propagation stock is becoming more evident. Haphazard methods of selection have caused varieties to "run out." This may be due to propagation of mutants or sports of the original line or to the propagation of diseased plant material. The carefully maintained stock block is the best method of assuring a reliable source of cuttings. The stock plants must be observed for habit of growth, flower characteristics, amount of flower production, and disease symptoms.

There are a few exceptions, but in general it is not important where the cut is made on the stem. The cut may be made at or between the nodes on the stem. Leaves should not be trimmed unless they are excessively large, as they contribute food to the cutting during the rooting period.

Moisture loss from the cutting is critical at all times. This water loss can be minimized if the cuttings are covered with a moist cloth or misted as soon as they are made. The cuttings should be stuck in the propagation bench as soon as possible, the medium firmed around the base of the cutting, and then thoroughly watered. The amount of firming that is needed depends on the type of medium. Sand should be firmed well before the cuttings are stuck, and then firmed somewhat after sticking. Vermiculite should not be firmed. Any medium, however, should be well watered after the cuttings are stuck.

8-8. With some plants stem (leaf bud) cuttings may be used for propagation as well as stem tip cuttings. This illustrates how Hydrangea stem and stem tip cuttings are prepared.

Cuttings should be removed from the propagation bench as soon as some root growth is evident. Most of the rooting mediums which are used contain no fertilizer, and if cuttings are kept in the propagation bench for long periods after they are rooted, they deteriorate rapidly. It is possible to supply fertilizer to the propagating medium, but invariably it is more satisfactory to remove the cuttings and either pot or plant them.

Rooted cuttings will become established more rapidly after planting if they are placed in somewhat reduced light and protected from drying by maintaining high air moisture and reducing air movement. They should be well watered after planting, but then the soil should be allowed to dry somewhat before the next watering. The thorough initial watering provides for good contact between the soil particles and the roots, and the somewhat drier conditions that develop later provide the good aeration that is necessary for rapid growth.

Propagation by grafting, or budding.   Grafting, or budding, is used with roses and some Camellias and azaleas. It is a method of producing a good-sized plant in a short period of time, and it also allows for the placement of a desirable flower type on a more satisfactory root system.

Special skills are required, and various kinds of grafting, or budding, are employed, depending on the species of plant, the facilities that are available, and the type of plant that is wanted. In any event, the problem consists of getting good contact between the inner bark of the two plant parts being grafted and maintaining this contact without any drying of the tissues or incidence of disease until the two parts have grown together. A grafting case is commonly employed in which moisture, temperature, and air movement can be controlled until a union is effected.

Air layering, or mossing.   Air layering is frequently practiced with foliage plants. A ring of bark about 1 inch wide is removed from the stem or a slanting cut is made below the top of the plant, the distance from the top being as great as the desired length of the new plant. In the case of heavy stems such as *Ficus*, small bamboo stakes are tied across the cut to support the stem. A ball of wet sphagnum moss is placed around the cut and tied with raffia or waxed string. The moss is then overwrapped with polethylene film or metal foil, which, because of its waterproof nature, prevents the moss from drying out. Some sort of tape should be used to keep an airtight seal where the film or foil is wrapped around the stem. When the sphagnum is filled with roots, the stem is severed below the root ball, the covering removed, and the plant is potted. For shipment as a rooted cutting, the film or foil is not removed.

The advantage of this system is that the "cutting" is attached to the parent plant; hence it forms roots rapidly and does not drop lower leaves, as would be apt to occur if the top of the plant were severed and placed in a propagation bench under mist or in a grafting or Wardian case.

8-9. Some plants are propagated by several means. Top: a started-eye, budded rose plant which has been planted in a greenhouse bench after the shoots have started to develop. Middle, left to right: manetti root stock; root stock trimmed and bark split; scion of rose variety to be reproduced; scion placed in contact with inner bark of root stock; and the resulting grafted plant. Bottom, left to right: rose un-rooted cutting and rooted cutting (own root). These are one-eye cuttings. Two-eye cuttings often are used.

9

DIAGNOSING
PLANT DISORDERS

Although many of the plant disorders are caused by rather common events, it is often difficult to make an orderly evaluation of what has happened. It is not unusual to find that no problem exists, and that the "disorder" is the result of faulty observation or poor interpretation of plant growth and development. If there is any question that a disorder exists, the plants in question should be compared with similar plants at the same place or at neighboring greenhouses.

If it is established that the disorder is real but the cause is not apparent, it may be helpful to determine when the disorder happened or whether a similar pattern of the problem exists. The time of occurrence in some instances can be established by observing the stage of growth of the plant that is affected, and it might be possible to link the disorder with unusual weather, pesticide or fertilizer applications, a worker's vacation, or other events. Very often there will be a certain pattern to the trouble—one portion of all plants is affected, only certain plants are involved, the trouble occurs only in definite areas of the bench or house, or the disorder may be located in treated houses and not in others.

Sometimes it will be helpful to evaluate whether the problem was present in the plant initially or whether it developed from the air or through the soil. This will help to establish the source of the trouble.

Unfortunately, it is often easier to make hasty conclusions than it is to reason and make an orderly evaluation of the problem. There is a common tendency to try to associate disorders with exotic rather than ordinary events. It is possible, too, that the trouble may have more than one cause, and this can lead to much confusion if only one source of the trouble is considered. Sometimes the right association of disorder and cause may be found simply by listing the events that occurred at about the time the trouble arose.

Troubles come frequently because someone read the wrong directions, used the wrong material, applied too much or too little, or used faulty procedures. In talking to the individuals involved, everything might sound all right, and the problem might not be apparent until mathematics is checked carefully, the correct source of materials verified, and proper procedures confirmed.

It is necessary to be suspicious of symptoms that can look alike and seek a definite determination of the source of trouble before taking corrective action. This may require the help of specialists or just another individual who has not been as close to the situation. If specialists are not known who can be of assistance, the county agricultural agent should be able to refer the problem to the proper person at the university or agricultural experiment station.

9-1. The effect of environmental conditions on leaf size. The rose leaf on the left is from a plant in optimum conditions. The right leaf shows the effect of unsuitable environmental conditions, which could be water deficiency from various causes: too high light intensity; deficiencies in some minerals, particularly nitrogen; or temperatures which are too high.

9-2. Dodder, a parasitic plant, is observed occasionally on outdoor plants but seldom on those in the greenhouse.

Some disorders are related to light. The quality, quantity, and daily duration of light have profound effects on the growth and development of plants, and variations in the light that is provided plants can cause some disorders. If the quantity of light is insufficient, plants may not flower or flowering may be delayed. Plants in low light intensity may have long stems, but they will be of small diameter and may not support flowers erectly. The leaves may be large but thin, and the lower leaves may wither and die.

Because the sun is a source of heat as well as light, it is difficult sometimes to separate the effects of light and heat. Many times the cause of disorder may be attributed to light when in fact it is due to a combination of light and temperature. Low light intensities are common in the winter, and the resulting low temperatures are adjusted with heat from artificial sources. In the summer the high light intensity may generate unduly high temperatures which contribute to the unfavorable effects on the plants. High light intensities can be expected to produce early flowering, a greater number of flowers, smaller leaves and flowers, lighter or bleached flower and leaf colors, and shorter but heavier stems.

The length of day has dramatic effects on the growth and development of some plants. The day-length effects that are most widely known are the ones on flowering. Chrysanthemums and poinsettias do not flower in long days, and many flowering disorders in these plants are related to improper day length. These plants produce leaves and increase in stem length in successive long days, but the growth terminates with flower buds when the plants are in a sufficient number of successive short days. When the day length is invariable, either the vegetative or flower development of the plant is normal, but if the day length fluctuates, abnormal flower development may occur. Many flower disorders in *Chrysanthemum* and poinsettia are related to unscheduled changes in day length. If there were a delay in the start of short days, the flowers would be well formed but flowering would be delayed a similar length of time; but if there were fluctuating day lengths, the flowers might be malformed and the time of flowering delayed.

Other effects of day length are long days causing earlier flowering and increased height in asters, snapdragons, and Petunias. In addition, Petunias normally branch in short days but grow to a single stem in long days.

Temperature can cause some disorders. Temperatures must be controlled very accurately in greenhouses; otherwise, many problems may arise. High temperatures are a common problem during the high-light-intensity periods of the summer. However, this is not the only time that the temperatures may be too high, as faulty management at other periods of the year may produce some high-temperature problems. Regardless of the time of the year, higher temperatures will generally result in earlier flowering but smaller flowers, smaller leaves, stems of smaller diameter, and reduced color of flowers and leaves. Some plants do not flower in temperatures that are too high. Chrysanthemums are a good example of this since some of the varieties that are commonly used for cropping in the winter will not flower satisfactorily in night temperatures above 60°F. Several Chrysanthemum varieties do not flower in the summer when night temperatures remain above 90°F, but they form flower buds (crown buds) which do not continue to develop until the advent of cooler temperatures. In the crown bud stage the stem continues to elongate below the flower bud, and when the flower finally does form, it is not of the desired quality because of the elongated stem (neck) below the flower.

Lower temperatures may delay flowering, but flower and leaf size and color are improved, and stems are of larger diameter. Some plants do not flower in temperatures that are too low, and typically the stem does not elongate but forms a rosette-type growth. The effects of temperature on moisture can produce decided differences in plant growth, and one of the most common effects is that soils stay wet longer in cool temperatures. When this occurs, the air is limited in the soil, and root growth is slow or may be terminated entirely. The constantly wet soil is also a more suitable environment for some of the disease organisms, and these may cause further damage to roots and stems. If heating is not properly coordinated with ventilation, moisture may form on flowers, leaves, or stem, causing a favorable situation for the germination and growth of several disease organisms.

The temperature effects on bulbs before they are planted as well as afterward must be considered. Most of the bulbs are given temperature treatments by the bulb producers to cause better growth and flowering after they are planted.

9-3.   Leaf spot on African violet caused by cold water on the leaves.

The effects of these treatments can be negated by the temperature in which the bulbs are kept until they are planted as well as the temperature they are given after planting. Prolonged storage of lily bulbs at cool temperatures before planting reduces the number of flowers that form and the size of the basal leaves, and increases the elongation of the basal portion of the stem. Keeping lily bulbs in too warm temperatures before they are planted may delay flowering. Too high temperatures are common with the first crops of *Iris* planted in the fall, and this can produce short growth and blasting of flowers.

Soil aeration, moisture, and minerals affect plant growth.   Conditions of the soil often are the causes of disorders in plants.   These may involve inadequate drainage so that the soil stays wet continually, with resulting poor aeration and lack of root growth, insufficient moisture, improper pH, pests, or deficiencies or excesses of minerals.   It must be kept in mind constantly that the entry of water and minerals into the plant is through the roots, and because absorption occurs primarily in the root hair area immediately behind the root tip, it is necessary to have continuous root growth to maintain this effective absorption area of the roots.   For many of the plant disorders the roots should be inspected first to determine whether they are growing actively, since such growth is an excellent indication that the soil drainage, aeration, moisture, pH, pests, and

9-4. The effects of too frequent irrigation, too heavy soil, or too much fertilizer on pot mums. Plants on the left with good root growth develop normally, but the plants on the right were in unfavorable conditions for root growth, causing shorter stems, smaller leaves, fewer stems, and slower flower bud development. (*Yoder Bros., Inc., photograph.*)

mineral excesses are not causes of the disorders. If the roots are growing actively, the only soil problem likely to exist would be some mineral deficiencies, and this is not too common. If the roots are not growing actively, it is then necessary to determine which of the several possibilities may be the cause or causes. No matter what disorder is apparent in the top portions of the plant, no solution is possible until the roots are in active growth.

Symptoms of deficiencies of various fertilizers have been studied over a period of years with plants in soil as well as in sand. From these experiments rather characteristic symptoms have been noted which are useful in diagnosing trouble from lack of fertilizer.

Chlorosis.   The term chlorosis is used to denote the loss of normal green color from the foliage whether it is on the older, more mature leaves or the younger foliage. The entire leaf may be affected, or just areas between the veins, in which case the yellowing is usually in irregular patches shading into the green color. Sometimes only the margin of the leaf or leaflets may be yellow, while the center of the foliage is almost a normal green.

Necrosis.   This refers to the death of the area severely affected by chlorosis. The areas are brown, sometimes black, and usually dried and somewhat shrunken. Necrotic spots or areas can also be caused by spray or aerosol damage, sunscald, and other such factors which may have no relation to fertilizer.

Regulated nitrogen deficiency.   In the culture of plants it might be assumed that a fertilizer deficiency should be avoided. To a considerable extent this is true, but surprising as it may seem, many plants are purposely maintained on a regulated nitrogen deficiency so that they are the kind of plant the grower desires. For example, a snapdragon kept on a regulated nitrogen deficiency will not develop excessive lateral growth of shoots but still will have stem and spike lengths to command a favorable price. Under higher nitrogen conditions the snapdragon becomes "grassy," meaning that the side shoots grow quite long and must be removed. Chrysanthemums will develop extremely brittle foliage under conditions of exceptionally high, but not injurious, nitrogen, and these leaves break readily when handled or shipped. A full supply of nitrogen for vine growth of sweet peas generally results in bud drop. These examples serve to illustrate that in some cases nitrogen fertilizer should not be supplied to the fullest extent for plant growth.

The first symptom of any deficiency is a reduction in growth, although it is not always possible to see this in the early stages in terms of reduced height or flower production. As the deficiency becomes more severe, the symptoms described below will be in evidence.

Nitrogen deficiency. Generally in nitrogen deficiency the entire plant becomes lighter green, but the effect is most noticeable on the older foliage. Gradually the oldest leaves lose their green color, and on most plants they become yellow. However, a red or bronze coloration of the lower foliage occurs with some plants. The leaves dry and turn brown under severe deficiency and do not drop.

The leaves are smaller and are borne rather stiffly, in a somewhat upright position on the stem. The stems are more slender and woody than on plants having an adequate supply of nitrogen. With some plants the stems are shorter, but in the case of the rose there are fewer shoots, although some long-stemmed flowers are produced. The flowers are smaller and may lack well-developed color. From 0 to 10 ppm (Spurway system) will generally result in such deficiency symptoms as these.

Phosphorus deficiency. In most soils it is doubtful whether a deficiency of phosphorus is severe. However, in the case of highly adsorptive soils where phosphorus is tightly held, or in the case of light, sandy soils where there is little possibility of retention, a deficiency may occur. A purplish coloration, developing first on the underside of the petiole and spreading to the main veins of the leaf, is characteristic of this deficiency. It may sometimes be noted on seedlings which have been germinated in a light soil and held too long before planting. In time, a deficiency will probably occur at 0 to 1 ppm.

Potassium deficiency. In potassium deficiency the margins of the leaves of the older foliage become yellow, and the chlorosis progresses toward the midportion of the foliage as this deficiency increases in severity. Necrotic areas or spots may appear on the margins in extreme cases of deficiency, and the leaves in the midportion of the plant will show symptoms. The older leaves may drop in very extreme cases of deficiency.

Sometimes chlorotic or necrotic spots or blotches appear in areas between the veins of the older leaves near the margin. In sand culture, death of the stem tips has been observed, but this would be an extreme case. Roots of plants in sand culture without potassium are long and stringy, indicating much reduced cambial activity but little inhibitory effect on the growing area of the tip.

Certain fumigants may cause marginal burning or chlorosis, and sometimes droplets of spray or fumigant may result in spots or blotches of chlorotic or necrotic nature. From 0 to 10 ppm is considered too low a proportion of potassium to soil.

Calcium deficiency. In sand culture a typical symptom of calcium deficiency is the development of short clubby roots followed in a matter of several

9-5. Leaf symptom of potassium deficiency. Interveinal speckling is followed by desiccation and death of the marginal tissue.

9-6. Typical leaf symptom of potassium deficiency in poinsettia.

weeks by their death.   Cambial activity of the roots occurs, but division of cells at the tip is materially reduced, giving rise to short, thickened roots.

The stems may be rather drastically reduced in length, and in severe cases the youngest foliage may develop chlorosis followed by death of the stem tip. In soil, such severe symptoms are seldom observed, but shortened stems and thick roots are common.   In many cases insufficient calcium is associated with a low pH of the soil.   Less than 100 ppm may cause difficulty.

Iron deficiency.   Iron deficiency is a rather common trouble, although an actual lack of iron may not be the primary cause.   When root growth is reduced or killed, chlorosis of the new leaves will appear rather quickly on some plants, the severity depending upon the extent to which the root system has been damaged.   As iron deficiency becomes more intense, necrotic areas appear on scattered portions of the yellowed leaves, and the affected foliage may drop.

Iron can become deficient in soil, but often the symptoms of this deficiency are induced by other causes, such as injury to the roots by overwatering or over-fertilization.   Unfavorable soil conditions, such as an alkaline reaction or too much calcium or phosphorus, can precipiate iron which may be present.   Nematodes, symphylids, or other soil pests can also induce iron chlorosis symptoms by interfering with root growth.

Boron deficiency.   The number of cases where boron deficiency is a limiting factor is few, and most of them are with certain rose and carnation varieties.   The new foliage is thick or leathery and quickly becomes chlorotic. The rose flowers are usually very malformed.   The stem tip dies, giving rise to

9-7.   Leaf symptom of deficiency of available iron.   This symptom may result from poor root growth for various reasons: unfavorable pH, excesses of other minerals, or an actual lack of iron.

growth of shoots immediately below, which in turn die at the tip, and a "witches' broom" effect is observed.

Magnesium deficiency.   In pronounced magnesium deficiency the lower leaves become yellow in blotchy irregular spots between the veins rather quickly. The remaining portion of the leaf is almost a normal green.

Manganese deficiency.   In manganese deficiency the top foliage becomes yellow between the veins, and eventually the entire leaf turns chlorotic. The chlorotic areas are rather small and scattered throughout the leaf blade, while the smallest veins remain green, giving a netted appearance to the leaf.

Sulfur deficiency.   It is doubtful that sulfur will become deficient, considering the amounts of it which are contained in many fertilizers.   In sand culture the upper foliage becomes chlorotic and the veins are usually more yellow than the surrounding tissue.

Remedial measures.   The correct fertilizer can be applied alone or in combination with others.   The rates of application and general precautions are given in Chap. 7.

Because deficiency symptoms can sometimes be confused with the effects of some other environmental factor or cultural practice, a thorough review of fertilizer application, soil testing, soil type, watering practices, and other procedures is warranted before hasty conclusions are reached.

An unfortunate belief among many growers is that when a plant does not grow under apparently favorable conditions, the trouble can be overcome by applications of fertilizer.   This practice has resulted in untold damage to or loss of crops, as more often than not the original trouble was too much fertilizer in the soil.   If additional fertilizer is applied when no more is needed, the results can be very injurious.

Sometimes the difference between a high but safe nutrient level and an injurious nutrient level is not very great, and the margin of safety may be extremely small.   Therefore it behooves the grower to test the soil in case of doubt to determine the advisability of fertilizer application.

Nitrogen excess.   In nitrogen excess the plants exhibit heavy, rank growth, with larger, dark-green leaves that are often crisp and break easily.   Additional nitrogen may inhibit root action, causing typical symptoms of iron chlorosis.   If the root system is killed, the plants wilt excessively and never recover.   This yellowing of the top foliage is very common in Chrysanthemums and snapdragons.   These plants may follow crops which have been heavily fertilized with nitrogen, and the roots of the young plants are burned when benched in this soil.   More than 75 ppm of nitrates is not safe.

Phosphorus excess.   Phosphorus excess may cause trouble with azaleas and Gardenias where considerable iron is needed and also with foliage and other plants where excessive phosphorus may precipitate minor or trace elements in the soil and bring about their deficiency in the tissue.   Overdoses of phosphorus precipitate the iron from the soil solution and make it insoluble and unavailable, causing iron chlorosis to develop.   More than 25 ppm may cause trouble.

Potassium excess.   Up to a certain point, excessive potash apparently is not injurious.   Greater amounts inhibit root action and may cause chlorosis, wilting, or immediate death of the plant.   Over 60 ppm is dangerous.

Calcium excess.   Usually the pH of the soil will rise when there is excessive calcium.   This causes iron chlorosis in many plants and has been called "overliming injury."   More than 300 ppm is high.

Iron excess.   In the normal pH range of soil, there is little danger of excessive iron since phosphorus or calcium will precipitate it from the soil solution.   At pH 5.0 or lower, iron becomes very soluble, and on Hydrangeas brown dots appear on the leaves, indicating that iron is being precipitated as water vapor is lost by transpiration.

Sulfate excess.   A low pH may often be characteristic of soils high in sulfates.   Sometimes high sulfates are encountered at pH 6.5.   More than 600 ppm is toxic to most plants.

Boron excess.   Excess of boron is often found in soil to which unleached cinders have been added or to which boric acid has been applied indiscriminately.   Certain water supplies may have rather high amounts of boron.   On roses, the serrations on the margins of the leaflets of the lower leaves turn black, and the remainder of the leaf turns yellow and drops.

Aluminum excess.   Aluminum excess is not troublesome except on Hydrangeas that are being blued.   Roots are burned, and the plants wilt.

Soluble salts excess.   The sum total of all soluble fertilizers in the soil constitutes soluble salts (Chap. 7).   Too much fertilizer in the soil injures or kills roots, and plant growth is severely reduced.

Remedial measures for excess fertilizer.   When fertilizer levels rise to the point where they become toxic, immediate steps must be taken to remove the excessive materials.

Excessive nitrogen can be leached from the soil by several heavy waterings (3 to 5 gallons per square foot).   Application of a straw mulch or incorpora-

9-8. Desiccation and death of the leaf margin due to insufficient water in the plant because of inability of roots to absorb water following damage from high concentration of soluble minerals (soluble salts) in the soil.

tion of chopped straw accomplishes the same end on beds which cannot be leached satisfactorily.   Ground corncobs may be used in place of straw.

Excessive phosphorus is overcome by addition of lime or iron sulfate. Phosphorus cannot be leached.

Excessive potassium is difficult to remove.   Leaching may wash some of it through the soil, but in clay soils removal may be almost impossible.

9-9. Snapdragons are particularly sensitive to high soluble salts. Root growth is limited, leaves are chlorotic, and there is little growth of stem. (*Yoder Bros., Inc., photograph.*)

Excessive calcium can usually be remedied by acidifying the soil (Chap. 7).

Excessive iron can be overcome by raising the pH or by adding phosphorus.

Excessive sulfates are removed by leaching and by avoiding the use of sulfate forms of fertilizers.

Excessive boron is difficult to overcome.   Leaching is practical but must be practiced every time the crop requires water.   Water glass, or sodium silicate, can be dissolved in water, at the rate of 100 cubic centimeters per gallon, and applied to the soil.   It will not harm the plants.

Excessive aluminum is overcome by raising the pH or by adding phosphorus.

Excessive soluble salts is overcome by leaching thoroughly.

Plant disorders can be caused by deficiencies or excesses in the air that is available to the plants.   Carbon dioxide and oxygen, two of the essential ingredients in the air for plants, are normally in sufficient supply.   However, it is possible that in cool weather, when the greenhouses are closed for long periods of time, their quantities may be too low for the best plant growth.   If carbon dioxide is added to the air at such times, some benefits may be expected, but it is possible that some disorders may arise because of misapplications or misuses.   The quantity of carbon dioxide added must be coordinated with the available light quantity and the amounts of minerals and moisture which are available to the plants. Excessive concentrations of carbon dioxide may cause flower malformation, flower bud formation on short stems, and the development of hard rather than succulent growth.   If carbon dioxide generators are used, it is possible that harmful gases might be produced as well, such as sulfur dioxide, carbon monoxide, and ethylene. It is also possible, if the air inlet is not properly regulated, that the oxygen supply in the greenhouse may become depleted.   Lack of sufficient oxygen in the air would be extremely harmful to plant growth.   Further combustion in the generator would not be complete, and toxic gases probably would be generated in addition to the carbon dioxide.   The disorders caused would vary with the gases that were present, but failure to flower, epinasty (bending down of leaves), petal and leaf burn, leaf drop, and possible death of the plants are some of the possibilities.

The amount of moisture in the air has an important effect on the growth and development of plants.   In dry air, plants will have smaller flowers and leaves, shorter stems, and fewer stems.   If the air is too moist, the plant growth may be too succulent, the stems may not support themselves erectly, or some plants may exhibit the disorder known as oedema.   Geraniums are very sensitive to moist air, and they are troubled with corky growths on leaves and stems, typical of oedema, when the ventilation is insufficient and the air is very humid.   Diseases are generally common in moist air as the pathogens can germinate and grow

OUACHITA TECHNICAL COLLEGE

more readily on the moist surfaces of the plants, and can invade the succulent tissues of the plants easily.

Fuel or illuminating gas once was a source of trouble to plants in greenhouses, but this problem was associated with ethylene and possibly other impurities in the manufactured gas that was widely used at that time. Natural fuel gas has no apparent effect on plants; and since natural gas now is used almost exclusively, the possibilities of disorders from fuel gas are remote.

Ethylene gas. Ethylene gas apparently is a by-product of metabolic processes and is given off in very small quantities by plants or their parts. Dropping of flowers after pollination is thought to be associated with ethylene vapors. Some flowers, like the snapdragon, apparently give off enough ethylene so that when packaged and in an airtight container, florets on some varieties drop quickly.

Apples and callas in quantity also give off enough ethylene to be damaging to carnations when placed in the same cooler. The carnation flowers close or may appear "sleepy," that is, the ends of the petals may curl inward.

Ethylene may occur in the air as a waste gas from certain types of manufacturing processes.

Sulfur dioxide. In very low concentrations sulfur dioxide is toxic to plants. Sulfur dioxide enters the leaf through open stomates and kills the cells nearby, thus causing patches of tissues scattered over the leaf to die and frequently affecting the margins. Middle-aged leaves are more susceptible to injury than old leaves, and old leaves are more susceptible than young leaves. Stems and buds are quite resistant, showing no injury until after the leaves are completely dead. Tissues along the veins are more resistant. Slightly wilted plants are much more resistant than turgid ones.

9-10. Fluorine damage to Gladiolus leaves. This gas is a by-product of some industrial processes. Other air pollutants also are responsible for some plant damages.

Damage from sulfur dioxide is commonly found in localities where coal is burned in large quantities, and particularly upon occasions when the atmosphere is heavily charged with moisture, forcing the gases to lower levels and into contact with plants.   Foggy days are particularly dangerous.

The common practice of using sulfur on heating pipes in rose houses to control mildew is responsible for leaf drop on some varieties.

Mercury damage.   Many plants are quickly damaged by vapors from metallic mercury.   This damage is manifested in roses by the peduncles of young buds turning yellow and later black, by half-matured buds turning brown, and by corollas abscissing from the receptacles without opening (Fig. 9-11). The color of flowers turns dark, and leaves are scorched.   Unless remedies are applied, plants remain stunted and eventually die.   Breaking of mercury thermometers or using bichloride of mercury on beds as a disinfectant is the usual way in which mercury may be released.   Control measures consist of removing all possible traces of mercury and covering the area where mercury was spilled or applied with a 2-inch thickness of iron filings.   Paint containing mercury as a fungicide should not be applied to rose houses.

9-11.   Mercury damage on roses.

2,4-D. The fumes of 2,4-dichlorophenoxyacetic acid and related compounds used as weed killers cause bending, curling, and other malformations of leaves, stems, flowers, or bracts. Metal cans containing weed killers rust, and the resulting distribution of fumes from such small amounts of material can cause severe damage. Lumber will absorb any of the material that is sprayed onto it, and if treated lumber is used for bench construction, the fumes have been known to injure plants.

Lawn fertilizers containing 2,4-D have no place in a greenhouse where they might accidentally be applied. Death of the plants is the usual end result. Fumes or "drift" from a spray applied along the side of a greenhouse may enter through the doors or side vents and cause trouble.

Therefore it is well to prevent trouble by keeping such sources of potential damage out of the greenhouse, boiler room, potting shed, or any place from which the fumes could conceivably enter a greenhouse.

Phenol compounds. Many materials containing phenol or its derivatives are toxic to plants. Tar, carbolic acid, pentachlorophenol, and many others of similar nature should never be used under glass. Treatment of wooden bench members with wood preservatives containing phenol compounds results in severe damage to the plants. For wood treatment, asphalt, though somewhat similar in appearance to tar, is perfectly safe, as are materials containing copper naphthenate.

Insects and allied pests are responsible for disorders in plants. Eternal vigilance and timely applications of effective controls will reduce losses from insects and allied pests to a minimum. Weeds in aisles or under benches are breeding places for a number of pests, and cleanliness is imperative. A generally overlooked area is that outside the greenhouse. Weeds harbor many pests which can enter through side or top vents and open doors at the ends of the greenhouses. Cleanliness and proper attention to the outside areas as well as under glass will reduce the sources of infestation.

Knowledge of the life cycle of pests is useful in applying controls, since there may be a vulnerable time in the life of the pest when it can be killed easily.

Some insects lay eggs which hatch into larvae or caterpillars that eat the plant tissues. These larvae later pass into a pupal stage in which they are sometimes protected externally by silken cocoons. They emerge as young adults in the form of moths, butterflies, beetles, and other forms, which may or may not cause further plant damage.

Other insects lay eggs that hatch into nymphs which resemble adults. Periodically they shed their external covering and grow larger, and the form of the insect between two such molts is called an instar. Leaf hoppers and grasshoppers are examples.

There are several considerations in the choice and use of pesticides.   The materials must not be harmful to individuals making the application or others in the vicinity, the crop plants must not be damaged, and the pests must be controlled successfully.   In order to choose the pesticide that will give control, first it is necessary to know definitely what pests are involved because many of the control materials are effective for only one or a few pests.   If the pest is not known, aid should be sought from specialists who do know it.   In the case of some pests several pesticides will give effective control, but with others there may be only one material that currently gives good results.   Many of the pests have the ability to mutate to forms which are not susceptible to certain pesticides, and immediate change to other controls should be made when this occurs.

The method of application may be dictated by the pesticide, as some of them are available in one form only.   If more than one method of application can be used for a specific pesticide, the one selected should give the best control of the pests with the least damage to the plants and the lowest cost.   Sometimes the method of application is determined by the stage of growth of the crops and the time and labor that is available.   It always is best to have several methods available for use as they are required.

Although there are many pests, there are relatively few which become

9-12. Leaf symptom of two-spotted mite (red spider) infestation. These pests usually feed on the undersides of leaves. They are small and difficult to observe, but the results of their feeding produce the characteristic speckling of the top surface of the leaves. Two-spotted mites are pests common to most greenhouse plants. (*Yoder Bros., Inc., photograph.*)

continuous problems. Five of the most common ones are discussed briefly below. The pests that can infest greenhouses will be listed in detail later. The red spider (two-spotted mite) typically locates on the underside of leaves. Red spiders are small enough so that they are barely perceptible to the eye, but their feeding on the undersurface of the leaf causes a telltale mottled appearance on the upper surface. The control problem with red spiders is most critical with roses, although these pests are problems with most crops in the greenhouse.

Aphids most often infest the stem tips and cause crippling of the young leaves and stems, and they are large enough to be seen easily. Most plants can be hosts, but aphids are most difficult to control on Chrysanthemums and lilies.

Slugs remain in moist atmospheres, and typically during the day they are under cover of leaves, pots, or soil. They feed on flowers and leaves after dark, leaving large holes in them, and a characteristic trail of slime marks their passage over soil and plants. Slugs are most common on bedding plants.

Thrips infestations are usually seasonal—in early summer and again in early fall, as they sail into greenhouses from field crops at those times—and they inhabit the flowers, where their activities and feeding produce brown streaks on petals and crippling and malformation of the flowers. Since thrips are small and not easily observed, damaged flowers are usually the first sign of invasion by this pest. Roses, carnations, and Chrysanthemums as well as other crops are subject to thrips in season.

9-13. Aphids on a rose stem. These pests usually infest the stem tip portions of plants.

9-14. White flies usually locate on the undersides of leaves, and they are a common problem to poinsettias, Ageratums, and Chrysanthemums.

White flies are common pests on Chrysanthemums, poinsettias, and Ageratums. They inhabit the undersides of leaves, and may go unnoticed except when they are disturbed and fly away in a characteristic flutter. The feeding activities on the undersides of leaves cause a characteristic mottling of the upper surfaces of the leaves and, in some instances, crippling of the leaves.

PESTS

Ants. Although their damage to plants is seldom serious, ants often eat seeds and small seedlings. Since they carry aphids and mealy bugs from one plant to another, it is desirable to kill them. Chlordane is the most effective control.

Aphids and plant lice. Aphids and plant lice are well-known insects that attack nearly all florist plants. They infest the younger growth of leaves or buds and cause injury by sucking the juices, which causes distortion of the tissues. They secrete a honeydew which drops onto the foliage below, and very often a black sooty mold grows on the area. Certain viruses are transmitted by aphids when they feed on affected plants.

In the greenhouse the female aphids, when they are mature, give birth to living young. The female lives only 20 to 30 days, but in that time may produce 60 to 100 other females, which after 6 to 7 days are mature and repeat the cycle. From this it is easy to see how aphid populations build up so quickly.

There are numerous kinds of aphids, some like the Chrysanthemum aphid which is specific to one crop, and others like the green peach aphid which is found on a variety of plants. They may be greenish, yellowish, pink, purplish, brown, or black, depending upon the species.

The most effective controls for aphids are Meta Systox-R, Diazinon, and Thiodan.

Root aphids are grayish in color and covered with a fine powdery wax. They are usually found on the roots of plants, but in heavy infestations they crawl up on the foliage. They suck the juices of plants and seriously weaken them. Bulbs of the Iris, tulip, lily, and other plants are sometimes infested before forcing, and under the high temperatures of the greenhouse the insects quickly multiply to epidemic proportions. Root aphids may also be troublesome on ferns, palms, and poinsettias.

Since ants carry aphids from plant to plant, complete control can only be obtained if both pests are eradicated. Soil sterilization or lindane, chlordane, or dieldrin soil drenches are effective control measures, but the latter treatment will not penetrate bulb scales, where the insects may be found in large numbers. Hot-water treatment should be given at the time of harvest. Iris bulbs and Gladiolus corms can be dusted with 1 percent lindane while in storage for control of aphids beneath the scales.

Bees. Pollination of snapdragons by bees causes the flowers to drop from the spike, and this can be very troublesome in spring. Screening of all the ventilators and doors is the standard remedy.

Birds. Sparrows are often troublesome in rose houses, where they pinch off the young flower buds. Screening of vents may be resorted to in extreme cases.

Black vine weevil (*Brachyrhinus sulcatus*). The adult black vine weevil is about ⅜ to ½ inch long and lives over winter in trash or dead leaves. The larvae also overwinter in the soil. In the spring adults may enter the greenhouse and lay eggs on the soil, and these hatch into grubs which feed on the roots or underground portions of plants. Azaleas, Camellias, and Cyclamen are the most common florist plants which are affected. Sterilization of soil or applications of DDT, dieldrin, or lindane to the soil will kill them.

Blister beetles (*Epicauta* spp.). Blister beetles vary in color from black to gray, some being striped. They are about four times as long as wide and not overly active, but they can quickly ruin the foliage or flowers. They are quite troublesome on asters and Chrysanthemums. Blisters usually appear on the fingers if the insects are crushed with the hand. DDT or parathion is effective.

Broad mite (*Hemitarsonemus latus*). The broad mite is quite similar to the Cyclamen mite, but it is found on the underside of the leaves rather than just in the crown. See Cyclamen mite for control.

Bulb mites. There are several species of bulb mites, and they attack the bulbs of the Narcissus, lily, tulip, hyacinth, and other miscellaneous plants. It has been assumed for years that mites were not particularly harmful and that they fed on dead tissue, but ever-increasing bulb troubles are believed to be due in part to mites.

The female deposits eggs in the tissue at the base of the bulb which hatch in a few days into six-legged larvae. After boring into the tissue, they feed for several days and then are quiescent for 2 days, after which they become eight-legged nymphs. These feed several more days, become quiescent for 1 to 3 days, and then emerge as adults, which mate and begin laying eggs. Depending upon temperature, the life cycle can be completed in 9 to 27 days, and large populations may occur. The adult can be seen with a hand lens; it is globular, almost transparent, and slow-moving. The injury causes reddish-brown spots or streaks on the bulb scales or flower stems which were within the bulb. Growth of the bulb is seriously checked if the infestation is heavy. Very often, springtails will be found in the region where mites have done a great deal of damage. Dipping bulbs for 10 minutes in 122°F water to which nicotine sulfate has been added in a 1 to 400 dilution will kill them but may cause some injury.

Chrysanthemum gall midge (*Diarthronomyia hypogaea*). Small galls on the foliage and stems are evidence of this pest, which can be serious enough to deform the growth. Female adults, which are flies, reddish to orange-yellow in color, lay orange-colored eggs on the upper foliage. The eggs hatch in 3 to 16 days, and immediately the young larvae enter the plant tissue and begin feeding. The presence of the insect causes a small growth of the tissue, which is the gall that increases in size as the larvae grow. Pupation occurs within the gall, and the adult emerges between midnight and early morning, leaving a white papery skin as evidence that it has matured. The life cycle from egg to adult is completed in about 35 days, and the adult dies in 1 or 2 days.

Control is rather easily accomplished with DDT, parathion, or lindane.

Corn borer (*Pyrausta numilalis*). The pink or flesh-colored larvae of the corn borer are often troublesome on geraniums and mums. The almost mature larvae over winter in corn stubble; in spring they pupate, and in June they emerge as adults. The females lay eggs at night on the underside of the foliage. The larvae bore into the stem and may cause it to wilt if the tunnel is sufficiently large to injure the vascular system. The stem may be so weakened that it will break off. The invaded stems should be destroyed and the plants protected in June by dusting with DDT. Overlapping generations may necessitate dusting at 5-day intervals until late in August.

Corn-ear worm (*Heliothis armigera*). In late summer and fall, the larvae of the corn-ear worm may do considerable damage to flowers of standard Chrysanthemums. The eggs are laid on the buds or upper leaves. The young larvae are only ⅟₁₆ inch long, but they develop rapidly as they feed and are commonly 1 to 2 inches long when the damage is first noted. The large feeding larvae are brown to green in color with indistinct markings of brown, black, or green. They occasionally attack carnations, Gladiolus, and geraniums. DDT is the most effective control material.

Cutworms. Cutworms are the larvae of some night-flying moths. The larvae are usually plump and shiny, about 1 to 2 inches long at maturity, depending upon the type. They cut off the stems of plants underground, and the climbing kinds eat the foliage or flowers. Carnation flowers appear to be especially attractive to cutworms, which hide in the soil during the day and damage the plants at night. Soil sterilization will kill them; otherwise they may be handpicked if they are few in number. Chlordane, dieldrin, or DDT on the plants are quite useful. Applying a 10 percent DDT dust liberally on the soil will kill cutworms that crawl through it.

Cyclamen mite (*Steneotarsonemus pallidus*). The adult mite cannot be seen without the aid of a lens, and it will be found either at the stem tip or in the basal portion of the flowers. It is almost transparent and somewhat glossy. The females lay eggs on the young leaves at the tip which hatch in 7 to 11 days. The nymphs have three pairs of legs at first and feed for about 7 days, after which they are quiescent for 3 to 4 days. Following this the eight-legged adult mite is produced, which lives 2 to 3 weeks.

The sucking of the mite on the very young tissues causes a distortion of the leaves or in some cases practically a complete cessation of new growth. With African violet, *Gloxinia*, and *Gynura*, the center, or crown, of the plant becomes whitish because of the development of the hairs without corresponding leaf growth. Other plants commonly affected are Cyclamen, Begonias, English ivy, snapdragons, Hydrangeas, and some foliage plants, though others are by no means immune. The new growth is generally crippled and twisted, with progressively smaller leaves, until growth may cease entirely. Because no pest is visible to the eye, diagnosing the trouble has often been difficult for florists.

Best control is with endrin sprays plus a spreader. Methyl bromide fumigation is effective but may injure the plants. Kelthane sprays are effective.

9-15. Cyclamen mite infestation on Cyclamen. These pests sometimes are found on snapdragons, Chrysanthemums, and English ivy. They are difficult to observe because they are so small, but the cupping and crippling of the terminal leaves are characteristic of their presence.

Cyclamen weevil.   See Black Vine Weevil.

Earthworms.   Though earthworms are not insects, they can be serious pests. They digest the soil in their paths, and when it leaves their bodies, it is puddled. When numerous, they honeycomb the soil and may injure the roots. Soil sterilization will control them; otherwise chlordane or DDT applications should be made periodically to the soil. Although saturated limewater is effective, it may cause the soil to become too alkaline. Mercury compounds may do more harm than good and should never be used in rose greenhouses.

Fuller's rose weevil (*Pantomorus godmani*).   Adults of the Fuller's rose weevil are grayish with an oblique whitish line on the wing cover. The females lay eggs on the branch tips, and the grubs fall to the ground and chew on the roots. They are most destructive to azaleas, roses, and Gardenias. Lindane on the soil will control larvae in the soil. Foliage dusts of lindane, DDT, or dieldrin will destroy adults before they lay eggs.

Fungus gnats (*various* spp.).   Fungus gnats are also called manure or mushroom flies. The adults are small flies about ⅛-inch long, either black or brown, with long wings and long, thin legs. The adults do not harm plants directly. The larvae are worms or maggots about ¼-inch long, and white or transparent with a dark head. Formerly it was thought that the larvae were saprophytes, but more recently it has been determined that they are definitely parasitic, and their feeding activities on roots cause damage to many greenhouse plants.

The adult fungus gnats can be controlled with Diazinon, DDT, or malathion. For control of the larvae, the soil should be drenched with DDT or lindane.

Grasshoppers. Grasshopper eggs overwinter in the soil and hatch into young nymphs which lack fully developed wings. Their damage to foliage and flowers is well known, and they can strip a plant of leaves in a short time if present in great numbers. Chrysanthemums are most seriously affected. Chlordane and dieldrin are the best controls.

Greenhouse orthezia (*Orthezia insignis*). The greenhouse *Orthezia* is an insect closely related to scales and mealy bugs. The nymphs are dark green, wingless, and about the size of a pinhead. The female, however, carries an egg sac attached to her body which is two or three times as long as the body. It is white-fringed, and the pest is easily identified from its striking appearance. It attacks the same kinds of plants as mealy bugs, and its control is the same.

Greenhouse white fly (*Trialeurodes vaporariorum*). The female white fly, which can lay as many as 100 eggs, attaches them to the underside of the leaves in a ring, or circle, on a very short stalk. These hatch in 10 to 12 days into small greenish nymphs which begin sucking the juices of the tissue. In 4 weeks they become adults which are four-winged and very white in color, and which fly when disturbed. They feed on the plants for a period of 30 to 40 days.

Damage may be severe if the infestation is heavy. A mottling of the foliage not unlike that caused by the red spider is evident. Foliage is often blackened by the sooty mold fungus that develops on honeydew in the infested area. A wide number of plants is host to this pest. DDT, parathion, Thiodan, and dibrom are controls.

Leaf-cutting bees (*Megachile* spp.). These honeybeelike insects cut almost perfectly circular areas from rose leaflets. They seldom become serious and can be controlled with DDT or parathion.

Leaf hoppers. Leaf hoppers are small mottled or speckled insects, green, yellow, brownish, or multicolored. They suck the juices of plants, sometimes causing serious trouble; they may also transmit virus diseases. Aster and Chrysanthemum yellows are transmitted by these pests. DDT and parathion kill them, but transmission of the virus is accomplished before the insecticides take effect.

Leaf miners.   Adult leaf miners are small winged insects which lay eggs on the leaf.   The larvae bore into the leaf and make irregularly shaped tunnels or blotches between the upper and lower epidermis which are generally light-yellowish-tan to brown in color.   Chrysanthemums and asters are often affected. Azalea leaf miner may cause the leaf to twist or to appear as if pinched between the thumb and forefinger.   As these larvae mature they fold the leaf together with threads and feed on the inner surface.

In the very late stages control is difficult if not impossible, but when the larvae are tunneling in the leaf, parathion, lindane, or malathion sprays penetrate the tissue and kill them.

Leaf rollers and leaf tiers.   This group of pests can be very destructive. The adults are moths which lay eggs on the foliage.   The eggs hatch in 5 to 12 days, and the larvae feed on the foliage, often leaving only the upper epidermis between the veins and giving the area a parchmentlike appearance.   Later the larvae tie one or more leaves together and pupate.   Some kinds chew into stems and small flower buds as well as foliage.

Chrysanthemums, roses, carnations, and asters are often damaged by these pests.   DDT, parathion, or malathion is effective when applied before the larvae have rolled up the foliage.

Mealy bugs (*Pseudococcus* spp.).   There are several species of mealy bugs which are closely related to scale insects.   The long-tailed mealy bug has four filaments protruding from the rear of its body, for which it is named, and it gives birth to living nymphs.

The short-tailed types which are most common include the citrus, coconut, and Mexican mealy bugs.   These reproduce similarly in that the female deposits 300 to 600 eggs in a cottony, waxy sac at the rear of her body over a period of 1 to 2 weeks.   When egg laying is complete, the female dies.   The sacs are generally found in leaf axils, in forks or branches, or under the leaves.   The eggs hatch in 10 days, and then the young, unprotected mealy bugs crawl over the plant and suck the juices.   Soon a waxy covering forms which protects them, and they move slowly over the various parts of the plant.   At this stage they are whitish to gray in color.   The males pupate and emerge as winged insects to mate with the females.   Males die shortly after mating and at no time feed on the plant.   About 30 days is required for one generation.   Ants carry mealy bugs in the greenhouse, and both pests should be eradicated.

A wide variety of plants is attacked. Malathion and parathion sprays are effective, and the latter may be used as an aerosol or a dust. Dithio aerosols are also useful. Applications every 7 to 10 days are necessary to kill the pests, and the insecticides are most effective on the younger pests.

Mice and rats. Mice and rats occasionally inhabit greenhouses and are particularly injurious to carnation flowers. Poisoned baits are quite effective, as is endrin sprayed in the runway.

Millipedes. Millipedes are brownish-colored, wormlike animals which have two pairs of legs on each body segment and are not true insects. They live in soil and feed on dead organic matter or live roots. Lindane soil drenches or DDT dusts are effective.

Dagger nematode. Root tips are attacked by the dagger nematode, which feeds in a somewhat similar fashion to the meadow nematode except that it does not bore within the root. It causes the root tips to stop growing and become somewhat stubby, and the plants to be stunted. These nematodes move about freely in the soil. See Root-knot Nematode for control.

Foliar, or leaf, nematode. The foliar nematode lives at the basal part of the plant. The small worms move from one leaf to another through films of moisture. They enter the leaf through the stomates and suck plant juices.

On Chrysanthemums, wedge- or pie-shaped brown areas develop between the main veins of a leaf, indicating the presence of this pest. The bird's-nest fern and other ferns are attacked, and portions of the fronds or leaves turn brown to the midvein. Swellings on the petioles of African violets can be caused by foliar nematodes, and the leaf blade is brown and discolored between veins when viewed from below. Browning of the margins of Melior Begonias is due to foliar nematode.

Parathion sprays are the best control since the material penetrates the leaf and kills the pest. The residue also is effective when the eelworm moves from leaf to leaf.

Meadow, or root-lesion, nematode. This rather common nematode does not cause any knots on the roots. It bores into the outer layers of the roots and root hairs and feeds on the cell contents, leaving minute openings in the root surface. Fungi or bacteria can enter the plant, and this, together with the destruction of the cells by the nematode, can cause the plants to be stunted or may kill them. Many of the roots may be involved when the infestation is heavy. See Root-knot Nematode for control.

9-16. Foliar nematode infestations often cause a characteristic pie-shaped section of dead leaf tissue.

Root-knot nematode.   Root-knot nematodes are eelworms which are too small to be seen with the naked eye.   The larvae hatch from eggs laid in the root and suck on the juices of the surrounding cells.   The irritation causes enlargement of the tissue, and a knot, or gall, is formed on the root.   The males are long and slender; the females are pear-shaped and may lay up to 500 eggs to the gall.

Affected plants are checked in growth, and the upper foliage may become chlorotic because of the impaired activity of the root system.   These pests are not necessarily confined to the roots, since they escape and move rather slowly throughout the soil.   Normal watering can leach them from the soil.   In greenhouses where water is collected from the drainage from benches, it is possible to spread root-knot nematodes to all parts of the range through the water system.

Although many plants are attacked, there are some which should be examined closely because they are particularly subject to them.   These are Chrysanthemums, Gardenias, African violets, Begonias, and Cyclamen.

Sterilization of the soil with steam is an effective control.   Methyl bromide penetrates unrotted roots and kills all stages of the pest, but when tear gas is used, roots should be allowed to partially decompose for best results.   There are some new chemicals that can be applied to the soil where the plants are growing that will kill the nematode without seriously damaging or killing the plant.

9-17. The results of a root-knot nematode infestation on Gardenia roots. Because of the extensive damage to the root system, the absorption of water and minerals will not be adequate for good growth of the plant. The visible effects on roots of infestations of other types of nematodes may be less spectacular, but the damage may be as real.

Vapam, VC-13, and Nemagon are useful soil-drench materials for controlling this pest.

Orchid weevil (*Diorymerellus laevimargo*). The adult orchid weevil is small, black, and shiny. It feeds on the flowers and young leaves, while the larvae or grubs eat into the new roots, causing them to die. DDT or lindane is effective.

Red spider, or two-spotted spider mite (*Tetranychus telarius*). A mite rather than a true insect, the red spider is probably the most troublesome of all pests under glass. The young and adults suck the juices of the leaves and petals, generally on the underside. Affected foliage becomes lightly mottled and eventually may turn a light bronzy color when the infestation is severe. A light webbing on the underside of the foliage is indicative of the beginning of a heavy infestation. Soon the webs may envelop the upper portions of the plant. Heavily infested foliage turns brown and dries, and a somewhat smaller population can have an equally bad effect on flowers.

The female adult lays 2 to 8 eggs per day individually on the surface of the foliage or flower and may produce 50 to 100 eggs during her lifetime. The eggs hatch in 4 to 5 days, and the first instar nymphs have three pairs of legs; all later instars have four pairs of legs. The females molt three times during their life, the males twice. Two dark spots can usually be seen on their bodies when they are viewed from above through a lens. The mites may be greenish, yellowish, or red in color and are quite small, about $\frac{1}{50}$ inch in length.

A generation is usually completed in 10 days at 80°F, in 20 days at 70°F, or in several months at cooler temperatures. All stages of a generation may be found simultaneously, and the rapidity with which they increase makes prompt application of control measures a necessity.

Red spiders are more difficult to kill on roses than on other plants. In addition, there are strains resistant to certain insecticides, and this further complicates control.

Possible control materials are Pentac, Morestan, aramite, Kelthane, and chlorobenzilate.

Roaches. Several kinds of roaches may be found in greenhouses, and the Surinam beetle, or roach (*Pycnoscelus surinamensis*), is common. They eat seedlings and cuttings and may chew the bark at the soil line on such woody plants as roses. DDT, chlordane, and parathion dusts or sprays are effective.

Rose midge (*Dasyneura rhodophaga*). The adult rose midge is a fly about $\frac{1}{16}$ to $\frac{1}{20}$ inch long, reddish to yellow-brown in color. The yellow eggs are laid in the buds behind the sepals or in the unfolding leaves of the young shoots, and they hatch in 2 days. The yellow-orange maggots feed for about a week, distorting the flowers and chewing the buds in the axils of the young leaves. They drop to the ground and pupate, emerging in about a week to mate and repeat the cycle.

Three applications of DDT to the plants, to soil in and under the benches, and to the walks in the greenhouse at 10- to 12-day intervals will effectively control them. Heavily infested buds and shoots should be pinched and destroyed. Parathion is also effective.

Rose stem sawfly (*Hartigia trimaculata*). The larvae of these wasplike insects are occasionally troublesome on roses. Eggs are laid in the stem and the larvae bore into the shoot, causing it to wilt.   Destruction of the cane is the best cure.

Scale insects.   There are numerous hard-shelled and soft-shelled scale insects which attack florist plants.   The first instar scale is unprotected and is most susceptible to insecticides.   Honeydew secreted by scale often may support a black sooty mold, which is unsightly.   Scales suck the juices of leaves and stems and weaken the plant.

Malathion sprays or dithio bombs are useful but must be applied regularly because they are most effective in killing the crawlers, or unprotected young. Parathion may kill some kinds of scale but is not effective on others.

Slugs and snails.   Slugs and snails are related to clams and oysters, and their bodies are soft and slime-covered.   Snails have a hard shell, but slugs are fully exposed.   They vary in length, depending upon the type, from ½ inch to 4 inches long.   They emerge at night and feed on leaves and petals.   A sticky secretion is given off from the body, which dries and leaves a shiny trail where it has crawled.   During the day they may be found under pots, bench litter, and other places where it is damp and dark.

Seedlings are often damaged, and many of the softer-foliaged plants are subject to damage.   Poisoned baits using metaldehyde as an attractant and chlordane as the poison are very effective.   Old metaldehyde loses its effect, and only fresh material will give control.

Sow bugs and pill bugs.   The sow bug and pill bug are not insects but are related to shrimp and crayfish and breathe through gills.   They are found only in very damp places.   They are light gray or slate-colored, about ½ inch long, and elliptical in shape.   Their backs are covered with plates, and they have seven pairs of legs.   The young develop from eggs in a pouch on the female, where they remain for 2 months.   They eat dead organic matter but also attack

9-18. Damage to leaves by slugs. These pests attack many kinds of plants and feed on flowers as well as leaves. They prefer a humid environment. Usually during the day they are in moist areas beneath pots, flats, or trash, and they feed at night. (*Yoder Bros., Inc., photograph.*)

the roots and stems of seedlings and cuttings.   Very often the Rhizoctonia fungus develops after injury from these pests, and the plant dies from rot.   About a year is required for maturity.   The pill bug rolls into a ball when disturbed, hence the name.   DDT, chlordane, or parathion on the soil is an effective control.

Spittle bug (*Philaenus leucophthalmus*).   Although not a serious pest, the spittle bug sometimes attacks Chrysanthemums and causes abnormal branching or distorted growth.   The nymphs suck the juices of the plant and hide in a froth, or spittle, which they excrete on the stems or in leaf axils.   Lindane or dieldrin is an effective control.

Springtails.   The springtail is an insect that feeds on decaying organic matter and is found in great numbers in most greenhouses.   In rare instances they may damage small seedlings.   They are less than 1/10 inch long and are usually white, cream, or tan in color.   They are wingless and cannot fly, but they have a forked muscular appendage at the end of the abdomen which enables them to jump surprising distances, considering their size.   They are objectionable but not necessarily harmful insects.   DDT, lindane, chlordane, or parathion will control them.

Strawberry root worm (*Paria canella*).   The strawberry root worm can become a serious pest on roses.   The adults are about ⅛ inch long and brown to brownish black.   The females lay eggs on the bench litter.   The eggs hatch in 10 to 14 days, and the grubs feed on the rose roots, causing a check in growth.   They become fully grown in 35 to 60 days and then pupate in the soil for about 2 weeks. The adults feed on the foliage, causing numerous small shot holes.   DDT applied as recommended for rose midge is effective.

Symphylids, or garden centipedes (*Scutigerella immaculata*).   Symphylids shun dry soil or sunlight and hence are not often seen.   They chew the roots of a wide range of plants.   The growth of the plant is stunted, and very few new white roots will be found.

The young symphylids hatch in about 2 weeks from eggs laid in clusters in the soil.   They have 10 body segments, 6 pairs of legs, and very short antennae, or "feelers."   As they shed their skins and grow to maturity, they are ¼ to ⅜ inch long, possess 14 body segments, 12 pairs of short legs, and antennae about one-third as long as the body.   A full generation is completed in a few months.   If clods of moist soil are broken apart, any symphylids present will quickly dart back into the moist, dark confines of the soil.

In raised benches steaming is an effective control since the symphylids will not crawl up or down bench legs.   Soil in ground beds with concrete bottoms may also be steamed with good control.   In ground beds with no bottoms, the pests move down as the soil becomes warmer during steaming and then return when the soil cools. Lindane applied to the soil as a drench is very effective in such cases and when potted plants are infested.

Tarnished plant bug (*Lygus lincolaris*). Adult tarnished plant bugs overwinter in trash and weeds, and in spring they lay eggs in leaves, stems, or flowers of various plants. The nymphs and adults feed by inserting their sucking mouthparts into the stems near the tip, causing abnormal branching of Chrysanthemums, asters, and other plants. It is believed that some toxic substance is injected which causes death of the tissue and resultant branching. The adults are about ¼ inch long, flattened, and somewhat oval in appearance; they are brownish in color, mottled with white, yellow, brown, or black in irregular patches. They are most troublesome on plants outside, but occasionally may cause damage in the greenhouse.

Dieldrin is a very effective control, as are parathion, chlordane, and DDT. New growth must be protected at all times by a light dust or spray covering.

Termites, or white ants. Termites differ from regular ants in that they do not have a slender waist. They are pale or cream-colored, soft-bodied, about ¼ inch in length, with well-developed heads and jaws. They tunnel in the soil and may enter the plant through wooden bench legs and bottoms. They bore into the stems of Chrysanthemums, geraniums, and other plants, and affected plants generally wilt and die. The pests avoid light and will generally remain undiscovered until the damage is done.

Swarming termites are in the reproductive stage, in which they have wings, and their bodies are nearly black. Plant damage is serious, and if the termites get into wooden building supports, they can cause collapse of the structure. DDT and chlordane are the chemicals most widely used to control them, but experienced personnel should be called in to treat the area. The soil may be drenched with either of these control materials as used for sprays, applying 1 to 2 pints per square foot.

Thrips. There are several kinds of thrips which are troublesome on florist plants both in the greenhouse and outdoors. The nymphs and adults rasp the tissue with their mouthparts and then suck the juices which flow from the injured cells. The damaged foliage is usually silvery or whitish underneath, and in severe infestations the injured foliage may turn brown. Petals of flowers are streaked, and roses may be malformed as a result of feeding.

The female deposits eggs in slits in the tissue, and these hatch in 2 to 7 days into nymphs which immediately begin feeding. Thrips are small, narrow insects that can be seen with the naked eye, but the small nymphs may escape detection. In 20 to 25 days they are mature, and the life cycle is complete. The adults may be tan, yellow, brown, or black in color, depending upon the species. The adults have wings which enable them to fly.

Dusts or sprays of dieldrin, lindane, malathion, DDT, or parathion are quite effective, as are the aerosol forms of parathion and malathion. Control measures must be applied periodically, since thrips damage a wide variety of plants and may enter through open vents or doors from weeds outside the greenhouse. Side ventilators can be screened with aster cloth which should be sprayed with dieldrin periodically.

White grubs (*Phyllophaga* spp.). White grubs are the larval form of May or June beetles. They chew the roots of various plants. They are usually brought in with soil from the field, and sterilization will control them. DDT, chlordane, dieldrin, or lindane applied as a soil drench is effective.

Wireworm. Wireworms are the larvae of click beetles and are generally hard-shelled, brown in color, and approximately 1 inch long. They chew the roots of plants and the outer scales of bulbs and are very destructive. Sterilization is quite effective, and lindane, chlordane, or dieldrin may be applied as a soil drench with good results.

PEST CONTROL MATERIALS

Aramite—2- (*p-tertiary butylphenozy*) 1-methylethyl 2-chloroethyl sulfite. Aramite is specific for the red spider and is used at 1¼ to 1½ pounds per 100 gallons of water with a spreader. It is compatible with captan, ferbam, zineb, or Karathane and can be used in the presence of sulfur.

The technical grade is a liquid which can be painted on steam pipes at the rate of 8 ounces for every 100,000 cubic feet. Vents should be kept closed the entire night of the fumigation. Applications should be repeated every 5 days until the infestation is eliminated.

Chlordane—1,2,3,4,5,6,7,8,8-octachloro-2,3,3a,4,7,7a-hexahydro-4,7-methanoindene. Control of ants, grasshoppers, plant bugs, crickets, termites, springtails, and roaches is quite easy with chlordane. The 40 percent wettable powders are used at 1 pound per 100 gallons with a spreader under glass, and twice this amount is used for outside crops. The 5 percent dust is also useful.

Chlordane mixed with metaldehyde is available as a bait for slugs and snails. Since metaldehyde loses its attractant powers when exposed to air, the container should be kept closed and small quantities ordered as needed.

Chlorobenzilate—2-hydroxy-2,2-bis (4-chlorophenyl) ethyl acetate. Red spiders are affected by chlorobenzilate. It is used at the rate of 1 pound of the 25 percent wettable powder in 100 gallons of water with a spreader.

DDT—*dichloro diphenyl trichloroethane.* A number of pests is controlled by DDT. Thrips, leaf rollers, orchid weevils, and other leaf-eating insects, sow bugs, pill bugs, rose and mum midge, leaf hoppers, white fly, corn-ear worm, and tarnished plant bug are the common pests for which it is effective. The 50 percent wettable powders are used at 1 pound per 100 gallons of water with a spreader, or at double this rate on outside crops. Dusts usually contain 5 or 10 percent DDT.

Oil sprays of DDT may damage the foliage on some plants. Only the purified grades of DDT dust or spray should be used on *Kalanchoe, Crassula,* and other succulents, and even then some damage may occur.

For soil pests DDT dust may be applied several times at monthly intervals.

Diazinon—*0,0-diethyl 0-(2-isopropyl-4 methyl-6-pyrimidinyl) phosphoro-thioate.* Diazinon is used primarily as a 50 percent wettable powder at the rate of 1 pound per 100 gallons of water for the control of aphids, thrips, Cyclamen mite, mealy bugs, leaf miner, scale, and carnation bud mite.

Dibrom—*1,2-dibromo 2,2-dichloroethyl dimethyl phosphate.* For the control of aphids, red spider, thrips, and white flies, the 8-pound emulsion is vaporized from steam lines at the rate of 1 fluid ounce per 10,000 cubic feet of greenhouse space.

Dieldrin—*hexachloro epoxy octahydro-endo, exodimethano naphthalene.* This material is used for the control of thrips, grasshoppers, spittle bugs, weevils, grubs, and other similar soil pests. It is used at the rate of 1 pound of the 25 percent wettable powder per 100 gallons of water. For thrips control the pads of cooling systems are treated by adding 1 quart of the 18.5 percent emulsion to the circulating water.

Dithio, dithiono, or sulfa tepp—*0,0,0,0-tetraethyl dithiono pyrophosphate.* Red spider adults, aphids, thrips, mealy bugs, and soft brown scale are killed by this material. It is available in aerosol form. Since the eggs of red spider are not affected, applications must be made every 3 days until the plants are clean. Scale and mealy bugs will need treatment weekly. The material is poisonous.

Endrin—*hexachloro octahydro-endo, endo dimethano naphthalene.* Specific for Cyclamen and broad mites, the 18 percent emulsion is used at 1 to 400 with a spreader. Because of its poisonous nature, precautions should be followed.

Kelthane—*1,1, bis(4-chlorophenyl)-2,2,2-trichloroethanol.* Kelthane is used for the control of red spider and Cyclamen mite. The 18.5 percent wettable powder is used at 1 pound and the 18.5 percent emulsion at 1 pint per 100 gallons of water.

Lindane—*gamma isomer of benzene hexachloride*.   Aphids, thrips, spittle bugs, springtails, and symphylids are killed by this material.   The 25 percent wettable powder is used at 8 ounces per 100 gallons of water with a spreader, and it is available as a 1 percent dust.

Soil-drench solutions can be prepared by placing 1 ounce in 30 gallons of water.   This solution can be applied to cover 100 square feet of bench space, or as a substitute for the watering of potted plants.   Soil applications are usually effective for 1 year.

Four ounces of the wettable powder can be mixed with enough water to make a thin slurry, and this is painted on steam pipes to fumigate 100,000 cubic feet of space for control of aphids or thrips.   Ventilators should be closed overnight.

Malathion—*0,0 dimethyl-S-(1,2-dicarbethoxyethyl) dithiophosphate*.   A wide range of pests is killed, and the material is safer to use than parathion.   The 25 percent wettable powder is applied at 1½ to 2 pounds per 100 gallons of water with a spreader, but for scale insects the dosage should be increased to 4 or 5 pounds.   Red spiders, aphids, thrips, scales, leaf rollers, army worms, cabbage loopers, and mealy bugs are among the more important pests controlled, but repeated applications are necessary.   Some rose leaf rollers are not affected by malathion.

Meta Systox-R—*0,0,dimethyl S-2-(ethylsulfinyl) ethyl phosphorothiate*.   Meta Systox-R is available only as an emulsion.   It is used at 1½ pints per 100 gallons of water for the control of aphids, white flies, leaf miners, and red spiders.

Methyl bromide.   Although this material is used more as a soil fumigant, chambers may be constructed for fumigation of pot plants to control numerous pests.   The difficulty lies in the injury which occurs if the dosage is too strong and in the lack of control when not enough material is used or the temperature is too low.   It is a method which has found only limited application.

Morestan—*6-methyl-2,3-quinoxalinedithiol cyclic carbonate*.   This 25 percent wettable powder is used at ½ pound per 100 gallons of water for the control of red spiders.

Nemagon—*1,2-dibromo-3-chloropropane*.   This control of nematodes can be used in soil in which some plants are growing.   For roses, infested plants and soil can be treated by drenching the soil with 70 percent emulsion at the rate of 2 gallons per acre.   This should be followed with heavy irrigation.   Two applications are recommended 1 month apart. For azaleas in peat moss the 70 percent emulsion is used at the rate of 2½ fluid ounces per 100 gallons of water. The peat is drenched at the rate of ½ pint per 6-inch pot.

OMPA—*octamethyl pyrophosphoramide.* Red spiders are controlled by this pesticide, as are aphids and foliar nematodes. It is a systemic material which is absorbed through the foliage and translocated to the younger leaves and stem. It is slow acting, and three or four applications at 1- to 2-week intervals may be essential. It is extremely poisonous.

Parathion—*0,0-diethyl 0-p-nitrophenyl thiophosphate.* This pesticide kills a wide range of pests, among the more important of which are red spider crawlers and adults, aphids, thrips, sow bugs, various leaf-eating pests, and rose or mum midge. It is available as an aerosol bomb, as a 15 percent wettable powder to be used at 1 pound per 100 gallons of water with a spreader, or as a 2 percent dust.

Unfortunately, serious damage may be caused by parathion on some plants. Bleaching of the flower color on poinsettias and pink or bronze Chrysanthemums often occurs. Foliage burn on ferns and white-flowered Cyclamen is almost a certainty, and yellowing of aster and Hydrangea foliage and leatheriness of Gardenia leaves develop as a result of its use. Succulents such as *Crassula* and *Kalanchoe* are severely damaged, as are seedlings of many plants, but covering the plants with newspapers is helpful when they are likely to be exposed.

In the presence of sulfur, parathion causes leaf drop on many rose varieties. It can be mixed safely with captan, ferbam, ziram, and zineb. Parathion is very poisonous.

Pentac—*bis(pentachloro-2,4-cyclopentadien-1-yl).* The 50 percent wettable powder is used at the rate of ½ pound per 100 gallons of water for the control of red spiders. Two applications should be made about 2 weeks apart. The results from treatment are not apparent for about 10 days to 2 weeks following an application.

Sevin—*1-naphthyl N-methylcarbamate.* For control of various caterpillars the 50 percent wettable powder is used at the rate of 1 to 2 pounds per 100 gallons of water.

Systox, E 1059, or demeton—*0,0-diethyl-0-(2-ethylmercapto-ethyl)-thiophosphate.* This systemic material is generally applied to the soil where it is absorbed by the roots and translocated to the younger tissue. It is somewhat faster acting than OMPA.

Two fluid ounces of the 26 percent emulsion placed in any convenient amount of water should be applied to cover 100 square feet of bench space, and this may give protection for 2 to 3 months.   For pot plants 1 fluid ounce in 15 gallons of water is applied to the soil as a substitute for watering.   On soft-stemmed crops it controls red spiders and aphids.

Tedion—*2,4,5,4'-tetrachloro diphenylsulphone*.   This spray material is specific for red spiders and is used at the rate of ⅛ pound of the 50 percent wettable powder per 100 gallons of water with a spreader.

TEPP—*tetraethyl pyrophosphate*.   Available as aerosol bombs and sprays, this material is most useful for red spider adults, aphids, thrips, mealy bugs, and white fly adults.   It can be mixed with the wettable powder of most fungicides. Undue wetting of the soil with the spray checks and stunts the growth of many plants.   TEPP is highly poisonous.

Thiodan—*hexachlorohexahydro-6.9-methanobenzodioxathiepin-3-oxide*. For white flies, aphids, and Cyclamen mites this 50 percent wettable powder is used at 1 pound per 100 gallons.

VC-13—*0,2,4-dichlorophenyl 0-0-diethyl phosphorothioate*.   This nema-cide can be used on soil where plants are growing.   Whether it will penetrate living roots and kill all nematodes within is not known, but it is useful in reducing the nematode population in a soil in which plants are growing.   A suggested rate is 1 quart in 100 gallons to cover 400 square feet of bed or bench area.   For pot plants, 1 teaspoonful in 2 gallons of water should be applied to three hundred 2½-inch pots, one hundred and twenty-five 3-inch pots, fifty 4-inch pots, or twenty 6-inch pots.   Applications may be repeated every 2 to 3 weeks.

Vapona—*2,2-dichlorovinyl dimethyl phosphate*.   Available in aerosol or emulsion form.   For treatment of aphids, red spiders, mealy bugs, leaf miners, and white flies, the 2-pound emulsion is vaporized from steam lines at 2 fluid ounces per 10,000 cubic feet of greenhouse space.

PLANT DISEASES

Diseases of plants may be caused by bacteria, fungi, and viruses which impair the usefulness of a plant or may even kill it.

Bacteria.   Bacteria are single-celled organisms which increase in number by division under favorable conditions.   They have no chlorophyll and obtain food from either living or dead organic matter.

Bacteria are most often spread by water, or they may be in or on the plant or its parts, and may be disseminated by propagation with infested plant material or water from infested areas. Some bacteria inhabit the soil, and invasion of the plant can occur through the roots or lower stem.

Fungi. Fungi are one of the lower, or simpler, forms of plant life which contain no chlorophyll and therefore cannot make their own food. They can live only by obtaining nourishment from organic matter, either living or dead. If the food comes from living plants, the fungi are parasites; otherwise they are known as saprophytes.

A fungus is composed of threadlike filaments called hyphae, several of which together are called a "mycelium." The mycelium may be visible on the surface of the plant as a kind of dense woolly mass, white, gray, brown, or black in color, or it may be entirely within the plant and not evident on the surface. For example, powdery mildew mycelia are quite visible on the outer portions of the plant, but fungi causing wilt diseases are internal and cannot be seen.

Fungi can reproduce by the breaking of the mycelium into several hyphae, but production of spores, which may be likened to seeds of higher plants, is the more common way. Several kinds of spores are produced by fungi. They usually develop in great numbers when the fungi are growing under favorable conditions, and thus the organism can spread quickly. Many of the spores are not resistant to adverse conditions and die, but resting bodies, called "sclerotia," composed of hyphae in compact groups which are supplied with food, sometimes form and can endure long periods of extremely unfavorable environment.

9-19. Culture-indexing of plants is a detailed laboratory procedure requiring highly trained personnel and specialized equipment. Here culture media are being placed into the autoclave for sterilization. (*Yoder Bros., Inc., photograph.*)

9-20. Placing carnation tissue in culture media under carefully controlled conditions so that any growth of pathogens can be observed and the plants from which the tissue was taken can be properly indexed. (*Yoder Bros., Inc., photograph.*)

Some spores or resting bodies can be carried by wind, while for others water is the chief means of spreading. Some fungi are found in or on seeds, cuttings, bulbs, or plants. Certain fungi also live and grow in the soil as saprophytes, becoming parasitic when susceptible plants grow in that soil.

Damage to the plant by the fungus consists of withdrawal of food from the cells by the hyphae, which penetrate within the tissue and seriously weaken or even kill the affected area or the entire plant, and also by poisons (toxins) formed by the fungus, which then pass into the host plant cells, killing them.

Viruses. Viruses are the least understood of all the causes of disease. They are exceedingly small entities which are visible only through the most powerful microscopes. They are capable of causing disorders within plants which are called "diseases."

Most viruses are spread from one plant to another through the feeding of insects which suck the juices of plants. Aphids and leaf hoppers are the most common carriers of certain kinds of viruses. Some viruses can also be spread by contact, particularly through cultural practices such as pinching or disbudding.

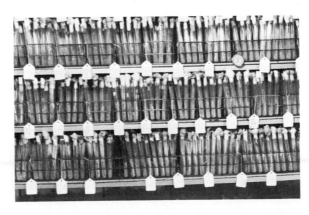

9-21. After the tissues from the plants being indexed are placed in the culture tubes, they are held at controlled incubation temperatures for a specified period of time before being "read." (*Yoder Bros., Inc., photograph.*)

Vegetative propagation of a plant having a virus disease is also a common means of spread.

Virus diseases are often known by such terms as mosaic, streak, and yellows, which aptly describe the appearance of the affected plant.

RELATION OF ENVIRONMENT TO DISEASE CONTROL

Organisms that live in the soil can be killed by steam or chemical sterilization, and prevention can be obtained in this manner. However, reinvasion of a sterilized soil very often results in the rapid growth of the disease organism and resultant damage to the plant. Steps must be taken to prevent reinoculation and keep the soil free of the organisms.

Certain soil organisms grow profusely when the moisture content is high. The spread of Rhizoctonia fungus through the soil can be reduced by keeping the surface of the soil dry through infrequent but heavy waterings, as contrasted with frequent light sprinklings.

The temperature and relative humidity of the air affect the growth of organisms. The Botrytis blight fungi thrive when the surface of the tissue is moist. Keeping relative humidity from reaching saturation either by day or by night is helpful in retarding the development of *Botrytis*. The powdery mildew fungi develop most rapidly at a relative humidity slightly less than 100 percent and are inhibited in the presence of free moisture.

Water splashed on the foliage spreads certain fungi and bacteria and in many instances is also essential for the germination of spores. Keeping the foliage dry will, for example, prevent the growth of the fungi which cause rust on carnations and black spot on roses.

Manipulation or regulation of the environment is the first step in control of many disease organisms. Disease organisms may enter on seeds, cuttings, plants, or bulbs that have been purchased for growing on, or they may develop on established growing stock when conditions are favorable. When diseased plants are found, appropriate control measures must be taken, and in certain cases destroying the plant or the diseased parts is the easiest method of control. Otherwise the source of the organisms remains, and they may be spread to other plants.

SPECIFIC DISEASES CAUSED BY FUNGI

Although identification of the causal organism of plant diseases is best obtained by means of culturing together with microscopic examination in the laboratory, some of the symptoms of attack are readily recognized. Knowledge of the organism and the factors that affect its growth is helpful in prevention and control.

Damping-off.   Seedlings are the principal victims of this trouble, caused principally by Pythium and Rhizoctonia fungi, which are common inhabitants of the soil.   In preemergence damping-off the seed is attacked by either or both organisms before it germinates, or the seedling is attacked before it breaks through the surface of the seedbed so that there is no emergence.   Many cases of "poor seed" are due to preemergence damping-off.   Seed-treatment materials such as arasan, captan, and semesan, plus sterilization of soil, flats, and pots, are effective in preventing this trouble.

Postemergence damping-off is due to the same organisms attacking the seedling after emergence in the region of the cortex, which is the principal supporting tissue.   The seedlings fall over although they are still green, and close examination of the stem reveals a disintegrated portion at or just below the surface of the germinating medium.   Seed treatment does not protect against postemergence damping-off, but applying Dexon, Terraclor, or Morsodren, as dusts or liquids on the surface of the seedbed, is often effective.

Planting seeds too deeply, use of too heavy a germination medium, over-watering, and not providing enough air circulation around the young plants are contributing factors which encourage growth of the damping-off fungi.

Leaf or flower blights.   *Rhizoctonia* may attack foliage of some plants, causing death of parts of the leaf, but it is not very common.   This organism does not produce spores, but rather spreads by contamination from the soil in a moist and warm environment.   The spread of this fungus is halted if the air is circulated to keep the foliage dry.   Terraclor or Morsodren may be used for control.

Botrytis is troublesome on the foliage of geraniums and tulips, and of the organisms which cause flower blight, *Botrytis* is the most common since it attacks

9-22. A Botrytis blight infection on a standard mum. (*Department of Plant Pathology, Pennsylvania State University, University Park, Pa., photograph.*)

a wide range of plants.   Chrysanthemums are particularly susceptible to *Botrytis,* as are Begonias, carnations, Hydrangeas, lilies, snapdragons, and tulips.

Botrytis spores are easily carried by air currents.   Spores germinate in high relative humidity over a temperature range of 50 to 90°F.   Regulation of temperature and relative humidity, as outlined in Chap. 4 and later in this chapter for powdery mildew under Mildews, is effective for control, and, in addition, water should be kept off the plants.   Circulation of the air by means of fans has proved to be the only satisfactory means of control on Chrysanthemums when summer night temperatures are so high that the use of heat is unnecessary.   Dusting is preferable to spraying because moisture in flowers is undesirable.   Zineb or captan dusts or sprays should be applied as often as twice a week if necessary when the flower buds are beginning to show color.   Under ideal conditions for growth of the organism, control by fungicides is very difficult.   When attacked by *Botrytis,* the ends of the flower petals usually appear water-soaked and transparent when held to the light.   This area eventually turns brown and may be lightly covered with a gray mold.

Ascochyta blight of Chysanthemums affects the buds.   They either do not develop or are one-sided, and the base of the petals turns brown or black.   Regulation of the environment as outlined for powdery mildew under Mildews is the best procedure.

Stem blight.   Glomerella blight of Camellias causes stems to wilt and die and may envelop the entire plant.   Shoots should be cut well below the apparent area of infection, and shears should be sterilized after each cut by dipping in rubbing alcohol.

Leaf or flower spots.   In some cases an organism may cause either a blight or a spot.   A number of organisms are responsible for these diseases, depending upon the particular plant.   Alternaria leaf spot is common on carnations, and black spot caused by *Diplocarpon* is a familiar leaf disease on roses.   Septoria leaf spot of Chrysanthemums is also called black spot, but a different organism is involved from that on the rose.   Other Septoria fungi may cause leaf spot on asters, azaleas, and carnations, and on these plants the affected area is generally purple or brown.   Cyclamen leaf spot can be caused by any of three fungi, *Glomerella, Ramularia,* or *Phyllosticta.*   Other fungi which can cause leaf spots are *Botrytis, Cylindrosporium,* and *Fusarium.*

Flower spot of azaleas, which is due to *Ovulinia,* is very serious in the South.

Spores of most of these fungi are spread by splashing water.   The foliage or flowers must be kept dry; therefore careful watering practices are imperative.   Spraying or dusting with captan, ferbam or zineb is recommended.

9-23. Septoria leaf spot infections usually are large and irregular.

Mildews. Powdery mildew fungi attack a number of important plants including African violets, Calendulas, Chrysanthemums, Hydrangeas, roses, snap-dragons, and sweet peas. The fungus organisms—*Erysiphe, Oidium, Microsphaera,* and *Sphaerotheca*—produce spores which are air-borne, so that careless ventilation can lead to quick spread of the fungus. The familiar whitish-gray patches of mycelia on either the upper or lower surface of the leaves or flowers, as well as on the stems, are evidence of the presence of this fungus.

In addition to using Karathane, Pipron, or sulfur, all of which are reasonably effective controls, attention must be given to ventilation and heating. Germination of the spores is greatest at relative humidities between 95 and 99 percent, but will occur at a moisture content of the atmosphere as low as 75 percent. In general, the most favorable temperature range for germination and growth of the fungus is between 63 and 77°F, but it varies according to the specific organism. Ventilation changes the air, allowing for entrance of an atmosphere which is generally lower in moisture content. Ventilation alone may not be sufficient to keep the relative humidity low enough to inhibit spore germination. Turning on heating lines throughout the house accelerates air circulation, and a slight rise in temperature results in a lowering of the relative humidity. Serious mildew infection usually indicates careless ventilation and heating practices, and whatever program has been followed must be changed if the fungus development is to be halted. Maintaining a small amount of heat in the greenhouse by use of relatively few lines per house, coupled with adequate ventilation, is a sound method of keeping mildew infection at a minimum.

9-24. Powdery mildew is the most prevalent disease of greenhouse roses. The leaf on the right exhibits the characteristic white, powdery, crinkled areas.

Downy mildew caused by *Peronospora* is a serious but rather rare disease of roses and snapdragons. However, the organism that attacks roses will not attack snapdragons and vice versa, because they are different species of *Peronospora*. Diseased rose leaflets fall while still green, and most commonly affected are the lower leaves on the stem bearing a flower. When a flower is cut in the usual fashion, allowing two 5-leaflet leaves to remain on the plant, the fungus in these two remaining leaves eventually causes them to drop, and a bare stem several inches long results. Shoots developing from buds on these stems may become affected, and soon the plant may be almost entirely defoliated. On

9-25. Powdery mildew infection in *Chrysanthemum*. The best means of prevention is regulation of temperature, moisture, and air circulation so that moisture is not present on the leaf surface.

snapdragons, patches of purplish mold appear on stems or the underside of the leaves. Both of these downy mildews develop most rapidly under cool, moist conditions.

Diseased leaves must be removed, and the environmental controls outlined for powdery mildew under Mildews should be followed. In addition, moisture should be kept off the foliage except when spraying with zineb, which is quite effective for control of downy mildew. Because the organism is found on the underside of the foliage, it is essential to direct the spray to this area.

Rusts.   Carnation rust is caused by *Uromyces*, while Chrysanthemums and carnations are affected by species of *Puccinia*. Rose rust is due to *Phragmidium*, and asters are attacked by *Coleosporium*.

Pustules, or blisters, which can appear on either surface of the leaf, rupture, exposing masses of orange-yellow to dark-brown or black spores, depending upon the stage of rust present. Splashing water and air currents spread the spores of these fungi, and care in watering will help prevent further distribution. The new growth of the plants should be lightly covered with captan, zineb, or sulfur to prevent germination of the spores which might be present.

Wilts.   Organisms which cause wilt diseases are commonly present in the soil even in the absence of host plants, and therefore effective soil sterilization and avoidance of recontamination are practical controls.

Verticillium wilt is a common trouble with Chrysanthemums when fresh or unsterilized soil is used together with cuttings from stock that has not been cultured. The leaves on one side of the plant or the entire plant may show symptoms. There is a loss of normal healthy green color, and the foliage is often somewhat yellow but may also be a gray-green. Wilting is mild, beginning with the older foliage, and as the plant continues to grow, additional leaves are affected, and the severity of the wilting increases. At flowering all foliage may be wilted and off-colored, and the flowers are usually small and lack good substance. Disease-free cuttings can be obtained from Chrysanthemum propagation specialists who have cultured the cuttings and propagate only from disease-free stock. *Verticillium* also is troublesome on cinerarias, particularly if potted in mum soil where the disease was evident. Plants of *Begonia socotrana* also are affected by this fungus. The use of steamed soil and pots and sterilization of the bench areas where the pots are placed are essential. With Melior Begonias, cuttings should be taken from healthy plants.

Fusarium wilt is common on asters and carnations, but different species attack the two plants, and the organism will not transfer from one kind of plant to the other. The organism can enter the plant through roots or cracks in the lower stem. The vascular system becomes plugged by the organism, and it is possible that toxic substances may be formed by the fungus. Wilting and death of asters are a certainty, but sometimes affected carnation plants may live several years, though they generally lack vigor. Cuttings taken from such plants are infected in many cases, which simply gives rise to further trouble and loss of production. Careful roguing of carnation stock plus effective soil sterilization is the best remedy. With cloth-house asters the soil must be sterilized or the house moved to a new location where asters were not grown previously. Treatment of seeds with corrosive sublimate or Semesan is recommended.

Sclerotinia rot attacks snapdragons, causing them to wilt and die. Water-soaked areas appear on the lower part of the stem, and a white mold forms. Black sclerotia, or resting bodies, may be found in the lower stem. The soil must be sterilized for control.

Anthracnose of snapdragons caused by *Colletotrichum* is generally found on the stems, and dirty-white sunken areas are indicative of its presence. Old areas or spots usually show small black dots in the center, which are the fungus fruiting bodies. The infected areas enlarge, girdling the stem and killing the plant. The stems must be kept dry, and weekly spraying with zineb is desirable.

Stunt.   Cyclamen stunt is due to *Cladosporium*. The organism enters the plant from the soil and causes dwarfing of the flower stalks and the petioles of the new leaves. Reddish-brown necrotic areas are evident if the thickened fleshy corm is cut through just underneath the base of the petioles. Sterilization of all soil, pots, flats, and bench areas is essential for eliminating this difficulty.

Stem and root rots.   Undoubtedly, the most prevalent organism in this category is *Rhizoctonia*. Care in various cultural practices is a great aid in preventing trouble. Deep planting, overwatering, and use of a heavy soil are factors which encourage the development of this fungus, and losses may be heavy. Rotting of the stem at or just below the surface of the soil is the usual symptom. This fungus attacks a wide variety of plants, and any of the florist crops can easily be infected. When individual specimens are attacked, the organism can spread to nearby plants through the soil. Application of Morsodren, or Terraclor as a soil drench is sometimes effective in halting the further development of the organism. Such treatment will not help plants which are already affected.

Fusarium root rot is a common trouble on carnations, while *Phytophthora* attacks the roots and stems of a number of plants. Root rot of calla and stem rot of aster are caused by *Phytophthora*. Losses from *Pythium* may occur in much the same manner as those from *Rhizoctonia* because it is a widely prevalent organism. Blackleg in geraniums is due to *Pythium*. *Thielaviopsis* is troublesome on poinsettias, geraniums, and sweet peas. For all these, sterilization and avoidance of soggy, poorly drained soil are essential.

Cankers.   Roses and Gardenias are attacked by various fungi which cause cankers either above or below the soil. *Coniothyrium, Cylindrocladium,*

9-26. Characteristic black stems from *Pythium* (black leg) on geraniums. (*Department of Plant Pathology, The Pennsylvania State University, University Park, Pa., photograph.*)

and *Cryptosporetta* cause death of rose canes, which can involve the entire plant unless remedial measures are taken. Pruning of the affected portion is the best means of control, and the shears should be sterilized by dipping in rubbing alcohol after each cut is made.

Phomopsis causes canker of Gardenias, and the stem near the soil may show longitudinal cracks. The inner stems are orange-yellow in color.

Stem cankers can be produced on azaleas by *Cylindrocladium scoparium*. This pathogen may invade cuttings in the propagation bench, causing basal stem rot and failure to root. With older plants the first symptoms of the disease may be wilting of the leaves, followed by the leaves turning brown or black and dropping. Infected plants cannot be cured, but the spread of *Cylindrocladium scoparium* to other plants can be controlled with Morsodren.

FUNGICIDES

Fungicides are chemicals that kill, retard, or inhibit the growth of fungi. The exact mechanism of their action is not clear, but it may be that the fungicide interferes with certain metabolic processes of the organism and thereby is effective in inhibiting growth. When the organism is inside the plant, fungicides applied to the external part are of no value, but there is a great possibility of developing systemic fungicides. Thus the common fungicidal materials are effective in killing the fungi which have not yet invaded the tissue and constitute a prevention of invasion rather than a control of infestation.

To be most useful, the fungicide should be effective yet safe, causing no damage to the plant to which it is applied. Furthermore, the residue should be as inconspicuous as possible. Greatest effectiveness is obtained when both the upper and lower surfaces of the foliage are covered, together with the stem and flowers, if present. When applying fungicides in a spray, spreaders are useful for coverage of all parts of the tissue since many of the florist crops have a somewhat waxy coating which causes water to gather in droplets. Fungicides for crops outside or under cloth should be applied before a rain since the spores are usually disseminated during rains. By the time a fungicide is applied after a rain, the fungus may have already invaded the plant so that the application is of little value.

One spraying or dusting is seldom sufficient; the new growth will need protection in the form of further applications.

Arasan—tetramethyl thiuram disulfide. Arasan is primarily a seed-treatment material. Other names are thiram and Tersan 75. Only a light covering is needed on the seed coat; excesses may interfere with germination or cause dwarfing, abnormal twisting, or discoloration of the young leaves. It may also be dusted lightly on the surface of the seedbed to control damping-off of seedlings.

Bichloride of mercury. Other names for this material are corrosive sublimate and mercuric chloride. It is useful for sterilizing the surface of bulbs, corms, rhizomes, and other such fleshy plant parts. The usual dilution is 1 to 1,000, or 1 ounce per 7½ gallons of water. Because it reacts chemically with metal, containers of wood, earthenware, or glass must be used. Bichloride of mercury dissolves slowly in cold water, and heating a small quantity of water to near boiling is suggested. The hot water should be poured into the nonmetallic vessel containing the chemical, and sufficient cold water added to make the required volume. It is poisonous to human beings if swallowed.

Bordeaux mixture. This very old fungicide is also useful in treating bacterial diseases. Various formulas exist, such as 2-2-50 and 3-3-50. The first number refers to pounds of copper sulfate, the second to pounds of hydrated lime, and the third to the number of gallons of water. The purpose of the lime is to neutralize free copper, which injures plants.

The chief objection to Bordeaux is the residue, an unsightly whitish deposit. It is seldom used except as a desperate measure.

Botran—2,6-dichloro-4-nitroaniline. For the control of Botrytis blight the 75 percent wettable powder is used at the rate of about ½ pound per 100 gallons.

Captan—N-trichloromethyl thiotetrahydro phthalimide. Captan is the common name for a newer class of fungicides. It is useful for many leaf spots, leaf diseases, and *Botrytis*. With a spreader the general rate of application is

1 pound per 100 gallons, although 2 pounds is suggested for use on plants outside or under cloth.   There is also a 5 percent dust.   It is one of the most effective fungicides and is compatible with many insecticides.

Cuprinol.   Cuprinol is copper naphthenate, and it is used only for treating wooden flats or benches to prevent rot.

Cuprocide—*cuprous oxide*.   Cuprocide is most generally used as a seed treatment.   A very light covering will protect against damping-off, but seed of plants in the cabbage family may be injured and should not be treated with this material.   If seedlings damp-off after germination, a light dusting or application of a solution of 1 teaspoonful per gallon of water is helpful.

Dexon—*p-dimethylaminobenzenediazo sodium sulfonate*.   The 35 percent wettable powder is used at the rate of ½ pound per 100 gallons for the control of *Pythium* and *Phytophthora*.

Ferbam—*ferric dimethyl dithio carbamate*.   Ferbam, a synthetic organic compound, was one of the first of a series of carbamates used by florists.   It is quite effective for various leaf spots, rusts, and blights but will not control powdery mildew.   Being black, it leaves a very undesirable residue, particularly when dusted or sprayed on light-colored flowers.   It is rather difficult to wet and must be stirred thoroughly in a small volume of water before placing in the sprayer.   It is used with a spreader at 1 pound per 100 gallons of water on crops under glass, but outside or in the cloth house, double that rate is suggested. The dusts are generally 5 or 10 percent.   Ferbam is compatible with a wide range of insecticides.

Karathane—*dinitro capryl phenyl crotonate*.   Various other trade names such as Arathane and Iscothan have been given to this material.   It is specific for powdery mildew, but has poor residual effect, so that periodic applications must be made.

If it is used too strong, the young shoots of some rose varieties will be speckled or spotted.   Karathane should be applied under conditions where it will dry rapidly, since damage is accentuated by slow evaporation from the plant. No more than 8 ounces per 100 gallons with a spreader is suggested, and often good control can be obtained with 6 ounces.   Karathane can be mixed safely with numerous insecticides.

Maneb—*manganese ethylene bis dithio carbamate*.   Maneb is useful for rusts, leaf spots, and blights.   It is used at 1 pound of the 50 percent wettable powder per 100 gallons of water with a spreader.

Morsodren—*methylmercury dicyandiamide*. For the control of *Rhizoctonia, Pythium,* and *Botrytis,* Morsodren is used at the rate of from 1½ to 3 fluid ounces per 100 gallons of water.

New Improved Ceresan—*ethyl mercury phosphate*. Specifically for soft rot of callas, New Improved Ceresan is used at the rate of 1 pound per 50 gallons of water with a spreader, and the callas are soaked for 1 hour. A nonmetallic container must be used since the material reacts with metal. The material is poisonous if swallowed.

Phaltan—*N-trichloromethylthiophthalimide*. Phaltan is used for the control of several leaf disease organisms. The 50 percent wettable powder is used at the rate of 1 pound per 100 gallons of water.

Pipron—*3-(2-methylpiperidino)propyl 3,4-dichlorobenzoate*. Pipron liquid concentrate is used at the rate of ¼ to ½ pint per 100 gallons of water for the control of powdery mildew.

Semesan—*hydroxymercuri chlorophenol*. Originally designed as a seed-treatment material, Semesan also can be used on propagation sand or as a soil drench for certain crops. A very light covering of the seeds is imperative since overdoses may prevent germination or severely damage the seedlings. Applications may be made to propagation sand or soil in the bench at 1 tablespoonful per gallon of water, or 3⅓ pounds per 100 gallons. Since it contains mercury, it should never be used on roses or in a greenhouse where roses are growing because of its very toxic effect on this plant.

Spergon—*tetrachloro-p-benzoquinone*. Spergon, sometimes called chloranil, is used for treatment of soft rot of callas. It is usually injurious when applied to other florist plants. It is used at the rate of 2 ounces of Spergon per 1 gallon of water, and the callas are soaked 3 hours.

Sulfur. Sulfur has been used as a fungicide for a great many years. It is most effective for powdery mildew but can also be used for rusts. To be useful as a dust, sulfur should be ground fine enough to pass through a 300-mesh screen. The wettable sulfurs used as sprays are also finely ground and contain a wetting agent to aid in the dispersion and suspension of the sulfur particles. Generally the wettable sulfurs are used at 1½ to 2 pounds per 100 gallons, and a spreader is desirable for coverage of the plant in spite of the wetting agent which is present. Flowers of sulfur is rather coarse, 60- to 65-mesh, and should be mixed with water to make a slurry which is painted on steam pipes. When the heat is applied, the sulfur vaporizes, covering the plant with a fine deposit. Dry flowers of sulfur is also used in a vaporizer. The constant vaporization of sulfur provides an invisible, light, yet adequate coverage of the rose plant.   If the sulfur ignites in the vaporizer, the sulfur dioxide fumes will injure or kill the plants in the greenhouse.   Flowers of sulfur is not suitable for use as dusts or sprays.

Sulfur will bleach or burn the flowers on many plants, particularly in warm weather.   Therefore the material should be applied, whenever possible, before the flowers appear and when temperatures are below 85°F.   Leaf drop on some rose varieties is common when sulfur is used, and applications of parathion in the presence of sulfur will usually cause excessive leaf drop on many rose varieties.

Terraclor—pentachloro nitrobenzene.   Terraclor is useful for control of *Rhizoctonia* in propagation benches and soil when used at 1 pound per 100 gallons of water.   The area should be drenched.

Tutane—2-aminobutane carbonated.   Tutane is used at the rate of ½ pint per 1 gallon of water for the prevention of *Botrytis*.

Zineb—zinc ethylene bis dithio carbamate.   Zineb is useful for control of various leaf spots, foliage and flower blights, and rust.   It is used at 1 pound per 100 gallons with a spreader in the greenhouse, and at double this rate outside or under cloth.   Since it is whitish, the residue is generally not too noticeable on most flowers.   Dusts contain 5 to 10 percent of the material.

SPECIFIC DISEASES CAUSED BY BACTERIA

It is fortunate that bacterial organisms are not as numerous as fungi, since bacterial diseases are more difficult to control.

Wilts.   Bacterial wilt of carnations is quite a common trouble where the temperature is warm.   *Pseudomonas*, the responsible organism, enters the plant from the soil, or it may be present in the cutting when it is taken from the parent plant.   The leaves wilt, the root system dies, and longitudinal cracks sometimes appear at the base of the stem.   When the stem is sliced, the inner portion may be sticky from the bacterial masses.   Death of the plant is a certainty.   Thorough soil sterilization is essential, together with selection of cuttings from wilt-free stock.

Stem and root rots.   Geraniums are affected by a bacterial disease of the lower stem, and the organism responsible is *Xanthomonas*.   Agri-mycin is useful.   A bacterial stem rot of Chrysanthemum stems due to *Erwinia* is common in hot weather, when the soil must be kept quite moist.   Wilting of the Chrysanthemum plants occurs, followed by their quick death, and there is no control once

9-27. Leaf spot symptoms of bacterial stem rot on geranium leaves. (*Department of Plant Pathology, The Pennsylvania State University, University Park, Pa., photograph.*)

invasion has occurred. *Xanthomonas* also causes rotting of the lower stem of stocks, which is sometimes called "bacterial blight."

Soft rot, caused by *Erwinia*, affects callas, Cyclamen, hyacinths, Iris, and other crops. A soft decay of the lower stems or the roots occurs. Rotted portions of callas should be removed before planting, and the bulbs soaked in Spergon or New Improved Ceresan, and then planted while wet.

Fasciation. Very numerous, thickened fleshy shoots with abnormal leaves which develop from the stem or surface roots of carnations, Chrysanthemums, geraniums, Pelargoniums, sweet peas, Petunias, and some other crops are caused by *Corynebacterium fascians*. Generally, affected plants are worthless and should be discarded. The organism is carried on seeds and can be spread by handling or watering. Sterilization of soil is recommended.

Galls. Crown gall is common on roses, Chrysanthemums, geraniums, Pelargoniums, sweet peas, and some other crops and is caused by *Agrobacterium*

9-28. Rose crown gall. (*Department of Plant Pathology, The Pennsylvania State University, University Park, Pa., photograph.*)

tumefaciens. The bacteria live in the soil and invade the roots or stems through wounds, with the result that the galls may be found at places other than the soil line. The organism is spread by water or, if the growth is cut off, by a knife which has been used for other cuttings. Generally little harm is done to the plants. Soil sterilization is the most effective prevention.

Leaf spots. Bacterial leaf spot of geranium is due to *Xanthomonas.* Small dark-brown dots, often with reddish borders, are noted between the veins, and on the underside of the leaf the affected areas appear water-soaked. Tissues between spots become yellow and die. Removal and destruction of the foliage are recommended, together with use of Agri-mycin sprays, and the leaves of the plants must be kept dry.

English ivy is affected with a black spot caused by *Xanthomonas,* but different from the one on geraniums. Destroying the badly diseased leaves is the best remedy. Other crops affected with bacterial leaf spots include delphiniums, Begonias, carnations, Gardenias, and some foliage plants.

BACTERICIDES

The mechanism of the action of bactericides is quite similar to that of fungicides. If the bacteria invade the plant, bactericides applied to the external part are useless, but the possibilities of using antibiotics as systemic bactericides are good.

Bactericides, like fungicides, should be safe and effective and should leave an inconspicuous residue. Complete coverage of the plant is necessary, and spreaders are useful on waxy foliage. Applications must be frequent enough to protect the new growth.

Agri-mycin 100. Agri-mycin 100 is an antibiotic material useful for control of bacterial blight on geraniums and foliage plants. It is generally used at 100 to 200 ppm.

Bordeaux mixture. The Bordeaux mixture is used as described earlier under Fungicides.

LF-10. LF-10 is a bactericide and fungicide for use primarily in propagation areas. It is used for hand or bench wash at 3 fluid ounces per 5 gallons of water and for spraying at 6 fluid ounces per 5 gallons of water.

SPECIFIC DISEASES CAUSED BY VIRUSES

Viruses usually cause mottled areas, or patterns, to appear on the foliage or flower, which often serve as a means of identification.

Mosaic.   Each of the mosaic diseases described here is caused by a different virus which will not spread to another kind of plant.   However, there are viruses which have a wide host range.

On geraniums the mosaic virus causes mottled light- and dark-green areas.   Sometimes the areas may be yellowish.   Lily and carnation foliage is also affected, but the areas are elongated into streaks in the younger foliage.   Carnation flowers show lighter streaks parallel to the veins, particularly in the red and pink varieties.   Aphids spread the mosaic virus of lilies and carnations.   Briarcliff roses show a yellow splotchy area on the foliage when affected with mosaic.   Moderate crippling of the young foliage is also a symptom on other rose varieties.   Some of the variegated azaleas and Camellias are affected with mosaic, producing a mottled condition on the foliage.   Variegation of *Abutilon* is caused by mosaic.

Streak.   Carnations are attacked by the streak virus, which is different from the mosaic virus.   Reddish or purple areas develop on the older foliage, and the leaves usually die.

Yellows.   The combination of the effects of the two viruses causing mosaic and streak of carnations is called yellows.   Typical symptoms appear for each, and the plant is markedly reduced in vitality.   Cuttings from such plants are worthless.

Aster yellows is caused by a single virus which is transmitted from plant to plant by the aster leaf hopper.   More than 70 kinds of plants are subject to this disease.   The chief symptoms include yellowing of the foliage, shortened internodes, formation of additional side shoots, and abnormal flowers.   Part or

9-29.   Heat   therapy   chambers used for the production of virus-free plants for propagation stock. (*Yoder Bros., Inc., photograph.*)

all of the flower may be greenish-yellow, and the size may be reduced. Affected plants should be destroyed. Aster yellows can be prevented by growing the plants in a cloth house so constructed as to exclude the leaf hoppers. Chrysanthemums are also affected by the aster yellows virus, and similar symptoms develop. Affected plants should be destroyed, since the cuttings will have the disease.

Stunt. The stunt virus, which attacks Chrysanthemums, causes a marked reduction in growth and a fading of the pink and bronze flowers. Often the affected plants will flower 1 to 2 weeks earlier than healthy stocks. The virus may be present in the plant for several months without symptoms developing, and apparently healthy stock may be affected, so that when cuttings are taken, all may be stunted. Discarding such stock and purchasing stunt-free cuttings is the only remedy.

Crinkle. Geraniums are subject to the crinkle virus, which is most apparent in winter when the weather is cooler. Small yellow spots appear on the foliage, which is often distorted or crinkled. The center of the foliage spots turns brown, and eventually the leaves may drop. As the weather becomes warmer, the symptoms do not show on the new growth, but the virus is present, though masked. Cuttings from such plants will show symptoms when cool weather prevails. Discarding the stock is the only remedy.

METHODS OF APPLICATION OF PEST AND DISEASE CONTROLS

Hydraulic spraying is the standard method of applying pest and disease controls, but there are many other means that can be used, each of which has some advantages. Although one primary method of application may be used at a greenhouse, there is an advantage in having alternate methods available because some control materials can be used only in one way, and because if labor or other considerations interfere, one method of application might be readily available when others could not be used.

Hydraulic spraying. The control material is mixed with water in a tank and pumped from the tank at pressures of 250 to 300 psi. The tank may be a large stationary installation with pipes to conduct the spray to the various greenhouses, or it may be small enough so that it can be wheeled through the greenhouses. The largest portable tanks hold 30 gallons, and usually they can be transported through the main walks of the greenhouse. A sufficient length of rubber hose is attached to the tank or to the spray lines in each house so that the individual doing the spraying can reach all sections of the greenhouse, and the hose terminates with a brass rod (tube) approximately 2 feet long, equipped with a shut-off valve and one or more nozzles.

Many of the control materials which are used do not dissolve in water but are in suspension, and even distribution of the material throughout the water in the tank is obtained by emulsions or wettable powders together with constant mechanical agitation of the water in the tank. It is important that the sprayer be equipped with a good agitator to keep the control materials from settling and being ineffective. The best dispersion of the control material throughout the water in the tank can be assured by first mixing the required amount of material in a few gallons of water in a bucket or jug and then thoroughly stirring the concentrated mixture into the entire tankful of water. At the time of mixing, the control materials are being handled in their most concentrated form, and if they are harmful or toxic to human beings, the best protective measures should be taken by the operator.

Wetting agents (spreaders) are used with sprays so that they flow over the surface of the plant and give complete coverage. Many of the control materials are compounded with wetting agents in them; but depending on the hardness of the water or the waxiness of the leaf, additional wetting agents may have to be used to get the best coverage of the plants. The amount of wetting agent to use is best determined by trial and error. If the spray remains in droplets on the leaves, additional wetting agent should be added until it just starts to flow over the surface of the leaf. Several wetting agents can be used satisfactorily; Multifilm X-77 is one of the better ones.

Hydraulic spraying is usually a two-man job, as one man drags the hose while the other directs the spray on the plants as he walks the length of each bench. For thorough coverage of the plants—undersides of leaves as well as top sides—it is necessary to use a nozzle positioned at a 45 to 90° angle to the spray rod and to direct the spray upward. If the plants are tall, it is necessary to use

9-30. Hydraulic sprayer with booms for treatment of Chrysanthemum fields. (*Dorcas Flowers photograph.*)

a sweeping motion from the base of the plants toward the top in order to give good coverage. In many instances the pest or the pathogen is not killed unless the spray contacts it. The effectiveness of a spray application depends to a large extent on the thoroughness of the operator. Actually, different spraying techniques should be used, depending on the pest or pathogen to be controlled. Red spiders usually locate on the undersides of leaves and may be more prevalent on basal leaves than top ones, while thrips and aphids often infest only the stem tip portions of the plants. Powdery mildew may be distributed generally over the plants whereas Botrytis blight may be limited only to the flowers. The operator needs to do something more than just spray—he needs to know what he is trying to control, where it is located, how to direct the spray in order to get coverage there, and how heavily to spray.

Cleaning sprayers. To avoid neutralizing the effectiveness of spray materials and to prevent injury from unsafe combinations of materials, the sprayer must be kept clean. After each spraying, wash the tank with clean water and allow it to run through the pump mechanism and hose and nozzle. Hot water is best. Never allow unused spray material to remain in the tank.

To remove oily scum from the sprayer, steam out the tank, wash with gasoline, or scrub with a wire brush. Trisodium phosphate at 1 pound per 25 to 30 gallons is best for cleaning, and hot water is recommended. This solution should be forced through the pump, hose, and nozzle back into the tank for 30 to 45 minutes to clean all parts and accessories of the sprayer. Then flush clean water through to wash out the trisodium phosphate and prevent corrosion. Use trisodium phosphate at least every 3 months, or more often if the sprayer is used continuously. Trisodium phosphate may be obtained at drugstores.

The weed killers containing 2,4-D and related compounds are useful for destroying weeds outside the greenhouse. The fumes of this material are very toxic to many plants, and it should *never* be used in the greenhouse. If 2,4-D has been used in a sprayer, the sprayer must be cleaned thoroughly before any standard insecticide or fungicide is applied. The usual methods of rinsing and cleaning sprayers will not remove 2,4-D. A solution of 5 pounds of ammonium nitrate to 100 gallons of water should be forced through the pump, hose, and nozzle back into the tank. Flush with clean water, repeat with ammonium nitrate, and flush again with clean water. Such treatment will usually remove the 2,4-D residue.

As compared to other methods of application, hydraulic spraying may be the most economical in cost of materials but the most expensive in labor. Possibly one of the worst features is that so much time is required to make an application that it is usually delayed until labor and time are available, at the expense of the welfare of the plants.

Table 9-1. *Spray-dilution Table*

t. = teaspoonful, T. = tablespoonful

	1 to 50	1 to 100	1 to 200	1 to 300	1 to 400	1 to 500	1 to 600	1 to 800	1 to 1,000	1 to 1,600
1 Gal.	72.5 cc or 5 T. plus ¼ t. or 2.56 oz	36.2 cc or 2 T. plus 1¾ t. or 1.28 oz	18.1 cc or 3¾ t. or .64 oz	12.2 cc or 2½ t.	9.1 cc or 2 t.	7.3 cc or 1½ t.	6.0 cc or 1¼ t.	4.5 cc or 1 t.	3.6 cc or ¾ t.	2.3 cc or ½ t.
2 Gal.	144.9 cc or 10 T. plus ¾ t. or 5.12 oz	72.5 cc or 5 T. plus ¼ t. or 2.56 oz	36.2 cc or 2 T. plus 1¾ t. or 1.28 oz	24.1 cc or 5 t.	18.1 cc or 3¾ t.	14.5 cc or 3 t.	12.2 cc or 2½ t.	9.1 cc or 2 t.	7.3 cc or 1½ t.	4.6 cc or 1 t.
3 Gal.	217.3 cc or 15 T. plus 1 t. or 7.68 oz	108.7 cc or 7 T. plus 2 t. or 3.84 oz	54.3 cc or 3 T. plus 2½ t. or 1.92 oz	36.2 cc or 2 T. plus 1¾ t. or 1.28 oz	27.2 cc or 1 T. plus 2¾ t.	21.7 cc or 1 T. plus 1½ t.	18.1 cc or 3¾ t.	13.4 cc or 1 T.	10.9 cc or 2¼ t.	6.9 cc or 1½ t.
5 Gal.	362.2 cc or 12.8 oz	181.1 cc or 6.4 oz	90.6 cc or 6 T. plus 1¼ t. or 3.2 oz	60.3 cc or 4 T. plus ¾ t. or 2.13 oz	45. 3 cc or 3 T. plus ½ t. or 1.6 oz	36.2 cc or 2 T. plus 1¾ t. or 1.28 oz	30.3 cc or 2 T. plus ½ t. or 1.07 oz	22.6 cc or 1 T. plus 1¾ t.	18.1 cc or 3¾ t.	11.3 cc or 2½ t.

Table 9-1. (Continued)

	1 to 50	1 to 100	1 to 200	1 to 300	1 to 400	1 to 500	1 to 600	1 to 800	1 to 1,000	1 to 1,600
10 Gal.	724.5 cc or 25.6 oz	362.2 cc or 12.8 oz	181.1 cc or 12 T. plus 2⅔ t. or 6.4 oz	120.8 cc or 8 T. plus 1½ t or 4.27 oz	90.6 cc or 6 T. plus 1¼ t. or 3.2 oz	72.5 cc or 5 T. plus ¼ t. or 2.56 oz	60.3 cc or 4 T. plus ¾ t. or 2.13 oz	45.3 cc or 3 T. plus ½ t. or 1.6 oz	36.2 cc or 2 T. plus 1¼ t. or 1.28 oz	22.6 cc or 1 T. plus 1¾ t. or .8 oz
25 Gal.	1,811.2 cc or 64 oz	905.6 cc or 32 oz	452.8 cc or 16 oz	302.8 cc or 10.7 oz	226.4 cc or 16 T. or 8 oz	181.1 cc or 12 T. plus 2½ t. or 6.4 oz	150.8 cc or 10 T. plus 2½ t. or 5.33 oz	113.0 cc or 8 T. or 4 oz	90.6 cc or 6 T. plus 1¼ t. or 3.2 oz	56.5 cc or 4 T. or 2 oz
30 Gal.	2,173.5 cc or 76.8 oz	1,086.6 cc or 38.4 oz	543.3 cc or 19.2 oz	362.4 cc or 12.81 oz	271.8 cc or 19 T. or 9.6 oz	217.5 cc or 15 T. plus 1 t. or 7.68 oz	180.9 cc or 12 T. plus 2 t. or 6.39 oz	135.9 cc or 9 T. plus 1½ t. or 4.8 oz	108.6 cc or 7 T. plus 2 t. or 3.84 oz	67.8 cc or 4 T. plus 4½ t. or 2.4 oz
50 Gal.	3,622.4 cc or 1 gal	1,811.2 cc or 64 oz	905.5 cc or 32 oz	602.8 cc or 21.33 oz	452.8 cc or 16 oz	362.2 cc or 12.8 oz	302.8 cc or 10.66 oz	226.4 cc or 8 oz	181.1 cc or 12 T. plus 2½ t. or 6.4 oz	113.2 cc or 8 T. or 4 oz

Aerosol.   Aerosols are used largely for control of pests, not diseases. The control materials in liquid concentrate form are placed in a strong container (bomb) together with a propellant, a substance that is liquid when confined under pressure but changes to gas when released at a lower pressure.   The aerosol applicator disperses such finely divided particles under pressure that by making one trip the length of a narrow house or two trips the length of a wider house, the entire air mass in the greenhouse becomes permeated with the control material.   The greenhouse must be completely closed during application and for several hours afterward.   The rate of application is based on the cubic contents of the greenhouse, the temperature, and the length of time the aerosol is dispersed in the greenhouse.   At the time of aerosol application, air movement outdoors should be low or the material will be distributed unevenly in the greenhouse or even forced through the laps of the glass.   Aerosols should be applied when a uniform temperature of 70°F can be maintained for several hours, and it is important that the aerosol container be brought to this temperature before use, as well as the air in the greenhouse.   In mild or warm weather it is easiest to maintain that temperature in the evening; however, during the winter it may be necessary to make the application in the afternoon in order to keep the house up to the proper temperature.   Control of temperature is very important, as the amount of dispersion of aerosols is greatly affected by it.

9-31.   Application of pesticide by means of an aerosol.   Note the protective clothing worn by the operator.   (*Virginia Chemicals, Inc., photograph.*)

The materials for aerosol application are relatively costly, but the labor and time used are very economical. Only certain materials can be dispensed by means of aerosols, and usually alternate means of application are needed to provide all the desired controls.

Vaporization from steam lines. Some materials can be vaporized from steam lines, and when this can be done, it is an efficient and economical method of application. Sulfur has been used in this way for years for the control of powdery mildew, and more recently, pesticides such as lindane, Tedion, Dibrom, aramite, Vapona, nicotine sulfate, and Pentac have been so used. Thin slurries are made from dry materials or wettable powders and painted on two or more pipes the length of the greenhouse depending on the width of the house, while liquid control materials are placed in oil cans, plastic squeeze bottles, or similar dispensers and skip-squirted on pipes the length of the greenhouse. The rate of application is based on the cubic contents of the greenhouse; a method of computing is to multiply the square feet of ground covered by 10 feet (the average height). An accurate mathematical computation of the air volume within a greenhouse can be made by multiplying length by width by height to the eave or gutter, and adding to this value one-half the product of multiplying length by width by height of the ridge above the eave or gutter. If the height of the ridge above the eave or gutter is not known, but the roof is standard pitch (6 inches rise per 12 inches in width), this measurement will be one-fourth the width of the greenhouse.

The control material should be applied to cold pipes, the ventilators should be closed, and the heat should be turned into the lines. Except in extremely cold weather this is a nighttime operation, and the ventilators are left closed all night. When it can be used, vaporization from the steam lines is an excellent method. Unfortunately, only a few materials can be used in this way and only during the heating season.

Fumigators. A few pesticides can be mixed with a combustible material; when this mixture is ignited, the pesticide is dispersed throughout the area. Fumigators containing nicotine, tedion-dithiono, and dithiono are the main ones that are used, and they are rated by the cubic contents that they will treat. The required number of fumigators is distributed equally throughout the greenhouse, the ventilators are closed, and the fumigators are lighted. The temperature and wind limitations are the same for fumigator applications as for aerosols. This type of application is convenient and requires very little labor, but the costs of materials may be more than for some of the other methods of application. It is possible to use fumigators as an alternate means of applying control materials, but they are not suitable as a sole means of control because of the limited number of materials that can be effectively dispersed from them.

Dusters.   Some greenhouse operators use dusters as the primary means of applying control materials, but more commonly dusters are used as an alternate method.   Dusting is an economical means of application, as the costs of material and labor are both low.   The disadvantages of dusting are that many materials that should be used cannot be obtained in the form of dusts, and that considerable residue is left on the plants.

There are dusters of different capacities and capabilities.   Some of the small, hand-operated ones are particularly helpful in treating infestations immediately in the areas where they occur.   This use should be more common because it allows local infestations to be treated promptly, preventing widespread troubles, with little or no effort or preparation.   Some dusters are power-operated, and the dust is dispersed in a high-velocity air stream.   These types of dusters can be used for treating large areas effectively, and they may also have a provision for misting by introducing liquid control materials into the air stream.   When these dusters are used for misting, the pesticide is placed in the concentrate tank at approximately 10 times the concentration used in hydraulic sprayers since dilution with air, when the pesticide enters the high-velocity air stream, results in about the same concentration as when the same pesticide is diluted with water in the hydraulic spray or tank.

Foggers.   Control materials are dispersed by foggers in heated and finely divided oil particles.   Treatments can be made rapidly, but specially prepared

9-32.   Application of pesticide by means of high-velocity air stream. The gasoline engine operates a blower which produces a high-velocity air stream. Good dispersion of dust or liquid is obtained by introducing either of them into the air stream. (*H. D. Hudson Manufacturing Co. photograph.*)

9-33. Flora-Fog, a thermal fog method for application of pesticides. (*E. C. Geiger photograph.*)

control materials are used in foggers, and generally they are more costly than the ones used for other means of application. The rate of application is based on the volume of the greenhouse, as with aerosol or vaporization methods.

Some plants are adversely affected by the oils that are used in foggers. The use of foggers is also limited because relatively few materials can be dispersed by this means.

Soil drenches. Soil drenching is a common method of application for the control of pathogens that infest the soil and the basal parts of plants, and in some instances it is used for the control of soil pests. A few materials are taken into the plants from the soil (systemics), in which case the entire plant may be treated effectively for pests by making an application of the proper material to the soil. Drenches should be applied to the soil at the rate of 1 quart of the drench per square foot of bench soil or ½ pint of drench per 6-inch pot of soil. When peat alone is used as a growing medium, 1 pint of solution per 6-inch pot is needed to adequately moisten the entire volume.

Read the label and take proper action. Many of the control materials are not only toxic to pests or pathogens but also harmful or toxic to human beings. Before a material is used, the label should be read thoroughly to make sure that the right material is being used, that it is being used at the right rate, and that proper protective measures are being taken. If the label does not make specific recommendations for the crop to be treated, get that information from a reliable source before using the product. The use of control materials on food crops is closely regulated because of the possibility of harmful residues being left on the crop and then ingested by animals or humans. There are fewer limitations on

9-34. Chemical treatment of Florida Chrysanthemum fields for control of pests and disease organisms. (*Dorcas Flowers photograph.*)

the use of these products on flower crops. If there are no recommendations on the label for the use of the pesticides on crops under glass, it should be determined whether the same rate is to be used under glass as outdoors. Commonly only about one-half the concentration of pesticide is used under glass as is used outdoors. The use of materials at the higher concentrations in greenhouses may cause damage to the plants.

As mentioned earlier, since many of the control materials do not dissolve in water, they are produced as wettable powders or emulsions (miscibles) that will remain in suspension and well dispersed throughout the water. Emulsions are made with oils, and under glass the oils can cause damage to many plants. Whenever possible, the emulsion form of control materials should be avoided in greenhouses. There is a temptation to use emulsions rather than wettable powders as less visible residue is left on the plants, but it should be realized that the

9-35. Chemical treatment of Florida Gladiolus fields for control of disease organisms and pests. (*Roman J. Claprood Co. of Florida photograph.*)

possibilities of toxic effects to the plants are greater.   Substances other than oils are used to keep some liquid formulations of control materials in suspension, and they are usually not harmful to plants.   These formulations may be referred to as aqua, flowable, or liquid concentrates, depending on the manufacturer.

Humans may be harmed by some control materials by contact or absorption through the skin, ingestion, or inhaling.   The label directions should be followed closely, and with some materials contact with the skin should be avoided by using rubber gloves, coat, and hat.   Ingestion or inhalation is prevented by the use of a proper respirator or gas mask.   In spite of these protective measures, the individuals involved should wash thoroughly after the application.   Pesticides vary in degree of toxicity to humans and other animals.   The relative toxicity of a pesticide may be referred to as its LD_{50}, which is the amount of the actual chemical in the pesticide product in milligrams used per kilogram of test animal (mg/kg) that kills 50 percent of the test animals.   Because pesticides may enter the animal through the mouth or nose (oral) or skin (dermal); both values are given in Table 9-2.

Table 9-2.   *LD_{50} of Several Pesticides*

TRADE NAME	ORAL LD_{50} (MG/KG)	DERMAL LD_{50} (MG/KG)
Aldrin	49.5	98
Tutane	4,000	
Aramite	3,900	
Guthion	12	220
Orthocide	15,000	
Sevin	675	*4,000
Morestan	1,450	*2,000
Mitox	3,200	
Chlordane	382	765
Chlorobenzilate	1,130	*5,000
Copper sulfate	300	
Acti-Dione	1.8	
Dicloran, Botran	*10,000	
DDT	115	2,510
Systox	4.3	13.1
Rotenone	62.5	* 940
Dexon	105	
Diazinon	92	677
Nemagon, Fumazone	173	
Vapona, DDVP	68	91
Kelthane	1,050	11,115
Dieldrin	46	75

* greater than

Table 9-2. (Continued)

TRADE NAME	ORAL LD$_{50}$ (MG/KG)	DERMAL LD$_{50}$ (MG/KG)
Cygon	215	505
Karathane	400	
DiSyston	4.5	10.5
Karmex	3,400	
Thiodan	30.5	102
Endrin	12.6	15.0
Fermate	11,000	
Phaltan	*10,000	
Heptachlor	131	222
Lead arsenate	100	2,400
Lindane	89.5	950
Malathion	1,187	*4,444
Manzate, Dithane M-22	6,750	
Metaldehyde	200	
Marlate	5,000	*6,000
Morsodren, Panogen, Panodrin	45	
Dibrom	430	1,100
Black Leaf 40	83	285
Omazene (Mathieson 466)	590	
Ovotran	2,050	
Terraclor	1,200	
Paraquat, Gramoxone	200	
Thiophos	8.3	13.9
Pentac, Hooker HRS 16	1,200	
Thimet	1.7	4.3
Pipron	2,500	2,500
Pyrethrins	*1,500	*1,880
OMPA, Pestox III	13.5	15.0
Sodium arsenite	30	
Agrimycin 17	300	
Dithio, Sulfa Tepp, Dithiono	5.0	
Meta-Systox-R	65	250
DDD, Rothane	*4,000	*4,000
TEP, Tetron	1.1	2.4
Tedion	*14,700	10,000
Arasan, Thylate, Tersan	780	
VC-13, Nemacide	270	
Zineb	5,200	
Ziram, Zerlate	1,400	

* Greater than.

Table 9-3.   *An Evaluation of LD_{50} Values* *

TOXICITY RATING	COMMONLY USED TERM	ORAL LD_{50} (MG/KG)	PROBABLE LETHAL DOSE FOR MAN
1	Extremely toxic	1 or less	A taste, 1 grain
2	Highly toxic	1 to 50	4 cubic centimeters 1 teaspoon
3	Moderately toxic	50 to 500	30 grams 1 ounce
4	Slightly toxic	500 to 5,000	250 grams 1 pint
5	Practically nontoxic	5,000 to 15,000	1 quart
6	Relatively harmless	15,000 and more	More than 1 quart

* From H. C. Hodge and J. H. Sterner in the *American Industrial Hygiene Association Quarterly.*

10

CUT FLOWER CROPS

Carnations, Chrysanthemums, and roses are the cut flower crops of the greatest economic importance; however, several other crops are produced commercially. Actually, the amount of production is affected by market demand, and the potential sales of the various crops can be affected by the general economy of the country, changes in customs and styles, and improvements in production procedures or varieties. The advent of year-round production of Chrysanthemums has made a radical change in the production of that crop, and the reduced use of corsage flowers has affected the amount of production of such crops as Camellias, Gardenias, and orchids.

ASTER (*Callistephus chinensis—Compositae*)

High-quality asters can be produced the year-round provided the seedlings are lighted during short days from the time that they emerge until flowering.

The same type of lighting as used for mums can be employed, but the light intensity required is less, so that the bulbs can either be spaced farther apart or be of lower wattage.   The primary effect of supplementary illumination during short days is causing the stems to elongate.   Asters will produce flowers in short days but on very short stems.   Asters at 50°F nights will be fully double with strong stems.   At higher temperatures they will grow reasonably well but will be weaker stemmed and have fewer petals.

Lighted asters can be used to good advantage by producing a crop earlier than the natural-flowering asters in the summer or as a short-term crop that fits into mum, snapdragon, or other rotations.   The summer crop is commonly produced in the cloth house.   The seed can be sown in the middle of March, the seedlings potted as soon as they can be handled, and the plants placed outdoors after frost in May.   The seedlings are lighted from the seed flat until they are set out in the cloth house.   About 4 months is required for flowering from seed sown in the spring, and as long as 5½ months is required for flowering from seed sown in November.   The Royal-type asters are considered the most suitable for forcing.

Asters should not be pinched since they are self-branching and 8 to 10 flowers are produced per plant.   Each shoot developing from the main stem is disbudded to a single flower.   The plants can be spaced 8 by 8 inches in the bench.

Fusarium wilt can be a very serious disease.   The organism is soil-borne, and thorough soil sterilization with steam is the best control.   Fusarium trouble is almost certain if successive aster crops are grown on the same soil without sterilization.   Some disease-resistant strains have been developed, but apparently there are different strains of the Fusarium organism, and asters resistant to the western Fusarium strain may be susceptible to the eastern strain, or vice versa.

Yellows is a virus disease that is transmitted from weeds or other host plants to the aster primarily by the leaf hopper.   A properly constructed cloth house will exclude the leaf hoppers.   Chance infestations can be controlled with DDT.

Rust may attack the plants if the foliage is kept moist by rain, dew, or careless watering.

Aphids, red spider, thrips, blister beetles, and leaf miner are the common insect pests.

CAMELLIA (*Camellia japonica—Ternstroemiaceae*)

Camellias have been grown to some extent in greenhouses in the northern states since the middle of the nineteenth century.   The cut flowers are used primarily for corsages, and young plants are occasionally sold as potted specimens.

Selection of plants and propagation.   Camellia plants do not grow rapidly, and since flower production is limited until the plants are large, it is often more practical to select plants from southern or western nurseries than to propagate from one's own stock.   There is much confusion in the names used for different Camellia varieties, and since some varieties may be given three or four different names, it is advisable to select the plants when they are in flower.

Camellias may be propagated by seed, cuttings, grafting, and layering; however, cuttings and grafting are most commonly used.   Either stem tip or leaf bud cuttings may be used.   The cutting is taken in the fall from the current season's growth and placed in a closed case with a bottom temperature of 72°F. Either sand or sand and peat can be used, and it takes from 60 to 100 days for rooting.   The rooted cuttings should be potted in a mixture of soil and acid peat.

Cleft grafting is the grafting method used most commonly.   It is possible to establish a plant more rapidly by this method.

Soil and fertilizer.   Camellias are grown in large tubs or boxes so that they may be spaced as they increase in size.   An acid soil (pH 5.0 to 5.5) is necessary for best growth, and a suitable soil mixture is composed of equal parts of soil and acid peat.

The use of fertilizer is restricted largely to the growing period during the spring and summer.   Fertilizer applications should be based on soil analysis. If the Spurway method is used, the following nutrient levels should be maintained: nitrates, 10 to 25 ppm; phosphorus, 1 to 5 ppm; potash, 10 to 20 ppm; and calcium, 100 ppm.   Sulfur or iron sulfate can be used to keep the soil on the acid side.   Ferrous sulfate is faster acting than sulfur.

Because of the slow rate of growth and the large soil volume as compared with the amount of water used, it may not be necessary to apply fertilizer to Camellias more than two or three times during the year.

Moisture, light, and temperature.   Camellia soils should be kept uniformly moist.   During the spring and summer the higher temperatures and the active growing condition of the plant require frequent applications of water, and syringing the plants and wetting down the walks is helpful.   When the temperatures are reduced in the fall, water should be applied less frequently.

High relative humidity at the time of flowering is helpful in inducing the opening of the flower buds.   The relative humidity can be raised by injecting either mist or steam into the house.

Except for the darkest period of the year, some reduction in light intensity is needed for Camellias.   A light shade on the glass can be used for fall and spring, and during the summer a cloth or netting shade inside the glass may be used as well as a heavy shade on the glass.   Camellia leaves burn readily if the light becomes too intense.

Flower formation occurs at temperatures above 60°F, and development of these buds to open flowers takes place at temperatures below 60°F.   As soon as the plants have flowered, the temperature should be raised gradually to 60 to

65°F. This allows new vegetative shoot growth to develop, followed by the formation of flower buds. As soon as possible in the fall the temperature should be maintained below 60°F, and the temperatures can be gradually lowered until they are maintained at 40°F during the flowering period.

Pruning, disbudding, and cutting. The primary objects of pruning are to control the size and symmetry of the plant, to limit the productive area of the plant, to improve the flower quality, and to remove weak or diseased growth. Pruning is done after flowering in the spring.

Disbudding is often practiced by removal of all the side flower buds, leaving only the terminal bud on each stem. This reduces the number of flowers, but it usually increases the size of flower. Disbudding must be done when the buds are about the size of a pea.

Camellias are commonly sold as tailored flowers. They are removed from the plant without any attached leaves, and then placed in a paper collar to which have been stapled Gardenia or Camellia leaves.

Pests and diseases. Scale, aphids, mealy bugs, and red spiders are common pests of Camellias. Malathion should control all these pests. Repeated applications may be necessary for scale.

Twig blight is caused by the fungus *Glomerella cingulata*. The symptoms are similar to fire blight of apples and pears. Branches, or even the entire plant, can be killed as a result of the girdling action. The affected branch should be cut back to the healthy wood.

Flower blight, caused by the fungus *Sclerotinia camelliae*, can be very destructive. Sanitation is the best control. Remove all diseased flowers from the plants as well as those that have fallen on the ground. Avoid overhead syringing just before the buds show color.

Flower bud drop may be caused by lack of sufficient relative humidity, dry soil, and too high or widely fluctuating temperatures.

Varieties. Camellia varieties are chosen for forcing because of some or all of the following flower characteristics: color, size, and form, time of flowering, productivity, and shipping and keeping qualities. Varieties that are commonly forced in the greenhouse are Alba Plena, Debutante, Pink Perfection, Elegans Chandleri, Herme, Jarvis Red, Otome, Prof. C. S. Sargent, Prince Eugene Napoleon, C. M. Hovey, and Mathotiana Rubra.

CALLA (*Zantedeschia aethiopica Godfreyana—Araceae*)

This plant is a native of Egypt which may be grown outdoors in mild climates or in greenhouses throughout the year.

It is propagated by means of division of the rhizomes. The rhizomes are potted in August, and flowering starts in the fall and continues in the winter and spring until the plants are dried off in early summer. They are started back in growth in late summer or early fall. The need for the dormant period caused by drying is questionable, as the growth and flowering would proceed in the summer if the plants were watered regularly.

Callas may be grown in beds or in pots. If they are in pots, they must be large enough to give adequate space for the large rhizomes and root system. Callas are subject to root rot, and the spread of this disease may be more easily controlled among plants in pots. With bed-grown callas it usually is easier to provide the uniform moisture conditions necessary for good growth.

Full sunlight should be provided, with the exception that if callas are grown during the summer, partial shade should be used. Growth and flowering are best at 55°F night temperatures, with the day temperatures about 5 to 10°F higher. There is no apparent effect of day length or temperature on flower formation and development.

Root rot of callas is common and may be caused by *Phytophthora* (dry rot) or *Erwinia* (soft rot). The rhizomes must be carefully inspected before planting, and any rotten spots completely cut out. The cleaned rhizomes should be soaked in 2 percent formaldehyde solution. Soil and containers must be thoroughly steamed before use. Red spiders, thrips, and mealy bugs are occasional pests on callas, but they are controlled by normal measures.

CARNATION (*Dianthus caryophyllus—Caryophyllaceae*)

The carnation is a native of southern Europe. Theophrastus wrote about carnations in his *History of Plants,* but it was not until the sixteenth century that carnations were widely used. The perpetual flowering type used for commercial purposes at the present time was originated by Dalmais in France in 1840 and introduced into the United States in 1856.

Carnations are propagated by means of rooted stem tip cuttings, and the main propagation is scheduled for the spring so that the young plants will be planted during the good growing conditions of spring and early summer. The plants are usually pinched once or more to produce a branched plant, and the time of planting and the method and amount of pinching determine when flower production will start. The carnation stem terminates with a flower after approximately 18 sets of leaves have been formed regardless of the day length, but growth and flower development are more rapid in high-light and high-temperature conditions.

Carnation plants could be cropped indefinitely, and in some instances the plants are grown for 2 or 3 years with continuous production of flowers. Such a system of management saves replanting costs and may increase production, but the quality of the flowers is not always as good with the older plants. In a 1-year rotation, the plants are benched in the spring; and flower production starts in the fall and continues until the plants are removed the following spring.

Standard carnation varieties produce large flowers of about 3 inches in diameter, and only a lone, terminal flower is allowed to develop per stem. The lateral flower buds should be removed (disbudded) as soon as they are large enough to be handled conveniently. Carnation production is primarily in the large, standard varieties; however, some miniature or spray varieties are grown. These are smaller flowered varieties, and the lateral flower buds as well as the terminal flower are allowed to develop so that a spray of flowers is produced per stem. Often the terminal flower bud is removed so that several of the laterals will be in flower simultaneously.

Propagation. Success or failure of the carnation crop starts with the selection of cuttings. The bases for selection are productivity, flower qualities, habit of growth, quality of the shoot, stage of development of the shoot, and disease or pest infestation. The first three of these characteristics will be known

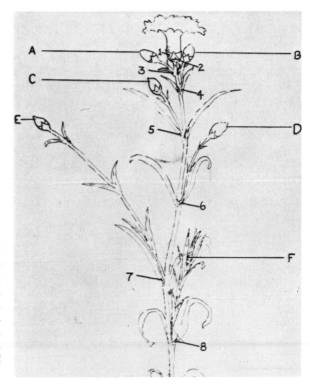

10-1. If standard carnation varieties were not disbudded, the lateral flower buds (*A–E*) would be at this stage of development when the terminal flower matured. These lateral shoots should be removed (disbudded) as soon as they can be handled. The shoot (*F*) at the eighth node should be vegetative. Shoots should not be disbudded below this point as succeeding flower crops develop rapidly from them. (*From Research Bulletin 786, Ohio Agricultural Experiment Station.*)

only if the plant from which the cuttings originate is observed carefully for several months and accurate records are maintained. This must be something more than merely taking cuttings from some plants of a given variety. Plants can and do change by mutation; and unless the growth and production of the plant are observed carefully, it will not be known whether good or unfavorable characteristics are being propagated.

The quality and the stage of development of the shoot are determined by the conditions that are provided for the stock plants and the management of them. The stem tip cutting must be of good diameter and have closely spaced leaves. The stock plants should be segregated, and they should be provided with the best growing conditions and care. The cutting must be in vegetative growth at the time that it is taken from the stock plant, and evidence of this is closely spaced leaves. The stock plants must be pinched and the cuttings harvested regularly when the shoots are long enough to make cuttings. If cuttings are made from long shoots, flower buds will have started to develop in the shoot tip. Such cuttings grow slowly and produce poor-quality plants.

If the stock plants are segregated, it is much easier to provide complete control of pests. Regular treatments will have to be made for the control of two-spotted mites, aphids, and possibly other pests.

There are several diseases of carnations, and most of the pathogens can be transmitted with the propagating stock. Virus, bacterial wilt, and Fusarium wilt pathogens may be present and growing within the stem tip without any external symptoms of the disease being evident. The presence of these pathogens can be determined by a detailed laboratory procedure known as culturing. Stock that is free of infestation is used for developing blocks of stock plants, and the stems that show evidence of disease during culturing are discarded. This procedure is known as culture-indexing. The presence of virus can be determined by the reaction of certain host plants to the sap or graft of the carnation being tested, but it is a long procedure. Virus in carnations can be eliminated by the use of heat therapy and meristem culture. Virus-free stock must be renewed frequently because reinfestation is possible by means of aphids or handling the plants.

Rhizoctonia is a soil-borne fungus that is usually not transmitted by the cutting if normal sanitary measures are used. Spores of the Fusarium stem rot organism, however, can be carried very easily on the surface of the carnation cutting, but the presence of neither of these pathogens could be expected to be determined by culturing. The elimination of Rhizoctonia and Fusarium stem rot pathogens from carnation stem tips being propagated is accomplished by the practice of strict sanitation and the use of some chemical controls. Terraclor is a specific control for *Rhizoctonia*, and captan is the best chemical to use for Fusarium stem rot.

The selection and production of high-quality carnation cuttings requires a degree of specialization that is not possible for the grower whose primary business is the production of carnation flowers. If he feels that he needs to propagate cuttings rather than buy them all from the specialist, he should at least obtain all his propagation stock from a specialist who can assure him that the stock has been carefully selected for best production and quality characteristics and that it is disease-free. It is then possible for the carnation grower to produce good cuttings with proper management and good growing conditions.

It is possible to set the time of propagation quite accurately if it is known when the carnations are going to be benched. The propagation date should be determined so that just the right amount of time is allowed for growing the young plants. The length of time between propagation and benching will depend on how the young plants are handled.

Plants that are placed in 2½-inch pots will have to be transplanted in a month for the best growth. If a 3-inch band is used, the plants will need moving within 2 months. For a June 1 benching the cuttings should be stuck in the propagation bench on March 1 if the young plants are going to be placed in 3-inch bands or on April 1 if 2½-inch pots will be used. If it is necessary to propagate earlier or to bench the plants later, some provision must be made for transplanting to larger containers.

When direct benching is practiced, the cuttings should be stuck 3 to 4 weeks before the benching time. Six-inch stem tips should be removed from the stock plants by breaking them sideways by hand. There is some danger of disease transmission if a knife is used. There is no need to break them from the plant at the node or the internode as either type of cutting roots very well.

If the cuttings cannot be stuck at once, they should be placed in refrigerated storage or under a moist cloth. If it is desired to hold them for several days or weeks, the cuttings will remain in good condition for periods of 2 to 3 months and possibly longer if the temperature is maintained between 31 and 33°F and they are protected from drying. This can be accomplished in several ways. A waterproof container is used so that some moisture will be retained around the cuttings, and usually some moisture should be introduced into the container. A layer of moist sphagnum in the bottom will suffice. Air movement in the container should be restricted so that drying does not take place; however, if a tight seal is used, air exchange is prevented, and the plant deteriorates rather rapidly. Regardless of the procedure that is followed, the cuttings should be inspected at weekly intervals to determine their condition.

Cuttings that are taken during the best growing season store the most satisfactorily. Usually the late winter and early spring cuttings are not suitable for long-term storage.

The storage of unrooted cuttings is very useful for building a supply of cuttings from a limited number of stock plants. The cuttings can be propagated in one lot, and that will allow the young plants to be started at one time, which assures better handling of cuttings and young plants.

The bottom pair of leaves may be removed to facilitate sticking, but other than that, no trimming is needed. Leaf trimming has been practiced in the past, but trimmed cuttings invariably root more slowly.

Carnation cuttings root in 3 to 4 weeks if they are placed in favorable environment, and it is not necessary to use growth substances. The propagation bench must provide for excellent drainage, and supplementary heat is usually needed so that the medium can be maintained at a higher temperature than the air. If the medium temperature is 60 to 65°F and the air temperature 50 to 55°F, the cuttings root readily.

Sharp silica sand and horticultural-grade perlite are excellent media. Other materials may be used very satisfactorily, depending on the requirements of the propagator. In very free-draining sand the cuttings should be watered thoroughly each morning. It may not be necessary to provide any means for adding moisture to the air; however, if the rooting is done during the high-temperature period of the year, it is helpful to mist the cuttings periodically during the day.

Whenever possible, intermittent mist should be provided for the propagation bench, and it should be controlled so that the leaves just remain wet. During warm weather and in good light, this may require about 5 seconds of mist every minute; during cooler and darker weather, a 5-second misting every 10 minutes may be sufficient.

The cuttings should not be covered directly, nor should they be placed in direct sunlight unless under mist. A removable muslin shade cloth that is placed a few feet above the cuttings is a good method for reducing the light intensity and at the same time allows adequate air movement. Maximum ventilation without direct drafts should be provided.

The cuttings should be removed from the propagation bench when the roots are about ½ inch long. If it is necessary to keep them in the bench for a longer period of time, they can be furnished a high-analysis complete fertilizer at the rate of 1 ounce per 2 gallons of water.

It is possible to store rooted cuttings for a few weeks in a refrigerator if the temperature can be carefully controlled. The procedure is essentially the same as that used for the storage of unrooted cuttings, but even in ideal conditions the rooted cuttings may not store well for more than 8 weeks. The best results are obtained with cuttings from the good growing periods of the year and under conditions of refrigeration where there is less than 1°F variation from the freezing point.

The manner in which the young plants are provided for in the early stages of growth is very important. Excellent results can be realized if the plants are placed in a large enough volume of soil, fertilized and watered regularly, and grown in the best light and temperature. This very often needs to be a studied program because the young carnation plants are competing with the various spring crops that are being finished. The crop that is being finished usually gets the attention.

An excellent job of growing the young plants can be done with any of the three methods, if they are properly handled. Direct planting is recommended as the method that requires the least amount of work for best results. Equally good results can be obtained with pots if the watering and fertilizing are handled carefully and the plants are not left in the small pots too long. Bands are usually easier to manage than pots.

Nurse-bed planting is a variation of direct planting. The rooted cuttings are planted in greenhouse benches in 3- or 4-inch squares. After about 2 months every other row is transplanted to another bench. This is an excellent method for starting carnation plants if the space is available. Another method is to plant the rooted cuttings approximately 3 by 3 inches apart in flats. Within 2½ months the plants should be benched, or they will become tall and leggy.

Regardless of the container, a good soil mixture is essential. Manure or peat should be incorporated at the rate of one part of the organic matter to three

10-2. Carnation plants may be started in the spring in 3-inch peat pots and then planted in the bench in early June. (*Jiffy Pot Co. of America photograph.*)

parts soil, and a 4-inch potful of superphosphate per wheelbarrow of soil should be added before the soil is steam-sterilized. The pots, benches, and any handling equipment should be steamed for control of soil-borne disease organisms. A greater amount of organic matter may have to be added to heavier soils.

After planting, the soil should be watered thoroughly and then allowed to dry somewhat between waterings. It is particularly important to space waterings properly when direct planting is used.

The fertilizer program should start as soon as active root growth is evident, which will be about 3 weeks after planting. A nitrogen and potash fertilizer should be furnished every 2 weeks until the plants are benched. Ammonium sulfate at 1 ounce per 2 gallons and potassium chloride at ½ ounce per 2 gallons of water can be used satisfactorily. If fertilizer can be supplied with each irrigation by means of an injector, nitrogen and potassium should be used at 200 ppm each.

Most growers now keep the carnation plants in the greenhouse at all times because there are many disadvantages to field culture. The latter is a laborious operation, and the control over disease and pests in the field is not satisfactory. Large plants can be produced outdoors, but the growth may be seriously checked when the plants are lifted and brought into the greenhouse. If planted in raised beds or benches in steamed soil, outside culture may be useful.

Planting, spacing, and supporting. Carnations should be planted as shallowly as possible to develop rapid root growth and give the young plants a faster start. There is also less possibility of infestation with the Rhizoctonia stem rot pathogen. The plants should be set so shallowly that quite a number of them topple at the first watering and need to be reset.

Plants should be spaced in the bench about 6 by 8 inches apart, or if only a single pinch is to be used, they may be spaced as closely as 6 by 6 inches. In some instances two rows of plants are planted together across the bench and the double rows are spaced about 12 inches apart. The advantages of this method of planting are that cutting of the flowers is facilitated, irrigation and fertilizer applications can be done more easily, there is improved airflow through the plants in fan and pad cooled houses, and possibly better light for the plants at the middle of the bench is provided.

Carnations should be supported so that the stems grow upright by using several layers of wire, or wire and string, grids. The first grid is placed about 6 inches above the soil, and the succeeding grids are gradually spaced farther apart until the top ones are about 12 inches apart. If wire and string grids are used, wire is strung the length of the bench between the plants, and string is laced across the bench beside each row of plants. As additional grids are added, upright columns are formed for the support of each plant. Welded wire fabric with 6- by 8-inch spacing may be used instead of wire and string grids.   If welded wire fabric is used, one or more of the grids are placed on the soil, and planting is done through them.   As the plants grow, the grids are raised to provide support.

Carnation plants weigh heavily on the support wires.   The wires must be stretched tightly the length of the bench and well anchored, and the grids must be supported about every 12 feet down the bench with stable metal or wooden supports.

Light and temperature.   The best growth of carnations is obtained in localities of high light intensity during the winter and cool temperatures during the summer.   Whenever possible, the carnation specialist should locate in an area that satisfies those conditions.   Regardless of the geographic location, it is important to construct the greenhouses so that the maximum amount of light can be utilized and the houses adequately ventilated.   Side ventilators should be provided if hot summer temperatures are normal for the area.   In moist areas of the country, fan and pad cooling for the summer is beneficial.

Excellent growth of carnations can be obtained at 50°F night temperature with 55 or 60°F daytime temperatures, depending on whether the day is cloudy or clear.   In some areas of the United States the glass never needs to be shaded. It is often necessary in other regions to provide some shade during June, July, and August so that the temperatures will be reduced for the best possible growth. Fan and pad cooling or misting is helpful in reducing the temperature and improving the quality of the stem and flowers.

Soil and fertilizer.   The most satisfactory soil is a loam of porous structure and high organic content.   Water percolates readily through such a soil, and aeration is good.   Carnation soils can be used for an indefinite period of time.   It is essential to add organic matter and to steam-sterilize the soil each time before the new plants are benched.   These practices ensure that the porous structure of the soil will be maintained and that soil-borne diseases and weeds will be eliminated.

The soil reaction should be maintained in the range of pH 6.0 to 7.0. Some experimental work has shown that the incidence of bacterial wilt was reduced in slightly alkaline soils.   Plant growth was not impaired, and the progress of the disease was slower at pH 7.0 as contrasted with pH 5.5.

The calcium in carnation soils should be maintained at the upper level of 200 ppm, which will usually require an application of calcium fertilizer before each planting.   If the pH needs to be raised, either hydrated lime or agricultural limestone should be used at the rate of 5 pounds per 100 square feet of soil; or gypsum is used at the same rate if the soil does not need to be made more alkaline.

There should be about 5 ppm phosphorus in carnation soils; and if the soil has been used before, additional phosphorus may not be needed. If the phosphorus supply is low, superphosphate should be added at the rate of 5 pounds per 100 square feet of soil before planting.

Nitrogen and potassium will need to be supplied regularly to the soil. The first application should be made as soon as the roots start to develop after planting, which should be with the first watering after planting. Dry fertilizer can be used on carnations, but liquid fertilizer is preferred as the plants are easily damaged by dry fertilizer that lodges on leaves or stems. Applying fertilizer by means of an injector with each irrigation is an excellent method of providing a uniform supply of nitrogen and potassium; or if fertilizer is applied periodically, the application should be made every 2 to 4 weeks. About 50 ppm nitrate nitrogen and 30 ppm potassium should be maintained in carnation soils.

Many soils are deficient in boron, and carnations are extremely sensitive to boron shortages. The symptoms of boron deficiency that are most apparent are malformations of buds and flowers, and short stems and excessive branching towards the tips of the stems. Boron may be applied to the soil with each irrigation through injection at the rate of ½ ounce of borax per 1,000 gallons of water, or it may be applied once a year at the rate of 1 ounce of borax per 100 square feet of soil. Greater amounts of borax should not be used, to avoid toxicity.

Moisture. Carnation soils should be thoroughly wetted when water is applied, but then the soil should be allowed to dry somewhat between waterings. This is particularly important in the early stages of growth. Subirrigation can be used successfully in the summer, but it is a questionable practice in the winter because the soil dries so slowly. Various nozzle or sprinkler systems may be used with carnations successfully.

Carnations can be grown in rather dry air; in fact, it has been considered that a humid atmosphere is detrimental. This belief was based primarily on the prevalence of rust disease in moist conditions, but rust is not the threat that it used to be when outdoor culture was practiced. Some care does need to be exercised, however, because of the stem rot diseases.

Air. Carnations should be grown in well-ventilated houses. Particularly if the house is not equipped with an air-cooling system, side ventilators as well as ridge ventilators are needed to provide maximum air movement and cooling during the summer.

During cold weather, when the greenhouse is closed much of the time, the carbon dioxide concentration in the daytime may fall below normal levels and limit photosynthesis. Maintaining a carbon dioxide concentration of 500 ppm or more by means of generators when it is cool enough outdoors to keep the greenhouse closed may give some increase in flower production and in the rate of growth and development. The degree of benefit from the addition of carbon dioxide is related to the suitability of other environmental conditions such as the amount of light, temperature, minerals, and moisture.

Continuous air movement provides uniform temperature, carbon dioxide, and humidity conditions throughout the house. Air-circulation fans supply positive, continuous air movement at all times; and they can be used to good advantage in the carnation house. Lower levels of carbon dioxide will be satisfactory when the air is circulated by fans since a constant supply to the leaf is assured.

Troubles. Splitting of the calyx is the most common problem with carnation flowers. Some varieties or selections split much more readily than others; hence the varieties that do not split excessively should be used. Apparently splitting is related to variable rates of growth caused primarily by temperature fluctuations or by changes from conditions unfavorable for good growth to those that are favorable due to management of fertility, moisture, or temperature.

Splitting is most common during the periods of the year when temperatures fluctuate rapidly and greatly, as in the fall and spring. Splitting can be aggravated at these times if the heating system is not being operated and the night temperatures drop lower than anticipated.

Various devices are used to prevent or repair calyx splitting, including rubber bands, ties, plastic collars, or pins that are placed on the calyx to hold it together. Their use is accepted in some markets without penalty, but in others the potential price is reduced.

Sleepiness is the condition in which the carnation petals cup upward. Many customers believe this indicates that the cut flowers have been stored too long before being marketed, but it is actually a symptom produced by ethylene gas that may affect either fresh or old flowers. Some of the most common sources of ethylene are fruits, vegetables, or greens that are stored in refrigerators, and decaying plant material in the vicinity of the carnation flowers. It is possible that some other gases or products of combustion may cause sleepiness in carnations.

Weak stems are common during the winter months. This is aggravated by reduced light because of dirty glass, excessive use of nitrogen fertilizer, and constantly wet soil. Cooler temperatures and a greater amount of light are aids in producing stronger stems in the winter.

Grassy growth and excessive development of side shoots is caused by a mutation, and cuttings should not be made from such plants because this characteristic will be reproduced in the new plants.

Diseases. Carnations are plagued by some very serious diseases, but the situation is much better if field culture is not practiced. When carnations were taken to the field, they invariably contracted rust, *Alternaria,* and one or more of the wilt diseases, to say nothing of various kinds of insect pests. Keeping the plants in the greenhouse for the entire period of growth has eliminated the source of infestation in many instances. The soil, benches, and handling equipment can be sterilized in the greenhouse to ensure that the plants will be placed in a disease-free environment.

The successful carnation disease-control program is based on selection of disease-free cuttings and thorough steam sterilization of sand, soil, benches, pots, and any equipment that is to be used around the plants. Proper ventilation and heating practices are helpful in the control of some of the diseases, and there are fungicides that can be used in some cases when the other measures of control fall short.

Rhizoctonia stem rot affects the plant at the soil line. The rotting of the tissues begins at the surface of the stem and proceeds to the inner portions. It may be just a week or two from infection until the plant is dead. *Rhizoctonia* develops rapidly in a constantly moist environment and at lower temperatures than bacterial wilt. The organism is soil-borne, and very often a careful sterilization program will eliminate the source of trouble. Planting shallowly and allowing the soil to dry somewhat between waterings will help keep this organism in check. If an infestation does occur, a soil drench of the immediate area with a suitable fungicide such as Morsodren or Terraclor is recommended.

Fusarium wilt (*Fusarium oxysporum f. dianthi*) is a fungus which grows in the water-conducting tissues of the stem. The plants may be infected for several months before definite wilt symptoms or death occurs. The progress of the disease is more rapid in hot weather than during the winter. When the wilting is first noticed, the roots usually show no evidence of rot. Since the organism grows in the inner tissues, it is possible to take cuttings that are infected but may not exhibit characteristic disease symptoms. A source of disease-free cuttings is essential, as well as thorough sterilization of soil, benches, and equipment. There are no effective chemical controls.

Botrytis blight is often serious on soft or white-flowered varieties. Portions of the petals appear water-soaked, and later a gray mold develops. The fungus thrives at a wide variety of temperatures but grows best in a humid atmosphere. Keeping the ventilators open with some heat to circulate the air is effective.

Bacterial wilt (*Pseudomonas caryophylli*) is a bacterial organism that thrives only at high temperatures. Very little trouble with bacterial wilt should be experienced in localities where night temperatures are below 75°F. This bacterium grows in the stem and produces symptoms that are quite similar to the Fusarium wilt symptoms; however, the roots are invariably rotted, and a sticky ooze is evident in stem and roots. The means of control are the same as for Fusarium wilt.

Fusarium root and stem rot (*Fusarium roseum*) is a fungus disease usually prevalent in the propagation bench or among the young plants. The rot starts on the surface and progresses inward. The organism may be introduced on the surface of cuttings, or it may be soil-borne. A stem rot or a root rot or both may occur. Careful sterilization and close attention to watering practices are the best means of control.

Rust is no longer a serious disease problem if the plants are kept constantly under glass. The primary source of infection in older methods of culture came from growing the plants in the field. Rust spores may not germinate unless there is free water on the plant.

Alternaria leaf spot and branch rot (*Alternaria dianthi*) have been eliminated along with rust because the plants are no longer field-grown. The same means of control are used.

Mosaic, streak, and yellows are virus diseases of carnations which have been so serious that some susceptible varieties have virtually been eliminated because of them. Earlier this had been ascribed to "running out" of the variety. Unfortunately, very often the symptoms of the disease are not noticeable at the time cuttings are taken. Thus it is very easy to propagate the disease in the new plantings. To eliminate the virus diseases, the stock plants must be closely observed over a long period of time to assure that the cuttings are not diseased.

Meristem culture is a procedure that may be used to produce carnation plants that are free of virus. It is a detailed laboratory technique in which the excised tip of the plant (meristem) is grown in aseptic conditions on nutrient media. The stem tips are taken from plants that have been grown at high temperature, and they are virus-free since the growth of the stem tip at high temtures is faster than the development of virus into the new tissues.

Pests. Red spider is the most serious pest on carnations. In winter the cool temperatures at which the plants are grown keep the population in check, but in spring with warmer weather they multiply rapidly. This pest is very serious in summer and fall when the temperatures are high. Young plants can be so heavily infested that the leaves dry up and the plants will be worthless.

Aphids disfigure the young growth and may cripple it severely.

Thrips cause streaks in the flowers, and generally they are most noticeable in periods of warmer weather. Affected flowers are unmarketable. Screening the side vents or covering the vents with cloth soaked or sprayed with dieldrin is useful in reducing the population. Regular spraying or dusting is essential.

Pinching. Carnation plants can vary considerably in rate of growth during the early stages. They should be pinched on the basis of stage of growth. Some plants will probably be at the right stage 4 weeks after planting, and others not until later. It may take 2 or 3 weeks to complete the first pinch on a block of plants.

When possible, the plants should be allowed to grow until the side shoots have cleared the leaves. That will often mean that the stem is in bud by the time the first pinch is made. Whenever possible, three cleared shoots and about

10-3. Position of pinch to be made before August 1 on carnation stems. In the early stages of growth, carnation stems are compact with leaves closely spaced and very little stem visible between sets of leaves (left). The shoots should be allowed to develop until internodal stem is visible, and the pinch should be made as indicated above six or more sets of leaves (right).

five sets of leaves should remain on the plant below the pinch. With the Sim varieties, that makes the pinch roughly 6 inches above the soil level. It is particularly important to pinch high on the Sim varieties during hot weather; harder pinching very often produces only one shoot per pinch.

Multiple pinching is the cultural method that is most commonly employed. It is sometimes referred to as double pinching or pinch and a half. The attempt is made to pinch the plants in such a manner that the resulting flower crops are produced during the periods of the year when carnations are in greatest demand. The carnation is used the year-round, but the demand is usually greatest from December through June. It takes about 5 months for a flower to develop from a stem pinched in mid-July. Stems pinched before then produce flowers in a shorter period of time, and the stems that are pinched later take a longer time to produce flowers. If the second pinches are going to be made in July, it is necessary to make the first pinch about May 1.

Not all the shoots grow at the same rate. When the first pinch is made the first of May, some shoots will develop sufficiently for a June pinch, and others in July and August or later. The top shoots develop most rapidly and usually receive the second pinch. The lower shoots are slower and very often are not pinched. The shoots that arise from the June pinches will start to flower in September.

A schedule that has given excellent results in the Middle West is as follows: stick the cuttings March 1, place the rooted cuttings in 3-inch bands March 25, make the first pinch May 1, bench the plants on 7- or 8-inch squares in early June, and start pinching the most advanced shoots in June. Pinching should continue until late July. After that time the shoots that are in flower bud can be pinched periodically. If the latter type of pinching is continued until September

10-4. Position of pinch to be made after August 1 on carnation stems. Pinching of carnation stems should be continued until early September, but from August 1 until that time only the stems which have started to form flower buds (right) should be pinched. This will eliminate early fall flowers but will increase flower production in January, February, and March. During this period, vegetative stems (left) should not be pinched as they will form flowers which mature from November on.

15, the very early fall flowers will be eliminated, but the late winter and early spring production will be increased, which provides for steady production from late November on.

This schedule was developed particularly to allow for benching the plants after the spring rush. It is especially difficult for the retail grower to bench carnation plants before June 1. Some adjustments can be made in the schedule, but later propagation and benching are usually not satisfactory because the last pinches then are made later and the flower production does not start until later in the winter.

Excellent plant growth can be expected from March through May because of the favorable light and temperature conditions at that time. If the rotation of crops can be worked out, it is best to bench the plants as soon as possible in the spring. The time of propagation is simply placed earlier to provide the rooted cuttings for the spring benching.

Several attempts have been made in many areas in recent years to control carnation cropping more accurately. It was hoped that the use of a single pinch would be more successful in the maximum production of flowers for any week of the year and that the total flower production from the pinch would be cut off in the shortest period of time. It now appears that the single pinch may have a few special applications of merit but is of limited worth as a general program.

The basic single-pinch schedule provides for sticking the cuttings 1 month before benching. The rooted cuttings are benched on 6- or 7-inch squares, and the plants are pinched about 1 month after benching. For December flowering the cuttings would be stuck about May 15, benched June 15, and given the single pinch July 15. Flower production from that pinch would peak in December, but with several varieties the total production would be spread over the period from October to March. For Ohio conditions, the return production from that peak December production would not occur until June and July. That is usually considered a doubtful market period for heavy production. The schedule can be shifted in either direction, but for Ohio, if one crop is produced during a good market, the return crop comes at a time of a poor market, and vice versa.

In most cases the first crop would be cut over such a long period of time that it would not be advantageous to cut the first crop and then discard the plants. There would be advantages in any short-term carnation schedule that would supplement production for a specific time of the year. For instance, particularly large quantities of red carnations can be used for Christmas and again for Mother's Day. The use of the single-pinch method for December production has been discussed. It could be used to supplement May production by planting the rooted cuttings about August 15 and pinching September 15. The total production from that pinch would be cut in a period of about 2 months, but the plants would have occupied bench space for 9 or 10 months.

Some use has been made of the no-pinch method for a short-term crop. The rooted cuttings are benched on 4-inch squares in January and not pinched for flower production in May. The plants can then be either transplanted to 8-inch squares for further growth or discarded.

The no-pinch system appears to have some possibilities, but it is by no means foolproof. Excellent cutting selection needs to be exercised. It is important that shoots be selected that are at the same stage of development. Random selection of cuttings will not be satisfactory. Cuttings made from long stems may have initiated flower buds already, and they will flower on short stems. Those that are taken from shorter stems usually are entirely vegetative and will form flowers on longer stems. Uneven flowering is prevented if the plants are pinched, but when the no-pinch method is employed, that equalizing effect does not exist.

An August 15 planting appears to be about right to supplement Christmas production. That is a short-term crop—about 4 months—but it does require planting during very hot weather. The young plants will need more careful handling than usual. Summer propagation of cuttings is a problem, but it is possible to use stored rooted cuttings. Preliminary findings indicate that at least at some periods of the year the stored rooted cuttings develop flowers more rapidly than those that have not been stored, which may be of minor concern with pinched plants, but may cause flowering on stems that are too short in the no-pinch method of production.

Flower development in carnations occurs at a faster rate during periods of high light intensity and high temperatures. Apparently the first stages of flower formation take place at about the same rate regardless of light and temperature conditions, but from that point on, the rate of development is dependent on weather conditions. In the Middle West this difference in rate of development may mean that the shoot that develops from a pinch will flower in 90 to 250 days, depending on the time of year the shoot is pinched.   Rapid flower development in periods of high light intensity accounts for the early crop in the fall when abnormally bright weather is experienced, and the slowdown in flower production during the dull days of winter is well known.

There is relatively little that can be done to modify the weather conditions sufficiently to cause a change in the rate of flower development.   However, adjustment can be made in the time of pinching so that the right amount of time is planned between pinching and flowering for that specific time of the year. For the Middle West it can be expected in general that about 90 days is required for flowering from a May pinch and about 150 days from an October 1 pinch. In areas where the summer light and temperatures are not quite as intense, the rate of flower development will not be as rapid at that time of the year.   Where the winter light intensity is greater, flower development will be more rapid than it is in the Middle West.

It is impossible to talk sensibly about the effect of pinching and weather conditions and their relationship to time of flower production unless there is a clear understanding of the method of pinching.   Flower production will be much slower on stems that are pinched to two leaves than on stems that are pinched higher, so that five or six sets of leaves are left below the pinch.   As described earlier, five or six sets of leaves should be left on the stem below the first pinch. The succeeding pinches should be made in much the same manner.   This is particularly important when the pinching is done during hot weather.   The plants will be built up more rapidly by this method of pinching, and flower development will be faster.

Rotations.   Various rotations of carnations can be used depending on the requirements for flower production.   If carnations are followed by carnations in one-year crops, the rooted cuttings or young plants are usually benched in late May or early June.   Flower production then starts in the fall and continues until the plants are removed in the next spring or early summer.   This rotation produces good-quality flowers during the time of the year when they are usually in greatest demand, but there is no flower production during the summer, although in most areas there is a continuing market for flowers during that period and carnations could be sold at a favorable price if they were produced.

There was a time when it was physically impossible to continue to grow carnations throughout the summer because of the excessive disease and pest infestations during the hot weather.   More careful selection of stock has virtually eliminated the disease problem, and the better miticides that are available control two-spotted mite effectively.   In addition, it is possible to grow good-quality flowers in the summer in the cooler temperatures of houses that are equipped with fan and pad or mist cooling systems.

A two-year rotation can be used in which half the area is planted each year, and this provides for flower production from the entire area from fall through spring and from half the area during the summer. It is possible also to have a portion of the area on a one-year rotation and the rest of the area on a two-year rotation. The amount of area on a two-year rotation would be determined by the quantity of flower production desired during the summer. Two-year crops save the cost of new plants and planting costs; but the plants may be tall and unmanageable, the quality of the flowers may not be as good, and it may not be possible to time crops as well as with one-year crops.

Carnations can be rotated with other crops, and snapdragons can be used best for this purpose. Whatever production area is needed for flowers in the summer is left in production until fall, and then it is followed by either one or two crops of snapdragons before being planted with carnations again. The benches vacated by carnations in late August could produce snapdragon crops in December and early May and be available for planting with carnations in late May. The carnation-snapdragon rotation works well; and if some snapdragons can be sold profitably in the winter, this may be the best way to produce good-quality carnations and still have summertime production. Rotations with Chrysanthemums are possible if the problem of providing 50°F temperature for carnations and 60°F temperature for the Chrysanthemums can be resolved.

Any rotation that is used must provide the right distribution of colors at the various times of the year. White and pink carnations are in greatest demand, and in most areas the year-round demand for all colors is quite uniform, with the exception of red. The market for red carnations is best at Christmas, Valentine's Day, and Mother's Day.

Cutting the flowers. Carnations should be cut when they are at the right stage of development, which can best be judged by observing the center of the flower. The center petals should be expanded so that the flower forms a hemisphere. Generally it is better to cut flowers tighter in the summer than during the winter. The flowers are usually cut from a given area two or three times a week.

It is best to use a knife in making the cut. Breaking the stem off very often injures the shoot developing at that node. The height at which the stem is cut is important and should be based on the effect that it has on the plant rather than on the length of stem on the cut flower. Cutting long stems in the fall is poor economy. The fall cut needs to be made high enough so that the plant is built up, and the return crop from a high cut will be considerably faster. Judicious cutting in September and October will increase the April and May crop.

If the plants are going to be discarded in July, the flowers may be cut with as long stems as desired after January. Stems from which flowers are cut at that time of the year do not have time to develop a return crop of flowers before the plants are discarded.

The proper height of cutting can best be described as in the area where the leaves are well spaced. If the cut is made down too far, it will be where there

10-5. Position for cutting carnation flowers. For the most rapid return crop and greatest yield, the flower stem should be cut as indicated above 2 or more lateral shoots.

is very little distance between leaves. It is usually advisable to cut above two side shoots whenever it can be done.

Varieties. Changes in the varieties that are planted take place rather rapidly. If the new introductions have desirable characteristics, they receive very wide acceptance very readily. In spite of this, it appears that the variety William Sim and its host of mutants will be very popular for several years. This group of carnations has many fine characteristics, and about their only fault is willowy stems in areas of poor light.

Another important carnation "family" arose through the variety Sydney Littlefied. The Littlefield carnations are not as widely planted as the Sim, and less color selection is available in the sports. The Littlefield varieties are large-flowered and strong-stemmed but are shorter growers than the Sim and less productive. A night temperature of 55°F increases production somewhat without materially affecting the quality of the Littlefield group.

New carnation varieties arise quite commonly from mutations, or spontaneous changes that take place in existing varieties. The result may or may not be desirable. If the mutant has some good characteristics, that portion of the plant which has changed can be propagated vegetatively by stem tip cuttings, and thus the new variety will be perpetuated and increased. The most notable example of mutations in recent years has been with the variety William Sim.

Mutation should not be confused with hybridization. New varieties can originate from either process, but hybridization is usually a planned act in which plants are crossed, seed is formed, and the new variety is obtained. The actual operation of crossing may be done in the winter or spring. Both the pistillate and staminate flowers should be bagged. The receptivity of the stigma is readily observed by the spreading of the two parts above the petals of the flower and by their becoming distinctly pubescent. With an abundance of sun the seed forms quickly and may be sown as soon as it is ripe. Germination takes place rapidly, so that the plants obtained from crosses in winter and early spring are as large as the plants produced from cuttings of that season. At least a 2-year trial is necessary to observe the proper qualities for dissemination.

There is some interest in producing various shades or tints of flower colors, and this is more common in some areas of the country than in others. It is possible to get various exotic or "decorator" tints in white carnations by placing the flower stems in dye solutions. The dye is absorbed by the stems and transmitted to the flower. It is possible to use many different dyes, but it is best to develop the methods individually that seem to be of most interest for the particular market. The same tint may be considered exotic by some and atrocious by others. The various dye manufacturers may use different trade or common names for the same dye, and it is best to refer to the dye by its generic name or color index number. A few of the dyes that can be used satisfactorily are:

For flower tint	Dye generic name	Dye index number
Pink	Red 1	18050
Pink	Red 33	17200
Orange	Orange 10	16230
Blue	Blue 9	42090
Yellow	Yellow 23	19140
Yellow	Yellow 34	18890
Green	Green 3	42085
Green	Green 5	42095

These dyes can be used at the rate of about 2 ounces to 1 gallon of water, and the flowers should be somewhat wilted when the stems are placed in the solution so that the dye will be absorbed more rapidly. Most uniform tint results from the immersion of the stems in the dye solution for about 12 hours. The use of a small amount of wetting agent such as Multifilm X-77 in the dye solution will increase the absorption of the dye.   Metal containers should not be used as there may be a reaction between some dyes and the metal.

Storage.   Carnation flowers can be kept in good condition for a longer time if they are well grown.   Flowers that are produced in adverse conditions do not keep as well.   After cutting, the flowers should be kept in cool temperatures as this greatly increases the useful life of the cut flower.   If the flowers are to be marketed promptly, they should be placed in vases of water as soon as possible after cutting and held at a uniform 40°F temperature until they are in the hands of the consumer.   Preservative solutions used whenever the stems are placed in water—at the greenhouse, the wholesale store, the retail shop, or in the consumer's home—will provide longer life.   It will be necessary for the flowers to be in warmer temperatures during grading, shipping, and selling, but this should be only for brief periods.

Immediately after cutting, if there is to be a delay in marketing, the flowers should be placed in a 31 to 33°F temperature in closed containers that do not absorb moisture but do allow the transfer of some air.   The stems are not placed in water before or during this storage period, and the flowers may be held in good condition up to 4 weeks.   When the flowers are removed from this storage, the stems should be recut and they should be placed in vases of a warm (80 to 90°F) preservative solution in an air temperature of 40°F.

Ethylene gas causes carnation flowers to look sleepy and age rapidly. The common sources of ethylene in storages are fruits, vegetables, some greens, and diseased or decaying organic matter.   Very small quantities of ethylene can cause a large amount of damage to carnation flowers, and care must be taken to see that the storage is clean and does not contain items that generate ethylene. Carbon dioxide generators that are not operating properly can produce ethylene or other toxic gases.

Marketing.   Carnations are usually packaged 25 flowers per bunch.   The standard grades for carnations (not including miniature types), as adopted by the Society of American Florists and the American Carnation Society, are:

MEASUREMENT STANDARDS

	BLUE GRADE	RED GRADE	GREEN GRADE	WHITE GRADE
Minimum flower diameter	2¾ in.	2¼ in.	No	No
Length overall	22 in. up	22 to 17 in.	17 to 10 in.	Any
Strength *	10 to 2	10 to 2	Unrestricted	

* The flower head will not bend lower than the ten or two on a clock if the base of the stem is held upright at six o'clock.

---

1. Bright, clean, and not badly wilted flowers and leaves.
2. Fairly tight.   Petals near center of flower are tight and unopened.
3. Symmetrical.   Flowers of shape characteristic of the variety.
4. No split calyx or mended splits except in white grade.
5. No buds or suckers.
6. No decay or damage.
7. Straight stems of normal growth and not more than slightly curved or crooked.

Carnations are sold by various methods—from retail greenhouses directly to the consumer, from wholesale greenhouses directly to flower shops, and from greenhouses through wholesale commission stores to flower shops.   Regardless of the method of selling, some sales efforts are required, and there are selling costs involved.   The average selling costs are 20 to 25 percent of the selling price.

Costs of production vary with the production methods that are used and the section of the country, but the total cost of production of carnations may be about $2 per square foot of bench space per year.   This includes administrative costs but not selling costs.   If 25 flowers per square foot of bench space were sold per year at a 10-cent average each and with a selling cost of 20 percent, the net return to the grower would equal the cost of production.

Carnations are used daily the year-round, but they are in greater demand for Christmas, Valentine's Day, Easter, and Mother's Day.   The price fluctuates with the market demand, and the holiday price often is about twice as high as it is at other times.

The American Carnation Society produces some promotional materials that are an aid in marketing flowers, and also represents the carnation producers in legislative and public relations matters.   Some special area groups are active in the promotion and public relations affecting the sales of carnations.   These groups are located in the areas of high carnation production such as New England, Denver, and California.

CHRYSANTHEMUM (*Chrysanthemum morifolium—Compositae*)

The *Chrysanthemum* is commonly supposed to be a native of Japan and serves to the present day as the national flower of that country.   However, according to Chinese history, the flower was cultivated in China more than 2,000 years ago, while the first available record of its use in Japan dates back to A.D. 1186, when the swords of the reigning Mikados were decorated with designs of the flower.

The earliest record of the introduction of the *Chrysanthemum* into Europe relates to its cultivation in Holland by a merchant of Danzig, Jacob Breynius.   In

1688 he described two types under the name of *Matricaria japonica* in red, white, purple, yellow, flesh, and crimson tints.

No reference to the cultivation of the *Chrysanthemum* in France is to be found before 1789, when M. Blanchard, a merchant of Marseilles, brought home three varieties from China, one white, one violet, and one purple, of which the last survived. In 1827 M. Bernet found perfectly matured seeds, and from these new varieties were obtained. This is the first record of successful production of seed, although many English and French gardeners made ineffectual efforts previous to that time.

John Salter gave a great impetus to the cultivation of the flower when he established a nursery at Versailles in 1838. He obtained a complete collection of the best kinds in France and Europe and began to raise seedlings, the most noted of which were Anne Salter, Marie, King of Crimson, and Queen of England.

In 1843 Robert Fortune was sent to China by the Royal Horticultural Society of London in search of rare plants. On his return in 1846 he brought back, among other curiosities, two small-flowered Chrysanthemums which were known as the Chusan Daisy and the Chinese *C. minimum*.

The importation of Japanese Chrysanthemums to England dates back to 1862, when Fortune introduced several varieties, some of which were spotted and striped, others of fantastic forms called Dragons, and one a beautifully marked white flower having the appearance of a pink rather than a *Chrysanthemum*. Others among them had petals like long thick hairs, red in color but tipped with yellow. Still others resembled the *Camellia* and vied with it in great size and brilliant coloring. At the same time the Japanese work *Phonsan Zowfu* pictured a considerable variety of forms, among them a narrow-petaled kind known as *C. striatum* and a single with small pink rays which may have been the wild form of *C. morifolium.*

The development of the *Chrysanthemum* before its introduction into England is not recorded. Hemsley stated in 1889 that "it is impossible to determine the parentage" of some of the double Chrysanthemums, and it is highly probable that some of them are hybrids of *C. indicum*, the small yellow, and *C. morifolium*. The same may be said of some of the early figures of double varieties of Chrysanthemums, which authors have identified with one or the other of the two wild species. The slender Chusan Daisy, the parent of all the pompons, for example, is probably of mixed origin, though it may be pure *C. indicum*. The true *C. indicum* is found in its wild state from Hong Kong to Peiping, the ray and disk flowers both being yellow. This species is not a native of India, and therefore Linnaeus' specification is inappropriate. It is a perennial shrubby plant, erect and rigid, growing to a height of 2 to 3 feet, with thin, flaccid, pinnately parted and acute-toothed leaves. The flowers are yellow. The rays are shorter than the diameter of the disk.

C. morifolium is found in Luchu Archipelago and the Chinese central province of Hupeh.   It is more robust than *C. indicum,* the leaves are thicker and tomentose, and the ray flowers are of a different color from the disk flowers.   The gracilis variety of *C. morifolium* is known only from the mountains near Peiping, from southern Manchuria, and from Japan.   The plants vary in color, having lilac, rose, and deep-rose ray flowers.   The Japanese specimens differ from the Chinese in having decidedly hairy leaves.

The early history of the cultivation of the *Chrysanthemum* in the United States is not available.   Doubtless it was introduced in America soon after its development in England in 1795, because the florists of that period were active in obtaining novelties from their Eastern correspondents.   It appears that the culti-vated *Chrysanthemum* was introduced into the United States much earlier than is ordinarily supposed.   By the time the Massachusetts Horticultural Society was incorporated in 1829, the interest in this flower had increased considerably. There were certainly 17 or 18 known varieties recognized.   From this time on, interest in the *Chrysanthemum* rapidly developed.

It was not until after the middle of the last century that the *Chrysanthe-mum* began to be regarded as a greenhouse plant.   Previous to that time it had been grown almost exclusively as a garden flower in regions where the fall season was favorable for its development.

Beginning with 1889, *Chrysanthemum* development in this country cen-tered about Elmer D. Smith, who introduced his first seedlings at an exhibit in Indianapolis in the fall of 1889.   The varieties shown were medium-sized, in-curved, and quite similar to those now grown as disbudded pompons.   In all, Smith originated, named, and disseminated over 500 varieties, many of which have stood the test of years and are still looked upon with favor.

Smith was followed by several hybridists who produced varieties of commercial value, and many new varieties are introduced each year.   The busi-ness of developing new Chrysanthemum varieties, producing disease-free stock, and selling rooted cuttings is one of the largest phases of the flower industry. Yoder Brothers, Inc., and later other organizations have been increasingly active in this field since the early 1940s.

There are many shapes, sizes, and colors of Chrysanthemum flowers, and they have excellent keeping qualities.   The Chrysanthemum cut flower is pro-duced in great quantities throughout the country for the daily market, but there is usually no increased demand for holidays.   The production of year-round Chrysanthemums is made possible by supplying artificially long or short days as needed for the growth and flowering of this plant.   The development of the practical application of daylight to Chrysanthemums was made by Laurie and his co-workers in 1930.

Chrysanthemums are propagated by means of stem tip cuttings.   The rooted cuttings are planted and grown in long days until the stem is of the proper length, and then short days are provided until the plant flowers.   After the flower

10-6. The use of black shade cloth to provide short days in the first attempt to flower Chrysanthemums in late summer at The Ohio State University, 1929 to 1932.

is cut, the plant is removed, the soil is reworked, and a new crop of rooted cuttings is planted for the next crop of flowers. Depending on how they are handled, approximately three crops of flowers can be produced per area per year.

Flower types.   The *Chrysanthemum* is actually an inflorescence of florets on a head.   Some of the florets which have distinct petals are known as ray florets; they are pistillate or contain only female flower parts.   The florets with extremely short petals are called disk florets, and they contain both male and female flower parts.   The flowers are classified by the kind and arrangement of florets.   Singles have one or more outer rows of ray florets with disk florets at the center, in a daisy-type arrangement.

Anemones have the same floret arrangement as singles, but the petals of the center florets are more developed, showing their tubular shape and forming a cushion.

Pompons have ray florets over the entire flower.   The disk florets are hidden by the ray florets, which form a formal, globular, or ball-shaped flower.

Decoratives have a floret arrangement that is similar to pompons, but the petals of the outer ray florets are longer than the inner ones, giving the flower a flatter appearance.

Incurved types are larger flowered varieties that have a floret arrangement somewhat similar to that of pompons.   The long petals of the ray florets curve upward and inward, forming a large, globular flower.

Reflexed types also have ray florets with long petals, but the outer florets reflex downward forming a less formal flower.

Spiders have tubular ray florets, and the outer florets are often much

10-7. Types of Chrysanthemum flowers.   Left to right from the top: incurved, spider, pompon, decorative, single, anemone.   (*Yoder Bros., Inc., photograph.*)

longer than the ones in the center.   In some varieties the tubes are hooked at the ends.

Fujis are somewhat similar in appearance to spiders, but the tubular ray florets are straight tubes and not hooked on the ends.   The center ray florets are approximately the same length as the outer florets, giving the fuji a brushlike appearance.

Classification of Chrysanthemum crops.   Chrysanthemums are classed also as standards, sprays, or disbuds by the type of growth or the method by which they are handled.   Standards are large flowers produced with one flower to a stem (all the lateral flower buds are removed or disbudded).   Incurved and reflexed flowers and to a limited extent spiders and fujis are used for standard production.   Standards may be grown as either single-stem or pinched crops; if they are pinched, the plants usually are pruned to only two stems per plant, as the goal is large flowers.   It is the large, incurved varieties that are produced in greatest quantity, with flowers from 4 to 6 inches in diameter and stems about 30 inches long.   Standards are produced the year-round in many northern and western greenhouses and on a limited basis outdoors in Florida.

Sprays are smaller flowered varieties that are produced with many flowers or a spray of flowers per stem; the lateral flower buds are not removed.   Several different flower types are grown as sprays, and the pompon type is the most common.   In some areas of the country the term pompon or pom is used interchangeably with or instead of the term sprays.   Single, decorative, and anemone flower types are all used as sprays, and they are more commonly grown as pinched crops with either two or three stems per plant.   Sprays are produced in some of the northern and western greenhouses the year-round, and they are grown outdoors from fall through spring on a large scale in Florida.   In other areas of the country, sprays may be grown outdoors or under cloth during the time of the year when temperatures are favorable for good growth.   Sprays are grown with about 30-inch stems and of medium weight, so that four to six stems may make a 9-ounce bunch.

Disbuds are grown with one flower per stem in the same manner as standards, but usually the flower is a size smaller and the stem shorter.   The smaller size may be due to the variety of *Chrysanthemum* that is used or to the method of growing.   The large-flowered types—incurved, reflexed, spider, and fuji—may be used for disbuds as well as some of the small-flowered types.   Some decoratives, anemones, pompons, and singles can be used for disbuds if they form a large enough flower when they are disbudded.   Disbuds are usually spaced closer together in the bench so that there will be more production of the medium-sized disbuds than there is of the large-sized standards.   Disbuds are produced in greenhouses primarily for local area sales.

Flowering in Chrysanthemum is controlled by length of day—or rather length of night.   During long days Chrysanthemums form leaves, and the stems increase in length, and during short days flowers are formed in the stem apex, and growth in length terminates with the flower.   In natural conditions the *Chrysanthemum* grows in length and produces leaves during the long days of summer; but in the shorter days of late summer and early fall, flower buds form, and the plant flowers.   Some Chrysanthemums form and develop flower buds more rapidly than others, and on the basis of this response the varieties are classed in groups according to the number of weeks required for flowering after the start of short days.   The fastest response to short days is 7 weeks, and the slowest response is 15 weeks.   The 7- and 8-week varieties are often used as garden plants in the North because in natural outdoor conditions they will flower in October

Table 10-1.   *Classification of Chrysanthemum Varieties and Date of Flower Bud Formation and Maturity*

Pinching date	Probable date of flower bud formation	Date variety matures	Classification of variety
July 4	Aug. 20	Oct. 5–Oct. 14	7-week
July 11	Aug. 23	Oct. 15–Oct. 23	8-week
July 18	Aug. 26	Oct. 25–Nov. 1	9-week
July 25	Sept. 1	Nov. 5–Nov. 14	10-week
Aug. 1	Sept. 4	Nov. 15–Nov. 23	11-week
Aug. 8	Sept. 8	Nov. 25–Dec. 1	12-week
Aug. 15	Sept. 12	Dec. 5–Dec. 14	13-week
Aug. 22	Sept. 15	Dec. 15–Dec. 23	14-week
Aug. 29	Sept. 18	Dec. 25–Jan. 1	15-week

before the killing frosts.   Farther south, the 9-, 10-, and 11-week varieties may be used for garden plants, as freezing weather occurs after their natural flowering period in November.   It is the 9-, 10-, and 11-week varieties that are used to the greatest extent in year-round mum programs in greenhouses.

For years Chrysanthemum flowers were produced only during the natural season, and flowering occurred from October to January by planting a selection from 8-week varieties through 15-week varieties.   Since it was learned that vegetative growth or flowering could be produced in the *Chrysanthemum* as desired by regulating the length of day artificially, Chrysanthemum flowers have been produced at any time of the year.

Some Chrysanthemums still are produced in the natural conditions of summer and fall, but the greatest proportion of the Chrysanthemum production is in carefully controlled light and temperature conditions the year-round.   The plants are started from rooted stem tip cuttings under long days to produce leaves and increase in stem length. When the stem is long enough, short days are furnished to produce flower buds followed by flowers. The *Chrysanthemum* is about a four-month crop from the planting of the rooted cutting to the production of flowers. After the crop is harvested, the remainder of the plant is removed, the soil is cultivated and steamed, and the rooted cuttings for the next crop are planted. Depending upon how they are handled, approximately three crops of flowers can be produced per area per year.

Propagation. Most Chrysanthemum flower producers purchase rooted cuttings from the specialist propagator because he has the facilities to produce disease-free, good-quality cuttings, and the right varieties at the time they are needed. Chrysanthemums are subject to many diseases, some of which can be transmitted with the cuttings. Most Chrysanthemum stock was infested at one time with Verticillium wilt and probably still would be if it were not for the procedure of culture-indexing designed by Dr. A. W. Dimock and developed for commercial use by Yoder Bros., Inc. Culture-indexing is a laboratory procedure designed originally to determine the presence of the Verticillium pathogen in plants and later adapted to include methods for determining the presence of several different pathogens. It is essential to have a procedure such as culture-indexing to identify disease-free stock, as the plant may appear to be perfectly healthy and yet harbor the disease organisms that will later produce the characteristic disease symptoms.

The specialist propagator also has facilities for selecting the best strains or clones of varieties. Plants sport or mutate continually. The striking mutations such as change of flower color are easily observed, but more subtle changes such as smaller flowers, fewer petals, less vigor, or greater or weaker stem strength may go unnoticed unless the stock is studied and the best characteristics are continually selected.

Most flower producers do not have the facilities for producing disease-free stock or selecting the best clones for propagation. If producers do not purchase all their cuttings from the specialist propagator, they should at least purchase their nucleus propagation stock from the specialist and replace this stock often enough to assure freedom from disease and the best selection of varieties.

Chrysanthemum stock plants should be grown at a minimum of 60°F and provided long days so that they continue to be vegetative. Varieties differ considerably in rate of growth, and this changes with the weather conditions of the various seasons of the year. Three-inch stem tip cuttings are taken from the stock plants when the shoots are long enough so that shoots with 2 or 3 leaves will be left on the plant. It takes about a month from the time a stem is pinched or a cutting is taken until the next crop of cuttings will be ready for removal from the plant. The shoots on the stock plants should not be allowed to grow for a long time before the cuttings are taken, as such stem tips may have started to form flower buds in spite of having been in long days.

In addition to providing the normally good temperature, light, moisture, air, and mineral environment for the stock plant, the planting and pinching of the stock plants must be carefully scheduled so that the right number of cuttings of the proper varieties is available at the right time. Scheduling may not be a big problem for a crop or two, but for a year-round program in which cuttings are planted weekly and varieties changed seasonally, it becomes a management problem fraught with many pitfalls.

Rooting the cutting is the lesser problem with Chrysanthemums since it is a rather routine procedure as compared to the many details involved in producing the supply of stem tip cuttings. Several materials can be used satisfactorily for the rooting medium, but mixtures of horticultural-grade perlite and German peat moss are used most commonly. Chrysanthemum cuttings are stuck about 1 inch apart in the rows, and the rows are spaced 2 inches apart. The cuttings are stuck just deep enough so that they remain upright.

The air temperature should be 60°F and the propagation bench temperature 70°F for rooting the *Chrysanthemum*. Other propagation procedures should follow the general practices outlined in Chap. 8. Chrysanthemums require about two weeks for rooting, and they should be lifted from the propagation bench when the roots are ½ inch long.

Chrysanthemum cuttings do not store as well as carnation cuttings, but either unrooted or rooted cuttings can be held satisfactorily for a few weeks at 31 to 33°F if all conditions are right.

Planting, spacing, and supporting. There are three primary concerns for the newly planted rooted cutting: minimizing water loss from the cutting, promoting rapid root growth, and having some nitrogen available for the plant. The best method of reducing water loss from the cutting is to mist the plants often enough so that the leaves remain moist, and in extremely hot weather a light shade may be placed above the plants. Root growth is aided by a favorable air supply in the soil. Shallow planting helps, and during the winter when soils dry slowly, the plants should be spot watered, leaving dry areas between the rows of plants. In cold weather additional heat around the newly planted area will dry the soil more rapidly and promote root growth. The young plants do not require a lot of nitrogen in the very early stages, but some is needed. If nitrogen is lacking at the time of planting, it should be supplied when the plants are watered in.

The amount of space that the plant is allowed in the bench is one factor that determines the amount of light that is available for the plant and possibly to a lesser extent the competition among plants for fertilizer and water. Within limits the farther apart the plants are spaced, the better the growth. Plants should be spaced at the distance that will produce the quality and quantity of flowers that can be sold at a profit.   A spacing of about 6 by 8 inches is used for plants that will be pinched and about 4 by 6 inches for plants that will be grown single-stem.   Actually the spacing should be varied from one season to another, allowing more space per plant during periods of inadequate light.

If the plants are grown single-stem, they are not pinched, and therefore only one stem per plant is produced.   This method of culture saves some growing time, and it is possible that better quality flowers can be produced, particularly during the winter.   Single-stem culture requires about twice as many plants as pinched culture, but the saving in production time about equals the cost of the additional plants.

Various methods can be used to support Chrysanthemums so that they will grow erect, but the most satisfactory system is welded wire fabric.   If varieties are used that grow to about the same height, a single layer of wire fabric can be used per bench.   At planting time the fabric is placed at the soil level, and planting is done through it.   As the plants grow, the wire fabric is raised so that the upper portions of the plants are supported upright.   When it is installed, the wire fabric is stretched as tightly as possible and fastened to bars at each end that can be moved up and down on the end posts.   About every 12 feet along the bench, upright members with crossbars are provided for support of the wire. These uprights also are the means for supporting lights and black shading cloth.

Light.   The *Chrysanthemum* will grow most rapidly under conditions of high light intensity.   In summer, shade on the roof makes the greenhouse a somewhat more desirable place to work, but will delay development of the plants. Plants grown under reduced light will be somewhat taller and thinner-stemmed and will have larger leaves.   If used, shade material on the roof should be very thin, and all of it should be off by late August.

In the winter, light is at a premium in greenhouses, and everything possible must be done to provide the greatest amount of light.   The quantity of light that the plants receive at any time of the year is one of the determining factors in the amount of photosynthesis that will take place in the plants, which affects the amount and quality of growth.   The best light-intensity range for photosynthesis in Chrysanthemums is probably from 3,000 to 10,000 foot-candles. As the light intensity in some winter days does not exceed a few hundred foot-candles, photosynthesis is limited at that time, and plant growth is reduced.

Chrysanthemums are affected also by the length of the daily light or dark period, a quality known as photoperiodism.   In the initial studies, the effects were ascribed to the length of daily light, and Chrysanthemums were called short-day plants because Chrysanthemum flower buds form and develop in short days. Later studies established that it would have been more appropriate to use the term long night rather than short day, but at least commercially, Chrysanthemums continue to be called short-day plants even though some of the procedures that are used are actually based on the effect of the dark period. More recently it has been learned that it is a blue pigment, called "phytochrome," in plants that actually changes in short or long days. It is this pigment, probably acting as an enzyme, that causes the photoperiodic effects. It has been demonstrated that the photoperiodic response is due not only to the daily length of day or night but also to the type or quality of light. The red end of the light spectrum, about 5800 to 7200 Å, produces the long-day response. Yet if plants are subjected to far-red light, about 7200 to 8000 Å, just the opposite effect is caused: the plants react as though they were in short days.

The commercial significance of the effect of light quality on Chrysanthemums is that the light that is rich in red rays should be used for extending the day length artificially. The incandescent lamp that is commonly used does provide that quality of light, but if fluorescent lamps are used, pink or red tubes will provide the red light needed. Theoretically it would be possible to produce short days for Chrysanthemums by irradiating them with far-red light during naturally long days, and it is possible that this or some related procedure may be developed in the future. Experimentally, far-red illumination has only been partially effective in producing the short-day effect in some Chrysanthemum varieties.

Low-intensity light is effective in providing the day-length response. Some Chrysanthemum varieties respond to intensities as low as 1 or 2 foot-candles; however, a minimum of 10 foot-candles of light is usually maintained when long days are furnished artificially. This amount of light is easily provided by several different lighting arrangements, but one of the most common is the use of 60-watt lamps spaced 4 feet apart and 2 feet above the plants. With such an arrangement the lights must be raised as the plants grow in height.

In long days Chrysanthemums form leaves and continue to grow in height. In order to produce this vegetative growth in naturally short days, the plants are supplied with artificial light sometime during the dark period daily. When this work was first started with Chrysanthemums by Laurie and associates, the artificial light was added at the end of the day to make a long day. Later work demonstrated that the long-day effect was really the effect of short nights— a daily dark period no longer than 9½ hours which can be provided by lighting for a rather long period of time at either end of the day or lighting for a shorter period during the middle of the night. Various methods are used commercially, but generally the lights are added each night of August and May for 2 hours; of September through October and March through April for 3 hours; and of November through February for 4 hours. In order to reduce the power load at any one time, half the area may be lighted immediately before midnight and the other half immediately after midnight.

There has been some interest in cyclic or flash lighting for Chrysanthemums. Several procedures have been used in a limited way. The one that has received some commercial acceptance provides a 4-hour lighting period each night, but the area is divided into five units that are lighted for 6 minutes every 30 minutes using a light intensity of 20 foot-candles. This procedure can reduce the total power load at any one time and may lower the total quantity of power that is used, but it must be realized that cyclic lighting is based on furnishing the minimum quantity of light. Slight variations in conditions may cause some problems; hence such a system can be used only if it is properly designed and supervised.

Chrysanthemums may be given partial shade during the time of the year when light intensity is high, in order to improve flower color and prevent petal burn. This partial shade is provided best by erecting cheesecloth or lightweight muslin above the plants as they start to flower. This is good procedure to follow in most areas of the country from May through September.

Artificial short days for Chrysanthemums during naturally long days are provided by placing black cloth over the plants. Black cotton cloth or in some instances black polyethylene are used for this shading, which must assure almost total darkness for the plants (2 foot-candles or less when the light intensity is 4,000 foot-candles). For the short-day effect, a daily dark period of at least 9½ hours must be provided, and commercially a daily dark period of 12 to 15 hours is used so that the cloth may be applied and removed by regular work crews. This method of applying the black shade cloth may be the most economical in the use of labor, but there may be some deleterious effects on the plants. Covering the plants with black cloth for too long a period daily may limit the amount of photosynthesis and may cause temperatures that are too high for the proper growth and development of the plants. This problem is compounded in areas that observe daylight savings time. After daylight savings time begins in the spring, if black cloth is applied at the same clock time as before, it will actually go on an hour earlier by sun time; this will reduce the effective light on the plants and increase the temperature under the cover. For best response of the plants, the black cloth should be applied daily at about 8 P.M. and removed at 8 A.M. This may be a problem if manual labor is used, but an automated operation can be performed under control of a time clock.

Black cloths are used over the plants beginning in early March and continuing to the end of September in order to have controlled short days. Some black cloth may need to be used during naturally short days to prevent chance lighting of areas that should be in short days; this is done best by using drop cloths between the areas lighted and the short-day areas.

Black cloth shading should be done daily during the period when artificially short days are being provided; however, it is possible to skip shading once a week without serious consequences other than delaying the flowering date by about the same number of days that are skipped. The only reason for skipping

TOO EARLY   TIME PINCHED   TOO LATE

10-8. The length of time between pinching and start of short days for Chrysanthemums must be carefully scheduled for best flower arrangement or formation. In spray mums it affects the height at which the terminal flower develops and the length of the lateral flower stems.

shading once a week is to give the shade pullers a weekly break. The black cloth treatment does not need to be continued until the flowers are cut, but with most varieties of standard mums it should be continued until the flower buds are as large as a nickel, and with sprays it should be continued until the flower buds show color.

When the length of day is manipulated mechanically, the environment is changed abruptly from long days to short days, but in natural conditions there is a gradual shift from one critical day length to the other—and in fact there is probably some shifting back and forth for a few days between long days and short days. The effect of abrupt versus gradual day-length transition has been a subject of speculation and some research, but it is believed that abrupt change may be as good as gradual. In some instances, however, a few short days are interspersed into the end of the long-day period, a custom known commercially as interrupted lighting. This procedure can increase the number of ray florets in standards during winter flowering, but the effect varies with varieties and some other environmental conditions. It is a procedure that has apparently been used to good advantage by some growers, but it has not been adopted as a general practice. There are some variations in the number of days of interruption that is used, but a common recommendation is 9 days of short days toward

10-9. Variable photoperiod causes delay in flower bud development and produces malformed or crown buds. The plant on the right received short days continuously. The plant on the left had some long days interspersed with the short days. (*Yoder Bros., Inc., photograph.*)

the end of the long-day period, followed by 12 days of long days and then short days to flowering.

Temperature. Although the *Chrysanthemum* has for years been called a "cool crop" because it flowers in the fall, many varieties will not form flower buds at cool temperatures. Depending upon the maturity date of the variety, flower buds form between mid-August and late September, at which time the night temperature should be maintained at 60°F to ensure proper bud formation. In the Middle West, the night temperature is generally at least 60°F, but occasionally the late varieties will be blind if no heat is used in cool September weather.

After the flower buds have developed to a size that is visible, the temperature may be lowered a degree every two nights to 55°F to enhance the quality of the variety. This reduction of temperature is of prime importance, particularly

10-10. For most rapid flowering, Chrysanthemums should be given short days each day after the treatment is started. (*Yoder Bros., Inc., photograph.*)

with many of the varieties which are in the 12- to 15-week groups.   Maintenance of a high temperature (60°F or higher) will actually delay development.   Thus with late varieties (12- to 15-week) the night temperature should be warm to form flower buds and then gradually cooled after buds are visible so that they will develop.   When grown too cool in September, flower buds will not form, the stems will be blind, and the growth will often be rosetted.   Heat delay has been commonly associated with hot summer temperatures, but it may be encountered in December with some varieties growing too close to the heating pipes or in a 60°F greenhouse.

In periods of warm fall weather the pink, bronze, and red varieties may fade.   If the air is kept too cool, many white varieties will become pink-tinged and yellow flowers turn bronze, but this may also be true of flowers that are too old.

Cooling greenhouses in summer with fan and pad or misting improves the quality of the growth.   The maintenance of a warm temperature at the time of flower bud formation is one of the key factors in successful culture of mums out of season.   Although there are a few varieties that form flower buds in cool temperatures, almost all the varieties must have a minimum of 60°F at night when short-day treatment is started.   In fact, in very dark weather a night temperature of 65°F is recommended to ensure uniform flower bud formation. As soon as the buds are barely visible, the night temperature can be lowered from 65 to 60°F.   With many of the 12- to 15-week varieties, night temperatures of 55 to 58°F will actually promote development of the buds, whereas a temperature of 60°F or higher will cause delay.   Quality of the flowers of many varieties is improved if the air temperature can be lowered to 55°F, but this may be impossible if there are plants in all stages of development in the same house.

In summer, delay caused by excessive heat is quite common on some varieties.   Night temperatures above 85°F are known to delay development (not formation) of flower buds.   This may be partially alleviated by uncovering the plants during the darkness and promoting the circulation and admittance of cooler outside air by fans.   Cooling by fan and pad or mists is effective in overcoming heat delay, but care must be exercised, or Botrytis blight may ruin the flowers as a result of the high humidity.

The pink, bronze, and red colors fade in hot weather, though there are some varieties which are more satisfactory than others.   It is believed that the color is prevented from forming by the high temperature.   Older flowers fade rapidly, particularly in hot weather.   In winter certain white varieties may show a pink tinge even at 60°F, which indicates it is too cool.

Soil.   The *Chrysanthemum* will grow best in a well-prepared soil.   It must be coarse and porous.   Addition of organic matter in the form of peat, chopped straw, or rotted manure will improve the structure and allow for full development of the plant.   No less than one-fourth organic matter by volume should be added, and if the soil is very heavy, increasing the amount to one-third will be beneficial.   Only the coarser grades of peat are satisfactory, and if the peat has been pulverized by a hammer mill, it will be too fine and not have the desired effect in improving the soil.

Whether the plants are in a raised bench or in a ground bed without a concrete bottom will make very little difference.   Somewhat longer stems, heavier foliage, and larger flowers can be expected on ground beds because of the more uniform conditions of moisture and nutrition.   Drainage of the benches or beds is of utmost importance since roots will not grow in poorly aerated soils.

Steam sterilization will kill the Verticillium wilt fungus which lives in the soil and severely damages many Chrysanthemum varieties.   Furthermore, steaming improves soil structure, kills weeds and weed seeds, and destroys other harmful fungi and bacteria.   It should be pointed out that cultured cuttings are only free of the Verticillium disease and not immune to it; therefore, planting cultured cuttings in wilt-infected soil will result in the plants becoming infected.

Chrysanthemums are easily injured by ammonia, which may be present in toxic quantities after soil is steamed, particularly if fresh or only partially rotted manure has been incorporated.   Browning or death of the tip of the stem or brown, rusty areas on the leaves is indicative that ammonia injury is occurring, and broadcasting 5 pounds of gypsum or superphosphate per 100 square feet on the soil, followed by an immediate watering, will quickly alleviate the difficulty.

Chrysanthemums grow best at a pH of 6.0 to 7.0.   When the soil is more acid, many varieties will be stunted in growth, and the upper foliage may become chlorotic.   Yellowing of the top foliage occurs when the pH is too high, and it is presumed that this is iron deficiency.   Overwatering or too much fertilizer in the soil will interfere with root action and also will cause chlorosis of the upper leaves.

Fertilizers.   When Chrysanthemums are grown in soil that is tested regularly, the following range of fertilizer is best, based on the Spurway system: nitrate nitrogen, 25 to 50 ppm; phosphorus, 5 to 10 ppm; potassium, 20 to 40 ppm; calcium, 150 to 200 ppm.

It has been found that if all the nitrogen the plant needs for good growth were applied during the first 8 weeks of its 15- to 16-week period in the bench, the quantity and quality of production would be equal to plants given uniform fertilizer throughout their life.   This points up the need for good root growth early to absorb the nitrogen, and also the futility of trying to compensate for improper culture by applying nitrogen heavily in the last 4 to 6 weeks of the crop.   With fertilizer injection, supplemental applications of nitrogen are very desirable during the first half of the life of the mum.

Although the *Chrysanthemum* will grow at Solu Bridge readings above 0.80 (1 part soil to 5 parts water), optimum growth is obtained if the readings are kept between 0.30 and 0.80.   Excessive fertilizer interferes with root development and subsequent growth of the tops.

The notion that Chrysanthemums are heavy feeders stems largely from the fact that fertilizer is usually applied every 2 to 3 weeks during the growing season.   This is necessary because the frequent watering in summer leaches the nitrogen from the soil, and it must be replenished regularly or the plants will be hardened or starved.   Many growers make a light application of a complete fertilizer every 10 to 14 days to maintain a supply of the elements needed for optimum growth.   If the soil is heavy and drainage poor, such frequent applications will usually lead to trouble from excessive fertilizer.

The choice of liquid or dry fertilizer depends upon individual preference. No matter which is used, the soil should be moist when fertilizer is applied, to avoid root injury and resultant damage to the crop.   If the fertilizer contacts the foliage, it should be syringed off, or it may burn the tissue.

Fertilizer deficiency symptoms.   When nitrogen is deficient in the soil, the plants are stunted and the leaves small, and their color is a light green.   The lower foliage turns yellow and then brown, and the stems become hard and woody.   The flowers lack size and the entire plant is stunted and hardened. Fungi attacking the root or stem may cause symptoms somewhat similar, but usually the plant wilts and it may eventually die, whereas with nitrogen deficiency it remains turgid and alive.

Marginal yellowing of the lower foliage is often indicative of potassium deficiency.   As it becomes more severe, the edge of the leaf turns brown and the yellowing progresses inward; the trouble moves from the lower foliage upward.   Some insecticides cause yellowing of the leaf margins, but such injury does not become progressively worse, nor does it continue to envelop more foliage, and this often distinguishes between injury from pest control materials and that from nutrient deficiencies.

Chlorosis of the upper foliage is often indicative of insufficient iron, but anything that interferes with root growth may cause a similar effect.

Fertilizer excess symptoms.   Overdosing with fertilizer may severely stunt plants or kill them outright, with no distinctive symptoms other than failure to grow, wilting, and eventual death.   However, when somewhat more than normal nitrogenous fertilizer material is applied, but not to the point of such toxicity, the leaves will become very dark green and crisp.   Such foliage is brittle and may break readily in transit.   Longitudinal cracks in the stem may appear when the plant is forced with too much nitrogen.

Moisture.   Chrysanthemums must be watered thoroughly immediately after they are planted in order to make certain that the soil in the vicinity of the roots is moist and that there is good contact between soil and roots. In the summer it is almost impossible to water too heavily, and the entire soil area must be thoroughly drenched. Because of the warm temperatures the soil will dry rapidly. In the dark and cool days of the winter the plants should be thoroughly watered after planting—but only in the immediate vicinity of the plants, leaving dry areas between the rows of plants. This is known as spot watering. Soils dry slowly in the winter, and spot watering when properly done provides adequate moisture for the plants while allowing the soil to dry rapidly. Root growth is more rapid in soils that are not constantly wet. New root development in Chrysanthemums should be evident within 3 or 4 days after planting. This is a critical period in the growth of the Chrysanthemum plants, and the irrigation procedures used shortly after planting can influence the future growth and development of the plants.

Until new root growth starts after planting, the water loss from the plants might be greater than the water intake. In order to prevent this, the air in the vicinity of the plants should be humid. The plants can be periodically sprayed or misted, or a tentlike structure made of plastic film can be placed over the entire bench for about a week after planting in order to maintain uniform moisture and temperature conditions. Growth is more rapid in such an environment, and more shoots develop.

Humid conditions as the plants come into flower can be the cause of serious infestations of Botrytis blight. Ventilating, ventilating while heating, and using air-circulation fans are some of the most effective ways of controlling high humidity.

Chrysanthemum soils should be allowed to dry somewhat between irrigations, but each irrigation must be thorough and heavy enough so that the water percolates through the entire soil mass. The thoroughness of the irrigation may be determined by observing the drip from the bench or by digging to the bottom of the soil after irrigating. Several different irrigation systems can be used successfully for Chrysanthemums. The perimeter pipe system in which nozzles are installed in plastic pipe placed around the entire perimeter of the bench is probably the most widely used system. Such a system when properly installed provides excellent irrigation and saves considerable labor time.

Air. Continuous air movement should be provided for Chrysanthemums to ensure more uniform temperature, humidity, and carbon dioxide, producing better plant growth; it also helps to control Botrytis blight on flowers. Good air movement results from the use of ridge and side ventilators at many times of the year, but there are many occasions when positive air movement with air-circulation fans is much superior to that from ventilation alone.

It is quite likely that there may be a reduction in the amount of carbon dioxide in the greenhouse during cold weather when the greenhouses are completely closed for long periods of time. Maintaining a minimum of 500 ppm carbon dioxide in the greenhouse atmosphere by means of carbon dioxide generators can increase photosynthesis with resulting improvement in plant growth if the other environmental conditions such as light, temperature, moisture, and minerals also are properly supplied. Some varieties of *Chrysanthemum* respond more favorably to additions of carbon dioxide than others. The benefits that can be expected from maintaining a favorable carbon dioxide level are faster and heavier growth, and apparently the most effect is obtained in the early stages of growth. The heavier growth leads to better quality flowers, and the faster growth results in less production time with possible savings in costs of production. The costs of installation of carbon dioxide equipment should be considered in this connection.

Troubles. Poor growth in the early stages is often caused by too much fertilizer, poor drainage conditions, or lack of fertilizer. If new roots are not growing, excess fertilizer or poor drainage or both should be suspected. In such a situation the top leaves may be yellow. If the root system is good, but there are little top growth and small greenish leaves, it is quite likely that there is a deficiency of fertilizer. The plants need some nitrogen continuously in the early stage of growth, and without it the top growth will be permanently stunted.

Various flower bud formation and development problems can be caused by unfavorable light or temperature conditions. If the plants are in short days but too low temperatures, flower buds may not be formed and the growth is compact or rosetted. If the plants are in short days but in too high temperatures, flower buds (crown buds) may be formed and the growth usually is elongated. Crown buds form more readily in some varieties than in others, but they will form in most varieties even in long days when the stem is allowed to grow long enough before short days are started. Formation of crown buds in plants within a few weeks after planting is an indication that the stock plants were not lighted properly or that the cuttings were taken from shoots that were too long.

Malformed flowers can be caused by diseases or pests, but they also can be caused by giving the plants various combinations of short and long days. Such situations arise from failures of electrical equipment, poor shading cloth, or failures of personnel to handle either lighting or shading properly.

Petal burn or sun scald is often confused with Botrytis blight, but they can be distinguished because *Botrytis* infests the tips of the oldest petals and burn occurs on the younger petals at the center of the flower. The burn usually appears as an arc or circle at the center of the flower because the petals at the same stage of development are affected. Burn is a problem with standard Chrysanthemums during hot weather, and it can be prevented by supplying light shade over the plants as the flower buds start to show color.

10-11. Sunburn on Chrysanthemum flowers. Some varieties are more susceptible than others. It can be prevented by placing a partial shade above the plants before the flowers start to open. The burn appears as an arc or circle on the flower, as florets of the same development are affected. *Botrytis* usually affects the oldest, outer florets, and sunburn the more recently formed florets toward the center of the flower. (*Yoder Bros., Inc., photograph.*)

Diseases.   Bacterial stem rot is most destructive in hot weather. Infected cuttings appear normal but soon begin to wilt, and the inner stem is hollow and blackened. A check in growth such as pinching appears to accentuate the trouble.

Botrytis blight, or gray mold, is a fungus causing the petals to turn brown and appear water-soaked. It is troublesome when the air is moist and so is best alleviated by using heat and ventilation plus circulating fans to keep the air moving.

Dodder is a parasitic plant found mostly on outside plantings. Unless destroyed, it will strangulate the plants.

Powdery mildew is prevalent under conditions of high humidity, particularly in dark weather. The white powdery fungus on the leaves is unsightly, and in severe cases the stems may be affected.

Root-knot nematodes cause gall-like knots on the roots and in general severely stunt the plants.

Rust appears as small blisters which erupt, exposing the brownish spores.

Septoria leaf spot, or black spot, is a fungus that causes irregular black blotches on the foliage. Infected leaves usually turn yellow and drop.

Stem rot caused by *Rhizoctonia* is common if the cuttings are planted too deeply, are overwatered, or are placed in very heavy soil. Rotted areas are noted at the soil line or below.

Stunt is a slow-moving virus disease that severely dwarfs the plants and causes fading of flowers of pink, red, and bronze varieties.

Verticillium wilt, or Siedewitz disease, is a vascular fungus that affects most varieties. Leaves on one side of the stem or the entire stem usually turn gray-green and wilt perceptibly. By the time the plant is in flower, the foliage is usually dead, and the flowers are small. *Verticillium* never kills the plant, and cuttings taken from infected stock will generally have the fungus within them.

Yellows is a virus that affects the flowers. A portion or all of the flower is yellow-green rather than the normal color, and the flowers are generally smaller. Aphids and leaf hoppers that feed on infected plants spread the trouble, as does handling the plants.

Pythium stem and root rot affects some varieties of *Chrysanthemum* much more readily than others. The use of the *Pythium*-susceptible varieties must be avoided in outdoor areas where the means of environmental control are not adequate. Soil and handling equipment must be thoroughly steamed, and Dexon drenches can be used to limit spread of the rot through the soil.

Ascochyta or ray blight is best known for the characteristic malformed flowers following an invasion of this pathogen, but other portions of the plant may be involved and the leaf symptom may resemble Septoria leaf spot. This organism germinates only if there is water on the plant and is therefore much more common on outdoor crops than in the greenhouse.

Pests. Aphids disfigure the young growth and are unsightly. There are various kinds and colors of aphids, and they are especially difficult to kill when they attack the stem tip and are protected by the enfolded leaves.

Chrysanthemum midge makes galls on the foliage and stems. Inside the galls of an affected plant are larvae which have hatched from orange-colored eggs laid by the female flies. The larvae feed about 28 days, and emerge to mate and repeat the cycle.

Cutworms eat the foliage or flowers. Of especial interest is the corn-ear worm, which in a short period of time can devastate a crop of standards in flower.

Cyclamen mite is found at the very tip of the stem, but it is too small to be seen without the aid of a magnifying glass. These pests cause malformation of the new growth, and in severe cases growth practically ceases.

Foliar nematode is an eelworm which moves from leaf to leaf through films of moisture. It enters the leaf through the stomates and causes development of brown wedge- or pie-shaped areas in the foliage between the veins. The damage usually is noticed in the basal foliage, and infested foliage usually dies. Keeping foliage dry prevents the worm's spread, but this is not always practical.

Grasshoppers chew the leaves and flowers and in severe cases will devour the young stems.

Leaf miner larvae tunnel through the foliage between the upper and lower epidermis and make irregular light-colored patterns in the leaf. The injured leaf may be split apart and separated into upper and lower surfaces.

Leaf rollers are whitish-green caterpillars that chew the underside of the foliage, leaving the upper epidermis, which dries until it looks like parchment.   They roll the leaves together by means of a web and emerge as brown moths to mate and repeat the cycle.

Mealy bugs occasionally infest mums and are easily distinguished by the white cottony masses covering the gray pests in the axils of the leaves.

Red spider is a serious pest because it sucks the juices from the leaves and causes a light mottling.   It also infests flowers and, if not controlled, can build up large populations in a short time.

Slugs and snails chew ragged holes in the foliage and occasionally attack the flowers.

Sow bugs chew the young stems and may attack the roots.

Spittle bugs are rarely troublesome but may sting the young growth and cause minor disfigurations.   A frothy white mass identifies this pest.

Symphylids stunt the growth through their injury to the root system.

Tarnished plant bugs sting the stem, causing excessive branching or even blindness.

Termites may become troublesome in wooden benches with wooden legs. They bore into the stems of the plants and cause wilting.

Thrips are a very serious pest at certain seasons.   They rasp the foliage and flowers and cause light-colored streaks on the foliage and deep-colored petals and brownish streaks on yellow and white petals.

White fly is unsightly.   The nymphs suck the juices of the leaves but seldom noticeably injure the plants.

Pinching, pruning, and disbudding.   The purpose in pinching is to produce a branched plant.   Chrysanthemums may be grown as either pinched or single-stem plants, and no matter which method is used, approximately the same amount of space is allowed per flowering stem.   Plants can be planted 6 by 8 inches apart, pinched, and pruned to two stems; in comparison, single-stem plants would be planted 4 by 6 inches.   To maintain the same spacing per flowering stem in a pinched plant pruned to three stems, the plants would be spaced 8 by 9 inches.

All the activities associated with producing Chrysanthemums are carefully scheduled so that the right-quality flowers are produced at the desired time.   One of these activities is pinching.   Time is allowed in the schedule for the plant to make enough terminal growth after planting so that the pinch can be made in the new growth.   A soft pinch should be used; remove as short a stem tip as possible.   Shoot growth from the leaf axils below the pinch will then be rapid and of good quality.   The length of time that long days are used after the pinch also is scheduled carefully so that the stem attains the proper length and is in vegetative growth at the time short days are started.   If the plants are given long days for too long a time after the pinch, flower buds (crown buds) start to form but do not develop completely. Crown bud formation is eliminated when the times of planting, pinching, long days, and short days are scheduled properly; and the terminal flower bud that forms during short days continues to develop during the short days to a mature flower.

Following pinching, several shoots develop, and these must be limited, depending on the amount of space that is allowed per plant. The top two or three shoots are usually of the best quality. For this reason, the cuttings are spaced widely enough apart at planting that there will be sufficient room for two stems per plant, and when shoots develop after the pinch, all but the two top shoots are pruned. In some instances three shoots are retained on the outside rows of plants if the good light conditions in this position justify it. Pruning should be done as soon as the shoots are big enough to be handled.

Disbudding is the process of removing flower buds that are not desired on the Chrysanthemum stem. A lone, large flower per stem is wanted in standards and disbuds; and in order to produce this, the lateral flower buds must be removed (disbudded). Disbudding must be done as soon as the flower buds can be handled because if they are left on too long, the size of the terminal flower is reduced, and it matures more slowly.

10-12. With standard mums the lateral flower buds should be removed (disbudded) as soon as they can be handled. Left: before disbudding. Right: after disbudding.

Some disbudding of spray mums may be done, but this is a selective type of flower bud removal to improve the arrangement of flowers in the spray. The most common disbudding on sprays is the removal of the terminal flower bud to make the lateral flowers more effective and to create a looser arrangement of the flower spray.

Rotations and cropping. Chrysanthemums may be grown during the natural season, making weekly plantings from late June until the middle of August and cutting flowers from late October to late December. Natural season crops require no artificial light or shade, which effects savings in production costs, but it may attract more growers into producing fall Chrysanthemums and thereby produce an oversupply and reduced prices. Natural season mums can be rotated with bedding plants, spring pot plants, or a spring crop of tomatoes. Natural season crops have their early growth in the warm temperatures of summer and early fall, and they are finished in the fall at about 50°F. The cool finish saves fuel and does improve the flower quality, but it delays flowering.

When it was realized that there were commercial possibilities in the use of artificial light or shade to control mum flowering, the first attempts were to lengthen the natural season by lighting some plants for flowering after the natural season and shading others for flowering before the start of natural season flowering. Gradually procedures were developed for flowering Chrysanthemums at anytime of the year. For flowering from late August until early October no artificial light needs to be used as the natural days are long enough, but black cloth must be used during this period when short days are needed. For flowering from mid-November until early April no black cloth shade needs to be used as the natural day length is short enough, but the plants have to be lighted

10-13. A planting machine used for Chrysanthemum cuttings (unrooted cuttings in this instance) in Florida. (*Dorcas Flowers photograph.*)

10-14. Newly planted Chrysanthemum fields in Florida. Note the electric lights for providing long days. (*Dorcas Flowers photograph.*)

during the early stages of growth.   For flowering at other times of the year both artificial light and shade have to be supplied.

When large-scale production of mums was started outdoors in Florida, flowers were produced from late November until May; and the plants had to be provided with artificial light but not black cloth.   Each year the flowering season has been extended, and so black cloth shading does have to be used for the spring and early summer crops.

In northern states crops cannot be planted outdoors until the first part of May because of frosts, and they may be safe from frost until early October. This allows for some outdoor production in the North from late August to October; however, the flowering season can be extended by starting a few crops indoors in pots and planting them outside in May, or by providing some protection from the frost in October and early November.

Outdoor production in any part of the country is better under tobacco cloth or plastic screen than it is in the open fields, and it is limited primarily to sprays, as standards are more susceptible to damage from rain, wind, and diseases.

Chrysanthemums are produced the year-round in many greenhouses throughout the country, and the objective often is to produce approximately the same quantity of flowers each week.   This becomes an interesting problem in management as varying lengths of time are required to produce Chrysanthemums, depending on the seasonal weather conditions.   It is not unusual to have to make some compromise between having the bench space occupied continuously and producing the crops at the time of greatest need.   In order to do the best job of utilizing the available space and producing flowers at the right times, it is necessary to develop a schedule for the mum production area about 2 years in advance.   This is an elementary but indispensable schedule that lists each planting unit, date of planting, date of flowering, date of replanting, date of second flowering, and so forth. It usually is satisfactory to allow 1 week between the scheduled flowering date and the date of replanting because the flowers should all be cut by the scheduled date, which provides one week for reworking and steaming the soil in preparation for the replanting.

Year-round scheduling of Chrysanthemums could be a simple operation if the same length of time could be used for each crop regardless of the time of the year. If, for instance, each crop required 18 weeks from planting to cutting, a 19-unit area could be planted weekly the year-round; and with a week between flowering and planting, a crop of flowers would be cut each week of the year. The growth of Chrysanthemums varies with weather conditions, and pinched crops require from 17 weeks for flowering in late summer to 21 weeks in midwinter. Single stem crops require 15 to 18 weeks. In order to produce a flower crop approximately weekly the year-round, about 20 units are needed for pinched crops and 17 units for single-stem crops. A unit can be a bench, several benches, or a house depending on the size of the operation.

Adequate lighting and shading must be provided for the entire area, and a minimum night temperature of 60°F is used.

Various rotations of mums with other crops may be used, but it is not practical to interplant Chrysanthemums in either carnation or snapdragon areas as the temperature requirements are different. Because Chrysanthemums are a short-term crop, it often is possible to produce a crop in an area vacated by roses or carnations between the time of removing the plants and the time for replanting.

Cutting flowers. Most growers allow the flowers to open too far before cutting. Cutting the stems while the flowers are slightly on the "green" side is preferred because it offers a better quality product for the customer. In general, spray types should be cut when the central flower is open and the surrounding flowers are well developed, and varieties which shed pollen badly will have to be cut before they become unsightly. Standards should be cut before the center florets are fully expanded.

Stems should be reasonably soft where the cut is made since very hard, woody tissue may not absorb water. Entry of water into hard stems is facilitated if the stems are slightly crushed with light blows from a hammer or mallet. The lower one-third of the foliage on the stem is stripped off to prevent leaves from fouling the water, and the stems are placed in water to "soak up." Warm water is absorbed faster, but the air temperature should be cool to harden the flowers. The flowers can be graded, bunched, and packed after several hours in water. Flowers to be stored dry at 31 to 33°F need not be placed in water unless they are wilted.

10-15. Pompons being flowered under plastic screen in Florida. Some Florida growers produce pompons in open fields—they do not use plastic screen at any stage. Other growers, as in this instance, apply plastic screen just before the buds show color. (*Dorcas Flowers photograph.*)

There are no universally accepted grading or bunching standards, and each grower uses his own judgment and ethics. The 9-ounce bunch has been used widely for the spray types, but bunches weighing 16 ounces are common, particularly in glut periods. Less than five stems per bunch is not acceptable to most retailers. Because of the wide variety of spray Chrysanthemums, it is difficult to establish a set of standards. The appearance of the bunch may govern the sale more than the weight or number of stems. Where stems are reasonably alike, no fewer than five should be placed in a bunch, and the bunch should weigh at least 9 ounces. The length of stem need not be over 30 inches for most purposes.

The grades for standard Chrysanthemums recommended for trial by the Society of American Florists are:

10-16. Machine for bunching pompons in Florida fields. (*Dorcas Flowers photograph.*)

Measurement Standards

	BLUE GRADE	RED GRADE	GREEN GRADE	YELLOW GRADE
Minimum flower diameter	6″	5″	4″	None
Minimum stem length	30″	30″	24″	24″

Inspection Standards

1. Similar varietal characteristics.
2. Bright, clean, and not badly wilted flowers and leaves.
3. Normal shape of flowers for the kind or variety, placed approximately at right angles to stem.
4. Fairly tight flowers, with center petals unopened and not exposing the center of the flower.
5. Free of injury, defect, dirt, or other foreign materials; free of discoloration, insects, diseases, or nutritional, chemical, or mechanical abnormalities which affect the appearance or shipping quality.
6. Fairly straight, stiff stems capable of supporting the flower in an upright position.
7. Foliage stripped from not more than the lower one-third of the stem.

Storage.   Although Chrysanthemums keep well at a cool temperature in water, their life can be extended by storing them dry at 31 to 33°F.   The flowers or bunches are laid in waxed boxes or boxes lined with sheets of polyethylene and are placed at the prescribed temperature, where they may remain for as long as 3 weeks.   The dry condition of the tissue plus the cool temperature reduces the rate of respiration and maturity.   When the flowers are removed from storage, the stems should be cut and they should be placed in 80 to 100°F water for several hours until soaked up, at an air temperature of 45 to 50°F, and then packed for shipment.   Stock infected with disease should not be stored since the trouble may spread to the entire contents of the box.   Only the best-quality stock should be stored because the plant material does not improve in cold storage.

Marketing.   For long-distance shipment, standards must be packed properly to prevent damage.   A cushion of rolled newspaper is placed on the bottom of the box, and the flowers are laid with the "necks" resting on the newspaper.   The next row of flowers is laid so the heads rest on the neck of those below, and strips of waxed paper are placed under all layers of flowers to prevent drying and injury.   When the stems touch the end of the box, the same system is started at the other end of the box, and the stems are inserted underneath the heads of the flowers at the opposite end of the box.   The center of the box is left open for cleats to securely fasten the stems and for ice, if needed.

The bunches of the spray types are laid in the box side by side, with one layer on top of the other from both ends until the box is filled.   If the bunches have been wrapped with cellophane or waxed tissue paper, there will be a minimum of entanglement of stems and flowers and resultant breakage.

In severely cold weather 20 or 30 layers of newspaper serve as insulation; there are also patented box liners which are better insulators than newspaper. Heavy cardboard boxes are better insulators than wooden boxes.

The cost of operation of a greenhouse area producing single-stem standard Chrysanthemums is probably about $3.50 per square foot per year, and the number of flowers sold from this area would be about 17 flowers per square foot per year.   If these flowers were sold on the wholesale market for an average price of $3.15 per dozen, the net return to the grower would be 21 cents per flower, which would not quite equal the costs of production.

The costs of operation of a greenhouse area producing pinched, spray Chrysanthemums would be about $3.25 per square foot per year, and the number of flowers sold from this area would be about 3¼ bunches per square foot per year.   If the sprays were sold on the wholesale market for an average price of $1.25 per bunch, the net return to the grower would be $1 per bunch, which would about equal the costs of production.   Costs of production should be lower and yields higher in outdoor operations in Florida, but monetary returns are also lower.

GARDENIA (*Gardenia grandiflora—Rubiaceae*)

The grandiflora varieties Belmont, Hadley, and McLellan's 23 have large flowers that are used primarily for corsages.   The veitchi *Gardenia* is smaller flowered and is used only as a potted plant.   The market demand for corsage flowers is for the holidays and the spring social season.

Propagation.   Tip cuttings, 3 to 5 inches long, are taken from the tops of the plants some time between November and March.   They can be rooted in sand or peat or in a mixture of the two.   One of the most successful methods is to pot the cuttings in peat and place them in a closed case with a bottom temperature of 75°F.   Rooting should take place in 4 to 6 weeks.

Canker can be troublesome.   It can usually be avoided if the cuttings are taken from the tops of the plants; and if the cut is made just above a set of leaves, no leaves will have to be removed before sticking the cutting, which reduces the possible places of entry of the canker organism.   Steaming the soil mixture and the pots is imperative.

Soil, fertilizer, and method of handling.   Benching is done in May and June.   The plants are spaced 15 to 18 inches apart in the row, with 18 to 24 inches between rows.   The plants may be staggered, three in one row and two in the next.   When plants are grown for 2 years, the middle plant of the three-plant row may be removed after the first year.   Boxes holding three plants are often substituted for benches.   This is helpful in preventing the spread of a nematode infestation.

A steam-sterilized mixture of equal parts of soil and acid peat is used.

Plant growth is best at a pH of 5.5 to 6.5.   It may be necessary to make applications of sulfur or iron sulfate periodically to maintain the proper pH. The appearance of chlorotic or yellow leaves on the new growth often indicates lack of iron.   However, it may also indicate overwatering, nematodes, or high pH.   A lack of iron can usually be corrected with applications of iron sulfate at the rate of 1 pound per 100 square feet.   Good results can also be obtained with chelated iron used at the rate of 1 ounce per 20 gallons applied to 100 square feet.

If superphosphate is incorporated with the soil initially, it may not be necessary to make further applications of phosphorus to the soil.   Too much phosphorus in the soil may cause an iron deficiency.   Additions of nitrogen and potash should be based on soil analysis.   Nitrogen should be 10 to 25 ppm, and potash 20 to 40 ppm (the Spurway system).

Moisture, light, and temperature.   Gardenia growth is best in a moist atmosphere.   It is good practice to have the house equipped with a nozzle or mist system so that the plants can be syringed or misted frequently.   High relative humidity when the plants are being forced at high temperatures is particularly helpful.

In the Middle West it is usually advisable to shade the glass during the early part of the summer so that the young plants become well established and start good growth.

Black-cloth shading for a 3-week period following July 20 will increase production for Christmas.

Flower buds form at temperatures below 65°F.   It is best to run the houses at 60 to 62°F except when a particular crop is being forced; higher temperatures may be an aid in hastening the development of the flowers.   Bud drop is common when the plants are forced.

Pruning and cutting.   The largest flowers of the best quality are obtained from 1-year plants, and from 20 to 30 flowers per plant may be expected the first year.   The plants may be grown on for the second year.   They are frequently cut back to 24 to 30 inches in May, and all thin wood is removed. Frequent syringing to hasten shoot development is necessary.   About 35 to 75 flowers may be expected on 2-year plants, but the size and quality are usually somewhat inferior.

The flowers are usually removed from the plant without any attached leaves and then placed in a collar of Gardenia leaves and wired so that they will be ready for use by the retail trade with a minimum of effort.

Extreme care must be used in handling the flowers as the slightest bruise develops into an unsightly brown area.

Pests and diseases.   Two-spotted mite (red spider) and mealy bugs are the most common pests.   Root-knot nematodes can be a serious problem. The following rules should be observed: make certain that any shipped-in plants are free of nematodes; steam-sterilize soil, boxes, or benches before planting; and plant in isolated boxes rather than in a bench so that chance infestations may be confined.

Canker (*Phomopsis gardeniae*) is the most prevalent disease.   The disease organism enters primarily through wounds.   Refrain from removing leaves or wounding the stem at the base.   Cuttings from the top of the plant are not likely to be infested with the organism.   Steam sterilization of the propagating medium and the soil can eliminate trouble from that source.

Leaf spots can usually be controlled by omitting syringing the plants and reducing the relative humidity.

GLADIOLUS (*Gladiolus grandiflorus—Iridaceae*)

This native of South Africa is now seldom grown in the greenhouse. Winter crops are produced in Florida, and summer crops in the northern states, with a gradual progression of crops between those periods in the intervening states.   This is all outdoor production.   The greatest acreage in Gladiolus production is in Florida in which the 1959 census reports about 7,500 acres producing 15 million dozen flowers.   The next largest area in Gladiolus production is North Carolina where approximately 2½ million dozen flowers are produced from over 1,100 acres.   From these outdoor production areas, Gladiolus are shipped to all parts of the country.

The *Gladiolus* forms a thickened underground stem that is commonly called a bulb but is technically a corm.   Propagation is by means of the bulblets (cormlets) which grow in clusters at the bases of the maturing bulbs.   From 40 to 120 bulblets are planted per foot of row.   About 8 months later they are dug, cured for 2 months, given a hot-water treatment for the control of some diseases and pests, dried and given cool temperature (about 40°F) for 2 to 4 months, and given warm storage (75°F) for a few weeks before being planted for the second season's growing period.   When the bulbs are dug after the second year's growth, they are cleaned and graded, dipped in a fungicide-pesticide, and placed in 40°F storage to terminate the rest period.   Before they are planted in the production fields it must be determined that they have had a sufficient time in cool temperatures to end the rest period.   The bulbs are then placed in 70 to 80°F temperatures for 1 to 3 weeks or until there is evidence of some root development.

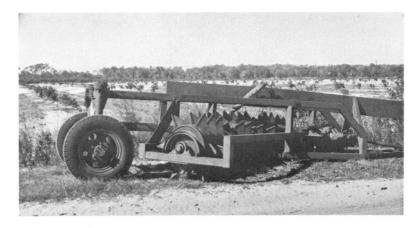

10-17. Machines such as this are used to windrow roots and limbs in cleaning land in preparation for planting gladiolus. (*Roman J. Claprood Co. of Florida photograph.*)

Gladiolus corms were formerly produced in the north and northwest states. More recently many of the corms have been propagated in Florida.

For flower production, No. 2 bulbs (1¼ to 1½ inches) and larger are used. In Florida, planting is usually done from September to February at the rate of about 3 corms per foot of row or an average of about 45,000 corms per acre.

10-18. Gladiolus fields being side-dressed with fertilizer. (*Roman J. Claprood Co. of Florida photograph.*)

Land must be chosen in a frost-free area, well drained but with irrigation water available, and free of diseases, pests, and weeds. If the land has not been under cultivation previously, it may be reasonably free of disease and weeds. Land used previously for crops of any kind should be treated chemically, if at all possible, for control of pests, diseases, and weeds. If the land cannot be treated, replanting to *Gladiolus* must be delayed as long as possible—at least 5 years.

Irrigation facilities must be available to supplement natural rainfall. Fertilizer must be applied regularly, and the kind and amount are dependent on the soil and the amount of moisture. Cultivation of Gladiolus fields is usually required to control weeds and improve the aeration of the soil. If weeds are not handled by cultivation or treatment of the soil before planting, herbicides such as dacthal or diuron may be used after planting. These herbicides are effective only against germinating seeds. Periodic applications for the control of pests and diseases usually are necessary during the growth of the crop.

The flowers should be cut when the floret buds swell and the petals begin to show. The stage of development for cutting the flowers is varied with the prevailing temperature. In warm weather, flowers are cut when three to four florets show color, and in cool weather not until five or six florets are at that stage. The flowers are shipped in tight bud, and all the floret buds develop and open satisfactorily when the stems are placed in water after they are shipped to the retailer. After cutting, Gladiolus are graded according to the number of florets, the overall length, and the weight and length of the flower head. The largest grade is labeled fancy, and the next grades by size are special, A, B, and C. The

10-19. Gladiolus being cut in Florida fields. (*Roman J. Claprood Co. of Florida photograph.*)

flowers are bunched in dozens, and they are shipped upright in hampers which hold from 10 to 24 dozen depending on the grade. If Gladiolus were shipped in the horizontal position, the tips might curve upward. This is a growth response known as geotropism which also occurs in snapdragons. This effect often can be observed in flower arrangements in which either Gladiolus or snapdragons are placed at the horizontal rather than upright position.

After flower harvest the corms are allowed to remain in the ground until they mature. This may be from 4 to 10 weeks after the flowers are cut. In hot, dry weather, irrigation must be continued during this period. About 2 to 3 weeks after digging, the corms are cleaned to remove the mother corm, roots, and cormlets. The corms are graded, given disease or pest treatments, and placed in 40°F storage for 2 to 4 months followed by about 75°F storage for a few weeks before replanting.

Several diseases are troublesome with Gladiolus. *Curvularia* may cause rather large rotted areas on leaves, stems, or corms, and infected florets may not open. The land should be treated chemically before planting or at least 3 years should elapse between plantings of Gladiolus on the same land. Irrigation should be done at the time of the day when the plants dry most rapidly, and sprays of zineb should limit the spread of the disease.

The Gladiolus Botrytis fungus may attack leaves, flowers, or corms. It may be particularly damaging on flowers as there may be no evidence of it when they are packed, but they may be completely ruined by the time they reach the destination. The leaf infection may produce small, circular, red-brown spots as well as larger light brown areas with the typical gray mold growth on some of them. Early infections on floret petals are clear, water-soaked, pinpoint-sized spots, and they are followed by larger rotted areas covered with gray mold. Corms infected with *Botrytis* have brown or black rotted spots with some gray mold in evidence, and the corms are soft and spongy. Because *Botrytis* thrives on old flowers and trash, a good sanitation program is essential. Sprays or dusts with zineb may limit the spread of *Botrytis*.

Stemphylium is a disease of the leaves that produces small, round, yellow, translucent spots which show on both sides of the leaves. No other round spot on Gladiolus leaves appears as bright when held against the light. Flower and corm size may be limited by this disease. Control may be obtained by spraying maneb.

The most destructive disease of Gladiolus is the brown rot of corms caused by *Fusarium*. It may cause stunting of the plant, yellow lower leaves, curvature of leaf growth, and small flowers with weak stems and conspicuous veins in the petals. If the land cannot be treated chemically, it should not be replanted to Gladiolus for at least 10 years. Wounding or bruising the corms should be avoided, and dipping or dusting the corms with some fungicides may be helpful.

Wireworms, cutworms, armyworms, thrips, red spider mites, nematodes, and leaf hoppers are common pests of Gladiolus. They are controlled only by persistent methods of treating the soil and thorough dusting or spraying.

IRIS (*Iris* spp., bulbous—*Iridaceae*)

Although the origin of *Iris* for forcing is uncertain, it is likely that the species *I. xiphium, I. tingitana,* and *I. filifolia* form the basis of our present-day varieties. Although *Iris* is a very profitable crop when grown well, blindness, or failure to flower, may occur.

West Coast Iris bulbs are dug in July and then kept at various carefully controlled temperatures, depending on how they will be used later, until shipment to the greenhouse operators. Those bulbs which are to be forced late in the season (for planting November 20 and later) are shipped after digging to distribution points around the country, where they are held at 86°F until 6 weeks before time for shipment to the greenhouse and then held at 50°F for the remaining period. These are known as retarded Iris. Bulbs that will be planted in greenhouses in October and early November are placed in 90°F temperatures within 5 days after digging, and held for 10 days to accelerate the formation and subsequent development of the flowers, since at harvesttime flowers are not yet formed. The bulbs are then shipped in controlled temperature carriers to various storages where they are kept at 65 to 70°F followed by 6 weeks of 50°F temperature immediately before shipment to the greenhouse. Bulbs shipped the first two weeks in October are called "special precooled" because they are the earliest dug and most mature; those shipped from mid-October to the third week in November are called "precooled."

Some growers still receive their Iris shipment in September and provide the cool storage treatments or plant the Iris in boxes which are buried outdoors for the cool treatment. It is now more common, however, for all the storage treatments to be handled by the bulb growers or distributors, and for the bulbs to be shipped to the forcer at the right time for planting. Continuous flower production from mid-December to May results from weekly plantings of Iris bulbs from the first week in October until March. Special precooled Iris are shipped the first 2 weeks of October. For the next 6 weeks precooled Iris are shipped, and for the remainder of the season bulbs which have been retarded and precooled are supplied. The Wedgewood variety may be forced most reliably during the entire period, and at a 60°F night temperature they flower from 10 to 11 weeks after planting. This is a short-term crop, and one which works in very well in small bench areas which may be available. This does not imply that Iris may be grown in any conditions. The best available light is required, and Iris must be kept well watered at all times.

Bulbs may be planted in boxes or flats, which must be at least 4 to 5 inches deep in order to provide the uniform moisture conditions required. Moving of flats at time of bud development may break roots and cause blasting of buds.   Whether they are planted in benches or boxes, the bulbs must be given adequate space.   Either 2 by 4 inches or 3 by 3 inches is satisfactory.   In some instances interplanting is used.   The first crop is spaced 2 by 6 inches, and if weekly planting is used, six equal-sized areas are planted at this spacing in 6 successive weeks.   In the seventh week, bulbs are planted midway between the rows of the first planting.   In the thirteenth week, bulbs are planted beside the bulbs in the area that was planted the first week, for by this time the flowers from the first planting have been cut.

Iris open well when they are placed in water if they are cut when the flower bud has opened just enough to show color.   This is a definite advantage if the flowers are to be shipped, as partially opened flowers pack much better than those in full bloom.   For local sales the flowers may be allowed to open more fully before they are cut.   Iris are usually bunched by the dozen.

NARCISSUS (*Narcissus* spp.—*Amaryllidaceae*)

There are many daffodils, or Narcissus varieties, but only a few of them are suitable for forcing.

The large-trumpet types have a cream- or yellow-colored trumpet as long as or longer than the corolla.   King Alfred is an example.

The medium-trumpet types have the trumpet one-third to one-half the length of the corolla.   Fortune is an example.

The short-trumpet types have the trumpet less than one-third the length of the corolla.   Mrs. R. O. Backhouse is an example.

N. jonquilla—Jonquils.   This group is characterized by round foliage, pleasing fragrance, and two to four flowers on a stem.   Odorous *regulosi* is an example.

N. tazetta—Paper White.   To this group belong the yellow and white hybrids of the bunch-flowered and star-shaped types.   Paper White (*N. lotus albus*) and Grand Soleil d'Or are typical.

N. poetaz.   These are hybrids between *N. poeticus* and *N. tazetta*, and Cheerfulness and Geranium are examples.

N. poeticus.   Poet's *Narcissus* has a white corolla and a small trumpet with dark red edge.   Actaea is an example.

N. bulbocodium—Petticoat *Narcissus*.   The trumpet is small, while the corolla is wide.   Sir Watkins is a typical example.

At the time of digging in the field, Narcissus bulbs have flower parts somewhat further developed than tulips, but they are not well differentiated.   The bulbs are stored at 90°F for 4 days to accelerate formation and subsequent development of the flower parts. Prolonged heat markedly reduces the stem length and flower size, so that the heat-curing process should not be continued beyond 4 days. Following this the bulbs are stored at 55°F until shipping.

Basal rot is a serious disease of *Narcissus*, and losses may be reduced in forcing by dusting the bulbs with Tersan before planting. One pound of the dust is used for 2,500 bulbs.

The bulbs generally arrive in early September, and they should be held at 55 to 60°F until planting, which in Ohio is usually mid-October. A field soil that is well drained should be used.

Bulbs that are to be precooled should be placed in flats or containers 4 to 5 inches deep, similar to those used for Iris. The bulbs are planted so that they almost touch each other, and they should be covered with soil so that the nose is about 1 inch below the surface. The boxes are then placed in a 50°F refrigerated storage that has a high relative humidity, and the soil should be watered thoroughly.

Bulbs may also be precooled dry in a 50°F refrigerated storage with high humidity, and this method of precooling is used by brokers or dealers. At least 6 weeks of precooling is necessary. Precooled bulbs shipped by the broker or dealer must be planted upon arrival and placed in a cool location, or the effect of the precooling treatment will be lost. Generally the bulbs arrive in mid-October. After the dry precooled bulbs are planted, the soil is watered well and the containers are placed in a 50°F refrigerated storage or buried outside in a well-drained area.

If the soil is frozen when the bulbs are brought in, it should be thawed gradually before forcing.

During the forcing period, the soil must never be allowed to become too dry, or the flower size will be reduced. Before the flower is completely open, if it is hardened off at 55°F the keeping qualities will be improved.

Experimental work on daffodils has shown that the bulbs may be stored dry for 12 weeks at 50°F, then planted in soil in a 60°F greenhouse. Although the customary rooting period before forcing has been eliminated, bulbs handled this way have only slightly shorter stems and will flower several days later than bulbs handled in the conventional manner.

Most Narcissus are used for cut flowers because the best varieties are usually too tall for pot plants. King Alfred is often suitable for pots when forced early, but it is usually too tall after Valentine's Day. Rembrandt is suitable at all seasons and has an exceptionally large flower. Texas and Van Sion are double yellows that are satisfactory, and Aerolite is a useful yellow trumpet for pots.

The double-nose No. 1 size Narcissus bulbs will generally average from 2 to 2½ flowers per bulb, while the double-nose No. 2 will average from 1½ to 1¾ flowers per bulb. Usually the highest bud count is obtained with later forcing.

Narcissus are attacked by root rot, basal plate rot, and neck rot, mites, mosaic, and nematodes.

Christmas.   King Alfred and Golden Harvest are preferred for this early forcing, and only large double-nose, precooled bulbs are suitable. The flats containing the bulbs are brought in December 1 and placed at 60°F. The flower bud should be clearly visible when the leaves are pulled apart, and the root system must be well developed or the bulbs will not force properly.

Early January.   The requirements for forcing at this period are similar to Christmas, but Rembrandt can be used in addition to King Alfred and Golden Harvest.

Midseason.   For this period precooled bulbs are not necessary, but at least 4 weeks at 60°F or 5 to 6 weeks at 56°F is needed for forcing. The boxes can be brought in beginning in mid-December.

Almost any variety may be brought into the greenhouse for forcing after January 15. In addition to those mentioned, the following varieties are very popular: for doubles, Texas and Twink; for large trumpets, Aerolite, Beersheba, Flower Carpet, Mrs. E. H. Krelage, and Queen of Bicolors; for medium and small trumpets, Fortune, Mrs. R. O. Backhouse, and Scarlet Elegance; for poeticus, Actaea; and for poetaz, Cheerfulness, Geranium, Laurens Koster, and L'Innocence.

Late.   For late March and early April the question is one of holding the bulbs back, not one of forcing them, as they develop in 10 to 14 days at temperatures prevailing at that time. Keep the flats in as cool a location as possible with very little light. A heavy covering of straw, leaves, or shavings is necessary to keep the temperature down.

The tazetta group does not require storage conditions for the formation of roots. Bulbs may be potted, flatted, or planted in a bench, and will flower easily for Christmas or before. During the winter 6 weeks is required for flowering from the time of planting, while in the spring, bulbs held in storage and planted will flower in half that time.

ORCHID (*Orchidaceae*)

The orchid family is one of the largest, with over 20,000 recorded species; however, most of these species are the exotics of the tropics and jungles, as only a few genera are used in commercial production. Cattleya, Phalaenopsis, and Cymbidium orchids are the only ones that are commercially produced in quantity in greenhouses, and in addition Cymbidiums and Vandas are produced commercially in outdoor semitropical areas.

Orchids are special-occasion flowers used mainly for weddings, formal or "dress-up" dances, Easter, and Mother's Day. Because the varieties flower at different times of the year and only once or twice a year, it has been necessary to use many different kinds for the production of flowers throughout the year. Flowering in *Cattleya* is controlled by day length and/or temperature, and the time of flower production can be adjusted by providing the proper photoperiod and temperature. Flower bud formation in *Cymbidium* takes place in cool temperatures, and these plants are grown in cool greenhouses or outdoors during the summer to promote flower bud formation.

Orchids have either sympodial- or monopodial-type growth. *Cattleya* is the best example of sympodial growth, but *Cymbidium* also is of this type. The sympodial orchids have a prostrate rhizome whose growth terminates periodically with an upright pseudobulb, leaf, and flowers. The flowers are terminal, and after the flowering a vegetative bud starts to grow at the base of the pseudobulb, forming a prostrate rhizome that terminates in a pseudobulb, leaf, and flowers. As this succession of growth—prostrate rhizome to upright flowering pseudobulb to prostrate rhizome—occurs, the plant eventually grows or extends over the edge of the pot and must be repotted.

Phalaenopsis has monopodial-type growth, in which the upright stem continues in uninterrupted terminal growth, producing closely spaced leaves as growth progresses, and periodically a flower stalk develops from a leaf axil. The monopodial orchids also form aerial roots from the stem as they proceed in their upward growth.

Propagation. Propagation of orchids by seed is a technical procedure that is handled best by the specialist. It is a means of developing new varieties, and some of the features sought in the new plants are heavier textured, larger, and longer lasting flowers; improved color; better flowering period; and faster and more vigorous growth and development. By knowing the characteristics of the parents, it is possible to predict the type of offspring with some degree of accuracy.

Propagation by seed is a time-consuming process: 4 to 8 years passes from the time of pollination until the flowering of the mature plant. The seed is sown on nutrient agar in aseptic surroundings, and the seedlings are transplanted to pots or small flats as soon as roots have developed.

The successful production of orchid seedlings requires detailed information, much experience, special equipment, and a devotion to the subject. It is a fascinating occupation that attracts many individuals, but most orchid growers would benefit from obtaining their seedlings from a reliable specialist.   For those that want to try propagation of orchids by seed, a good reference is *The Orchids,* by Carl L. Withner, published by the Ronald Press Company.

If the seedlings are obtained from the propagator in the seed flasks, a small wire hook may be used for their removal from the flask.   They are planted in either fir bark (⅛- to ¼-inch size) or a mixture of ½ fir bark, ¼ German peat, and ¼ perlite in small flats.   After planting, the seedlings should be drenched with Morsodren for disease control.   Uniformly moist conditions must be provided, and the seedlings should be misted frequently or covered with polyethylene film until the plants are established.

Orchid seedlings are grown at 70°F and in partially shaded locations that provide from 1,000 to 2,000 foot-candles of light.   Faster growth and good-quality plants can be obtained by extending the day length to 18 hours with electric lights that furnish 2 to 5 foot-candles of light.

The plants should be fertilized regularly when they are established in the flats, using 20-20-20 or lower analysis at the rate of 2 ounces per 100 gallons of water with each irrigation.

When the plants are large enough they are transplanted to small clay pots, and they are then transplanted to larger pots as growth requires.

Cattleya and other orchids that form pseudobulbs can be propagated by division.   The division is made so that there are at least four good pseudobulbs with each section, and they are then potted.   If virus is present, it is possible to transmit it with the knife or shears that is used to make the division.   To avoid contamination, the tools should be sterilized between each cut by steam or by dipping them in a solution of calcium hypochlorite.   The growth of the divisions may be slow depending on the condition of the pseudobulbs.

With *Cymbidium*, divisions of one or more of the pseudobulbs are started in a mixture of sand and peat at 65°F and in moist surroundings.   When the leaves are 6 inches long, the young plants are potted.

Phalaenopsis can be propagated vegetatively from growths formed on the flowering stem and known as offsets.   The flowering stem may be cut into sections of at least one node, its surface may be sterilized in a calcium hypochlorite solution, and it may be planted in a fine potting mixture.   Offsets form at the nodes, and when the roots of the offset are about ¾ inch long, it is removed from the flowering stem and potted.

Meristem culture is a detailed laboratory procedure that can be used for the vegetative propagation of orchids.   The advantages of meristem culture are that a large number of individuals can be propagated from a single clone selection in a short period of time and that the propagation of virus-free stock may be coupled with the procedure.   Actually meristem culture is a method of propagation by division, but the divisions are tiny sections of a growing point (meristem).   The sections are handled in aseptic conditions, and they are started in growth in a nutrient culture.   It appears that meristem culture is one of the most important developments in the commercial production of orchids.

Potting mixtures.   The same potting mixture may be used for *Cattleya* and *Phalaenopsis* except that for *Phalaenopsis* the pH of the mixture must be adjusted to 6.0 with limestone, and the plants are potted more loosely than Cattleya plants and watered more frequently.   The roots of the monopodial-type *Phalaenopsis* are structurally different from the roots of the sympodial-type *Cattleya,* and root growth is best with slightly different treatment.

Osmunda fiber was used for years as a potting medium for orchids, but more recently various mixtures of bark and peat have been used.   When osmunda was used, it was necessary to pot the plants very firmly; and the potting procedure occupied much of the total labor time.   The osmunda was firmed with stick in hand, or in some instances potting machines were fabricated that did the firming faster.   Much less firming and consequently much less potting time are required when fir bark mixtures are used.

The requirements of the potting mixtures for orchids are good aeration, uniform moisture conditions, and a source of supply of minerals.   When osmunda fiber was used, it was considered that orchids should not be supplied fertilizer, as the osmunda did contain a small amount of nitrogen.   However, subsequent experimental and commercial trials of growing orchids in gravel or haydite that were fertilized regularly demonstrated the basic requirements of the potting medium, which led to the use of various potting materials and regular additions of fertilizer.

A good potting mixture is made from poultry-litter-grade German peat moss, ¼-inch fir bark, shredded redwood bark (Palco wool), and horticultural-grade perlite.   The proportions for a common mixture are 18 cubic feet fir bark, 1 bale peat moss, ¼ bale shredded redwood bark, and 3 cubic feet perlite.   These materials must be moist but not wet before mixing, and they are mixed with a shovel before being passed through a shredder.   Because of the difference in weight of the various ingredients, the mixture must be discharged downward from the shredder in order to remain well mixed.

For a coarser mixture a greater proportion of fir bark may be used.   Such a mixture has better aeration but has to be watered more frequently.   A coarse mixture should be firmed more when potting to produce suitably uniform moisture conditions for the roots.   Apparently a pest problem is related to the coarseness of the fir bark mixture, too, as small bush snails that feed on orchid roots can be harbored in a coarse mixture.   Control of this pest is easier in finer potting mixtures.

Because the rhizome of *Cattleya* is prostrate and grows horizontally, this orchid is potted toward one edge of the pot; and eventually the leading growth of the rhizome reaches the other edge of the pot.   It is necessary then to repot the plant.   The rhizome is cut into sections each containing 4 or 6 pseudobulbs, and each section may be repotted.

Because the growth of *Phalaenopsis* is continuously upward, the plant eventually becomes too large and must be replaced with younger plants that have been started from offsets or seed.

Orchids are classed often by their position of growth in their natural habitats.   Some orchids grow on tree trunks or branches above ground level and are classed as epiphytes.   Other orchids grow in or on the ground in natural conditions and are classed as terrestrial.   *Cattleya* and *Phalaenopsis* are epiphytes, and *Cypripedium* is terrestrial.   Some orchids may be found as either epiphytes or terrestrials, and *Cymbidium* is one of these.   Commercially *Cymbidium* may be grown in ground beds or in large pots or tubs, and the medium is more of a terrestrial mixture.   Cymbidium potting mixtures must be well drained but retain moisture, and they are commonly made from mixtures of German peat moss, leaf mold, and sharp, coarse sand.   The pH should be maintained at pH 5.5 to 6.0.

Although *Cymbidium* has sympodial-type growth, the horizontal extension of the rhizome is slight; and the plant can remain in the same tub for a long time without division and repotting.

Moisture and fertilizer.   Orchids are grown in coarse, well-drained mixtures, and they must be maintained moist.   Irrigation must be frequent enough to keep the mixture moist and heavy enough to provide some leaching with each watering, and with *Cattleya* and *Phalaenopsis* the irrigation method must be such that thorough watering is accomplished without getting water on the upper portions of the plants.   If watertight benches are available, subirrigation of the pots may be used.   If proper breakers are used, irrigation systems using small-diameter, black polyethylene tubing can probably be installed.

The air moisture content should be maintained at approximately 70 percent relative humidity for young plants and plants in leaf; however, for plants that are in bud and flower, too much air moisture may promote some flower diseases.   Continuous air movement with air-circulation fans and the proper regulation of heating lines and ventilators can provide suitable humidity.

Orchids do not grow rapidly, and large quantities of minerals are not required.   Various fertilizers and rates of application are used at different greenhouses; but if the irrigation is thorough with some leaching, a 20-20-20 fertilizer may be used with alternate irrigations at the rate of 5½ ounces per 100 gallons of water.

Light.   Orchids grow best in light intensities from 1,000 to 3,000 footcandles.   At higher light intensity the leaves become yellow and may develop burned areas, and at lower light intensity the leaves are dark green and the development of the plant delayed.   In many localities a partial shade needs to be provided to reduce the amount of light for orchids. Light intensity can be regulated by lath shades on the roof, shading compounds sprayed or painted on the roof, or plastic screen suspended over the plants in the greenhouse. Generally some shade must be provided between February and November.

Flowering in *Cattleya* can be controlled with day length: delayed by long days and promoted by short days. Commercially, day length is controlled primarily to delay flowering to coincide with a better market period. If a variety flowers in natural conditions in February, it may be given artificially long days to delay flowering until Easter; or a variety that flowers naturally in October may be delayed in flowering until Thanksgiving or Christmas by providing artificially long days.

It is possible to predict with some accuracy the natural flowering period of a seedling by knowing the flowering characteristics of the parents, and the lighting procedure to time flowering for a certain period also can be predicted. The length of time required for flower bud initiation and development varies with the variety, but with several of the varieties flowering occurs 90 to 120 days after the start of short days. To delay flowering, lighting then would have to be started at least 17 weeks before the time of natural flowering, and lighting would be discontinued about 17 weeks before the time of desired flowering. It is theoretically possible to produce vegetative growth or flowering by providing the temperature and day-length conditions as needed, and by doing this a variety could be flowered at any time of the year. Commercially it has been more practical to use several varieties or groups of varieties and flower them within a few weeks of the natural flowering period.

Seedlings which are produced from the same cross will have similar characteristics including the time of natural flowering, but they will not be exactly the same. The time of flowering of a group of seedlings can vary by a few months. As vegetative propagation by means of meristem culture comes to be used more commonly, it will be possible to have large numbers of exactly the same clone; and timing of flowering will possibly be more responsive and other characteristics will be identical for the entire group of plants that are produced from a single individual.

Artificial lighting to provide long days can be supplied to orchids in the same manner as it is to Chrysanthemums; and if black cloth shading is needed, it is also done in the same way.

Flowering in Cymbidiums apparently is not affected by day length, and the time of cropping is controlled solely by temperature.

Temperature. *Cattleya* should be grown at a 60°F night temperature and about 10°F warmer during the day; however, in some instances temperatures about 5°F lower are used during the flower-forming stage as this promotes flower initiation in some varieties.

When possible, *Phalaenopsis* is grown in temperatures about 5°F warmer than those used for *Cattleya*.

Summertime temperatures should be kept below 95°F as leaves may be burned in higher temperatures. Orchid houses are commonly shaded to reduce the temperature in periods of high light intensity, and fan and pad or mist cooling is desirable.

Cymbidiums are grown in cooler temperatures—generally 5 to 10°F cooler than those used for *Cattleya* whenever possible. Fan and pad or mist cooling systems are helpful for the warm period of the year. Flowering of *Cymbidium* is promoted by cool temperature, and as soon as possible in the fall the temperature is maintained at 45 to 55°F.

Air. Continuous air movement should be provided as this helps to maintain the uniform temperature and the needed moisture conditions. High humidity when Cattleyas are in bud and flower provides conditions that are suitable for development of some flower diseases.

Flowers are injured by smog, ethylene, or other air impurities that are found in industrial areas, and the best solution in such a situation may be to move to an area where the air is not contaminated.

Some trials have been made with orchids in atmospheres with increased carbon dioxide, but the results have been inconclusive.

Troubles. Black areas on the leaf are caused by the sun's heating the leaf area to a point where the tissues are killed. Shade on the roof or cloth shades under the glass will prevent this.

In periods of high humidity, particularly in spring and fall when heat is not used at night, the yellow pigmented areas in the throats of Cattleya orchids often turn black several days after cutting. This may be due to a fungus. Control is accomplished by use of additional heat plus ventilation. It is advisable not to refrigerate the flowers for a period of 12 hours after cutting if this difficulty is experienced.

In periods of hot, humid weather an exudate may appear on the lips of dark orchids which causes a discoloration and collapse of the tissue and ruins the flower. Heat and ventilation at night will prevent the trouble. It is often necessary to keep the night temperature higher than normal to provide the circulation of the air.

"Dry sepal" of *Cattleya* is a problem when humidity is high, particularly in industrial areas where smog is prevalent. Certain varieties of Cattleya orchids are highly susceptible, while others are quite resistant to dry sepal damage.

Cold injury on Cattleya orchids is characterized by the throat turning brown, the end of the column turning black, and the petals and sepals becoming water-soaked in appearance. Flowers of the Cattleya, Cymbidium, Cypripedium, and Vanda orchids should be stored at a temperature range of 50 to 55°F with the optimum at 55°F.

Deformed flowers of many Cattleya hybrids are caused by continued temperatures of 55°F or lower during bud development, which may occur during attempts to delay the development of the flowers. This condition should not be confused with deformities which are hereditary.

Wilting of the flower, if not due to old age, is generally caused by pollination, usually by bumblebees.

Pests. Scale, snails, and thrips are the worst orchid pests. The best controls are metaldehyde dusts for snails, aquamalathion for scale, and dieldrin for thrips. Aphids, mealy bugs, slugs, and millipedes may be troublesome also.

Diseases. There are several virus diseases, and what is known as the Cattleya virus is one of the more serious. The flower color is streaked or broken, usually rendering it unsalable, and the plant will eventually die. The virus can be transmitted by a knife when cutting rhizomes or roots, and infected plants should be discarded. The Cymbidium mosaic virus causes loss of vigor on Cattleya plants, and symptoms appear on the leaves as lighter colored green streaks or areas which later turn brown or black and often are sunken. The flowers are not affected.

Botrytis causes a red-brown area to develop and occurs when there is drip on the plants in cool or cold weather.

Root rot is a serious fungus disease on *Cattleya* and is prevalent when the medium is kept too wet and cold (below 60°F).

Brown rot attacks the crown of *Cypripedium* and *Phalaenopsis* and is evidenced by a soft rot at the base of the leaves. Standing water in the crown should be avoided by watering early in the day and maintaining a lower humidity at night.

Cutting. The Cattleya flower should be cut from 3 to 5 days after the bud dehisces or splits depending on whether the weather conditions are favorable for rapid development. Cutting is facilitated if the plants are tagged each day as the buds split, and the flower on the tagged plant then is cut 3 to 5 days later. After cutting, the flower stems are placed in water at an air temperature of 55 to 60°F. Orchid flowers should never be placed in temperatures lower than 50°F because transparent "water spots" may appear on the petals or the flowers may wilt.

Phalaenopsis flowers are cut when they are fully open, either individually or as an entire spray. If the spray is cut above the bracts on the lower stem, a new flowering shoot will develop.

Cymbidium flowers can be cut individually, but more often the entire spike is removed and the individual flowers are cut at the time of grading and packing. The flower stems should be placed in water after cutting; and if they are kept in an air temperature of 55°F, they will keep for several weeks. Of all the cut flowers, the *Cymbidium* has the best keeping qualities.

Shipping. For shipping, the flower stems are inserted through gum rubber caps into small tubes filled with water. The opening of the rubber cap must be sufficiently large so that it does not restrict water movement in the stem. The tubes are taped or sewn to the bottom of the boxes, with the flowers on crumpled or shredded wax paper. Enough shredded wax paper is used around the flowers so that they do not rub on each other or on rough surfaces in transit.

ROSE (*Rosa hybrida—Rosaceae*)

Our present-day varieties are all hybrids which have been derived from crosses between *R. gallica* and *R. chinensis,* from which came the Hybrid Chinese. *R. chinensis* was also crossed with *R. centifolia* to produce *R. Edward.* This in turn crossed with *R. gallica,* which resulted in *R. bourbon.* A triple cross of the Hybrid Chinese, *R. bourbon,* and *R. damascena* in two successive generations developed our present-day hybrid perpetuals. To secure continuity of bloom, a further cross of the hybrid perpetuals with *R. chinensis odorata* resulted in the hybrid tea, which is the type largely used for forcing purposes, as it combines the necessary qualities of productiveness, fragrance, attractiveness of bud, and multiplicity of colors.

The hybrid tea rose forms a large terminal flower per stem, and if any lateral flower buds form, they are disbudded. The demand for red roses is greatest, and some yellow, pink, and white hybrid tea roses are grown also. Roses are in particular demand for holidays, and the plants are handled in such a way that greater production is realized at those times.

Some floribunda roses are grown. They are smaller flowered varieties that may produce a lone terminal flower per stem, or lateral flower buds may form and be retained so that there is a spray of flowers per stem. Several of the floribunda varieties have better keeping qualities than the hybrid teas, and because of this the demand for them has increased. Light pink is the most popular color, followed by red, yellow, and white. Typically only about 10 percent of the rose range may be used for floribunda production, but that would account for more than 10 percent of the total flower production, as floribunda plants may produce up to twice as many flowers as hybrid teas.

Roses usually are planted in the spring, and flower production may start 2 to 3 months after planting. Rose stems form leaves and increase in length in the early stages of growth. Eventually flower parts start to form in the stem tip, and growth terminates with a flower. When the flower is cut, new shoot growth starts in the axils of the leaves below the cut, and the growth and flowering cycle is repeated.   Growth and flowering are faster in good light and warm weather, but flowers are formed in the rose at any time regardless of the day length or season.   Rose plants may be pruned or cut back during the second and third summers in order to keep them within height limits, but other than that the plants are cropped continuously for approximately 4 years before they are discarded and replaced with new plants.

Propagation.   Roses are reproduced vegetatively by means of cuttings, grafts, and buds to produce the plants for the production of flowers.   Each method has good features, and equally good results can be obtained with any method, depending on how it is handled.   However, budded plants are used more commonly than rooted cuttings or grafted plants because they can be handled better in typical situations that exist.   Budded plants are dormant when they are received from the propagator, and they remain dormant and in good condition when properly refrigerated.   They may be kept dormant in refrigerated storage from December until June or planted at any time during that period with good results, and this provides a flexible planting program that is needed in many instances.   Rooted cuttings and grafted plants are actively growing plants—or at least they should be, and the only way that good plants can be produced is by providing the best growing conditions at all times.   This is particularly important in the early stages of growth.   The time of propagation must be coordinated carefully with the time of planting so that the plants can be kept growing actively all the time.   It is not possible to delay planting and still achieve good results with either rooted cuttings or grafted plants, but when they are handled properly, they can be just as good as budded plants.

Sexual propagation is used only for the production of new varieties. Rose breeding requires special techniques and equipment, and it can be handled only by the specialist.

Budded plants are produced in a year's time on the West Coast or in Arizona, and they may be either started-eye or dormant-eye plants.   *R. manetti* is used for the understock; hardwood cuttings of this plant are lined out in the fields in December, the budding is done from late May to August, and the mature, budded plants are dug in December.

A well-drained nonpacking soil with a fair grade to facilitate irrigation is preferred.   Numerous fine roots form in fine, sandy soil, while fewer, large roots form in heavy clay soil.   The former type of soil is preferred at the time of budding and digging, but generally it requires more irrigation.   The rows are best lined in the direction of the prevailing wind to prevent the started-eye from breaking off at the union, especially the first shoot.   The cuttings are planted in December as soon as they are made, with a spacing of 3 inches in rows 4 feet apart.   No furrowing is required for irrigation at the time of planting; it is usually done after a couple of good showers. Lines for planting are made by means of markers drawn along by a horse or tractor. The cuttings are merely pushed into the soft ground with about 1 inch exposed and foot-tramped along the side to ensure firmness. Weeding and cultivation begin in the spring as soon as the ground becomes workable, but care must be taken not to disturb the cuttings or rooting will be hindered. Irrigation is usually not necessary until the middle of May; then it is done by making a ditch alongside each row with a single plow and a horse. At this stage, the cuttings are well established with a foot or more of top growth so that a little disturbance by ditching will not affect growth. Moisture is retained to a greater extent if cultivation is not practiced until a week after irrigation.

Budding may start as early as the latter part of May, that is, as soon as the bark starts "slipping" and the cuttings have attained fair size. If budding is done too early, the process will be difficult and the cuttings dislodged or the roots injured. If done too late, the bark is too thick and will cover the bud. The process is continued throughout the summer until the middle of August. The plants budded from early May to July 15 will be grown as started-eyes, and the later ones, from July 15 through August, will be used for dormant-buds.

The bud wood of the desired variety is obtained from either outdoors or the greenhouse, making sure it is ripe and free of mosaic. It is cut into lengths of 10 to 12 inches and stripped of all thorns, and the leaves are cut off, allowing a short petiole to remain, while being careful not to injure the bark near a bud. A knife is used if difficulty is encountered in removing the thorns. The scions are then wrapped in moist burlap or plastic bags to prevent desiccation.

Stocks to be budded are furrowed 3 to 4 inches deep on each side by a single plow, a previous irrigation being required if the ground is too hard. Too deep furrowing will cause the wind to blow the stocks over and injure the roots. The budding process is done in groups of three—by a hoer, a budder, and a tier. The hoer scrapes the soil away from the plant and cleans the clinging soil from the bark by a burlap strip tied to the end of a stick. The budder, carrying his bud stocks in a small box protected from the sun, makes the cut and inserts the bud. The tier follows and ties the bud with small rubber strips which decay and fall off in about 3 weeks. The first application of water is given 10 days after the budding and is continued periodically throughout the growing season.

The tops of the plants budded from May through July 15 are cut off about 1 inch above the inserted bud. This is done 3 weeks after budding in order to force the bud into growth. The stock tops may be partially cut through and then bent over, which allows food from the top to nourish the root. The stock top is later completely severed. The shoot that develops is pinched to three eyes to force out bottom breaks. This plant becomes the started-eye or started-bud type of plant, so named because the eye or bud that was inserted was forced to start or grow during the summer. The tops of the late-budded plants are not removed until the plants are dug, and because the eye or bud did not grow during the summer, the plant is known as a dormant-eye or dormant-bud.

All plants are dug in December, graded, and packed for shipment to greenhouse operators. With started-eye plants the XXX grade is preferred, as there should be several heavy shoots per plant. The tops of the dormant-bud plants are used as hardwood cuttings for the next year's plants. Mosaic is spread rapidly as a result of this random used of hardwood cuttings. Even though a manetti cutting is free of mosaic when stuck in the field, if the bud that is inserted is infected with mosaic, the disease spreads through the manetti plant, and when it is used as stock the following year, all plants budded on it will be infected. Because certain types of mosaic lower the vitality of the plant, the use of selected stool blocks free of mosaic and the use of mosaic-free buds are practices which would meet with approval of the forcers of greenhouse roses. Producers of plants estimate that from the time the cuttings are stuck until the plants are shipped, losses may run about 50 percent. This is due to failure of cuttings to root, failure of buds to unite and grow, breakage, pests, and other factors.

Occasionally some budding is done in the flower production greenhouses, and this is called "top budding" as buds of new varieties are inserted in the top portions of producing plants so that the flower qualities of the new varieties can be observed, or in order to increase bud wood of the new variety. The bud is inserted in a T cut and tied with a rubber strip, and 3 weeks after budding the shoot above the inserted bud is cut off to start growth in the new bud.

Grafting of rose plants is a greenhouse operation that is used by some operators to produce a portion or all of the plants that they need for replanting their greenhouses. In some instances they also graft additional plants for resale to other rose growers. *R. manetti* usually is used for understock, and it is obtained from West Coast or European growers. The grafts are made from February through April. The plants are set in closed cases or under mist until the graft knits, and then they are placed in regular greenhouse conditions to produce some top growth before planting. Grafting can be a very successful method of propagation if it is carefully timed so that the plants are benched as rapidly as possible, good growing conditions are provided at all times, and plant growth is continuous and unchecked.

The *R. manetti* understock is potted in 2½- or 3-inch rose pots (the rose pot is deeper than its diameter). Potting may be done just before grafting, or it may be done a few weeks before grafting so that root growth has started before the graft is made.

The scion wood for the splice grafting should be selected from the flowering shoots. The upper end of the scion will contain a bud accompanied by a leaf, although the leaf area is normally reduced to four leaflets. The scion is usually one to three eyes in length. Larger scions are not recommended. Hook scions, which are made from that portion of the stem from which a flower has previously been cut or where a pinch has been made, will produce larger plants, and when planted in the bench, they will break from the base much more easily than the more common one-eye scions. The scion wood should be of medium texture and free from pests; it should be kept moist during the grafting operations. Scion wood should not be taken from plants recently sprayed with oil sprays sometimes used to control red spider. Foliage when so treated is softened, and when placed in the grafting case often turns yellow and drops from the scion. As a result, the graft fails to unite.

The top of stock is first cut off with pruning shears, 1½ to 2 inches above the soil, and then a slanting cut is made with a sharp knife as close to the pot as possible. The cut at the base of the scion is made at a similar angle. The scion and stock are then joined together so that the cambium layers, on one side at least, are in contact. It is important to keep ⅟₁₆ inch of the cut surface of the scion above the top of the understock. The graft is tied firmly with raffia, rubber strips, or waxed string. The grafted plant is watered so that the cut surface will not dry out before reaching the case.

The bark graft is useful in cases where the stocks are much larger than the scions. It is performed by first cutting off the stock 1½ to 2 inches above the soil, then making a vertical cut about 1 inch long at the top of the stock extending into the cambium. The scion is sliced in the same way as described for splice grafting, and it is inserted between the bark and the cambium of the stock in the area of the vertical cut. The top of the understock should be cut on a slight slant, and the scion is placed into the understock on that side which is at the base of the slanted cut. This will allow moisture to run into the graft union and prevent drying. Tying is done with rubber strips or raffia.

After the graft is made, the plants must be kept in a warm and moist atmosphere, and these conditions are provided in either a closed grafting case or an open bench with intermittent mist. A temperature of 75°F should be maintained, and the graft union must be kept uniformly moist. These conditions are obtained in grafting cases by plunging the pots into moist peat moss and covering the case with panes of glass. The case is kept completely closed for several days, and then opened gradually as the graft knits. With plants in benches under mist, the misting is reduced gradually as the graft knits. From 3 to 4 weeks is required in the grafting case or under mist, and the plants should be benched within 4 weeks following that. For best results with grafted plants, the graft should be made 2 months before the plants are to be benched. If the plants are to be benched June 1, the graft should be made about April 1. If any more time than that is allotted, it is not possible to keep the young plant in good growing condition in the small pot, and the growth of the grafted plant after planting will be slow and of poor quality.

Rooted cuttings of roses are commonly called "own-roots." This term arose and is in general usage because it acknowledges that the rooted cutting has the roots of its own variety, but the roots of grafts or buds are *R. manetti*. There are controversies on whether roses grow better on their own or manetti roots. This may be an academic question as rose soils are heavily mulched, and roots form above the graft or bud so that even grafted or budded plants grow on their own roots, too.

Some rose growers use rooted cuttings for a portion or all of their rose plant requirements. Two eye cuttings are used, and they root in about 5 weeks with a bench temperature of 70°F and an air temperature of 60°F. Several rooting materials are satisfactory, and mixtures of perlite and peat moss are commonly used. The cuttings are spaced 1 inch apart in the row with 3 inches between rows. Rose cuttings should be furnished as much light as possible without drying the cuttings. Intermittent mist systems should be used whenever possible because they provide the needed uniform moisture without excessive shading of the propagation area.

Either unrooted or rooted rose cuttings can be held in 31 to 33°F storage up to a few weeks with satisfactory results, and this can be an aid because the cuttings can then be collected for a period of time before being stuck or planted. If the cuttings are placed in plastic bags which are not sealed, they will have good air-moisture environment during storage.

The rooted cutting may be potted or planted directly in the bench. If the cuttings are potted, they must be planted within 3 weeks after potting to avoid hardening because of limited area for root growth. When the cuttings are planted directly in the bench, they are usually provided with better growing conditions, and the end results are better.

Roses are propagated sexually only by the hybridizer in an attempt to develop new varieties. As the color develops in the petals, the mother-plant flower is emasculated (the anthers are removed) to prevent self-pollination; and when the stigma is sticky, pollen from the staminate parent is transferred to it. The pollinated flower is then covered with a plastic bag until the seed begins to form.

In natural conditions rose seed does not germinate until the second year after sowing, but the hybridizer shortens this time by a cold-storage period. The seed is removed from the hips (rose fruits) by crushing and fermentation, and the clean seed is then disinfected and stratified in moist peat moss at 35 to 45°F for 4 to 6 months.

Planting, spacing, and supporting. The time of planting is based on the availability of bench space and on the development of good plant growth in sufficient time for flower crop production. Bench space becomes available primarily when old, producing rose plants are removed, and in many instances the most economical time to remove them is in May after the Mother's Day crop has been harvested.   The removal of the old plants is very often timed to follow one of the holiday crops, which may be Christmas, Valentine's Day, Easter, or Mother's Day.   Rose plants are kept in production for about 4 years, and about one-fourth of the rose range is replanted each year.   Cropping and work is better spaced if the replanting is done over a period of a few months in the spring.

An Easter crop of flowers can be produced from plantings made in late December and January, and a Mother's Day cut can be made from plants benched in January and February.   This first crop, however, must not be taken if the general growth and development of the plants are not satisfactory.   Flower production starts during the summer in plants benched later in the spring.

In most areas growing conditions in the spring are the best for starting rose plants; however, if either fan and pad or mist cooling is provided, roses can be planted during the summer and produce good growth.   The primary objective is to develop rose plants with good, heavy canes and large leaves, as such plants produce the best growth during the poor light conditions of the winter.

Rose plants are spaced about 12 by 12 inches, and there is no advantage in deep planting.   Plants that are shallow-planted form roots more readily than ones that are planted deeper; and since mulches are applied later to rose soils, shallow planting prevents the plant from being buried too deeply in the mulch.

Some budded rose plants have such a large root system that some pruning of roots may need to be done before planting, but as large a root system as can be handled in planting should be retained.   The roots should be spread in the soil rather than knotted or bunched together.

After planting, the plants must be watered in well, but during the dark and cold weather in December and January they should be spot-watered—leaving dry areas between plants.   The entire soil area is then watered thoroughly at the second irrigation.   When planting takes place later in the season during good light and temperature conditions, the entire soil area should be thoroughly watered with the first irrigation.

The air around the plants must be maintained as moist as possible.   This provides a more suitable atmosphere for shoot development in the dormant budded plant, and it maintains the leaf and stem growth in grafted plants or rooted cuttings until new root growth supplies water to the plants.

Budded plants may be planted in the dormant stage directly from refrigerated storage, or they may be "sweated out" for a few days by being kept moist at 60°F until the eyes start to swell.   There are some advantages to both methods of handling, but with either one it is important to keep the tops of the plants moist.   After planting, the air can be kept moist around the plants by misting periodically or by covering the plants.   More uniform air moisture is usually maintained by covering unless a mechanically operated mist system is used, as it is virtually impossible to mist regularly enough with hose in hand.   Various covers may be used successfully.   The plants may be covered directly with either sphagnum moss or straw, or clear plastic or light cloth may be supported just above the plants. This is a critical period in which much better results follow with uniform humidity. The plants must be observed very carefully, and as shoot development takes place, the cover is removed gradually. Not all the plants may develop at the same rate, and it is necessary to cover the slower plants individually when the cover is removed from the entire area.

Grafted plants and rooted cuttings are actively growing plants at the time they are planted. They need to be in moist air for several days after planting, but they cannot be covered directly. It is best to mist regularly, cover with a light cloth above the plants, or use a combination of the two methods.

Rose plants need some nitrogen in the early stages of growth. If the nitrogen in the soil is low at the time of planting, a fertilizer containing nitrogen should be applied with the first irrigation.

A method of support is needed to keep rose stems erect, and either individual plant stakes or a series of grids are used. When stakes are used, a galvanized No. 9 wire stake is inserted in the soil beside each plant and attached at the top to a wire that is stretched the length of the bench. As the stems develop on the rose plant, they are tied individually to the stake. When grids are used, they may be either welded wire fabric or wire run the length of the bench between the rows of plants with string laced across the bench between the plants. The first grid is installed about 18 inches above the soil, and succeeding grids are placed at about 15-inch intervals above the first. As the rose stems develop, they are guided into the upright columns formed by the grids.

Light. Light is generally considered the most important limiting factor in the growth of plants in the greenhouse. The intensity of light is highest in summer, and it is at this time that the greatest number of roses is produced by the plants unless they are cut back during this period. Under the low light conditions of winter, fewer flowers are produced.

Day length has no apparent effect on the growth and flowering of roses.

As the sunlight increases or decreases, depending upon the season, growers modify the practices of watering, fertilizing, cutting, and pinching. Cultural practices vary from season to season, depending upon light and its effect on temperature. Fertilization with nitrogen is frequent in spring, summer, and fall because of favorable light conditions for growth. Reduced light in winter is associated with lesser amounts of fertilizer. Excessive use of fertilizer at this time causes damage because reduced watering and absorption by the plants result in nitrogen accumulation in the soil.

Because of the high light intensity and the resultant rise in temperature in summer, many growers in the Middle West apply a shading compound to the roof. A reduction of light intensity to about 6,000 to 8,000 foot-candles from about 10,000 to 12,000 foot-candles is apparently satisfactory. The temperature is reduced, relative humidity is increased, and generally the stems will be longer with somewhat darker green leaves. Too much shade seriously reduces growth, and mildew infections can become serious. Shade is often applied lightly in early May, is increased in June and July, and should be removed by late August. When the greenhouses are cooled by means of fan and pad, mists, or high-pressure fogs, little or no shade is needed on the roof. Such a condition is favorable for growth because of the high light intensity together with the cool temperatures.

Cutting and pinching practices depend upon light intensity because of their effect on food manufacture. In spring, summer, and early fall it is not always necessary to allow two 5-leaflet leaves to remain on the plant. Cuts can be made leaving knuckles, or stubs, on heavy wood from March to October, but in winter such a practice usually would result in blind shoots. As the light intensity decreases in the fall, it is important with most varieties that two 5-leaflet leaves remain on the shoot to make food for additional flowers. Very often shoots are pinched in the fall to add foliage to the plant.

The light intensity within the greenhouse also affects the plants. In an east to west house, rose plants in the south row of a bench produce more flowers than plants in any other row. The plants in the north row are next in production, followed by the inner rows. The production from plants in wide benches with five or more rows of plants across will not be great because of the increased number of inner rows.

Temperature. Most rose varieties are grown at a night temperature of 60°F because at that temperature the quality and quantity of roses produced are considered satisfactory. At lower temperatures growth is slower and production is reduced, but the quality of the flowers is higher. At higher temperatures growth is increased and production is greater, but the quality is not as good. Temperature affects the rate of all physiological processes, such as photosynthesis, respiration, and amino acid and protein formation in the plant, and their effect on growth is governed by the temperature maintained in the greenhouse.

The temperature on sunny days is generally maintained 10 to 15°F warmer, if possible, than the night temperature. The purpose of this is to allow for greater food manufacture in the leaves. It is believed that at temperatures above 85°F the rate of photosynthesis levels off; therefore such high temperatures are undesirable. With a reduction of light intensity on cloudy days, the temperature is raised no more than 5°F because of the reduced rate of photosynthesis.

Respiration occurs both day and night and proceeds at a faster rate as the temperature increases. Therefore loss of food can result in poorer quality roses if night and day temperatures are not regulated properly.

The synthesis of proteins and amino acids, which are vital constituents of cells, takes place in the presence of a favorable supply of carbohydrates and some form of nitrogen, so that regulation of temperature affects the materials from which new growth is made.

The rate at which temperatures should be changed from night to day, and vice versa, is not known. As the sun rises, the greenhouse is heated, and there is no difficulty in reaching the desired temperature. In fact, on bright sunny days it is usually impossible to keep the temperature from going beyond the desired point unless the greenhouse is cooled by fan and pad, mists, or fogs. Bringing down the air temperature in the evening may require quite some time in warm weather because the structure, benches, soil, and plants are warm and it may be difficult to dissipate this heat by nightfall. In cold weather lowering the temperature to the desired point is no problem.

The temperature of the water applied to the soil appears to have little measurable effect on the plants. Warm water is not effective in increasing production, and cold water drops the soil temperature several degrees for only a matter of a few hours.

Soil.   Since roses remain in the bench for a period of several years, thorough preparation of soil is imperative. When new soil is to be brought into the benches, a system of field preparation, as suggested in Chap. 6, is advised. In addition, organic matter should be added to the soil in the bench regardless of the adequacy of preparation in the field.

When rose plants are removed from the bench, it is the usual practice to add some kind of organic matter rather than laboriously to change the soil for the next planting. For years manure has been used with good results, but as it is becoming scarce, other materials can be substituted quite satisfactorily. Coarse peat moss is an excellent material since it is low in fertilizer and quite resistant to decomposition. Ground corncobs have also been mixed with soil, but there is danger of nitrogen starvation caused by the growth of microorganisms as the cobs decompose. Chopped straw or hay can be used, but they deteriorate rapidly and their effect is very temporary. Peanut hulls, chopped sugar cane, rice hulls, and cottonseed hulls may be used, if available.

Rose soils must remain coarse and porous, and with some soils it will be helpful to incorporate ¼- to ½-inch-grade haydite or calcined clay. The amount to add varies with the soil. Heavy, clay soils will benefit from larger additions.

Whatever mulch remains on the soil when the plants are removed can be incorporated, but unless the mulch was recently applied, it probably is quite decomposed and as such adds little but bulk to the soil.

When either peat or manure is added, the amount should be at least one-fourth by volume. It should be incorporated throughout the entire body of soil where roots will develop.

The improved growth of plants benched in steamed soil compared to similar soil not steamed makes steam sterilization a necessary step in soil preparation.

Mulches are used for a number of purposes in rose houses. Primarily, they reduce soil moisture loss by evaporation, but they also prevent the running together and resultant packing of the soil particles at the surface when water is applied, by acting as a barrier between the water and soil. Mulches also keep the soil somewhat cooler in summer. Roots will permeate a mulch, and the mulch therefore adds to the area where roots can develop. As mulches decompose, carbon dioxide is released into the greenhouse atmosphere, and this may keep the carbon dioxide concentration in rose houses at a favorable level.

The chemical changes induced by a mulch are dependent upon the type of material used. Peat may lower the pH somewhat, but it usually does not affect the fertilizer levels. Well-rotted manure has little chemical effect, but fresh manure will cause a rise in nitrates. Corncobs generally bring about a rapid depletion of soil nitrogen, and the rose plants may become starved and hardened unless some form of nitrogen is added periodically.

When the mulch material stimulates growth of microorganisms, soil structure is improved. Corncobs illustrate this effect, as does reasonably fresh manure.

Manure, peat, ground or whole corncobs, peanut hulls, cottonseed hulls, rice hulls, sugar cane, and other similar materials are satisfactory. No matter what material is used, it should be applied to a depth of several inches. When the mulch becomes thin because of decomposition or washing, it should be replenished to avoid exposure of the soil to forceful streams of water. Alternate use of the various mulch materials is a practice of some growers, while others mix the materials and apply them together.

Practically any organic material can serve as a mulch provided it is properly managed with respect to needed fertilizer for the plants and frequency of watering. Mulches may be applied soon after the newly benched plants are established and growing satisfactorily.

Fertilizer. Phosphorus and calcium fertilizers should be added to rose soils before the plants are benched. Superphosphate may be used at the rate of 5 pounds per 100 square feet of soil for the phosphorus source, and either agricultural limestone or hydrated lime may be added at the rate of 5 pounds per 100 square feet of soil as the calcium source if the soil needs to be made more alkaline. If no adjustment in pH is needed or if the soil should be more acid, calcium sulfate (gypsum) should be applied at the rate of 5 pounds per 100 square feet to supply the needed calcium.

At the time of planting, the supply of other minerals in the soil should not be excessive, but there should be some nitrogen available since the new plants require nitrogen for growth as soon as new roots start to form. If there is little nitrogen present in the soil at the time of planting, the plants should be given a liquid fertilizer solution containing nitrogen when they are watered in after planting.

When phosphorus and calcium fertilizers are added to the soil before planting, fertilizers containing nitrogen and potassium may be used for the regular fertilizer program. The soil should be tested regularly and fertilizer added accordingly to maintain 50 to 100 ppm nitrates, 5 to 10 ppm phosphorus, 20 to 40 ppm potassium, and 150 to 200 ppm calcium. Various methods of applying fertilizer may be used successfully, but one of the best is a fertilizer injector that supplies minerals with each irrigation. Rose plants in leafy, vegetative growth use large quantities of minerals, and the fertilizer application program must take this into account. Injection of fertilizer at each watering, using 200 ppm each of nitrogen and potassium, fulfills the fertilizer requirements.

Regardless of the supply of minerals in the soil, the minerals will not be of use to the plants unless the root systems are growing actively. The rose grower must continually observe the root growth in order to evaluate whether soil, irrigation, and drainage conditions are being maintained that are suitable for continuous growth of roots. If root growth is poor, that condition must be corrected before any benefits from applications of fertilizers are possible. In some instances pests such as nematodes infest the roots, and they must be controlled effectively if good root growth is to be obtained.

Iron should be added to rose soils about once a year, and this may be in the form of either ferrous sulfate at the rate of 1 pound per 100 square feet of soil or chelated iron at the rate of 2 ounces per 100 square feet of soil. In some instances boron needs to be applied to rose soils. It is provided by making a single application of borax at the rate of 1 ounce per 100 square feet of soil. In some areas magnesium is deficient in the soil, and application once or twice a year of magnesium sulfate (Epsom salts) at 1 pound per 100 square feet will correct the problem.

Moisture. Rose soils should be watered thoroughly with each irrigation, using ½ gallon of water per square foot of soil. If the soil is coarse and drains well and the bench drainage is good, the water will percolate rapidly through the soil. The soil should be allowed to dry somewhat between irrigations, and the rose grower must constantly inspect the root growth to make sure that the roots are growing continuously. If the soil is constantly wet because of poor soil or bench drainage or because of too frequent irrigations, root growth may stop because of the lack of sufficient air in the soil.

Rose soils can be irrigated satisfactorily with hose in hand, but this requires more labor time than is normally available. Several different irrigation systems can be used successfully, and the cost of investment is returned promptly in savings in labor time.

In the past it has been common practice to syringe rose plants with forceful sprays of water, in order to add moisture to the air surrounding the plants, to wash pests from the leaves, or to help control powdery mildew. Syringing has been replaced largely with mist systems to increase the air moisture, pesticides that give more effective control, and better means of control of powdery mildew.   It is an interesting historical note that the frequent syringing did give fair control of two-spotted mite and powdery mildew, but it also was very effective in spreading infestations of black spot.   When syringing was discontinued, black spot became a disease of little importance in the rose greenhouse.

A high air-moisture content (relative humidity) should be maintained in rose houses, as new shoots will start in growth faster, stems will grow longer, and leaves and flowers will be larger if it is.   Typically the greenhouse air is too dry during the daytime in summer and during both night and day during the heating season.   In cold weather the moisture from the air is deposited on the inner side of the glass as water droplets or ice, and the greater the differential in air temperature between indoors and outdoors, the drier the air will be in the greenhouse. High-pressure-mist systems can be used effectively to increase air moisture, and they have the added benefit of reducing the air temperature during the summer.

Air.   Ventilation in the rose greenhouse is very critical because it is through continuous air movement and regulation of temperature and relative humidity that powdery mildew is kept in check.   It is necessary to keep the plants warmer than the surrounding air so that there is no deposition of moisture on the plants, as the slightest film of moisture on their surface provides the conditions that are suitable for an infestation of powdery mildew.   When heat declines, solid objects such as plants lose heat more rapidly than the surrounding air; and for this reason it is standard practice in rose houses to start heating in the afternoon before the sun goes down, but to continue ventilation.

Continuous air circulation by means of properly placed fans can provide more uniform temperature and relative humidity conditions around the plants, and houses equipped with side ventilators as well as ridge ventilators have better air movement.   Fans can, however, rapidly spread mildew spots if an infestation starts, and control may be very difficult.

When the ventilators are closed for long periods of time during cold weather, it is possible to reduce the carbon dioxide supply in the air and limit photosynthesis because of it.   This may not be quite the problem with roses in greenhouses as it is with some other crops since rose soils are usually heavily mulched, and the decaying organic mulches do produce some carbon dioxide. Maintaining the carbon dioxide in the greenhouse air at about 500 ppm during the day by use of generators may cause some increase in quality and quantity of flowers produced when other conditions such as light, temperature, minerals, and moisture are satisfactory.

Troubles.   The normal flowering shoot on a greenhouse rose possesses fully expanded sepals, petals, and reproductive parts.   The failure to develop a flower on the apical end of the stem is a common occurrence; such shoots are termed "blind." The sepals and petals are present, but the reproductive parts are absent or aborted. Blind wood is generally short and thin, but it may attain considerable length and thickness when it develops at the top of the plant.

The first evidence of change from a vegetative shoot to a flower bud is a broadening and thickening of the stem tip as seen under the microscope. The flower parts form in the order of sepals, petals, stamens, and pistil. When a cut or pinch is made on a shoot, the bud immediately below becomes the terminal and begins growth. Between 16 and 18 days after a cut or pinch, this bud usually shows the presence of sepals and petals. From the practical standpoint, when a shoot that develops as a result of a cut or pinch is 1 to 1½ inches in length, the flower bud is formed. The length of stem is governed by the enlargement of the cells within this short stem plus the inherent character of the variety.

The cause of blind shoots is not known. Investigatons have shown that, under normal conditions of growth, the amount of blind wood varies from 35 to 40 percent at any time of year and on any plant, whether planted in an outer or inner row of the bench. Various nitrogen and potassium fertilizer levels have neither induced nor retarded blind-wood production. Severe defoliation will often temporarily increase the percentage of blind wood, and it is possible that some hormonal mechanism is responsible for blindness rather than the direct results of such environmental factors as light intensity, temperature, and nutrition.

Chlorosis of the upper foliage can be caused by lack of one or more fertilizers as well as excesses, but injury to the roots from overwatering may induce similar symptoms. Nematodes on the roots may induce a light chlorosis, but more often stunt the growth. Some insecticides and fungicides may injure the leaves of the younger growth and cause yellow blotched areas or spots to appear.

Bullheads are malformed flowers in which the center petals of the bud remain only partly developed and the bud appears flat. They are common on very vigorous shoots, particularly bottom breaks, and it is possible that there is a lack of carbohydrate to develop the petals. The cause of bullheading is as yet unknown, however. Thrips infestation will also cause malformed flowers.

A problem with some yellow varieties is that the petals may be green or a dirty white instead of a clear yellow. Raising the night temperature several degrees will reduce the number of off-colored flowers. Occasionally the pink or red varieties develop bluish-colored flowers. This is very often associated with use of organic phosphate and various other kinds of insecticides.

Leaf drop is experienced frequently and can usually be traced to some check in growth. Extreme dryness followed by resumption of normal watering will cause the rapid yellowing and drop of older foliage. Fumes are also responsible, and undetermined factors in the use of aerosols for insect control have caused undue foliage drop. Certain organic phosphates in the presence of sulfur on the plants cause a rapid shower of older foliage. Sulfur fumes from the material applied to heating lines for mildew control and the products of combustion from the smokestack are also responsible. Varieties differ in their "shedding," too. Black spot results in leaf drop, and when mildew is extremely severe, the leaves will fall in due course of time. Loss of roots due to any cause can result in foliage loss.

Mercury toxicity is rare, but mercury is without question the most dangerous material which can be brought into the rose house. There is one case on record in which the rose benches were painted with a bichloride of mercury solution for sterilization, and roses were then planted. The growth was so poor that the range was eventually dismantled. Zimmerman and Crocker have conducted experiments to show typical symptoms. They showed that the sterilization of bench boards with bichloride of mercury may cause damage to all plants in the house. Thermometers, humidiguides, and temperature-control instruments which are standard equipment should be placed in a location that renders them inaccessible to moving objects. Mercury thermometers should have no place in a rose house, as there are accurate types that do not contain mercury. When mercury is spilled, it spreads in very numerous small droplets which add up to a very large surface area. Since mercury is a liquid, it evaporates, but at a very slow rate. Therefore the mercury vapors would be present in a rose house for many years. Paints containing mercury as a fungicide should not be used.

The symptoms of mercury damage are quite specific and are easily recognized. The stem below the flower, or peduncle, on young shoots turns brown, and the fall of petals is common. On Columbia-type roses, such as Better Times, Briarcliff, and others, the pink or red color of the petals is first muddy, then becomes decidedly blue, and in severe cases is bleached to a dirty white. Growth is stunted, and the drop of all foliage except leaves on the youngest of shoots is common. The production of bluish-red flowers is the outstanding characteristic of mercury damage.

The only control known is to remove as much as possible of the soil in and under the bench in which the mercury is found or suspected. This should be discarded, but not in the vicinity of the rose range. Iron filings—the finer the better—neutralize the mercury by formation of an amalgam which does not vaporize. Mixed metal filings may be used, but iron is preferred. These should be scattered to a depth of at least 1 inch over all areas where the presence of mercury is suspected. Since mercury is a heavy liquid, it spreads over a wide area when dropped, so that thorough inspection of the soil for a considerable distance is warranted.

Boron and zinc toxicities have been discussed in the section on Fertilizer Excess Symptoms.

Limp necks on roses are most noticeable in the retail store or with the ultimate customer. The area of the stem just below the flower "wilts" and will not support the head. Sometimes this is due to insufficient water absorption;

cutting off the lower 1 to 2 inches of stem and placing the cut stem in water at 100°F with a preservative will revive the flower.   Lack of sufficient carbohydrates undoubtedly has some relation to this difficulty.

Diseases.   Powdery mildew is very common and is recognized by the whitish powder on the leaves, stems, and petals.   Air currents spread the spores readily.

Downy mildew is rare but causes drop of green leaves near the base of the shoot bearing the flower.   Exacting regulation of temperature and relative humidity is important in its control.

Black spot causes loss of foliage, but if the leaves are kept dry, the spores can neither spread nor germinate.

Canker organisms of various kinds cause death of stubs from cuts, and the entire plant can be killed if the infected wood is not removed.   Galls may appear on the lower stems or roots.

Black mold is a disease of the grafting case, and a blackened condition of the graft union is evidence of the disease.   Infected plants die.

Verticillium wilt causes yellowing of the stems, and infected stems should be removed well below the visible area of trouble and destroyed, as should stems infected with canker.

Viruses cause mottling or distortion of leaves but in general are not thought to be exceptionally damaging.

Pests.   Red spider is the most serious pest in that resistant strains develop and new insecticides are constantly being sought to control them.

Aphids are unsightly but generally cause little damage.

Thrips can be responsible for bullheads or otherwise malformed flowers.

Leaf rollers of various sorts chew the leaves and petals, while sow bugs and roaches feed on the stems.   Leaf-cutting bees remove circular pieces of the foliage.

Sawflies may bore into the canes and cause wilting, and removal and destruction of the cane are suggested.

Root-knot and other nematodes will seriously reduce the vigor of the plants.

Rose midge damages the flowers and feeds on the buds in the axils of the upper foliage.

Scale occasionally is a problem.   The sugary secretions drop on foliage below, and black sooty mold fungus will grow profusely.

Strawberry root worm adults puncture numerous small holes in the foliage, while the larvae chew the roots.

Pinching.   Rose plants are pinched in various ways to produce branched plants, larger diameter canes, cropping of flower production, and longer stemmed flowers.   The type and method of pinching are determined by need.

The objective with the newly benched plants is to develop several good-diameter canes from the base of the plants, and this can be controlled considerably by the way the pinching is handled.   Typically the rose plant starts to develop one or two heavy shoots from the base of the plant and several shoots of small diameter.   The diameter of the shoots can be increased if they are pinched at an early stage.   The decision on the quality of the shoot needs to be and can be made at an early stage—when the shoots are approximately 1 inch long.   If the tip of the shoot is removed just above the second or third 5-leaflet leaf as it is unfolding, the leaves on the shoot will develop to the largest possible size; and the shoots that grow after the early pinch will be of greater diameter than the original shoot.   With small-diameter stems, it may be necessary to make two or more successive early pinches to produce the size cane that is desired.   This early pinch is often called a "roll-out" since only the very tip of the shoot is removed.   Some shoots that are pinched early will not form new shoots, but this is not of consequence as the large leaves that form following the early pinch improve the photosynthetic capacity of the plant.   Since the early pinch on newly benched plants must be made at the right stage, all the plants must be inspected and pinched daily after growth starts in the plants.

The heavy shoots that develop naturally should be allowed to grow until the flower bud is just visible, and then they should be pinched above the top 5-leaflet leaf.   This type of pinch is commonly called a "soft pinch."   Hard pinches

10-20.   Early pinch (roll-out) on rose.   The pinch should be made above two or three 5-leaflet leaves which are just unfolding.   When pinched at this stage, the leaves below the pinch attain maximum size, and the shoot that develops will be larger in diameter than the one pinched.   This pinch should be used at any stage in the plant's development if heavier canes and larger leaves are desired.

are made lower on the stem, leaving two 5-leaflet leaves below the pinch, which is at about the same place where flowers are cut.

The decision on when to stop pinching and start flower production should be based on the quality of growth that exists in the plant and on the future growing conditions. Growing conditions are much better from spring through early fall than they are in the winter, and it is to be expected that the quality of the shoots that develop in the winter will not be as good as those that grow earlier. Flower production can be started sooner with plants that are started in early spring than with those that are started later, as there will still be a period of good growing conditions after flower production starts. When flowers are cut from the plant, leaves are removed also, which means that the plant must be of sufficient size by fall to have enough leaves remain on the plant after the flowers are cut. The size and number of leaves on the rose plant during the time of the year when light conditions are poor will materially affect the amount of food manufactured in the plant.

Pinching to improve the growth of the plant must be continued during the time of flower production, and this pinching is limited to shoots that are not heavy enough or long enough. Small-diameter stems should be given the early pinch—just the tip is removed when the shoot is about 1 inch long. When this type of pinching is practiced religiously, there should be no small-diameter canes on the plant. Stems of medium diameter that were not given the early pinch

10-21. Soft pinch on roses is made to the first 5-leaflet leaf on stems just starting to form flower buds. This pinch is used in timing crops for holidays or to increase the flower stem length.

should be soft pinched to avoid production of short-stemmed roses, for which there is generally limited sale. It is necessary to do selective, early, and soft pinching on producing rose plants to maintain good-quality growth.

Pinching is used to time crops for holidays or to shift flower production from one period to another. Rose growers in each locality know from past experience the length of time required for a rose to develop following a pinch. In order to increase flower production for holidays, they pinch the proper number of weeks before the holiday. Usually a record is kept of the number of flowers cut and the number of pinches made during this period so that it will be possible to estimate the number of flowers that will be cut for the holiday. Either a soft or a hard pinch is used. Actually the length of time required from pinch to cut varies with the weather conditions, and the pinch dates are based on averages. If the weather is better than usual, the holiday crop is produced too early, and if the weather is not as good as the average, the flower crop will be delayed and may be too late for the holiday. The rate of development of the flower buds must be watched closely during this period, and the temperature must be adjusted to speed or delay the development as needed.

If rose plants are pinched so that they will crop for a holiday, they will recrop following the holiday. If the crop will not be needed at that time, some selective pinching must be done to distribute the flower production more evenly.

Flower production timing. In late spring or summer, 5½ to 6 weeks is required for the production of a flower from a cut or pinch. In winter it takes approximately 8 weeks, and proportional lengths of time are necessary for spring and fall production. It is important to remember that a soft pinch requires from 3 to 7 days longer to develop a flower than does a hard pinch or cut.

The variations in temperature in a greenhouse must also be considered. If one end of the house is several degrees cooler than the other, pinching must be started 3 to 7 days in advance at the cool end.

The development of the shoots themselves is quite variable. Roses with stem lengths between 15 and 24 inches mature faster than do the shorter or longer grades. Usually the shorter-stemmed roses are produced on the thinner and weaker wood, which probably accounts for the slower growth, and it is presumed that the flowers on the longest-stemmed roses are not formed as soon as those of medium length, and hence require additional time to mature.

For a Christmas crop, the plants should be soft-pinched from October 17 to 21 and hard-pinched from October 21 to 25 in the latitude of central Ohio. Varieties differ, but these dates will apply for this locality.

A portion of the crop that is cut for Christmas often comes back for Valentine's Day on February 14, although this is not to be taken as a certainty. Easter occurs at a different date each year, but approximately 7½ weeks should be allowed when it is early and 7 weeks when it is late. A considerable number of Easter cuts will come in for Memorial Day if Easter is neither very early nor very late. By counting back from a specific day, the grower can pinch and bring his crop in at the desired time. The crop can be delayed or hastened by gradually lowering or raising the temperature as much as 8 or 10°F at night. The night temperature should not be raised or lowered more than 2°F in any one night. Extremely warm, sunny weather in the late fall may cause the Christmas crop to develop too rapidly, while long periods of cloudy weather may delay it. During the last 15 to 20 days considerable attention must be given to night temperatures.

Pruning. One or more times during the period the rose plants are in the bench, they must be pruned back rather severely to prevent them from growing so tall that cutting, tying, and other operations become inefficient. Two methods are used: (1) direct pruning and (2) the gradual cutback. Both have their advantages and disadvantages; it is quite likely that both methods should be used in the rose range, not necessarily for comparison but for their adaptability to the general management of the range.

Direct pruning, or cutback. Usually sometime after Mother's Day, when roses are not needed in such large numbers, the plants can be pruned. Formerly, severe drying was allowed, until the foliage wilted, but this is no longer practiced. Instead, the plants are simply cut back to the desired height, and the frequency of watering thereafter is reduced because of the limited use by the pruned plant. The height to which the plants are cut back the first time should not be less than 24 inches for most varieties because the wood is generally quite hard below this point. If after cutting back, forks, or branches, remain in preference to single canes, so much the better. Each time the plants are pruned, the cuts should be made about 6 inches above the previous cutback to keep in somewhat softer wood, which "breaks" more readily. Relative humidity should be kept high by syringing frequently, closing side vents, using high pressure mist, and providing a roof shade, to encourage development of new shoots.

Gradual cutback. Gradual cutback is often called "knife pruning" since the stems are cut with a knife when the flowers are taken from the plant. The gradual pruning, or cutback, is a modification of the direct cutback since not all stems are cut off at once. The gradual cutback can be started with the Easter crop, followed again by further removal for the Mother's Day crop. By Mother's Day it is possible to have completely cut back the plants so that few flowers are present. No matter how rapidly the gradual cutback is practiced, it is important that not all cuts be made at the same time. Some shoots are in flower at the time others are breaking out following the cutback. The plants should not be cut lower than 24 inches in height.

This method of pruning requires more skill and time than the direct cutback, but it has the advantage of not completely eliminating production for a period of several months, as occurs with the direct system.

A combination of the two methods may be followed: The first year after planting, the roses are cut back gradually. The second year after planting they are direct-pruned. The third year after planting they are again cut back gradually. They are often removed when they are 4 years old.

Cutting flowers.   Close examination of a typical flowering stem of most greenhouse roses will reveal that approximately in the center section of the stem there are two to five leaves bearing five leaflets and immediately above and below them are several three-leaflet leaves. With reference to the buds at the axil, or base, of these leaves, it will be noted that the buds on the lower one-half or two-thirds of the flowering stem of vigorous shoots are either blunt or rounded, while the buds on the upper section of the flowering stem are pointed. The shape of the bud in the axil of the leaf serves as a guide when cutting flowers. Stems with flowers should rarely be cut to a leaf that has a pointed bud at its base. Such buds usually develop into flowering stems without the normal distribution of foliage or a series of scalelike leaves. The stems with flowers should be cut to a leaf that has a rounded or blunt bud at its base. The general rule observed by most rose growers in cutting the stem is to allow two 5-leaflet leaves to remain

10-22. Cutting rose flowers. With roses it is generally good practice to cut "up" (leaving two 5-leaflet leaves below the place of cutting—top arrow) in the fall and winter, as this retains a sufficient number of leaves on the plants for adequate food manufacture in the low-light-intensity period of the year. In the spring and summer, due to good growing conditions, the flower stems may be cut "down" (below the "hook"—bottom arrow).

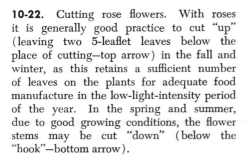

below the cut. This is practiced except where soft pinches have been made. In that case the cut can be made below the soft pinch, again allowing two 5-leaflet leaves to remain on the stem. Some varieties are often cut to a stub or "knuckle" on the more vigorous shoots because they break faster and production is increased.

If the flowering stems were cut "up" each time, allowing two 5-leaflet leaves to remain, some of the more vigorous shoots would be much too high after several months' time. On such shoots, it is common to cut as described, then the next time cut to the leaf immediately below the hook. When the bud in the axil of this leaf develops into a mature flower, the stem is cut in the usual way. This is sometimes called "going up two and down one" and serves to prevent the more vigorous shoots from becoming too tall. The less vigorous shoots are generally handled in the usual way.

The stage at which the flowers are cut differs with the variety. The yellow varieties can be cut somewhat tighter than most pink or red types, and the buds will open and unfold normally. Flowers cut too tight fail to open for

10-23. Left to right: malformed flower commonly called "bullhead"; loss of terminal growth or blindness; a well-developed rose flower.

the customer.   Most red and pink varieties should be allowed to develop to a stage where one or two of the outer petals begin to unfurl.   In most cases the sepals will be at right angles to the stem axis, or pointing downward.

Beginning in early August it is desirable to allow as much foliage as possible to remain on the plant after cutting flowers, to build up the plants for winter.   This means cutting up, except in the case of very vigorous shoots.   In the spring, from mid-Februray on, as light intensity increases, the "up-and-down" cutting system is useful on many shoots.   At all times it is desirable to try to maintain a zone, or area, where the majority of flowers are cut.   If some flowering stems are very high and others quite low, cutting is more difficult.

Knuckle cuts usually are made in the spring and fall.   They are flowering stems cut to a hook, or crotch, allowing approximately ¼ to ½ inch of stub to remain.   There are usually numerous latent buds present which can be seen with the naked eye, and these develop into strong shoots when the wood is heavy. If weak, thin wood is knuckle-cut, the breaks will be short and blind.   In case numerous shoots develop from a knuckle cut, the weak, thin growths should be removed.

Storage.   If the flowers are to be shipped without delay, the stems should be placed in lukewarm water containing a preservative as soon as they are cut and in 40°F air temperature for about 12 hours before shipment.   At the wholesale store and at the retail shop the flowers should be kept in preservative solution and in a 40°F temperature.

If it is necessary to delay marketing the roses, they may be held satisfactorily from a few days to as long as 2 weeks at 31 to 33°F when proper procedures are used.   They are not placed in water after cutting, but instead are put in a nearly airtight container that does not absorb moisture.   The temperature and moisture conditions must be carefully regulated.   Upon removal from storage the stems should be recut and placed in warm (80 to 90°F) preservative solution in an air temperature of 40°F.   From that time until they are sold, they should be in preservative solution and 40°F temperature.   Fewer problems with limp necks and keeping quality occur when these practices are observed.

The consumer should be instructed in the use of preservative solutions for roses in the home, and should be encouraged to use them.

Marketing.   Standard grades for roses have not been adopted, but the methods that are in general usage base the grade on length of stem.   There is little uniformity among the various regions of rose production.   Some methods base grades on 2-inch increments starting at 10 inches, others use 3-inch increments starting at 9 inches, and others, in order to reduce the number of grades, use 4-inch increments starting at 14 inches.

Stem length is measured from the cut end of the stem up to and including the tip of the flower petals.   In all grades the flowers should be uniformly developed, the stems should be straight and of sufficient strength to support the flower without undue bending, the flowers should be uniform in color, the foliage should be clean and unblemished, there should be no bullheads, and the flower buds should be of the size characteristic of the variety.   All roses that do not meet these standards may be bunched together as "utility" or "work" grade.   The stem length on these grades should be reduced only to the extent that the flower is adequately supported.

There are two common methods of packing roses for shipment.   The one used in the eastern states, called "sheeting," consists of laying roses in rows on sheets of parchment or waxed paper, one row on top of the next, the buds of each row below those of the previous row, with ice covering the stems.   This method reduces bruising, but it is inconvenient because of the necessity of lifting these layers of flowers out for display on commission house counters before sale.

The second method of bunching roses in bundles of 13 or 25 is much more universally used throughout the rest of the country.   The roses are either bunched in round bundles and then wrapped in parchment paper, or else they are spiral-wrapped by placing the heads together on the proper size paper and then rolling the paper with the roses to make a round pack.   The spiral pack reduces bruising to the minimum.   To prevent breakage of stems and looseness of pack, at least two ties are made: one around the wrap below the flower heads, and the other close to the base of the stems.   Some growers use a lightweight grade of asphalt paper around the base of the stems.   Handling is facilitated if the paper is heavy enough to prevent thorns from penetrating.

In place of waxed or parchment paper, the use of cellophane is suggested for greater sales appeal.   The MSAD 86 type of cellophane will not discolor roses and may be cut in sheets of the desired size.   The cellophane may be tied with string, held together with Scotch tape, or heat-sealed by lightly rubbing the cellophane with a sealing iron.   No matter what type of wrapping is used, it should extend 2 inches beyond the tips of the buds.

The cost of operation of rose greenhouses is about $2.50 per square foot of bench area per year, and the average number of hybrid tea roses that could be sold from this area would be about 28 flowers per square foot per year.   If these roses bring an average net return of 9 cents each, the costs of production will be met.

The production of floribunda roses per square foot is greater than the production of hybrid teas, and it could be expected that about 40 flowers would be sold per square foot of bench space per year.   If an average net return of 6½ cents each were realized for the floribundas, the return would exceed the costs of production.

Roses, Inc., started in 1937 by Joseph Hill and Alex Laurie, is an organization of commercial rose growers that functions primarily in the areas of promotion and public relations, and in addition sponsors some experimental work with roses. Through Roses, Inc., the rose producers do have a means of presenting a united front in marketing and legislative matters. For many years much of the research work on rose culture was sponsored by grants from this organization.

SNAPDRAGON (*Antirrhinum majus—Scrophulariaceae*)

The snapdragon is a perennial plant, native to the Mediterranean region. The flower is a spike inflorescence in which the lower florets open first, and, at the time of cutting, the florets are at all stages of development from fully expanded at the base of the spike to tight buds at the graceful tip of the spike. Not many spike-type flowers are grown commercially, and since they add interest and appeal to the flower arrangement, there is a constant demand for snapdragons.

Snapdragons are propagated from seed, and approximately 1 month after sowing, the seedlings are the right size for transplanting. The rate of growth and flowering of snapdragon is affected by light intensity and temperature, and plants growing during the summer will flower in as short a time as 7 weeks after they are benched. Snapdragon plants grown single-stemmed during the winter require about 22 weeks from the time they are benched until they flower.

Most snapdragons are grown as single crops; after the flowers are cut, the plants are discarded. However, in some instances two or possibly three crops of flowers are cut from the same plants before they are discarded. The main period of flowering snapdragons is during the winter and spring; but because of the good F-1 hybrid varieties which are available for all seasons of the year, year-round flowering of snapdragons is quite common.

Flowering in the snapdragon apparently is controlled by a combination of light quantity, temperature, and day length. Some varieties have a high light requirement and will flower satisfactorily only in the summer, while others have a low requirement and can be used for winter flowering. Snapdragons are classified into four groups according to their flowering properties at various times of the year.

Group 1 varieties flower satisfactorily in the low-light, low-temperature, and short-day conditions of winter; and they are grown at 50°F night temperatures for flowering from mid-December through April. The group 1 varieties flower in as short a time as 15 weeks after benching at the first of the season or in as long a time as 22 weeks at the end of the season.

Group 2 varieties flower best in the late fall conditions from mid-November to mid-December and in the late winter conditions from mid-April through mid-May, but they may be used also for flowering during the entire period from mid-November to mid-May. The group 1 varieties apparently are insensitive to day length, but the group 2 varieties, like mums, will flower in a shorter period of time during the winter if they are given long days for about 2 months in the early stages of growth. Group 2 varieties should be grown at 50 to 55°F night temperatures, and the length of time for flowering after benching will be 12 to 15 weeks in late fall and 22 to 17 weeks in late winter.

The group 3 varieties, known as the fall or spring types, are flowered from May through mid-June and from mid-September to mid-November. These varieties are grown at 60°F night temperatures, and they are quite sensitive to long days. Their length of time for flowering after benching is from 17 to 12 weeks in the spring and from 9 to 13 weeks in the fall.

The snapdragon varieties in group 4 are used for flowering in the summer as they require high light, high temperature, and long days. The length of time for flowering after benching varies from 12 to 7 weeks in the period from mid-June to late August, and they may be flowered satisfactorily until mid-October.

This group classification for snapdragons is based on average conditions in Ohio. If the weather conditions are different from these, the use of the groups should be adapted to the weather conditions that can be expected.

Propagation. Propagation from seed is practiced, except on rare occasions when double varieties are propagated by cuttings. The seed is very small and must be sown on the surface of a finely screened medium.

Good results can be obtained with several mediums. If soil is used, it should be a light mixture with peat and sand, and the fertilizer content must be low. Shredded sphagnum, neutral peat, and vermiculite can also be used. Regardless of which material is used, it should be screened so that the seed can be sown on a smooth surface that maintains a uniform moisture supply. Since the medium has little fertilizer in it at the time the seed is sown, some fertilizer will have to be supplied after the seed germinates and true leaves are formed. Peat-lite mixtures of peat and vermiculite may be used successfully for seed germination.

Subirrigation of the seed flat usually is best. The medium is thoroughly wetted without danger of washing the seeds on the surface. The flats should be placed at 65 to 70°F under intermittent mist or a plastic or glass cover until the seed germinates, at which time they are moved to a 60 to 65°F temperature.

Damping-off in the seed flat can best be handled by doing a thorough job of steam sterilization before sowing, then sowing the seed thinly. One trade packet will generally be sufficient for two flats, and it is usually best to sow in rows. After germination strict attention must be given to moisture and ventilation. If the surface soil is kept constantly moist after germination, some damping-off can be expected.

Transplanting should take place as soon as true leaves form. Excellent results can be obtained from direct planting to the growing bench. This method is used most often with single-stem culture. If the plants are transplanted to flats, pots, or bands, they must be benched before they draw up or become hardened.

Snapdragon seed is packed 2,000 seeds per trade packet. The number of good seedlings that can be obtained per seed packet depends on the quality of the seed and the conditions that are provided during germination, but it is safe to plan on producing 800 good-quality seedlings per packet of seed. Production of fewer than this is usually due to some mishandling of propagation procedures.

Snapdragon seedlings should be transplanted as soon as they can be handled; however, if this cannot be done, the next best plan is to hold them in temperatures of 31 to 33°F until they can be planted. They can be held at this temperature several weeks and will be in better condition than if they remained in the seed flat in "growing temperatures."

Planting, spacing, and supporting. The snapdragon seedlings should be planted as soon as they can be handled, when the plant is less than an inch high and the leaves are just unfolding. The plants grow and develop much more rapidly when they are transplanted at this early stage than they do when the seedlings are larger. The tiny plants should be handled by the leaves during planting to avoid damaging the stem. The plants should be watered well after planting; however, if the planting is done during the winter, the plants or the rows of plants should be spot-watered, leaving dry areas between the rows.

Either a pinched or a single-stem crop has its advantages. If the plants are grown single-stem, 2 to 3 weeks can be gained, the quality is very often more uniform, and the crop cuts off in a shorter period of time. The principal disadvantage in single-stem culture is the number of seedlings required. About four times as many seedlings are necessary for a single-stem crop as for pinched plants.

10-24. Snapdragons should be planted as soon as the seedlings can be handled (approximately 1 month after sowing the seed). Left: a flat of snapdragon seedlings at the right stage for planting. Right: recently planted snapdragon seedlings. The penny in the foreground is for size comparison.

The initial investment in seed is greater, and more labor is required for planting. In most instances, however, the advantages of single-stem culture are much greater than the disadvantages.

For pinched-plant culture the plants should be soft-pinched to three or four sets of leaves. Either two or four shoots will develop following the pinch, depending on the stage of development of the lateral shoots at the time the pinch was made. The correct time of pinching is determined by the variety and by the weather conditions that can be expected. Snapdragons flower much more rapidly in the high-light-intensity–high-temperature periods of the year. The best-conceived pinching schedules can be sadly lacking if the anticipated weather conditions do not materialize. For instance, abnormally bright, hot autumn weather can cause the "Christmas crop" to be produced for Thanksgiving Day.

Spacing of about 8 by 8 inches is used for snapdragons that are pinched; however, snapdragons that are grown as a single-stem crop are spaced from 4 by 4 inches for flowering in the summer to 4 by 6 inches for the winter crop.

If varieties are used that reach about the same height, a single grid can be used to support the tops of the plants and keep them erect. The grid can be made from string laced across wires that are stretched between the rows of plants the length of the bench, or it can be welded wire fabric. The grid may be placed at ground level for planting and raised as the plants grow.

Soil and fertilizer. Snapdragon soils should be porous, well drained, and thoroughly steam-disinfested. The addition of poultry litter grade peat moss, straw, or manure will make soils more porous, and particularly fine- or heavy-textured soils can be improved by the addition of materials such as haydite, coarse perlite, or calcined clay.

The pH of the soil should be about 6.5, and if any adjustments are needed, they should be made before planting. There should be 5 ppm phosphorus in snapdragon soils, and if an addition is needed, superphosphate should be applied before planting at the rate of 5 pounds per 100 square feet of soil. If calcium is below 150 ppm, either limestone or gypsum should be added to the soil before planting, at the rate of 5 pounds per 100 square feet of soil. With the phosphorus and calcium requirements satisfied before planting, fertilizers containing nitrogen and potassium should be applied periodically during the growth of the crop. The total fertilizer content of the soil should be low at the time of planting, but the young plant needs some nitrogen in the early stages of growth. If there is little nitrogen in the soil at the time of planting, some should be provided when the plants are watered in or at the first irrigation after that. The nitrates should be maintained at 25 to 50 ppm, and potassium at 25 to 30 ppm. Applying fertilizer with each irrigation by means of an injector is a good method to use with snapdragons.

Light. Snapdragons need to be partially shaded from the sunlight only in the early stages of growth in the seed flat, and after that growth is best in full·light. In most areas of the country, the winter light conditions are not good enough at best, and every effort should be made to provide the best light possible for the plants. Growth and development of snapdragons are more rapid in high-light and high-temperature conditions, and flowering of snapdragons may be ahead of schedule in unusually bright seasons and delayed if the weather conditions are darker and cooler than usual.

The effect of day length on snapdragons varies with the variety, and flowering in some varieties can be advanced in long days and delayed in short days. Some advantages may be gained by the artificial adjustment of day length for flowering snapdragons at some times of the year, but it has been more satisfactory to flower them only during the "natural season" according to the group classifications.

Temperature. Snapdragons are usually considered to be a 50°F night temperature crop. This is because they are more commonly grown during the winter, and the varieties that are used at that time of the year grow and flower best at that temperature. Snapdragons which are flowered in the spring or fall should be grown at 60°F night temperatures, while for summer flowering 65°F night temperatures can be used. The day temperature should be maintained about 10°F higher than the night temperature.

Growth of the young plants for the first 4 to 6 weeks is best at 60 to 65°F night temperatures at any time of the year; and when it is possible, that temperature should be used for the young plants of the winter crop as well.

In many areas of the country summer temperatures are higher than desired for the best growth of snapdragons. A 10 to 20°F reduction in day-time temperatures is possible with fan and pad cooling systems, and this is sufficient to produce better quality snapdragons during the summer.

Moisture. Root growth is poor in soils that are constantly wet, and root and stem diseases are more prevalent. If coarse and porous soils are used for snapdragons, the soil will drain readily so that overwatering problems will be minimized. The soil should be allowed to dry somewhat between irrigations, and this is particularly important in the dark and cool weather in the winter. Root rot organisms thrive in constantly moist soil even if it is well aerated, and the continued use of peat moss as a soil conditioner can lead to trouble.

Some leaf and stem diseases are more common in snapdragons if the relative humidity is high. Adequate ventilation and heating while ventilating should be done to keep the air moisture level at a satisfactory level.

Air.   Continuous air movement is best as that provides the most uniform temperature, humidity, and carbon dioxide conditions throughout the air mass. The use of ridge and side ventilators can produce good air movement in the snap-dragon house most of the time; however, air circulation fans will provide for continuous air movement all the time, and a better supply of carbon dioxide in the area of the leaf is assured when air is circulated by fans.

If other environmental conditions are suitable, maintaining 500 ppm carbon dioxide in the greenhouse atmosphere by means of generators during the cold weather may produce heavier stems, faster growth, and earlier flowering.

Troubles.   Chlorosis of the tip foliage indicates a root problem.   The most common cause is poor drainage resulting in poor root growth; however, too much fertilizer in the soil or root pests can be the cause.

A wilt that occurs in snapdragons at about the time the flower buds are well developed has not been associated definitely with a particular pathogen, and it may be caused by either pathogens or physiological situations or a combination of them.   It occurs primarily during the poor growing conditions of winter, and it is believed that poor root growth at that time is due to low temperatures, low light intensity, and too wet a soil.   There is a possibility that Pythium root rot may be involved in some instances.

Floret drop or shatter is not as much of a problem as it once was because resistance to shattering is one of the characteristics that hybridists have bred into the new varieties.   Other than the genetic factor, the primary causes of floret drop are pollination of bees or other insects and the effect of gases such as ethylene.

Hollow stems may occur in the winter, as a result of the low light intensity at that time.   The condition can be remedied if the temperature is reduced, irrigations are spaced farther apart, and less nitrogen fertilizer is applied.

Floret skip is a problem that arises only if the snapdragons are subjected to unusually cool temperatures during formation of the spike.

Foliar die-back has no known pathogen, but it may be caused by soil or root conditions during the winter.   Some of the leaves about midway in the stem die gradually from the tip, and when the condition progresses as far as the stem, the portion of the stem above the position of the affected leaves wilts.

Diseases.   *Rhizoctonia* and damping-off are very common diseases of snapdragons, and they occur primarily in the early stages of growth.   Soils and handling equipment must be carefully steam-disinfested, plants set as shallow as possible, irrigations spaced well, and continuous air movement provided. Terraclor is a specific control for *Rhizoctonia,* and Morsodren can be used for either *Rhizoctonia* or damping-off.

Botrytis or gray mold can attack snapdragons at any stage of growth, and typically it produces a stem rot some place above the soil line—often midway on the stem. The spores of *Botrytis* are very common in the greenhouse, but their presence can be reduced if good sanitary measures are used, as this pathogen thrives on trash. The area should be carefully steamed before planting, and good air movement and low relative humidity should be provided while the crop is being grown. This disease is easily controlled if heating and ventilating practices are good. A chemical control is either zineb or Botran, but the latter may cause some plant injury.

Powdery mildew should not be a problem if heating and ventilating are properly handled, and rust is even less of a problem as rust resistance has been bred into many of the varieties. Rust will germinate only if there is water on the plants, and this usually does not occur unless the greenhouses are in very poor condition or the watering practices are improper.

Pests. Aphids are the most common pests, and they often cause twisted or misshapen leaves at the tip of the plant. The best control for aphids is Meta Systox-R sprays.

Cyclamen mites are occasional pests on snapdragons. They are so tiny that they are often overlooked, but their effects can be seen on the plants, as they cause small cup-shaped leaves and severely reduced growth. Either endrin or Kelthane can be used for the control of Cyclamen mites.

Two-spotted mites or red spider can be a problem at any time, and thrips do infest snapdragons in season. These pests, however, are rather easily controlled with several different pesticides.

Rotations and cropping. Because of the different seasonal light and temperature conditions, the snapdragon varieties must be used that grow and flower well in each season. Table 10-2 gives the planting and flowering dates for single-stem crops throughout the year. Approximately 1 month is needed to produce a seedling of the right size for planting, and therefore seed should be sown about 1 month before each planting date. The timing listed here is based on average weather conditions in Ohio. If there are more light and higher temperatures where the snapdragons are to be grown, flowering will be faster, and the varieties in groups 2, 3, and 4 can be used earlier in the spring and later in the fall.

The rate of flower development and the time of flowering in snapdragons are affected greatly by temperature and light. If the weather conditions vary from the average, the time of flowering will be advanced or delayed accordingly.

Table 10-2 can be used for scheduling year-round flowering with snapdragons, and a minimum of 9 units is needed to provide uniform flowering throughout the year.

Snapdragons may be rotated with other crops. A winter crop of snapdragons can be followed by spring bedding plants, or carnations that are removed

Table 10-2. *Snapdragon Variety Classification and Dates for Planting and Flowering*

DATE OF PLANTING	WEEKS IN BENCH	DATE OF FLOWERING	VARIETY CLASSIFICATION
July 10	10	Sept. 15	Group 3
July 25	10	Oct. 1	Group 3
Aug. 1	11	Oct. 15	Group 3
Aug. 10	12	Nov. 1	Group 2
Aug. 15	13	Nov. 15	Group 2
Aug. 25	14	Dec. 1	Group 2
Sept. 1	15	Dec. 15	Group 1
Sept. 4	17	Jan. 1	Group 1
Sept. 7	19	Jan. 15	Group 1
Sept. 15	20	Feb. 1	Group 1
Sept. 20	21	Feb. 15	Group 1
Oct. 3	21	Mar. 1	Group 1
Oct. 15	22	Mar. 15	Group 1
Nov. 1	22	Apr. 1	Group 2
Nov. 20	21	Apr. 15	Group 2
Dec. 15	20	May 1	Group 2
Jan. 15	17	May 15	Group 3
Feb. 10	16	June 1	Group 3
Feb. 25	15	June 8	Group 3
Mar. 10	14	June 15	Group 3
Apr. 1	12	June 22	Group 3
Apr. 10	12	July 1	Group 4
Apr. 20	11	July 8	Group 4
May 1	11	July 15	Group 4
May 25	10	Aug. 1	Group 4
June 5	10	Aug. 15	Group 4
July 1	9	Sept. 1	Group 4

in the fall can be followed by a crop of snapdragons before the area is replanted to carnations.   Many other rotations are possible.

Snapdragons are often grown outdoors in the North during the summer. If the first planting is in late April or May, two crops can be produced before frost in the fall.   The quality of the flowers is much better if the plants are grown under cotton cloth or plastic screen.

Cutting.   The flowers are cut when the bottom florets are completely expanded and the tip florets are in tight bud.   For single cropping, the stem may be cut at any suitable length, as the plants are discarded after the flowers are cut; however, if a second crop of flowers is to be produced from the same plants, the cut should be made above four sets of leaves.   The flower stems should be placed in water immediately after cutting, in a 40°F air temperature.

Snapdragons can be stored dry at 31 to 33°F for up to 3 weeks, but this is seldom done as floret drop may result from ethylene generated by the flowers in storage.

Snapdragons are graded by spike and stem length and bunched by the dozen. Although standard grades are not widely used, the grades suggested by the Society of American Florists are listed below:

GRADE DESIGNATION	MINIMUM NUMBER OF OPEN FLOWERS	MINIMUM LENGTH OF STEM, INCHES
Blue	15	36
Red	12	30
Green	9	24
Yellow	6	18

If snapdragons are to be shipped for any length of time, they must be positioned upright, or the flower tips will crook. This is a geotropic effect: when the stems are laid horizontally, the tips soon turn upward. If snapdragons are shipped, they are placed upright in hamper-type containers. Because of this shipping problem, snapdragons usually are sold locally and are not shipped for long distances.

White and light pink snapdragons are used in the greatest quantities, while yellow and dark pink varieties are grown in lesser amounts. Red, bronze, and lavender colors are used seasonally according to the demand.

Marketing. The cost of operation of a snapdragon area the year-round is probably about $2 per square foot per year, and the production that could be expected from the area would be approximately 2 dozen flowers per square foot of bench per year. If the snapdragons were sold on the wholesale market at an average price of $1.25 per dozen, the net return to the grower would meet the costs of production.

STEPHANOTIS (*Stephanotis floribunda—Asclepiadaceae*)

S. floribunda is a vigorous-growing vine with thick, leathery leaves and clusters of white star-shaped flowers. It is fairly common outdoors in the deep South and is grown commercially in the greenhouse for its heavy production of flowers. The flowers have exceptionally good keeping qualities, are very fragrant, and are excellent for make-up work.

Cuttings can be made from half-matured wood any time of the year. It is usually more convenient, however, to make them at the same time gardenias are propagated, which is December through March. Since only a few plants are usually required, they can be put in the propagating case with gardenias. Cuttings should be made 4 to 6 inches long and potted directly in a sand and peat mixture, the same as for gardenias.   It is advisable to use one of the rooting powders to hasten rooting.   A temperature of 70°F should be maintained in the grafting case day and night.   Cover the case during sunny days with several layers of aster cloth or light canvas to provide shade.   Keep the humidity in the case high by syringing, and make sure the rooting medium is kept moist.

After the plants are well rooted, they can be either shifted to larger sized pots or planted directly in tubs or large boxes.   Some provision must be made for the vines to twine on a trellis or other structure.   The area that a single plant will cover is considerable.   Stephanotis can be grown in almost any part of the greenhouse, especially in odd corners or crosshouses where other plants usually do not do well.   This does not imply that plants in unfavorable conditions of light and temperature will do as well as those grown under ideal conditions, but this plant will tolerate adverse conditions.

Since the native habitat of *Stephanotis* is Madagascar, the plants grow best at 60°F or higher with high humidity.   The usual flowering season is from April through most of September.   The flowers are produced on the current season's new wood.   Occasionally flowers are produced in small quantities during the winter.   Some growers feel that additional light of 4 hours' duration in winter induces earliness of flowering.

The soil for mature plants can be anything from the sandy types to clay, with a good proportion of organic matter.   A heavy mulch of peat or manure is essential during the late spring through early fall to prevent too rapid drying. *Stephanotis* requires large quantities of water.

Almost any commercial or organic fertilizer is satisfactory, but of course some discretion must be used.   As to type of soil, the pH seems to be unimportant. This plant can be grown well within a range of pH 5.0 to 8.0.

The chief pests of *Stephanotis* are nematodes, scale, and mealy bugs. Even with heavy infestation of nematodes, this plant does well, so this pest is not important except that if it is present, it is a source of infection for other crops; in this respect its presence can be serious.

11

FLOWERING POT PLANTS

Most of the pot plant crops are produced for a specific season of the year or for certain holidays, and about the only ones that are grown in quantity for periodic flowering throughout the year are Chrysanthemums, African violets, and, to some extent, azaleas. Poinsettias, Christmas Begonias, and Cyclamen are flowered in December, primarily for Christmas; and Hydrangeas, roses, Calceolarias, cinerarias, lilies, and gloxinias are forced mainly for the spring holidays.

These are all short-term crops, each of which occupies the greenhouse space for portions of the year rather than continuously. Most of the pot plant growers attempt to produce the assortment of plants that are in demand throughout the year, and rotations must be developed by each grower that will produce the plants required while making full use of all the available greenhouse space. There are very few pot plant growers who produce only one or two kinds of crops, and they rotate their areas with the various seasonal or holiday pot plants. There is much flexibility with pot plant crops because they can be started in small pots and shifted to larger pots as they grow, and the plants can be set pot to pot and spaced farther apart as they become larger. The pot plant crops are mobile —they can be moved from area to area as required. This flexibility and mobility can be used to good advantage in making some rotations; but if the schedule is planned too closely, the plants may not get shifted to the next size pot on time or the spacing might not be done as soon as it is required.

The pot plant range should have benches about 30 inches high, and they may be up to 6 feet in width if they can be worked from both sides. The arrangement of benches should allow for easy movement of wheeled carts in the greenhouse because this facilitates the movement of the pots, and in a pot plant range a considerable proportion of the labor is expended in moving pots—from the potting area to the benches, from one bench to another while spacing the pots, from a greenhouse of one temperature to one of another, and from the greenhouses to the sales or shipping area.

In addition to the greenhouses the pot plant range must have a potting and shipping area that is large enough and accessible to the greenhouses. The potting area must provide storage space for soil, soil additives, fertilizers, and pots; and it must contain soil-mixing and soil-sterilization equipment as well as tables where the potting is done. The shipping area should be large enough so that plants can be brought in from various greenhouses and grouped or staged by order for loading on the truck in proper sequence. The shipping of pot plants must be done promptly regardless of the weather, and this is possible only if the staging and loading can be done inside for protection from inclement weather.

Soil. The pot plant grower must have an unlimited supply of soil because it is sold with the plant. In many areas the best source is the topsoil from construction sites. If some care is exercised in choosing the soils, and some supervision is given so that subsoil is not included with the topsoil, these can be good sources for potting soil. Fortunately, good topsoil is a poor base for roads or buildings and is therefore constantly available from construction sites.

Regardless of the source of the soil, it is important to get as much information as possible about the previous use or treatments that the soil might have had. Field soils may have been treated with herbicides to control weeds in the field crops, and it is possible that these materials may be harmful to the greenhouse crops. If soil from greenhouse cut flower crops is being used, it may contain more fertilizer than desirable; and with any soil an analysis should be made before use so that the desired adjustments in pH and minerals can be made.

Most soils will have to be amended to make them suitable for use with pot plants. These amendments are made to improve the soil air-moisture relationship and to make adjustments of pH and minerals. The uniform moisture and air conditions needed in the soil are provided most easily in soils which are coarse and porous, and which drain readily. Most soils can be satisfactorily amended to this condition by adding coarse, organic matter such as poultry-litter-grade peat moss, chopped straw, peanut hulls, or other similar materials. If the base soil that is used is particularly heavy, adding ¼- to ½-inch grade haydite, perlite, or calcined clay, as well as the organic matter, will be helpful. The relative amount of material that should be added to the soil depends on the soil that is used, the irrigation and fertilization methods employed, and the plants that will be grown.

Any adjustment that is needed in pH, phosphorus, and calcium should be made at the time the soil is being mixed. Soils that are too acid should have ground limestone or hydrated lime added to them at the rate of about a 4-inch potful per wheelbarrow (2½ bushels) of soil. If the soil test indicates a low supply of phosphorus, superphosphate should be added at the same rate. If it is not necessary to adjust the pH or add phosphorus, calcium should be added by applying gypsum at the rate of a 4-inch potful per wheelbarrow of soil.

Soils must be thoroughly mixed, but they must not be shredded so that they are too fine. In too many instances the soil is so finely shredded that the benefits from addition of coarse materials are completely lost. Small batches of soil can be mixed thoroughly by turning the pile several times by shovel. Larger batches of soil can be mixed with rotary, tumbling mixers.

In some areas of the country, because of particular soil problems, mixtures that contain no soil are used for pot plants. These are often combinations of peat moss and sand or mixtures of peat moss with either perlite or vermiculite. The advantage of these mixtures is that they can be reproduced uniformly each time, and methods of irrigation and fertilization do not have to be adjusted to changes in soil. They do have to be compounded carefully, and a complete supply of minerals included if the basic materials that are used do not contain the required minerals.

Fertilizers. The pH of the soil and the requirements for phosphorus and calcium should be handled at the time the soil is mixed, as discussed earlier. In most instances no further adjustment of pH or additions of phosphorus or calcium will be required for the duration of the crop.

Root growth will be poor if there is too much fertilizer in the soil at the time of potting; however, some nitrogen is needed in the early stages of growth, or else plants will be stunted if there is none available in the soil. The best way to assure a supply of nitrogen for the young plants varies with the situation. In some instances it is better to add a small amount of nitrogen to the soil at the time of mixing, and in other instances the nitrogen requirements can be satisfied by watering in the plants with a fertilizer solution.

The general fertilizer program should be started as soon as new root growth is visible, which should be in less than a week after potting. Fertilizer should be applied to pot plants in liquid form as it can be applied more evenly, and considerable labor saved. If fertilizer can be supplied by means of an injector with each irrigation, this is the best method to use generally because a uniform supply of minerals is assured. If phosphorus was added to the soil before potting, only nitrogen and potassium need to be used for the general fertilization program. The amount of fertilizer to apply with each irrigation when an injector is being used is from 100 to 200 ppm each of nitrogen and potassium, depending on the soil, the method of irrigation, the plants, and the weather conditions. To supply 100 ppm nitrogen with each irrigation, using an injector with a proportion of 1 to 100, approximately 6¾ ounces of fertilizer containing 20 percent nitrogen would be used per gallon of the fertilizer concentrate solution, and twice as much would be used to supply 200 ppm. If liquid applications of fertilizer are going to be made periodically instead of with each irrigation, the applications should be made at about weekly intervals with no more than 3 pounds of fertilizer containing 20 percent nitrogen per 100 gallons of water.

At the time of fertilizing, the soil must be moist, or the concentrated fertilizer solution will burn the roots as it penetrates the dry soil. The presence of moisture will dilute the fertilizer as it permeates the mass of soil in the pot. If in doubt, water the soil lightly first to ensure that it is sufficiently moist before applying fertilizer. Absorption of fertilizer by the plant is very rapid when conditions favor rapid evaporation of water vapor from the leaf. Occasionally fertilization during such a period will cause damage to soft or young leaves because of too great a concentration within the tissue. Portions of the leaf blade will appear first water-soaked, then wilted, and later brown and dried up. Applying too strong a solution burns the roots and causes the plant to wilt, drop leaves while green, or even die. Liquid fertilizer splashed on the leaves, stems, or flowers is likely to burn by causing withdrawal of water from the tissue, and it should be washed off.

Irrigation. In spite of its being botanically untrue and grammatically questionable, the old saying, "The man with the hose grows the plants," emphasizes the importance of the proper use of water in the growth of plants. This cannot be stressed enough. The good grower not only knows when to irrigate, but even more important he knows when not to irrigate. Irrigation practices must be determined by how freely the soil drains, temperature, light, air movement, and the kind and size of plants. Regardless of the equipment used for applying the water, some individual must make the decision on the frequency of watering and the amount of water to apply. If soil and pot drain freely, the irrigation problems are much simpler than they are with soils which drain slowly.

There is some confusion in irrigation terms as used in greenhouses. Frequently when the term overwatering is used, it is incorrectly related to the amount

11-1. Irrigation of pot plants by means of small-diameter plastic tubes is efficient and economical. (*Stuppy Supply Co. photograph.*)

of water that is applied at a time rather than to the frequency of irrigation. Most instances of "overwatering" are related to applying water too often, and very often too small a quantity of water is being used per irrigation in spite of it being referred to as "overwatering."

Soils must be kept uniformly moist for good root growth, but if they are saturated, the air supply in the soil is so low that it limits root growth. Coarse and porous soils drain rapidly and will have an adequate air supply immediately after irrigation. Such soils can be irrigated frequently without a problem. Soils that are heavy and closely packed drain slowly, stay wet longer, and have a lower supply of air in the soil for an extended period after irrigation.

The pot plant grower should spend about as much time looking at the roots as he does at the tops of the plants. Enough plants should be knocked out of pots each day to learn whether they are growing actively. If they are, it will be evident by the presence of white root tips on the surface of the soil ball. The most common cause of poor root growth is lack of air in soils that stay too wet because they are watered too frequently.

Watering pot plants properly with hose in hand is a slow process, as the rate of water flow from the hose must be slow so that the freeboard space above the soil in the pot can be filled with water. If the flow of water from the hose is too forceful, water and soil will splash out of the pot. The pots are watered one at a time by directing the end of the hose close to the soil in the pots. A 6-inch pot requires about ½ pint of water with each irrigation. Soils dry at dif-

11-2. Pot plants should be placed on benches which drain readily. Well-spaced wooden bench bottoms are satisfactory. (*Yoder Bros., Inc., photograph.*)

ferent rates, and the good grower attempts to irrigate only the pots that require it each time.

One of the greatest labor savers in the pot plant range is the small-diameter plastic tube system of irrigation developed by Chapin. There are several adaptations of the basic system, but they all involve supplying each pot with water through a small-diameter (0.045 inch) plastic tube that is fed from a water main or manifold on the bench. Several hundred pots can be watered in the time required to water just a few by the hose-in-hand method, and the plants are irrigated just as well as or better than they are by the manual method. Such a system can be automated by the use of electric water valves and a weighing device that activates the valves when the soil in the pots is getting dry (the total weight of the pot plant is less) and closes the valves when the soil is well irrigated (the total weight of the pot plant is greater).

Pots. Pots are made from several different materials, and the suitability of the pot depends on the use to which it will be put. Clay pots are available in all sizes, and through the years they have been used successfully for all purposes. Clay pots are porous, providing some exchange of moisture and air through the pot, and this is considered to be beneficial for the moisture-air relationship in the soil. Two objectionable aspects of clay pots are that they are heavy and that algae grow on the sides, necessitating cleaning them before sale. When clay pot manufacturers treat the outside of the pots with silicone, the algae growth is markedly reduced.

Plastic pots are made from several different materials and may be either rigid or flexible. Because they are lighter than clay pots, they are commonly used for pot plants that will be shipped. Plastic pots are impervious to moisture and air, which may be a problem with soils that drain slowly or if irrigation is too frequent. Algae growth on the sides of the pots is not a problem, and there-

11-3. Clay pots are sized by the top inside diameter, and standard pots are as deep as they are wide. The top row shows standard pots from the 1-inch to the 6-inch size. At bottom left is an azalea or three-quarter pot. At bottom center is a bulb pan which is approximately one-half as deep as it is wide. (*Cleveland Pottery Co. photograph.*)

fore the plastic pots do not have to be cleaned before the pot plants are sold. Plastic pots become deformed in high temperatures and cannot be sterilized with steam. If the pots were to be reused, they would need to be sterilized by some other means.

Pots made from peat and wood fiber are useful in smaller sizes for seedlings or rooted cuttings. The pot is planted together with the plant. This saves the operations of knocking the plants out of small pots and sterilizing and storing the pots, and it reduces the disturbance of the roots. Peat pots are somewhat fragile to handle, and usually trays are required so that several pots can be moved at once.

The so-called "standard" pot is most universally used. Such a pot is as wide at the top as it is high (for example, 2½ inches high and 2½ inches across at the top, or 6 inches high and 6 inches across at the top). They are available in all sizes from 1 inch up to 14 and 16 inches. Pans begin usually with the 5-inch size and are half as high as they are wide (for example, 6 inches across at top and 3 inches high). Pans are useful with poinsettias and also for germination of seeds. Three-quarter pots and azalea pots are generally similar in that they are three-quarters as high as they are across (6 inches across and 4½ inches high). The three-quarter, or azalea, pot is not as widely used as it should be. For example, many pot plants, such as azaleas, primroses, Calceolarias, and Chrysanthe-mums, look more balanced in an azalea pot than in a standard pot. In addition, less soil is used, which makes a lighter plant to move and carry. Azalea pots have a wider base than a standard pot and are not as likely to fall over. Rose pots are useful when potting *R. manetti* stock and for growing small plants or cuttings. Since they are taller than they are wide, they provide more soil for development of a larger root system and require less frequent watering. They are rarely over 3 inches across the top.

Potting or shifting. Except when seedlings or cuttings are being pricked off or potted, the soil should seldom be screened as the lumps are beneficial in preventing the soil from becoming too tightly packed. When a shift is being made to a slightly larger pot, soil must be screened so that it may be worked into the space between the soil ball and the side of the pot. It is desirable to use potting soil that is low in nitrates. If nitrates are high, the young roots will be burned or severely stunted, causing their growth into the new soil to be slow. It is always easier to add nitrogen to the soil after the plants are established than it is to leach it out, as the latter process requires many applications of water be-cause the drainage is small when the total volume of soil is considered.

The moisture content of the soil at the time of potting is important from the standpoint of ease and convenience. Too wet a soil will be packed too tightly, and too dry a soil will not be firmed well enough and also will be difficult to wet again. The correct moisture content is determined by squeezing the soil in the palm of the hand, and if it forms a ball which will just hold together, it is satis-factory.

When shifting, it is the usual practice to set the plant at the same level in the soil as it was in the smaller pot. Cyclamen are sometimes raised slightly to prevent rotting of the crown. Burying the old soil ball in the larger pot is not recommended.

Usually one man or a crew of men does all the potting, which is advan-tageous in that all plants will be uniform in respect to depth and firmness of the new soil. Indiscriminate and haphazard potting methods result in extreme vari-ation in compaction of the soil, which makes watering a nuisance. Some pots will dry out more rapidly and require frequent touching up with the hose, while the soil in others will be so compact that the soil will drain poorly and dry too slowly for the health of the plant.

Firm potting is desirable, as little is to be gained by a very loosely packed soil. Poor contact between the soil particles and the roots causes slow growth. Soil should rarely be packed or pounded, however, unless palms or rose grafting stock are being potted and anchorage is desired. As to judging when potting is being done right, experience is the best guide, and practice makes perfect.

Experienced potters have a system depending upon whether they are right- or left-handed. For a right-handed potter, the new pots and drainage (broken pieces of pot) are on his right, the soil mixture is in front of him, and the plants to be shifted are on his left. A flat is usually placed on top of the soil pile in which the newly potted plants are to be placed. Assuming the plants are already knocked out of the old pots, the usual method of procedure is as follows. With his right hand the potter places the pot in front of him and puts in the drainage. He lifts the plant with his left hand and simultaneously runs his right hand into the soil pile, palm upward (or nearly so). Some soil is placed in the pot with the right hand, the plant is then placed correctly in the pot with the left hand, and more soil is added with the right hand; meanwhile the left hand is turning the pot, if a large pot is being used. While there are all sorts of variations, depending on the type of plant material and other factors, these basic fundamental movements will be followed generally. The reverse order in regard to pots, plants, and methods will be found more convenient for left-handed persons.

In firming the soil, the pot should not be revolved slowly with the thumb and forefinger of both hands, pressing on the soil surface with the thumbs. This practice firms the soil at the top of the pot, which is the wrong place. Instead, using the thumb and forefinger of each hand, press down near, but not on, the stem of the plant, so that the soil will be firmed in the region of the roots. Lift the pot, tap sharply on the bench, and then place the pot in the flat.

Potting rooted cuttings directly into the finished pot is practiced with the *Chrysanthemum* and the poinsettia. Cuttings are placed in a 5- or 6-inch azalea pot, and the plants are shaded until they become established. Soil must be low in fertilizer, especially nitrogen, and the soil must be run on the dry side until the plants are established. Select uniform cuttings with respect to quality of root system and appearance of the stem and leaves in order to obtain uniform pot plants when they are finished.

Staking and wrapping. Begonia, Calceolaria, Chrysanthemum, and poinsettia pot plants may require staking to assure that the stems remain upright, but most of the other pot plants do not require it as they are either shorter or the stems are more sturdy. Lightweight bamboo stakes dyed green or 14-gauge wire stakes enameled green are useful. Methods vary with the plant and the type of growth, but Begonias and Calceolarias may be supported by a single stake placed at the center of the pot with the stems tied to it. If Chrysanthemums are staked, it usually is with four stakes at the edge of the pot with green string attached to each stake and encircling all the plants. Poinsettias are staked by placing a stake in the soil beside each stem and tying the stem to the stake. Staking should be done before the plants are fully developed.

The necessity for staking is determined in part by the method of marketing. Plants that are shipped some distance may require staking while those that are sold locally may not.

Pot plants must be wrapped to provide protection and facilitate handling during shipping, and various methods are used depending on the size of the plants, the distance to be shipped, and the method of transportation. The plants may be wrapped individually and handled individually or placed in trays or flats so that several plants can be carried at once. Paper or clear plastic sleeves are made in various sizes so that they can be pulled up and around a plant readily. The clear plastic sleeve may not be as durable as the paper sleeve, but it displays the plant while protecting it.

If pot plants are to be shipped in shelved trucks, the individually wrapped plants may be placed on the shelves, pot to pot, without further wrapping. If the truck is not shelved, plants must be boxed for stacking in the truck. Depending on the type of plant and the method of boxing, the plants may or may not be individually wrapped before they are boxed.

The bracts of the poinsettia flower are easily bruised or broken, and each flower should be wrapped individually before the plant is wrapped.

Irrigation of the pot plants must be scheduled carefully. The plants must be watered before wrapping so that they will have sufficient moisture during transit and will not wilt. However, enough time must elapse between irrigation and wrapping so that the pots drain well before they are packed to keep the boxes and vehicles from getting too wet.

Pot plants arrive at the destination in better condition if they are shipped in refrigerated vehicles in the summer and heated ones in the winter. Great care must be taken in shipping pot plants during freezing weather. The plants must be well wrapped and the shipping containers insulated, but it is virtually impossible to provide enough insulation to prevent the plants from freezing if they are placed in freezing temperatures for longer than a few minutes. Very often the damage from cold temperatures occurs while the plants are on a loading dock awaiting transportation.

Marketing. It is considered generally that because of the size and weight of pot plants, shipping costs for long distances would be prohibitive, and the economical area of sales is based on how far the customer can conveniently drive to pick up plants or on how far the pot plant grower can afford to deliver the plants in his own vehicles. With improvements in transportation and highways, the distance that pot plants can be transported economically has increased. In spite of this, the major market for pot plants probably always will be relatively local.

Some pot plant growers market their entire production through their own efforts, by delivery of orders as they are sold or by operation of regular delivery routes within a certain radius of their greenhouses. Many wholesale commission houses handle some pot plants, but the biggest proportion of the plants is sold directly from the growers to the retailers. Marketing costs are about 25 percent of the selling price whether the plants are sold directly or through a commission house.

Pot plant rotations.   Pot plant crops are much more adaptable to rotations than cut flowers, as they are short-term crops.   They may be spaced at various distances, and they can be moved from area to area.   Because of the high degree of adaptability there are many different possible rotations, but very detailed planning is required to develop good rotations, as several different pot plant crops are grown in each pot plant range, with each crop requiring increasing space as it grows.   It is a complex problem to fit all of the crops into the space available so that the plants have the space and conditions that are needed and so that maximum use of the greenhouses is still made.   It is easy to develop convenient rotations which do not make maximum use of the greenhouse space, but adequate financial return from the area is not realized unless all of it is used intensively.

Pot plant rotations must be made for each specific situation, but to illustrate some of the possibilities—and some of the problems—a rotation is presented here for a greenhouse range that contains a glasshouse with 30,000 square feet of bench space: about 45,000 square feet of ground area covered with glass, with 15,000 square feet in walks and 30,000 square feet in benches.   In addition to the glasshouse area there is 16,700 square feet of bed space in plastic houses (approximately 25,000 square feet under plastic) and 20,000 square feet of bed space outdoors for growing plants during the summer.

The first consideration in making a rotation is to develop a workable schedule for the production of pot plants that can be marketed at a profit.   If this can be done and at the same time the entire greenhouse space can be fully occupied, the plan for rotation is completely successful.

The year-round pot mum program consists of 500 six-inch pots per week, and they are placed about three pots per square foot for 3 weeks in an area where light and/or mist is available, which means that 166⅔ square feet per crop is required, or a total of 500 square feet in the entire area.   They are then shifted to an area at finish spacing of 1¼ square foot per pot, requiring 625 square feet per crop or a total of 6,870 square feet for the 11 weeks that the pots may be in this area before being marketed.   The total area required for the year-round mum program is 7,300 square feet of bench space; however, in order to make some space available during the critical period in March, April, and May, the pots are shifted gradually at that time in order to gain some space for the holiday pot mums. Five mum cuttings are used per 6-inch pot, and the average cost of the plants to start is 30 cents per pot.

The off-season azaleas are grown in the greenhouse for the entire time except for 6 weeks in refrigerated storage.   This program schedules 100 plants for flowering each week from May 1 to December 1: 100 five- by six-inch azalea plants are planted in the greenhouse benches 6 by 6 inches apart each week from September 1 to April 1, requiring 25 square feet of bench space per crop or a total of 300 square feet for the 12 weeks they will remain there.   The plants are then potted and spaced at ¾ square foot per pot or 75 square feet per crop or a

Table 11-1. *Rotation for a Greenhouse with 30,000 Square Feet of Bench Space* *

SQUARE FEET OF BENCH SPACE

CROP	JAN.	FEB.	MAR.	APR.	MAY	JUNE	JULY	AUG.	SEPT.	OCT.	NOV.	DEC.
Mums—year-round	7,300	7,300	7,000	6,600	7,000	7,300	7,300	7,300	7,300	7,300	7,300	7,300
Azaleas—off season	1,200	1,200	1,900	1,900	1,900	1,900	1,900	1,900	1,900	1,900	1,600	1,200
Poinsettias	.....	.....	.....	.....	3,800	9,000	9,000	11,000	18,000	16,000	15,000	15,000
Azaleas—natural season	8,000	8,000	.....	.....	.....	.....	.....	.....	.....	.....	1,000	3,000
Hydrangeas	1,000	2,000	6,000	7,500	3,000	.....	.....	.....	.....	.....	.....	.....
Lilies	1,000	1,500	1,500	1,500	.....	.....	.....	.....	.....	.....	.....	1,000
Mums—holiday	5,000	7,000	11,000	12,500	11,800	.....	.....	1,000	2,500	4,800	5,100	2,500
Tulips	1,000	1,000	1,000	.....	.....	.....	.....	.....	.....	.....	.....	.....
Hyacinths	1,000	1,000	1,000	.....	.....	.....	.....	.....	.....	.....	.....	.....
Gloxinias	.....	.....	.....	.....	2,500	11,000	11,000	8,000	.....	.....	.....	.....
Total	25,500	29,000	29,400	30,000	30,000	29,200	29,200	29,700	30,000	30,000	30,000	30,000

* In addition to the glasshouse with 30,000 square feet of bench space, there is a plastic house with 16,700 square feet of bed space used for storage of azaleas (15,000 square feet) from October through March, and Hydrangeas (1,700 square feet) from October through January, for growing azaleas (15,000 square feet) during the summer, for forcing azaleas (8,000 square feet) in March, April, and May, and for forcing mums (3,000 square feet) in April. There are an outdoor area of 20,000 square feet of bed space for growing azaleas and Hydrangeas and an outdoor area of 6,000 square feet of bed space for the storage of tulips and hyacinths from October to January.

total of 900 square feet for the 12 weeks that the plants will remain at that space. The total growing area needed is 1,200 square feet of bench space. The plants are placed in refrigerated storage for 6 weeks, and at 3 pots per square foot a total of 200 square feet of bench space in storage is required. Azaleas require about 6 weeks at forcing temperatures and they are spaced at 1 square foot per plant. The forcing area required would be 100 square feet per crop and 700 square feet for the entire program. The estimated shipped-in cost for the 5- to 6-inch plants to start the program is 50 cents per plant.

This rotation plans the production of 48,000 poinsettias in 2¼-inch pots for resale in early fall to other growers and 10,000 poinsettias in 6-inch pans to be forced for the Christmas market. The 2¼-inch plants would be rooted directly in peat pots spaced at four per square foot for a total of 12,000 square feet. In order to supply the cuttings that are required, 600 stock plants would be started in May. The estimated cost of plant material prorated per cutting is 3 cents. The 10,000 six-inch pans require 30,000 rooted cuttings, as they are planted 3 per pan, and 400 stock plants would be started in May to supply these cuttings. The cuttings are stuck in the propagation bench at 9 square inches in late August and September, which will require 2,000 square feet of propagation bench area. The rooted poinsettia cuttings are potted in 2¼-inch pots, and in early October three plants are panned per 6-inch pan. The finish spacing on the 6-inch poinsettia pans is 1½ square feet per pan. Poinsettia stock plants are started in May at a spacing of 4 square feet each and spaced to the finish spacing of 9 square feet each in June through September. The estimated cost of the plant material (stock plants) prorated per 6-inch pan is 10 cents.

It is planned to produce 30,000 natural season azaleas in 6-inch pots of which 1,000 will be forced for Christmas, 8,000 for January, 8,000 for February, 8,000 for March and April, and 5,000 for May. These plants will be started from 5- to 6-inch plants received in May, and half will be grown in the plastic house and the other half outdoors at a spacing of 1 square foot per plant. By October the azalea plants will be placed in the plastic house for storage at a spacing of 2 plants per square foot. The azaleas are forced at 1 square foot each, and the December, January, and February plants are forced in the glasshouses and the March, April, and May plants are forced in the plastic house. The shipped-in cost of the plant material is estimated at 50 cents per plant.

A total of 5,000 Hydrangeas, 3 canes in 6-inch pots, is planned, of which 3,000 would be forced for Easter and 2,000 for Mother's Day. Approximately 5,000 square feet of bed space would be required outdoors, as the plants should be grown during the summer at 1 square foot each. From October to January the Hydrangeas will be stored in the plastic houses at 3 pots per square foot. For forcing, the plants are started at three pots per square foot and spaced to 1½ square feet per pot for finishing. The estimated cost of the plant material is 10 cents per pot.

The rotation plans 3,000 lilies to be forced for Easter in 6-inch pots, and they are started at three pots per square foot and finished at two pots per square foot. The estimated cost of plant material is 45 cents per pot.

A total of 18,600 pot mums in 6-inch pots would be produced for the holidays of which 3,200 would be forced for Thanksgiving, 2,000 for Christmas, 4,000 for Easter, and 9,400 for Mother's Day. Finish spacing for the pot Chrysanthemum is 1¼ square feet per pot, and five cuttings are used per pot with an estimated average cost of 30 cents per pot for plant material. In order to accommodate a portion of the pot mum crop in April, 3,000 square feet of space is used in the plastic houses in addition to the glasshouse space.

The tulips would be panned seven per pan in October, set three pans per square foot outdoors, and covered with soil, straw, or other material to prevent freezing but keep the bulbs uniformly cool. This would require an area of 3,000 square feet of bed space for the 9,000 pots to be forced. The tulips would be brought in for forcing in three lots in January, February, and March, and as they are set three pots per square foot, 1,000 square feet of bench space is required. The cost of the bulbs is estimated at 55 cents per pan.

The hyacinths would be handled in the same manner as the tulips with the differences that they are panned 3 per pan and that the cost of the bulbs is estimated at 45 cents per pan.

Gloxinias would be grown only in the summer by buying 2-inch banded plants in May, potting them in 6-inch pots, and giving them an initial spacing of three pots per square foot. The rotation plans for 7,000 pots, which would require 2,500 square feet of bench space for the initial spacing and 11,000 square feet for the finish spacing. The estimated plant costs are 20 cents per pot.

Developing a rotation on paper is one thing, and putting it into effect in the greenhouse is another, as some unplanned problems do arise. One common problem is the usability of the bench space. A bench that contains 400 square feet will hold 400 pot plants spaced one per square foot when the plan is developed on paper, and it will actually hold 400 pot plants if its dimensions are 4 by 100 feet, as the plants will be placed four across the bench and 100 rows down the bench. If a 400-square-foot bench has dimensions of 3½ by 113 feet, however, usually only 339 plants would be placed on it for a one-per-square-foot spacing, as the plants would be placed three across the bench with 113 rows of plants down the bench. This by no means indicates that plans should not be made because they are not entirely reliable, but it does illustrate that after the plan is made, the usability of the space should be verified before the plan is put into effect.

The whole pot plant production program revolves around the production of plants for the holidays, primarily Christmas, Easter, and Mother's Day. Every square inch of space is used at these times, and it is not unusual to find that plants are spaced too closely in order to get a larger number of plants into the available space, or that a portion of the plants are grown on temporary shelving above the benches.   Although either practice is questionable, it is possible to use them with some degree of success if good judgment is exercised.

There are two periods of the year when pot plant ranges are likely to have bench space that is not being fully used—in the summer and in January and February.   At those times some short-term crops can be forced if there is a market for them.   In this rotation a crop of gloxinias and 2¼-inch poinsettias are planned for the summer, and azaleas, tulips, and hyacinths are scheduled for forcing in January and February.

The scheduled rotation must be somewhat flexible so that changes can be made as needed, but before a change is made it should be determined what the long-range effect will be.   Sometimes the change that seems desirable at the moment will prove very unsatisfactory when the results of future crops are considered.

There are various reasons why the number of plants sold does not equal the number of plants planned.   This number varies from crop to crop and year to year, but through the years it is estimated that the loss is about 5 percent for most pot plants.   For lilies the estimate is 15 percent and for tulips and hyacinths 10 per cent.   The important point in this discussion is not the amount of loss, but that there is a loss.   Too many plans are made on the basis that the entire quantity planned will be sold, but this seldom occurs because of cultural problems, diseases, pests, physical injury to the plants, and poor market conditions.

In this analysis of income it is estimated that selling costs for pot plants average 25 percent of the selling price.   The selling cost is subtracted from the total selling price in determining the gross income from the crop.

The total gross income per year from the pot plant range in this example is $163,292.   The total bench and bed area involved in the range is 56,700 square feet—30,000 square feet in glasshouses, 16,700 square feet in plastic houses used primarily for storage but rated the same as the glasshouses in computing income, and a glasshouse equivalent of 10,000 square feet in outdoor beds, as this area is charged at one-half the glasshouse rate.   The gross income per square foot of bench space per year would be $2.88.   It is possible that the plastic house area used primarily for storage should be rated less than the glasshouse area, and if this were done, the gross income per square foot would increase.

In order to make a comparison of income among the various crops that were grown, the original plant costs were subtracted from the gross income, and the gross income per month was determined by dividing this amount by the number of months the crop was in production.   Dividing the gross income per month by the average amount of bench space used by each crop per month gives the gross income per square foot per month.   The greatest value in presenting this analysis may be in suggesting a method of comparing relative incomes from greenhouse crops rather than in the actual values that were determined in the example.

Table 11-2. *Gross Income from a Greenhouse with 30,000 Square Feet of Bench Space*

| CROP | NUMBER OF PLANTS | | SELLING PRICE | | LESS SELLING COSTS † | GROSS INCOME PER YEAR |
	PLANNED	SOLD *	EACH	TOTAL		
Mums—year-round	26,000	24,700	$1.65	$40,755	$10,189	$30,566
Azaleas—off season	3,000	2,850	2.50	7,125	1,781	5,344
Poinsettias, 2¼ in.	48,000	45,600	.22	10,032	2,508	7,524
Poinsettias, 6 in.	10,000	9,500	2.25	21,375	5,344	16,031
Azaleas—						
natural season	30,000	28,500	2.00	57,000	14,250	42,750
Hydrangeas	5,000	4,750	2.50	11,875	2,964	8,911
Lilies	3,000	2,550	1.75	4,463	1,116	3,347
Mums—holiday	18,600	17,670	1.65	29,156	7,289	21,867
Tulips	9,000	8,100	1.50	12,150	3,038	9,112
Hyacinths	9,000	8,100	1.50	12,150	3,038	9,112
Gloxinias	7,000	6,650	1.75	11,638	2,909	8,728

Total gross income per year. $163,292

* The difference between plants planned and plants sold is estimated to be 5 percent with the exceptions of 15 percent for lilies and 10 percent for tulips and hyacinths.
† Selling costs for pot plants are estimated to be 25 percent of the selling price.

Table 11-3. *Income per Square Foot per Month for Several Pot Plant Crops*

CROP	GROSS INCOME PER YEAR	INCOME LESS PLANT COSTS	INCOME PER MONTH	BENCH SPACE PER MONTH, SQ FT	INCOME PER SQ FT PER MONTH
Mums—year-round .	$30,566	$22,766	$1,897	7,192	$0.26
Azaleas—off season.	5,344	3,844	320	1,725	0.18
Poinsettias, 2¼ and 6 inch	23,555	21,115	2,629	12,100	0.22
Azaleas—natural season	42,750	27,750	2,313	15,042	0.15
Hydrangeas	8,911	8,411	701	2,883	0.24
Lilies	3,347	1,997	399	1,300	0.31
Mums—holiday ...	21,867	16,287	1,629	6,620	0.25
Tulips	9,112	4,162	832	1,800	0.46
Hyacinths	9,112	5,062	1,012	1,800	0.56
Gloxinias	8,728	7,328	1,832	8,125	0.22

AFRICAN VIOLET (*Saintpaulia ionantha—Gesneriaceae*)

The African violet is a native of tropical Africa and was given its generic name in honor of Baron Walter Von St. Paul who discovered the plant. It tolerates the low light, warm temperature, and relatively dry air in the home and makes a very satisfactory flowering houseplant.

Saintpaulias are produced the year round in 2¼- to 4-inch pots, and many of the plants are purchased by the housewife for use in the home although some of the larger sizes are used for hospital or other gifts. The use of these plants is not associated with any particular holiday, but sales are better generally in the spring than at other times of the year.

African violets flower the year-round with no effect of day length on flowering. The leaves and flowers arise from a compact stem producing a crown type of growth. The plants increase very little in height as they grow, but they do expand in width as new plants form at the base.

Propagation. Plants are propagated by leaf cuttings taken with a petiole about ½ inch long to help anchor the leaf in the propagation medium. Young plants develop slowly from long petioles stuck deeply in the rooting medium. Mature leaves may be taken any time of the year, and for a 4-inch plant from 8 to 10 months should be allowed from the time of propagating.

A mixture of equal parts of sand and peat or sand, vermiculite, and peat is preferable to sand alone because it does not dry as fast and retains fertilizer. Ordinary greenhouse flats are filled with the rooting medium, and leaves are stuck close but not touching each other, so that there are several hundred in a flat. The flats may be placed overhead on racks in a 65°F house. Rooting will occur in 3 to 4 weeks, but shoot formation and development to a size convenient to handle take 8 to 12 weeks. Growth substances hasten rooting but often delay shoot development.

Nematodes may infest the petioles, and generally there are swellings present. Such leaves should not be used for propagation, because there is no control except to discard the plants. All flats, rooting mediums, pots, soil mixtures, and bench areas should be steamed to prevent nematode infection.

Seed may be used with only a few varieties which reproduce true. The majority of seedlings from a cross will be different from the parent and constitute the major source of new varieties. Extensive breeding by amateurs has led to the introduction of far too many varieties because of reluctance to discard inferior sorts.

The seed is fine and should be sown on the surface of a screened, well-prepared medium that is watered from below. At a temperature of 70°F, germination will occur in several weeks time. The plants are pricked off to flats approximately 1 inch each way and, when crowded, are placed in 2½-inch pots and later shifted to 4-inch pots, where they are flowered and evaluated.

Since African violets are so readily propagated by seed or leaf cuttings, today there are numerous varieties which are identical, or nearly so, yet have different names. Many varieties should be discarded because they are poor; some are satisfactory as small plants, but deteriorate after reaching the flowering stage in larger pots. The large-flowered, heavy-leaved kinds are presumed to be tetraploids.

Light. Regulation of light intensity is very important. Optimum growth and flowering will be obtained at 1,100 foot-candles of light during the brightest part of the day. More than this level of light will cause compact growth and bleaching or burning of the foliage. Too little light induces stretching of the petioles and reduction of flowering. The African violet grower should purchase an inexpensive light meter so that light intensity can be maintained at the optimum range at all seasons.

Regulation of the intensity can be accomplished by several means. Applying shading compounds to the roof should begin in early March, and as the sunlight increases in intensity, additional shading material is used. By June the glass should be completely covered with shading compound. In late September some shade can be brushed or scraped off, and by late November, in Ohio, most of it should be off because of the prevalence of dark cloudy weather. Cheese-cloth, muslin, and other similar cloth suspended on wires overhead may be used alone or in conjunction with shading material on the roof to regulate light intensity.

When the only source of light is fluorescent lamps, growth of the African violet is very satisfactory. The plants have heavier, darker green leaves with attractive pigmentation underneath, flowering is much more profuse, and in general the plants are far superior to those produced under the most optimum conditions in the greenhouse. Leaves allowed to root and form small plants under fluorescent light and then grown in the greenhouse produce mature plants faster than if grown in the greenhouse from propagation. Therefore fluorescent lights can be quite useful in propagation where great numbers of leaves occupying a relatively small area can be lighted. The added growth obtained makes this a feasible undertaking.

The light intensity should be 600 foot-candles, and the length of exposure per day should be 15 to 18 hours. The standard cool-white tubes have proved somewhat superior to soft-white, or daylight, fluorescent tubes, although the latter may be used. Green fluorescent lights are useful if an equal number of white tubes are used in conjunction with them. Gold and blue fluorescent tubes are not satisfactory, and mercury-vapor lights generate too much heat.

To obtain 600 foot-candles over a 4-foot bench, two industrial fixtures, each holding two tubes, should be suspended side by side, 12 inches above the tops of the plants. The 40-watt tubes are 4 feet long, and the area covered will be 16 square feet. Instead of fixtures, strips which have the ballast and receptacle for the tubes may be mounted on plywood painted white for maximum reflection. If these strips are spaced 6 inches apart, the optimum light intensity can be obtained at reduced initial cost. Limited tests have shown that African violets can be lighted for 24 hours (continuously) if given 400 foot-candles of light. This eliminates the need for a time switch to operate the lights and promotes longer life for the tubes, which wear out faster when turned on and off.

The fluorescent light itself is not solely responsible for the improved growth of the plants. It is true that optimum light intensity is obtained for 15 to 18 hours, which is quite different from greenhouse light intensities, but usually environmental conditions in a room without sunlight do not vary so greatly, and growth is accelerated from the more uniform environment.

Temperature. At temperatures lower than 60°F, the African violet grows very slowly, may get mildew, and will have hardened, brittle, downward-curled foliage. Best growth is obtained between 65 and 70°F, though maintenance of a 62 to 64°F temperature is more economical and quite satisfactory. At 80°F the plants grow well and flowering is profuse, but the petals are faded and small.

Potting and spacing. When the shoots at the base of the petiole are about 1 inch long, the leaf with the attached plants is carefully lifted and placed in a 2½-inch pot. Such plants will become multiple-crowned (all shoots develop). Single-crowned specimens are produced by separating the crowns at the time of initial potting or after the plants have developed to some extent in 2½-inch pots. Single-crowned plants have leaves that spread out like spokes in a wheel and are difficult to ship because of leaf breakage. Multiple-crowned plants grow into a salable plant more rapidly and ship rather easily.

The small pots are placed pot to pot in the bench, and they are kept at that spacing until time for repotting. When the leaves of the young plants extend to the edges of the pots, the plants are removed from the bench and repotted. They are shifted to the size in which they will be finished, usually either 3-inch or 4-inch azalea pots.

After repotting, the plants may be placed pot to pot on the bench, or they may be placed at the finish spacing. The method of spacing is determined by the amount of available space, the number of plants to be grown, the quality desired, and the available labor. Labor will be conserved, and plant growth will be better if the plants are set at the finish spacing. The spacing used varies with the type of plant desired, but it is about 4 inches for 3-inch pots and 6 inches for 4-inch pots.

Troubles. Overwatering the African violet generally kills the roots, and the plant will have a gray-green appearance. Very often the crown will rot if kept too wet. The soil should be allowed to dry, but not to the point that the plants wilt.

The temperature of the water is very important. If the water is somewhat cooler than the leaf temperature, irregular spots, streaks, or rings develop that are white or cream-colored. The chlorophyll in the leaves will never develop in that area again. If the plants are watered early in the morning when the leaf temperature is at its lowest point, cool (not cold) water usually is safe. Warming the water to a temperature of 80°F by means of steam or hot water is the safest procedure to eliminate danger of leaf spotting. Watering before 10 A.M. will ensure that the crowns and foliage will be dry by night, which is an effective way of reducing the danger of rot or other diseases developing.

Petiole rot occurs where the petiole contacts the edge of the pot and is due to injury from the minerals that have accumulated in the pot. This is not common in production when new pots are used, but it can be a problem after the plants have grown for several months in the home. There is no pathogen involved, and the control is to prevent the leaves from touching the pot edge by covering the edge with aluminum foil or other material.

Diseases. Botrytis blight may affect leaves or flowers, and the best means of control are sanitation and adequate spacing of plants. Increasing ventilation or using air-circulation fans will help also.

Root and crown rot are caused by the Pythium pathogen, and soil, pots, and handling equipment must be sterilized thoroughly before use. This pathogen thrives in soils that are constantly moist.   The use of well-drained soil coupled with well-spaced irrigations provides more favorable conditions.   Dexon 35 can be used as a soil drench.

Powdery mildew may infest the leaves of African violets, but this should be no problem if heating and ventilating are done properly, which provide air movement and lower humidity.

Pests.   Aphids and mealy bugs can be troublesome.   Probably the most serious pest is the Cyclamen mite, which sucks the juices of the youngest leaves and causes them to be curled upward and dwarfed.   The leaves also have a dense whitish pubescence on the upper surface when mite has infested the plants. Flowers are malformed, and soon the plant ceases to produce flowers, because the mite sucks juices from the young inflorescences, which prevents their development.

Thrips cause light streaks on the flowers of the darker-colored varieties. They pollinate the flowers, which drop quickly, and seed pods form.

Nematodes, both root-knot and foliar, attack the African violet.   Knots or galls may form on the roots, while swellings of the petiole or discolored brown areas appear between the main veins of the leaves, indicating their presence. Nematode-infested plants should be destroyed, and pots, soil, and bench areas steam-sterilized.   Nematodes can leach from the soil in a pot and infest the bench area, so that infested plants constitute a serious hazard.

The Pritchard mealy bug lives on the roots of African violets and is a small (⅛ inch or less in length) white insect covered with waxy threads.   Several hundred may infest the plant roots, and losses can be great.   Aldrin 25W at 1 pound per 100 gallons as a soil drench is a useful control, as is an endrin soil drench.

AZALEA (*Rhododendron* spp.—*Ericaceae*)

The azalea varieties which are grown by florists originated from either the *Rhododendron indica* (Belgian) or the *Kurume,* and for years a variety was classified as belonging to one or the other type.   There has been much breeding done of azaleas, resulting in hybrids with characteristics that vary considerably from either type, and more appropriate classifications now might be large-flowered types and small-flowered types, rather than trying to identify the variety with an exact type which may be far removed.

Another way of classifying azaleas is as early, midseason, or late varieties. This is determined by the length of cool period required for maturing the flower buds.   The early varieties require a shorter cool period than the late varieties.

Azaleas grown in natural conditions produce leaves and increase in stem length during late spring and early summer, and growth in stem length terminates with the formation of flower buds in late summer.   After flower buds are mature, if the plant is placed in temperatures below 50°F for several weeks in late fall, the plants will flower a few weeks after they are placed in 60°F temperatures.   In natural conditions azaleas can be flowered in the winter and spring, but by artificially supplying cool temperatures earlier in the fall, some varieties can be flowered as early as December.

If temperature and possibly day length are adjusted artificially, the type of growth and the development of some azaleas can be regulated so that they may be flowered at any time of the year.   Some growers produce azaleas the year-round by these means.

A few growers produce azaleas entirely on their own place from propagation through flowering; however, more commonly the northern grower starts with small plants bought from growers along the Gulf of Mexico, in Florida, or on the East Coast or the West Coast.   The small plants are grown outdoors in these favorable climates, but some of the growers have greenhouses for propagation, and plastic houses and screen or slat houses for growing on.   For winter and spring flowering, the northern greenhouse operator receives the growing-on plants in the spring, grows them outdoors or in greenhouses during the summer, holds them in cold frames or cool greenhouses in the fall, and forces them into flower during the winter and spring.

Propagation.   Most florists buy their stock because propagation is an exacting procedure.

Cuttings can be used for all the kurumes and pericats, while only some indica and rutherfordiana types are handled in this way.   From June through August, cuttings 2 to 4 inches long are taken from the growing-on stock, very often at the time of pinching.   Very soft wood may rot, and the firmer half-ripened wood is therefore best.   The lower leaves are stripped to facilitate sticking, and flower buds are removed.   A mixture of sand or perlite and acid peat, equal parts by volume, will be satisfactory, and the bottom heat should be 65°F, with a somewhat cooler air temperature if possible.   Shading of the roof will reduce the temperature and aid in maintaining a high relative humidity, which should be 60 to 80 percent.   Mist propagation is very successful, but no shade should be used.   Within 5 to 10 weeks most varieties will be rooted, but some additional time may be needed for some indica and rutherfordiana types.

Light.   From fall through spring, azaleas are grown in full sunlight, but in summer they are usually partially shaded by either slats or plastic screen.   The partial shade in summer not only reduces the light and temperature but makes it possible to provide more uniform moisture conditions around the plants.

There have been conflicting reports on the effects of day length on azaleas, but apparently this has been caused by differences in varieties, temperatures, or other conditions.   Some varieties are affected by day length because they form leaves and increase in stem length more readily in long days, but stem growth terminating in flower buds occurs faster in short days.

Leaf drop can occur in azaleas held in dark refrigerators in the fall at 40 to 50°F, but this can be reduced if the plants are provided with long days artificially while they are in the refrigerator.   In 35°F storage, leaf drop is no problem, regardless of day length.

Temperature.   Azaleas should be grown at a minimum night temperature of 60°F with day temperatures approximately 10°F warmer, as formation and development of leaves and flower buds proceed satisfactorily at these temperatures.   At cooler temperatures growth is very slow, but at slightly warmer temperatures growth proceeds faster.

After flower buds have formed and reached an advanced stage of development, they will not continue to develop until they are placed in temperatures of 50°F or below for several weeks.   The length of the cool period needed to mature the flower buds varies with the variety of azalea and the growing conditions.   It may be as short a time as 4 weeks or as long as 8 weeks.   Actually in many localities the outdoor night temperatures in the summer will be below 60°F some nights, and this will delay flower bud formation.   If the cool temperatures occur after the flower buds are formed, they do contribute to the maturing of the buds; and the plants will require fewer days of cool temperature storage.   It may be expected that plants grown in greenhouses in which the the temperature is carefully regulated will require a longer period of cool treatment for maturing the flower buds than plants that have been grown in the variable outdoor temperatures.   Plants sprayed with growth regulators to increase the number of flower buds will require a longer cool period and a somewhat longer time to force than untreated plants.   Temperatures from 35 to 50°F can be used for maturing azalea flower buds.   If the plants are to be stored for the minimum length of time, it is usually at 50°F, as they force a little more quickly after storage at this temperature than at cooler temperatures.   If the plants are to be held in storage for a longer time, 35°F temperature is used, since leaf drop is less of a problem.

Azalea flower buds are very sensitive to cold temperatures in the fall; and if the plants are grown outdoors in the country where early freezes are possible, great care must be taken to protect the plants from even short periods of frost.   In the northern states the azaleas will need to be moved to a protected area by the middle of September or earlier.

For forcing azaleas into flower, a minimum of 60°F night temperature is used, with the day temperature approximately 10°F warmer.

Soil.   Azaleas are grown in a wide variety of soil types in the various outdoor areas where they are produced, but in the greenhouses German peat moss generally is used.   The poultry-litter grade is best as its coarse, lumpy structure provides the air-moisture relationship needed for good root growth.

The soil should be acid—about pH 5.0 to 5.5.   Since German peat moss is acid in reaction, acidifying it is not necessary, but adding limestone or hydrated lime may be necessary, if the pH is below 4.0, at the rate of 3 pounds per 6-cubic-foot bale or 1 to 2 pounds per 100 square feet of area.

Potting and spacing.   Azalea cuttings should be transplanted from the propagation bench to peat moss in flats or benches, spacing them about 1 inch apart in the row with 2 inches between rows.   The plants are pinched as soon as possible after planting; and when leaves of adjacent plants touch, they should be transplanted to benches and spaced about 4 by 4 inches.   The plants should be pinched shortly after planting; and when they have grown enough to occupy the allotted space, they either are transplanted to benches at 6-inch spacing or potted in 6-inch azalea pots.

The size of most potted plants is expressed as the size pot in which it is grown; however, azaleas are sized by the diameter of the head of the plant. Plants that are 6 by 6 inches or 6 by 8 inches are potted in 6-inch azalea pots, and this is the size plant that is sold in the greatest quantity.   Not all the plants in a given lot attain the same size, and the 3- by 5-inch or 4- by 6-inch plants may be potted in 4-inch azalea pots, or two plants may be potted together in a 6-inch pot. Larger plants are potted in correspondingly larger pots, and 14-inch plants are potted into about 10-inch azalea pots.

While in the growing, vegetative stage, azaleas must be spaced so that they have room in which to increase in size.   Plants that are grown too closely together will develop odd-shaped heads.

Budded azalea plants, brought in for forcing into flower, may be spaced with heads almost touching as the plant does not increase in size greatly while the flowers are developing.

Troubles.   Chlorosis of the tip leaves usually indicates a lack of available iron in the plant, which may be caused by a lack of available iron in the soil or by a damaged root system which is not able to transfer the iron from the soil to the upper parts of the plant.   If the roots are growing actively, an application of chelated iron or iron sulfate will correct the situation.   If the roots are not growing well, the cause for this poor growth must be corrected first.   The most common causes of poor root growth in azaleas are inadequate drainage with constantly wet soil, too much fertilizer in the soil, nematodes of various kinds, and fungus diseases.

Bypassed flower buds—caused by vegetative shoots starting in growth immediately below the flower buds—may be a problem during the forcing period. If they are allowed to continue in growth, the flower buds on those stems will not open—they will be bypassed.   If the vegetative shoots are removed when they first appear, the flower buds will open normally. Most bypass growth can be prevented if conditions for flower bud formation are good while the plant is grown. Then the flower buds form not only in the terminal position in the stem but also in the lateral position, immediately below the terminal, and the stems have clusters of flower buds with no possibility of bypass shoots forming.

Leaf drop does occur, and this is associated usually with root damage because of either extremely dry or extremely wet soil or because of the use of too much fertilizer. In addition, the lack of light or presence of ethylene in storage may cause some leaf drop.

Bronzing of the leaves can be caused by cool temperatures, and it is more pronounced when the light intensity is high and the nitrogen supply is low.

Loss of roots can be caused by poor soil drainage or keeping the soil too wet, by too much fertilizer in the soil, or by allowing the soil to dry too much. If peat moss becomes too dry, it is difficult to wet; then the soil ball should be submerged in water briefly. If coarse poultry-litter-grade peat moss is used, drainage usually is not a problem. An application of fertilizer can damage the roots if the soil is dry when applied, and it is good practice to irrigate just before fertilizing.

Diseases. Phytophthora root rot is caused by *Phytophthora cinnamomi* and is most prevalent in soils which are poorly drained or are irrigated too frequently. Diseased plants should be rogued and the soil moisture conditions improved. In addition, Dexon 35, used as a soil drench, controls this root rot. *Cylindrocladium* is a fungus attacking the lower stem or roots. It grows best at warm temperatures under moist conditions. There is no control, but Morsodren will protect uninfected plants. Losses from the fungus can be great and are often ascribed to other fungi. Laboratory culturing will identify the organism.

Flower spot caused by *Ovulinia azaleae* can be a serious problem for azaleas. In the early stages the spots are pinhead size and are white to rust in color, and as the infestation progresses, the spots enlarge to irregular blotches with the collapse of the entire flower. The affected flowers dry and remain on the plant, as contrasted with the normal flower drop of old flowers. This pathogen forms sclerotia that can overwinter in the soil. Infected flowers should be completely removed from the area as soon as possible, and the area should be sterilized if it is to be used for azaleas the following year. If an infestation does occur, spraying with zineb at the rate of 1 pound per 100 gallons of water 2 to 3 times a week should give control.

Leaf spots caused by *Septoria azaleae* and other fungi are most troublesome when the leaves remain wet for extended periods. The leaf spotting is usually followed by leaf drop. If there is any evidence of leaf spot, the plants should be sprayed with either ferbam or zineb at weekly intervals, and overhead syringing should be stopped.

Rhizoctonia stem rot occurs primarily when the soil is too heavy, the plants are set too deeply, or irrigations are too frequent. These conditions should be corrected, and Terraclor can be used as a soil drench.

Pests.   Nematodes have become increasingly serious pests, and the best control is careful sterilization of soil and all handling equipment. Plants infested with nematodes cease growing because of the severe damage to the roots, leaves are off-color, and the plants may wilt permanently. Infested plants in peat moss can be treated by drenching with 2 to 2½ fluid ounces of Nemagon EC 2 per 100 gallons of water at the rate of 1 pint per 6-inch pot. In mineral soils half that quantity of Nemagon should be used in making the drench.

Azaleas may be infested with two-spotted mites, aphids, thrips, Cyclamen mites, or mealy bugs, but normal control measures are usually effective. Leaf miners are controlled with Diazinon or Meta Systox-R, and leaf rollers should be treated with Sevin.

Cropping and rotation.   Azaleas may be flowered in their natural season from December to May, or they may be flowered off-season from May to December by growing them under carefully regulated conditions. The standard practice for producing azalea plants to be flowered during the natural season (December to May) is to schedule as much as possible of the operation to coincide with suitable weather conditions, available greenhouse space, and the length of time needed to form and develop flower buds. Plants to be flowered in December must be brought into forcing temperatures (60 to 65°F) approximately 6 weeks before, or about November 1, which must have been preceded by at least 4 weeks of temperatures below 50°F for maturing the flower buds. After azalea shoots are pinched, about 12 weeks is required for the new shoots to grow and the flower buds to form and develop. This means that the shoots would have to be pinched by July 1 in order to have sufficiently well-developed flower buds to be placed in cool temperatures on October 1. In order to have plants with enough growth on them to be pinched in late June, small azaleas are shipped in from southern or coastal propagators in May and grown in the greenhouse for a few weeks before their growth is continued either in the greenhouse or outdoors. Plants to be flowered later than December are grown on the same schedule because this allows for growth in the summer and cool storage in the fall and winter until the plants are brought into the greenhouses for forcing.

Azaleas may be either bed- or pot-grown during the summer; however, if they are bed-grown, they should be dug and potted soon enough in August so that root growth will be well established in the pot before the plants are placed in storage in the fall.

Weather conditions are generally favorable for growing azaleas outdoors in most parts of the country during the summer. Temperatures are about right, but in some areas where night temperatures are below 60°F periodically, flower bud formation in some varieties will be slow or fail to appear. In the Midwest the summer light intensity is too high and the humidity too low for the best azalea growth, and the plants should be placed under partial shade of lath or plastic screen with some provision for misting or spraying.

To provide the cool temperatures (below 50°F) which are needed to mature the flower buds, the azaleas are placed in cold frames or cool greenhouses before chance of freezing in the fall. The plants are kept in these cool locations until they are brought into greenhouse forcing temperatures (60 to 65°). Because a minimum time of 4 weeks is needed in cool temperatures before they can be forced, the plants which are to be flowered early in the season often are placed in refrigerated storage to assure uniformly cool temperatures. Although the plants that are in cool temperature storage are not in an active state of growth, they are not completely dormant, and they do require some moisture and light. The soil should be moist but not wet. In cool greenhouses or cold frames the glass will have to be shaded to limit the temperature during the day, and this will give a sufficient amount of light. In refrigerated storage, the plants should be given 10 foot-candles of light artificially for 12 hours each day.

In most areas of the country it is difficult to hold azaleas cool enough in natural conditions so that they can be flowered for Mother's Day or later. They could be held satisfactorily in refrigerated storage, but it is generally considered uneconomical to use refrigerated storage for that length of time. For flowering in the off season from May to December, some azalea specialists produce plants specifically for that period by growing the plants at a minimum of 60°F until the flower buds are formed and well developed, and then place the plants in refrigerated storage until the flower buds are matured. The production of off-season azalea plants requires a constant source of small plants, greenhouse space to provide the uniform growing and forcing temperatures required, and refrigerated storage.

A limited number of varieties are used for off-season flowering, as this simplifies scheduling. Some adjustment in time needs to be made depending on the season in which the plants are being grown. Approximately 5 months is required for formation and development after the young plants are received, 6 weeks of refrigerated storage for maturing the flower buds, and 3 to 6 weeks for forcing the plants in the greenhouse.

Growth regulators. Some chemicals retard the growth of azaleas and, when properly used, develop buds quicker and more uniformly. Cycocel at 2½ ounces per gallon of water or B-Nine at 4 ounces per gallon can be used as a spray, and the spray should be applied when the shoots are approximately 1 inch long after a pinch. The sprays should be applied to run off from the leaves to well-watered plants with dry leaves, and water should be kept off the leaves for at least 24 hours following the application. Two applications should be made about a week apart.

These materials are of maximum value only when used in addition to providing the best temperature and day length conditions for formation of flower buds. Some bad effects may be expected if they are used at too great concentrations, too often, or under wrong conditions. However, when used according to label directions, they may be helpful.

Either Cycocel or Phosfon can be used as a soil drench to retard vegetative growth and improve flower bud formation, but this not a common practice. Cycocel applied as a spray is easier and more economical, and the results are as good as with a soil drench. It is more difficult to schedule the use of Phosfon and to regulate its effect.

Experimentally in some situations it has been possible to use the potassium salt of gibberellic acid to mature azalea flower buds instead of using cool temperature treatments. It appears, however, that commercial use is not practical.

BEGONIA (*Begonia socotrana—Begoniaceae*)

B. socotrana is a semituberous-type *Begonia* that is commonly called "Christmas," "Melior," or "Norwegian" *Begonia*. It is produced almost entirely for the Christmas market, although some plants are sold later in the winter.

Propagation. These late fall and Christmas flowering varieties are propagated by leaf cuttings with a long petiole in November and December. Medium-sized mature leaves from healthy plants are stuck in sand and spaced so they do not touch, to prevent rot from developing. With a bottom heat of 70°F, rooting will occur in a month's time, but potting should be deferred until the new shoots develop, which may be 8 to 10 weeks after the leaves are stuck in the sand. Growth substances hasten rooting but may delay shoot growth.

Light. The Christmas Begonias are normally grown in natural light conditions, as the plants will flower at the time of greatest market demand. However, vegetative growth is promoted in long days and flowering in short days, and the plants can be lighted or shaded to produce the type of growth needed. If vegetative growth of the young plants is wanted earlier in the spring, long days can be provided by lighting the plants each day. If flowering earlier than Christmas is desired, the plants should be shaded with black cloth in the fall. The plants flower 8 weeks after the shading is started.

During the high light period of the summer, the plants should be given partial shade with a spray application on the glass or a light cloth suspended above the plants.

Temperature. Night temperatures of 60°F should be provided, with day temperatures about 10°F warmer for most varieties of Christmas Begonias, but the Norwegian Begonia varieties should be grown about 5°F cooler.

Potting and spacing. The rooted cuttings are potted in 2¼-inch pots and are set pot to pot or spaced just enough so the leaves do not touch. In late spring the plants are shifted to either 4- or 6-inch pots, depending on the available bench space. If they are shifted to 4-inch pots, they should be transplanted to 6-inch pots by late summer. The plants must be spaced so that the leaves do not touch, as leaf rot will occur in the moist surface between the leaves in contact.

Although Christmas Begonias are self-branching, some pinching should be done to shape the plants and make them more uniform.

The 6-inch plants should be spaced on 12-inch centers for finishing, and the plants should be staked. The best staking method is to place 3 or 4 light stakes at the edge of the pot and encircle the plant with light, green cord. When this is done early enough in the fall, the stakes and cord will be hidden by leaves at the time of sale.

Diseases. Most of the Begonia diseases can be controlled if normal sanitation is practiced, and if moisture, ventilation, and temperature are regulated so that leaves and stems do not remain moist. Bacterial leaf spot is caused by *Xanthomonas begoniae,* which first appears as small, round spots on the leaves. As the disease progresses, large areas of the leaves may become infected and appear water-soaked. Some leaf drop may occur, and if the disease progresses to the stem, the entire plant may wilt. Diseased leaves should be removed and destroyed promptly. Continuous air circulation should be provided and moisture kept off the leaves.

Botrytis blight or stem rot usually gets its start in cuts or damaged areas of the leaves or stems or in old or aging flowers and leaves. The pathogen is *B. cinerea,* and it develops rapidly in moist conditions. Large areas become diseased in the leaf, and the entire leaf may turn black. When the stem is infected, it may be completely girdled, causing the death of the entire plant. Sanitation, control of moisture and air movement, and spraying with either zineb or captan may keep this pathogen in control.

Powdery mildew should not be a problem unless ventilation and heating are so neglected that moisture forms on the leaves. In addition to correcting cultural practices, sulfur may be vaporized or sprays with Karathane or Actidione PM may be used.

Pythium stem rot should not be a problem if soil, pots, and handling equipment are carefully sterilized, and if the irrigations are spaced so that the soil dries somewhat between waterings. Dexon 35 may be used as a preventive soil drench.

Pests.   Christmas Begonias may be infested with either root or foliar nematodes.   The best control of root nematodes is sterilization of soil, pots, and all handling equipment.   Foliar nematodes can transfer from plant to plant if the leaves touch each other.   They produce large brown areas toward the margins of the leaves, and can be controlled with parathion or Meta Systox-R sprays.

Two-spotted mites, aphids, thrips, and Cyclamen mites are controlled with normal measures, although some pesticides are toxic to Begonias.   Adequate trials should be made with each control material before large-scale application.

CALCEOLARIA (*Calceolaria hybrida—Scrophulariaceae*)

Calceolaria flowers are brilliant yellows, reds, and bronzes, and they are pouch-shaped, which gives the plant the common name of pocketbook plant.   In natural conditions they flower in late spring, and if their keeping qualities were better, they would be of considerable commercial worth.   Unfortunately they wilt readily in normal home conditions.

Propagation.   Seed of *C. hybrida* is sown in July and August, and since it is very fine, care must be used in preparation of the medium and watering. The seedlings must be shaded rather heavily and protected from camel crickets, sow bugs, and other such pests.   Damping-off, aggravated by overwatering, can be very serious unless adequate air circulation is provided.

When of convenient size to handle, the seedlings are pricked off to flats, spaced 2 to 2½ inches apart each way, and they are allowed to grow until they touch each other.   A mixture of two parts soil and one part each of sand, peat, and manure will be useful for the seedlings and mature plants.   Overwatering is a common trouble with *Calceolaria* in flats.

Light.   As the plants are maturing in the spring, they must be given some partial shade because the flowers are burned easily in full sunlight.

Although the start of flower formation is not dependent on length of day, the development of the flowers is faster in long days.   To provide artificially long days, 100-watt lamps are spaced 4 feet apart and 2 feet above the plants, and they are operated each night for 4 hours.   For Valentine's Day flowering the plants must be lighted from mid-November, and for flowering in March and April the lighting must be started about 3 months before the plants are needed in flower.

Temperature.   In the early stages of growth, the plants may be grown at 60°F, but as soon as possible in the fall the night temperature is maintained at 50°F with day temperatures 10°F higher.   Flower buds do not start to form in Calceolarias unless the temperature is below 60°F.

Potting and spacing.   From the transplant flat the Calceolarias are potted to 2¼- or 3-inch pots and set pot to pot.   When the leaves touch adjacent ones, the plants are shifted to 5- or 6-inch pots and set pot to pot or at the final spacing. If they are set pot to pot, they must be shifted to the final spacing soon enough to assure good light and air movement conditions at all times.   The final spacing of Calceolarias should be about 12 inches.

Calceolarias should be staked, and this is best handled by using a single light stake at the center of the pot and tying the main axis of the plant to it.

Troubles.   Chlorosis of the tip leaves may be caused by poor root growth in the young plant because of poor soil drainage, too frequent irrigation, or too much fertilizer in the soil.

Diseases.   Stem rot can be a problem if the plants are potted too deeply, if soil drainage is poor, or if the soil is kept too wet.   Correcting these cultural practices and providing better air circulation around the plants should keep stem rot of Calceolarias in control.

Pests.   The most common pests are aphids, thrips, and white flies, and they can all be controlled with normal pest-control measures.

CHERRY *(Solanum pseudocapsicum—Solanaceae)*

Known commonly as the Jerusalem, or Cleveland, cherry, this is a cheap plant for Christmas sales.   Seeds are sown in January or February, and the plants are grown in a 55 to 60°F house.   In late May they can be placed in 5- or 6-inch pots and placed in frames or plunged outdoors, or the plants can be placed in beds for later potting.

During the summer the fruit is set.   Overdoses of nitrogen promote excessive vegetative growth and poor fruiting.   Bed-grown plants are potted in late August and placed in a 52 to 54°F house, where the fruits will be well developed by Christmas.

CHRISTMAS CACTUS *(Zygocactus truncatus—Cactaceae)*

This genus is native to Brazil where it grows in large clusters as an epiphyte on trees.   If grafted on *Pereskia* or other upright-growing, slender-stemmed cacti, so that the pendant branches are elevated above the pot, the Christmas cactus makes a very showy plant for Christmas use.   For small plants the leaflike branches may be cut and propagated easily in sand, provided too much moisture is not used.   A porous soil with some peat moss makes a satisfactory potting mixture.

Christmas cactus is grown at 60°F, and at this temperature flower buds are formed in short days. At 55°F flower buds form regardless of day length, but at temperatures above 70°F flowering does not occur.

CHRYSANTHEMUM (*Chrysanthemum morifolium—Compositae*)

Within recent years no other potted plant has increased in demand as much as the potted *Chrysanthemum*. It is comparatively easy to grow compact, graceful specimens economically, and in addition the *Chrysanthemum* keeps exceptionally well in the home and is available in a comparatively wide range of colors.

Chrysanthemums are grown the year-round in carefully controlled temperature and day-length conditions to produce vegetative growth or flowering as desired. Rooted stem tip cuttings are potted directly into the pot in which they are going to be finished—either four or five cuttings per 6-inch pot. The plants may be grown in long days for several days to produce leaf growth and increase in stem length; they are then pinched and placed in short days until flower buds are well developed. From potting to flowering, the pot *Chrysanthemum* is about a 3-month crop.

Chrysanthemum varieties that are suitable for use as pot mums must flower on relatively short stems, branch readily, form a well-shaped plant, and have flowers of the size, shape, and color that are desired. It is mainly the large flowered varieties that are used, and the lateral flower buds are removed (disbudded), producing a lone, large flower per stem.

There is a good market demand for Chrysanthemums the year-round as well as for some of the holidays. The best holidays for pot mums are Easter and Mother's Day, but some additional plants are produced for Valentine's Day, Thanksgiving, and Christmas. The 9-, 10-, and 11-week varieties are used the year-round, and in addition the 7- and 8-week garden varieties are grown as pot plants for Mother's Day and Decoration Day.

Potting, pinching, and spacing. Before potting, the rooted cuttings should be graded for size so that each pot will have cuttings of uniform size. The cuttings should be potted as shallowly as possible because that provides the best soil air-moisture relationship for rapid root growth. If the cuttings are planted at an angle, with the top of the cuttings extending over the edge of the pots, each cutting has a greater area in which to grow, more shoots develop per cutting, and the plant is larger and better formed. After potting they are set pot to pot, and if the plants are to be furnished long days artificially, it is most economical to do it at this close spacing. Growth and development of the young plants will be best in a warm (65°F minimum) and moist atmosphere. Uniformly moist air can be provided with an intermittent mist system or by

11-4. Pot mums should be started in warm temperatures (65 to 70°F) and high humidity. Using intermittent mist or plastic film enclosure for several days after planting is good practice. (*Yoder Bros., Inc., photograph.*)

enclosing the area in clear plastic film or a combination of the two. In such an environment root growth is rapid, the new leaves attain maximum size, and more shoots develop when the plant is pinched. The plants should be in this moist atmosphere for approximately 1 week and then given standard greenhouse conditions.

When the plants have been lighted as long as necessary (from 0 to 3 weeks depending on variety and time of the year), they should be spaced, at the final distance of about 1¼ square feet per pot. It is possible to space the pots several times, gradually giving them more space as the plants grow, but it is seldom that this spacing gets done on time. Gradual spacing may conserve some space, but it does require more labor. Since the closely spaced plants cast shade on adjacent plants, they do not develop as well. Actually the amount of final spacing allowed the plants and the method of spacing can be used to adjust the size of the finished plant. In some instances the plants are grown closer together so that a greater number of plants of smaller size may be produced per unit area to satisfy a market demand for plants of that quality.

Chrysanthemums are pinched to produce branched plants. The pinching is done in such a way that the maximum number of shoots develop following the pinch. The plants should be pinched after they have made enough growth so

11-5. Chrysanthemums flower sooner and more uniformly if they are supplied short days each day. Left: Chrysanthemums given short days 5 days a week. Center: Chrysanthemums given short days 6 days a week. Right: Chrysanthemums given short days every day of the week. (*Yoder Bros., Inc., photograph.*)

11-6. Delay in disbudding causes delay in flowering in Chrysanthemum. Right: Chrysanthemums disbudded as soon as the lateral buds could be handled. Left: Chrysanthemums disbudded about 1 week later. (*Yoder Bros., Inc., photograph.*)

that the pinch can be made in the new growth.   Just a small amount of stem tip should be removed in making the pinch, and this is called a "soft pinch" or "roll-out." If the plants have been grown properly and the pinch is well executed, there will be about 10 leaves below the place of pinch.

Growth regulators.   Height control in pot mums is of constant concern because the finished height must be within certain limits above the top of the pot, and the varieties of Chrysanthemums that are grown differ in their height potential.   The varieties are classed as short, medium, or tall, and various procedures are used to finish all varieties at the same height regardless of their growth characteristics.

Because Chrysanthemums form leaves and increase in stem length in long days, and because flower buds form and stems terminate with flowers in short days, the day length that is provided can be used to influence the finished height of the plants.   Before short-growing varieties are provided with short days, they are grown in a sufficient number of long days to increase the length of the stems. Tall-growing varieties may not be given any long days in an effort to terminate stem growth with a flower as soon as possible.

Height control by means of day length is a good standard practice, but additional control of height can be provided with some chemicals.   Either B-Nine or Phosfon is an effective growth retardant, and they can be used to produce

11-7.   Some growth chemicals may be used to regulate the height of pot mums.   The plant on the left was sprayed with B-Nine about 2 weeks after it was pinched.   (*Uniroyal Chemical Division photograph.*)

shorter pot mums.   B-Nine is used as a spray and usually at a concentration of 0.25 percent (6 ounces B-Nine per gallon of solution) or 0.5 percent when high temperatures cause greater elongation.   The plants are sprayed about 2 weeks after pinching, and in some instances a second spraying may be used 1 or 2 weeks later or at the time of disbudding.   Phosfon can be used as a soil or pot treatment, but it is not in common practice because of uncertainty of results.

Troubles.   New root growth should be evident 2 or 3 days after planting. Failure of new roots to develop rapidly may be due to heavy soil that drains poorly, too frequent irrigation, too much fertilizer in the soil, too deep planting, or too low temperature.   When new roots develop slowly, stem growth will also be slow, and not as many shoots will develop after the pinch.

Plants that are too short are due to several different causes.   If the root growth is poor, it is not possible to have good stem growth because the plant will not obtain the water and fertilizer needed for growth.   If the root growth is good but the stem growth is not, it is possible that the plants had insufficient nitrogen available in the early stages of growth.   This can produce stunting from which the plants do not recover.   Another possible cause of short plants is the failure to provide enough long days for the necessary increase in stem length.

Plants that are too tall can be caused from too many long days after the pinch, inadequate spacing of plants, growing the plants in shaded locations, and too high temperatures (above 90°F).   If too high temperature is the cause, flowering will be delayed as Chrysanthemum flower buds do not continue to develop at high temperatures.

Uneven flower bud development may be a problem during the winter, and it can be caused by too low night temperatures.   Some varieties flower uniformly at 65°F but develop unevenly at 60°F or below.   Failure to form flower buds can occur at night temperatures below 60°F with some varieties.

Crown buds form in hot weather (temperatures about 90°F), and they do not continue to develop into flowers until the temperatures become lower. During this delay in flower development the stem continues to elongate, the plants become too tall, and the stems have a stretched appearance.   The temperatures may be reduced in Chrysanthemum houses by use of fan and pad or misting systems during the daytime.   Night temperatures can be reduced by maximum ventilation, by air-circulation fans, by applying the black shade cloth later in the day (7 P.M. standard time), or by raising the sides of the black shade cloth after dark to increase air movement through the plants.

The development of too few shoots per plant after the pinch can be caused by unfavorable conditions in the first 2 weeks after the cuttings are potted. Some of these conditions are poor root growth, insufficient nitrogen in the soil, too cool night temperatures, dry air, and too hard a pinch.

Flower malformation usually is the result of poor control of day length, or fluctuation of short days and long days.

For discussions of flower types, propagation, light, temperature, air, diseases, and pests, refer to the section on Chrysanthemum in Chap. 10.

Cropping and rotations.   Various schedules, designed to adjust the height of plants, are used for cropping pot mums.   The height desired varies with the market area.   Then, too, the plants do not reach the same height in every greenhouse in spite of being grown on the same schedule, because growing conditions or methods of handling may vary.   Propagators or sellers of Chrysanthemum cuttings suggest schedules which are suitable for average conditions, and each grower should adjust the schedule as needed for his particular situation.   The schedule should allow enough time before pinching so that the pinch can be made in new growth and leave about 10 leaves below the pinch.   For short- and medium-growing varieties long days are always provided for this growing period before the pinch.   Short-growing varieties are given at least a week of long days after the pinch in order to give them additional stem length, but medium-growing varieties are usually given short days immediately after the pinch as they then will finish at about the right height.   Tall-growing varieties may or may not be given any long days before the pinch, and they are seldom given long days after the pinch as that would make them taller than desired.   Short days for tall-growing varieties often are started about a week before the pinch in an effort to reduce the height at which the plants finish.

Chrysanthemums do not grow as rapidly in the cool and dark weather of the winter as they do in better light and warmer temperatures.   The schedules that are used for pot mums must take this into consideration and provide for more long days before the start of short days for plants grown in the winter.

The time of flowering of Chrysanthemums is determined by the time of starting short days.   The different variety classes or response groups flower in a set length of time after the start of short days regardless of when they are planted or when they are pinched—10-week varieties flower about 10 weeks after the start of short days.   It is the 9-, 10-, and 11-week varieties that are used mostly for year-round flowering.   If crops are produced at regular intervals throughout the year, no adjustment needs to be made in time of planting of the various response classes or short-, medium-, or tall-growing varieties, as there will be some of each kind of flower at all times no matter when they were planted or how long they take to flower after the start of short days.   However, for holiday crops when all the plants are required to be in flower at the same time, the different response classes must be planted and handled so that all are in flower exactly for the holiday market.   Scheduling pot mums for the holidays is an interesting problem in management, as the 10-week varieties must be planted 1 week before the 9-week varieties, and the short-growing varieties have to be planted earlier than those that grow tall.

The keeping qualities of pot Chrysanthemums are better in the flower shops and in the homes if the flowers are allowed to develop fully in the greenhouse before they are sold; however, this is not common knowledge to the people buying the plants. In some market areas the customers insist that the flowers be in tight bud at the time of sale, and in other areas various stages of flower development are requested. This may not be a problem for year-round sales, as flowers at all stages of development are available, but for holidays the grower must be able to have the entire crop at just the right stage of development for his particular sales area. At holidays there is generally a greater demand for plants with fully developed flowers than there is at other times, as the plants are used immediately for maximum display.

It is possible to grow pot Chrysanthemums in the natural season in the fall without the use of either lights or black cloth, but this is seldom done, as exact scheduling is not possible, height control is variable, and the possible savings are slight.

In the spring, the garden varieties (7- and 8-week response class) can be flowered in May in natural conditions without the use of either lights or black cloth. The garden varieties make good Mother's Day items as the individual plants can be cut back and planted outdoors after the holiday, and they may flower again in the fall and for several years thereafter. Because many of the garden varieties are not large-flowered types, the stems are not disbudded, resulting in a spray of flowers on each stem. Some garden varieties are flowered in 3-inch pots and used in combination planters for Mother's Day or Memorial Day.

In some instances large-flowered mum varieties are grown single-stem in pots—the plants are not pinched. This produces fewer but larger flowers per pot, and they make an entirely different quality plant. The market demand for single-stem pot mums varies with the sales area, but in general it is greatest for the spring holidays.

In a year-round pot mum program, the pot mums rotate with themselves, and a uniform quantity of pots is produced throughout the year. Many different methods of moving and spacing pot mums are used; and because of this, space requirements do vary. If it were desired to produce 500 six-inch pot mums each week, the pots would be lighted in one area while spaced pot to pot, and then moved to another area and placed at the finish spacing of 1¼ square feet per pot until they flower. This would require about 300 square feet of bench space in lighted area and about 7,000 square feet of bench space for short days until the plants flowered. The potential production would be about 3.7 six-inch pots per square foot of bench space per year.

Pot mums produced for the spring holidays must be rotated with some other crop, and the most likely pot plant crops with which to rotate are poinsettias and azaleas. The Easter pot mums would occupy the bench space shortly after it was vacated by the poinsettias in December, and the Mother's Day pot mums could use the bench space in which azaleas had been forced in January and February. It is possible to rotate the spring pot mums with cut flower crops such as cut Chrysanthemums or roses, but this might involve additional labor and less desirable growing conditions for the pot mum crop.

CINERARIA (*Senecio cruentus—Compositae*)

The cineraria is an inexpensive flowering plant for sale from January to May.   Seed sown in June will produce flowering plants in January, a July 15 to August 1 sowing will flower in February, and a September sowing will flower for Easter.   A number of compact strains with numerous flowers are available. Since the seeds are small, care should be exercised in the selection of a suitable medium for sowing and preventing the seed flat from drying out.

The seedlings are transplanted to flats when large enough to handle and are grown there until ready for either 2½- or 3-inch pots.   Seedlings may be planted 3 inches apart in the transplant flat.   When they become crowded, they are shifted directly to the finishing pot, saving considerable labor, though additional space is needed in the early stages.

All soil, flats, and pots should be steam-sterilized to prevent Verticillium disease, which causes the plants to wilt, from which they never recover and eventually die.   The disease becomes apparent between the time the plants are half grown and maturity.   A mixture of three parts soil and one part well-rotted manure or peat can be used.   Azalea pots of the 5- or 6-inch sizes are preferable to standard pots.

Fertilizer should be applied every 2 or 3 weeks when the plants are established to obtain large dark green specimens.   Spacing is necessary to prevent the plants from becoming leggy.   Because cinerarias develop a large leaf area, they must be watered frequently, and in the spring when the sunlight is intense, the plants may wilt even if the soil is moist.   A night temperature of 45 to 50°F is best.

Since the plants grow rapidly, the cost of production is comparatively low. This makes cinerarias suitable for cheap sales.

Cinerarias are subject to aphids, red spider, leaf rollers, white fly, and thrips.   Stem rot is often caused by too deep planting, and Verticillium wilt is a serious disease.

CYCLAMEN (*Cyclamen persicum—Primulaceae*)

The *Cyclamen* was at one time the most popular plant for Christmas, but the newer varieties of poinsettias have almost entirely supplanted *Cyclamen* for this holiday.   Because the *Cyclamen* has rather poor keeping quality in the average home, it has fallen in favor and is gradually being supplanted by the azalea and the pot mum.   In spite of these limitations, however, there is a demand for well-grown Cyclamen plants.

Propagation. The plants are propagated by seed sown from August until December, with the later sowings intended for smaller plants. For the seed flat, use a mixture of equal parts of soil, sand, and peat or leaf mold. Susceptibility of *Cyclamen* to root-knot nematodes and other soil pests makes it desirable to sterilize all soil, flats, and pots. Leaf mold is often the source of infestation of root-knot nematodes.

The seeds are large, and the seedlings remain in flats for a considerable time. They may be sown individually about 1 inch apart, using a special board studded with rounded nails as a marker to make depressions into which the seeds are placed. At 55 to 60°F, germination will take place in 4 to 8 weeks.

Young plants. After two or three leaves have developed, the young plants are ready for transplanting. Although the plants may be placed in 2½-inch pots, they dry out rapidly, and planting them 3 inches apart in either flats or benches is preferred. Crowding the plants causes the petioles of the leaves to elongate, and the plant becomes leggy. Several applications of a complete fertilizer when the plants are small will keep them growing. In March or April the plants are shifted.

With a gradual shift, the small plants in 2½-inch pots are placed in 3- or 4-inch pots in spring, and in July or August they are repotted in 5- or 6-inch pots, depending on the size of the plants. The gradual shift requires considerable labor but enables the grower to produce a larger number of plants in a relatively small area. Allowing the plants to become pot-bound and hard is usually the cause of poor specimens, which are common. The production of plants for shipping must necessarily be confined to the smaller pots.

With the direct shift in March or April, young plants in small pots and flats or benches may be placed directly in finishing pots. Larger plants may be shifted to the 6-inch size, and the smaller specimens to 4- or 5-inch pots. A soil low in nitrates will allow the root system to become established quickly in the large volume of soil. Overwatering after shifting will check the development of the plants. The direct shift is useful for production of large specimen plants where there is sufficient greenhouse space.

General culture. Whatever system of shifting is used, the hypocotyl (commonly called "bulb," or "corm") should be elevated so its top is above the surface of the soil. Crown rot may occur with deeper planting. A mixture of two or three parts soil, one part sand, one part peat, and one part well-rotted manure or leaf mold is ideal. When plants are well established in the pots, applications of a complete fertilizer every 2 or 3 weeks are necessary during the spring, summer, and fall. During the summer, plants should be in a rather heavily shaded greenhouse and spaced so that the leaves do not touch. Frequent overhead syringing is beneficial, but water standing overnight in the crown of the plant may cause rot. Allowing the plants to wilt before water is applied checks their growth, especially in summer.

In late September the shade should be removed and the night temperature maintained at 50°F. Staging the plants by placing them on inverted pots provides aeration and reduces the danger of disease. Prior to October all flowers should be pulled for better development of the plant. Applications of fertilizer may be reduced beginning in October, but the plants should not be allowed to become hard and starved. Overhead syringing should be eliminated.

It is possible to carry the plants over for the second year or longer by resting them after flowering, but it is not practiced commercially. Cyclamen may be propagated vegetatively by cutting the hypocotyl in sections with a leaf or two attached and rooting the sections in sand. If the propagating is done in January, this method will reduce the time necessary for maturity from 15 to 12 months, but it is seldom practiced.

There are a number of named varieties in the trade, but red, salmon, pink, and white are the preferred colors. Variegated and double or fringed types are seldom in great demand.

Pests. Red spider, aphids, thrips, and mite must be controlled. Mite causes the leaves and flowers to curl or become distorted. Thrips cause a scabby condition on the underside of the foliage, and colored flowers are streaked with brown. Occasionally the black vine weevil becomes a pest, and it chews the roots off the hypocotyl, or corm.

Diseases. A disease called "stunt" produces reddish-brown areas in the hypocotyl and shortens some of the leaves and flower stems. This peculiar growth is referred to as the "two-story" disease, since the leaves are borne in two separate heights. The "corm" has reddish areas within. After the plant is infected, no control is known, but steam sterilization of the soil and pots prevents the trouble. Crown rot is evidenced by a white fungus growth at the base of the leaves and is more noticeable in the cooler weather when moisture stands in the crown. Brown or black areas developing at the margins of the leaves are leaf spot, and infected foliage should be removed and destroyed. Root-knot nematodes cause knots to develop on the roots, and the plants should be discarded. Steaming the soil and pots is the best prevention.

FUCHSIA (*Fuchsia hybrida—Onagraceae*)

The *Fuchsia* has declined in popularity as a specimen plant, but it is useful for combination pots in the spring.

Plants not sold in the spring and stock plants reserved especially for propagation are grown during the summer in a shaded greenhouse or lath house.

In late summer they may be carried on the dry side or dried off to rest them for 1 month.   In September or October they may be started by removing some of the old soil and repotting them in a mixture of three parts soil and one part well-rotted manure or peat, placing them in the same size pot.   The plants should be cut back, and if possible some foliage allowed to remain.   If the shoots are free of insects, the severed portion may be used as cuttings for an early propagation. A complete fertilizer should be applied each month to the stock plants when they have become established.   The night temperature should be maintained at 60°F for stock plants.

Cuttings are taken from November through March and may be rooted in sand, sand and peat, or vermiculite.   When rooted, the cuttings are placed in 2½-inch pots at a night temperature of 52 to 55°F.   In January or early February, three plants in the 2½-inch pots are placed in a 6-inch pot, and if they are pinched, these will make bushy specimens for spring sale.   Single-plant specimens are obtained from plants propagated early and shifted to a 4-inch pot in December or January and then to a 5-inch pot in March.

Bushiness and compact growth on pot specimens are obtained by pinching.   For Mother's Day the plants should be pinched 8 to 9 weeks before they are wanted in flower, and for Memorial Day a pinch is necessary 6 to 7 weeks prior to the date.   Fuchsias may be rooted as late as March and will make satisfactory unpinched plants for combination pots.

There is limited demand for hanging baskets.   In February, three to four plants of suitable varieties are placed in a 6-inch basket, and they are pinched as previously described to induce branching.   It is recommended that stock plants be renewed yearly by selling them each spring as large specimen plants.

There are many varieties of Fuchsias.   Among the doubles some of the better types are Bagdad, Giant Double Pink, Pride of Orion, and Gladiator. Singles includes Mrs. Marshall, Black or Purple Prince, Glendale, and Display. The single varieties Pink Beauty, Little Beauty, and Lord Byron are recommended for Mother's Day, since they are early.   Varieties suitable for hanging baskets are Inca Maiden, Gay Senorita, Cascade, and Hallowe'en.

Fuchsias can be infested by red spider, mealy bugs, aphids, and white fly.

GLOXINIA (*Sinningia speciosa—Gesneriaceae*)

Gloxinias may be started from seed or tubers.   Usually seed is sown in December, January, and February for flowering plants in spring and summer, but recently the gloxinia has been popularized as a suitable plant for any season, so that seed can be sown any time.   About 6 to 8 months from sowing, the plants will be in flower, if conditions have been provided for rapid growth.

Since the seeds are extremely small, they should be sown on the surface of a screened medium and watered from below.   The seed flat or pan should be placed where the night temperature is near 70°F for most rapid germination and early growth.   Direct sunlight is injurious, and the seed flat and seedlings should be protected with a moderately heavy shade.   Steam sterilization of flats or pans and mediums is helpful in preventing damping-off, and subirrigation is advised to prevent disturbing the small plants.

When the seedlings are large enough to handle, they should be pricked off to transplant flats, spaced about 1 to 1½ inches apart each way, using a well-sharpened pencil.   A mixture of two parts soil, one part sand, one part well-rotted manure, and one part peat, passed through a ¼-inch mesh wire screen, is suitable.   Care must be exercised in watering and in the regulation of light intensity at this stage of their growth.

When the leaves touch each other, the plants can be placed in pots.   For shipping purposes the 2½-inch size is used; otherwise 3- or 4-inch pots are recommended because the larger volume of soil does not dry out as quickly.   The soil mixture suggested for the seedlings can be used throughout the entire life of the plants.

When the root system is well developed, the plants can be shifted to the finishing pot, which could be a 4-, 5-, or 6-inch size, depending on the vigor of the specimen.   Since gloxinias are not tall, azalea pots are much more in proportion than are standard pots.   The young plants grow rapidly and must be fertilized frequently to obtain dark green leaves.   Any complete fertilizer is satisfactory, but the solution should not be allowed to remain in the crown of the plant, or it will burn the leaves.

Watering is an important factor in the culture of gloxinias because if it is allowed to remain on the crown of the plant overnight, losses from stem or crown rot will occur.   Light intensity must be regulated in the same manner as for African violets, except that 2,400 foot-candles of light at noon is optimum.

Gloxinias develop large, ungainly leaves which necessitate spacing the plants to prevent them from stretching or becoming leggy.   These leaves are rather brittle, which makes shipping a difficult procedure, but brittleness can be reduced somewhat by keeping a high relative humidity and a night temperature of 70°F.   At temperatures lower than 60°F, growth practically ceases.

Lighting gloxinias often results in earlier flowering if the plants are grown at 60°F.   This is apparently the effect of light and heat on food manufacture rather than any photoperiodic effect on the plant.   Either 100-watt incandescent lamps 4 feet apart and 2 feet above the plants or standard cool-white fluorescent lamps may be used.   They should be turned on after sundown and continued for 4 or 5 hours.   Light is most effective if it is started as soon as the seeds germinate.

Gloxinias grow well in an opaque structure, using fluorescent lights as the sole source of light, as described for African violets.   Because the gloxinia takes so much space it is doubtful whether the culture of these plants in an opaque structure would be practical, except for the production of small plants in flats since they are grown quite close together. Flowering specimens will grow quite easily from seed in as little as 4 months under fluorescent lights.

If the old plants are not sold at the end of summer, they can be dried off and rested by turning the pots on their sides. They may be left in the pots or shaken free of soil and placed in dry peat and stored at not less than 50°F. After January, they can be started in growth.

New or leftover tubers are best started by placing them in a flat of moist peat and keeping them at 70°F. As soon as a few leaves begin to unfold, the started tubers can be placed in the finishing pot and handled as described for seedlings. Tubers started in January will flower in spring; those started in March will flower throughout the summer.

Mite is the most serious pest, and crown or stem rot causes loss of plants.

HYACINTH (*Hyacinthus orientalis—Liliaceae*)

When hyacinths are received in the fall, those which have been treated for early flowering should be potted at once or placed in a 55°F storage until potting. Untreated bulbs should be unpacked and spread out in layers in flats or shallow boxes and kept at a temperature of 65 to 70°F. If bulbs are left in the shipping cases, any rot that may be present will spread very quickly.

Hyacinths are potted with one bulb in a 4-inch pot, two bulbs in a 5-inch pot, or three bulbs in a 6-inch pot in a soil that is porous for good drainage. The nose of the bulb is placed about ½ inch above the surface of the soil. If the soil is acid, some lime should be added. Varieties which produce large, heavy spikes will need staking, and green sticks may be inserted into the bulb, and the stems tied with green twine.

In "spitting," or "toppling," the flower spike appears to have been cut off; it is a rather common trouble with hyacinths being forced. It can be caused by too early planting (before October 15), too high a soil temperature outside, poor drainage in the area when the bulbs are buried outside, and exposure to a cold temperature when dug from outside beds or brought out of storage for forcing.

Christmas. Only the 19-centimeter, or larger "special" or "prepared," bulbs are suitable for this early forcing. The special bulbs (sometimes called "Herald") are grown in Holland in soil over heating pipes. This extra heat hastens maturity of the plant and causes earlier formation of the flower parts. Prepared bulbs have been stored at 80°F for several weeks after digging, which also accelerates the formation of the flowers.

The bulbs should be potted in late October and placed in a 50°F storage. An outside storage is recommended only for early forcing when bulbs can be covered with a deep mulch or put in a shady location where temperature variations can be kept at a minimum.

Between November 25 and December 1 the bulbs should be brought into a 58 to 60°F greenhouse for a week and then raised to a temperature of 65 to 70°F if desired when sufficient roots have developed and the tops are at least 1 inch long. The pots may be placed under a bench where there are heating pipes, or on top of a bench where they may be shaded with black cloth or newspapers until the shoots are 1 to 1½ inches long, and then exposed to full sunlight. The plants should be kept at 58 to 60°F with some bottom heat, and after flowers show color, the temperature should be reduced to 50°F, which hardens the plants before sale.

Midseason. Bulbs to be flowered from late January until mid-March need not be planted until late October or early November. Prepared bulbs are not necessary for this forcing period, but large-sized bulbs produce the best plants. The bulbs are potted and handled as described, but are not brought into the greenhouse until very late December or early January and at intervals thereafter. From 3 to 4 weeks should be allowed for maturity at 60°F early in the season, but later in the forcing period, at 65 to 70°F, this may be reduced to 2 weeks.

Late. Bulbs to be forced for late March and April can be stored at 65 to 70°F and planted the first 2 weeks of December. They must be covered well because if the soil freezes, they will not make roots. Their culture is the same as described. Without cold-storage facilities it is difficult to hold hyacinths for a late Easter since they force rapidly.

Varieties. The list of hyacinth varieties for forcing has not changed appreciably within the past few years. No plants should be forced unless they show well-developed roots and have at least an inch of top growth. The dates for bringing in hyacinths are as follows:

December 1, 15, and 25: Bismarck (blue), Pink Pearl, L'Innocence (white), prepared or special bulbs.

January 1: Bismarck (blue), Dr. Lieber (blue), Ostara (blue), Lady Derby (pink), L'Innocence (white), Edelweiss (white), Pink Pearl (rose), and Nimrod (pink).

January 15: Gen. DeWet (pink), Grand Maitre (blue), Ostara, Lady Derby, and Prince Henry (yellow).

February 1 and 15: City of Haarlem (yellow), Gertrude (pink), LaVictoire (red), Marconi (rose), Myosotis (blue), Ostara and Duchess of Westminster (blue).

March 1 and later: King of the Blues, Carnegie (white), Queen of the Blues,

Queen of the Pinks, and Queen of the Whites.   These varieties are best for late forcing.

HYDRANGEA (*Hydrangea macrophylla—Saxifragaceae*)

Hydrangeas are produced only for the spring pot plant market.   The plants are propagated in late spring from rooted stem cuttings, grown outdoors during the summer, and placed in cool temperatures in late fall until the flower buds mature and the leaves drop.   The dormant plants are brought into the greenhouse to start forcing for Easter flowering in late December or early January, depending on the date of Easter.   For Mother's Day, forcing is started in late January.

The production of Hydrangea plants is limited to areas that have fairly cool summer temperatures, as the growth of the plants and the formation and development of the flower buds are best in a temperature range of 55 to 65°F.   There is an advantage, too, in being able to use natural cooling in the fall for the cool-temperature treatment of the plants.

The Hydrangea flower is a large, globular cluster of pink, blue, or white flowers.   The sepals are the showy and colorful parts of the flower, and the petals are rather inconspicuous.

Propagation.   Cuttings of Hydrangeas are taken in February, March, April, and May from blind wood on Easter or Mother's Day plants or stock plants reserved especially for this purpose.   The notion that cuttings of blind wood will not produce flowering plants is erroneous, and it is not necessary to sacrifice flowering wood for the sake of propagation.   Where stock is scarce, leaf bud cuttings will be found fully as satisfactory as stem cuttings.   With leaf buds the cuts should be made about 1 inch below the node and ¼ inch above, splitting the stem in half, with each half bearing a leaf.   Some trimming of leaves is necessary to conserve space and to prevent severe wilting.   Sterilized sand, or sand and peat, in an open bench with a bottom heat of 65°F and an air temperature of 55 to 60°F is recommended.   For the first few days covering soft cuttings with cheesecloth or newspaper may be necessary to maintain high relative humidity and reduce wilting, unless a mist system is used.   The cuttings should be ready to pot in 3 to 4 weeks.   Cuttings taken in April or May can be placed directly in 5- or 6-inch pots.

When smaller plants are desired, propagation in June and July is feasible.   Cuttings are made from the plants propagated earlier, which are pinched in June or July.   When the plants are pinched, the portion of the plant removed is rooted rather than thrown away.

There are disadvantages in using the plants being forced into flower as the source of cuttings.   It may not be possible to obtain the quantity of cuttings needed, and the cuttings must be taken earlier than the plants can be handled conveniently in the greenhouse. These problems can be overcome by using either softwood or hardwood cuttings from the West Coast. Unrooted softwood cuttings should be obtained in April or early May, rooted in about 3 weeks, and then potted in 5- or 6-inch pots. The cuttings should be lifted from the propagation bench promptly when the roots are ½ inch long, as cuttings that are left in the propagation bench too long are adversely affected by the lack of nitrogen and grow slowly after potting.

Unrooted hardwood canes obtained from the West Coast in January or February are cut into about 2-inch sections, each bearing a node or joint and stuck in the propagation bench for rooting. With this type of cutting it is possible to get too many shoots developed after potting, and the young plants should be pruned to 1 or 2 good shoots.

Light. Hydrangeas are grown outdoors in the summer; and in most parts of the country, best leaf size and plant growth occur in the partial shade of lath or plastic screen. However, this partial shade should be removed in August, and the plants should be finished in full sun for the best development of the flower buds.

When the plants are forced into flower in the winter and spring, they should be placed in the best available light. If bright and hot weather develops at the time of flowering, partial shade will improve the intensity of flower color and cause less wilting of the plants or burning of the leaves and flowers.

Flower bud formation in Hydrangeas is not dependent on length of day, but buds do form faster in short days than in long ones. In natural conditions Hydrangea flower buds form in September, and the day length is naturally short at that time.

If the plants are in long days during forcing, the internodes will be longer. This is one of the reasons why Hydrangeas for Mother's Day are taller than those forced for Easter.

Temperature. Hydrangeas are grown outdoors during the summer and early fall without control of temperature other than some reduction given in summer by partial shade, or protection from frost in the fall by covering cold frames with sash. If the plants were grown in controlled temperature conditions, the night temperature should be 60°F with day temperatures about 10°F warmer. Growth of the plant and formation and development of the flower buds are best at these temperatures. Flower bud formation is slow and questionable at temperatures above 65°F or below 55°F. Because most Hydrangeas are grown under natural conditions, the time of flower bud formation in the fall will vary depending on the weather and the resulting temperature.

By early November the Hydrangea flower buds should be fully developed, and the plants should then be given 6 weeks of cool temperatures to mature the flower buds. This cool temperature should be uniform and below 50°F; a temperature range of 40 to 45°F is best. Cold frames, sheds, refrigerators, or cool greenhouses can be used for cool treatment of Hydrangeas, but at least a portion of this period should be in the dark so that the plants will shed their leaves, which helps to mature the flower buds.

The plants must be given adequate protection from freezing temperatures in the fall, but slow cooling to temperatures well below freezing is not detrimental. In many areas of the country, killing frosts are possible any time after early September.

For forcing Hydrangeas into flower, 60°F night temperatures should be used with day temperatures about 10°F warmer. The plants will flower in about 4 months at these temperatures. In some instances plants that are to be flowered for Mother's Day are started at 50°F night temperatures, but this is a questionable practice as the internodes increase in length and the plants are taller at this temperature than at 60°F.

Fertilizer and flower color. Except for white-flowered types, Hydrangea flower color can be controlled by the amount of aluminum that is available in the plant. Aluminum is generally present in soils, but it will not be available to plants in alkaline soils nor in soils that have an excess of phosphorus. Aluminum and other minerals cannot be taken into the plant even if they are available in the soil unless the roots are growing and functional.

Hydrangea varieties differ in the effect of aluminum on flower color, but in general the flower is blue if aluminum is available in the plant, and pink if it is not available. The color potential of each variety is known, and the varieties that develop the best colors are selected for treatment.

Flower color can be controlled with fertilizer treatments given during the forcing period; but for more reliable results, the plants should be treated in both the growing period in the summer and the forcing period in winter and spring. If the native soil that is used is definitely acid in reaction, the flowers will generally be blue unless the soil is made more alkaline or fertilizers high in phosphorus are used. In areas of alkaline soil, Hydrangeas typically have pink flowers unless the soil is made more acid or some aluminum fertilizer is added to the soil.

For pink flowers, choose varieties that have the potential for good, clear pink flowers, and use fertilizers that contain phosphorus for growing and forcing the plants. The soil pH should be maintained in the range of 6.0 to 6.5, and this may require the addition of limestone or hydrated lime to acid soils.

For blue Hydrangea flowers, select the varieties which produce the best blue colors. Some varieties do not have good, blue flowers regardless of treatment. No phosphorus should be added to the soil or fertilizers very low in phosphorus should be used, and the pH of the soil should be maintained at about 5.0.   In areas where the soil is alkaline, periodic applications of iron sulfate will be required at the rate of 3 pounds per 100 gallons of water or aluminum sulfate at the rate of 7 to 10 pounds per 100 gallons of water.   If aluminum sulfate has to be supplied during the summer or if the native soil is acid, about three applications of aluminum sulfate will be sufficient during the forcing period; however, if no aluminum sulfate was used in the summer or the native soils are alkaline, at least six applications of aluminum sulfate should be made during forcing, starting as soon as new root growth is observed and at about 10-day intervals thereafter.

Potting and spacing.   Various methods of potting and growing Hydrangeas are used, but regardless of the methods, large enough pots should be used so that the plants can grow actively.   From the propagation bench the rooted cuttings should be potted directly into 5- or 6-inch pots or started in 3-inch pots and then shifted to the larger pots as soon as they are established.   There must be no delay in shifting to larger pots, and it should be done within 3 weeks after the cuttings are potted.   The time of propagation must be scheduled so that the plants can be handled in the best possible way after propagation.   Most pot plant greenhouses are completely filled with plants being forced for the spring holidays until mid-May, and there just is no room for handling young plants until the finished plants are sold.   If the Hydrangea cuttings are stuck in the propagation bench the last week in April, the plants can be potted in 3-inch pots about the middle of May, shifted to 5- or 6-inch pots in early June, and moved outdoors later in June as soon as new root growth has been made following transplanting.

The plants in 3-inch pots can be spaced pot to pot as well as after shifting because in either instance they will not remain there long enough to require additional space.   Outdoors the plants are spaced on about 12-inch centers, and the pots may be plunged or set on the ground.   Hydrangeas require a great quantity of water, and growing the plants in large pots provides a more uniform moisture supply.   If the plants are grown in 4-inch pots, and an irrigation system is not available, or if the natural conditions in the locality are dry, it is better to plunge the pots.   If the pots are plunged, it must be in a well-drained area so that the plants do not remain in saturated soil following heavy rains.

The plants must be protected from freezing temperatures in the fall by placing them in cold frames or in greenhouses.   Whenever possible, this should be the same area in which the plants later will be given their cool temperature storage.   Pot-to-pot spacing is used, but the plants must be watered, fertilized, and given uniformly suitable temperatures, as they are in active growth and at an important stage in the formation of the flower buds.

From November to mid-December or later the Hydrangeas must be in cool temperatures (below 50°F) to mature the plants, and during this period they are set pot to pot in cold frames, cool greenhouses, sheds, or refrigerators.   In order for the plants to mature properly, the leaves must drop, and this is hastened by placing the plants in complete darkness.   Because of the dormant condition of the plants and the cool temperatures, very little maintenance of the plants is required in storage.   The fallen leaves must be removed to prevent disease infestations, 40°F temperature maintained as uniformly as possible, the plants watered sparingly, and continuous air circulation provided in order to prevent bud rot from *Botrytis*.   Leaves should not be induced to drop before late October or flowers may be poorly developed.

When the dormant Hydrangeas are removed from storage in preparation for forcing at 60°F night temperatures, they can be set pot to pot or at final spacing, whichever is better because of available space and labor.   If the plants are to be shifted to larger pots for forcing, they should be started in the same size pot they were grown in and then shifted when new root growth has started. If irrigations are well spaced, new roots should be evident about 1 week after the plants are started.   Root growth starts slowly when the plants are shifted to larger pots immediately from storage.   The final spacing for 3-cane hydrangeas in 6-inch pots is approximately 1½ square feet per plant, but this differs with varieties as some make larger plants than others.

Troubles.   Blindness is the failure of flower buds to form in the stems, and this can be caused by any conditions that are unfavorable for flower bud formation.   The most common causes of blindness are not enough active leaf area (too few leaves, not large enough leaves, or damaged leaves), too cool or too warm temperatures in late summer and early fall, generally poor growing conditions including inadequate supply of minerals, and too late pinching.

Summer flowers develop in some stems, and this usually is related to the stage of development of the stems used for cuttings.   In some instances summer flowers form in stems that are pinched early.

Burned leaves can occur in plants at any stage of growth if the plants wilt in the bright sunlight, and this can be prevented by adequate irrigation and syringing plus the use of shade over the plants.   In most areas of the country the outdoor growing area in the summer should be equipped with a good nozzle system so that the plants can be misted or syringed frequently.   Burned leaves should not be a problem during the forcing period in winter and spring if the plants are not allowed to dry out and are protected from the direct rays of the sun when near maturity.

Chlorosis of the leaves is generally considered to be caused by a lack of available iron in the plant.   However, it may be caused by poor root growth, insufficient iron in the soil, too alkaline soil, or an inadequate supply of nitrogen. Most soils should receive a few applications of iron sulfate (ferrous sulfate) at the rate of 3 pounds per 100 gallons of water during the summer.   Chlorosis, common in plants at the start of forcing, is invariably due to poor root growth.   At this time there is a temptation to make an application of iron, but no fertilizer should be applied until root growth is good.

Poor root growth can be caused by soils that are saturated or have too much fertilizer in the soil. The problem is most common just after the dormant plants are brought in for forcing and usually is caused by too frequent irrigation.

Slow development of the plants in forcing and short stems with small flowers are caused by an insufficient length of time in cool temperatures before forcing. The most common reasons for too short a cool period are (1) abnormally warm falls during which it is impossible to keep the storage area cool enough and (2) an early Easter date for which the plants are removed too soon from storage.

Hydrangeas often are too tall for Mother's Day, and there may be several reasons for this: (1) The plants may be forced slowly at temperatures below 60°F, which causes increase in stem length. (2) Hydrangea stem length is greater in the long days of later spring. (3) The plants may not be adequately spaced because of the large number of Easter plants being grown. (4) Some varieties of Hydrangeas grow tall even in the best-regulated conditions, and the height of these plants can be reduced with growth chemicals. For shorter growth in the summer, the plants should be sprayed with a 0.75 percent solution of B-Nine in late July when the shoots are 1 to 2 inches long following the pinch. For shorter growth during the forcing period, the plants can be sprayed with a 0.50 percent solution of B-Nine about 2 weeks after forcing starts, when four or five pairs of leaves are visible.

Diseases. Botrytis blight or bud rot can occur in cool storages, and this is a particular problem with the variety Merveille. The control of bud rot includes the removal of fallen leaves promptly as they are sure to become badly infected with *Botrytis* and therefore a source of inoculum for infection of the buds; the careful use of water so that the area does not remain wet; providing continuous air movement with air circulation fans; and spraying with Botran or zineb.

Powdery mildew is more common in the fall with the combination of cooler night temperatures and reduced air movement because the plants have been set closer together. Some heat and increased air movement provide the best control. The plants may be sprayed or dusted with sulfur, or other powdery mildew controls may be used. Septoria leaf spot is caused by a fungus, and purplish blotches appear on the leaves usually in the late summer and fall. Spraying or dusting with fungicides that control leaf-spot diseases will be effective.

Pests. Two-spotted mites and aphids are the principal pests, and they are easily controlled with ordinary precautions. Particular care should be taken to assure that the plants are entirely free of pests before they are placed in frames or greenhouses in the fall as an infestation will spread rapidly in warm temperatures and among the closely spaced plants. The Cyclamen mite may also infest the shoot tops, causing malformed growth.

Pinching and cropping. Plants propagated very early must be pinched twice to prevent them from becoming too tall. The first pinch is made some time in April or May, and the second pinch in June or early July.

It is erroneously believed that late pinching causes blindness of shoots; in reality it is not the pinching itself but rather the failure of the plants to develop shoots properly following the pinch. It may be desirable to pinch late-propagated plants in late August or early September to make them branch and reduce their overall height. Provided the plants have been fertilized properly and growth is satisfactory, little blindness will result because of a pinch made at such a late date.

When shoots are pinched, at least two pairs of good leaves should remain on the stem. If the foliage is small or injured, additional pairs of leaves should remain or shoot development may be slow and blindness may be troublesome.

On vigorous plants a number of shoots will develop after pinching. As soon as these are convenient to handle, all unwanted stems should be removed. The demand is greatest for specimens with two or three flowers, and limiting the number of stems on each plant can be done at this time.

If there were a market demand for Hydrangeas at any time of the year other than in the spring, the plants probably could be produced for flowering at any time by using controlled temperatures in greenhouses and refrigerators, but this would increase the costs of production considerably. Because of the rela-

11-8. Hydrangea flower buds should be about the size of a nickel 6 weeks before Easter.

tively poor keeping quality of Hydrangeas in the home unless careful attention is given to watering, it is doubtful whether there would be much demand for out-of-season plants. The cropping schedule that is used for Hydrangeas is based on using natural conditions for producing the plants and controlled greenhouse conditions for forcing the plants into flower. At 60°F temperature approximately 13 weeks is required for flowering after the dormant plants are brought into the greenhouse; however, longer periods are commonly used, as the plants often are started at 60°F but finished at 50°F. The plants develop more slowly at the cooler temperature, but they are of better quality. Depending on the date of Easter and the temperatures that will be used, the dormant plants must be brought into the greenhouse forcing temperatures between late December and the middle of January. For Mother's Day flowering, forcing of the dormant plants will have to be started between late January and early February.

If the dormant plants are going to be available and ready for forcing from late December on, the cuttings must be rooted by April, the plants pinched by July, and the plants with well-developed flower buds placed in cool storage in early November. This is the minimum length of time required when light, temperature, moisture, minerals, and other conditions are suitable. If optimum environmental conditions are lacking, additional time may be required.

KALANCHOE *(Kalanchoe blossfeldiana—Crassulaceae)*

K. blossfeldiana, introduced by Robert Blossfeld, a German hybridizer, has a scarlet flower, and by means of manipulation of day length can be flowered at any time of the year.

Kalanchoe can be propagated by leaf cuttings with or without a piece of stem attached or by stem cuttings, but seeds are more satisfactory since plants from seeds are more vigorous and grow more rapidly. Leaf cuttings with a piece of stem attached taken in January will develop into salable plants by the following winter. Cuttings should be stuck in sand, and after they are well rooted, they are placed in 2½-inch pots. Stem cuttings can be taken in June and July and will make small late-flowering plants.

Seeds are sown in January for the largest plants, and a July sowing will make small plants suitable for late flowering. A light soil is best and it should be steam-sterilized to prevent rot. Seed germination will occur in 10 to 14 days at a temperature of 65 to 70°F. Overhead watering may cause considerable loss of the small plants, and subirrigation of the seed flat is advised.

When seedlings are large enough to handle, they are pricked off to other flats or to 2½-inch pots with two plants in a pot. When ready for shifting, three of these small specimens may be placed in a 6-inch azalea pot. Any well-drained soil is satisfactory, and the plants should be given a complete fertilizer every 3 or 4 weeks. Plants pinched in June or July will be more compact than unpinched plants, though they may not flower as early. Tops of pinched plants can be used for stem cuttings.

Kalanchoes may be planted in frames or a cloth house. They should be lifted and potted in late August, taking care not to overpot since the root system is small.

The plants should be grown at 60°F in full sun to prevent elongation of the flower stems. At 50°F the growth is slow. Stem rot is a very serious disease; to avoid this trouble, the soil and pots should be steam-sterilized, the plants should not be syringed overhead, and high potting should be practiced. Mealy bugs are also a serious pest. Commercial DDT should not be used on Kalanchoes because of leaf and stem injury which will cause death of the plants, but the purified grades are relatively safe.

The *Kalanchoe* normally flowers in the spring, but it is a short-day plant and reduction of the day length causes earlier flowering. For earlier flowering, black cloth can be applied daily from 5 P.M. to 7 A.M. according to the following schedule:

Shading period	Date of flowering
July 20 to September 20	October 20
August 15 to October 1	December 1 to December 15
September 1 to October 20	December 25

Plants may also be shaded in spring for summer flowering, allowing approximately 3 months from shading to maturity.

There are several useful varieties. Tom Thumb and coccinea are dwarf, while the hybrid blossfeldiana and related types are long-stemmed and sometimes used as cut flowers. There is also a yellow-flowered type.

LILY (*Lilium longiflorum—Liliaceae*)

The pot lily is flowered only for Easter. The plants are started from bulbs that are produced on the West Coast, in the southern United States, or in Japan. The bulbs are dug in the fall, and most of the lily bulbs are given temperature treatments before being shipped to the pot plant growers in late November. Depending on the date of Easter, the lily bulbs are potted in late November or December. In some instances the bulbs are shipped to the growers directly from the bulb fields, potted immediately, and given temperature treatments after potting.

Propagation. The propagation of lilies is an operation for specialists. Lilies are propagated primarily from scales separated from the parent bulb or stem bulblets produced underground. The scales are planted in the fall in rows about 6 inches apart. Bulblets are formed in the first growing season, and they are dug and replanted in the field. The mature bulbs are dug the following fall and graded by size in inches of circumference from the smallest size 6½ to 7 inches, to the largest, 10 to 11 inches. The smaller bulbs produce smaller plants with fewer flowers than do the larger bulbs.

Digging of the bulbs is done about the first week in October on the West Coast. Earlier digging is not done by the bulb growers because the bulbs continue to develop and increase in size in the fall, and later digging cannot be done or there would not be time to plant the new crop of stem bulblets before the start of the general rains in late fall. In southern fields the bulbs are harvested as early as late August.

Light. In the greenhouse, lilies should be grown in the best available light. If the light intensity is too low because of weather conditions, overhead structure, or too close spacing, the plants will be tall and have few flowers, and the lower leaves may turn yellow and wither.

The length of day apparently has little or no effect on flower formation in lilies, but plants provided with long days will be taller than those in short days and will flower earlier. Commercially the day length is seldom adjusted to control height as the cost of treatment is not considered worth the results that are obtained; however, if the lilies were consistently too tall or too short, either black cloth treatment or artificial lighting could be used. The treatments, to be effective, must be provided from about the time the stem emerges from the soil until the flower buds are clearly visible. Lighting to hasten flowering is used, but it must be started at least 6 weeks before maturity if there is to be any marked effect.

Temperature. The temperature that the bulbs are given after digging and even the temperature that exists in the later stages of growth in the field affect the growth and flowering of the lily when it is forced. If the bulbs are in temperatures of 40°F or below for 4 to 6 weeks after harvest, they produce flowers in the shortest time. The plants from these bulbs also have fewer leaves and fewer flowers than plants produced from bulbs kept in warmer temperatures. The earliness of flowering of bulbs that have had cool-temperature treatment is desirable, but the reduction in the number of flowers is a drawback. Another characteristic of plants that develop from bulbs which have had cool-temperature treatment is the formation of small leaves at the base of the plant, and the general appearance of these plants is objectionable because of it. Bulbs which have received just the minimum amount of time (about 6 weeks) in cool-temperature treatment will flower in a short time (about 120 days at 60°F), with a suitable number of flowers and good development of basal leaves.

The amount of cool temperature that the bulbs receive is complicated by the possibilities of cool temperatures while the bulbs are still in the fields and the necessity of a variable length of time between digging and the start of forcing for Easter because of the changeable date of this holiday. For an early Easter there is just enough time between digging and potting to allow for 6 weeks of cool storage of the bulbs and time for shipment to the forcer. For a later Easter date it may be possible to keep the bulbs at 70°F for a period after digging to be followed by 6 weeks of cool storage before shipment to the forcer.

In some instances the bulbs are shipped directly to the forcer from the fields after digging, and the bulbs are potted immediately and placed in cold frames or cool greenhouses. These structures are operated at natural temperatures which would be quite warm in early fall and just above freezing in late fall. The natural temperatures that are available are cool enough to produce early flowering, and there are less reduction of number of flowers and better formation of basal leaves than in plants produced from bulbs that were given cool treatments before potting. This method of handling lily bulbs does require that the potted bulbs be maintained for a longer time, and the early flowering effect is dependent on weather conditions that may not be favorable for some years.

Lilies should be forced at 60°F night temperatures with day temperatures about 10°F warmer. At lower temperatures growth and development are slower, and at higher temperatures they are faster. If the plants are behind schedule, they can be supplied 70°F night temperatures, but these temperatures must be started in January or early February. Plants which develop too rapidly may be placed in a 40 to 50°F refrigerator at the stage when the buds are well developed (white, puffy stage) but before they start to open.

Potting and spacing. Lily bulbs are shipped so that they will be received each year at the right time for potting. For an early Easter date the bulbs are shipped for arrival in late November, and for a later Easter they should be received in December. If there is a delay in potting after receiving the bulbs, they should be kept in moderate temperatures from 40 to 60°F. Soil for lilies should be well aerated, but the use of too much peat moss should be avoided since it holds moisture which can cause problems from root rot.

Lily bulbs should be placed down in the pot rather than at the surface, and after potting they should be set pot to pot on the greenhouse bench and watered. They may remain at this spacing for 3 or 4 weeks, and then may be spaced once or more to the final distance of from two to three 6-inch pots per square foot. Some lily varieties have large leaves and need more space than other varieties, but generally large bulbs produce larger plants that will require more space than will plants from smaller bulbs.

There usually is some variability in growth of a lot of lilies, and when the plants are being spaced, the shorter plants should be placed at the sides of the bench, and the taller plants toward the center.

Troubles.   Environmental conditions on the West Coast sometimes cause the lily to sprout in the field, a stage of early growth of the stem that normally is dormant until forced by the florist.   Sprouted bulbs, in general, are satisfactory, and they should be potted so that the sprout is buried in the soil, if possible. The sprout must never be broken off because then a new stem must form and develop.   Desprouted bulbs take considerably more time to force, and the bud count is reduced.

Croft lilies are subject to a physiological disorder known as leaf scorch, which is characterized by half-moon-shaped brown areas developing near but not at the tip of the leaves on the midportion of the plant.   This usually becomes apparent in early February in severe cases.   Since leaf scorch is more severe in acid soil and at low nitrate levels, enough lime or limestone should be added at the time of soil preparation to raise the pH to the neutral or slightly alkaline

11-9. Lily root rot is evident in plants on right. Top: comparison of the plants as they are knocked out of pots. Bottom: roots after removal of the soil.

range.   In addition, the incorporation of well-rotted manure or peat, one-fourth by volume, is recommended to promote conditions favorable for root growth. Superphosphate may be incorporated, if desired, but in spite of the fact that nitrogen deficiency accentuates leaf scorch, complete or chemical fertilizers should not be added to the potting soil because of the danger that high soluble salts might injure the roots.   Dried blood, a slowly available source of nitrogen, may be incorporated, but it is not necessary.   Leaf scorch also is accentuated if the roots are injured or killed by overwatering or other causes.

The problem of too few flower buds may result from using too small bulbs, storing the bulbs too long before forcing, blasting of the flower buds, or allowing the bulbs to become dry in storage.   Blasting of the flower buds may be caused by lack of water in the plant because of poor roots or insufficient irrigation, low light intensity, and extremely high forcing temperatures.

Yellowing and eventual drying of the lower leaves may be due to insufficient light (very often the result of spacing the plants too closely together) or lack of nitrogen.   This can be prevented by spacing the plants more promptly and supplying nitrogen fertilizer regularly after the tip of the plant emerges through the soil.

11-10.   Loss of lower leaves of lilies can be caused by a deficiency of nitrogen, by the plants being placed too close together (shade from adjoining plants reduces light intensity), or by poor root growth.

Diseases.   The most prevalent causes of root rot are *Rhizoctonia* and *Pythium,* but other pathogens are often found in diseased roots and may be associated with the trouble.   The soil and all handling equipment must be thoroughly sterilized before use with lilies.   Coarse, porous soils will drain more readily, favoring active root growth and limiting the development of the root rot pathogens.   If root growth is poor because the soil has been saturated, root growth will be promoted by knocking the plants from the pots and setting them back in the pot lightly to increase the air around the surface of the soil ball.   If Pythium or Rhizoctonia organisms are involved in the root rot, they can be controlled with a soil drench of ½ pound each of Terraclor 75 and Dexon 35 per 100 gallons of water applied at the rate of ½ pint per 6-inch pot.

Botrytis blight is caused by *Botrytis elliptica,* and it produces circular or oval spots on leaves or flowers.   In damp conditions the spots become covered with gray mold.   The best control is to reduce the humidity of the air by heating while ventilating and by increasing air circulation.   Moisture should be kept off leaves and flowers.

There are several virus diseases of lilies, but because of continuing efforts among the bulb growers to propagate from virus-free stock, and because of control of insects that transfer virus in the fields from plant to plant, severe effects of virus diseases are not common in bulbs used for forcing in greenhouses.

Pests.   Aphids are common pests of lilies, and one of the best controls is Meta Systox-R used as a spray.   Aphid infestations occur primarily on the stem tips.   If the flower buds are involved, splitting of the flower may result.

Nematodes can infest lily bulbs, and root rot is usually associated with the nematode infestation.   Excellent measures for control of nematodes are used in the lily fields with the result that the presence of nematodes in the bulbs is negligible.

Timing and cropping.   When lily bulbs are forced at 60°F night temperatures, approximately 120 days is required from the time of potting to flowering. Less time is needed with higher temperatures and more time with lower temperatures.   For an early Easter (in late March) the lily bulbs must be potted in late November and placed in conditions suitable for root development.   It is often inconvenient to find space in the greenhouse for lilies at that time as they are commonly rotated with poinsettias that are still occupying the bench space. Root development is good at 50°F, and it is feasible to place the newly potted bulbs for 2 to 3 weeks in an area that has a uniform temperature between 50 and 60°F.   This also allows for additional precooling which results in faster forcing later on.   The pots must be well irrigated after the bulbs are planted, but at this early stage they do not necessarily have to be in good light conditions, as the growth will be limited to root development.   Stacking of the newly potted lilies under benches is a questionable procedure as this will compact the soil in the

11-11. Croft lily bud stage of development at 60°F. Left: 6 weeks before Easter. Right: 4 weeks before Easter.

bottom pots, and the temperature may be variable because of heating lines under or on the sides of the benches.

For a late Easter (in late April) the lily bulbs can be potted from mid-December to immediately after Christmas and placed on benches recently vacated by poinsettias.

It is unusual for all the lily bulbs being forced to grow and develop at the same rate, so that the slower plants must be placed in warmer temperatures and the fast ones in cooler temperatures. This necessitates shifting some of the lilies from houses of one temperature to houses of another temperature from week to week—which leads to the standing jest among lily growers about the pots being worn thin on the bottoms from constant moving.

PEPPER (*Capsicum frutescens—Solanaceae*)

There is a limited demand for peppers at Christmas. The pepper plant is produced in a similar manner to the Jerusalem or Cleveland cherry except that it should be grown in pots. The plants are pinched in early July to make them bushy and compact. Seed sown in June will be ready by Christmas if three plants are placed in a 5- or 6-inch azalea pot and not pinched.

POINSETTIA (*Euphorbia pulcherrima—Euphorbiaceae*)

The poinsettia was introduced into the United States from Mexico about 1825 by the first United States ambassador to that country, J. R. Poinsett. Initially it was used as an interesting exotic plant in conservatories and botanical gardens, but later it was grown for cut flowers commercially. Early in the 1900s Albert Ecke started to specialize in the production of poinsettia cut flowers in

the Los Angeles area, and his descendants have been instrumental in the succeeding years in developing new varieties and promoting the culture of poinsettias
throughout the country.

The poinsettia "flower" consists of the small and rather inconspicuous
yellow flowers at the center which are immediately subtended by large and
colorful bracts. The most common bract color is scarlet red; and since the
poinsettia flowers in natural conditions about Christmas time, the primary use
of the plant has been for that holiday. Poinsettias with white or pink bracts
have been selected or developed, but the greatest market demand is for red
poinsettias at Christmas.

Poinsettias are propagated by means of stem tip cuttings which are
rooted during the summer or in early fall for plants to be forced for Christmas.
The plants propagated in midsummer are used for producing large plants in
tubs for cathedral or store decorations, or they may be grown as pinched plants.
The majority of poinsettias are rooted in late August and early September and
grown single-stem without pinching so that a large individual flower develops
per stem. The number of plants used per pot is determined by the size of the
pot and by the results desired, but usually three- plants are placed in a 6-inch
pan with correspondingly more plants in larger pans.

Propagation. The grower of poinsettia pot plants may produce the cuttings in his greenhouses or buy them from the specialist propagator. If he does
produce them himself, he needs a source of supply of stem tips. These come
from stock plants grown from field plants shipped in from California, from car-
ried-over stock plants held dormant in the greenhouses, or from stock plants
started from rooted cuttings planted in the greenhouses in the spring.

The field-grown stock plants are produced in southern California as the
natural weather conditions there are good except for the lack of rainfall from
spring through fall, when the plants are irrigated regularly. These plants are
started from rooted cuttings planted in early spring, and the mature stock plants
are dug and shipped either 2 or 3 years later, depending on growing conditions
and the desired size of plants. The plants flower in natural conditions in the
field from November to January, and at this time they are inspected for flowering
characteristics. Later in January the weather becomes cooler, and the plants
lose their leaves and flowers, and become dormant. The plants that are to be
shipped are cut back in February, and before growth resumes in March the
plants are dug, graded, and packed for shipping. The time of shipping is coordinated with the time of Easter so that the growers receive the dormant stock
plants as soon as possible after Easter. Most of the growers who produce
poinsettias are very busy with the various Easter pot plant crops, and they are
not able to give any attention to the poinsettia stock plants until after the Easter
plants have been disposed of.

11-12. Poinsettia stock plants being dug in Southern California in March. (*Paul Ecke, Inc., photograph.*)

The stock plants from California usually arrive in early April, and they should be planted immediately. If they cannot be planted upon arrival, they should be kept in unopened boxes at a minimum temperature of 60 to 70°F. Storing the plants in open boxes dries them and reduces production. Using small pots or small tubs for containers does not give satisfactory results because of the limited area for root development, and the rapid drying of the small soil volume reduces plant vigor. Any container is satisfactory provided it is large enough and has sufficient drainage. Standard wooden butter tubs are useful for one large stock plant or two of a smaller size. Orange crates, half-bushel baskets, or similar large containers are satisfactory. Individual stock plants may be placed in large tubs, but 8-inch palm tubs are too small. Large clay flower pots are not desirable because the soil dries rapidly and growth is checked. The larger the container, the greater the production of cuttings.

Soil for stock plants should be prepared by mixing three parts soil and one part well-rotted manure or peat. The addition of a 4-inch potful of super-phosphate to a wheelbarrow is recommended, and the mixture should be steamed.

Immediately after potting, the plants should be placed in a 70 to 80°F greenhouse. Growth of roots and shoots on the plants can be hastened by means of a high temperature coupled with high relative humidity. Frequent syringing is beneficial, and placing cheesecloth, aster cloth, or plastic over the tops will maintain a high relative humidity around the plants. When the shoots start to develop, the temperature is dropped to 60°F.

Sometimes when the stock plants first begin to grow, they may not produce normal stems. There may be self-branching stems, or false flowers. When this abnormal condition is noted, the stems should be cut off, leaving as much normal new growth on the stock plant as possible.   Normal stems will develop from the buds at the base of the leaves on the new growth.

After the plants produce 8 to 12 inches of new growth and are at the right stage for the first pinch or the first crop of cuttings, fertilization should begin.   Every other week some form of nitrogen and potash should be applied, but any complete fertilizer will also be satisfactory.   A manure or peat mulch, applied after the first crop of cuttings has been taken or after the plants have been soft-pinched, will maintain a more uniform soil moisture.

Regular fertilization will produce new growth, from which cuttings are made.   There is an erroneous belief that fertilization makes the cuttings too soft to root well.   Crowding the stock plants softens the cuttings by limiting light, and only the top cuttings which are exposed to the greatest amount of light should be used for propagating material.   After the last cuttings are taken, which is usually in late September, the stock plants may be discarded or grown at 60°F until they flower.

Stock plants.   Stock plants may be carried over yearly, but they should be allowed to flower at 60°F before drying off, usually in January.   After drying off, the plants are placed under a bench or in any convenient location at a temperature of 60°F.   The soil should not be allowed to dry until the stems begin to shrivel, because this would reduce the vitality of the stock.   Carrying over stock plants is not as satisfactory as buying new stock yearly, because careless handling during the dormant season reduces the number and vigor of the cuttings.

If the stock plants are started from rooted cuttings planted in the greenhouses, the spacing that is used depends on the length of time that the plants will be grown.   Cuttings planted in May or June should be spaced about 12 inches apart.   The procedures that are used for stock plants started in this manner are the same as those used for the field-grown plants.

The new growth on the stock plants should develop to a length of 8 to 12 inches before it is soft pinched or a cutting taken.   Soft pinching as the canes become heavy induces greater vigor in the stock plants and causes development of a greater proportion of the cuttings later in the season.   When the second breaks appear, they should grow long enough so that when the next cuttings are removed, two good leaves remain on the shoot from which the cutting is taken. This practice should be followed with every batch of cuttings except the last, to build up the plants so that strong cuttings will be produced during the life of the plant.   The thicker the cuttings, the larger the flower; and thin, wiry cuttings will never produce the exceptionally large, perfect flowers wanted by the public. Thin wood on the stock plants should be allowed to grow and develop before it is either pinched or used for cuttings.   Removal of the heavy cuttings, which are at the top of the plant, allows light to fall on the shoots underneath, and they will become noticeably heavier in about a week's time.

The cuttings should be taken early in the morning when the plants are turgid. They should be about 4 inches long, and it is not necessary to make the basal cut through or just below a node or joint. A lower leaf may be removed to facilitate sticking the cuttings, but as much foliage as possible should remain because the leaves contain food which is necessary for formation of roots. Heavy stem cuttings may be taken as late as September 21, but it is more common to stop propagating by mid-September. Approximately 28 days elapses after a cutting is taken before the shoot grows sufficiently to produce another cutting.

Poinsettia cuttings may be rooted in benches or directly in pots, but regardless of method, the principles involved are the same. Bench and pot must drain freely, and the air-moisture relationship in the rooting mixture must be good. The rooting material must be coarse enough so that it drains readily, maintaining good aeration. For propagation benches, horticultural-grade perlite or coarse sand and peat moss are commonly used for rooting. For rooting in pots, light soil mixtures such as equal parts of soil, peat moss, and horticultural-grade perlite should be used. The mixture which is used in pots must be suitable not only for rooting the cuttings but also for the growth of the plant later, and if too light a mixture were used, it might be difficult to supply water and fertilizer frequently enough to the finished plant.

Serious disease infections are possible in poinsettias, and the propagation area must be sterilized carefully and the best sanitation procedures used. If disease does start in spite of good sanitation measures, some specific chemicals can be used for control, but the pathogens must be identified first so that the proper control material will be applied.

Poinsettias should be spaced in the propagation bench so that there is a minimum overlapping of leaves. The rows of cuttings in the propagation bench should be about 5 inches apart, with the cuttings stuck about 2 inches apart in the rows. If cuttings are rooted in pots, the pots must be supported in some kind of rack, with plants spaced on about 4-inch centers.

A mist system should be provided in the poinsettia propagation area as moisture then can be supplied as needed, more light can be allowed in the propagation area, and the cuttings root faster and are of better quality. Propagation areas which are not equipped with such systems must be shaded heavily in order to reduce the moisture loss from the cuttings before roots form, and such low light intensity causes soft and stretched growth in the cuttings as soon as roots start to form. When a mist system is used, the cuttings must be fertilized once or twice during propagation, as the frequent misting leaches minerals from the cuttings. If fertilizer is not supplied during propagation, the leaves will be yellow-green in color, and the lower leaves may drop prematurely.

The temperature of the propagation bench should be maintained uniformly at 70°F, and the air temperature should be 60°F at night and 70°F during the day. Failure to maintain these temperatures causes delay in rooting.

Because poinsettias are propagated in late August and September when the heating system may not normally be operated for other crops, special arrangements must be made to provide the heat that is required for the propagation area.

It is considered generally that 3 weeks is required for poinsettias to root, but some varieties root in as short a time as 2 weeks, and others require 4 weeks. The rooted cuttings should be lifted from the propagation bench when the roots are about ½ inch long, and at this time some of the cuttings may be callused only. The callused cuttings may be potted rather than being restuck in the propagation bench as they will root promptly in the pots, particularly if placed under mist for a short period.

Light.   Poinsettias should be grown in full sunlight, and this includes the stock plants grown in the summer as well as the potted plants produced in the fall.   Shade from adjoining structures, gutters, and overhead obstacles should be avoided.

Flowering in the poinsettia is controlled by the length of day.   In long days the plants develop leaves and increase in stem length, and in short days flower buds are formed, and the stems terminate in growth with flowers.   Under natural conditions flower buds start to form in poinsettias late in September, and depending on weather conditions and the variety, the plants flower in late November and December.

Some varieties in natural conditions flower too early for Christmas, and for these it is possible to provide long days artificially in the fall before flower buds form, and thereby to delay flowering as desired.   The artificially long days should be started about September 20, and they may be continued until about October 5 to 10.   There are several variables that must be taken into consideration in making the decision on how long to provide artificially long days.   Plants propagated earlier flower earlier than those propagated later.   If weather conditions in the fall provide much sunlight and warm temperatures, the plants will flower earlier than they would in less favorable weather conditions.   Some varieties of poinsettia flower earlier than others.

Many homeowners wonder why their poinsettia never flowers in the home after the first year.   This is invariably because the plants are kept in rooms that are lighted artificially each night so that the poinsettia plant is never in the short days required for forming flower buds.

Temperature.   Poinsettias are generally considered to be a 60°F night temperature crop, but some temperature manipulation is used.   The field-grown stock plants should be started at 70 to 75°F night temperatures if high humidity is also provided, and after growth has started, the night temperatures are maintained at 60 to 65°F with the day temperatures about 10°F higher.   In some areas of the country where the day temperatures in the greenhouses during the summer exceed 95°F consistently, fan and pad cooling systems will provide better growth of the poinsettia stock plants.

In the fall the poinsettia pot plants should be provided 62°F night temperatures, with daytime temperatures about 10°F higher. At lower temperatures growth and flowering are slower and at higher temperatures they are faster, so some adjustment of temperature is used, depending on the rate of development that is needed. At lower temperatures soils stay wet longer, and root and stem rot can be more prevalent. At temperatures above 65°F flower bud development will be delayed if the day length is not short enough, but it will be more rapid if day lengths of 9 hours are provided artificially. In the later stages of flower development (from the middle of November and on) flower development is faster with increase in temperature. Bract size of poinsettias can be increased markedly if the night temperature is maintained at 65°F from mid-October to late November. This causes earlier flowering, necessitating lighting of the plants until about October 10.

Potting and spacing. When the poinsettia cuttings are rooted directly in 2- or 2¼-inch pots, they are spaced on about 4-inch squares and will remain at that spacing until they are panned, which should be from 4 to 6 weeks after they were stuck in the pots. Cuttings that are rooted in propagation benches should be placed in 2¼-inch pots when the roots are about ½ inch long, and the pots should be spaced on about 4-inch squares until they are panned from 2 to 4 weeks later.

Cuttings propagated earlier to be used for pinched plants or for larger specimens should be potted into 3-inch pots as they will remain in the pot for a longer time before panning.

Irrigation and fertilization must be provided regularly while the poinsettias are in the small pots so that growth will proceed without check. The plants may or may not be treated with a growth retardant, depending on how long they will be in the small pots, how early they were propagated, the height of finished plant that is desired. Plants in 3-inch pots should be spaced on about 6-inch squares.

Poinsettias should be planted in the finishing pot early in October. This is called "panning" as the poinsettia pot is either a bulb pan or an azalea pot rather than the standard pot. Single-stem poinsettias are planted at the rate of three or four plants per 6-inch pan, four or five plants per 7-inch pan, and correspondingly larger numbers of plants in larger pans or tubs. In most instances rooted cuttings are grown in small pots until they are established and then they are panned; however, sometimes the rooted cuttings are planted directly in the pan. This does save some labor and time, and good results can be obtained with direct planting. However, it does require closer attention to the moisture requirements of the plants until they are established in the pans, and the finished pan may not be as uniform because of the different rates of growth of the cuttings in each pan. Grading the cuttings by size and planting cuttings of the same size in each pan is a good method of producing finished pans with plants of approximately the same height.

After panning they may be set pan to pan and then spaced gradually as the plants grow, or the pans may be set at the final spacing at once. Poinsettias in 6-inch pans should be given about 1½ square feet each, and the larger pans will require more space accordingly.

Troubles. Leaf drop is a characteristic of poinsettias and is more common in some varieties than in others, but regardless of variety it can be controlled under proper cultural conditions. Several events or conditions are known to promote leaf drop, and these probably are responsible for the problem because of their effect on the minerals and/or water supplies in the plants. A deficiency of nitrogen in the plant is a common cause of leaf drop which may be due to an insufficient supply of nitrogen in the soil or to very little uptake into the plant because of poor root growth. The most common causes of poor root growth are too frequent irrigation, root diseases, and the application of too much fertilizer. If the irrigation practices are not changed as rapidly as the weather conditions change in the fall, the poinsettia soils will be kept too wet. Root growth will cease, root diseases may get started, and leaves will drop.

Bypass bud or split tip is a problem with some varieties in which a flower bud starts to form in the stem tip but does not continue to develop. Shoots then grow from the leaf axils below this partially formed flower bud, producing a branched plant. Stock plants of these varieties should be grown at 65°F night temperatures, and the stem growth in length should be limited by pinching or taking cuttings from short shoots on the stock plants. Propagation of these varieties should be as late as possible since early propagation allows too long a period of growth with the partial formation of flower bud and branch development below the bud.

Plants which are too tall are the result of too early propagation, and this should be corrected in succeeding years by later propagation. If some early propagation still must be used, the plants can be treated with growth regulant chemicals for control of height.

Too early flowering can be controlled by later propagation, by providing long days artificially in late September and early October, and by supplying cooler temperatures during the forcing period.

Diseases. Loss of cuttings or plants is a common trouble, and at least three fungus organisms are known to be responsible for stem rot, root rot, or both. They are *Rhizoctonia, Pythium,* and *Thielaviopsis.* Isolations made from a number of diseased specimens showed that *Rhizoctonia* in Ohio caused more than 90 percent of the losses.

Rhizoctonia generally attacks the stem at the surface of the propagating medium or soil. Overwatering the cuttings in the propagation bench or the plants in pots or pans causes rapid spread of the organism and widespread losses due to stem rot. In the cutting bench an ever-widening area of dying or dead cuttings is typical of *Rhizoctonia*. In the panned specimens one plant may die, and this is often followed by death of the other plants, although the organism may not always spread. The leaves on an infected plant usually curl upward at the edges, gradually turn yellow, and then fall off, beginning with the oldest foliage. At potting or panning, too deep planting leads to stem rot because the stem at the newly established soil line is soft and easily invaded by the Rhizoctonia fungus.

If drainage is poor or the medium is too fine in the propagation bench, rot of the basal end of the cutting can be caused by *Rhizoctonia*. Rhizoctonia root rot of the plants is associated with too heavy a soil, poor drainage, or overwatering.

Losses can be reduced by steam or chemical sterilization of the propagation medium and by taking care that the rooting medium is not kept too wet. Pots, pans, and all soil mixtures should be steam-sterilized, but losses can occur through reinfection and careless culture. Regulation of the moisture content of the surface of the soil is very important. This is accomplished by watering heavily enough to moisten the entire soil mass and then allowing the soil to dry normally before watering again. Frequent light waterings should be avoided. Chemical treatment of the sand or soil with Morsodren or Terraclor is recommended.

Pythium is a fungus which often attacks seedlings, causing the loss known as damping-off. It may attack poinsettias. Control is the same as outlined for *Rhizoctonia*, except that Dexon is the most effective chemical. Benlate

Thielaviopsis is a root rot fungus that grows best between 55 and 60°F. Roots on infected plants die and quickly turn black. Lower leaves on infected plants curl, turn yellow, and fall, as with *Rhizoctonia*.

Steam sterilization of soil, pots, and bench areas where plants are to be placed is the best method of control. *Thielaviopsis* is often found on geraniums and may live over in the sand or gravel in the bench, so that trouble may be experienced where these crops are grown in the same house even though at different seasons.

Maintaining the night temperature at 62 to 64°F will usually reduce losses from *Thielaviopsis* since it grows best at temperatures of 60°F or just below. Losses can be reduced by the warm temperature, but lights are usually necessary to delay flower bud formation and resultant maturity of the plants. In December, cooling the plants, which have been growing at normal night temperatures, may result in losses from *Thielaviopsis*. Ferbam is a useful drench.

Symptoms of a bacterial disease appear as water-soaked longitudinal streaks on the stem which crack open and reveal a yellow-colored ooze which is made up of masses of the bacteria. The stem usually dies. The disease organism may be transferred with a knife, and there is no control except the destruction of the infected plants and steam sterilization of the pots and soil. It is not a common trouble.

Poinsettia scab is usually confined to the tropical areas, and it may appear at any time of the growing season on either the cuttings or the stock plants. At first the stem turns somewhat purplish, and a small elongated canker appears, with the long axis of the canker parallel to the stem. The canker gradually enlarges, and if it girdles the stem, the foliage turns yellow and drops off, and the stem dies back from the tip. The center of the canker in the later stages is depressed and often covered with velvety-gray to gray-brown spores. The depression in the canker often develops into a crack, and the stem may break. Leaf lesions, or cankers, are smaller than those on the stem and are confined to the petiole and the midrib and smaller veins of the leaf. The leaf cankers closely resemble cankers found on citrus leaves, which are called "citrus scab." The poinsettia leaves are distorted and wrinkled in the area of the canker. If the petiole is attacked, the leaf will usually fall. Unfortunately, no control is known, and the infected stems should be cut well below the area of infection and burned. If they are not burned, spores will form and may blow into the greenhouse, causing reinfection.

The lesions caused by scab somewhat resemble a blisterlike raised area found on many poinsettia stems in late November and December. This is apparently a normal growth phenomenon and is no cause for alarm.

Pests. Relatively few insect or allied pests attack the poinsettia. Plants carried over the winter season in the greenhouse often become infested with mealy bugs and scale. Mealy bugs prove troublesome, especially after bracts show color, since most insecticides bleach the color of the bracts. Every effort must be made to clean up any infestation of mealy bugs by the middle of November.

Scale is a nuisance, and the sugary secretions are an ideal medium for the sooty mold fungus. This dirty-black condition of the foliage is very objectionable. Insecticides for scale control must also be applied before color appears in the bracts because of the danger of bleaching.

White fly is a pest that must be controlled before the bracts appear. Root aphids occasionally may be found in the soil and are recognizable as white or gray woolly masses around the roots. Growth of the plants is stunted, and in severe cases the lower leaves will turn yellow and drop.

Cropping and timing. There has been some interest in flowering poinsettias for some other holidays besides Christmas, but this plant continues to be the Christmas plant and is cropped almost solely for this period. The greatest amount of production of poinsettia pot plants is in 6-inch pots or pans with three or four single-stem plants. In order to flower the plants at an acceptable height, the cuttings must be stuck in the propagation bench from late August to mid-September. If a sufficient quantity of cuttings is to be available for sticking at that time, the stock plants must be planted early enough and pinched regularly.

Cuttings that are propagated earlier can be used for larger plants or for pinched plants. The larger pots or tubs should have taller plants, and these come from the earlier propagations. A quantity of the larger plants is used for store decorations as well as for churches and cathedrals, and larger and taller plants are required for these displays. The earlier propagated cuttings flower earlier than those propagated later, but this is satisfactory as their use in store decorations starts in late November.

Poinsettias are not often produced as pinched plants; but if they are, the cuttings should be propagated about 2 to 4 weeks earlier than those which will be grown single-stem and not pinched. Pinched plants to be finished in 6-inch pots are stuck in the propagation bench in late July or August and can be given a hard pinch as late as August 15 or a soft pinch by September 1. Plants that will be pinched should be potted in 3-inch pots or larger from the propagation bench as they will remain in the pots longer before panning than the plants with single stem.

There is no good method for producing single-stem plants in 6-inch pots or smaller, using cuttings that are stuck before late August. The growing period is too long before flower formation, and the plants either finish too large or are stunted from lack of water or fertilizer in the early stages in an effort to limit growth.

There are height limits for poinsettia pot plants. These vary with the market area in which the plants are sold, but plants in 6-inch pans should be about 12 inches above the pans. The best way to adjust the height of the finished plant is to schedule the time of propagation so that the plants have the right amount of time to grow and increase in stem length before the time of flower formation. Since in natural conditions flower buds start to form in late September, the cuttings for plants to be finished in 6-inch pans should be stuck in late August or early September. Plants for larger pans should come from earlier propagations, and plants for smaller pans can be propagated later.

If the plants are supplied with artificially long days in late September and early October to delay the start of flower formation, the time of propagation must be delayed accordingly in order for the plants to finish at the same height as they would in natural conditions. High temperature also causes stem elongation, and maintenance of 65°F nights to increase bract size can induce taller plants.

Some growth regulant chemicals can be used to retard the growth of poinsettias and produce shorter finished plants. Cycocel can be used as a soil

drench or foliar spray and B-Nine is used as a spray.   There are several variations in methods of use, and until a routine is established at each individual greenhouse, it is best to make some trials based on label recommendation.   As a soil
drench or foliar spray, Cycocel is used at the rate of 1 quart per 10 gallons of
water.   This solution is applied to the soil at the rate of 6 fluid ounces per 6-inch
pan or to foliage run-off as a spray.   A spray application of Cycocel uses less
material per treatment but does not give quite as satisfactory results in height
control as a drench.   In some instances the leaves have been injured from foliar
spraying.   B-Nine can be used only as a spray, and the recommended concentration commonly is 12 fluid ounces of B-Nine per gallon of solution.   It is less
effective than Cycocel as a spray in controlling height.

The use of growth regulant chemicals must be in anticipation of the
growth that will result.   It is impossible to wait until the plants get too tall, and
then successfully adjust their height by treating them.   Since the amount of
growth a plant makes is dependent on the weather and other environmental conditions, treated plants may be too tall if better than average conditions follow or
too short if unfavorable conditions follow.   More than one treatment may be
needed, but when the plants are treated too late in the season, the size of the flower
will be reduced.   Growth regulant chemicals for the control of height should not
be used on poinsettias later than the middle of October.   A reduction to one-half
the above-mentioned concentration of either Cycocel or B-Nine is suggested when
it is necessary to spray in October or in early November if the temperature is
unduly high.

It is important to have poinsettias in flower at the right time for the
Christmas market, and usually in natural day-length conditions they flower a
few days to a few weeks too early.   Flowering can be delayed by propagating the
plants later, providing artificially long days in late September and early October,
or growing the plants in cooler temperatures.   The time of propagation also
affects the height to which the plants grow, and later propagation can be used
to delay flowering only if shorter plants are desired.   Poinsettias grow and develop more slowly in cool temperatures than they do in warmer ones, and the
adjustment of temperature has been used commonly to time flowering.   If it is
determined in late November that flowering will be too early, the temperature
may be reduced gradually to about 55°F at night.   This does delay flowering,
but it also provides conditions suitable for stunted root growth and root rot followed by leaf drop.   Actually the hazards of using the lower temperatures in the
later stages are greater than the benefits.   In natural day length conditions poinsettias start to form flower buds in late September, but if the plants are given
long days artificially after about September 20, they will not start to form flowers
until the artificially long days are discontinued.   Depending on how long the
lighting is continued, the plants may flower too early, at the right time, or too late.
If a choice must be made between stopping lighting too early or too late, it would

be best to discontinue lighting too early, as a plant which is too mature will sell more readily than one that is not in flower.   In many instances it is found that if the plants are given artificially long days from September 20 to October 5, they will be at about the right stage of flower development for Christmas sales.   The use of growth regulators does not affect the date of flowering.

ROSE (*Rosa hybrida—Rosaceae*)

Pot roses are very satisfactory for spring sales because they can be planted in the garden, where additional flowers may be obtained the same season.

Polyanthas or baby ramblers, hybrid teas, hybrid perpetuals, and climbers are used, and XXX is the most desirable grade.   Rose plants should be purchased from a reliable nursery which specializes in their culture.   Upon receipt late in December, all but the climbers should be trimmed 8 to 10 inches above the crown, and only the weak canes are removed from the climbers.   Pruning varies with different varieties in the same group, and low pruning produces a smaller number of flowering shoots but makes longer stems.   Low pruning is advocated for hybrid teas for exhibition, but low pruning on polyanthas will make top-heavy plants.   All weak stems are removed at pruning.   The size of the roots determines the size of pot for potting, whether 5-, 6-, or 7-inch.   A slightly acid, fibrous soil is desirable.

After potting, the plants should be stored in a cool location, such as a 40°F greenhouse, shed, or cold frame.   In the latter, the canes are covered with straw to prevent drying, but periodic examinations of the plant are necessary because mice cause damage.   In January the plants are brought into the greenhouse and placed close together.   Frequent overhead syringing encourages growth of the buds, and covering the plants with burlap or straw is desirable to raise the relative humidity.   The temperature and time of starting growth depend upon the Easter date.   Plants started January 1 in a temperature of 45 to 48°F flower in late March; plants started January 15 will bloom in April.   The temperature should be raised gradually to 54 to 56°F by 1 month after starting, and after 6 weeks the temperature should be up to 60°F.   During the forcing period, especially at cool temperatures, mildew may become serious.

After the temperature is at 60°F, a complete fertilizer should be applied regularly until the plants are sold.

On polyanthas that develop exceptionally heavy stems, a pinch 7 to 9 weeks before Easter is recommended.   Buds should develop on the polyanthas 6 weeks before Easter and should show color about 2 weeks before the date required.   On hybrid teas and hybrid perpetuals, the bud should appear 4 weeks before Easter and should show color a week to 10 days before the holiday.

Plants of hybrid teas and polyanthas which fail to develop flowers at the desired time can be pruned back to two good 5-leaflet leaves, and they will come back into flower in 6 weeks.   This may be practiced also with the leftover plants from Easter to flower them for Mother's Day or Memorial Day.

The recommended polyanthas include Erna Teschendorf, Gloria Mundi, Triomphe d'Orleans, Dick Koster, Margo Koster, Snowbank Chatillon, Donald Prior, Orange Rosette, Baby Rambler, Verdun, Bernice, Gruss an Aachen, Pink Gruss an Aachen, and Miss Edith Cavell.

The best of the hybrid teas are Countess Vandal, Dame Edith Helen, Etiole de Hollande, E. G. Hill, Mme. Edouard Herriot, President Hoover, Texas Gold, Souvenir de Claudius Pernet, and Talisman.   All hybrid teas are hard to time exactly, and under unforeseen conditions of extreme sunlight many flower much too soon.

Hybrid perpetual varieties include Frau Karl Druschki, American Beauty, and Magna Charta.

The better climbers are Crimson Rambler, Eugene Jacquet, Excelsa, Dorothy Perkins, Rosary, Tausendschoen, and Paul's Scarlet Climber.

Red spider, aphids, thrips, black spot, and mildew are troublesome.

TULIP (*Tulipa suaveolens* and *T. gesneriana* hybrids—Liliaceae)

Perhaps no flower has been more closely allied with the economy of any country than has the tulip with Belgium and Holland.   The tulip craze which ended in 1637 was historic in that the desire for the flower was so widespread.

Tulip popularity has suffered greatly in recent years because of its relatively short keeping quality.   However, a good many tulips are forced both as cut flowers and for potted plants.

There are various kinds of tulips available for forcing.   Single Early tulips generally lack substance, but some of the Double Early types are useful after Valentine's Day.   Mendel tulips are hybrids between Duc Van Tol and Darwins and are suitable for forcing in January for Valentine's Day.   Triumphs are crosses between the Early tulips and the Darwins.   They have the strong stems of the Darwins but flower somewhat earlier and have good keeping qualities. Darwins are the aristocrats of all tulips, possessing strong straight stems, outstanding colors, and excellent substance and keeping quality.   Breeder tulips flower with Darwins but have oval-shaped flowers of pastel color.   The origin of Cottage tulips is uncertain, but they have oval flowers on medium stems with a wide range of colors.   Lily-flowered tulips belong to the Cottage group and are so named because of their resemblance to lilies.   Broken tulips have an irregular distribution of colors and may be found among the Breeder, Cottage, and Darwin types.   Rembrandts are broken Darwins.   Parrot tulips have fringed petals and bizarre colors but do not force satisfactorily.   The species of tulips that are useful in rock gardens are not suitable for forcing.

Tulips are dug when leaf primordia are present but the flower bud has not been formed, and bulbs are stored at 65 to 68°F to hasten formation of flower parts. If tulips are heated at high temperatures as Iris are, the flower parts will be killed.

The bulbs generally arrive in early October. A limited number of cut flower varieties can be precooled either in soil at 50°F or dry at the same temperature for 6 weeks, after which time they must be planted and placed in a cool location. Bulbs not to be precooled should be held at 60 to 70°F until planting about mid-October. The 12- to 13-centimeter size is best for forcing.

Manure should never be mixed in tulip soil, nor should it be used as a cover for the bulbs outside. *Botrytis* may develop as a result of the use of manure, and this disease is very destructive. Bulbs that show evidence of rot should not be planted.

A well-drained field soil is very satisfactory for tulips. If grown for cut flowers, tulips may be planted in ordinary greenhouse flats. The flat should be filled halfway with soil, and the bulbs set in, almost touching each other. Soil is then filled in around the bulbs, but their noses can be left uncovered.

For pot plants, 6 or 7 bulbs are placed in a 6-inch pan, 8 or 9 in a 7-inch pan, and 11 or 12 in an 8-inch pan. The first leaf develops on the flat side of the bulb, and if it is desired to have leaves droop over the pot, this flat side is placed next to the pot rim. Soil is generally placed in the pots, and the bulbs are pushed down until their noses are barely visible.

The flats or pots are placed in a 50°F refrigerated storage with high relative humidity, or buried outside. Precooled bulbs are best in a cool storage since the outside soil temperature is often too warm. Do not pot or flat precooled bulbs outside on a warm sunny day since the high temperature may nullify the effect of the precooling treatment. As a precaution against *Botrytis,* the pots or flats of tulips can be dusted with ferbam, zineb, or captan when they are placed in storage. Some tulips are suitable for early forcing, while others are best for late, and the development of the tops and roots should be used as a guide. No tulips should be forced which do not have several inches of top growth and a heavy root system. For pot plants forced early, American-grown or specially precooled Dutch tulips should be used. Precooled bulbs often can be brought in for forcing 2 weeks earlier than bulbs not precooled.

The flats or pots are generally brought into a 55°F house for 10 days, then transferred to a 60°F location where they will force in 4 to 6 weeks. They can be forced in 4 to 5 weeks if brought directly to a 60°F house, but higher night temperatures soften the flowers. Bottom heat is beneficial provided it is not too intense. The shoots should be covered with black cloth or newspapers for several days if brought in when the sunlight is bright. This helps to stretch the stem in addition to preventing sunburn. When the growth is 2 to 3 inches high, it is advisable to spray with a solution of either ferbam, zineb, or captan at 1 pound per 100 gallons with a suitable spreader for prevention and control of

Botrytis, or tulip "fire."   This disease can be recognized by the minute yellowish spots surrounded by water-soaked areas that appear on the leaves, stems, and flowers.   A gray fungus growth may be visible in the center of these areas during periods of high relative humidity.   If this occurs, give more air, spray as directed above, and keep water off the foliage and flowers.   It is a good practice to water early in the day so that the foliage will be dry by night.   The ventilators must be opened wider to dissipate the high relative humidity which is instrumental in promoting growth of the Botrytis organism.   Sometimes *Botrytis* is troublesome in storage.   Little can be done until the following year when sulfur or sulfur candles can be burned to kill fungus organisms before the bulbs are put in storage. Sulfur dioxide fumes are lethal to plants.

Recent experimental work on forcing tulips indicates that the bulbs may be stored dry at 40°F for 6 weeks, then flatted and kept for 6 weeks at 48 to 50°F, and then brought into a 60°F greenhouse.   An even more radical, yet successful, procedure consists of storing the bulbs dry for 12 weeks at 45°F, then planting and forcing at 60°F.   These procedures are experimental and are recommended on a trial basis only.   The Copland varieties cannot be handled by either of these two methods.

For pot plants there are only a few varieties that force easily before Valentine's Day, but after this date some of the Mendel, Triumph, Cottage, and Darwin types force satisfactorily and can be brought in as needed beginning in mid-January.

12

FOLIAGE PLANTS

Foliage plants are used for indoor gardens because of the pleasing effects of the leaves and stems. These are plants with environmental requirements that allow them to remain in good condition in the home or in public buildings for at least several weeks and possibly several months. In many instances because of insufficient light within buildings, temperatures that may be either too low or too high, and low relative humidity, the plants may not grow actively but will just maintain themselves. There are advantages in this as the plants then do not out-grow the containers or locations in which they are placed.

Indoor gardening is possible on any scale. Tremendous quantities of small foliage plants are used in small planters which are commonly called "dish gardens." These may be gift items, but often they are purchased by the consumer for use in the home. Larger foliage plants are used as points of interest in the home, as screens, or to soften harsh, straight lines in modern homes. Many homes are designed with permanent planters or indoor garden areas.

Public buildings usually are designed to include indoor gardens. These may be huge areas in which 40-foot palm trees and other large plants are used. Sometimes the foliage plants are used to add warmth and beauty to an otherwise cold and impersonal structure, and other times they are used to provide an exotic atmosphere.

Many of the foliage plants originated in the tropics. Most of the foliage plants are native to mild climates and many of them actually came from various tropical areas around the world. They are truly exotics. In spite of originating in tropics or other mild climates, the foliage plants may have come from different elevations which produce contrasting environments. As far as possible the native environment should be provided for the plants in their new location.

The commercial grower of foliage plants is interested in supplying the best possible growing conditions for the plants because he is desirous of producing more and larger plants. These conditions may be reproduced in outdoor areas in some sections of the South and in greenhouses in the North. In most instances the consumer cannot provide good growing conditions in the buildings in which the plants are placed, so that the manner in which the plants are handled by grower and consumer must be quite different.

Foliage plants are grown in the South and finished in northern greenhouses. The stock plants of many foliage plants are grown outdoors in the South or possibly in some protective structure, and rooted cuttings or small plants are shipped to northern greenhouses for growing on. The way in which the plants are handled depends on the locale and the type of plants. In southern Florida the plants are grown outdoors or under plastic screen. *Sansevieria, Citrus, Ficus,* and some of the palms may be grown entirely outdoors, while Philodendrons, Aglaonemas, Dracaenas, crotons, Dieffenbachias, Nephthytis, and Pothos may be grown in plastic screen houses. Greenhouses are used in a limited way for the production of foliage plants in southern Florida. Plastic-covered houses are widely used, however.

In central Florida the general procedure is to grow the stock plants in slat sheds or plastic screen houses and root and grow on the plants in greenhouses. In recent years the slat sheds and plastic screen structures have been modified so that they may be covered with plastic film in the fall in order to prevent damage from freezing and to provide warmer growing temperatures in the winter. In addition many of the growers provide supplementary heat by means of steam boilers or other heaters. Aglaonemas, Sansevierias, and palms

12-1. A slat shed used for growing Philodendron totem poles in southern Florida.

12-2. *Philodendron cordatum* rooted in greenhouses in central Florida.

12-3. *Philodendron cordatum* being rooted in greenhouses in central Florida.

12-4. Plastic screen houses and greenhouses for the production of foliage plants in southern Florida. (*Vosters Nurseries and Greenhouses, Inc., photograph.*)

12-5.   Foliage plants growing in a slat shed in Florida.   (*Vosters Nurseries and Greenhouses, Inc., photograph.*)

may be grown entirely in slat sheds or plastic screen houses.   The stock plants of *Dieffenbachia, Maranta, Nephthytis, Peperomia, Philodendron,* and *Pothos* are grown in heated slat sheds or plastic screen houses, and greenhouses are used for propagation and finishing.

12-6.   *Pittosporum tobira* growing in open fields in a southern Florida nursery.   (*South Florida Nurseries, Inc., photograph.*)

12-7. Croton stock plants in a plastic screen house. (*South Florida Nurseries, Inc., photograph.*)

The foliage plant operations in Puerto Rico are in slat sheds (the sheds are sometimes covered with palm leaves instead of slats) or plastic screen houses. Dracaenas are grown in quantity, and several other types of foliage plants are produced. The Puerto Rican grower supplies unrooted and rooted stock to Florida growers and rooted cuttings and 2¼-inch plants to northern greenhouse operators.

The main sources of ivies, cacti, and succulents are in southern California. Some of the stock plants are grown outdoors or in partially protected areas, but most of the production is in greenhouses.

Some foliage plants are produced in southern Texas, in outdoor areas or with some protection. The propagation is largely done in greenhouses.

12-8. Fifteen acres of plastic screen house used for foliage plant production, viewed from above. (*South Florida Nurseries, Inc., photograph.*)

12-9. Slat sheds are commonly covered with plastic film during the winter to provide warmer temperatures. (*South Florida Nurseries, Inc., photograph.*)

A portion of the foliage plants which are produced in the South is sold directly to stores that place them on display for immediate sale to the consumers. This type of selling has been more common among some of the Florida producers and operators of chain stores. It is a method for handling a large volume of plants but is not without problems. Some growers supply poorly

12-10. Emergency means of heating slat sheds or plastic screen houses are required in Florida to protect foliage plants from freezing during occasional cold weather.

12-11. Some Florida growers use wind machines to prevent freezing of foliage plants in periods of cold temperatures. (*Vosters Nurseries and Greenhouses, Inc., photograph.*)

grown plants, and very often the plants are not watered or properly cared for in the stores.

Northern greenhouse operation varies with the size of the plants. Most of the small foliage plants are used in dish gardens. The greenhouse operator buys rooted cuttings or small potted plants from southern growers for making the gardens. In some instances the rooted cuttings are planted directly in the dish gardens, and at other times they may be potted first. The most popular dish garden plants are *Philodendron cordatum, Nephthytis, Peperomia, Dracaena godseffiana* and *sanderiana*, Neanthe bella palms, *Sansevieria*, ivies, boxwood, cacti, and succulents. The dish gardens may be sold within a few days after they are planted. Making dish gardens can be established as a production line project, but some attention must be given to using the proper plants together, selecting containers of consumer interest, and arranging the plants in good design.

The large foliage plants may be obtained from the southern growers in the size in which they will be sold to the customer, or they may be purchased in a smaller size for growing on in the greenhouse and later sale. Usually the plants are shipped in at the size wanted for sale, grown a few weeks in the greenhouse until they are well established, and then sold.

Some of the most popular large plants are those grown on bark slabs or poles and called "totem poles." These are produced in sizes from 2 feet and up. *Philodendron pertusum* is used most commonly, but other large-leaf Philodendrons are grown as well. The totem poles may be grown in Florida and shipped to the northern greenhouses for resale, or they may be grown in the greenhouse by planting at the base of poles small plants obtained from the South.

Light. The best growth of most foliage plants is produced with approximately 1,000 foot-candles of light. However, Sansevierias and Peperomias should be supplied about 2,000 foot-candles, and *Aglaonema simplex* does best at about 700 foot-candles. In outdoor areas such as Florida and Puerto Rico, the plants are shaded by slat sheds or plastic screen houses. In northern greenhouses shading compound may be put on the glass or cloth, or plastic screen may be installed above the plants.

There is no apparent effect of day length on foliage plants.

In the home or public buildings the problem is not usually one of reducing the amount of light but of providing enough. Most of the foliage plants require at least 30 foot-candles of light daily for 12 hours. In some situations it will be necessary to install lights over the plants so that they will get sufficient light.

Temperature. Foliage plants should be provided 70 to 75°F temperature if it is possible. Florida is the location in the continental United States that comes closest to these temperatures in the winter; however, there are many times when the temperatures are lower than that, and freezing temperatures may even be experienced. Covering the slat sheds in central Florida with plastic film and heating them have kept the plants from freezing, and in addition, because warmer temperatures can be maintained during the winter, plant growth is more rapid and production is greater.

Temperatures below 60°F are unusual in Puerto Rico, and it is questionable whether supplementary heat would be of economic worth there.

The northern foliage plant specialist is aware of the temperature requirements of these plants, and he maintains the necessary heat. The growers who attempt to grow foliage plants in 60°F houses together with other crops soon learn that they do not grow at that low temperature.

If homes and public buildings were operated at a "healthful" 68°F, the temperature would be about right for foliage plants. Very often the temperatures are maintained considerably higher, with harmful effects to plants and humans. Even in buildings which are heated properly there may be some locations not suited for plants such as over hot radiators or in cold windows or doorways.

Moisture. With the exception of such plants as Peperomias, Sansevierias, cacti, and succulents, high humidity should be provided for foliage plants (75 to 80 percent). The soil should be irrigated regularly so that it remains uniformly moist.

Homes and public buildings have very low humidity during the winter. Some improvement in foliage plant growth could be expected if the humidity could be raised, but this is not practical in such buildings.

Because of the low light intensity in homes and public buildings, foliage plants grow very slowly and their requirements for water are not great. Customers should be advised to water foliage plants infrequently. Watering them too frequently at home is probably the most common cause of their early demise.

Soils and fertilizers. Foliage plants, with few exceptions, grow best in highly organic soils. At least half the soil mixture should be acid peat moss or leaf mold, and even more if the basic soil is fine (clay or silt). Addition of organic fertilizers to the soil mixture is conducive to quick development, and once a good root system has been produced, light applications of liquid nitrogenous fertilizers are desirable. The majority of the tropical foliage plants will do well in acid soils (pH 4.0 to 5.0). Rooted cuttings or small potted plants should be potted in moist soil and not watered immediately. The first watering should be made when new roots have started to develop.

Foliage plants in the home or public buildings usually do not require frequent fertilizer applications, as their growth is too slow. Too liberal application of fertilizer to such plants can cause damage to the roots and subsequently to the tops of the plants.

ARALIAS (*Araliaceae*)

The plants known in the trade as Aralias are in the Aralia family but in various genera.

A. balfouriana (*Polyscias balfouriana marginata*) originated in New Caledonia and has grayish-green leaves with white border. It is propagated by stem cuttings and used mainly as a small plant in dish gardens.

A. elegantissima (*Dizygotheca elegantissima*) is a native of New Hebrides and is propagated from seed. It is a graceful plant with narrow, palmately compound leaves. Its feathery texture can be used to advantage as either a small or large plant.

A. seiboldi (*Fatsia japonica*) came from Japan. It has dark-green, star-shaped leaves. The smaller plants may be used in dish gardens, and the larger plants as specimens. It is propagated by cuttings.

ASPIDISTRA (*Aspidistra elatior—Liliaceae*)

Because of its ability to withstand the most adverse conditions, this Chinese plant is often called the iron plant. It is propagated by division of the plants in the spring. Any well-drained soil is satisfactory, provided a temperature of at least 50°F is maintained and an abundance of water is provided. When the plants are partially starved, variegated foliage will often result.

BOXWOOD (*Buxus microphylla japonica—Buxaceae*)

The boxwood is a native of Japan with small, bright-green leaves. It is propagated by rooted cuttings and is used in dish gardens as a tiny tree.

BROMELIADS (*Bromeliaceae*)

The bromeliads are used to a greater extent in Europe than in America, although they have become more common in the trade here in recent years. They are excellent keeping plants in the home and in public buildings. Many of them have highly colored foliage, and some have rather spectacular flowers. Flowering may be induced in some bromeliads by treatment with calcium carbide, acetylene, or beta hydroxyethyl hydrazine. The calcium carbide treatment is probably the most practical commercially. The calcium carbide is mixed with water at 5 grams per 1 quart of water. After bubbling ceases (about 10 minutes) the solution is poured into the cup of the plant formed by the rosette of leaves. About 24 hours later the calcium carbide solution is poured out and replaced with water. This treatment is used only on mature plants, and they flower 6 to 8 weeks afterwards.

Aechmea fasciata variegata has a rosette of leathery, gray-green leaves with silver bands. It has a striking inflorescence of rose colored head with blue flowers.

Billbergias have narrow, upright leaves often banded or mottled. The flowers are pendant and usually blue.

Cryptanthus leaves usually make flat rosettes and many of them are highly colored.   The small plants are suitable for dish gardens.

Neoregelia spectabilis is commonly called Fingernail Plant because of the characteristic red tips on its olive-green leaves. The flowers are blue, and other species have striking color combinations on their leaves.

Vriesia splendens major is known as Flaming Sword because of the flaming red inflorescence. The blue-green leaves form a rosette and are barred in black.

CACTI (*Cactaceae*)

Several genera are grown commercially, and there are many types and forms. Propagation by seed is most common with cacti; however, in some instances plants are propagated by cuttings. In the past cacti were collected in the arid land of southwestern United States and Mexico. Cacti will exist under very unfavorable conditions, but for best growth it is necessary to water when dry and fertilize occasionally. The most important genera are *Astrophytum, Cephalocereus, Cereus, Mammillaria,* and *Opuntia.*

CHINESE EVERGREEN (*Aglaonema* spp.—*Araceae*)

The most common form is *Aglaonema simplex,* which requires little light and will do well in the average home either in containers with soil or in shallow dishes of water. It is propagated by single-node divisions of stems or by tip cuttings. The short divisions are set or scattered in peat and produce salable plants in 6 to 12 months, depending on the size wanted. Fungus troubles are serious. Temperatures of 70 to 75°F are desirable. An 85 to 90 percent reduction of light is necessary to maintain dark-colored leaves. Nitrogenous fertilizers during the growing season speed growth. The so-called variegated Chinese evergeen (*A. commutatum*) has a deep olive-green leaf coloring with silver marking along the midrib and veins. It is propagated and handled in a manner similar to that recommended for *A. simplex.* *A. costatum* and *A. roebelini* are two other species grown commercially. The latter is generally sold under the genus *Schismatoglottis.* *A. costatum* is a low grower, while *A. roebelini* is tall, with gray-green leaves marked with silver.

CITRUS (*Citrus mitis* and other spp.—*Rutaceae*)

C. mitis came from the Philippines. It is commonly known as Calamondin or dwarf orange. Calamondins are propagated from cuttings, and they are grown as specimen pot plants and sold when they are in fruit. Meyer lemon and Ponderosa lemon are Citrus species that are also used. These make larger specimen plants. Meyer lemon is also grown in the variegated form.

DIEFFENBACHIA (*Dieffenbachia* spp.—*Araceae*)

These showy plants, with thick succulent stems and variegated foliage, come from the West Indies and South America. They are propagated in a warm (75°F) house from pieces of the stems containing one or more eyes. The pieces should be laid on the propagating bench in a medium of peat and barely covered. When rooted, they can be potted directly into 5-inch pots in a light soil with about one-fourth peat or leaf mold added.

Dieffenbachias are susceptible to stem rot and to some leaf diseases. It is difficult to obtain disease-free cane for propagation purposes, and clean stock will remain that way only if the strictest sanitation measures are followed. Disease infestations often limit the commercial production of Dieffenbachias. The two in greatest use are *D. exotica* and *D. amoena*. *D. exotica* may be used as small plants in dish gardens or as a large specimen plant depending on the size it is allowed to attain.   The leaves are olive green splashed with cream white. *D. amoena* is a large plant which may be used only for specimen purposes.   Its leaves are emerald-green with regular, white markings extending outwards from the midrib.   Both of these Dieffenbachias hold their lower leaves well and give good service in the home or public buldings.   Other *Dieffenbachias* used to some extent in the trade are *D. picta*, which has grass-green leaves with ivory-white blotching that is not as extensive as it is on *D. exotica*.   *D. picta Rudolph Roehrs* leaves are almost entirely yellow with some white blotches and a dark-green border and midrib.   *D. picta superba* is quite similar to *D. picta* but with more variegation and heavier leaves, and *D. bausei* has the most colorful leaves, of yellowish-green spotted with dark-green and white, but it is more subject to leaf drop than some of the others.

DRACAENA (Dracaena spp.—Liliaceae)

These South African tropical plants are used as specimens for their foliage, and also in made-up baskets and boxes.   The more common species in use are *D. deremensis warnecki, D. fragrans massangeana, D. godseffiana, D. marginata,* and *D. sanderiana* (from New Zealand).

All the species mentioned are propagated by cuttings from ripened stems.   The old stems are cut in pieces from 1 to 2 inches long (or the whole length of the stem is used); then the cuttings are placed just below the surface of the medium of peat and kept there for several weeks at a temperature of 80°F. They do best when placed in a grafting case with high humidity.   At the axil of each leaf a new shoot will develop; it should be severed and rooted.   This is a quicker process than that in which one awaits the development of roots from the base of the new shoot before removing the plants from the peat.   The potting soil should be a fibrous coarse loam mixed with one-half leaf mold or peat. High air humidity and temperatures from 70 to 75°F are best for Dracaenas.

ENGLISH IVY (Hedera helix—Araliaceae)

These hardy, climbing plants, native of Europe, are extremely useful for ground-cover work and as vines for the home, the porch box, or the hanging basket.   The plants are readily propagated by long- or short-stem cuttings taken at any time of the year.   Cuttings started in the spring will make bushy plants for spring sales.   During the summer they may be lined out in the field, then potted in the fall, and grown in a temperature from 50 to 60°F.   Variegated specimens are available but slow-growing and hard to propagate, and they frequently make leggy and unsightly plants unless considerable time is spent in training them.

EUONYMUS (*Euonymus japonicus—Celastraceae*)

Several varieties of *Euonymus* are used for dish gardens. They originated in Japan. The leaves are small and variegated green and yellow. *Euonymus* is propagated by stem cuttings.

FATSHEDERA (*Fatshedera lizei—Araliaceae*)

F. lizei is a hybrid between *Fatsia japonica* and *Hedera helix*. It has a dark-green, star-shaped leaf and is used primarily as a small plant in dish gardens. It is propagated from stem cuttings.

FERNS (order *Filicies*)

Ferns are indispensable in any collection of plants, no matter how select. For commercial purposes, therefore, the ferns constitute an important group of foliage plants, serving the purpose of individual plants for home use or for decorative effects, and of fillers in combination with many other plants. Conservatories and botanical collections may also contain many groups, such as the tree ferns exemplified by *Alsophila australis, Cyathea dealbata, Dicksonia antarctica,* and *Lomaria gibba;* the gigantic nonarborescent forms of *Acrostichum aureaum, Adiantum trapeziforme, Asplenium caudatum, Blechnum braziliense, Cibotium schiedei, Davallia divaricata, Nephrodium macrophyllum, Polypodium aureum,* and *Woodwardia orientalis;* and the variegated, the crested, the trailing, the transparent, and the viviparous kinds. The most important commercial genera are the *Nephrolepis* and *Adiantum,* together with the general group of table ferns, including *Pteris, Cyrtomium, Aspidium,* and *Asplenium.*

BIRD'S-NEST FERN (*Asplenium nidus—Polypodiaceae*)

The bird's-nest fern is an attractive Brazilian fern with large light-green leaves and prominent black venation. Its culture is similar to that of table ferns, except that care should be taken to prevent water from accumulating in the crown, which causes rotting of the leaves.

BOSTON FERN (*Nephrolepis exaltata—Polypodiaceae*)

The original native form growing wild in subtropical regions is no longer used, having been superseded by numerous sports. The first one discovered in 1896 was named *N. exaltata bostoniensis.* In 1900 a bipinnate form appeared and was called *N. piersoni,* which sported again into a tripinnate form known as

N. elegantissima and its variety *N. compacta*. This variety later gave rise to a four-pinnate form, *N. superbissima,* and its dwarf counterpart, *N. muscosa.* Other distinct sports which have come into commerce include Scotti, Teddy, Jr., Roosevelti, Whitmani, and Norwood.

The culture of the Boston fern and its relatives is simple. They are propagated by runners which develop from stock plants in all directions, are lifted and potted in 2½-inch pots, and then are shifted as needed until specimen plants develop in 6-inch pots or larger. To secure the runners, ferns are planted out early in the summer in a house of 60°F, in a light soil mixed with about one-fourth peat or leaf mold. By fall the new plants may be potted and will produce satisfactory plants in about 8 to 12 months. Occasionally, growers plant the runners in a bench and allow them to reach a size large enough to be potted in a 6-inch pot. This procedure will produce a much larger plant, but care must be taken that the plants establish a satisfactory root system in the pots before they are offered for sale.

Humidity is essential, as is heat, in the production of ferns. At no time, however, should bottom heat be applied. During the summer months shade should be supplied and frequent application of nitrogenous fertilizers should be made.

Browning of the fronds is most often caused by overwatering, a dry atmosphere, or fumigating with cyanide. White fly, scale, and mealy bugs are the most serious pests.

MAIDENHAIR FERN (*Adiantum cuneatum croweanum* and *A. farleyense—Polypodiaceae*)

The maidenhair ferns are natives of South America. They are extremely useful for cutting purposes but somewhat less valuable as pot plants for sale. Propagation is carried on by two methods—spores and divisions of the crowns. The spores may be sown at any time of the year, although they are commonly sown in the spring, requiring at that time about 8 weeks to develop the first true fronds from sowing. If sown in the fall or winter, 4 weeks longer is usually necessary. The spores should be scattered evenly on the surface of light sandy soil mixed with sterile peat, preferably in pots, but pans or flats can be substituted. The soil medium should be thoroughly soaked before sowing, and the container should be covered with glass immediately after the operation.

Placed in a temperature of 65 to 70°F, with no water applied at the top, the prothallia will develop rapidly. As soon as they make their appearance, the glass may be removed and overhead watering can be practiced. Further culture consists of planting four or five of the young plants in clumps in a pot, spaced about 1 inch apart and grown at 60°F. Later, usually 8 months from sowing time, these plants are potted in individual pots in a soil compost of heavy fibrous loam mold.   *A. farleyense* requires a temperature of 65 to 70°F and a great deal more humidity than *A. cuneatum*.   Propagation by division consists of cutting the fronds, drying the plants partially, and then cutting the solid mass of roots and crown into several sections, potting into 3- or 4-inch pots, and starting into growth.   Like the Boston ferns, *Adiantum* suffers from bottom heat and requires good drainage.   Nitrogenous applications in liquid form should be applied during the summer.

PTERIS FERN (*Pteris cretica* and other spp.—*Polypodiaceae*)

These small-growing, attractive ferns, native of tropical regions, are very useful as pot plants and fillers.   The species commonly used are *P. cretica alba*, *P. lineata*, *P. wimsetti*, *P. tremula*, and *P. cretica wilsoni*.

The plants are propagated by spores, in the spring, similarly to *Adiantum*, but require only about 6 months from sowing to potting.   The same treatment of temperature and humidity also applies, except that it is possible to drop the temperature to 55°F with success after the plants have become established in pots.   To develop spores, let the stock plants become pot-bound and keep them on the dry side.   *Cyrtomium falcatum* and others grouped as table ferns require similar conditions.

FICUS (*Ficus* spp.—*Moraceae*)

The genus *Ficus* is of importance economically, being cultivated for fruits and for ornamental purposes, and the plants are commonly called rubber plants.   *F. elastica* is native of Southern Asia.   Green and variegated, it is used extensively as a house plant.   Other species grown to a lesser extent for similar purposes are *F. benghalensis*, *F. nitida*, *F. philippinensis*, *F. pandurata*, *F. pumila*, *F. rubiginosa* (*australis*), *F. religiosa*, and *F. belgica*.   *F. belgica decora* is most popular.

The plants are propagated by mossing and by cuttings in the spring. Mossing is the better method.   If cuttings are used, the top 6 or 7 inches should be taken, cutting below a node and inserting the end deeply in sand where bottom heat of 80°F is provided.   Because of their large evaporating surface, the leaves are usually drawn together about a stick.   High humidity and close atmosphere are necessary for rooting, but only a moderate amount of water should be used in the propagating medium.   Under constant-mist propagation in full sunlight, rooting of cuttings takes place readily.   Perfect drainage is essential.   The mossing operation has been described in Chap 8.

Rubber plants thrive best in a temperature of 70°F and high humidity, but during the winter will exist in temperatures as low as 50°F. A fibrous loam mixed with one-half peat moss makes a satisfactory medium for potting. Small pots and an abundance of water are necessary.

F. repens and *F. repens minimus* are climbing plants from India. They root readily from stem cuttings taken any time of the year and grow rapidly in a temperature of 60°F. The leaves are small, and they do exceptionally well under average house conditions.

FITTONIA (*Fittonia* spp.—*Acanthaceae*)

These are evergreen herbaceous plants of dwarf habit, with compact foliage covered by a beautiful variegated, netted venation that stands out prominently from the ground color of the leaves. They are very useful for filling hanging baskets or for covering the surface, both top and bottom, of baskets containing other plants. The two species found most commonly are *F. argyroneura*, which has a ground color of pale green profusely netted with silver-white veins, and *F. verschaffelti*, which has deep-green leaves with red veining. The plants have succulent stems and they root easily. Light soil with plenty of peat or leaf mold and sand added is best for good growth. These plants are readily propagated by cuttings of any length and can be rooted easily in a medium of one-half sand and one-half peat. High humidity is desirable, and partial shade is needed.

GRAPE IVY (*Cissus rhombifolia*—*Vitaceae*)

Grape ivy is a very satisfactory trailing plant, especially well adapted to average house conditions. It is propagated at any time of the year by stem cuttings two or three nodes long, with a bottom heat of 60°F. Salable plants will be produced in 10 to 12 months. Abundance of water, a light fertile soil, and a temperature of 55 to 60°F are desirable, as is partial shade.

HOYA (*Hoya carnosa* variegated—*Asclepiadaceae*)

Hoya is a vine with large, green leaves bordered in cream white. It is propagated by stem cuttings. The small plants are used in dish gardens, or specimen plants are produced by growing one or more plants on a trellis or pole. They are very susceptible to pests, particularly mealy bugs.

NEPHTHYTIS (*Syngonium* spp.—*Araceae*)

Syngoniums (*Nephthytis*) are climbers that do very well in the home or office. They fit into planters, dish gardens, or on poles and will stand air conditioning as well as abuse.   S. *podophyllum* (*Nephthytis liberica*) is a fast grower with large leaves, while its sport, Little Gem, or Emerald Gem, is more suitable for smaller containers.   Several variegated types are available; some are small, such as Ruth Fraser, and others are more vigorous, such as Tri-leaf Wonder and Green Gold.   Another species which resembles the variegated types mentioned is S. *hoffmani,* and still another is S. *wendlandi,* with velvety leaves and silver striations.   Of all these, S. *podophyllum* and its variegated forms are the best commercially.   They are propagated by single-node stem cuttings.   The leaf at the node is removed when the cuttings are stuck upright into a peat medium.   The removal of the leaf dwarfs the plant and causes development of small leaves.

The cuttings are stuck about ½ inch apart and allowed to remain until two leaves have developed; then they are transplanted to other beds about 2 inches apart.   It takes about 3 months to produce a salable rooted cutting with four to five leaves, although often a plant is pulled sooner, with only two to three leaves.   The temperature needed is 75 to 80°F, with greater light than is needed for Philodendrons, to produce high variegation.   When they are grown in the dark, the colors seem faded.   Most of the stock is produced in Florida, where the stock plants are grown outdoors under slats and rooted under glass.

NORFOLK ISLAND PINE (*Araucaria excelsa—Pinaceae*)

This graceful, coniferous evergreen from Norfolk Island is used as a specimen plant for the home, thriving well under trying conditions.   The plants may be propagated by seed, but the specimens so produced have long internodes between the branching tiers and are not attractive.   The recommended method is to use cuttings made from the leaders.   These are best taken in the fall and are easily rooted in a shaded grafting case, where high humidity and a temperature of 70°F can be maintained.   Cuttings from side shoots will produce one-sided specimens.   A light soil mixed with one-half peat is satisfactory.   The temperature during the winter may range from 50 to 55°F.   Plants should be grown on the dry side during the winter months.   Shifting should be watched carefully, as these plants grow to be large trees in their native habitat, and root growth should be restricted to keep them dwarf enough for plant sales.

PALMS (*Palmaceae*)

The greatest quantity of palms that are used are the small, seedling Neanthe bella (proper classification is *Chamaedorea elegans*) palms which are used in dish gardens.   For this purpose the Neanthe bella palms are purchased when they have three to five leaves and are about 6 inches tall.   Some Neanthe bella palms are grown on, to larger specimen plants.   The palms more commonly used as specimen plants are *Kentia fosteriana, K. belmoreana, Areca lutescens,*

Phoenix roebelini, and *Cocos weddeliana.* All palms are grown from seed by specialists in subtropical states (Florida, California) and shipped to the growers and retailers. Kentias are often made-up specimens containing three plants to a pot.

Their general culture is simple. Those kept for rentals should be grown at a temperature of 55°F, those for sale at 65°F. The reason for the difference in temperature is that the former are subject to abuse when rented and should be hardened to exposure, drafts, and lack of water. Their life is usually comparatively short (2 to 4 years) unless good care is taken by wrapping them before shipping in winter, and also by making sure that they are properly watered when away from the greenhouse and not subjected to extremes in temperature.

During the summer an abundance of water at the roots and high humidity in the air are necessary, as well as reduction of light by shading. During the winter less water is needed, and the shade should be removed. Since palms are usually grown in comparatively small pots and not shifted oftener than once a year, nitrogenous applications during the summer are essential. The best soil for palms is coarse and heavy, but good drainage is absolutely essential. An addition of peat to the soil, especially for palms used for decorations, will be beneficial.

Thrips, mealy bugs, and scale are the worst pests, but syringing and an occasional good scrubbing will keep them under control.

PANDANUS (*Pandanus utilis* and *P. veitchi—Pandanaceae*)

These native plants of South Africa and Australia are exceedingly useful as decorative specimens and as focal points in porch box decorations and urns. Their adaptability to trying conditions of the home makes them exceptionally good for such purposes. Propagation is accomplished by suckers and seeds. Suckers should be removed in the spring and rooted in a fairly dry medium with a bottom heat of 70°F. Seeds may be started in pots of light soil with bottom heat provided. A fibrous loam soil mixed with one-half peat moss is satisfactory. High humidity during the spring and summer months and winter temperatures of 65 to 70°F are necessary. Reduction of watering during the winter months is essential to prevent rotting at the roots. Lack of shading and partial starvation will produce variegated specimens, while overwatering will cause *P. veitchi* to fade out to white and eventually die.

PEPEROMIA (*Peperomia spp.—Piperaceae*)

These fleshy-textured plants, native of South America, are useful in planters and dish gardens. Two species are in commerce—*P. obtusifolia,* which is green, with its variegated strain *P. obtusifolia variegata,* and *P. sandersi* (the watermelon Peperomia, so named because of its silver bands that resemble those of a watermelon). The plants are propagated by leaf or stem cuttings with bottom heat. The top temperature need not exceed 60°F, although quicker rooting is obtained at higher temperatures. The low water requirement and light fertilization must be observed for success, and sandy soils are best. Sharp sterilized sand or perlite is best for propagation, although other mediums may be used. These plants require about half the shade of the majority of tropical plants. There are other species and varieties which have found limited acceptance in the trade.

Stem rots caused by *Rhizoctonia* and *Pythium,* as well as leaf diseases (*Phytophthora*), are common.

PHILODENDRON (*Philodendron* spp.—*Araceae*)

This genus provides the most popular plants for the home. Some of the species are climbers and require supports (totem poles, mossed stakes, cypress knees, cypress bark, cork bark, tree fern stems); others are allowed to trail down; and some are self-headers and grow upright. The most common and acceptable species is *P. cordatum.* It is used in small pots, in planters, in dish gardens, and on totem poles. It does well under home, office, or public place conditions and it is rather tolerant of light, shade, warmth or coolness, and dry or wet soil. It is propagated by one- or two-eye cuttings which are stuck in peat or mixtures. If fibrous sphagnum peat is used (sedge peat is too fine and compacts and dries out readily), it may be mixed with perlite to provide better aeration. However, such a mixture in pots larger than 3 inches is too loose for shipping, and the plant is difficult to repot unless pot-bound; hence the most satisfactory medium for initial potting in small pots is sphagnum peat. A temperature of 75 to 80°F is ideal for propagation, with humidity averaging 75 to 80 percent. Under such conditions a new plant with three leaves can be produced in 6 weeks. The ideal conditions for such propagation are found in the favorable Florida climate. Artificial heat and humidity in northern climates cannot be reproduced inexpensively, so that the usual time for such propagation is increased at least threefold. The plants are usually sold as three- to five-leaf rooted cuttings or in small pots, singly or two or three together. They are shipped to the northern growers, who grow them to finished size.

Larger specimens of other species of climbing Philodendrons are sold as rooted tips or in 4-inch pots. These are later attached to poles and sold as specimen plants for large homes, offices, and public places. Most of these are propagated as tips with aerials which are potted direct in pots of peat.

P. pertusum is used in the greatest quantities. It has rounded leaves which are deeply cut or split and sometimes perforated. This species is very popular for use as large specimen plants or totem poles, and it commonly is called "split-leaf *Philodendron.*" *Monstera deliciosa* is closely related to pertusum and by some is thought to be its mature form. It has larger leaves and they are more perforated. Other large-leafed Philodendrons in common usage are *P. panduraeforme,* which has fiddle-shaped leaves; *P. hastatum,* which has been largely replaced by *P. Emerald Queen* as they have somewhat similar arrow-shaped leaves and Emerald Queen is less subject to diseases; and *P. dubium,* which has deeply lobed leaves.

Some of the Philodendrons have red pigmentation. *P. micans* is small-leafed somewhat like *P. cordatum* but with a green-bronze leaf of velvet texture. Some of the large-leafed Philodendrons are *P. Red Emerald* and *P. mandaianum* with red pigment primarily on the undersurfaces of the arrow-shaped leaves. *P. Florida* has deeply lobed green leaves with red petioles.

P. selloum is a self-heading-type *Philodendron,* and it is about the only one of this type used for greenhouse production. It makes a large plant with big leaves, and usually it is more suitable in larger buildings than it is in the home. *P. squamiferum* is a self-header that is used to a limited extent. It has anchor-shaped leaves with red pubescence on the petioles.

PILEA (*Pilea cadierei—Urticaceae*)

The green and silver variegated leaves give the *Pilea* the common name of Aluminum Plant. It is easily propagated from stem cuttings, and the plants are used in dish gardens.

PITTOSPORUM (*Pittosporum tobira—Pittosporaceae*)

The Pittosporum is a native plant of China and Japan, and it has dark-green, long, ovate leaves. It is propagated by stem cuttings. Small plants are used in dish gardens, and larger plants as specimens. There also is a variegated form.

PODOCARPUS (*Podocarpus macrophylla maki—Taxaceae*)

The *Podocarpus* grows upright and has dark-green, needlelike leaves. It is propagated from seed and cuttings, and small plants are used in dish gardens. Large plants may be used for specimens, and sometimes they are sheared to various shapes.

POTHOS (*Scindapsus aureus—Araceae*)

The *S. aureus* is commonly known as *Pothos,* and several types are popular. *S. aureus* and *S. aureus wilcoxi* are two that have light-green leaves with yellow streaks or blotches. The variety Marble Queen, sometimes called "Silver Marble," has white streaks or blotches and is in great demand.

Propagation of *Pothos* is similar to that of *Philodendron* except that it is often stuck in 2¼-inch pots as an unrooted cutting. If the single-eye cutting is stuck so that the petiole (leaf stem) is below the surface of the rooting medium, the leaf may turn yellow and drop off. This is especially true with potted cuttings. A pecularity known as "leaf skipping" is often serious. As the shoot develops from the eye, only a petiole will form at one or more nodes, and no leaf ever develops. Such plants are not salable. This leaf skipping is associated with extreme heat or too much shade. The time required for production of plants is similar to that for *Philodendron*. Florists often have difficulty in the winter with rooted cuttings of *Pothos* produced in the South. The plants apparently arrive in good condition, but after potting they die within a relatively short time. To prevent this, the plants should be potted immediately upon arrival in a mixture of equal parts of soil, sand, perlite, and peat. They should be watered thoroughly with water at a temperature of 60 to 70°F and placed in a 75°F shaded greenhouse. The plants should be covered with a light cloth and syringed frequently, but kept dry at the roots. The greater the amount of variegation, the less frequently the plants should be watered. Drafts at this stage may be fatal. Stock is produced in a similar manner to that recommended for *Philodendron*.

SANSEVIERIA (*Sansevieria trifasciata—Liliaceae*)

This old-time favorite of the dish garden is still an important plant in the home. It is tolerant of the dry conditions of the home and will stand much abuse, except when it is overwatered or chilled suddenly. The varieties in the trade today are S. *trifasciata* and its sports, S. *trifasciata laurenti* and S. *trifasciata hahni*. Through error, the correct species name, trifasciata, is not used commercially; S. *trifasciata* is known as S. *zeylanica*. The plants are grown for stock in half shade and are propagated by division of the rhizomes for S. *trifasciata laurenti* and by rooting leaf sections for S. *trifasciata*. For dish gardens the "rosettes"—small plants with three to five leaves—are prized. When Sansevierias are subjected to sudden chilling with high moisture, they develop wet, sunken areas which dry up and make the plants unsalable.

SCHEFFLERA (*Schefflera actinophylla—Araliaceae*)

Schefflera is commonly called "Umbrella Tree" because of its characteristic form at maturity. The leaves are shiny, bright-green, and palmately compound. It is propagated from seed, and the seedlings may be used in dish gardens. More commonly Scheffleras are used for large-size specimen plants. Red spider is a troublesome pest.

SUCCULENTS

Succulents are plants with fleshy leaves and stems of several different genera and families. There are many shapes and types, and the succulents are used mainly as points of interest in dish gardens. Some of them are propagated from seed, and others by cuttings. The most popular genera are *Aloe, Crassula, Echeveria, Haworthia,* and *Sedum.*

ADAPTABILITY OF FOLIAGE PLANTS

Foliage plants vary in their use and ability to withstand adverse conditions, as indicated below:

Plants that will grow in water

> *Aglaonema simplex* (Chinese evergreen)
> *Syngonium* (*Nephthytis*)
> *Philodendron cordatum*
> *P. panduraeforme*
> *Scindapsus aureus* (*Pothos*)

Plants that stand abuse

> *Aglaonema simplex* (Chinese evergreen)
> *Aspidistra elatior*
> *Dieffenbachia amoena*
> *Dracaena fragrans massangeana*
> *Ficus elastica*
> *Peperomia obtusifolia*
> *Philodendron cordatum*
> *Sansevieria trifasciata*
> *S. trifasciata laurenti*
> *Syngonium podophyllum* (*Nephthytis*)

Plants that do reasonably well in the home in addition to the above

> *Cissus rhombifolia* (grape ivy)
> *Dieffenbachia picta*
> *D. picta Rudolph Roehrs*
> *D. exotica*
> *Ficus benghalensis*
> *Hedera helix* (English ivy)
> *Philodendron*—all climbers and self-heading varieties
> *Sansevieria hahni*

Plants that do well under extremely dry conditions

>   Bromeliads
>   Cacti
>   *Peperomia*
>   *Sansevieria*
>   *Scindapsus* (*Pothos*)

Plants for totem poles

>   *Philodendron*—all except self-heading varieties
>   *Scindapsus* (*Pothos*)

Plants that require the minimum of light

>   *Aspidistra elatior*
>   *Aglaonema simplex* (Chinese evergreen)
>   *Crassula arborescens*
>   *Dieffenbachia amoena*
>   *Ficus elastica*
>   *Philodendron cordatum*
>   *P. panduraeforme*
>   *Schefflera actinophylla*

13

BEDDING PLANTS

The bedding plants are those that are used for flower gardens in the landscape. Some of the plants are perennial and continue to grow year after year. The production of perennial plants is largely an outdoor operation, and is not involved in this discussion. Bedding plants as discussed in this chapter are those handled as annuals. Most of them do not live through the winter, and new plants are set out each spring. The planting time may be February or earlier in the South and as late as June in the North, and the bedding plants must be scheduled carefully so that they are at the right stage of growth and size for planting. Actually the time of planting is based primarily on the last date that frost can be expected for the area; however, if the spring is cooler or warmer than usual, planting is delayed or advanced accordingly.

Many of the bedding plants are propagated by seed. This is an economical method of propagation if proper conditions are provided. The bedding plants propagated by seed that are used in the greatest quantities are petunias. Geraniums and a few of the other bedding plants must be propagated by cuttings in order to produce the desired plants.

Light.

The growth of most bedding plants will be best in full sunlight. Plants grown in shaded locations, closely spaced, or in poor light will be too tall with weak stems and will flower more slowly.

Most bedding plants can be started and grown for a few weeks solely in artificial light. Fluorescent light should be used at about 1,000 foot-candles, and this can be obtained by placing the tubes about 4 inches apart and about 6 inches above the plants. The light should be provided for a minimum of 16 hours daily. Excellent plant growth results in the early stages, but as the plants become larger, they are more easily managed in sunlight.

The length of day affects the kind of growth and the rate of flower formation of some bedding plants. The effects of length of day on the growth and flowering of Petunias are covered in the discussion of that crop.

Temperature.

The production of bedding plants is known generally as a cool-temperature operation. In some instances cool temperatures are used simply because the physical facilities will not provide warmer temperatures. Warm temperatures and accurate control of them must be provided for the propagation of bedding plants, but only a relatively small area is involved, as the seed flats and cuttings do not occupy much space. Rigid temperature control during propagation is indispensable. After propagation the plants should be grown in cooler temperatures, and the more closely these temperatures are regulated, the better the growth and timing of flowering.

Usually bedding plants are grown at 50°F night temperatures with day temperatures about 10°F warmer. At these cool temperatures growth and flowering are slow, and stems are short, compact, and of good diameter. Geraniums and some of the other plants must be grown at 55°F night temperatures or warmer in order to produce satisfactory growth.

More recently there has been interest in growing many bedding plants at 60°F night temperatures in order to produce them in a shorter period of time.

Soil, fertilizer, and water.

A reliable source of soil is required for bedding plants since the soil is sold with the plants. The soil must be well prepared so that it is porous and drains well. The bedding plants that are propagated by seed should be transplanted when the seedlings are very small, and for good contact between soil and the small root systems, the soil must be finely shredded. To compensate for the fineness of the soil, a sufficient amount of peat moss should be added so that the soil remains porous after shredding.

Artificial soil mixtures of peat moss with perlite, vermiculite, or fine sand may be used. These have the advantage of being uniform from season to season, and they can be handled in the same fashion, but fertilizer must be incorporated uniformly in these mixtures.

Soils which have not been used previously in the greenhouse will usually benefit by additions of phosphorus and calcium fertilizers at the time of mixing. Superphosphate should be used as the source of phosphorus and dolomitic limestone as the source of calcium if the soil is somewhat acid in reaction, or gypsum if the soil is neutral or alkaline. Applications of nitrogen and potassium fertilizers then must be made regularly after planting. If some nitrogen fertilizer cannot be supplied shortly after planting, a small amount should be incorporated into the soil at the time of mixing as some nitrogen is required by the plants at all stages of growth.

If soils have been used previously in the greenhouse, excess of fertilizer may be expected. This must be corrected before planting, or the young plants may be seriously damaged from the excess fertilizer.

Fertilizers are most efficiently applied in the liquid form to bedding plants, and this can be done by means of an injector with each irrigation or periodically by other means. Fertilizer should not be withheld in order to delay the growth of plants which are ahead of schedule. This produces poor-quality plants, and they grow and develop very slowly after they are planted in the garden.

Watering. Bedding plants are generally grown at a time of year when increasing light intensity and temperature cause rapid drying of the soil. Frequently, the plants are severely checked because they suffer periodically from lack of water. While it is true that dry soil will cause the growth to be compact, very often this is carried to excess, so that too much additional time is required to produce a salable plant. This is particularly true of geraniums.

Overwatering causes chlorosis on a great number of annuals used for bedding. When they are grown in flats, boards nailed too closely together may swell, to the extent that water will drain only at the edges of the flat. Plants near the edge will be nearly normal, while those at the center will be dwarf or yellow.

Newly planted seedlings must be watered with nozzles that provide a fog or fine mist so that plants or soil are not washed from the containers. As the plants grow, coarser nozzles can be used. It is usually most satisfactory to use an irrigation system with nozzles that provide a uniform spray of water for the entire area. The small-diameter plastic-tube irrigation systems can be used to advantage for geraniums in 4-inch or larger pots.

Growth regulant chemicals. Some chemical treatments can be used to produce shorter, more compact plants. B-Nine is the material most commonly used. It can be used effectively on Petunias, marigolds, Verbenas, asters, and Salvias. A 0.05 percent solution should be sprayed on the plants just before they start to stretch. An application should be effective from 4 to 6 weeks, and if needed, a second application may be made.

Diseases. Geraniums are troubled with several diseases not common to the other bedding plants, and for that reason geranium diseases are included in the discussion of that crop.

The disease known as damping-off is most common with bedding plants. The pathogens involved may be *Rhizoctonia, Pythium,* or *Phytophthora.* They may produce seed decay, stem rot, or root rot, and in extreme instances they may invade the upper portions of the plants. Usually stem rot occurs at the soil line, and the plants topple and wither. The pathogens grow rapidly in the warm and moist environment provided for the seedlings, and as long as the conditions are favorable the plants become infested and die in an ever-increasing circle from the point of infestation. Control of damping-off results from eliminating the pathogens, providing environmental conditions less suitable for the growth of the organisms, and treating with chemicals that limit the growth of the organisms.

If steam is available, it should be used to eliminate these pathogens in the soil, containers, benches, and handling equipment before they are used for bedding plants. Chemicals such as methyl bromide or Vapam may be used for treating the soil and the surroundings in place of steam, but steaming is the most satisfactory treatment when it is available. After treatment, care must be taken not to reinfest the area. Some of the most common ways in which pathogens are reintroduced are bringing in infested plants, putting feet on benches or containers, and using contaminated tools, irrigation equipment, or containers. LF-10 is useful for treating tools and potting benches, and for washing hands.

The growth of the damping-off pathogens is favored in constantly moist conditions. It is possible to control damping off by less frequent irrigation, better drained soils or containers, or more air circulation. Depending on the situation, improved air circulation may be obtained by sowing the seed more sparsely or spacing the plants farther apart, removing obstacles from around the plants, increasing ventilation, or using air-circulation fans.

If damping-off does occur, in addition to limiting the moisture and increasing the air circulation, the soil should be drenched with a combination of Dexon 35 and Terraclor 75, each at ½ pound per 100 gallons of water, or Morsodren at the rate of 3 fluid ounces per 100 gallons of water.

Botrytis blight caused by *Botrytis cinerea* is common in bedding plants, but in contrast to damping-off, the infestation starts in the upper portions of the plants and grows downwards. This pathogen develops most rapidly in moist areas on aging or injured tissues. It is commonly called "gray mold," because in the advanced stages the affected portions are covered with a mass of gray spores.

The best means of control are the elimination in the greenhouse of trash such as old stems, leaves, and flowers, as the source of Botrytis spores, and the prevention of moisture from forming on the leaves and stems of the bedding plants. Irrigation earlier in the day and more ventilation and air circulation coupled with better spacing of plants are the best means of keeping them dry and less susceptible to a Botrytis infestation.

Pests.   Bedding plant pests are usually controlled with various materials. Slugs are common, and the area should be treated with Slugit spray or with metaldehyde baits.   The best control for aphids is Meta Systox-R.   Two-spotted mite on bedding plants usually can be controlled by several different materials—parathion, Kelthane, aramite, Pentac, or Morestan.   White fly should be controlled with either Diazinon, Dibrom, Thiodan, or lindane, while dieldrin is the best treatment for thrips.

Containers.   For years annual bedding plants were grown approximately 100 per flat, and plants were dug from them at the time of sale.   Injury to the plants and inconvenience have brought about sweeping changes in containers used for bedding plants.

Small containers made of thin plastic, aluminum, paper, or a paper composition product that will hold 6 to 12 plants at maturity are preferred.   Several of these containers can be placed in a conventional flat with no waste space.   At the time of sale, the individual container is taken from the flat; the plants are removed by the customer when he requires them at the time of planting.

Pots made of peat and paper are also used.   While somewhat fragile, they offer the advantage that no knocking out of pots is necessary since the entire unit of pot and plant is set out in the planting.   Pots made of aluminum or plastic may also be used.

13-1.   Peat pots together in strips improves handling in production as well as sales.   Here unrooted geranium stem-tip cuttings are being dibbled into the pots for rooting. (*Jiffy Pot Co. of America photograph.*)

13-2. Growing bedding plants in market-size containers has been a great sales stimulus. This container holds 1 dozen plants and is made of molded wood fiber. Containers of several sizes and materials are available. (*Jiffy Pot Co. of America photograph.*)

Containers should be placed on boards, fine gravel, sawdust, or similar material, rather than directly on soil, which becomes muddy and into which roots grow readily, encouraging rank, soft growth.

Rotation and structures.   Depending on the crops, how they are handled, and the area of the country, structures of some kind will be required for the

13-3.   An integrated family of plastic containers in which the plastic flat holds four dozen 2-inch pots, two dozen 3-inch pots, or either six or eight plastic packs. (*American Plant Container Co., Inc., photograph.*)

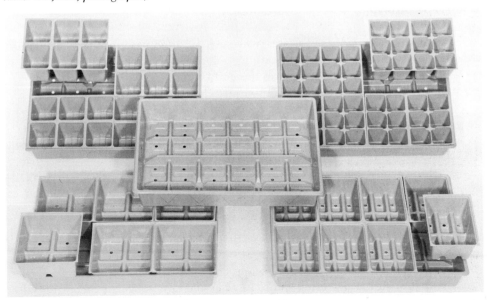

production of bedding plants from about January to June. The greatest requirement for space in northern greenhouses comes from the middle of March to June. Because of this, bedding plants do not rotate well with pot plant crops as most greenhouses are filled to overflowing with spring pot plant crops at that time of the year. If the pot plant grower desires to produce bedding plants also, he generally uses temporary structures for the bedding plants. Cold frames were used earlier, but they have been largely replaced with plastic film houses because temperature and moisture are more easily controlled and less labor is required for handling the crops. Although these may be temporary structures or used for only a portion of the year, they should provide adequate means for controlling temperature and ventilation for the best results.

It is possible that year-round structures could be used by rotating Christmas crops such as poinsettias and azaleas with bedding plants; however, cut flower crops such as Chrysanthemums and snapdragons make a better rotation.

Geraniums should not be grown in cold frames as a greater degree of control is needed than can be provided in such structures.

Marketing. Many improvements have been made in the marketing of bedding plants. The quality of the bedding plants has increased, the plants are grown in the size and units that the customers desire and can use conveniently, more information is available on how to use bedding plants and what the effect of each type of plant will be, and the sales areas have become more numerous, accessible, and attractive.

ACALYPHA (Acalypha spp.—Euphorbiaceae)

Acalypha marginata is a free-growing handsome variety which has a leaf with a reddish-brown center and a carmine edge.

A. obovata has green leaves in the early stages, edged with creamy white, and with age the edge assumes a crimson hue.

Stock plants can be lifted in the fall and kept cool until January when the plants may be cut back and placed in a temperature of 60°F with high humidity. They produce a crop of cuttings which will root readily with bottom heat, and satisfactory plants can be produced by bedding time in May.

Stock plants should be kept well syringed to keep down red spider. Well-branched specimens of both these varieties are frequently used for porch boxes and for pot plants.

AGERATUM (Ageratum houstonianum—Compositae)

This plant is a blue-, pink-, or white-flowered tropical American herb used extensively for outdoor flowering and to some extent as a pot plant for spring sales.

The plants may be grown from seed or cuttings. Seed sown in February will produce marketable plants in 4-inch pots in May, if grown in a temperature of 50°F. Cuttings may be taken in January from stock plants, lifted in the fall before frost, and carried in a cold house. Only 2 to 3 weeks is necessary in the propagation bench. After they are placed in 2½-inch pots the plants should be pinched to obtain bushiness, and they will be flowering and ready for sale in about 4 to 5 weeks. Aphids, red spider, and thrips are serious pests.

ALTERNANTHERA (*Telanthera amoena—Amarantaceae*)

The alternanthera is a very dwarf South American plant, with long lance-olate leaves, sometimes elliptic, acuminate, and colored green, yellow, and red. Alternantheras are used largely for ribbon bedding because of their compact growth, ease of shearing, and high coloration. They should be propagated in the fall by cuttings or division of plants. By either method they may be set in shallow flats and grown in a temperature of 60°F with reduced moisture at the roots. They should be potted in April for planting outside in late May.

ASPARAGUS (*Asparagus plumosus* and *A. sprengeri—Liliaceae*)

These graceful plants, native of South Africa, are used in hanging baskets, as fillers for window boxes and plant baskets, and as individual specimens.

Seed should be sown early in the spring, after soaking for 24 hours. Germination takes from 30 to 50 days. Seedlings should be planted in light but fertile soil and grown in a temperature of 60°F. Satisfactory plants are produced in about 12 months. The use of nitrogenous fertilizer is recommended during the summer. Ammonium sulfate in liquid form at the rate of 1 ounce to 2 gallons of water at biweekly intervals is satisfactory. These plants should have partial shade during the hot months to prevent yellowing of the foliage.

BEGONIA (*Begonia* spp.—*Begoniaceae*)

Begonia semperflorens. The ever-flowering, or wax, *Begonia* is used in combination pots or bedding in spring and as a cheap specimen plant at any season. Propagation is by seed or stem cuttings. Seed sown in June will make 2½- or 3-inch plants for Christmas or 4-inch plants for Valentine's Day. September sowings finish as 4-inch plants for spring. Late December and January sowings will make 2½- and 3-inch plants in spring. The same soil mixture suggested for tuberous-rooted Begonias is ideal, although the semperflorens type will grow well in three parts soil and one part manure or peat.

The plants are pinched to make them bushy and compact. Complete fertilizers applied every 3 to 4 weeks keep the foliage lustrous. The temperature should be 50 to 55°F.

There are numerous varieties in the trade. For pink flowers with green foliage, Adeline, Appleblossom, Prima Donna, Masterpiece, and Pink Pearl are suggested; for red flowers with green foliage, King of the Reds, Ball's Red, and Red Pearl; for pink flowers with bronze foliage, Luminosa, Carmen, and Indian Maid. Other varieties are Westport Beauty, a double pink; Geneva Red, a double red; and Geneva White, a double white.

Red spider, aphids, mealy bugs, white fly, and leaf roller are common pests. Mites cause cupping of the young growth and browning and withering of the unopened flower cluster. Root-knot nematodes are a serious pest, and steaming soil, pots, and bench areas is the best control. The semperflorens withstand sprays, dusts, and aerosols and are not as tender as other types.

Begonia tuberhybrida. These are sold as specimens or for bedding plants in shaded areas. The flowers of the large types may be used for corsages. Seed is sown in January, and since it is fine, the medium should be screened and the seed flat or pot watered from below. The germination temperature should be 65 to 70°F. As soon as the seedlings are large enough to be handled conveniently, they are pricked off an inch apart each way to flats. When crowded, they should be shifted to 2½-inch pots, then later to 5- and 6-inch pots, where they are fertilized regularly and kept under a moderate shade. The plants stop growing in the fall because they are a long-day type, and they can be ripened by reducing the moisture. The pots may be placed in a 45 to 50°F house, and in winter the tubers are removed, cleaned, and started in growth again in 5- or 6-inch pots. A mixture of equal parts of soil, peat, leaf mold or rotted manure, and sand should be used.

Since seedlings are so difficult to handle, most florists buy tubers grown in California under lath. When started in January, flowering plants may be expected in early spring; and tubers started in March flower in summer.

The best way to handle tubers is to bury them upright in flats of moist peat at 70 to 80°F. As soon as several leaves are unfolding, place them in 5- or 6-inch azalea pots, using equal parts of soil, peat, rotted manure or leaf mold, and sand. When established, apply a complete fertilizer every 3 to 4 weeks. Tuberous-rooted Begonias do best at 55°F with high relative humidity. Spacing will prevent undue elongation. A light to moderate shade will be necessary to prevent burn of the foliage and flowers. The tuberous-rooted *Begonia* is a long-day plant and can be lighted to extend the flowering season if desired.

Stem rot is troublesome, and painting or swabbing the area with a thin paste of zineb or captan is advisable. Avoid deep planting, and stake if necessary.

CALADIUM (*Caladium bicolor—Araceae*)

This South American perennial has beautifully marked leaves, rising from large rhizomes. The rhizomes are usually potted in March in 3- or 4-inch pots in coarse loam and one-fourth leaf mold and manure and are grown in a temperature of 60 to 65°F with bottom heat. Watering should be done sparingly until good roots develop. Later shifting to 6-inch pots will produce brilliant plants during summer, provided that slight shade, high humidity, and sufficient moisture at the roots are maintained. When the leaves begin to dry up in October, watering should be gradually decreased. In about 4 weeks the pots should be placed on their sides in a temperature of 60°F and water withheld, but not so stringently that the plants become bone dry.

CANNA (*Canna indica—Cannaceae*)

Clumps may be lifted in the fall with soil adhering and stored at a temperature of 45 to 50°F until January or February. At that time the clumps are separated, and each piece should have at least one eye and 3 to 4 inches of thickened root. These are placed in sand at a temperature of 65 to 70°F, with the eyes about 1 inch below the surface. The sand should be kept moist, and when the leaves are 4 to 6 inches long and the roots well developed, the pieces may be placed in 3- or 4-inch pots for later sale.

CHRYSANTHEMUM (*Chrysanthemum morifolium—Compositae*)

The *Chrysanthemum* is being used extensively as an item for mixed or combination pots and also as a spring flowering plant to enjoy in the home and then plant in the garden to flower in the fall. The production of flowering specimens of both garden and greenhouse varieties in small pots is covered in Chap. 11.

COLEUS (*Coleus blumei—Labiatae*)

These showy-leaved herbs of tropical Asia and Africa are used for carpet bedding and for edging formal beds. They can be propagated at any time of the year, but stock plants should be lifted before frost in the fall. If they are grown in a temperature of 60°F, they will produce an abundance of cuttings throughout the winter. Cuttings taken as late as April will make excellent plants in 4 weeks.

The plants are hybrid in character, and interesting variations in foliage color may be obtained by sowing seed in late January for spring sales. These variations can be perpetuated by subsequent vegetative propagation.

The red-leaved varieties can be grown as pot plants or for filling plant baskets for Christmas. Cuttings taken in September, and pinched to induce branching, will produce satisfactory plants in 4-inch pots in December.

CORDYLINE (Cordyline [Dracaena] indivisa—Liliaceae)

Cordyline indivisa thrives at a temperature of 50°F and is raised from seed sown in the spring. During the first season the seedlings should be grown entirely under glass, but the following summer they will make satisfactory plants if set out in the field. They should be lifted in September and potted in 4- or 5-inch pots. *Cordyline indivisa* is especially valuable for points of emphasis in window boxes, hanging baskets, and urns.

CROTON (Codiaeum variegatum—Euphorbiaceae)

These very attractive South American tropical plants are used as specimens and in combination with other plants in boxes and baskets. They are not very satisfactory houseplants unless a sufficiently humid atmosphere and a high temperature are provided.

Two methods of propagation are used. Cuttings of young shoots may be taken in February and March and rooted in a humid case with a top temperature of 70°F and additional bottom heat. A fibrous soil of one-fourth sand mixed with well-rotted cow manure or peat is a satisfactory potting medium, if drainage is provided.

A second method of propagation consists of mossing the top growths and potting the plants as soon as a mass of roots forms in the moss.

High humidity and a 70°F temperature are necessary. Unless these conditions are provided, the lower leaves will drop, and unsightly specimens will result. Fluctuations in temperature are also detrimental. Shade is necessary during the summer, as well as constant care in the control of red spider and mealy bugs, which are serious pests.

DAHLIA (Dahlia variabilis—Compositae)

The small-flowered types that grow to a height of 18 to 24 inches are used for bedding purposes. Seed sown in early March will make plants large enough to bed out in May. In the extreme heat of summer the Dahlia flowers may not develop, a condition similar to "heat delay" of Chrysanthemums.

ECHEVERIA (Echeveria secunda glauca—Crassulaceae)

These succulent, glabrous, dwarf plants, native to Mexico, form compact rosettes and are used for ribbon bedding and edging.

Old plants should be lifted in the fall for stock, planted closely in deep boxes, and kept fairly dry and cool. Leaf cuttings are taken in November and December. Each leaf should be taken individually with an axillary bud and inserted in sand, which should be kept rather dry until the roots develop and the new shoot begins to show. Rooting will occur in about 4 weeks at 60°F, and the young plants will be of satisfactory size for bedding in the spring.

Echeverias often stool, forming small rosettes at the base of each stem. These may be separated from the parent plant in the fall and grown in flats in a warm house; they will be bedding size in the spring.

FLOWERING MAPLE (*Abutilon hybridum—Malvaceae*)

The flowering maple is a shrubby plant, native of warm regions, with drooping, bell-shaped flowers ranging in color from white to crimson. Abutilons have a limited sale, but make satisfactory plants for combination boxes in the spring. Either seed or cuttings are used for propagation. Cuttings may be taken in the spring from plants lifted in September, cut back, and grown on in a temperature of 55°F. Fall propagation may also be practiced. Seed may be sown in the spring. Bottom heat is necessary for both the cuttings and the seed. Porous soil of comparatively low fertility is the most satisfactory medium. High nitrogen content may cause failure to flower. Pinching is necessary to secure compactness of growth.

Mealy bugs, red spider, thrips, and aphids are serious pests.

FUCHSIA (*Fuchsia hybrida—Onagraceae*)

The *Fuchsia* is often used in combination pots or porch boxes. Cuttings taken in early February will make nice 2½-inch plants for use in May if grown at 55 to 60°F. Culture of the plants as larger specimens is covered in Chap. 11.

GERANIUM (*Pelargonium hortorum—Geraniaceae*)

The primary market for geranium plants is in the spring, and they are used for planting in the gardens. In some instances geraniums are forced at other times of the year and used as flowering plants in the home or as gifts for hospital patients, and the market demand for them has been increasing, especially in the South.

Geraniums can be propagated by seed, and when suitable varieties are developed which can be propagated this way, it will no doubt become a common method of reproduction. Vegetative propagation by means of rooted stem cuttings is used in order to reproduce the varieties that have the most desired growth and flowering characteristics. The majority of the plants are finished in 4-inch pots, though there is demand for smaller sizes. Depending on temperature and other conditions, the 4-inch plant will be in flower and ready for sale from 3 to 4 months after the rooted cuttings are potted; and since most of the plants are needed from the middle of May until early June, the rooted cuttings should be potted in January and early February. Actually, because of conditions that exist or methods that are used, some growers start their geranium plants earlier than this, particularly when they are to be used as specimens for Mother's Day.

Propagation.   For propagation by rooted cuttings the geranium grower must have a source of supply of cuttings, and most of these are needed in December and January. In order to supply his needs at that time, the grower either maintains his own stock or gets the cuttings from outside sources. Southern California weather conditions are suitable for the growth of geranium plants outdoors the year-round, and many of the geranium cuttings originate from this area. These are largely outdoor operations although the cuttings may be rooted in structures. California geranium cuttings may be furnished as unrooted, callused, or rooted cuttings, but the majority of them are shipped as unrooted or callused cuttings. Unrooted cuttings are used because of the lower cost or because the grower wants to root the cuttings on his own place. Callused cuttings are used because there may be less loss than with unrooted cuttings, and they may become established and grow as fast as or faster than rooted cuttings.

Geranium cuttings from any source must be handled promply to avoid leaf drop and the start of some diseases. California geranium cuttings are shipped to all parts of the country via air freight satisfactorily, but on arrival they must be unpacked and handled promptly.

Because the California geranium stock is grown outdoors, weather conditions sometimes cause delays in shipping or affect the quality of the stock. In spite of the usually ideal southern California weather, there may be periods of extreme heat in the fall which affect the growth of the plants, there is danger of frost in the winter, and cuttings cannot be shipped during rainy weather since they deteriorate rapidly in the confines of the shipping container. Disease control in outdoor areas is not as easy as in greenhouses—and disease control in geraniums is a problem even in the best conditions. The best-regulated operations treat the fields before planting, select the stock carefully, and take all possible measures to maintain disease-free stock.

If the greenhouse operator in areas of the country where frosts are expected in early fall has geranium stock plants outdoors, he must harvest all the cuttings from the plants before frost. This might require that the cuttings be taken as early as September in many localities. Since this is much too early to start 4-inch geraniums for most purposes, it is not possible to produce geraniums economically from stock grown outdoors in the North.

When geranium stock plants are grown in greenhouses, they usually are

13-4. A geranium stem (leaf bud) cutting is made by cutting a section of the stem with a leaf and the bud in the axil of the leaf.

started in early summer, and the best stock is selected for this purpose. The grower who uses his discarded and rejected plants from spring sales as the source for his geranium stock plants invariably has poor results. The selected stock should have the best flower and growth characteristics for the variety and should be free from disease. The finest source for geranium stock plants is the specialist propagator who can supply cuttings from culture-indexed stock of carefully selected plants.

Several methods of growing geranium stock plants in greenhouses are used, but basically they are variations of two procedures. In the first, only stem tip cuttings are used and these are harvested periodically from fall through spring. The other procedure calls for both stem tip and stem sections or leaf bud cuttings (stem section cuttings), which are harvested from late December to March. Each method has its advantages. Considerably more cuttings may be obtained per plant from the second procedure, by using about half of each type of cutting. Stem sections require a somewhat longer growing period than stem tip cuttings to develop the same size plants, and this may be a problem in some instances. There is a definite advantage, however, in having cuttings available in quantity at the proper time to start plants for finishing in 4-inch pots. The procedure used is to allow the terminal stem to continue in growth after the initial pinch, with continuous pinching of lateral stems. This produces upright growth of the plant with numerous short lateral stems. The plants are staked to keep them erect. Approximately the first of December, the terminal stem is pinched for the first harvest of stem tip cuttings about the middle of January. Stem tips and stem sections then are taken in February. If earlier cuttings are desired, the terminal stem is pinched correspondingly earlier. Stem section cuttings should not be taken until there is new growth in the axils of the leaves to provide more uniform shoot development after rooting.

Geranium stock plants may be planted directly in the ground or placed in large cans or baskets. If planted in the ground, they should be spaced about 12 inches apart each way. The soil for the stock plants must be coarse and well drained whether the plants are in the ground or in containers. If the phosphorus is below 5 ppm and the calcium below 150 ppm, superphosphate and either dolomitic limestone or calcium sulfate should be incorporated into the soil at the rate of 5 pounds each before planting. After the plants are established, they should be regularly supplied with nitrogen and potassium fertilizers.

Geranium stock plants should be given 55°F night temperatures, with day temperatures about 10°F warmer. The plants should be allowed to produce a flower after planting to verify the variety, but following that, the flower buds should be removed as they form. As the plants grow, large leaves form toward the base of the plants, and some of these should be removed periodically in order to improve the air movement and light for the stems in that area.

A geranium cutting should be about 4 inches long, but shorter cuttings can be used when stock is scarce. The cuttings may be allowed to wilt without injuring them, and if they are soft, drying the cut end by exposure to air for 6 to 12 hours reduces loss from damping-off. Only the lower leaves should be removed, to facilitate sticking. Removal of too many leaves reduces the speed of rooting and the vigor of the root system, though some space in the propagation bench may be gained. To ensure that the stock plants have sufficient leaf area to develop food for new stems, no fewer than three perfect leaves should remain on a shoot from which a cutting is taken. Not allowing enough leaf area to remain on the stock plant reduces its vitality, and cuttings taken from hard wood do not root readily. Leaf bud cuttings are very satisfactory, but more time is required to produce a plant.

Treatment with a growth substance decreases the time required for rooting, which is usually 4 weeks. Sand is an ideal rooting medium, and it should be steam-sterilized to prevent troubles from damping-off. Vermiculite is an excellent rooting medium but can be easily overwatered. Perlite is a satisfactory medium. After the cuttings are stuck, they should be given a heavy watering and then carried somewhat on the dry side. Further watering may not be necessary for as long as 2 to 3 weeks, depending on the fineness of sand and the season; however, the cuttings should not be allowed to become so dry that they wilt severely. Cuttings can be rooted under intermittent mist, provided there are no foliage diseases and the rooting medium drains well.

Geraniums can be rooted very well directly in pots if a well-drained soil is used. Commonly, 2¼-inch peat pots are used; and after the plants are well rooted, they can be shifted directly to 4-inch pots.

The propagation of geraniums by seed is of considerable interest primarily because of the greater possibilities of disease control. When varieties are developed that have good commercial characteristics and can be propagated by seed, the propagation procedures for geraniums will change radically. The timing for producing a 4-inch geranium plant is about the same for plants started from cuttings or seeds—the cutting would be stuck or the seed would be sown at approximately the same time. Although geranium seed germinates with difficulty unless it is especially prepared, the treated (scarified) seed germinates promptly and the seedlings can be pricked off to small pots within 2 weeks after sowing.

Light. Geraniums should be grown in full light and without shade of any kind, with the possible exception of bright and hot periods in late spring when the plants are in flower. A light shade at that time will maintain good flower color or prevent burning of flowers of the softer varieties.

There are no apparent effects from the length of day on the flowering of geraniums.

Temperature. A night temperature of 55°F with day temperatures about 10°F higher should be used for geraniums, and if faster growth and flowering are desired, 60°F night temperatures may be used to good advantage. Growers who attempt to produce geraniums at the 50°F or lower night temperatures which may be used for other bedding plants find that the flowering and growth of geraniums are very slow at that temperature, and the leaves may be bronzed or edged with red.

Soil, moisture, and fertilizer. A porous, well-drained soil should be used for geraniums, and this is usually best supplied by adding chopped straw, strawy manure, or peat moss. The soil should be tested before use, and if phosphorus or calcium is low, it should be incorporated into the soil before potting by adding superphosphate and dolomitic limestone or calcium sulfate at the rate of a 4-inch potful to each wheelbarrow of soil (2½ bushels).

When geraniums are irrigated and fertilized properly and regularly as required, growth and development of the plants are rapid and of good quality. Irrigation can be done with the small-plastic-tube system, which saves much labor and also keeps moisture off leaves and flowers, thus reducing the possibilities of

13-5. Small-diameter plastic-tubing irrigation systems can be used to good advantage on 4-inch geraniums. (*Chapin Watermatics, Inc., photograph.*)

disease. When phosphorus and calcium are incorporated into the soil before potting, fertilizers containing nitrogen and potassium should be used regularly after the plants are established in the small pots. Supplying fertilizer by means of an injector with each irrigation is an excellent method for maintaining the required quantities of minerals in the soil. Some florists believe use of nitrogenous fertilizers prevents flowering, but failure to flower in winter is generally due to poor light conditions.

Air. Apparently the quantity of carbon dioxide in the greenhouse air in the winter and early spring is not enough for the best growth and development of geraniums. The maintainance of carbon dioxide at 500 to 750 ppm has produced faster growth and flowering of 4-inch plants and a greater number of cuttings from stock plants. The amount of benefit from the additional amounts of carbon dioxide will depend on the amount of light, minerals, and water that are available to the plants.

Geraniums also benefit from adequate ventilation and air movement. This helps to limit infestations of *Botrytis* and the occurrence of oedema by decreasing the air moisture (humidity) in the vicinity of the plants.

Potting and spacing. Geraniums may be rooted directly in pots; and when this is done, it is usually in 2¼-inch peat pots set pot to pot. Within a month

13-6. Geraniums appear to be one of the most responsive plants to increased quantities of carbon dioxide in the atmosphere, resulting in faster growth and earlier flowering. (*Yoder Bros., Inc., photograph.*)

after the cuttings are stuck, either the pots should be spaced or the plants repotted.

Cuttings which are rooted in benches should be placed in 2¼-inch pots and set pot to pot until they are established. They should then be shifted to 4-inch pots within a month. It is also possible to place rooted cuttings directly into 4-inch pots, but care must be exercised in watering in the early stages while the plant is becoming established.

Plants in 4-inch pots may be set for final spacing after potting, or they may be set pot to pot and then spaced out as the plants grow. If the space is available, the advantages in setting them at the final spacing immediately are that the plants are assured of good light conditions (no shading from adjoining plants) and that the labor of spacing the pots is eliminated. The finish spacing of 4-inch pots should be about 6 inches, which is 4 pots per square foot of bench. Some adjustment must be made for bench widths that do not accommodate the correct number of pots across the bench for that spacing.

Troubles. Oedema is a common problem in geraniums, and it is identified by the corky areas that develop on the undersides of leaves and occasionally on leaf petioles or the stems of plants. The cause of oedema is a surplus of water in plants which are in humid conditions and do not transpire enough moisture to the surrounding air. The development of oedema will cease with lower humidity, and this usually can be accomplished simply by providing more ventilation and better air circulation. Irrigating in the morning rather than in the afternoon will help also.

Diseases.   The most prevalent disease of geraniums throughout the country is Botrytis blight caused by *Botrytis cinerea*.   This pathogen exists primarily on older plant tissues such as older florets at the center of the flower, lower leaves, and fallen or discarded portions of plants.   The most common symptoms are petal or leaf spots or rots that are brown in color and often irregularly shaped.   The Botrytis organism also may produce stem rot in geraniums.   Usually this starts in a cut or damaged area or at the place on stems where leaves or flowers are removed.   In a moist atmosphere the involved area may be covered with a mass of gray-colored spores.   Spores of *Botrytis* are very common in greenhouse environments; however, their incidence is reduced considerably if plant refuse and trash are not allowed to accumulate in the greenhouse or around it.   The spores germinate and grow rapidly on moist surfaces of the plants; thus, keeping moisture from the leaves and flowers by careful irrigation practices, good ventilation, and adequate spacing are essential means of control.   Spraying or dusting the plants with zineb or Botran will limit the germination and spread of this pathogen.

The stem rot disease of geraniums caused by *Pythium* is called blackleg, and this is appropriate as the involved area typically is coal-black in color.   The propagation area, soil, containers, tools, and handling equipment must be thoroughly sterilized if this pathogen is to be controlled, and cuttings must not be taken from infected plants as the disease organism may accompany the cuttings.   Dexon or captan sprays or soil drenches may limit the development of this pathogen before it enters the plant, but they are ineffective in helping the infected plant to recover.

Bacterial stem rot and leaf spot are caused by *Xanthomonas pelargonii*, and it may produce dark-brown, rotted areas on the stem or circular spots on the leaves which enlarge into irregular shaped areas followed by the wilting and death of the leaf or the entire plant.   Because this pathogen can be transmitted with the cuttings, it is very important to know that the source of cuttings is not infected.   The best method for making this determination is a detailed laboratory procedure known as culture-indexing.   Not every cutting is cultured, but the stock from which the cuttings are taken is cultured and then handled in such a way that the cuttings are free of this pathogen.   The use of cuttings from culture-indexed stock must be coupled with strict sanitary measures to keep the cuttings from being infected subsequently with disease organisms of any kind.

Although possibly less common than other stem rot diseases of geraniums, stem rot produced by *Rhizoctonia solani* does occur.   It is a soil-borne organism, and thorough steaming of soil, benches, tools, and handling equipment is essential for control.   Typically a brown rotted area develops on the stem at the soil line, and this is followed by wilting of the plant and death.   Morsodren soil drenches can be used to control the spread of this organism from one area of the soil to another.

There are several virus diseases of geraniums, and their control lies primarily in the selection of virus-free stock for cuttings. This can be done quite successfully by careful and systematic observation of the visual symptoms of the plants to be used for stock. Devising practical laboratory methods to determine the presence of virus in geraniums could be a significant step forward in the control of geranium diseases.

Pests. Ordinary control measures usually are sufficient to keep pests in check on geraniums. Geraniums are infested with some of the pests that are common on other crops, and in addition they are sometimes troubled by two pests that are rather rare. Termites may tunnel in the stems, causing wilting and possibly toppling of the stems. Because termites may inhabit wooden structures and then transfer to the geraniums, replacing wooden benches with concrete or transite can remove the source of this trouble.

The geranium plume moth is a pest of more recent origin. The adult is a small, tan-colored moth, and it lays its eggs on the undersides of leaves. The young caterpillars burrow into flower buds, leaves, and stems. This pest can be controlled with DDT, parathion, lindane, or Thiodan, but repeated applications are necessary.

Pinching and cropping. In most marketing areas the customers demand that geranium plants have at least one flower on them at the time of sale; therefore, the plants must be started and handled in such a way that they are not only large enough and well-shaped but also in flower when they are marketed. The rate of growth and flowering of geraniums is dependent on many factors. Aside from the varieties that are used, the temperature in which the plants are grown and the amount of sunlight that is available are responsible for their rate of growth and flowering. Because of the variability of the weather, many growers start their geraniums earlier than required for average weather conditions so that the plants will be in flower in time if the light and temperatures are below normal. If the weather conditions are above average, rapid development and flowering of the plants may not be a problem, as the first flower can be removed when it is too old and the second flower may be at the right stage of development at the time of sale.

Geraniums may or may not be pinched, depending on the variety and the type of desired growth. Some varieties branch well without pinching if they are given sufficient space. The Irene varieties that are commonly used branch well, and they are grown often without pinching. Generally a branched plant is most desirable, and if the variety does not branch readily, it should be pinched. If just the tip of the plant is removed (soft pinch), the plants may be pinched as late as March 1 for flowering before Memorial Day. In some instances it may be worth while to remove enough of the stem tip in making the pinch so that the tip can be used for a cutting (hard pinch). When this is done, approximately 3 inches of the tip is removed, allowing at least two leaves to remain on the stem. Geraniums to be flowered before Memorial Day should be hard-pinched by February 1 as shoot development is not as fast after a hard pinch as after a soft pinch.

GLOBE AMARANTH (*Gomphrena globosa—Amarantaceae*)

Gomphrena grows rather slowly as a small plant; hence seed should be sown in late January or early February for sales in May as well-developed plants. The night temperature should never be less than 55°F. *Gomphrena* does well in hot weather.

IRESINE (*Iresine herbsti* and *I. lindeni—Amarantaceae*)

Iresines are South American herbs with red foliage, used largely for borders and ribbon bedding. Their culture is similar to that of *Coleus*.

LANTANA (*Lantana camara—Verbenaceae*)

This native of southern United States is a very showy shrubby plant, useful for spring sales and for bedding. The stock plants should be lifted and potted in September, pruned back, and carried in a cool house of 40°F. Specimen plants will be produced, and they will bloom in May. Ordinarily, cuttings are taken early in the fall from outdoor plants or from the potted stock plants grown in a warm house. Softwood cuttings root easily in sand or sand and peat, provided bottom heat of 65°F is supplied and transpiration is reduced to a minimum. Cuttings usually root in 3 to 4 weeks. They are generally pinched and will be flowering in 2½-inch pots approximately 6 to 8 weeks after pinching. The plants do best in medium-heavy soil and a temperature of not less than 60°F. Red spider, mealy bugs, thrips, and white fly are troublesome pests.

MARIGOLD (*Tagetes—Compositae*)

The French, or dwarf, marigold is especially useful for bedding purposes or combination pots. The tall African kinds are cut flower types. Seed of the French marigold varieties sown in early January will be in flower in 2½-inch pots in April, while sowings made February 1 will flower in early May in 2½-inch pots. For Memorial Day, an early March sowing is satisfactory.

Most French marigolds do not flower well during extremely warm days, and as a result they often stop flowering in late July and early August. This is probably similar to heat delay with Chrysanthemums. Flowers appear in profusion in cooler weather and continue until frost.

PANSY (*Viola tricolor—Violaceae*)

Pansies are very useful for early bedding. Seed is sown in August, and the seedlings are transplanted to cold frames about 6 inches apart each way in September. An application of a complete fertilizer is desirable after the plants are established. The plants can be mulched with straw after cold weather begins and cold frame sash can be placed over them, but it should be covered to prevent winter sun from heating the frame and causing the plants to start growing too early. The mulch may be removed in March, and the plants will be in flower in early spring.

PETUNIA (*Petunia hybrida—Solanaceae*)

Petunias are the most popular bedding plants grown from seed. There are good reasons for this, as they are available in a wide range of colors and they make a maximum show with a minimum of care in the garden.

Significant advances have been made in recent years in breeding Petunias, and excellent F_1 hybrids have been produced in all colors and classes. The F_1 hybrids are used almost exclusively, as the flower and growth characteristics are much better than those of the selfed varieties. Petunias are classed by some of their flower characteristics. The Grandifloras are the large-flowered varieties and the Multifloras have smaller flowers but a greater number of them. There are single and double forms of both these classes. The California Giants have huge flowers, and they are single only. It is the single Grandifloras and the single Multifloras which are used in quantity in landscape plantings.

Propagation. Petunias are propagated by seed. Because the seed is tiny, it must be sown on the surface of the propagating medium, which should be finely screened to assure good contact with the seed. At 70°F, Petunias will germinate in about 1 week. Some Petunia varieties must receive light before they will germinate, but this usually is not a problem as the seed should be sown on the surface of the medium where light is available. Uniform moisture conditions must be provided for the germination of Petunia seed; and since the seed is on the surface, the seed flat must be misted regularly or covered. After germination the temperature should be maintained at 60°F, and the seedlings should be transplanted promptly when the first true leaves develop.

Light. Petunias are affected by day length as well as by the quantity of light they receive. After the plants are pricked off from the seed flats, they should be grown in full sunlight. Petunias in shaded locations will be tall and have stems of small diameter.

Petunias in short day lengths—10 hours or less—produce short, compact, branched plants that do not flower rapidly. In long days—13 hours or longer—

they develop a single elongated stem and flower early. The temperatures at which the plants are grown also affect the nature of the growth. The Petunias that are sown early in the spring—January and February—are in naturally short day lengths in their early stages of growth and can be expected to develop as compact, well-branched plants. Plants that are started in March and later in natural conditions may be elongated, single-stem plants which flower early because of the long day lengths at that time. If tall, single-stem Petunias have been a problem, consideration should be given to providing short days (10 hours or less) artificially for about 1 month after the plants are pricked off, or the plants can be soft-pinched to induce branching.

Temperature.   Growth and development of Petunias will be best if they are in 60°F night temperatures for about a month after transplanting, followed by 50°F night temperatures until they are sold. Many Petunias are grown at 50°F with cooler night temperatures after transplanting. This produces short, compact, well-branched plants, but flowering is delayed and the plants develop slowly after they are planted in the garden.

It is possible to grow Petunias in a shorter period of time if 60°F night temperatures are used continuously; but if this is done, artificially short days and growth substances may need to be used in order to produce short and well-branched plants.

Cropping.   Petunias may be grown in pots for use individually or in Paks or flats for general bedding purposes. The potted Petunias are used more commonly in early May for Mother's Day gifts, either alone or in combination planters with other garden plants. The doubles, the California Giants, and the larger Grandifloras are most popular for these purposes. They may be finished in 2¼- or 3-inch pots depending on how they will be used. If the plants are grown in 50°F night temperatures, the seed should be sown about December 15 to have the plants in flower for early May. When warmer temperatures are used, the seed may be sown later. The Petunia seedlings may be transplanted directly from the seed flats to the pots in which they will be finished, but if they are to be finished in 3-inch pots, they may be pricked off to flats first and then transplanted to the pots.

Petunias that are to be sold in Paks or from flats should be sown from mid-February to mid-March if they are grown at 50°F night temperatures. If they are grown at warmer temperatures, they may be sown later, and cooler temperatures require earlier sowing.

SANTOLINA (*Santolina chamaecyparissus—Compositae*)

Santolina is a half-hardy, silver-foliaged plant, native of Mediterranean regions. It is very useful for edging, enduring much shearing and withstanding

13-7. Petunias in 3-inch peat pots make a good item for early May and Mother's Day sales. (*Jiffy Pot Co. of America photograph.*)

dry conditions.   Cuttings made in the fall will produce excellent plants in 2½-inch pots by spring if grown at 50°F.

SILK OAK (*Grevillea robusta—Proteaceae*)

This very popular fern-leaved plant from Australia is commonly used in combinations and window boxes.   The plants are raised from seed which, if sown in March, will produce salable plants by the following spring.   Grown in a light, cool greenhouse (50 to 55°F) in light, well-drained soil, the plants make excellent specimens for decorative effects.

VERBENA (*Verbena hortensis—Verbenaceae*)

Though Verbenas can be sown in early March for spring sales, better plants with several flowers may be had by sowing in early February and carrying at 55°F.   Pinching will make compact, bushy plants of the taller grandiflora types, although naturally dwarf varieties are available.

VINCA (*Vinca spp.—Apocynaceae*)

The common periwinkle, or *Vinca rosea,* is an annual with white, pink, or red flowers, a very useful bedding plant which stands extremes of heat and dryness well.   Since the plant grows slowly when small, seed should be sown along with *Gomphrena.*

V. major is a common vine, or trailing plant, which is used for window boxes and hanging baskets. The plants are propagated by cuttings with two buds, made in September; when rooted, they are potted in light soil in 2-inch pots and shifted to 3-inch pots in January. As they grow, they are usually placed on the edge of the bench so that the pendulous growths can hang down. A temperature of 50°F is desirable. Plants propagated in the spring may be lined out in the field, then lifted in the fall and potted in 3- or 4-inch pots, producing bushy specimens by May.

OTHER BEDDING PLANTS

There are a great many other plants, particularly annuals, that are very useful for bedding or cut flowers. Seed can be sown in late February or early March, and there will be sufficient time to develop plants ready for sale by mid-May. A list of the more common plants follows: *Alyssum,* aster, balsam, Bells of Ireland (*Molucella*), *Browallia, Calendula, Campanula,* castor bean, *Celosia, Centaurea, Clarkia, Cleome, Cosmos, Delphinium, Dianthus, Exacum,* heliotrope, hollyhock, *Impatiens, Kochia, Lobelia, Nasturtium, Nicotiana, Nigella, Phlox, Portulaca, Salvia,* snapdragon, *Torenia,* and *Zinnia.*

14

MARKETING

Flowers and plants are purchased by the public in various types of retail outlets: flower stores which handle only flowers, plants, and accessories; retail greenhouses; and general retail stores which handle flowers and plants in addition to many other types of merchandise. The flower store is the most common retail outlet for flowers and plants. Flower stores vary considerably in size and capabilities, but they should be able to take care of any request from selling a single flower to handling the largest wedding. They produce nothing, and all their merchandise is therefore purchased for resale. Flowers and plants are purchased from wholesale commission florists or directly from wholesale greenhouse operators. The flower shop proprietor may visit the wholesale store or the greenhouse in order to obtain his supplies, he may order by telephone, or he may purchase from trucks operated on regular routes by the wholesalers. Most retailers use all methods of procurement at various times. In many instances the holiday pot plants are bought directly from the grower.

It is possible to get into the retail flower business with a minimum amount of capital, information, and ability. That many do get into it is illustrated by the fact that in most market areas approximately 50 percent of the entire retail business is done by about 10 percent of the retail florists. The ill-prepared and the lazy do not stand a chance of success in the flower business. This is a dynamic affair in which the manager must not only like to smell the flowers and work with them but must have real ability in presenting them for sale, as well as being a shrewd purchasing agent, a clever advertiser, a good manager of personnel and money, a sound merchandiser, and an adept credit manager. There are many opportunities in the retail flower business for industrious individuals who are well schooled in business principles as well as in some of the arts of handling flowers.

Retail greenhouses operate in much the same way as retail shops, except that they produce a portion of their own merchandise. The retail greenhouse is probably even more useful in the display of plants, particularly for the holidays, and in the perpetuation of the belief that all the flowers are "greenhouse fresh" even though they may have been purchased through the same wholesale channels as the retail store operator uses. Most retail florists, whether they have only a shop or a shop and a greenhouse, are associated with one of the national or international services through which flowers and plants can be supplied readily to any part of the country or world. A considerable portion of the retail florist's business is a result of the flowers-by-wire services. These are the Florists Telegraph Delivery Association, Teleflora, Florafax, and Western Union.

Most of the flowers and plants sold by retail florists are special-occasion flowers—for holidays, funerals, weddings, anniversaries, and special events. Only a very small share of the florist's total sales are flowers for the home for everyday uses.

The general stores which commonly handle flowers and plants are either grocery stores or variety stores. Usually they do not have a complete florist's service. They do not design funeral pieces or install decorations, but they may have pot plants or packaged flowers which can be carried conveniently by the customer. The flowers and plants purchased in these outlets are largely used in the customers' homes rather than for gifts. These stores may carry a general line of foliage plants most of the time with special promotions periodically in packaged flowers or pot plants, or they may have pot plants primarily for the holidays. They usually buy directly from the wholesale growers. The local growers may service individual stores in the vicinity, or, in the case of chain stores, the grower may deliver only to the warehouse for distribution from that point.

The producer is vitally concerned with flower and plant sales.   It is not being too practical to acknowledge that the producer is in business to make a profit.   In order to do this, he must not only produce the right product in quantity, but he must make sure that it is marketed in such a way that he gets the best return.   Various methods may be used successfully, but regardless of the method the grower must spend as much time on the sales portion of the business as he does on the production end, if not more.

The retail grower is in a difficult position.   He wears two hats, and very often the head under the producer's hat is too generous to the head under the store operator's hat.   Somehow procedures must be established so that the produce from the greenhouses is "sold" to the store.   Usually the retail greenhouse production should be scheduled so that small quantities of a large selection of flowers are produced continuously.   This makes sensible marketing possible as the retail shop may be expected to "buy" the entire production each day and supplement its needs with plants and cut flowers from wholesale florists.   The retail grower who schedules large quantities of a single crop periodically not only makes profitable marketing impossible for his crop but may ruin sales for wholesale growers who supply that item regularly.   Some retail growers try squeeze-play marketing in which they insist that unless the wholesaler can move some of their excess crop, they may transfer future purchases for their shop to another wholesaler.   No one gains by this sort of merchandising, and responsible wholesalers will not become involved in it.

Some retail growers have developed single crops which they produce well and market profitably.   This is possible only because the grower carefully surveyed the market and knew that there would be a ready demand for his crop at the time of maturity.

Wholesale growers may elect to sell their produce directly to retail florists or other retail outlets, or they may use a sales agency.   There are several variations of each type of marketing.   Throughout the country pot plants are more generally marketed directly than are cut flowers.   Because of the difficulty in packaging and the weight, it usually is considered that pot plants must be marketed locally.   Notable exceptions to this are the direct marketing of pot mums from Florida and California to several areas of the country.

The sales agencies generally used by the growers are wholesale commission houses to which the produce is consigned.   The flowers are offered for sale together with flowers consigned from other growers, and periodically the commission house submits report of sales and dumpage to the grower together with payment for the flowers sold, less the commission.   Some wholesale commission houses operate separately and have no direct connection with any producer.   Several large producers of flowers and plants have established wholesale commission houses in which they sell their own produce as well as stock consigned from other greenhouses.

Some of the exceptions to the standard marketing patterns are the Boston and San Francisco markets and the cooperatives in Colorado. In Boston the growers cooperate to the extent of furnishing a market area which all use, and of furnishing the general management of the building, but each grower leases the stall space he desires and maintains salesmen for his own crops. In San Francisco many of the growers sell their own flowers from stalls in a common marketplace frequented by wholesale as well as retail sellers. Some of the growers in the Denver area formed cooperatives primarily for marketing flowers, although they do some purchasing through the cooperative and also obtain some other services. These are primarily one-crop sale organizations which sell carnations. They may sell to various wholesale commission houses, but much of their effort is geared to making sales directly to retail florists throughout the country.

The auction type of marketing used in some areas of Europe appears to have some advantages for the producer—advantages which are lacking in marketing methods used in the United States. It is at the auctions that the wholesale merchants obtain the stock which they will sell to the retailers. The growers bring their flowers and plants to the market early in the morning, the grade is verified by an official, and the stock is identified by lot number and placed on display. The auction proceeds rapidly; the flowers are brought in by lot, the clock is started at a price known to be too high, the wholesalers watch from tiered seats, and the first wholesaler to press his button, stopping the progress of the clock, purchases the lot. The clock indicates the price and buyer, and the auction starts on the next lot. Because the wholesale merchants can view all the flowers and then compete with all the other merchants in buying, the price is readily established by supply and demand, and the best-quality flowers receive the top price. The psychology of going from the high price down is good. There is no second chance to buy that lot of flowers; the first man to press the button makes the purchase. The clock moves rapidly, leaving little time for contemplation. The merchant knows very well that if he wants a specific lot of flowers, he must have a fast button finger or go without. There are, no doubt, some undesirable features of marketing by auction, but it does appear to be an excellent method for selling flowers to wholesalers. After the buyer has purchased the flowers which he needs at the auction, he sells them to retailers in much the same way as it is done in this country.

Growers who specialize in the production of certain types of plants may sell their product to other growers through companies variously termed brokers, jobbers, or dealers. Such items as rooted cuttings of a wide variety of plants (Chrysanthemums, carnations, poinsettias, foliage, and many others), dormant plants (poinsettia stock, roses, azaleas, Hydrangeas, etc.), and other kinds of plant material can be sold and distributed from one grower to another. Jobbers have sales representatives soliciting the growers, and the plant material is shipped direct from producer to grower without passing through the hands of the jobber who collects a commission for acting as sales agent. A few items—bulb stock and flower and vegetable seeds—may be purchased by jobbers for distribution, and jobbers may also handle supplies needed by growers in production of floral crops. These include pest-control materials, fertilizers and injectors for their application, tools, shading cloth, and a host of other items which are generally purchased directly by the jobber.

Marketing through wholesale commission houses. Some growers have the time, ability, and facilities to sell flowers as well as produce them, but many need the marketing help which is available in the wholesale commission houses throughout the country. The wholesale commission houses receive flowers and plants from growers on consignment, sell them to retail florists, and then periodically pay the grower, subtracting a commission for their services.

All the wholesale commission houses carry a complete line of cut flowers, and in addition some of them also have pot plants and retail shop supplies. Very often some of the wholesalers in a locality specialize in certain items. One house may be best known for roses, another for greens, and another for supplies. Most wholesale houses carry as complete a line as possible in order to take care of all the needs of each retailer.

The earliest wholesale commission houses obtained flowers only from local growers for sale to local retailers, but as shipping facilities improved, flowers came to be shipped in from various areas of the country. The development of railroads throughout the country made it possible to ship flowers successfully for several hundred miles. Later, as air freight service became available and refrigerated and insulated truck shipping was started, it became possible to ship anywhere in the United States rapidly and economically. Shipment of flowers overseas via air freight has become more commonplace and is likely to increase. In addition to the general line of flowers the wholesale house may obtain from local growers, they may ship in spray Chrysanthemums and Gladiolus from Florida; carnations from New England, Colorado, or California; roses from California, the East Coast, or various locations in the Midwest; greens from Oregon and Washington; and orchids from a few widely separated growers in various parts of the country and as far away as Australia.

Usually the commission house manager attempts to procure the best local stock and supplement it with flowers obtained from other sources. In order to do this he must successfully market all the crops from the best growers so that they will continue to consign to him. Close cooperation is required between grower and wholesale house manager so that crops will be produced at the right times. The grower must know the market demands for his flowers, and the manager must be advised regularly of the kind and amount of flowers which the grower will have available. Only under pure happenstance will grower and wholesaler be able to work together successfully on any other basis. Actually

Consignment Report　　　　　PHONE 585-5365

A. RASMUSSEN & SON, Inc.

715 S. SEVENTH STREET
LOUISVILLE, KENTUCKY 40203

TOTAL SALES..	1929 10
COMMISSION 20.	385 82
NET SALES....	1543 28
EXPRESS	
ALLIED	15 43
REMITTANCE ..	1527 85

SOLD FOR

John Doe Co.,
250 E.Main St.,
Anywhere,U.S.A.

REPORT ANY ERRORS IMMEDIATELY

DATE	Pompy	Mums	Large Mums	Snaps		EXPRESS
CARRIED OVER	73	25				
10-4	162 hu	600	7 dg	28 dg		
10-5		150				
10-6	119	600	1 C	21		
10-7	173	700	9			
10-10	176	800	9	26		
TOTAL RECEIPTS	703	2875	35	75		
SALES	578	2848	35	67		
THROWN OUT	16	5	0	0		
ON HAND	109	22	0	8		
10-4	107	134 75	558	195 30	7	24 50	25	50 00		
10-5	32	40 00	192	67 20			3	6 00		
10-6	144	177 25	619	216 65	10	35 00	21	41 75		
10-7	96	114 75	688	246 80	8	23 00				
10-8	35	41 75	2 nedy	1	3 50				
10-10	164	169 00	789	276 15	9	31 50	18	35 25		
	578	677 50	2848	996 10	35	122 50	67	133 00		
CARRIED FORWARD							
GROWER NO.		REPORT FOR PERIOD ENDING				
51		10-10-66				

14-1. Consignment report from wholesale commission house to grower. Usually the report together with remittance is made weekly.

the grower in planning the production in his greenhouse must base it on the market demand for those crops, and the best source of this information is the manager of the wholesale house. If there is no apparent market for the crops, other flowers in greater demand should be grown or a plan for development of the market should be in hand.

Consignment of flowers has good and bad features. The wholesaler probably stocks more flowers than he would if he had to purchase them outright for resale—and having them on hand may cause greater quantities to be sold. Sometimes more flowers are sent to the market than can possibly be sold, and this usually depresses the price. There probably would not be too many flowers on hand if they were purchased by the wholesaler rather than consigned to him. The consignment system is a bit too cozy for many individuals. It can produce a false feeling of well-being for both grower and wholesaler, with the unfortunate result that neither really works at selling flowers. This does not occur among alert, aggressive, or ambitious growers or sellers.

When a grower consigns his flowers to a wholesale commission house, he really is hiring the wholesaler to be the sales agent for his crops. This relationship must be understood by both parties, and the grower must hold the wholesaler responsible for the desired results. In practice, some wholesalers become retailers' purchasing agents, and the grower must be close enough to the marketing situation to know whether he is being fairly served.

Some of the most successful growers use controlled consignment in which they set the minimum price for which their flowers can be sold, and request that all unsold lots be returned to them rather than dumped. This system may work well if the grower has top-quality stock and keeps well informed on market conditions.

There is a trend away from the consignment system and toward the purchase of flowers by wholesalers. This has good features for both producers and sellers. When the flowers are purchased, the producer becomes directly involved in the transaction. The relationship between producer and wholesaler is more clear-cut and generally better understood by both parties. The producer sells his own flowers, and his customers are wholesalers. The producer sets the price, and the wholesaler either buys or declines, depending on need, quality, and price. Having purchased the flowers, the wholesaler then establishes a resale price based on his purchase price and attempts to sell them to his retail store customers. This is a business procedure that places price setting and responsibility for sales in the hands of the producer. The wholesaler actually is a customer in this procedure, rather than a sales agent as he is in consignment selling.

The practice of selling flowers to wholesalers arose among many of the California and Florida producers when they started in business, and it has since spread to some other areas. It is possible that some wholesalers do not stock as many flowers obtained by purchase as they would if the flowers were obtained by consignment, and prices may be higher. Of course, if all flowers were sold to wholesalers, the indiscriminate and blind shipping that some large producers practice in consignment selling would be eliminated.

Flowers are sold at wholesale commission houses directly to retailers visiting the market, by means of the telephone, or via truck routes which bring the stock to the retail shop. The methods used vary considerably in different areas. There was a time when the retailers made all their purchases while visiting the market early each morning. With improvements in communication and transportation, however, the retailers' buying procedures have changed. Some retailers make all their flower purchases by telephone or from trucks which stop at their shops two or three times a week. This places much responsibility on the salespeople using the telephone, as they must be the eyes and nose of the customer and cause him to be as stimulated as he would be by a trip to the market. In most wholesale houses each salesman maintains a list of "his" customers and calls them several times a week to keep them advised of market conditions and incidentally make some sales. Depending on the size of the operation, the telephone company may be able to suggest improvements in telephone equipment and the use of it.

Whenever possible, the wholesaler establishes the truck route so that most of the load is sold before the truck starts on its trip. Some additional stock may be carried on the truck in anticipation of additional sales, but truck routes cannot be operated successfully on speculative sales. Some of the trucks bring flowers back to the market from greenhouses along their route for sale the next day.

When the flowers arrive at the wholesale commission house in the morning, they are unpacked and identified with the grower's number. (The grower is assigned a number when he starts consigning to a particular wholesale store, and it is used for any stock that he brings in.) When a sale is made, the grower's number, as well as a description of the flowers and the price, appears on the sales slip; thus a record is maintained for each grower's stock. Various methods of display are used, depending on the type of flowers and the customs of the area. Since most of the stock should be sold within a few hours after it is received by the wholesaler, the flowers may be laid on tables, except that roses are commonly placed in vases of water in refrigerators. By late morning the flowers which remain unsold are placed in vases of water in refrigerators. The refrigerator is an integral part of the wholesale house. It makes it possible to keep flowers in much better condition. The walk-in refrigerator has been a big aid to proper handling of flowers, and more recently see-in refrigerators make it possible for the salespeople to be stationed at telephones outside the refrigerators but see and describe the flowers within the refrigerators to their customers. Most of the refrigerators are operated at 40 to 45°F, but for longer term storage some of them may be kept at 33 to 35°F. The minimum temperature for orchids is 50°F, to prevent chilling damage.

A minimum amount of wrapping and boxing is required for flowers which are purchased and taken from the market by the retailer. Flowers which are to be shipped require better protection. They must be packed well enough so that they can be stacked with other cartons and not damaged if weight is placed on them or if they are tossed about. They must be given adequate protection from extreme temperatures. In warm weather, if refrigerated transportation is not available, crushed ice should be packed with the flowers, and the carton should be insulated to retain the cool temperatures around the flowers. In cold weather the cartons must be well insulated to prevent freezing. In spite of the best packing, the flowers will be safe from freezing for only a few minutes if the carton is placed in low temperatures. Great care must be taken in selecting the best means of transportation. Many times the temperatures on the vehicle are satisfactory, but the carton may be left too long in extreme temperatures on a loading dock.

Local deliveries are usually adequately controlled by the wholesaler's own personnel, so that damage in transportation is negligible. Shipping to neighboring towns is best handled by bus as this service is available in communities of any size, and it is rapid. Long-distance shipping may be done with good results via either air freight or insulated and refrigerated truck.

Truck routes operated by wholesale commission houses use insulated and refrigerated trucks so that the flowers are protected from temperature extremes at all times of the year. Some of the flowers are transported in vases of water, and all of them must be packed in such a way that they will remain in good condition yet be available for delivery along the route.

Some wholesale commission houses sell supplies as well as flowers, others handle no supplies, and a few sell only staple supplies such as ribbon and wire. It is possible that a good line of supplies increases the potential customers for flowers. If the supplies can be handled at a profit, there is a definite advantage

14-2. A flower order packed at a wholesale commission house for shipment to a retail shop.

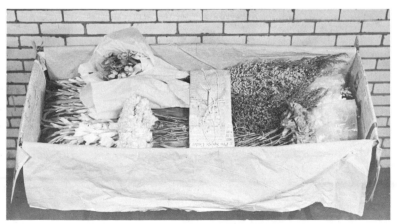

in having them for sale. Actually the supply business is quite different from the flower business. The merchandise is purchased rather than consigned, and for a complete line of supplies a few hundred thousand dollars may be tied up in supply inventory. These are nonperishable items with an unlimited shelf life, but many of them remain on the shelf too long because fashions or fads change rapidly. Some wholesalers believe the supply stock must be turned over three times a year in order to have a sound business. Thus an inventory of $100,000 should develop at least $300,000 worth of supply business a year.

The rate of commission on consigned flowers is 20 to 25 percent of the selling price. Most wholesalers report to their growers once a week, declaring the amount of flowers sold and dumped, the amount of commission being withheld, and the net return to the grower.

Selling directly from the wholesale greenhouse to the retail shop. At the local level direct selling is practiced more often with pot plants than it is with cut flowers. Some pot plant growers deliver plants as they are ordered within a 50-mile distance of their greenhouse. Others operate regularly scheduled truck routes within about 100 miles of their greenhouse. In some instances the retailers come to the greenhouse to select their plants and transport them to their shop.

It has been considered generally that pot plants are too heavy and difficult to package for long-distance shipping; however, larger trucks, better roads, and insulated and refrigerated truck facilities have made it possible to ship pot plants very nearly across the country economically.

Locally, cut flowers are not sold directly as a standard practice, but large quantities of flowers are sold directly from several areas of the country, such as spray mums and Gladiolus from Florida, carnations from Denver, and standard mums, carnations, and roses from the San Francisco area. The selling is handled by long-distance telephone, and transportation is by air freight or insulated and refrigerated truck.

Preparation of flowers for market. The sales potential for some of the best-grown crops can be ruined simply by the way the flowers are presented for marketing. The most successful growers prepare the flowers for market very carefully so that the best possible price may be realized. This starts with cutting the flowers at the right stage of maturity. Keeping quality and the general display value of the flower may be greatly affected by the stage of development at which it is cut.   The right time to cut varies with the kind of flower; some are cut in tight bud, and others when they are fully developed.   The time of cutting must be determined by the effect on the usefulness of the flower.   There is a common tendency to cut flowers too soon when the market demand is good, and too late when the demand is low.

Flowers must be graded so that those of the same kind and quality are bunched together. Various grading procedures have been used or proposed, and there has been some acceptance of Standard Grades as proposed by the Society of American Florists. Any grading procedure is only as good as the integrity of the individuals using it. Many growers have developed their own grading procedures and standards through the years and used them successfully in presenting their flowers for marketing. Such growers will use Standard Grades successfully, too, when they are adopted. The grower who uses Standard Grade labeling in name but not actually in practice will not benefit the industry or himself. The standards must be established for each kind of flower because of the different qualities involved, but regardless of kind, the flowers must be fresh, not diseased or malformed, and cut at the right stage of development. Then grading standards are based on size of flower, length of stem, strength of stem, and other qualities which may pertain to specific kinds of flowers.

Methods of bunching flowers vary with the growers and the market areas. Generally the wholesale bunch contains either 12 or 25 units depending on the flower. Roses are placed in bunches of 13 or 25, carnations are bunched 25 in a pack, and snapdragons and standard mums may be bunched by the dozen. Spray Chrysanthemums are bunched by weight, as this is a more practical method of designating quantity than the number of flowers.

The wrapping for the bunch of flowers should provide maximum protection and display. Usually, clear plastic film is used since the same degree of protection may be provided as with paper, and in addition the flowers are attractively displayed. The grade designation should be on each bunch, and if the grower's name or trademark is used, the retailer may readily identify stock of the same quality in future purchases.

Before the flowers are marketed, they should be "hardened" by placing them in vases of water in cool storage (40 to 45°F) for a few hours. The usual routine is to cut, grade, and bunch the flowers, and then place them in vases of water in the refrigerator overnight.

Packaging of the flowers for shipment to the market depends on the distance from the market and the method of shipment. Flowers taken to the local market often are trucked in vases of water. Flowers to be shipped any distance must be well packed so they are not damaged in transit. The bunches of flowers are placed in the carton with stem and head ends alternating, and paper rolls or pillows are used to support and cushion the flowers. If each bunch of flowers is not protected by a wrapping, waxed tissue paper is placed around the flowers for protection. The packaging material must not absorb water from the flowers; waxed cartons must be provided, and parchment or waxed paper used for direct contact with flowers. The packaging used and the method of shipment must assure protection from temperature extremes. Refrigerated or iced facilities must be used in warm weather, and insulated or heated ones in cold weather. Some protection can be provided by insulating materials used in packaging, but this is very limited, short-term protection if the package is exposed to extreme temperatures.

Keeping qualities of cut flowers.   In spite of having been separated from the plant, cut flowers have life.   True enough, the termination of that life is inevitable a few days to a few weeks after the flower is cut, but during this period the flower is living and may continue to develop and increase in size.   The death of the flower occurs when its food or water supplies are exhausted.   Anything done to increase the keeping qualities (life) of the cut flower is based on adequately maintaining its food and water supply.

The potential length of life after it is cut varies with the different kinds of flowers.   Under a given set of conditions roses might remain in good condition 5 days, carnations 7 days, Chrysanthemums 14 days, and Cymbidium orchids 28 days after they are cut.   The flower does not necessarily distinguish among times spent with wholesaler, retailer, or consumer.   Its potential life is the same regardless of ownership, but the ultimate consumer will not enjoy enough of that life if the flower has dallied too long en route to him.   The keeping quality in the hands of the consumer is of most concern, and shortening the time from greenhouse to consumer is an excellent method of increasing the keeping quality of any flower.   This is generally well understood by the individuals in the industry, and efforts are made to handle cut flowers rapidly.

The flower contains food and water at the time it is cut, but these will become depleted if new supplies are not added.   The food supply varies considerably in the flower, depending on the conditions in which it was produced.   Flowers grown in insufficient light, dark cloudy weather, or temperatures which are too high have a lower food supply and do not keep as long as those produced in more favorable conditions.

After the flower is cut, it should be placed in cool temperatures to reduce respiration and transpiration and to conserve the food and water in the flower.   Flowers live longer in cool temperatures.   A dramatic difference in keeping qualities may be demonstrated between room temperature (70°F) and a 40°F refrigerator.   Some further benefits in keeping qualities are possible with some cut flowers when they are kept at temperatures just above freezing.   The proper use of temperatures continuously must become something of a religion if the best job is going to be done to conserve the keeping qualities of cut flowers.   Of course it is not possible for the consumer to exercise rigid temperature control, but he should be guided and counseled to display the flowers in as cool a location as possible.   Some consumers do not realize that placing cut flowers in front of hot air registers or in direct sunlight will reduce their keeping qualities.

Cut flowers require a continuous supply of water.   This may be approached from two directions: supplying adequate water to the flowers regardless of other environmental conditions, and reducing water loss from the flowers by cool temperatures or high humidity. Both approaches should be used. High humidity around the flowers is best provided by wrapping them in a moisture-proof film. The use of transparent plastic film around bunches of flowers protects them from physical damage, reduces moisture loss, and improves the display value of the flowers.

Water may be supplied adequately to cut flowers only if the stem is able to absorb water and there is sufficient water available. The stems should be recut before they are placed in a vase of water. Water can enter the stem where leaves or thorns have been removed or the stem sliced or lightly crushed; hence the vase must be deep enough so that the stems are immersed deeply in water to cover these areas. Warm water (110°F) should be used as it is absorbed more readily than cooler water. Clean water and vases must be used. Water and containers that are used repeatedly for cut flowers become fouled with bacterial growth, and when this occurs, the stems also become infected and plugged so that water is not absorbed effectively. Cut flower containers should be cleaned regularly and treated with sodium hypochlorite or LF-10 solutions, and fresh water should be supplied each time the containers are used. Plugging of water-conducting tissue can also occur from breakdown of cells near the cut or wound on the stem.

Unfortunately many retailers make flower arrangements without concern for the water requirements of the cut flowers. Apparently they have no conception of or concern about the effects of water on the keeping quality of flowers. Flowers placed in small vials of water or stuck into blocks of absorbent material in shallow containers are doomed to death from desiccation within a few hours. There is no possible way for even the informed and interested consumer to add water often enough to such containers to keep the flowers in good condition.

Some excellent commercially prepared cut flower preservative mixtures are available, and no doubt improvements will continue to be made in these products. Most of these provide food for flowers plus an acidifier and possibly some growth regulators. These preservatives should not be used instead of proper temperature and moisture control but in addition to it. Keeping cut flowers in preservative solutions at all stages—wholesale, retail, and consumer—will be helpful.

Ethylene gas has an aging effect on flowers. It may produce sleepiness in carnations, petal drop in roses, leaf drop in many flowers, and floret drop in snapdragons. The most common sources of ethylene are imperfect combustion of fuel, decaying plant material, florists' greens, and some fruits and vegetables. Flowers must not be stored in the same areas as fruits, vegetables, and florists' greens. Old flowers and plants must be eliminated from flower storage areas as they may produce ethylene. Combustion products from vehicle exhausts or the boiler may have harmful effects on flowers.

15

COSTS OF PRODUCTION

There are many concepts of costs of production—not only of actual values per product but of methods for deriving them. The methods vary all the way from elementary ones that assume that the costs of production equal the amount of money disbursed currently to highly sophisticated and involved methods that project, prorate, and assign costs in the finest details. Actually many growers are willing to assume that the costs of production for the crops which they grow are the same as cost figures reported by some other grower. The only good method is the one which provides each individual grower with the complete costs involved in producing each of his crops.

Through the years it has become necessary to keep more detailed business records and make more voluminous reports to the government. It is necessary in most instances to employ an accountant to make the reports in an acceptable form. It is essential that the manager or owner of the business understand and fully appreciate that many of the accountants may do an acceptable job of making governmental reports but may have only slight interest in or knowledge about keeping some business records or analyzing them. The government, the accountant, and the owner of the business have their individual interests in the business. The primary interest of the government is in analyzing each business to determine whether it pays its proportionate share of the tax. It is possible that the accountant who is used will become involved only in the part of the business which requires governmental reports. The owner of the business must be highly interested in all phases of the business, and usually this will require keeping some records not required by the government. The analysis of these records leads to management decisions which affect the welfare of the business. The case in point here is costs of production. This is not the responsibility of the government or of accountants, but it is essential information which management must develop so that decisions may be made which will lead to the profitable operation of the business—and incidentally the ability to pay tax and accountants. Management must choose the method of determining the complete costs of production for each crop.

Costs vary with the expenditures and the quantity produced. The cost of production per unit is the total cost for the crop divided by the number of units produced for sale. Because expenditures and yield both may vary with each crop, it is necessary to keep continuous records of both so that an accurate production cost figure will be available to compare with the income on the crop. This is the only way in which it can be determined whether the crop in question produces a profit.

Production or yield records are rather easily taken, but it is necessary to establish the exact manner in which they are to be kept. The yields of the various kinds of crops must be recorded separately, and in some instances it will be desirable to segregate the yield by variety. This record should be the number of units offered for sale rather than the number of flowers cut or the number of pot plants grown per bench. The methods of reporting yield and income must be made in the same manner so that meaningful comparisons may be made readily.

It is difficult to establish a workable method for keeping accurate cost records. The system must be foolproof enough that all the costs are assigned and to the right crops, but it must be simple enough to operate so that only the minimum amount of labor and time are required to maintain it. There is no one system of keeping cost records which will be suitable for all greenhouses. Each owner or manager must devise the system which best suits the purposes of his business. Some of the costs for a crop are the proportionate shares of the costs of conducting the entire business.   Other costs can be charged directly to the crop, as they pertain solely to it.

The specific costs which can be assigned directly to each crop are labor, plants, seeds, bulbs, soil, pots, special equipment or power, packaging or wrapping, and transportation.   With some crops the amount of labor is static, and the same labor costs are incurred each week.   With most of the crops, however, the amount of labor which is used varies, and a system must be designed for charging the labor to the proper crop.   In some instances each worker may be required to list the amount of time worked on each crop per pay period, and in other situations the foreman may keep this record.   Once the routine is established, it is not difficult to maintain the labor-crop record.

The general costs for the entire business may be prorated to each individual crop based on the area occupied per crop.   This may be either the area under glass (which includes walks as well as bench area), or it may be bench area.   Both methods have merit.   In the discussions in this book, bench area per crop is used.   Keeping records of the space occupied is easy for long-term crops such as roses and difficult for pot plant crops which are continually moved and spaced.   The best plan seems to be to take inventory of the entire range once a month and charge the area to the crops according to the space used at that time.   All the area must be accounted for and charged to some crop each month.   If any idle area cannot be charged properly to a specific crop, it then must be prorated to all the crops.   Some of the general costs for the entire business which must be prorated to each crop are heating system, labor, irrigation system, taxes, structure, cooling system, vehicles, communication, repair and maintenance, fuel, power, watchman, bad debts, insurance, office and storage buildings, refrigeration, handling equipment, general labor, administration including the owner's salary, interest on invested as well as operating capital, fertilizer, and pesticides.

Most greenhouses will have all these cost items, and some have others. All costs must be included.   Either by design or through error some costs are commonly omitted.   These are structure, owner's salary, and interest on invested and operating capital.   Depending on governmental regulations, the cost of structure is depreciated over a period of years rather than assume it all in a single year.   Permanent structures are usually depreciated in 20 years and temporary structures in a shorter period of time.   If the business has been operating within costs, at the end of the depreciation period funds will be available for replacing the structure.   In the minds of some, the owner's salary is part of the profit.   Actually, however, it is a definite cost of the business, and any residue which may remain after the total costs are subtracted from the total income is the profit which may go to the owner in addition to his salary.

In order to have and operate a business, a certain amount of capital is required.   It is generally realized that capital is required to provide structures and some equipment, but too often the requirement of operating capital is forgotten or ignored. Supplies and equipment must be purchased, payrolls met, and credit extended. For a greenhouse range of 30,000 square feet (20,000 square feet of bench space), it is possible that the capital invested in land, structures, and equipment might be approximately $150,000. Depending on the crops and other factors, the potential gross income from such a greenhouse might be about $60,000 per year. Most of this gross income would be paid out in various costs including the owner's salary. Hopefully all costs would be met, and there would be a remainder left known as profit. The operating capital required for such a business might be approximately $15,000. This is money that is tied up constantly in current expenses and extended credit. Depending on how the products are sold, the capital involved in credit might be about $5,000 on the total amount of business. These are not bad debts but current accounts. For the 20,000 square feet of bench space, it might then be possible to need about $165,000 to provide the necessary structures, equipment, and operating capital. At 5 percent interest this would be $8,250 yearly to be included in the costs of production.

Labor is the largest item in cost of production. The expenditure of funds varies with each greenhouse, but invariably the single item contributing the most to the cost of production is labor. Usually pot plant crops require more labor than cut flowers. In areas of higher wage scales, the labor cost is higher. In some large greenhouse ranges, where the owner actually functions solely as an executive, it is possible that the expenditure for labor in proportion to the total cost will be higher and the administrative and owner's salary expenditure correspondingly lower, whereas in smaller greenhouses the owner works as a laborer as well as an administrator. On the other hand, larger ranges may have more labor-saving equipment which reduces the expenditure for labor. For the greenhouse of 20,000 square feet of bench space referred to above, the distribution of costs might be as follows:

ITEM	PERCENTAGE OF TOTAL COSTS
Labor	37
Administration and owner's salary	15
Interest on invested and operating capital	13
Structures and equipment (depreciation)	10
Fuel	10
Plants	5
Repairs	5
Other items	5
Total	100

Means of reducing costs of production. Unfortunately the means used commonly for reducing costs is simply to ignore some of the costs. This produces a false cost figure, creating the impression that the business is operating at a profit when in fact it may be losing money on each sale.

It is no more possible to operate a business without invested and operating capital than without structures or labor. If the owner is using his own money to operate the business, he must charge to costs a fair rate of interest on this money. To some individuals it is clear that the interest on money borrowed to finance the business is a cost of production, but they see the use of the owner's own funds as a convenience which does not enter into the costs. The owner who operates on that basis is not getting the return on his funds that he should.

Structures and equipment must be charged to costs on a depreciation schedule so that at the end of the depreciation period funds are on hand to replace them. Repairs must be made continually so that the best use and life are obtained from structures and equipment. Individuals who ignore these costs are commonly referred to as "living off the greenhouse." It is possible to operate a greenhouse on this basis for a limited time, but eventually structures and equipment become unusable and there is no money for repair or replacement.

There are really only two ways in which costs of production may be reduced. One is to produce more units of equal quality in the same space, and the other is to reduce expenditures. Both routes should be explored in the attempt to reduce costs of production. The discussions on various crops throughout this book include methods of producing more units of equal quality per given area; and hopefully, if some of these suggestions can be used without increasing expenditures, costs per unit may be decreased.

Discussions of methods of reducing costs often get no further than saving labor. Since this may be the largest single item of expense, savings in this category certainly should be investigated—but not to the exclusion of the other costs. The analysis of labor costs is a complex subject which must delve deeper than the hourly rate paid and the total hours worked. Labor hired at a low rate may be less productive per dollar than higher priced help. Equipment and machines may replace some labor but may actually save labor only if management makes sure that the replaced individuals are either released or placed on other productive work. In some instances the high cost of labor is a direct result of lack of planning or instructions by the owner or manager. There are possibilities of saving labor costs if management will expend the thought and time required for solution.

In the example used earlier in this chapter, the capital investment was based on the erection of the most durable structures and permanent equipment. This requires the maximum invested dollar, but usually the repair and depreciation rates are lower. It is possible to save some interest on invested capital by building on more reasonably priced land and erecting semipermanent structures. Young people interested in an "operation boot strap" venture may be able to get into business with a plastic film range to be replaced later with more permanent structures as funds become available. This is possible because not as much capital is required for a plastic house, and the costs of production may be lower because of savings in interest on the money invested.

An even bigger "savings" is effected by an individual starting in business who works extremely long hours for a very low salary. This may reduce the costs of production sufficiently so that there is money available to put back into the business for improvement of facilities or expansion. It must be recognized, however, that this is only a temporary expedient, and if the business is to flourish, a more realistic view of costs of production will have to be taken.

INDEX

INDEX

of the Hohenzollern dynasty in Germany was heralded by a woman wearing white. In mythologies around the world and across millennia, women wearing white have been endowed with supernatural powers and strength.

Though Belgian men were most certainly involved in resistance work, women—from young girls to grandmothers—were recruited for all manner of tasks, including intelligence gathering, sabotage and even assassination. Their bravery knew no bounds. As I read more about La Dame Blanche (and interested readers might start with *Female Intelligence: Women and Intelligence in the First World War* by Dr. Tammy Proctor, professor of history at Utah State University), I kept wondering how it might feel to have been a girl in her early teens who was called upon to serve her country—and then approached again in womanhood to join the Belgian resistance as war ravaged Europe in WWII.

With my series featuring psychologist-investigator Maisie Dobbs, which comprises seventeen novels thus far, I have created the story arc of a woman from her pre–WWI girlhood, through the Great War, the Depression, the Spanish Civil War, and now to the Second World War. With the series, I wanted to explore how it might be for each of the cast of characters to live through a defining period of the twentieth century, anchoring them in the big and small events of their day. When I started thinking about *The White Lady*, I knew that within one novel I wanted to do something similar, and asked myself, "How would it be if a woman had been required to kill in two wars? And how would it be if I followed her journey from adolescence to womanhood, and then set her down amid the world of organized crime in postwar London?"

One of the worst winters on record heralded the start of 1947. Wartime organized crime was still rocketing, though the kingpins were finding it harder to make the same level of big money once Allied soldiers returned home. But they were helped by the fact that many guns came back to Britain with returning troops, and the American military, in particular, left plenty behind when their men sailed back to the USA. At the same time, homelessness was rife in Britain's cities, and in London the new prefab housing being constructed in a hurry to accommodate a war-weary citizenry would never meet demand. Most people agreed that postwar rationing, indeed postwar life on so many levels, was worse than when the bombs were dropping.

In her "grace and favor" home, Elinor White finds a fragile calm in the countryside, more than anything hoping to break free from her past. But she puts any chance of peace on the line when she is drawn into the brutal underworld her neighbors—a young couple, Jim and Rose Mackie, and their daughter, Susie—have left London to escape.

There is another part to this author's story. There was a point when I realized that to craft a story about a woman familiar with the use of firearms, I should probably know what it's like to hold a gun. It's something I'd never done before and will never do again. My first "lesson" was simply in handling the weapon safely—and it was a crucial lesson, because I realized how easy it would be to make a devastating error if it were a real handgun (and not one used with blanks for recreational target practice). The way people around me ducked when I held the weapon told me I would never be proficient in the handling of a gun. I was supposed to have a second lesson where I actually fired the handgun, just to feel what it was like—but for me one lesson was more than enough! Just fifteen minutes on the basic handling skills was more pressure than my emotions could stand. Handing back the gun with a sigh of relief, I decided my imagination had already brought me a long way on my journey as a storyteller—it would have to do the rest.